Handbook of Research on Global Perspectives on International Advertising

Ipek Krom
Istanbul Esenyurt University, Turkey

A volume in the Advances in Marketing, Customer
Relationship Management, and E-Services
(AMCRMES) Book Series

Published in the United States of America by
  IGI Global
  Business Science Reference (an imprint of IGI Global)
  701 E. Chocolate Avenue
  Hershey PA, USA 17033
  Tel: 717-533-8845
  Fax: 717-533-8661
  E-mail: cust@igi-global.com
  Web site: http://www.igi-global.com

Library of Congress Cataloging-in-Publication Data

Names: Krom, Ipek, 1976- editor.
Title: Handbook of research on global perspectives on international
  advertising / Ipek Krom, editor.
Description: Hershey PA : Business Science Reference, [2022] | Includes
  bibliographical references and index. | Summary: "This book of
  contributed chapters gives a global perspective on international
  advertising from countries/regions from around the world, giving an
  overview of the advertising industry from the perspective of
  geopolitics, socio-politics, economics and culture of the
  country/region"-- Provided by publisher.
Identifiers: LCCN 2021060984 (print) | LCCN 2021060985 (ebook) | ISBN
  9781799896722 (hardcover) | ISBN 9781799896746 (ebook)
Subjects: LCSH: Advertising--Cross-cultural studies. | Advertising--Case
  studies.
Classification: LCC HF5823 .G5628 2022 (print) | LCC HF5823 (ebook) | DDC
  659.1--dc23/eng/20220207
LC record available at https://lccn.loc.gov/2021060984
LC ebook record available at https://lccn.loc.gov/2021060985

This book is published in the IGI Global book series Advances in Marketing, Customer Relationship Management, and E-Services (AMCRMES) (ISSN: 2327-5502; eISSN: 2327-5529)

British Cataloguing in Publication Data
A Cataloguing in Publication record for this book is available from the British Library.

For electronic access to this publication, please contact: eresources@igi-global.com.

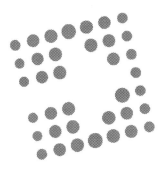

Advances in Marketing, Customer Relationship Management, and E-Services (AMCRMES) Book Series

Eldon Y. Li

National Chengchi University, Taiwan & California Polytechnic State University, USA

ISSN:2327-5502
EISSN:2327-5529

MISSION

Business processes, services, and communications are important factors in the management of good customer relationship, which is the foundation of any well organized business. Technology continues to play a vital role in the organization and automation of business processes for marketing, sales, and customer service. These features aid in the attraction of new clients and maintaining existing relationships.

The Advances in Marketing, Customer Relationship Management, and E-Services (AMCRMES) Book Series addresses success factors for customer relationship management, marketing, and electronic services and its performance outcomes. This collection of reference source covers aspects of consumer behavior and marketing business strategies aiming towards researchers, scholars, and practitioners in the fields of marketing management.

COVERAGE

- Electronic Services
- Mobile CRM
- Customer Relationship Management
- Text Mining and Marketing
- Cases on CRM Implementation
- Cases on Electronic Services
- Relationship Marketing
- B2B marketing
- Web Mining and Marketing
- Database marketing

IGI Global is currently accepting manuscripts for publication within this series. To submit a proposal for a volume in this series, please contact our Acquisition Editors at Acquisitions@igi-global.com or visit: http://www.igi-global.com/publish/.

Titles in this Series

For a list of additional titles in this series, please visit: www.igi-global.com/book-series

Examining the Future of Advertising and Brands in the New Entertainment Landscape
Blanca Miguélez-Juan (University of the Basque Country (UPV/EHU), Spain) and Gema Bonales-Daimiel (Complutense University of Madrid (UCM), Spain)
Business Science Reference • © 2022 • 335pp • H/C (ISBN: 9781668439715) • US $250.00

Critical Perspectives on Diversity, Equity, and Inclusion in Marketing
Ayantunji Gbadamosi (University of East London, UK)
Business Science Reference • © 2022 • 325pp • H/C (ISBN: 9781668435908) • US $240.00

Disruptive Innovation and Emerging Technologies for Business Excellence in the Service Sector
Vipin Nadda (University of Sunderland, London, UK) Pankaj Tyagi (Chandigarh University, India) Malini Singh (Amity University, India) and Priyanka Tyagi (Chandigarh University, India)
Business Science Reference • © 2022 • 285pp • H/C (ISBN: 9781799891949) • US $250.00

Cases on Academic Program Redesign for Greater Racial and Social Justice
Ebony Cain-Sanschagrin (Pepperdine University, USA) Robert A. Filback (University of Southern California, USA) and Jenifer Crawford (University of Southern California, USA)
Information Science Reference • © 2022 • 361pp • H/C (ISBN: 9781799884637) • US $215.00

Adoption and Implementation of AI in Customer Relationship Management
Surabhi Singh (IMS Ghaziabad, India)
Business Science Reference • © 2022 • 272pp • H/C (ISBN: 9781799879596) • US $240.00

Handbook of Research on IoT, Digital Transformation, and the Future of Global Marketing
Hatem El-Gohary (College of Business and Economics, Qatar University, Qatar) David Edwards (Birmingham City University, UK) and Mohamed Slim Ben Mimoun (Qatar University, Qatar)
Business Science Reference • © 2021 • 471pp • H/C (ISBN: 9781799871927) • US $325.00

Management and Marketing for Improved Competitiveness and Performance in the Healthcare Sector
José Duarte Santos (Polytechnic Institute of Gaya, Portugal) and Inês Veiga Pereira (ISCAP, Polytechnic Institute of Porto, Portugal)
Business Science Reference • © 2021 • 355pp • H/C (ISBN: 9781799872634) • US $250.00

IGI Global
PUBLISHER of TIMELY KNOWLEDGE

701 East Chocolate Avenue, Hershey, PA 17033, USA
Tel: 717-533-8845 x100 • Fax: 717-533-8661
E-Mail: cust@igi-global.com • www.igi-global.com

I would like to dedicate this book to my mother, whose kind and caring support has helped me make my way to my academic career...

Editorial Advisory Board

List of Contributors

Table of Contents

Section 1
International Advertising in Africa

Section 2
International Advertising in America

Section 3
International Advertising in Asia

Section 5
International Advertising in Oceania

Detailed Table of Contents

Section 1
International Advertising in Africa

Chapter 1
Nurdan Güven Toker, Haliç University, Turkey

This study takes Egypt as a case to understand the dynamics of political advertising in competitive authoritarian regimes. The sample universe of the study was formed from the political advertisements published in the last two years on the official Facebook accounts of President Abdel Fattah Saeed Hussein Khalil el-Sisi and the Nation's Future Party he supports. Advertisements were examined in the axis of 12 criteria determined in the axis of sociological analysis methodology. During the examination process, critical theory, which examines the dynamics of authoritarian systems, was also utilized. In the study, it is argued that political advertisements in Egypt are designed in a way that can establish both consent and coercion.

Chapter 2
Başak Özoral, Istanbul Commerce University, Turkey
Mehmet Sinan Tam, Bandırma Onyedi Eylül University, Turkey

Political advertising is a form of campaigning that allows candidates to directly convey their message to voters and influence the political debate. South African political parties (African National Congress and the Democratic Alliance) also adopted the use of social media networks as an effective tool for political campaigning purposes and to encourage the public to engage in political discourse. The chapter investigates how both the South African public and the political parties are using YouTube for discussion, debate, and opinion formation during the 2019 South Africa elections. Sociological analysis method is used in the research. The subject is especially about Aristotle's concept of rhetoric, promises of political messages, and political persuasion in written form. The findings part of the study shows that the most prevailant issues in the election campaigns were corruption, failure to keep promises, and the effort to create a new leader identity in the DA party. By ANC, independence, Mandela's contributions and past actions, and the importance of voting were mentioned.

Chapter 6

Poshan Yu, Soochow University, China & Krirk University, Thailand
Yuejia Liao, Independent Researcher, China
Ramya Mahendran, Independent Researcher, India

This chapter focuses on the development of social media advertising in China, especially influencer marketing through social media posts. More specifically, this study examines how the personal traits of social media influencers, the characteristics of the content posted by them, the form of advertising, and the users' personal preferences influence the effectiveness of these influencers' advertising. Through this research study, the authors conclude that social media influencers in China act as great assets to advertising and in recent times have gained the attention from many brands. During COVID-19, social media usage increased dramatically and helped influencers increase their followership. In an ever-accelerated pace of this digital and social era, it is worthy for brands to rethink how to collaborate and partner with these influencers. It is also significant for influencers to think about how to maintain long-term relationships and garner meaningful interactions with their fans and fellow influencers.

Chapter 7

Mehmet Sinan Tam, Bandirma Onyedi Eylul University, Turkey
Kazım Babacan, Karadeniz Technical University, Turkey

Because of its dense population and rising economy, many companies in India appeal to their consumers through advertising agencies. In the Indian advertising sector, the agencies that became dominant were British agencies until 1947 and local agencies starting from 1947. When the country gained its independence in the 1990s, foreign advertising agencies again became dominant in the country with the new economic approach adopted. This research aims to explore the advertising practices in the prime-time zone on Indian television channels with a special focus on the prime-time zone advertisements of the ABP News TV channel, which broadcasts continuously on YouTube and has the most followers. In the research, it is concluded that health advertisements are broadcasted more frequently on TV than in other sectors. Performance and quality are frequently emphasized in the advertisement content, and the positioning strategy is more frequently adopted by advertising agencies.

Chapter 8

Meltem Özel, Istanbul Esenyurt University, Turkey
Onur Karakaş, Kocaeli University, Turkey

In this chapter, the adaptation strategy, which is one of the global advertising strategies, is used in the analysis of advertisement. The adaptation approach is based on the fact that nations located in different geographies in the world are structurally and culturally separate from each other, and advertising messages are reshaped according to these differences. The approach aims to cooperate with the country's local agency and adapt the advertisement to the country's cultural characteristics. The study aims to determine how cultural differences are emphasized in global advertising strategies and how these differences are adapted in ads.

Chapter 9

Ipek Krom, Istanbul Esenyurt University, Turkey

This research aims to analyze the American impact on Japanese advertising through the use of celebrity endorsement strategy. In order to reach this aim, at first the geo-politics, economy, history, and culture of Japan is analyzed. In the research, three soft cell Japanese advertisements are chosen, in which American Hollywood and pop music icons are starring. According to the results of the research, the use of American celebrities adds popularity, attractiveness, likability, sympathy, and sexual appeal to the products as well as humor appeal to the advertisements in order to draw attention. Although Japanese cultural elements can be found in the advertisements like the masculine culture, samurai heroism, and the appreciation of the Japanese working class, the advertisements are generally under the consumption imposition of American culture with higher-status symbols, upward capitalist social comparison, and sexual objectification of women.

Chapter 10

Suzana Dzamtoska Zdravkovska, American University of Ras Al Khaimah, UAE
Sabir Haque, American University of Ras Al Khaimah, UAE

A thriving media ecosystem today requires a vibrant content production ecosystem. The MENA region today boasts several established and emerging media ecosystems. Key criteria essential for establishing a healthy media production workflow are location, production, infrastructure and support, incentives and investment returns, city infrastructure and safety, as well as access to talent. This chapter aims to establish UAE as a hotspot for film and TV production, making it a regional hub for television advertising production. The study includes the new framework of UAE media strategy, looking close into the media regulations which have revolutionized the media-free zones in all the emirates of the UAE. The research approach is of an exploratory and descriptive nature involving a problem-centered interview (PCI) that offers a structured interview procedure investigating individual perspectives on the UAE film and TV advertising industry.

Section 4
International Advertising in Europe

Chapter 11

Ceren Gül Artuner Özder, Beykent University, Turkey

Through this research, an attempt is made to understand how Croatian coastal cities Dubrovnik and Split, with rich historical and cultural heritage, promote, market, and advertise this heritage through the official websites of local tourism organizations. In this context, after examining the general discourses on the homepage of the official websites of these cities, the discourses they adopt to promote their historical and cultural wealth in order to create a destination image are analyzed using content analysis. To do this, key concepts are discovered, and themes are determined, under which these concepts are collected inductively. The coding process is performed based on the concepts extracted from the data.

Then, the two destinations, the official sites, and the sites to which they link are analyzed on the basis of the themes and concepts, discussing their weaknesses and strengths, identifying gaps, and making improvement proposals.

Chapter 12

Árpád Ferenc Papp-Váry, Budapest Metropolitan University, Hungary
Réka Kerti, Budapest Metropolitan University, Hungary

The advertising industry is an essential part of the Hungarian economy, which had an important role in rebuilding it after the COVID-19 pandemic. The industry is quick to adopt online and technological innovations. Digital media spend was the highest in 2020, and global partners such as Google and Facebook took the biggest slice. The case study introduces a recent EFFIE Hungary award-winning campaign with an unusual consumer review driving idea that relied on digital channels. The chapter fills gaps in the literature as well as provides essential information for global advertising teams.

Chapter 13

İlkay Erarslan, Beykent University, Turkey

Social advertising is an important element that influences attitudes, beliefs, and behaviors. It also aims to make an impact by drawing attention to the fundamental social problems of different countries. In international digital marketing campaigns, International Women's Day is one of the contents used in advertisements with the corporate support of brands. The present research aims to examine what expressions were used to describe the admiration for the March 8th Women's Day-themed social advertisement in the Russian advertisement of Nike and whether the advertisement was perceived as feminist in the audience's verbal expressions. Considering the resource and time constraints, a YouTube sample was included. In the study, the content analysis technique was used and the main female characters as well as the expressions expressing admiration for the advertisement were analyzed.

Chapter 14

Merve Çelik-Varol, Beykent University, Turkey
Nazlım Tüzel-Uraltaş, Marmara University, Turkey
Erdem Varol, Marmara University, Turkey

In this study, the commercial film titled Let's Turn Off the Taps of the Finish brand, which has been awarded the Silver Award in Crystal Apple in the category of Media Use–Television Section in 2020 will be analyzed. One of the advertisements of the "Tomorrow's Water" campaign, which is an awareness movement led by Finish Turkey and supported by National Geographic Turkey, Let's Turn Off the Taps draws attention to the risk of Turkey becoming water-poor soon and aims to raise awareness about this problem. In addition, Taner Ölmez, the leading actor of the The Miracle Doctor series, took part in this commercial, and the commercial was shot in Lake Kuyucuk. The commercial, which draws attention with the slogan "The end of the water is seen" broke a new ground in Turkey and brought a different dimension to the scenario integration work by bringing together the TV series The Woman and The Miracle Doctor broadcast on Fox TV.

Chapter 15

Onur Serdan Çarboğa, Istanbul Bilgi University, Turkey
Ece Nur Kaya Yıldırım, Ege University, Turkey

To comprehend how British advertising gained its unique identity, this study reviews historical events and phenomena such as imperialism and Brexit, discusses the cultural structure of British society, and considers the advertising industry's political-economic structure. It utilises a modern branch of critical discourse analysis called multimodal discourse analysis and extensively studies the HSBC TV commercial titled 'Home To So Much More', focusing on how its visuals create and represent Britishness and the British way of making advertisements.

Section 5
International Advertising in Oceania

Chapter 16

Mehmet Cihan Toker, Istanbul Esenyurt University, Turkey

Settled at the crossroads of politics and advertising, political advertising has an idiosyncratic nature that makes it both an embraced and criticized phenomenon. On the one hand, it is considered an integral part of democracies because it enables voters to make their political choices more consciously; on the other hand, it is thought that voters gradually lose their faith in the political process and in politicians, especially due to negative advertising in political campaigns. This chapter aims to explain the paradoxical character of political advertising in the context of Australia. In this route, firstly, Australia's historical development and political and socio-cultural structure are examined. Then, legislative regulation of political advertising in Australia is examined in the context of compatibility with democratic ideals. Lastly, political advertisements featured by the Australian Labor Party and Liberal Party of Australia towards the 2022 federal elections are examined through quantitative content analysis.

Foreword

I must state that my interest and excitement has increased since Ipek Krom, with whom we worked as a graduate student, shared the idea of publishing a book with a global perspective on international advertisements and intercultural advertising, which she has started working on in 2021.

Unfortunately, most people do not realize that advertising can be studied scientifically and fail to appreciate how effectively science can be used to debunk myths. Scientific methods can be used to investigate the psychology of advertising, the psychology of consumer judgement and decision making since consumers are frequently unable to explain how an ad influenced them or why made a particular vote or purchase. Fortunately, scientific methods can be used to uncover mental process of ad's influences that affect consumer with or without their knowledge. This what we find most fascinating about scientific advertising research, and this what this book is all about.

The scientific and global perspective is used throughout this book because research has shown that training in sciences (a) helps students to become critical thinkers (i.e., to not believe everything they read or hear) and improve their creative problem-solving skills, (b) helps managers to develop better decision-making skills, which are important to anyone who wants to be an effective manager in todays complex and extremely competitive market place, (c) helps researchers understand and apply the concepts of major approach to companies and marketing situations. *Handbook of Research on Global Perspectives on International Advertising* is filled with interesting examples, visuals, and practices.

This book is designed to provide the advertising professions, marketing managers, researchers and students with an understanding of the international and intercultural advertising function with the modern business environment. It discusses the principal problems faced by advertisers and advertising agencies and examines the approaches, policies, and broad procedures used by them to arrive at profitable solutions.

Many companies must focus on foreign markets to survive. Most European nations are relatively small and without foreign markets would not have the economies of a scale to compete against larger U.S. and Japanese companies. The dramatic economic, social, and political changes around the world in recent years have opened markets in Asia, Europe and China. The growing markets of the Far East, Latin America other parts of the world present tremendous opportunities to market of consumer products and services as well as business-to-business marketeers. Advertising and promotion are important parts of the marketing programs of firms competing in the global marketplace. Many companies have run into difficulties developing and implementing advertising programs for international markets. Just as with domestic marketing, companies engaging in international marketing must carefully analyze the major environmental factors of each market in which they compete, including economic, demographic, cultural, and political/legal variables. Another important aspect of the international marketing is the culture of each country.

In this connection sociological and psychological factors that play a role in purchasing decisions and behaviors, culture and subculture also affect the daily lives of individuals like an "invisible hand". In this respect, intercultural advertising and multicultural advertising studies are focused on cultural differences in parallel with the requirements of the day are new global and international advertising practices.

While international advertisements communicate with different consumers in different countries, multicultural advertisements are advertisements for consumers with different cultures within the same country. For this reason, cultural characteristics and values affect the determination of elements such as message tone, emotion and style of global advertisements and creative works.

In *Handbook of Research on Global Perspectives on International Advertising* the use of advertising, and its creative practice as a way of communication was discussed through culture theory. For this purpose, it was attempted to investigate how a culture was created through the ways advertising are used especially in visual-based mass media. It was emphasized that visuals strengthen expression and communication and also guides the perspectives of societies and people. Here, whose literature was reviewed, it was pointed out that the intercultural advertising affects the audience's mental world and is of importance in the establishment of communication, and it was focused on the role of mass media in this process.

Each chapter begins with an introduction intended to contextualize the creative projects within it. The projects are then examined individually in greater detail throughout of chapter. It also offers a global perspective to the advertising function. Recent changes in agency ownership, and in agency structures, the growing importance of multinational advertising, and the cultural and ethnic nature of the global market are all discussed through the text. It is rare that companies selling any products or services, even those sold exclusively in the USA can be successful without some intercultural perspective. Some of the major marketing disasters of recent years have been caused by an ignorance and insensitivity to the cultures and customs of other groups within our society or in other countries.

If you are considering running an International Ad campaign, this book is an excellent way to impose boundaries and formats on the Net or Television and other media, briefly, international advertising should be about creativity, open standards, and freedom of form. It will teach you 30-second commercials, planned campaigns, a studied approach to buying and selling.

Remember, in general, instead of seeing one powerful global economic and political model, we now see a shifting mosaic of concerns fighting for attention, interest, desire and action of our customer, our voter. The role of technology and social media such as YouTube and its influencers has been significant in that it has brought all these issues closer to us. Hence it has become far more difficult for the powerful to control the public, or its many online 'friends' around the world. For example, of international advertising execution area in 2019 South African Elections, Oceania 2022 Federal election period and Brexit of the United Kingdom from the European Union on 31 January 2020 and the Arab Spring show emerging technology works hand in hand with the actions of activists and protesters. Bringing all the information and images by ads right to our keyboards or touchscreens certainly helps to start shifting the thinking of the collective consciousness. At the same time, the experience and opinion of users voiced to others is a continuous background to all international advertising and promotional work. It is so powerful that it can markedly affect the position of a brand in the marketplace. In other words, advertising research is pervasive- the *brain* and the *brawn* of any advertising agency.

As you see all the cases and readings dealing with the special issues for instance "how cultural difference are used in International Advertising? What is the role of celebrity using and its effect of consumer in a different culture?". For that reason, analyses through distinct research methods are used such as an exploratory and descriptive approaches, or content analysis as well as social and psychological approaches to understand how visual and message design for market and consumers in Political Advertising, Social Advertising, and Tourism Advertising besides of International Advertising.

In short, the advertising contained in this book show that over the past fifteen years the emergent technologies have become integral to image capture, image making and image dissemination. Creative disciplines are merging and the individual has greater strength through connectivity. At the same time, it recognizes that advertising is both an art and science. The authors hope that we have offered you insights into the profession and at the same time conveyed our sense of anticipation and enthusiasm over this ever changing but never dull business.

Finally, we always welcome comments and suggestions from users of this edition, as it is through such feedback that we can continue to provide an up-to-date and useful product.

Funda Savaş Gün
Doğuş University, Turkey

Preface

International advertising can be explained as advertising across the borders of a home country. In terms of cultural as well as the social, political, economic structure of a home country; the advertisement sector is familiar with questions like how to address the target audience, what kind of messages to deliver, which creative strategies to use or how to increase the sales of the goods. However, when a foreign country is the subject of matter, all these familiar questions become unknown. So as to speak, without the necessary information about the country profile and market know-hows, multi-national companies can become back to fish out of water in foreign markets. As Hofstede states, some cultures are collective like Japanese and Chinese, whereas American culture is much more individualistic. Although the creative advertisement strategies that works in Japan like the celebrity endorsement strategy, which is often used in soft sell advertisements portray an American influence, Japanese advertisements are still very specifically of Japanese cultural origin. On the other hand, since the country is of Islamic origin, the Iranian people have three types of cultural identity including the Pre-Islamic Iranian national identity, Post-Islamic Islamic identity and the modern identity as a result of the entry of modernization to Iran. Even considering the global advertisement campaigns in Iran, the multi-national companies need to consider the geographical and cultural characteristics, gender roles, religious roles and various social rituals like the eating habits. Although Australia is an English-speaking country, knowing the advertisement regulations, knowing the ethical dimensions of advertising and the current digitalization trends following the Covid-19 pandemic in this country is an important part of entering this international market. Especially in terms of political advertising in Australia, Government campaigning as well as the truth factor used in advertising continue to be a part of debates. What is more in today's digitalization era following the information era and Covid-19 Pandemic, the styles of doing business have changed to a greater extent. The rising of multi-national companies, globalization, and free movement of goods, have raised interest in the subject matter of international advertising. International advertising is closely related with international marketing. International marketing is the marketing of goods in international markets. For reasons like profit-based interest in foreign countries in search of alternative markets, international commerce agreements that ease the circulation of goods, low demand of goods in local markets and preventing economical turbulences, the multi-national companies have been showing a growing interest in international marketing. As a result of globalization, the world has become a single global market. On the other hand, the consumers of international markets are still very different from each other. Therefore, the emerging of the global market segments, have raised questions to consider regarding the standardization and adaptation processes in international advertising. Standardization strategy focuses on transferring standardized messages through advertising. Meanwhile, adaptation strategy considers the different cultural and structural dynamics of a certain country. While multinational companies might need to use the standardization strategy in advertising to some extent, it is also important to consider each culture on its own dynamics. Underestimating the different culture and structure of a specific international market, results in the failure of multi-national companies across their borders. Although some valuable research has been done by important sociologists like Hofstede and Schwartz that portray the cultural dimensions and values of different cultures in order to examine the differences and similarities of different countries as well as researches regarding international markets, research in the field of international advertising is still limited. Consumers in different countries are very different from each other. They speak different languages, have different values, have different cultures, have different expectations and purchasing intentions. The success of an international advertising campaign, depends on research on the cultural, geo-political, socio-economical, historical structure of a certain country, an international marketing analysis as well as a thorough analysis of the international advertising practices. In order to gain brand awareness, brand trust and brand loyalty in an international market, international advertising need to be localized. Considering the globalization and glocalization processes each country experiences in our world, has motivated us to cover international advertising from a global perspective. Therefore, each chapter in this book starts with a background information about a different country including its geopolitics, socio-culture, economy and history. Next, the chapter gives information about the advertising industry in these countries. Furthermore, each chapter in this book focuses on a specific advertising research analysis on the current advertising structure of the market including case-study analyses of award-winning campaigns, provides an insight to the international advertising practices as well as advertising strategies used in different countries. The chapters in the book cover various subjects like adaptation strategy, advertising strategies, celebrity endorsement strategy uses, creative revolution in advertising, cultural codes, cultural dimensions, destination image building, digital advertising, engineering of consent and coercion, feminist advertising, film and TV advertising production, global advertising strategies, globalization and glocalization, international advertising, negative advertising, political advertising, political advertising in authoritative regimes, political persuasion, post Covid-19 Pandemic period advertisements, postmodern advertisements, post Covid-19 Pandemic influencer marketing, prime time advertisements, rhetoric, social media influencers, purchasing behavior, social advertisements, tourism advertising, as well as award-winning and cult advertisement cases in countries in five different continents across the globe including Australia, China, Croatia, Colombia, Egypt, Hungary, India, Iran, Japan, Russia, South Africa, Turkey, U.A.E., U.K., and the U.S. *Handbook of Research on Global Perspectives on International Advertising* has been written by the contributions of 26 valuable academicians and independent researchers with multi-national backgrounds. The target audience of this book is academic researchers, academicians, instructors, marketing and advertising experts as well as students. The sections of *Handbook of Research on Global Perspectives on International Advertising* are divided into five including five different continents and the chapters are listed in alphabetical order according to country name. I hope that the readers will enjoy learning about the international marketing practices from countries across five different continents: Africa, America, Asia, Europe and Oceania. In order to portray a profile of the book, let us consider the sections and the chapters listed in these sections of *Handbook of Research on Global Perspectives on International Advertising*:

In the first section of "International Advertising in Africa," the first chapter is on international advertising in Egypt. The chapter is called "Political Advertising in Egypt: Engineering of Consent and Coercion" and focuses on political advertising practices in authoritative regimes unlike most of the political advertising studies that focus on political advertising practices in democracies. The chapter analyzes political advertising works of Sisi in Egypt through using the sociological analysis method under the scope of uses and gratifications theory. The goal of the study is to explore how the ads of Sisi try to gain the gratification of electorates by benefiting from sociological and cultural issues.

The second chapter in this section is about international advertising in South Africa. The article is called "Using YouTube in Political Persuasion: 2019 South African Elections." The chapter focuses on political advertisements on YouTube. After giving a background information regarding the social structure of the country and information about the advertising sector, the article investigates how both the South African public and the political parties use YouTube for discussion, debate and opinion formation in federal elections. The article uses sociological analysis method and focuses on Aristotle's concept of rhetoric, promises of political messages and political persuasion in written form.

In the "International Advertising in America" section of the book, the third chapter on international advertising in Colombia called "Colombian Advertising Industry: The Effects of Social Context on Advertisement Outcomes" analyzes the advertising industry in Colombia starting with an overview of the country profile including internal armed conflicts and the related illegal drug production as well as the situation of the advertising industry in the post Covid-19 Pandemic period. It focuses on the advertising industry on Colombia and in the research part it focuses on the analysis of two Cannes Lions Award-Winning campaign case studies regarding the demobilization of paramilitary and guerilla combatants.

The fourth chapter called "The Effects of Different Developments in Advertising: An Overview of American Advertising" portrays an overview of the USA in terms of geography, socio-politics, culture as well as advertising industry. As the history of advertising in the USA has had a remarkable impact on the history of advertising, the chapter focuses on the development of advertising in the USA including the changing perceptions and creative revolution. Furthermore, it studies the latest technological developments in advertising. Next, it focuses on three different American advertisement case-studies that had an impact on the development of advertising in the USA from past to present and analyzes them using case-study method including cult advertisement campaigns of Volkswagen's "Think Small" and Dove's more recent "Speak Beautiful."

In the third section of the book called "International Advertising in Asia," the fifth chapter is called "Advertising in China: An Analysis of Ads During the COVID-19 Period" and focuses on the country profile, international advertising in China as well as the post Covid-19 pandemic period advertisements through a linguistic and visual analysis based on the affect dimension of Martin and White's appraisal theory. The article studies the most frequently used elements in advertisements during the Covid-19 Pandemic as well as the most frequently used expressions and visuals in these advertisements on the linguistic and visual base of appraisal theory.

The sixth chapter in this section is called "Research on Social Media Advertising in China: Advertising Perspective of Social Media Influencers" is also on international advertising in China; however, it portrays a special focus on influencer marketing and social media influencers. It discusses the social media influencer marketing sector before and after the Covid-19 Pandemic period and portrays the social media influencers' impact on consumers' purchasing behavior through conducting a survey analysis.

The seventh chapter is about international advertising in India and is called "A Study on the Prime-Time Television Advertorial in India." The article gives an overview of the country profile as well as information about advertising industry in India. The research focuses on prime-time zone advertisements of the ABP News TV channel, which broadcasts on YouTube and has the most followers. The research carries a content analysis regarding the advertising strategies used in Indian TV advertorials, the values emphasized as well as the sectors that frequently advertise to the prime-time commercials.

The eighth chapter is about international advertising in Iran and is called "Adaptation Strategy in International Brands: An Examination in Iranian Advertising." The chapter starts with a background information on Iran including the country's socio-politics, economy and culture. Next the article talks about advertising industry in Iran. The article makes use of adaptation strategy and Hofstede's Cultural Onion Model for the analysis part and aims to determine how cultural differences are portrayed through global advertising strategies and how these differences are adapted in advertisements.

The ninth chapter of International Advertising in Asia is about international advertising in Japan. In the article called "The Use of Celebrity Endorsement Strategy and American Impact in Japanese Advertising: The Case of American Celebrities," the country profile is given with a geopolitical, socio-cultural and historical perspective with a special focus on Japan's relationship with the USA. Background information is given about the advertising industry and Japanese consumers. The article focuses on celebrity endorsement strategy and its uses in Japanese soft sell advertising practices. The article analyses different Japanese advertisements in which world-famous American pop stars and Hollywood icons star and studies the American impact on Japanese advertising.

The tenth chapter in this section is called "TV Commercial Space in the UAE: A Regional Hub for Advertisement Production" and is about international advertising in UAE. The article gives a background information about the country profile as well as media and advertising industry. The chapter introduces UAE as a hotspot for film and TV production and makes it a regional hub for TV advertising production. The article moves on with a descriptive interview analysis of prominent head of the advertising and film production sector. In the analysis part the research focuses on key questions like making UAE a regional center for film, TV and social media, the impact of pandemic on the advertising and TV sector and challenges for the advertising sector like media regulations, cultural sensitivities as well as transition to digitization.

In the "International Advertising in Europe" section, the eleventh chapter is on Croatia. In this article called "Tourism Advertising and Destination Image Building Through Cultural Heritage in Croatia: A Comparative Study of Dubrovnik and Split," after giving a historical, geographical, ethnical, religious, cultural and linguistic background of the country, it is aimed to understand the historical and cultural heritage of Croatian coastal cities Dubrovnik and Split as well as how these cities promote, market and advertise their heritage through the official website of local tourism organizations. With a special focus on tourism advertising in Croatia, this article studies the role of effective advertising in destination image building for Dubrovnik and Split through conducting a content analysis on the official tourism websites of Dubrovnik and Split and the weaknesses and strengths of these websites are discussed in terms of promoting these cities.

The twelfth chapter is called "The Hungarian Advertising Market and an Award-Winning Effie Case Study as Good Practice" and is about international advertising in Hungary. The article focuses on advertising practices in Hungary and especially on digital media, which had an important impact on rebuilding the Hungarian economy in the post Covid-19 Pandemic period. Next the article introduces an Effie Hungary Award-Winning advertisement campaign and talks about the key insights, the strategy, the activation of the idea and the factors that contribute to the success of the campaign.

The thirteenth chapter in this section on international advertising in Russia is called "Research on the March 8ᵗʰ Women's Day-Themed Advertisement in Russia." The article gives background information about the economy-politics of the country, the advertising industry as well as women's rights in Russia. Next the article focuses on a Women's Day themed social advertisement of Nike and analyses whether the advertisement was perceived as feminist through carrying a content analysis and analyzing the verbal expressions as well as main female characters and expressions used.

The fourteenth chapter in the international advertising in Europe section is called "A Scenario Integration Study in Brand Communication: 'Let's Turn off the Taps Advertising Case'." The article is about international advertising practices in Turkey and starts with an overview of the county profile as well as brief information about advertising history and advertising industry. Next the article focuses on a postmodern social advertisement of the international Finish brand, which is a Silver Crystal Award winning advertisement and analyzes it through content analysis method. The advertisement was shot in Lake Kuyucuk and it draws attention with the slogan "The End of the Water is Seen," that broke a new ground in Turkey by bringing a new scope on social advertisements.

The fifteenth chapter in the International Advertising in Europe section is called "From an Empire to Brexit: Globalization and Glocalization in British Advertising" and is on international advertising in the UK. The article discusses the country profile of UK and focuses on the unique identity of British advertising through studying the history and development of advertising in UK. In the research the advertisement campaign called 'Home To So Much More' with close affinity to the Brexit phenomenon is analyzed using a multimodal discourse analysis and the British cultural codes and whether the advertisement typify British advertising is studied.

The last section of *Handbook of Research on Global Perspectives on International Advertising* focuses on "International Advertising in Oceania." The sixteenth chapter called "Political Advertising in Australia: Marketing of 'Who/What to Vote For'" is about political advertising practices in Australia with a special focus on the impacts of negative advertising. After giving a brief country profile and information on political structure along with media and advertising industry and the political advertising regulations, the article considers the nature of political advertising in Australia towards 2022 Federal elections. In the research part the article focuses on the nature of Australian political advertisements using content analysis method and explores the common features, distinctive differences, subjects emphasized and strategies used in these advertisements.

The chapters of *Handbook of Research on Global Perspectives on International Advertising* cover international advertising practices from a research analysis-based perspective with a special focus on international advertising know-hows in international markets. When firms enter a foreign market, with the intention of international marketing as well as international advertising, they need to consider this market from multidimensional perspectives including the different geopolitics, socio-culture, economics, ethnicity, language, history, advertising industry and international marketing dynamics. Although there are researches in international advertising in the social sciences literature; not many of them cover international advertising on country/region base thoroughly. I expect that *Handbook of Research on Global Perspectives on International Advertising* will address the need in academic literature regarding international advertising in terms of following current trends in the post digitalization, globalization, glocalization and post Covid-19 Pandemic period in international markets, providing a know-how to international advertising to multi-national corporations, as well as researchers and academicians. I hope that this first edition of the book becomes a local guide and insight into international advertising practices in different cultures across the globe.

Ipek Krom
Istanbul Esenyurt University, Turkey

Section 1
International Advertising in Africa

Chapter 1
Political Advertising in Egypt:
Engineering of Consent and Coercion

Nurdan Güven Toker
https://orcid.org/0000-0002-4868-0717
Haliç University, Turkey

ABSTRACT

This study takes Egypt as a case to understand the dynamics of political advertising in competitive authoritarian regimes. The sample universe of the study was formed from the political advertisements published in the last two years on the official Facebook accounts of President Abdel Fattah Saeed Hussein Khalil el-Sisi and the Nation's Future Party he supports. Advertisements were examined in the axis of 12 criteria determined in the axis of sociological analysis methodology. During the examination process, critical theory, which examines the dynamics of authoritarian systems, was also utilized. In the study, it is argued that political advertisements in Egypt are designed in a way that can establish both consent and coercion.

INTRODUCTION

Academic studies on political advertising mainly focus on countries with a democratic regime. The emergence of such a tendency among researchers can be linked to an assumption that only democratic regimes provide a fertile ground for the professional development of political advertising since democracy is based on free competition which is the equivalence of the commercial market. The role of political advertising in authoritarian regimes, on the other hand, is considered within the perspective of propaganda and examined mostly by researchers in the field of political communication. The apathy of researchers can be tied to the fact that the leaders or parties in authoritarian regimes do not feel a strong necessity to convince people and change their preferences. Thus, they do not have much interest in applying marketing and advertising techniques in their political campaigns. Sure, this is a questionable argument but there is a more important point that should be noticed. Traditional authoritarianism has been replaced by a new type of authoritarianism since the end of the Cold War and the collapse of the Soviets. This new system, named competitive authoritarianism or electoral authoritarianism, is a hybrid regime between

DOI: 10.4018/978-1-7998-9672-2.ch001

democracy and authoritarianism. Formal democratic institutions exist and are considered the single legitimate means of gaining power. However, the incumbents appeal to undemocratic measures like abusing the state resources to get an advantage vis-a-vis their opponents (Levitsky & Way, 2010, p. 5).

The enormous transformation in communication technology, especially the development of digital media medium, increased the awareness of citizens toward democratic principles, so the weight of democracy has increased in this mixture. While continuing to use coercive means, authoritarian leaders and parties now have to respect the competitive nature of the system and be more willing to win voters' consent. As a natural outcome of this transformation, professional and scientific marketing and advertising techniques have gained importance in the political field.

Egypt is an important case exemplifying the situation depicted. The country is governed by a semi-presidential system established following the resignation of President Hosni Mubarak in the Egyptian Revolution of 2011. The power period of Abdel Fattah Saeed Hussein Khalil el-Sisi, the current president of the country, can be described as competitive authoritarianism. Compatible with the regime type, the number of studies on political advertising in Egypt is quite limited. Of course, the fact that the characteristics of the country's past regimes are closer to authoritarianism also plays a role in this. When looked at the literature, it is seen that the researchers are interested most in the role of media in political process. They tried to shed light on the ambitions of the incumbents of controlling the press and lack the key elements of a democratic regulatory system to ensure and protect the independence, transparency, and accountability of the media (Elmeshad, 2021; Rozgonyi, 2014; Mendel, 2011; Sakr, 2012; Khodair, AboElsoud, & Khalifa, 2019). As a study conducted on political advertising specifically, it is possible to mention only the study by Gaweesh (2015, p. 17) in which television advertisements broadcasted during the parliamentary elections in 2012 were examined. Gaweesh's findings reveal that the political campaigns of Egyptian politicians' appeal to emotions as much as, sometimes even more than rationality. Most preferred emotional appeals are nationalism, identity, religion, nostalgia, enthusiasm, and revolution. These findings will be compared with the findings of this study.

In this study, the political advertisements used by Sisi and Nation's Future Party (NFP), also known as Mustaqbal Watan Party, will be analyzed. The methodology of research is determined as the sociological analysis based on the "uses and gratifications" theory formulated by Berger (1991). Besides, in order to understand the essence of the relationship between competitive authoritarianism and political advertising, works of intellectuals belonging to critical theory current one of whom the main concern is authoritarian regimes, are utilized in the analyzing phase. The goal of the study is to explore how advertisements try to gain the gratification of electorates by benefiting from sociological and cultural issues.

COUNTRY PROFILE

Politics is a social fact that is derived from the relationship among humans, and, therefore, almost everything related to politics contains a social aspect. Besides, it is strongly bounded with the history, culture, political and socio-economical structure of the country. Therefore, an analysis of political advertisements cannot be held in a healthy way without considering the cultural, political, and socio-economic structures of the country. In this context, a background will be tried to be presented in the first part of the study.

Brief History

Egypt is one of the earliest civilizations of human history and, with no doubt, it owes its fame in part to its historic influence over other civilizations including ancient Hebrews, Mesopotamians, Syrians, classical Greece, and Rome. It has at least 5,000 years of recorded history, and many Egyptians claim for it even more.

The civilization was politically united under the rule of the first pharaoh in 3150 BC. This political unity lasted for the next 3,000 years. The country was captured by Alexander the Great in 332 BC, then became a province of the Roman Empire in 30 BC. After the division of the Roman Empire, stayed in the side of the Eastern Roman Empire until the Sassanian invasion in 618. This period lasted short because it was recaptured by Byzantine Empire ten years later (Grimal, 1994). The destiny of the country changed by the conquest of Arab armies under the leadership of Umar, the second caliph, in 639. This new era can be marked by the Arabization and Islamization that was to take several centuries (Marsot, 2007).

Egypt came under the rule of the Ottoman Empire in 1517. In 1798, Napoleon Bonaparte tried to occupy the country. Although he managed to defeat the Egyptians on land, he was obliged to leave the country after the defeat received in the face of the British Navy. Mehmet Ali Pasha, who was appointed as the governor at the beginning of the 19th century, carried out a modernization program that the Ottoman sultans would take as an example. After the struggle with the Ottoman Sultan, Egypt gained autonomy during his reign (İslami, 2016, pp. 189-193). In 1882, Britain occupied Egypt and brought a forceful conclusion to almost a century of Great Power rivalry. While Egypt remained a province of the Ottoman Empire, and the dynasty founded by Mehmed Ali continued the throne, the country came under the auspices of Britain (Daly, 1998, p. 239). In 1922, Britain granted Egypt formal independence and sanctioned the promulgation of a democratic constitution within a year. With Egyptians assuming increasing control over their state, the age of liberal politics, spanned between 1923 and 1952, began (Botman, 1998, pp. 285-286).

This period featured a political system characterized by western-style constitutionalism and parliamentary government. However, the period between 1923 and 1952 can be marked by political instability due to the competition between the monarchy and elected political actors, especially the Wafd Party (Botman, 1998, pp. 307-308). A new period began for the country with the Egyptian Revolution of 1953. In the revolution, King Farouk was toppled by a coup d'etat initiated by the Free Officers Movement and the constitutional monarchy was abolished. In 1956, President Nasser announced a new Constitution which introduced a presidential system of government. All presidents until 1981 came from the Free Officers Movement and they governed the country with authoritarian policies. Secularism and nationalism can be defined as the backbone of their ruling period. The Muslim Brotherhood movement was banned and reactionary movements were suppressed with rigid measures. The Suez Canal was nationalized and Egypt became the standard-bearer of Arab Nationalism, especially during the reign of Gamal Abdel Nasser. As a reflection of this policy, the United Arab Republic was established with Syria in 1958. Although Syria withdrew from the union after a military coup in 1961, Egypt continued to use the name United Arab State until 1971. Another important issue that should be mentioned is the historical rivalry between Israel and Egypt. There were four wars between the two countries in 1948, 1956, 1967 and in 1973 (Marsot, 2007).

After the assassination of Enver Sadat on October 6, 1981, another soldier, Husni Mubarak, became the head of state and was elected four times in a row in the elections held in 1987, 1993, 1999 and 2005, in which the participation of the opposition was restricted. His period of power can also be classified as authoritarianism. After the Arab world protests that started in Tunisia in 2011 started in Egypt on January 25, 2011, he resigned on February 11, 2011, by handing over his duty to the army and the constitutional court.

The mass uprising of 2011 is one of the critical turning points in the history of modern Egypt and understanding the dynamics of the revolution and aftermath is very crucial for the evaluation of today's Egypt. Firstly, it should be indicated the revolts were, in a sense, the volcanic eruption of political and social gradually accumulating discontent stemming from the authoritarian rule of Hosni Mubarak lasting thirty years, social end economical inequalities, corruption, and clientelism (El-Mahdi & Marfleet, 2009; Bakr, 2012). The uprising in Tunisia was just the earthquake that triggered this explosion. Another important point that should be underlined is the transformative effect of the media. The spread of mass media and the increase in the number of news agencies and international news channels that deliver news from all over the world caused the political and social expectations of the masses to change. Especially the role played by the Al Jazeera, which broadcasts in Arabic and English, in the change of political culture in the Middle East and North Africa has attracted the attention of many researchers (Sultan, 2013; Abdelmoula, 2015). On the other hand, the biggest piece can be given to the digital media medium, especially the social media platforms such that some observers tend to identify the Arap Spring as the Facebook revolution or Twitter uprising (El-Nawawy & Khamis, 2020; Eltantawy & Wiest, 2011). Thanks to this new virtual activism, political discontent was fertilized and turned into an organized movement.

Foreshocks of the revolution had begun to be seen in the early 2000s. The protest cycles can be traced to the creation of the Egyptian Movement for Change called Kefaya (Enough) which lasted between 2004-2006. Another protest wave occurred almost simultaneously, but it was much more social and effective. People coming from different sectors of Egyptian society, such as workers, teachers and civil servants, were expressing demands of an economic and financial nature. The mobilization of labor increased dramatically until the 2011 revolution (Abdalla, 2012, p. 86). The slogan (Bread, Freedom and Human Dignity) of the 25 January uprising reveals the connection with the early protest cycle. Protesters called for Mubarak to step down immediately and for free elections to be held for a democratic regime. As stated above, Mubarak could not resist the protests and handed over the duty to the Supreme Council of the Armed Forces. Before going to the elections, a temporal constitution that introduced some democratization measures such as judicial supervision of elections, limitations on the presidency, and easier conditions for nomination in presidential elections was presented to the referendum and approximately 77% of the voters were in favor of the constitution.

The parliamentary elections were held in the most liberal atmosphere in Egyptian political history in 2012. The victory of the Muslim Brotherhood (MB) in the elections was surprising to some observers, but, on the other hand, it was the result of a long-term political struggle. MB was founded by Hasan al-Banna in 1928 and became one of the largest and most influential organizations of Islamic revivalism current. Although the movement spread to other Muslim countries, the largest organization has been in Egypt and has left remarkable marks on the political history of the country. Putting a parenthesis here and having a glance at these traces will be very beneficial in terms of understanding the transformation in the political landscape of the country.

The grand ideal of the organization is the establishment of an Islamic state ruled by Sharia. However, as many researchers stressed, MB is a modernist movement and should be treated differently from Salafi movements in many aspects (Lynch, 2010; Wictorowicz, 2006). For instance, contrary to Salafi's purification of Islamic understanding, MB has shown a more inclusive approach by which the Islamic principles can be reconciled with the needs of the time. As a natural outcome of this comprehension of religion, democratic participation is seen as a legitimate way of political struggle. However, this does not mean that the MB never resorted to violent activities. The movement was associated with numerous bombings and assassinations in the past. The movement, which was banned by the state and tried to be suppressed with severe measures, made various attempts since the 1980s to turn into a political movement and to be active in the political arena, so it allied with the Wafd Party in 1984, and the Labor and Liberal Party in 1997. The democratic participation strategy, which accelerated with the 17 seats won in the 2000 elections, reached its peak five years later with the gain of 20% of the seats in the parliament. Participating in the elections with independent candidates due to bans, MB had become Egypt's largest opposition group. In order to prevent the development of the movement in the next elections, Hosni Mubarak again resorted to severe measures and hundreds of MB members were arrested. The failure of the MB candidates to win even a single seat in the first round of the 2010 election brought along widespread allegations of irregularities. The organization, together with other opposition parties, decided to boycott the second round of the elections. The pressures against the opposition resulted in people taking to the streets on 25 January.

MB participated in the parliamentary elections in 2011 and 2012 as the Freedom and Justice Party and the Democratic Alliance front led by this party won approximately half of the seats. However, in the process that began with the ousting of Mubarak, a number of Salafi political parties were also formed and they established the Islamist Alliance led by Al-Nour Party. They won about 25% of the seats in the election and became the second-largest group in the Parliament (Ranko & Nedza, 2015). According to this composition of the parliament, Islamist forces had taken over 70 percent of the parliament and had the majority of the 100-member constituent assembly, which was tasked with preparing the new constitution. This view of the new political landscape disquieted especially the liberal and secular circles. Despite their previous commitments, the MB's nomination of Mohamed Morsi in the presidential elections in 2012, reinforced the concerns that the movement would become too strong.

The concerns gradually turned into protests against MB and Morsi was elected as the president by getting 51.73% of the votes in the second tour. Despite the boycott by secular, liberals, and Coptic Christians, the ratification of the constitution by the constituent assembly increased tensions. These groups felt that the constitution did not sufficiently guarantee freedom of expression and religion. By the increase of turmoil in the country and the number of people lost their lives in the conflicts, the army warned Morsi on 1st of July and announced that if he did not accept the people's demands within 48 hours, it would intervene and prepare "its own road map". This road map was put into force two days later with a coup d'état. The country was divided into two. Supporters of Morsi gathered in Nahda Square and protested the coup for more than one month, but the demonstrations were suppressed by severe measures of security forces on 14th of August. Members of MB, which was first banned and then declared a terrorist organization by many neighboring countries as well, had to flee to countries such as Qatar.

The current president of the country, Abdel Fattah Saeed Hussein Khalil el-Sisi, got the presidency after the 2013 coup d'état. He was the chief of the Egyptian Armed Forces and was involved in the coup. On March 26, 2014, in response to calls from supporters to run for the presidency, Sisi retired from his military career and announced that he would run as a candidate in the 2014 presidential election. The election, held between 26 to 28 May, featured one opponent, Hamdeen Sabahi, saw 47% participation by eligible voters, and resulted in Sisi winning in a landslide victory with 97% of the vote.

Geography, Ethnic and Religious Composition, Culture and Language

The historical and civilizational importance of the country is strongly related to its geographical position. Settled in the northeast corner of Africa, it occupies the land between the Red Sea and the Mediterranean Sea. Therefore, it can be said that it is located in the middle of commercial and migration routes. With the opening of the Suez Channel, which connects the Mediterranean Sea and the Red Sea, in 1869 strategic importance of the country increased significantly.

Egypt is 636 miles long (1,024 km) from north to south and 770 miles wide (1,240 km) from east to west. With an area of 387,050 sq miles (1,002,450 km$^{2)}$ it takes up a 30th of Africa's total land and is the 29th largest country in the world. The fate of the country also depends on the Nile River, which brings life with it as it crosses the whole country from south to north. Without the river, almost all the land would be desert, and only a few people would live there (Goldschmidt Jr., 2008).

Thanks to the Nile, Egypt is a vibrant country with more than 90 million inhabitants. With this population rate measured with 2017 census, it is the second most populous country in the Middle East and the second-most populous on the African continent (Population, 2022). Ethnically, Egypt is a homogeneous country. Many Egyptians are descended from the Arab settlers who came to the region after the Muslim conquest in the 7th century. While many Egyptians refer to the majority ethnic identity as "Arab", many others prefer the term "Egyptian". Ethnic minorities include the Berber-speaking community of the Siwa Oasis, the Bedouin Arab tribes of the Sinai Peninsula and the eastern desert, and the Nubian people clustered along the Nile in the southernmost part of Egypt. There are also sizable minorities of Beja and Dom. Religious minorities include Shi'a, Jews, Sufi Muslims, Jehova's Witnesses, Ahmadis and Quranists. Besides, the country hosts around 90,000 refugees and asylum seekers, mostly Palestinians and Sudanese (Egypt, 2022).

For millennia, Egypt has been home to different cultures. After the Pharaonic era, it came under the influence of Hellenism and Christianity. After the conquest of Arab armies under the leadership of Umar, the Arabization and Islamization period began that was to take several centuries. Today, many aspects of Egypt's ancient culture exist in interaction with newer elements, including the influence of modern Western culture, itself with roots in Ancient Egypt. With its ancient history, cosmopolitanism, strong Islamic traditions, modern pan-Arab political and intellectual history, and relative freedom, Egypt is the cultural capital of the Arab world (Overview of Culture & Arts, 2022).

Islam is one of the prominent cultural components of Egypt. According to article two of the 2014 constitution, Islam is the religion of the state and Arabic is its official language. Besides, the principles of Islamic Sharia are the principal source of legislation (Constitution of the Arab Republic of Egypt, 2014). Therefore, some advertising campaigns can be banned according to the Egyptian Standard Specifications of Advertising Requirements (Eyada, 2018), however, it is possible to speak of a transformation. For instance, gender representation has shown significant change in the stereotype of women particularly in digital advertising. Contemporary advertising in Egypt represents women as strong partner in almost every field of life. Also, women are represented in untraditional contexts like sports venues and work environments rather than domestic traditional contexts. Same contexts are used for women and men that reflect equal gender ranking representation (Abboud, 2020, p. 608).

Political and Economic Structure

In constitutional terms, Egypt is a republic and governed by a semi-presidential system. The executive authority is shared between the president and the government, but the large rights given to the president like dissolving the parliament turn the system into a semi-presidential system from the parliamentarian system. Legislative power is carried out by the bicameral parliament.

Elections are the core component of the system and are held under the audit of National Elections Commission. Presidential elections are held every six years with a two-round system and the next election should be held in 2024. Parliamentarian elections are held every five years with a direct and secret voting system. Women are allocated at least one-fourth of the total number of seats (Constitution of the Arab Republic of Egypt, 2014).

Currently, there are over 100 registered political parties in Egypt, yet, the number of the parties which managed to get at least one seat in the parliament is only fifteen. The most effective one of these parties, also supported by the President, is the Nation's Future Party has 149 seats in the Senate and 316 seats in the House of Representatives. It is not possible to say that any party can have an effective role in the system, including the Republicans People's Party, New Waft Party, and Homeland Defers Party, having the highest number of seats after the NFT.

The current president of the country, Abdel Fattah Saeed Hussein Khalil el-Sisi, got the presidency after the 2013 Egyptian coup d'état. Sisi administration can be defined as an example of the competitive authoritarian regime. Although elections seem to be held regularly, the Sisi administration effectively uses state power to suppress its opponents. For instance, many political figures involved in a new coalition to run in 2020, including Zyad Elelaimy, Hisham Fouad, Omar El-Shenety and Hossam Moanis, were arrested on June 25, 2019, on charges of "bringing down the state" (Masr, 2019). Similarly, public funds are used for strengthening the image of Sisi. For instance, as will be mentioned in the further parts, public funds were spent for a documentary video in which president Sisi was portrayed as a savior and this video was released from the official Facebook account of the president. In the end, despite the competitive nature of the system, president Sisi and the NFP dominate the political system by controlling both the execution and legislation.

When we look at the economic structure, we see that Egypt has a developing economy. According to the data of the World Bank, the per capita income of the country is around 3500 $ (GDP per capita (current US$) - Egypt, Arab Rep., 2022). Besides, it is the 31st largest economy in the world with 365.2 billion dollars GDP (GDP (current US$), 2022). In the International Monetary Fund's global economic report, the Egyptian economy is expected to achieve a rising growth momentum until 2027. However, inflation is expected to rise from 6.4% in 2021 to 7.4% in 2025 with the increase in domestic market demand. The economic contraction during the Covid-19 Pandemic period caused the unemployment rate to rise to 9.7% (World economic outlook, 2022).

Advertising Industry and Media

Advertising was not an unknown occupation in the mid 19th century in Egypt. However, the advent of advertising in the press after 1882 (especially during the 1890s), brought commerce into the public sphere in an entirely new way and print journalism grew radically that coinciding with an impressive economic boom as Egypt became integrated into the global market of capitalism (Shechter, 2003, p. 44).

Newspaper and magazine advertisements have been important marketing tools in Egypt until recent years. Although total newspaper circulation is relatively small, the print media manage to get a great share of high-value advertisers because of the concentration trend of press readership among the high class (The Report: Egypt 2013, 2014, p. 277). However, the market share of television advertising has risen radically since 2010, well above press advertising (Statista, 2022). The increase in the number of private TV channels since 2010 has an important role in this rise. The country has three national and more than 20 private TV channels today. Besides, Egyptians can watch also more than six hundred satellite channels including European, North American, and Turkish. Diversity in the media environment has also contributed to the formation of a more competitive market by affecting consumer expectations. As a natural consequence of this situation, there are many professional advertising and marketing companies operating in the national and international fields in Egypt; Switch Communication, AZ-Studios, Local SEO Search, Yellow Media, FP7 Cairo, Big Move Agency, and New Step Media are some of the leading ones to be mentioned.

Internet and social media seem to be the next favorite advertising landscape. The number of internet users increased around 22% between 2019 and 2020 and reached 42 million. The number of active Facebook accounts has reached more than 38 million users and Instagram accounts have reached more than 11 million users in 2020 (Kemp, 2020) and we can state that the Covid-19 Pandemic period has a significant impact on this rise. There have been significant changes in the consumption and trade habits of people who had to be confined to their homes. Examining the role of social media platforms in commercial life in Egypt, Eldin at all (2021) showed that social media provides micro, small, and medium enterprises with massive opportunities such as becoming more present to the customers or achieving multiple forms of growth in the most efficient way.

As seen in Arap Spring periods, digitalization provides an important transformation not only in the commercial field but also in the political field (Karagiannopoulos, 2012). It is possible to see that the internet and social media have become the main tools used in political communication; the strict measures applied on the media and press can be considered as the main reason for this situation. Thanks to the press law and penal code, the government and presidency are equipped with strong tools to control the media (Rozgonyi, 2014; Mendel, 2011). Egypt ranks 168th in the freedom of expression index of the Reporters Without Borders (Freedom of expression index, 2022). This appearance of the media can be considered an indicator of the competitive authoritarian regime.

POLITICAL ADVERTISING IN EGYPT

Methodology

Politics is a social fact that is derived from the relationship among humans, and, therefore, almost everything related to politics contains a social aspect. Since politics by its nature is a social phenomenon, the products or offerings of political marketing should be compatible with people's perception of social things. Various research on consumer attitudes concerning politics stresses the specificity of human reactions to political objects as opposed to consumer goods (Cwalina & Newman, 2015, pp. 8-9). Thus, the social structures should be taken into consideration in the analysis of political advertising as well. In that regard, the methodology employed in the research is determined as the sociological analysis based on the "uses and gratifications" theory.

The sociological analysis focus on components of social life like culture and gender relations. Yet, it is possible to speak of a diversity in the employment of sociological analysis. Researchers can apply to different theories or theorists such as Marx, Weber, Giddens, Durkheim, interactionism, structuralism, or functionalism while employing sociological analysis. In addition, there is no specified criteria that should be followed when employing any of these methodological paths. To come over this diversity, John Scott (2011, p. 2) offers eight key principles to be followed in sociological analysis that can be applied to all disciplines in social sciences such as culture, nature, system, space-time, structure, action, mind, and development. Berger (1991) also provides some criteria similar to Scott's when formulating the sociological method for media analysis. Besides, he combines sociological analysis with the "uses and gratifications" theory in order to acquire findings related to advertising techniques like consumer attitude, perception of the product and etc. When we look at the studies, it is seen that the sociological analysis method offered by Berger is particularly efficient in terms of the analysis of commercial advertisements (Krom, 2020). Yet, as stated above, the dynamics of political marketing are different in some senses which leads us to consider another mythological construction. In this study, while applying Berger's sociological analysis technique, at the same time, critical theory, which makes the dynamics of authoritarian systems one of the main topics of discussion, is utilized. The intellectuals of the critical current (such as Theodor W. Adorno, Herbert Marcuse, Franz Leopold Neumann, Willhelm Reich, Leo Löwenthal, and Erich Fromm) move from conceptualizations of Karl Marx's alienation and Georg Lukács' reification (Fuchs, 2018, p. 4). Then, they shed light on the instrumentalization of sociological issues for the interest of the ruling elites.

The sample universe of the study consists of 55 video advertisements released on the official Facebook accounts of President Sisi Abdel Fattah Al-Sisi (The official page of President / Abdel Fattah Al-Sisi, 2022) and NFP (Mostaqbal Watan Party-the official page, 2022). In determining the sample population, the videos published in the last two years were taken into account, since the previous parliamentarian election was held in 2020. The transcription of the videos' content was held through Sonix, a commercial software, and they were translated into English with the help of a student of whom Arabic is the native language.

The main argument of the study is based on a proposition about the nature of the competitive authoritarian regime. Since the one dimension of the competitive authoritarian regime is acquiring power through elections, gaining the consent of the people is crucial for political agents. On the other hand, authoritarian policies may cause discontentment among people and this fact leads authoritarian leaders to convince people in the way that voting for them is an obligation. Moving from this proposition, this study argues that political advertising in such regimes functions for creating both consent and coercion at the same time.

This proposition brings along another question. If coercion is one of the components of political advertising in the competitive authoritarian regime, why are people influenced by these advertisements? As a matter of fact, we can say that this question is one of the fundamental issues of uses and gratifications theory. Berger (1991) enumerated some answers that help us to understand the psychological patterns behind this relationship such as "affirming moral, spiritual and cultural values". Since the policies of politicians directly affect people's lives, being informed about these policies can be accepted as a central motivation that leads people to be interested in political advertisements. However, some other answers should be found to understand the psychological patterns that provide gratification from advertisings of a political actor whose policies are not compatible with our worldview.

To examine the validity of the argument stated above and to seek the psychological motivations that provide gratification, four research questions are determined. The research questions are as follows:

RQ 1: What are the common features of political ads released by Sisi and NFP?
RQ 2: Which social components come to the fore in the advertisements?
RQ 3: How are the social issues treated to achieve the consent of the people?
RQ 4: How do the advertisements create a coercive effect on people to vote for the authoritarian leader?

ANALYSIS AND FINDINGS

In the analyzing phase, twelve criteria were determined according to the sociological analysis formulation of Berger. These criteria are alienation, anomie, minorities, class (socio-economic), leadership, gender, culture, lifestyle, race, role, stereotype, and political messages. Advertisements will be analyzed under these headlines from the perspective of critical theory.

Alienation

Alienation is one of the key concepts to understanding the arithmetic of advertising in competitive authoritarian regimes. It means, literally, no ties and refers to a feeling of estrangement and separation from others (Berger, 1991, p. 79). There are different interpretations of the causes and social reflections of this state of consciousness. From Marxist interpretation, it refers to separation from one's genuine or essential nature and causes from capitalist production relations. According to Marx, workers' experience of alienation begins with alienation from the product of their labor and continues with alienation from the process of labor, then from fellow workers. In the end, they alienate themselves and become a mere commodity (Marx & Engels, 1970). Adorno and Horkheimer, two important critical theorists, took this interpretation of Marx on a more general basis. They argued that popular culture is turned into a factory producing standardized cultural goods that are used to manipulate mass society into passivity. Thanks to the development of mass communication media, consumption of the pleasures of popular culture becomes a daily routine that makes people submissive, no matter how difficult their economic circumstances. In their interpretation, this is also a process of alienation of people from themselves (Adorno & Horkheimer, 2014).

Political actors' efforts of alienating people to themselves -in other sense to their real needs- by manipulating the social and cultural values and disseminating by media and other ideological apparatus have become one of the prominent concerns of critical theorists. They draw attention, especially, to the fact that authoritarian and populist leaders try to strengthen their own positions by alienating people from values such as freedom of expression and judicial review by using values. Bertell Ollman (2011, p. 333) argues that the values created on the axis of patriotism and become a daily routine through political activities such as carrying a hat and waving the flag, cause individuals to become estranged from their human nature and become patriotic comrades who are expected to renounce their basic rights such as life.

The analysis of the political advertising of Sisi and NFP reveals that the most applied tools used in that sense are nationalism and patriotism. His campaign slogan is "long live Egypt" and is seen with the image of Sisi in almost every advertising video. Another strategy employed is the use of the Egyptian flag as much as possible. The video titled "Part of the reception of President Abdel Fattah El-Sisi upon his arrival to the homeland after his participation in the activities of the United Nations General Assembly" is an interesting example illustrating this advertising strategy. Although the content of the video has no nationalist message and sense, it begins with a waving Egyptian flag, then shows the dialog of the president with people. The use of nationalism and patriotism is a very fertile advertising strategy that provides consent and coercion simultaneously. The electorate (political consumer) who prefer purchasing the product presented by political actors will feel comfortable themselves though this exchange produces uncomfortable results. On the other hand, those who are reluctant to purchase the same product may feel uncomfortable themselves because their preference can be interpreted as betrayal and, this produces coercion over them.

Another advertising model that should be mentioned from the perspective of alienation is the showing of the material aid campaigns. Numerous advertisements are released showing the distribution of aid packages, prepared on behalf of Sisi, to low-income people. Another example of this kind of advertising is the video of the car granting campaign to needy people. Needless to say, all the videos begin with the image of president Sisi on the right and the party emblem that includes the Egyptian flag on the left. Also, we meet with these images in every second of the video and the aid packages, trucks, and scenes are all covered by the pictures of the president and the Egyptian flag. People are seen in their happiest moments and they express their thanks to the president. The masterpiece of this strategy is the advertising titled "The Future of the Nation Party presents the president's gift to the Egyptians by distributing 5,000 electrical appliances to families in need". In the video, the aid distribution scenes are combined with the conflict scenes of troubled years and scenes showing the Sisi period's giant investments.

This advertising strategy contributes to the alienation of electorates from basic individual rights. It instills the idea that whatever the others say about my political path (referring to claims about the authoritarian character of the regime and arguments that this kind of such regimes brings unhappiness and they are doomed to fail.), I will bring happiness to every home because I act with patriotic motivations. This advertising strategy provides both consent and coercion because it gives the message that if you do not vote for the Sisi and NFP you will be deprived of these kinds of gifts.

Anomie

The word anomie, first used by the French sociologist Emile Durkheim, is of Greek origin. It means invalidation of laws, instability resulting from a breakdown of standards, and chaos. In Durkheimian sociology, the term is used to explain the state of society in which common values and common meanings are no longer valid, and new values and meanings have not developed. This state of society causes negative emotions like lack of purpose and despair.

The state of anomie is also a source of anxiety for people -especially those who have authoritarian personality traits that Adorno et al (1950) describe- and authoritarian leaders utilize this emotion in their political campaigns very effectively. They present authority as the prescription of the anomie and make people remember the chaotic days of the past frequently to sustain people's consent (Heywood, 2017, p. 114). Actually, this strategy also has a twofold effect that provides consent and coercion simultaneously, because not consenting to the authority of the leader means preferring chaos.

The documentary video, named "A homeland's tale", can be considered one of the masterpieces of this strategy. In the video, Sisi is portrayed as a savior from the chaos that the country dragged into after the Egyptian revolution in 2011. The period after the revolution is picturized with the rise of religious reactionism, armed turmoil in the streets, bombings, ruins, collapse of the health system, electric cut-outs, and political deadlock. The power period of Sisi, on the other hand, is described as the order, stability, and economic flourish with the scenes of new buildings, road constructions, and industrial production. This positive image of Sisi's leadership continues to be strengthened by other videos introducing development projects.

Minorities

Egypt presents an ethnically homogeneous structure. In the context of minorities, Christian and Jewish minorities come to the fore more. As stated above, Islam is the official religion, and Sharia is considered the frame for law. However, Christian and Jewish minorities were granted some autonomy in some communal and private issues such as regulating their personal status, religious affairs, and selection of spiritual leaders (Constitution of the Arab Republic of Egypt, 2014). The granting of relative autonomy to the Christian and Jewish communities can be evaluated in terms of preserving the image of ancient Egypt. In terms of political communication, minorities are also used as an image of tolerance. We see that Sisi also benefited from this communication technique in the video showing the speech he gave at the Christmas Mass held at the "Nativity of Christ" cathedral.

Class (socio-economic)

The studies on the political economy of competitive authoritarian systems have not reached a consensus in terms of the class politics of the incumbent leaders and their parties. The analysis of the political advertising of Sisi and NFP reveals that the lower class is prioritized. Although, Sisi tries to touch every segment of the society in his campaign, the lower class -in the economic sense- seems to be the backbone of the target electorate. The large number of ads related to aid campaigns can be considered an illustration of this fact. On the other hand, the advertising of big infrastructure investments aims to give positive messages to the middle and upper class.

Leadership

The most distinctive feature of the examined political advertisements is that they all contribute to building the image of a strong and capable leader. The leader-centered campaign is a common strategy used in established democracies as well. However, the comprehension of the strong leader image seems different in the Egyptian case. Sisi is portrayed not only as a strong leader but also as a savior. This image instills the idea that the country will drag into the troubled years back in the absence of Sisi. Sure, this belief provides also a strong legitimizing ground for Sisi's all kinds of policies including suppressive measures applied against dissidents and his political rivals.

Four different strategies are determined in the construction of the leader image. The first strategy is to make people remember the troubled years and the second, advertising giant investment projects. Third, introducing the services provided by government facilities, such as the Covid-19 vaccine, as a gift from the president to his people. A video related to vaccination is titled as a gift from the president. Fourth, he is presented as a leader who changes people's lives with a single touch. For example, an advertisement describes how he changed the lives of a low-income family he came across on the street by donating a car.

Gender

Since Sisi came to power after a military coup against the rule of the Muslim brothers, he had to maintain a relatively secular stance. However, Islam is one of the strongest components of the cultural structure of the Egyptian people. Looking at the gender relations in advertisements, it is seen that a balance is sought in this axis. Although women and men appear together in advertisements, the relationship between them is as much as cultural dynamics allow. When we look at the advertisements about the aid given to low-income families, it is seen that women are mostly used. Thus, it is ensured that the emotional reaction desired to be obtained with advertising is increased.

Culture

Cultural symbols like pyramids, deserts, and traditional wearing are used in the advertisements to give the message that the Sisi is a man of Egyptian culture who respects to values of the people. This image serves also for strengthening his nationalist and patriotic image. From the perspective of critical theory, such a strategy is used to disassemble the fact that ruling elites prioritize the interest of the high class.

Lifestyle

In the political advertisements examined, a temperate lifestyle that is characterized by conservatism, traditionalism, and ordinary income generally comes to the fore. It is noteworthy that the advertisements were shot in the neighborhoods where low-income families lived. Considering that the national income per capita in Egypt is around three thousand five hundred dollars, we can say that this is a very appropriate choice. Failure to meet people's rising expectations is a major threat to the political elite. Describing the acceptable citizenship model on low-income people, in a sense, lowers people's life expectancy. In terms of critical theory, it makes people easy-to-manage commodities.

Race

It is not possible to speak of an ethnic diversity in the advertisings. It should be kept in mind that Egypt acted as the banner bearer of Arab nationalism in the past, especially in the time of Gamal Abdel Nasser. Besides, nationalism is one of the strongest components of Sisi's campaign. As a natural consequence of these facts, Arabic race comes to the fore in the advertising, but it is not possible to say that they carry racist messages.

Role

The most prominent role defined in political advertisements is acceptable citizenship. The major components of this role are having a patriotic conscious, satisfying with ordinary incomes, and having a traditional way of life. The role attributed to the woman is also compatible with the acceptable citizenship imagery. The woman generally seen in the role of housewife with traditional clothes. The wearing styles generally reflect moderate Islam understanding.

Stereotype

Stereotypes can be positive, negative, or mixed. Yet, regardless of the kind, they are detrimental to social relations because they present oversimplified and overgeneralized images coded with some biases. What is more, stereotyping can be used as a political strategy, especially by populist leaders, to manage the electorate through manipulation (Corbu & Negrea-Busuioc, 2020). It is seen that both positive and negative stereotypes are created in the advertisements examined. The people used in the scenes about the MB movement are stereotypes that remind political Islam, which is presented as detrimental to the future of the country. This stereotype production feeds a negative opinion in terms of the highly religious segments of the country. As for the stereotypes used in a positive way, we see ordinary people, especially seen in charity distribution videos. Adherence to traditions, satisfaction with the services provided by the state, and being low-income are the main characteristics of these people and form a stereotype of *persona grata*.

Political Messages

The political messages are formulated mainly around strong leadership, nationalism, patriotism, development, survival, and troubled days of the past. In a sense, each advertisement has both positive and negative messages. While positive messages are more aimed at gaining consent, negative messages, on the other hand, are constructed on the axis of fear with the goal of coercion.

CONCLUSION

In this study the political advertising in Egypt is examined to obtain some findings related to the dynamics of competitive authoritarian regimes. Based on the proposition that although the system based on competitive elections, political elites in the competitive authoritarian regime needs some kinds of compelling mechanisms, it is tried be illustrated that political advertising in such regimes functions for creating both consent and cohesion at the same time. In that regard, political advertisements are examined around four research questions.

The first two research questions were about the common characteristics of the political advertisements and social components that were covered more. The common characteristic determined as follows: All the advertisements are designed for the creation and maintaining of strong leadership image. It is interesting that although NFT was competing for the seats in the parliament and Sisi is not an official member of the party, all the election campaign designed around Sisi. Another common characteristic is that the political advertisement mainly addresses to low-income people. Lastly, cultural issues especially Egyptian flag is used as much as possible to stimulate nationalist and patriotic emotions.

The other two research questions were about the ways used for getting the consent of people and establishing coercive mechanisms. One of the findings obtain in the research is that the messages and strategies used in the advertisements functions to engineering of both consent and coercion simultaneously. For instance, the stimulation of nationalist and patriotic emotions through the use of Egyptian flag encourages people to vote for the leader and the party. On the other hand, it brings along a cognitive accounting about whether not voting for the leader and the party is a kind of betrayal to the country or not. Another instance is the advertisement about material aids given to low-income people. These advertisements also motivate the electorate to vote in a positive sense. Yet, on the other hand, it threatens people subliminally with the missing out from these aids in case of not being elected of the leader again. Lastly, making people remember the troubled days of the past and presenting the leader as a savior is another strategy employed in the campaign. preferences and a serious threat, so functions as coercive impulse.

From the perspective of uses and gratifications theory, the findings reveal that the use of nationalist and religious symbols and messages, directs people with the motivation of "affirming moral, spiritual and cultural values" and also "gaining identity". Sure, "gaining information about the world", "participating in history", "satisfying curiosity and be informed" are also important motivations that Berger indicated and valid for the political advertising. On the other hand, the most interesting finding achieved in the sense of uses and gratifications, making people remember the troubled days is one of the most effective techniques which stimulates the motivation of "to be purged of unpleasant emotions" and bring along the gratification of people even though they are not in favor of the main political path of the leader.

FUTURE RESEARCH DIRECTIONS

Political advertising has an important role in the construction and maintenance of competitive authoritarian systems. However, the number of studies in this area is quite limited. It will be very productive to compare the findings obtained in this study with the studies to be carried out in Egypt's different economic and political conditions. Similarly, comparative studies in which other countries with competitive authoritarian systems are included in the analysis framework will provide very useful information in order to understand the characteristics of these regimes.

REFERENCES

Abboud, D. G. (2020). Exploring evolving trends of gender representation in digital advertising in Egypt. *Journal of Architecture, Arts and Humanities*, 5(21), 594–610.

Abdalla, N. (2012). Social protests in Egypt before and after the 25 January revolution: Perspectives on the evolution of their forms and features. In L. A. Secat & H. Gallego (Eds.), *IEMed Mediterranean Yearbook: Med.2012* (pp. 86–92). European Institute of the Mediterranean.

Abdelmoula, E. (2015). *Al Jazeera and democratization: The rise of the Arab public sphere*. Routledge. doi:10.4324/9781315720272

Adorno, T., Frenkel-Brunswick, E. L., & Sanford, N. H. (1950). *The authoritarian personality*. Harper and Brothers.

Adorno, T. W., & Horkheimer, M. (2014). *Aydınlanmanın diyalektiği*. Kabalcı Yayıncılık.

Bakr, N. (2012). The Egyptian revolution. In S. C. Calleya & M. Wohlfeld (Eds.), *Change and opportunities in the emerging Mediterranean* (pp. 57–81). Mediterranean Academy of Diplomatic Studies.

Berger, A. A. (1991). *Media analysis techniniques*. Sage Publications.

Botman, S. (1998). The liberal age, 1923-1952. In M. W. Daly (Ed.), *The Cambridge History of Egypt: Modern Egypt, from 1517 to the end of the twentieth century* (Vol. 2, pp. 285–308). Cambridge University Press. doi:10.1017/CHOL9780521472111.013

Constitution of the Arab Republic of Egypt. (2014). Retrieved from State Information Servise: https://www.sis.gov.eg/UP/Dustor/Dustor-English002.pdf

Corbu, N., & Negrea-Busuioc, E. (2020). Populism meets fake News: Social media, stereotypes and emotions. In *B. Krämer, & C. Holtz-Bacha, Perspectives on populism and the media: Avenues for research* (pp. 181–200). Nomos. doi:10.5771/9783845297392-181

Cwalina, W. F., & Newman, B. I. (2015). *Political Marketing: Theoretical and Strategic Foundations.* Routledge.

Daly, M. W. (1998). The British occupation, 1882-1922. In M. W. Daly (Ed.), *The Cambridge History of Egypt: Modern Egypt, from 1517 to the end of the twentieth century* (pp. 239–251). Cambridge University Press. doi:10.1017/CHOL9780521472111.011

Egypt. (2022). Retrieved from Minority Rights Group International: https://minorityrights.org/country/egypt/

El-Mahdi, R., & Marfleet, P. (2009). *Egypt: The moment of change.* Zed Books. doi:10.5040/9781350219830

El-Nawawy, M., & Khamis, S. (2020). Political Activism 2.0: Comparing the Role of Social Media in Egypt's "Facebook Revolution" and Iran's "Twitter Uprising". *CyberOrient*, 6(1), 8–33. doi:10.1002/j.cyo2.20120601.0002

Eldin, H. F., Shahin, M., & Miniesy, R. (2021). The impact of social media adoption on financial & non-financial growth of MSMEs: An empirical comparison of Facebook and Instagram in Egypt. In Egypt's future outlook: The search for a new balances (pp. 1-36). The British University in Egypt.

Elmeshad, M. (2021). *The Political Economy of Private Media in Egypt.* SOAS University of London.

Eltantawy, N., & Wiest, J. B. (2011). Social media in the Egyptian revolution: Reconsidering resource mobilization theory. *International Journal of Communication*, 1207–1224.

Eyada, B. (2018). An empirical study of banned advertising in Egypt and violated morals. *International Design Journal*, 8(2), 27–37.

Freedom of expression index. (2022). Retrieved from Reporters Without Borders: https://rsf.org/en/index

Fuchs, C. (2018). Authoritarian capitalism, authoritarian movements and authoritarian communication. *Media Culture & Society*, 40(5), 1–13. doi:10.1177/0163443718772147

Gaweesh, K. (2015). Televised political advertising in egypt: The case of 2012 parliamentary elections. *The Scientific Journal of Department of Public Relations and Advertising*, 10(2), 1–22. doi:10.21608jocs.2015.88997

GDP (current US$). (2022). Retrieved from The World Bank: https://data.worldbank.org/indicator/NY.GDP.MKTP.CD?most_recent_value_desc=true

GDP per capita (current US$) - Egypt, Arab Rep. (2022, May 23). Retrieved from The World Bank: https://data.worldbank.org/indicator/NY.GDP.PCAP.CD?locations=EG

Goldschmidt, A. Jr. (2008). *A brief history of Egypt*. Facts On File.

Grimal, N. (1994). *A History of Ancient Egypt*. Wiley-Blackwell.

Heywood, A. (2017). *Political idologies: An introduction*. Palgrave.

İslami, İ. (2016). Political History of Modern Islam. *LIRIA International Review, 6*(1), 189–206.

Karagiannopoulos, V. (2012). The Role of the Internet in Political Struggles: Some Conclusions from Iran and Egypt. *New Political Science, 34*(2), 151–171.

Kemp, S. (2020, February 17). *Digital 2020: Egypt*. Retrieved from Datareportal: https://datareportal.com/reports/digital-2020-egypt

Khodair, A. A., AboElsoud, M. E., & Khalifa, M. (2019). The role of regional media in shaping political awareness of youth: Evidence from Egypt. *Politics & Policy, 47*(6), 1095–1124.

Krom, İ. (2020). Reklam ve algı yönetimi: Toplumbilimsel analiz çerçevesinde 2019 yılında en çok hatırlanan reklamlar. In Ö. U. Yurttaş (Ed.), *Reklam Perspektifleri* (pp. 175–204). Nobel Yayınları.

Levitsky, S., & Way, L. A. (2010). *Competitive authoritarianism: Hybrid regimes after the cold war*. Cambridge University Press.

Lynch, M. (2010). Islam divided between Salafi-jihad and the Ikhwan. *Studies in Conflict and Terrorism, 33*(6), 467–487.

Marsot, A. S. (2007). *A History of Egypt: From the Arab Conquest to the Present*. Cambridge University Press.

Marx, K., & Engels, F. (1970). *Manifesto of the communist party*. Foreign Languages Press.

Masr, M. (2019, June 25). *Arrests target political figures involved in new coalition to run in 2020 parliamentary elections*. Retrieved from Mada: https://www.madamasr.com/en/2019/06/25/feature/politics/arrests-target-political-figures-involved-in-new-coalition-to-run-in-2020-parliamentary-elections/

Mendel, T. (2011). *Politics and Media: Transition in Egypt*. Internews. Retrieved May 23, 2022, from http://hrlibrary.umn.edu/research/Egypt/Internews_Egypt_MediaLawReview_Aug11.pdf

Mostaqbal Watan Party-the official page. (2022, May 10). Retrieved from Facebook: https://www.facebook.com/mostqbalwataneg/videos/321794412854914/

Ollman, B. (2011). *Yabancılaşma*. Yordam Kitap.

Overview of Culture & Arts. (2022). Retrieved from State Information Service: https://www.sis.gov.eg/section/10/497?lang=en-us

Population. (2022). Retrieved from state Infromation Service: https://www.sis.gov.eg/section/10/9400?lang=en-us

Ranko, A., & Nedza, J. (2015). Crossing the Ideological Divide? Egypt's Salafists and the Muslim Brotherhood after the Arab Spring. *Studies in Conflict and Terrorism*, 1–23.

Rozgonyi, K. (2014). *Assessment of Media Legislation in Egypt.* European Union. Retrieved from https://www.menamedialaw.org/sites/default/files/library/material/medmedia_egypt.pdf

Sakr, N. (2012). Social media, television talk shows, and political change in Egypt. *Television & New Media*, *14*(4), 322–337.

Scott, J. (2011). *Conceptualising the social world: Principles of sociological analysis.* Cambridge University Press.

Shechter, R. (2003). Press advertising in Egypt: Business realities and local meaning, 1882-1956. *The Arab Studies Journal, 10/11*(2/1), 44-66.

Statista. (2022). *Retrieved from Distribution of advertising expenditure in Egypt from 2008 to 2015, by medium.* https://www.statista.com/statistics/388242/advertising-expenditures-share-by-medium-egypt/

Sultan, N. (2013). Al Jazeera: Reflections on the Arab Spring. *Journal of Arabian Studies: Arabia, the Gulf, and the Red Sea, 3*(2), 249-264.

The official page of President / Abdel Fattah Al-Sisi. (2022, May 14). Retrieved from Facebook: https://www.facebook.com/AlSisiofficial?hc_ref=ARSy4Df0jHID2YDbXqaMVkJ5mcgJMe7kBz4n6SnJm9 KNVfzCwjMBkcnIEaRM2n6wLH0&fref=nf&__xts__[0]=68.ARCMs9EXsue6ebQYJY7KNGrlhT-gPDw19zkP0LpO1hUfhcOnHY7ELgg_RlMZJ7c6YVIa1iafKRdjorJGIZH0dey3EQ0XARBDCmS-AOwS6t1jGDTI120-KqyK

The Report: Egypt. (2013). Oxford Business Group.

Wictorowicz, Q. (2006). Anatomy of the Salafi movement. *Studies in Conflict and Terrorism, 29*(3), 207–239.

World economic outlook. (2022, April). International Monetary Fund.

Chapter 2
Using YouTube in Political Persuasion:
2019 South African Elections

Başak Özoral
ⓘ https://orcid.org/0000-0003-3075-6362
Istanbul Commerce University, Turkey

Mehmet Sinan Tam
ⓘ https://orcid.org/0000-0001-9897-0803
Bandırma Onyedi Eylül University, Turkey

ABSTRACT

Political advertising is a form of campaigning that allows candidates to directly convey their message to voters and influence the political debate. South African political parties (African National Congress and the Democratic Alliance) also adopted the use of social media networks as an effective tool for political campaigning purposes and to encourage the public to engage in political discourse. The chapter investigates how both the South African public and the political parties are using YouTube for discussion, debate, and opinion formation during the 2019 South Africa elections. Sociological analysis method is used in the research. The subject is especially about Aristotle's concept of rhetoric, promises of political messages, and political persuasion in written form. The findings part of the study shows that the most prevailant issues in the election campaigns were corruption, failure to keep promises, and the effort to create a new leader identity in the DA party. By ANC, independence, Mandela's contributions and past actions, and the importance of voting were mentioned.

INTRODUCTION

Political parties or candidates who want to have the vote and support of the voters try to persuade and influence them. The parties or candidates manage this through conveying their services, projects and political ideas to the voters by using the media (newspaper, television, internet, etc.) or outdoor advertising

DOI: 10.4018/978-1-7998-9672-2.ch002

spaces. "Persuasion" (Jamieson, 1996, p. 4), which necessitates the imagination of a spectrum ranging from "influence" at the moderate end to "force" at the other end, plays an active role in ensuring the acquisition and maintenance of political power. Again, persuasion is always taken into account in the message design phase of all political communication activities.

The development of democracy, the prominence of elections, the appreciation of legitimacy and similar developments have increased the importance of persuasion in the political communication process. Political communication is now seen as the use of methods such as public relations, advertising, social media (YouTube & Instagram) and propaganda, which enable the candidates to gain the support and trust of individuals (Damlapınar & Balcı, 2014, p. 33; Güven, 2020, pp. 44-45). Political advertising can mobilize a person to participate in an election and persuade a person to vote for a particular candidate. The ultimate goal of political campaigns is to influence the election (Gordon et al., 2012, pp. 391-403). Bailenson et al. compares the relative effects of partisan, issue, gender, physical and facial similarity, as well as candidate familiarity, on voters' assessments of candidates (Bailenson et al., 2008, pp. 935-961). He states that he is inclined to choose candidates whose physical characteristics, face and demeanor are closer to him. Despite all the professionalization in the production of political messages and the increase in the possibility of presenting messages through different media, it should be kept in mind that politics is always carried out through political speeches. From the past to the present, rhetoric has managed to preserve its existence firmly (Reisigl, 2008, pp. 96-97).

Youtube campaigns are important platforms to persuade voters through facial expressions and speaking manners, making candidates physically visible. Political Youtube videos contain both verbal and visual elements. Adding audio elements such as music and sound to this, increases the impressiveness and persuasiveness function of the advertisement. With the spread of the internet by removing the limitations on space along with smart mobile phones, individuals are in an open position to messages at any time and from anywhere. According to Uztuğ (2004, p.17), the possibility of repeating and broadcasting political advertising messages in many channels ensures the retention of the message. You can not only reach the voters who are interested in politics and support the political party/candidate, but also the voters who are not interested in politics or the opposing side voters. A political candidate can correct his/her negative impressions, if any, through the opportunity to express himself/herself by participating in the party program, which includes his/her future goals, past practices, tone of voice, gestures, body knowledge and clothing selection, and through answering the criticisms and questions directed to him/her using Youtube videos. In this context, political advertisements on Youtube not only contribute to the formation of a positive image, but also provide the political information and political motivation that the voters need.

In South Africa, political parties were trying to use Youtube effectively in the 2019 general elections. Political advertisements published on Youtube, which is an important source of political information, are one of the important components of the political campaign process, as they are one of the factors that affect the political choice of the voters. Two of South Africa's leading parties, the African National Congress (ANC) and the Democratic Alliance (DA), were also parties that used Youtube as a political advertising tool along with other online platforms in the 2019 elections. Undoubtedly, speeches made by political party leaders within the framework of rhetorical principles contain persuasive expressions. This study aimed to present a periodic cross-section of the intensities of use of rhetorical persuasion components by the ANC and DA parties. In the selected Youtube content, it has been examined how the codes of service to Black Africans, especially change, improvement, well-being, ethnic or multiculturalism and security are represented and shown in the produced narrative. On the other hand, when the common themes that the leaders mentioned in their speeches were examined, significant relationships were found between the persuasion components they used. Accordingly, in the common themes discussed, it was seen that the logos (rational attractiveness) component of persuasion was used more intensely by the ANC, and the logos and pathos (emotional attractiveness) persuasion components were used more by the DA. It is prominent that the component of ethos (credibility of the source) is used in both parties.

BACKGROUND

The Geographical, Cultural, Economical, and Socio-Political Structure of South Africa

Geography and Culture

Africa is the second largest continent in the world. Her territory covers 471,000 square miles, an area slightly larger than that of California, Arizona, Nevada, and Utah together. This great continent is the cradle of Human civilization. Africa has a population of more than 700 million in fifty-four countries where more than 1,000 languages are spoken. The Republic of South Africa is a country located at the southernmost tip of Africa. It has the Atlantic Ocean to the southwest and the Indian Ocean to the southeast. It is bordered by Namibia, Botswana and Zimbabwe to the north, and Mozambique and Swaziland to the northwest. Lesotho, a small kingdom, is located in the Republic of South Africa. South Africa is an extraordinary country blessed with natural beauty and a rich cultural heritage. The climate in South Africa is transitioning from a temperate to a subtropical climate. The nature, which offers wonderful views, has fertile plains and forests. (De Blij & Muller, 1992, pp. 440–42).

Due to the special geographical location of South Africa, the country has become a region where states and peoples from both the East and the West live together. The country's special strategic location, rich mines, fertile lands are the main reasons for immigration and occupation from Europe and Asia. Thanks to its natural resources and industrial development, South Africa is the most developed country in Africa. However, in the historical process, the wealth of the white minority and the poverty of the black local people have continued as a serious contradiction and have been an indicator of inequality in the country. (De Blij & Muller, 1992, pp. 440–49). Climate, geography and culture vary from region to region in South Africa. Africa has different cultures and traditions. Home of approximately 49 million people of different ancestry and races, South Africa uses 11 official languages, along with the indigenous languages of Xhosa, Sotho, Venda, Tsonga, Pedi, Shangan and Ndebele, as well as English and Afrikaans. These indigenous languages are only as similar to each other as German is to Spanish (Davenport & Sanders, 2000, pp. 379–396). As a matter of fact, centuries of migration naturally provided a rich influx of other cultures into this mix. Around one million people of Asian origin, mostly from India as contract workers, are also added to the country's population. In addition, about three million hybrids, most of whom settled in the eastern Eastern Cape region, are also part of this mosaic. Its origins are based on relationships, marriages between slave workers and white owners, and even between the indigenous Khoikhoi and Xhosa people (Afolayan, p.10-11).

Although Africans take care to preserve their traditional social norms and cultures, the severe impact of globalization is particularly evident on the young population. However, influences from other continents are quite strong and globalization is especially affecting the culture of youth. Media is one of the most important tools of this change. Social norms and values are especially effective in male-female relations and their roles in society. South African culture has a very patriarchal feature. While women's opinions are not considered important in the family, they are expected to do the heavy work. The multi-functional work and labor of women in society is ignored. In business life, managerial positions are not often provided to women. Moreover women in leadership positions are not taken into account by their male colleagues because they are women (Mabokela & Mawila, 2004, pp. 396-416) However, since 1994, South African culture, like all soceties, has been going through of transitions. The aim of this effort is to erase the ravages of colonialism and apartheid and rebuild the social structure.

Religion is a central aspect of life, culture, and society in South Africa. South Africa has never had an official state religion. The country's constitution explicitly states everyone's right to freedom of conscience, religion, thought, belief and opinion. However, the government actively promoted Christianity throughout much of the 20th century and it remains the most widely followed faith today. Table 1 shows the percentage distribution of beliefs in South Africa.

Table 1. Religion – All South Africans

Religion	Number	%
Christianity	35 750 641	79.8%
Islam	654 064	1.5%
Hinduism	551 668	1.2%
Judaism	75 549	0.2%
Other beliefs	283 815	0.6%
No religion	6 767 165	15%
Undetermined	610 974	1.4%
Total	44 819 774	100%

Source: (The Arda, 2015)

As mentioned above, this multi-ethnic, multilingual and multi-continental structure constitutes South Africa's cultural mosaic of diverse traditions and lifestyles. Rituals and ceremonies unique to different ethnic and religious groups living in the country have an existential meaning and importance. Verbal culture is a prominent feature of South Africa's indigenous society. Literacy became widespread in South Africa after the arrival of Europeans, but the paintings found on rocks and caves are examples of artistic expressions of local peoples depicting nature and their lives.

Economy in South Africa

South Africa is classified as an upper middle-income country, with real GDP per capita currently at US$5,916, up from US$4,652 in 2000. The uneven and, at times, sluggish growth in average income levels, however, has meant a moderate decline in poverty, from 40 percent of the population in 1995, to 26 percent in 2013, using the World Bank's $2- a- day poverty line (Bhorat et al., 2016, pp. 231-232) With a current population of almost 53 million, this equates to about 13.7 million people living in poverty in South Africa. The per capita poverty rate in South Africa has risen from 31 percent in 1995 to 53.8 percent today. This headcount ratio was calculated using the upper line of a newly reconstructed national poverty line, but the national lower-line working poverty rate of 37 percent, poverty undoubtedly remained high. Therefore, despite the optimistic outlook for the South African economy as the country transitioned to democracy in 1994, economic growth has been moderate over the past two decades. (Bhorat et al., 2016, pp. 231-232). In fact, while the widely implemented social welfare system has succeeded in reducing inequalities in access to public services and housing, poverty has remained stable and unemployment rates remain high.

Socio-Political Structure

The effects of colonialism, discrimination, and the regime of apartheid on local black people have left their mark on South African history. Not long but, just 14 years ago, South Africa was the only officially racist country of the 20th century until it ended its racist policy at the end of 1990. The country had brutal laws for blacks. Every two votes cast by black was equal to one white vote. Blacks were not allowed in many places. They could not be represented in the parliament, they could not form a party. They could not be candidates in the elections. It was a country dominated by a purely white minority.

D. F. Malan, who came to power after the Second World War (1948) and advocated extreme racist views, passed some laws to develop apartheid policy, and the scope of racial discrimination was expanded to include not only blacks but also other races other than whites in the country. Marriage between whites and non-whites was outlawed, and racial segregation was systematically enforced everywhere, from schools to workplaces, from trains to movie theaters J. C. Stridjom (1954-1958), who became prime minister after Malan, and H. F. Verwoerd, who was killed in 1966, furthered the same policy. However, it did not take long for such extreme racist behaviors to meet with strong opposition, and the African National Congress of South Africa (ANC) organization of blacks, which was founded in 1912 but could not show much presence, started a boycott of non-compliance with the law. Even though the black leader Mandela, who would later change the country's fate, was imprisoned, the freedom struggle that started in 1982 spread throughout the country and the regime ended as a result of international pressure. (Lodge, 1987, pp. 2-3). In 1990, the famous black leader Nelson Mandela was released, declaring that blacks would be granted the right to vote and that minorities would be protected. On April 27, 1994, it was decided to hold the first national elections according to the proportional representation system. While the African National Congress of South Africa won the majority in the elections held on this date, a black and white government was formed for the first time under the chairmanship of Nelson Mandela, after 342 years of power of the white minority. (Lodge, 1987, pp. 2-3).

The ANC's firm adherence to the principle of anti-racist democracy provided a solid foundation, thanks to which all political parties were able to form an interim constitution between 1991 and 1993 at the World Trade Center near Johannesburg. Mandela at the first free and fair elections in 1994, and has been re-elected at every election since, though with a reduced majority every time since 2004. The ANC was once seen as a beacon of hope in post-apartheid South Africa. But more than two decades on, the party has been mired in countless corruption scandals and infighting (Sander & Govender, 2018). In 2019, the ANC received 57.5% of the total vote, showing its worst performance in all national elections. A struggling economy and corruption have eroded the ANC's popularity. ANC leader, President Cyril Ramaphosa, called on the people to build a united South Africa (Keane, 2019).

The official opposition to the ruling African National Congress (ANC) is the Democratic Alliance party (Afrikaan: Demokratiese Alliansie, DA). The DA is a centre-left party and has both centre-left and centre-right policies. The DA, which was founded in 1959 and is against apartheid, has experienced many mergers and different names have represented the party. DA generally includes various liberal tendencies (Rohanlall, 2014, pp. 9-10). In addition to running several major metropolitan municipalities, the DA administers the Western Cape, one of South Africa's nine provinces, since the 2009 general election, winning a larger majority in the 2014 election but losing some support in the 2019 election. As of 2014, the party has support from predominantly Afrikaans and English-speaking people (80% of its voters), over 35 (65%) and whites, coloreds and Indians (50%) (Gerber, 2019).

ADVERTISING IN SOUTH AFRICA

According to the writer John Berger, who is also famous for his ideas on advertising, advertising aims to create jealousy in the consumer, so that the consumer wants to buy the advertised product. In his well-known book, Ways of Seeing, he says that the advertising industry "offers us to transform ourselves or our lives by buying more and more of it (Berger, 1990, p. 131)." This definition is controversial for Africa, because the desire of the middle class in Africa is to achieve middle class life in more developed countries. The African advertising industry offers consumers the possibility of a better and improved lifestyle. According to a report by McKinsey, a global research institute, "The most popular business sector in Africa in the near future appears to be the emerging consumer market (McKinsey & Company, 2017)." The report focuses on the five main consumption areas in Africa and growth is expected in these areas: clothing, financial services, groceries, internet and telecommunications. Africa is the continent with the highest population growth rate in the world and is the second most economically developing region in the world after Asia. This makes the continent extremely attractive for consumer-oriented companies. On the other hand, there are many issues that encourage this consumption. In the development of this global consumption culture; colonization and missionary activities of the British and other European superpowers and the programs of channels such as CNN and MTV broadcasting in the country with cable network programs are decisive (Oyedele & Minor, 2012, p. 93). In addition to consumption culture, especially multiculturalism and nationalist discourses are prominent in the advertisement content published in South Africa (Johnson et al, 2010; Oyedele & Minor, 2012). This situation reveals that the adaptation strategy, which is the strategy of the slogan of thinking globally and acting locally, is quite effective in the country.

Revenue from the advertising industry in South Africa rose notably in 2019, but advertising spend in television and video still covers the highest values of the advertising market. However, the online advertising industry is growing and it is expected to surpass television advertising in the near future. Looking at the distribution of the advertising industry in South Africa, 80% of the advertising agencies are international holdings (Shand, 2020). In addition to the adaptation of the advertising agencies operating in the country to this change in the field of advertising, these agencies also need to focus on stereotypes, linguistic ethnocentrism, empowerment of black people, multicultural advertising communication, advertising discourse and strategies for conflicting cultures and green advertising that has come to the forefront in recent years (Hugo-Burrows, 2004; Mazirri, 2020). These six items listed can be listed as the biggest handicaps of agencies operating in the country, especially international advertising agencies. Because the main concept in advertising is that the right message reaches the right target audience and creates a change in attitude and behavior. Advertisers and agencies should always keep the above-listed issues in their briefs in South Africa, where there are many cultures and minorities, and especially in a sensitive climate in terms of sensual differences at the end of the apartheid period.

It has been seen that the most prominent item in the efforts of companies to reduce their costs during the Covid 19 quarantine period is the advertising sector. As television and digital are used more during the pandemic, there have been remarkable changes in the way consumers meet with advertising content.

Advertisers tend to use more digital channels while trying to reduce their costs (Shand, 2020). In addition to the changes and transformations in the advertising field, there are also changes in the persuasion and action of the masses. In advertising activities, it is important for the masses to act behaviorally for the desired or expected target as well as convincing the target audience. Here age, gender, social class, personality etc. many individual and social characteristics come into play (Krom, 2019, p. 187). A key feature of South Africa is the terrific fragmentation of its consumer markets. The apartheid policy, which has been implemented for many years, has caused the society to consist of many ethnic layers. These groups are also separated by income differences. Each major racial group in turn is divided into subgroups. The majority of Bantu tribes enjoy similar living conditions. Among whites, the 60% African-speaking majority have adopted a lifestyle that differs from the English-speaking minority in details. This can be an important feature in some markets (for example, Africans generally prefer to have fun at home, while many English-speaking South Africans choose to take their guests to or from a restaurant, showing the difference in their spending capacities and consumption habits (Thorelli, 1968, pp. 40-48).

Figure 1. Advertising spending in South Africa from 2018 to 2021 (in million South African rand)
Source: (Guttman, 2021)

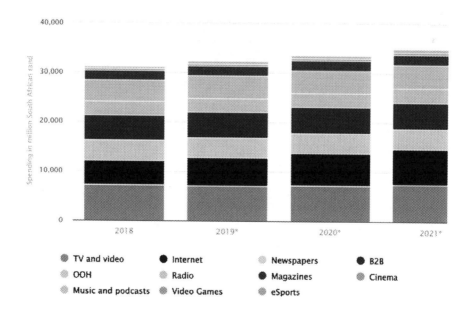

The entire advertising market in South Africa in 2019 is estimated to be worth 30.4 billion South African rand (approximately 2.05 billion U.S. dollars), and TV and video advertising spending is projected to account for the largest share of that amount, around 21 percent. The internet is said to be the second largest medium in the country. However, looking at 2018-2023 compound growth rates, TV's 1.8 percent CAGR in the period will be exceeded by internet's 12.4 percent CAGR, which means that by the end of 2023 internet advertising will be higher than TV advertising for the first time.

Internet Advertising in South Africa

The influence of internet advertising in South Africa is increasing day by day, it is expected to reach a value of over 580 million US dollars by 2023, reaching 25 percent of the total advertising market in the country. At the same time, mobile and internet advertising revenue is expected to reach 50 percent. This ratio shows how important mobile platforms are for the future of the South African advertising industry. This explains the fact that some of the biggest advertisers in South Africa are telecommunications companies such as Vodacom or Mobile Telephone Network (Guttmann, 2021). According to Statista, South Africa's advertising market was just under Rs 40 billion in 2018, with TV and video ad spending accounting for around 21% of this market and the internet being the second largest media platform.

According to PwC's Entertainment and Media Outlook Report, 2022 will see a significant change in these numbers as internet advertising is predicted to outnumber TV advertising for the first time (PWC, 2019, p. 72). SA's internet advertising revenue will also reach R9.4 billion in 2022, with search revenue accounting for 75% of that revenue (up from 66% in 2017) (Pygmaconsulting, n.d.).

The PwC report mentions 'Convergence 3.0', which involves an emergence of "ever-expanding super-competitors" within the advertising industry as a whole (PWC, 2019, p.42; p.165). These super-competitors will need to build relevance, and at the right scale, in order to remain competitive. More importantly, business models will need to be completely reinvented: think new revenue streams and memberships.

According to data from the Global Web Index, every year more South African users access the web, especially social media, with one third of the time South Africans spending more than eight and a half hours online each day. It should be noted that in the near future, the advertising industry will also change, becoming "personalized, automated, comprehensive, experiential and measurable". Internet advertising can get ahead of TV advertising, but it also brings some problems. According to The Media Online, mobile usage and internet advertising are growing rapidly, but with South Africa's demographic and the reach of free TV, the gap between mobile and TV is much larger than in developed markets. Mobile advertising is on the rise, but South Africa is still somewhat problematic (Bratt, 2019).

Digital will undoubtedly have a big impact in the near future, but we have to take into account that South Africa's internet infrastructure is less developed compared to the rest of the world, it has a lower percentage of the population with internet access and lower data costs. Costs are still too high. However, South African markets generally follow global patterns, meaning that by 2022 the broadcast advertising landscape may look very different than it does now (Bratt, 2019).

Looking specifically at Southern Africa and South Africa, penetration rates are a mix of relatively low (51% for internet, and 38% for social media), to comparatively high (162% for mobile over 100% due to dual SIMs and multiple connections) (Businesstech, 2019). South Africans spend over 8 hours a day online and a third of that time is spent on social media

According to the report, South Africa's social media activity is also one of the fastest growing in the world, where the country ranked 17th for its relative growth (seeing a 28% increase in activity year-on-year) and tied for 9th for net growth, having added 5 million new users since January 2018. South Africans also spend more time using social media platforms than the global average, with the report recording the average time spent at 2 hours 48 minutes each day. South Africans have an average of 8 social media accounts (Businesstech, 2019).

The Internet, whose content and technology is mainly tied to the United States, is predominantly English as a result. It is a transnational public sphere, as internet platforms are one of the lowest-cost areas to media today. Internet access in South Africa is very high, the Internet has growth potential and the potential impact on its users is much greater. All these reasons show that the influence of the internet in political advertising is very strong and will be used even more.

Political Advertising in South Africa

In South Africa, which carries out political advertising activities under a set of rules in local and national election processes, a set of rules has been introduced for all kinds of promotional content to be made by parties during the election process. Here, some issues such as the obligation to have a license for the traditional media, the limitation of party election broadcasts to a maximum of 60 seconds, and the fact that the content of the advertisements are not illegal, criminal and provocative are particularly highlighted (Goverment Gazette, 2014, pp. 6-9). In the periods when TV was not very common, the criteria for conducting political advertising activities through newspapers with legal, correct and honest content were sought (Pottinger, 1987, p. 38). In studies examining policy advertising in South Africa, the party leadership identity is used to a limited extent in TV commercials in the country, advertising texts and scenes are used to focus on the country's main social problems, and it is desired to persuade the audience, especially in an emotional context.

It has been explained that the actors played in these advertisements are chosen from among the more disadvantaged segments, and the images of children, women and the disabled are kept in the foreground in the contents of political advertisements (Sindane, 2010, p. 144). On the other hand, it has been observed that emotional appeals such as uncertainty, anger and fear are used mutually, especially by rival parties, so that political discussions in rallies occur in advertisements in this way (Fourie & Froneman, 2003). From this perspective, it can be said that the findings of this research, which examines the political content on the Youtube platform, are in line with the results of political advertising broadcast on South African Televisions. It can be stated that they are in a holistic line in line with the messages, strategies and targets that will support each other.

The biggest handicap of political advertising was that it brought politics to a liberal line instead of pluralistic and controversial democracy (Sindane, 2014, p. 24). Because the budget problem in preparing political advertising content for traditional media channels is an important problem that should not be ignored for smaller and new parties. For this reason, although political advertising is seen as legitimate to use as a means of making political propaganda, over time this situation has turned into a commodification tool in the capital order. However, it can be argued that the introduction of social media channels into our lives and the fact that not only parties and leaders, but also voters express their opinions through these networks, pave the way for the emergence of the idea of pluralism and participation, which is the most important argument of democracy. Of course, the existence of bots and fake accounts on these platforms and the existence of channels/pages/personal social media accounts that are forcibly closed should not be forgotten.

Recently, it is possible to see traces of social media political advertising in South Africa, as in every country. The two leading parties (ANC and DA) in the country use social media platforms in their political advertising activities. Here, it is seen that not only in producing the advertisement content, but even the advertisement itself is turned into a propaganda tool by the Youtube users. Here, users to Youtube ads of ANC and DA parties; Mandela has been found to react with the belief that change will happen with voting, nationalist/racist expressions, and negative and positive rhetoric (Tyali & Mukhudwana, 2020).

ANC and DA parties used radio, newspaper, flyer and TV platforms to convey their political promises to the target audience in previous election periods. Among these two parties, the party that allocated the most budget to political advertising activities was generally the ANC. While the ANC frequently spread the same theme in their political advertisement content through different media outlets, DA gave positive advertising messages for change, innovation and a new order with either slogan-like political discourses or negative advertisements that criticize the power (ANC) harshly or assertive discourses (Teer -Tomaselli, 2006). It can be stated that in developing such a strategy, the DA never came to power alone and tried to create a social ground that it was the only party that would come to power in the future.

The most important thing that stands out in political advertisements is to persuade the target audience to the political messages expressed. One of the most obvious methods that leaders or parties will resort to at this point is undoubtedly Aristotle's rhetoric. The concept of rhetoric has been used since ancient times. Many definitions and technical uses of rhetoric have been proposed throughout history (Covino Joliffe, 2014, p. 327). Rhetoric is not only limited to writing or oratory, but has become visible with a unique style in almost every medium of communication. Not only in the dimension of communication, but the three most well-known concepts of rhetoric, ethos, pathos, and logos, have been defined and named with different concepts by many thinkers and writers, especially Plato, unlike those defined by Aristotle (Meyer, 2017, p. 17-19). Persuasion is at the forefront in Aristotle's rhetoric. The components that will realize this persuasion are ethos, pathos and logos (Dow, 2015). At the beginning of the usage areas of rhetorical persuasion is politics. As a matter of fact, this idea is also seen in the book series called Aristotle's Politics (Fortenbaugh, 1992, p. 222).

Emotions are included in Aristotle's pathos variable. Aristotle gave more weight to many negative emotions such as fear, anxiety, war, phobic situations, pain, hunger, anger, thirst (Nussbaum, 1996). Aristotle persistently included the logo in his texts as "logical proof" and in his work called Rhetoric, the concept that he discussed the most, as opposed to ethos and pathos, was logos (Braet, 1992, pp. 309-310). Ethosta, which is another concept and focuses on the believability of the speaker, is made dependent on the speaker's or the author's understanding of his/her own life and character very well in order to convince others (Halloran, 1982, p. 60).

POLITICAL PERSUASION IN YOUTUBE ADS OF ANC AND DA PARTIES

In this study, which is about the 2019 general elections of the Republic of South Africa, the advertisements on the Youtube channels (African National Congress, 2019; Democratic Alliance, 2019) of the ruling (ANC) and main opposition (DA) parties were determined based on the homogeneous typology of the sample (Etikan et al., 2016, p. 3). Based on the problematic of how the sharing of advertisements on the Youtube platform of both parties is practiced in the context of political persuasion, the research data has been evaluated.

In this paper, which aims to reveal the role of advertisements in political persuasion in the Republic of South Africa, one of the most developed countries of the African continent, the advertisement contents of the ruling and main opposition parties on the Youtube platform in the pre-election period were examined by sociological analysis method. Sociological analysis is an analysis method that can be applied in every field of social sciences and acts on the basic social values that can be seen in almost every field of social life. This analysis method was used by thinkers such as Marx, Weber and Durkheim (Bottomore & Nisbet, 1978, pp. 7-10). Although the term social science was coined by Auguste Comte, especially Durkheim's studies were decisive in shaping sociological analysis (Tiryakian, 1978, p. 203). Berger evaluated the analysis of media contents with the method of socio-scientific analysis under three headings. The first one is an analysis based on 16 concepts from gender to culture, from anomie to lifestyle. Second, the evaluation of media content from the perspective of uses and gratifications. The last one is the analysis using the content analysis technique (1993, pp. 77-94). In the research, the research data were evaluated based on the sociological analysis typology that Berger first put forward.

The data of the research was also examined by using Aristotle's rhetorical triangle (ethos, pathos and logos), which is frequently used in the field of political communication, and how advertisements are used in political persuasion. In Aristotle's rhetorical triangle; ethos includes the speaker's reliability, credibility, and pathos. Pathos is the ability to manage the emotions and logos of the interlocutor, to present the arguments put forward by the speaker on a logical basis, including critical, analytical skills, good memory and purposeful behavior. (Shabrina, 2016, p.13; Mshvenieradze, 2013, pp. 1939-1940).

Techniques and Strategies Used in Advertising

It has been determined that in the content of Youtube advertisements prepared by the ANC and DA party, the advertisements last for a maximum of one minute and 30 seconds, and the places in the advertisements are prepared using street, workplace, home, school and green screen effects. At the point of advertisement time, the DA party shared longer-term content. Youtube story feature is only used by the ANC party and a new story is shared every day 60 days before the elections. While a simpler narrative and scenes were preferred in the Youtube contents of the ruling party, many scenes were used together in the main opposition party to keep the audience's attention constantly alive. In the commercial dubbing, ANC directly used the voice of the commercial actors and the female voice-over, while DA included the tension music, the male voice-over and the speeches of the party leader. Both parties shared their advertisements on Youtube, not only verbally but also by including English subtitles in the videos. In the ANC, the event setup was generally built from within the social life, whereas in the DA, the moment of voting at the ballot box, news footage of past events in the country and the speeches of party leader Mmusi Maimani were used and conveyed to the audience.

When a general evaluation is made, it can be easily stated that while DA follows a more globalist approach by including images of many segments in its advertisements, whereas ANC emphasizes more nationalist and nationalist discourses in its advertisement content. It has been observed that DA also includes images of the party logo in its advertising content. It can be said that DA also gives importance to the messages related to corporate identity in Youtube content. It has been determined that subliminal and implicit messages are given through some visuals in the advertisements of DA. Such scenes were placed to remind the voters of the old issues that came to the agenda in the country. On the other hand, the party has targeted the voters under the age of 30, who will cast new votes based on young characters in general, in their Youtube content. This premise has been tried to be instilled with implicit messages, with a thoughtful fiction from the style of music used here to the clothes worn. ANC, on the other hand, used local motifs more frequently in their advertising content.

There were differences in using the advertising strategy in the advertising content shared on Youtube by both parties. The ANC party has conveyed its messages to the voters by positioning almost every situation from social peace to employment, from security to social justice over the party identity. Here, messages are constructed within the framework of party ideals and ideals rather than messages about the party leader. In the DA, on the other hand, it was seen that the fear messages were heavily constructed for the ANC party leader. It has been determined that leader identity and discourses are used in advertisements rather than party identity. The DA also brought the rhetoric and gaffes of ANC party leader Cyril Ramaphosa to the attention of the electorate with humorous appeal. On the other hand, in the advertisement content, positive or negative political advertisements for political power and political advertisement types for class/section and demographic groups were also used (Eroğlu Yalın, 2006, p. 173).

Analysis of Youtube Advertsing Content of ANC and DA Parties Within The Framework of Sociological Analysis

There are 16 titles in the analysis content put forward by Arthur Asa Berger for the analysis of media contents (Berger, 1991, pp. 79-85). Each title here is evaluated on its own. In the study, the advertisement posts of the ANC and DA parties on Youtube channels were evaluated with the method of sociological analysis, by adding a title that is thought to be related to the research topic with the nine titles put forward by Berger.

Anomie: There was an uprising in all the content shared by the main opposition party. The norms that the DA party rejects here refer to the actions taken by the government. In particular, it has tried to position the government as the cause of corruption, income inequality and conflicts within the country and to present itself as the party that stands against these norms.

Minorities: At first, the whites and Muslims were seen as minorities by both parties. In the advertisement, the Muslim minority was represented by a man in white clothes, a white cap and a beard. Another minority consisted of white-skinned people. Especially with the emphasis on living in peace, images and discourses that life with this minority is possible and acceptable have been constructed. Despite the presence of similar minority groups in the advertisements of both parties, other minority segments were given more space in the DA.

Class (Socio-Economic): The ANC party mostly gave messages about the middle class. The segment played in the advertisement contents is also in this class. In the content prepared by the DA party, images of people who are low or not included in any class gained intensity. There is a clear difference in the advertisements of both parties in terms of class purchasing power. In ANC, a profile that reaches its wishes and ideals and satisfies at this point is presented, while in DA, the portrait of the South African people who cannot meet even their most basic vital needs (eating, drinking, shelter, security, etc.) and living in chaos is presented to the audience. On the other hand, in a content prepared by the ANC party, the influence of the ANC party on young girls and children living freely on the street without their parents was conveyed in the local language by an old woman voter. This situation implied that a positive class transition took place in the country along with the government.

Gender: Here, the gender played in Youtube advertisement content is predominantly men, and the "…. It has been seen that women are one step ahead in the content named "is voting ANC". In the contents shared by the main opposition party, it has been determined that women are the gender that is frequently oppressed and oppressed, and that the ruling class tries to convey the segment that improves welfare and quality of life compared to the past, through the female identity. On the other hand, it has been determined that both parties use objects or child extras related to children on their Youtube channels.

Culture: Traces of cultural difference were also seen in advertisements. In addition to the traces of village and urban culture, messages within the framework of multiculturalism were consciously reflected in the advertising contents of both parties. In addition to multiculturalism, cultural integration was tried to be instilled in the audience with elements of national identity (Mandela, Flag, Colors).

Lifestyle: Since the characters in the ANC advertisements belong to a higher class than the advertisement personalities in DA, the western lifestyle is presented to the audience in the images of the lives of the individuals here. In DA advertisements, on the other hand, a life style compatible with the African continent was prioritized. It has been noted that the setting of the place where the characters in the ANC advertisements live is more luxurious and ostentatious than DA.

Race: ANC party advertisements, while black ethnicity is used extensively in advertisement content, it is seen that other ethnic (White, Indian and Coloured) origins are included more in DA party besides black characters. Both parties belong to non-black ethnicities; war and peace, chaos and peace dilemmas.

Role: In the advertisement content, people with the roles of women, men, children, parents, housewives, workers and students have acted. While there are people with more specific roles in ANC advertisement content, more general characters (such as male and female) in DA are made visible on the Youtube channel.

Stereotype: Stereotypes are frequently used in the advertisement content shared by DA on Youtube. Here, it has been tried to instill in the audience that Ramaphosa is an opportunistic politician, by revealing that the leader of the ruling party acts with his own personal interests.

Political Messages: ANC; Security, social assistance, education, employment, minority rights, corruption, past actions, social peace and tranquility and generally positive message contents were addressed to the voters. DA, on the other hand, tried to persuade the electorate with negative message content related to change, turmoil, corruption, poverty, empty promises and promises of the government, and moments of conflict in the country.

The Rhetoric of The ANC and DA in The Framework of Political Persuasion

The data in the study was also tried to be explained by Aristotle's rhetoric of persuasion, which is prominent in studies on politics. The rhetorical triangle introduced by Aristotle; It consists of the headings ethos, pathos and logos.

Ethos (Credibility): Ethos focuses on the speaker's character traits (McCormack, 2014, p. 136). When the personalities used in the advertisement are evaluated, it can be said that DA preferred to convince the voters based on the charisma of the party leader and the ANC based on the image of Mandale and the party. On the other hand, the DA often focused on the promises that the ANC party did not keep before, giving clear messages to the audience that the rival party did not have any source credibility. ANC, on the other hand, tried to maintain its credibility by presenting the promises made in the previous elections (such as free education) to the attention of its audience.

Pathos (Emotion): Emotional persuasion was often exercised by the opposition party in advertisements shared on Youtube. It has been found that the party that often reaches its audience through the pathos variable in its advertisements is DA, where not only variables such as sadness, fear and anxiety, but also nationalist discourse and elements related to national identity are included in the advertisements.

Here, he especially emphasized the colors and flag of the country in the emotional scenes he built on national values. In addition, the words and images of the relatives of the people who lost their lives in the conflicts in the country and the images about corruption were shared on the Youtube channel with dramatic music. ANC, on the other hand, shared content that prioritizes the sense of loyalty by making use of Mandale's national identity. Thus, the party tried to keep its ties with Mandele, the country's symbol name and the first president after apartheid, alive in line with national identity values. On the other hand, a dramatic discourse was also used that the difficulties experienced by the advertising actors disappeared day by day with the ANC party.

Logos (Logic): In the advertisements published by the ANC party, more personal-oriented messages were given to the voters. For example, by giving the name of the advertisement character at the beginning, with the slogan "Is Voting ANC", the reasons for voting for the ANC party have been tried to be explained by presenting logical reasons in an individual context. What stood out here was stability, prosperity and trust. The government has made a logical dialogue with the audience that it actually voted for these three things with this election, that what would happen in the opposite case, could be experienced again with what the advertising characters conveyed in their past experiences. In the logical proposition presented to the audience by the DA, the chaos, economic situation and corruption discourses in the country were highlighted and the voters were tried to be persuaded through more generally accepted discourses.

CONCLUSION

Within the framework of the sociological analysis presented by Berger, the advertisements shared by the ANC and DA parties on the official Youtube channels in the South African 2019 elections were examined. In these advertisements; the DA party has positioned itself as the party that stands against these norms by citing the corruption, income inequality and conflicts that the opposition party has put forward against the government. It has been seen that both parties include minorities, and especially whites and Muslims are reflected as minorities. In the advertisements shared by the ANC party, mostly upper-class images were found. While both parties are giving their messages in a way to reveal gender differences, it has been determined that DA in particular focuses on discourses that women are the oppressed and oppressed segment. From a cultural point of view, it was found that the descriptions of village and urban culture were included by both parties, ANC built a western style of life in the advertisement content, and DA fictionalized the advertisement contents by adhering to the local motifs of the African continent. At the race point, it was determined that ANC included black ethnicity and DA included extras from many ethnicities in their advertisement posts. While ANC acted from individuals with more specific roles, DA, on the contrary, wrote advertisement texts based on more general characters. DA stood out in the stereotypes used and tried to match the ruling party leader with an opportunistic politician stereotype. In this study, which focuses on the general elections held in the Republic of South Africa in 2019, the advertisement contents shared by the ANC and DA parties on Youtube channels were examined. It has been determined that both parties prepared professional content for Youtube, these contents prepared on Youtube remained at very low viewing figures, and Youtube was used to adopt party propaganda in the local elections held in 2019 and 2021.

The apartheid practiced by whites in South Africa was also reflected in the 2019 elections. While the DA party associated the dilemma of us and the other with the development of the country, not with sensual colors, the ANC constructed its messages by emphasizing the historical experience (apartheid) implicitly. It has been seen that DA positions corruption as the biggest discrimination and presents this issue with fear and humorous appeals. Therefore, it can be stated that the view put forward by Dean that parties build the pathos more out of fear is confirmed in this study (2010). In the contents shared by the ANC, positive political discursive expressions such as stability, prosperity, trust and development are positioned with the identity of the party.

In the research, it has been seen that the opposition (DA) constructs its political messages at the point of pathos and logos, and the government (ANC) intensively at the point of logos. The research has figured that DA constructs the pathos technique intensely with a sense of fear, realizes the logical proposition using news images, and ANC tries to impose the discourse. By offering the services it previously offered to its voters, it is tried to impose the idea that "it has done it before, it will do it again" according to the logic of the voters. Although it was seen that the ethos dimension of persuasion was not built very intensely by both parties, it was determined that DA used the discourses of the party leader and the previous discourses of the ANC party, and the ANC tried to increase its credibility by referring to Mandela and his past actions. Therefore, in convincing the voters in the country; It can be stated that fear of the future, news reflected in the media, promises that are made (unfulfilled) and a leader-oriented attitude are adopted.

It may seem normal to persuade some segments by starting from the personalities who have the role of opinion leaders in certain areas. However, in the Republic of South Africa, it has been observed that the voters are not only tried to be persuaded in terms of political promises, but also political persuasion is tried to be realized at the point of voting behavior. The prominent thing here is the image/identity of the leader. As a matter of fact, as a result of the election, it was determined that the participation rate in the elections remained at a very low level compared to the elections of previous years, and the election in 2021 was the election with the lowest participation in the history of the Republic of South Africa (Cele & Vecchiatto, 2021). In the elections held in 2019, it was revealed that especially the young people did not act to vote (Schulz-Herzenberg, 2020, p. 17). In this context, parties/policy makers in South Africa need to focus on advertising content for the act of voting, apart from convincing the voters of political promises.

FUTURE RESEARCH DIRECTIONS

In this research, which deals with the elections held in the Republic of South Africa in 2019, the advertisement contents of the Youtube channels of the ANC and DA parties were examined. It is suggested by the researchers to examine the other social media applications of the parties in question, other than Youtube, and the advertising studies in traditional channels. On the other hand, it is recommended to conduct field studies on the effectiveness and (failure) of advertisements not only on the parties with a source position, but also on the electorate.

REFERENCES

Afolayan, F. (2004). *Culture and customs of South Africa*. Greenwood Press.

African National Congress. (2019). *MyANC Youtube channel*. Retrieved 04/28/22 from: https://www.youtube.com/c/MyANC/videos

Bailenson, J., Iyengar, S., Yee, N., & Collins, N. (2008). Faical similarity between voters and candidates couses influence. *Public Opinion Quarterly*, *72*(5), 935–961. doi:10.1093/poq/nfn064

Berger, A. A. (1991). *Media analysis techniques*. SAGE.

Berger, J. (1990). *Ways of Seeing*. Penguin Books.

Bhorat, H., Naido, K., Oosthuizen, M., & Pillay, K. (2016). South Africa demographic, employment, and wage trends. In H. Bhorat & F. Tarp (Eds.), *Africa's lions, growth traps and opportunities for six african economies* (pp. 229–270). Brookings Institution Press.

Bottomore, T., & Nisbet, R. (1978). Introduction. In T. Bottomore & R. Nisbet (Eds.), A history of sociological analysis (pp. 7-16). Basic Books.

Braet, A. C. (1992). Ethos, pathos and logos in Aristotle's rhetoric: A re-examination. *Argumentation*, *6*(3), 307–320. doi:10.1007/BF00154696

Bratt, M. (2019, June 27). *Mobile advertising soars, but South Africa still a bit sore*. Retrieved 05/07/22 from: https://themediaonline.co.za/2019/06/mobile-advertising-soars-but-south-africa-still-a-bit-sore/

Businesstech. (2019, February 1). *South Africans spend over 8 hours a day online – and a third of that time is spent on social media*. Retrieved 05/08/22 from: https://businesstech.co.za/news/internet/296716/south-africans-spend-over-8-hours-a-day-online-and-a-third-of-that-time-is-spent-on-social-media/

Cele, S., & Vecchiatto, P. (2021). *South African voter turnout slumps in municipal elections*. Retrieved 05/01/22 from: https://www.bloomberg.com/news/articles/2021-11-01/voter-turnout-slumps-in-south-african-municipal-elections

Covino, W., & Joliffe, D. (2014). Writing about writing a college reader. In E. Wardle & D. Downs (Eds.), *What Is Rhetoric?* (pp. 325–346). Bedford / St. Martin's.

Damlapınar, Z., & Balcı, Ş. (2014). *Siyasal iletişim sürecinde seçimler, adaylar, imajlar*. Konya, Türkiye: Literatürk.

Davenport, R., & Sanders, C. (2000). *South Africa: A modern history*. St. Martin's Press. doi:10.1057/9780230287549

De Blij, H. J., & Muller, P. O. (1992). *Geography, realms, regions, and concepts*. John Wiley & Sons.

Dean, D. (2010). Fear, negative campaigning and loathing: The case of the UK election campaign. *Journal of Marketing Management*, *21*(9-10), 1067–1078. doi:10.1362/026725705775194111

Democratic Alliance. (2019). *Democratic Alliance Youtube channel*. Retrieved 04/28/22 from: https://www.youtube.com/c/DemocraticAllianceSA/videos

Dow, J. (2015). *Passions and Persuasion in Aristotle's Rhetoric*. Oxford University Press. doi:10.1093/acprof:oso/9780198716266.001.0001

Eroğlu Yalın, B. (2006). Siyasal iletişimin reklam boyutuna ilişkin kuramsal bir inceleme. *İstanbul Üniversitesi İletişim Fakültesi Dergisi, 25,* 169-180.

Etikan, İ., Musa, S. A., & Alkassim, R. S. (2016). Comparison of convenience sampling and purposive sampling. *American Journal of Theoretical and Applied Statistics, 5*(1), 1–4. doi:10.11648/j. ajtas.20160501.11

Fortenbaugh, W. W. (1992). Aristotle on persuasion through character. *Rhetorica, 10*(3), 207–244. doi:10.1525/rh.1992.10.3.207

Fourie, L. M., & Froneman, J. D. (2003). Emotional political advertising: A South African case study. *Communicare, 22*(1), 187–211.

Gerber, J. (2019, October 9). Explained i what is the DA's federal council. *News24.* Retrieved 04/28/22 from: https://www.news24.com/news24/SouthAfrica/News/explained-what-is-the-das-federal-council-20191009

Gordon, B. R. G., Lovett, M. J., Shachar, R., Arceneaux, K., Moorthy, S., Peress, M., Rao, A., Subrata, S., Soberman, D., & Urminsky, O. (2012). Marketing and politics: Models, behavior, and policy implications. *Marketing Letters, 23*(2), 391–403. doi:10.100711002-012-9185-2

Government Gazette. (2014, February 17). Regulations on party election broadcasts, political advertisement, the equitable treatment of political parties by broadcasting licence and related matters, *Independent Communications authority of South Africa, 584*(37350), 1-17. Retrieved 05/19/22 from: https://www.icasa.org.za/legislation-and-regulations/party-elections-broadcasts-and-political-advertisement-and-related-matters-regulations-2014

Guttmann, Y. A. (2021, Mar 15). *Advertising spending in South Africa from 2018 to 2021.* Statista. Retrieved 05/02/22 from: https://www.statista.com/statistics/386540/advertising-expenditures-by-medium-south-africa/

Güven, A. (2020). Siyasal toplumsallaşma aracı olarak youtube: "Mevzular" örneği. In A. Güven (Ed.), Youtube Türkiye'de kültür, siyaset ve tüketim (pp. 1-53). İstanbul, Türkiye: Kriter.

Halloran, S. M. (1982). Aristotle's concept of ethos, or if not his somebody else's. *Rhetoric Review, 1*(1), 58–63. doi:10.1080/07350198209359037

Hugo-Burrows, R. (2004). Current trends and future challenges in the South African advertising ındustry - An ıntroductory review. *Journal of African Business, 5*(2), 39–52. doi:10.1300/J156v05n02_03

Jamieson, H. (1996). İletişim ve İkna. Anadolu Üniversitesi Yayınları.

Johnson, G. D., Elliott, R. M., & Grier, S. A. (2010). Conceptualizing multicultural advertising effects in the "new" South Africa. *Journal of Global Marketing, 23*(3), 189–207. doi:10.1080/08911762.2010.487420

Keane, F. (2019, May 11). *South Africa election: ANC wins with reduced majority.* Retrieved 05/03/22 from: https://www.bbc.com/news/world-africa-48211598

Krom, İ. (2019). Reklam ve algı yönetimi: Toplumbilimsel analiz çerçevesinde 2019 yılında Türkiye'de en çok hatırlanan reklamlar. In Ö. U. Yurttaş (Ed.), Reklam perspektifleri (pp. 175-204). Ankara, Türkiye: Nobel Akademik Yayıncılık.

Lodge, T. (1987). State of exile: The African National Congress of South Africa, 1976-86. *Third World Quarterly, 9*(1), 1–27. doi:10.1080/01436598708419960

Mabokela, R. O., & Mawila, K. F. N. (2004). The impact of race, gender, and culture in South African higher education. *Comparative Education Review, 48*(4), 394–416. doi:10.1086/423359

Mazirri, E. T. (2020). Green packaging and green advertising as precursors of competitive advantage and business performance among manufacturing small and medium enterprises in South Africa. *Cogent Business & Management, 7*(1), 1–21. doi:10.1080/23311975.2020.1719586

McCormack, K. C. (2014). Ethos, pathos, and logos: The benefits of Aristotelian rhetoric in the courtroom. *Washington University Jurisprudence Review, 7*(1), 131–155.

McKinsey & Company. (2017, 12 April). *The Rise of the African Consumer*. Retrieved 05/20/22 from: https://www.mckinsey.com/industries/retail/our-insights/the-rise-of-the-african-consumer

Meyer, M. (2017). *What is rhetoric*. Oxford University Press. doi:10.1093/oso/9780199691821.001.0001

Mshvenieradze, T. (2013). Logos ethos and pathos in political discourse. *Theory and Practice in Language Studies, 3*(11), 1939–1945. doi:10.4304/tpls.3.11.1939-1945

Nussbaum, M. C. (1996). Essay on Aristotle's rhetoric. In A. O. Rorty (Ed.), *Aristotle on emotions and rational persuasion* (pp. 303–321). Universities of California Press.

Oyedele, A., & Minor, M. S. (2012). Consumer culture plots in television advertising from Nigeria and South Africa. *Journal of Advertising, 41*(1), 91–108. doi:10.2753/JOA0091-3367410107

Pottinger, B. (1987). Political advertising in South Africa: Promise and pitfall. *Communicare, 6*(2), 36–43.

PwC. (2019). *Outlook: 2019-2023 An African perspective* (10th ed.). Retrieved 05/14/22 from: https://africa.mediaoutlook.pwc.com/dist/assets/pdf/AEMO_entertainment_and_media_2019_final.pdf

Pygmaconsulting. (n.d.). *The change of the advertising medium in South Africa*. Retrieved 05/10/22 from: https://pygmaconsulting.com/the-change-of-the-advertising-medium-in-south-africa/

Reisigl, M. (2008). Analysing political rhetoric. In R. Wodak & M. Krzyzanowski (Eds.), *Qualitative discourse analysis the social science* (pp. 96–120). Palgrave, Mcmillan. doi:10.1007/978-1-137-04798-4_5

Rohanlall, L. (2014). *Party ideology in South Africa*. Retrieved 05/04/22 from: https://wiredspace.wits.ac.za/jspui/bitstream/10539/15787/2/thesis%20361561_05%20SEP%202014 pdf

Sander, F., & Govender, S. (2018, December 5). *South Africa: The rise and fall of the ANC*. Retrieved 05/07/22 from: https://www.dw.com/en/south-africa-the-rise-and-fall-of-the-anc/a-4260392

Schulz-Herzenberg, C. (2020). *The South African non-voter: An analysis, The Midpoint Paper Series*. Konrad-Adenauer-Stiftung.

Shabrina, I. (2016). *Persuasive strategies used in Hillary Clinton's political campaign speech* [Undergradute thesis, Universitas Islam Negeri Maulana Malik Ibrahim]. Retrieved 04/29/22 from: http://repositori.uin-alauddin.ac.id/16843/1/NURHIDAYATILLAH.pdf

Shand, K. (2020). *The Advertising Industry in South Africa 2020.* Retrieved 05/21/22 from: https://www.whoownswhom.co.za/report-store/advertising-industry-south-africa-2020/

Sindane, S. (2010). *The rise of political advertising on television in South Africa and its implications for democracy* [Doctoral dissertation, University of the Witwatersrand]. Retrieved 05/1922 from https://citeseerx.ist.psu.edu/viewdoc/download?doi=10.1.1.927.2315&rep=rep1&type=pdf

Sindane, S. (2014). The commodification of political advertising on television during the 2009 general elections in South Africa. Global Media Journal African Edition, 8(1), 1-29.

Teer-Tomaselli, R. (2006). The SAGE Handbook of Political Advertising. In L. L. Kaid & C. Holtz-Bacha (Eds.), Political Advertising in South Africa (pp. 429-444). Sage Publication. doi:10.4135/9781412973403.n26

Thatelo, M. T. (2017). *A social semiotic analysis of the verbal, non-verbal and visual rhetoric of the 2009 and 2014 African National Congress (ANC) political television advertisements: a comparative qualitative content analysis study* [Doctoral dissertation, University of South Africa]. Retrieved 05/20/22 from: https://uir.unisa.ac.za/bitstream/handle/10500/25218/dissertation_mopailo_ma.pdf;jsessionid=9A4E731D7B4E1061473263969B568E89?sequence=1

The Arda. (2015). *South Africa – Religious.* Retrieved 05/15/22 from: https://www.thearda.com/internationalData/countries/Country_207_2.asp

Thorelli, H. B. (1968). Its multi-cultural marketing system. *Journal of Marketing*, *32*(2), 40–48. doi:10.1177/002224296803200207

Tiryakian, E. A. (1978). Emile Durkheim. In T. Bottomore & R. Nisbet (Eds.), *A history of sociological analysis* (pp. 187–236). Basic Books.

Tyali, S. M., & Mukhudwana, R. F. (2020). Discourses on political advertising in South Africa: A social media reception analysis. In M. N. Ndlela & W. Mano (Eds.), Social media and elections in Africa, volume 2 challenges and opportunities (pp. 245-270). Palgrave Macmillan. doi:10.1007/978-3-030-32682-1_13

Uztuğ, F. (2004). *Siyasal iletişim yönetimi.* İstanbul, Türkiye: Media Cat.

KEY TERMS AND DEFINITIONS

2019 General Elections of the Republic of South Africa: Fourteen parties participated in the election held on 08.05.2019 in South Africa. In the election, ANC became the first party and DA became the second party. As a result of the election, the ANC decreased the number of seats in the parliament compared to the previous elections, while the DA increased the number of seats.

African National Congress: The ANC party was founded in 1912, but faced prohibitions in many periods of its political life. After the bans, Mandela became the head of the party and he also became a national symbol of the country.

Aristotle's Rhetoric: Aristotle stated that three important elements are dominant in persuading the masses. These are the ethos that reveals the credibility of the source, the pathos that activates the emotions of the audience, and the logos that reveals the logical propositions.

Coloured: Coloured, formerly Cape Coloured, a person of mixed European ("white") and African ("black") or Asian ancestry, as officially defined by the South African government from 1950 to 1991.

Democratic Alliance: The party that changed names many times was renamed the Democratic Alliance in 2000. Continuing its political life along the liberal line, the party entered the election with Mmusi Maimani in the 2019 election, but at the end of the following year, Jhon Steenhouisen became the head of the party.

Political Advertisements: It is a type of advertisement used by policy makers to persuade the electorate, especially during election periods. Here, the ossified, indecisive and opposing voters are tried to be persuaded in favor of the party and the leader with political promises and discourses.

Sociological Analysis: The sociological analysis method used in researching sociological issues was proposed by Arthur Asa Berger in examining media contents. There are 16 independent titles in this analysis method.

YouTube: The US-based company was founded in 2005. Youtube is currently broadcasting in hundreds of countries. One of these countries is the Republic of South Africa. The general logic of this social media platform is to create and share video content.

Section 2
International Advertising in America

Chapter 3
Colombian Advertising Industry:
The Effects of Social Context on Advertisement Outcomes

Andres Barrios
Universidad de Los Andes, Colombia

Burcu Sezen
ⓘ https://orcid.org/0000-0001-5492-6085
Universidad de Los Andes, Colombia

ABSTRACT

This chapter analyzes how a country context shapes advertising creativity. To do so, the chapter explores the situation of the advertising industry in Colombia (South America), a country recognized by the social focus of its advertisement. The chapter presents an overview of Colombia's socioeconomic situation, the internal conflict development, and the effects of the evolution of COVID-19. Then, a description of the country's advertising industry, media investments over the last years, and effects of the COVID-19 pandemic will follow. The chapter comprises a case study analysis employing two Colombian award-winning advertising campaigns to understand how the country's context has influenced the advertising is developed. The chapter concludes by summarizing the key learnings of the analyzed cases and by presenting suggestions on possible academic research in the country's context.

INTRODUCTION

A key factor in advertising is creativity (Smith and Yang 2004). Previous studies have analysed using a micro lens approach how individual factors shapes advertising the creative process (e.g., Hackley and Kover 2007; Leung and Hui 2014). This chapter takes a macro lens approach analysing how a country context shapes advertising creativity. To do so, the chapter analyses the current situation of the advertising industry in Colombia (South America), a country recognized by advertisement social focus. The chapter presents an overview of Colombia's socioeconomic situation, the internal conflict development, and the

DOI: 10.4018/978-1-7998-9672-2.ch003

effects of the evolution of COVID-19. Then, the country's advertising industry's composition regarding investment and digital advertising development is described. Third, the chapter uses case study analysis employing two award-winning advertising campaigns to understand how the country's context has influenced the advertising outcomes. Finally, the chapter concludes by summarizing the key learnings of the cases analysed and by presenting suggestions on possible academic research in the country's context.

OVERVIEW OF COLOMBIA

Colombia is a medium-sized country, with 440,831 square miles, located in the northern portion of the South American continent. It borders Venezuela, Ecuador, Peru, Panama, and the Pacific and Atlantic Oceans. The country's location on the Ecuadorian line provides tropical weather and grants important fauna and flora biodiversity. The country is known for being the second most biodiverse in the world, with 51,330 species registered in the country, after Brazil. Colombia is the third-most populous country in Latin America, after Mexico and Brazil, with over 50 million inhabitants and about 81.6% living in urban areas. The country's population age average is 31.5, and its literacy is over 95% (DANE, 2020). Most of the population follows a Christian-related religion (90%).

The World Bank positions Colombia as an upper-middle-income economy (World Bank, 2020). The 2020 GDP reached USD$ 271,547 billion. The primary sector of the economy represented 12.9% of GDP. Coffee, bananas, flowers, sugar cane, cattle, and rice make up the main agricultural products, while the primary mining and energy resources include coal, oil, natural gas, iron ore, ferronickel, and gold. The secondary sector contributed 17.6% of GDP. Textiles, chemicals, metallurgy, cement, cartons, plastic resins, and beverages stand out in the industrial sector. The tertiary sector accounted for 69.5% of GDP, emphasizing services, especially tourism (Mincomercio, 2021). Before the pandemic, Colombia had a stable GDP growth of around 4 to 6% (DANE, 2021). This situation led to an important reduction in the unemployment rate, decreasing from 18% in 2010 to 9.6% in 2019, as well as a decrease in the population below the monetary poverty line (US$ 5.5/day) from 40.7% to 27% in the same period. However, economic prosperity did not equally benefit all groups within the population. The GINI index has been around 0.5 for the last ten years (World bank, 2021). This situation puts Colombia among the Latin American countries with the highest level of inequality.

Colombia has had a protagonist position in the political scenario of its internal armed conflict and the related illegal drug production. In 1964, the country entered an armed conflict with guerrillas and paramilitary groups. Between the 80s and 90s, the conflict took a drastic turn as violence escalated, fuelled by illegal drug production and trafficking (Ballentine and Nitzschke, 2003). Guerrillas entered this illicit market, firstly by "taxing" drug producers and then by becoming producers and traders themselves. Subsequently, a right-wing paramilitary group -- Autodefensas Unidas de Colombia (United Self-defenders of Colombia, known as AUC) -- entered the conflict. Initially envisioned as an alliance of legal landowners with private security forces to deter or combat the guerrillas, this group morphed into a group of 11,000 mercenaries hired by drug dealers to protect their illegal businesses (ACNUR 2002). The internal armed conflict directly victimized 8,792,781 people, 22% of the country's population (UARIV, 2019). In 2008, paramilitary groups signed a peace agreement with the Colombian government, which resulted in the demobilization of approximately 31,000 members (Colombian Presidency, 2008). Then, in 2016 the FARC group, the most prominent guerrilla group in the country, reached a peace agreement with the government, and 17,500 combatants voluntarily handed over their weapons.

Despite these advances, other armed groups took the management of the drug trafficking business, and the country remains the second country in terms of narcotics cultivation areas globally (UNODC, 2021).

Colombia is developing its technology infrastructure by increasing the internet penetration rate. Currently, 40 million people (80% of the country's population) have internet access, mainly from mobile technology, 82% with 4G speed, followed by fixed technology, 18% with 39.4 Mbps speed (Portafolio, 2021). Among the Colombian population, 34.73 million (68%) have adopted the internet, mainly accessing (94.8%) from their mobile phones. Colombians spend on average 10 hours a day on the internet. The most common activity on the internet is watching TV (4 hours), using social media (3 hours 45 minutes), reading newspapers (1 hour 44 minutes), listening to music (1 hour 42 minutes), and listening to the radio (1 hour and 15 minutes) (Alvino, 2021).

Finally, the Covid-19 crisis hit Colombia in March 2020, and its effect on its society has been nefarious. More than five million people have been diagnosed with the virus, and over 128,000 people have died (Worldometers, 2021). As of November 2021, Colombia had applied 51 million vaccine doses (WHO, 2021), and the country decided to reopen all economic sectors. The different restrictions provoked by the pandemic severely affected the country's economy, especially tourism. In this sector, the number of non-resident visitors (1.38 million) decreased 69.4% compared to 2019. In 2020, the country's GDP decreased by 6.8%, unemployment reached 15.9%, and people under the poverty line reached 42.5% due to the pandemic (DANE, 2021). Despite these adverse effects, the International Monetary Fund recognized the dynamism of the Colombian economy and estimated that real GDP would increase by 5.15% in 2021 (IMF, 2020).

Advertising Industry in Colombia

The Colombian law defines advertisement as "all forms and content of communication intended to influence the consumption decisions" (Consumer Protection Law, 2011). Companies that develop such content belong to the advertising industry. The Colombian advertising industry involved 1068 companies in 2020, and employed 23.380 people (EMIS, 2021). Despite the number of companies, a small group of large international companies holds a significant market share (85%), and a large group of small companies aims to increase its share (15%). Some sources attribute this high concentration to Colombian companies' tendency to work with integrated agencies that solve all their communication needs, instead of specialized agencies (Scopen, 2021).

The sector's total investment in 2020 was USD$ 1.18 billion, which places Colombia in third place within South America after Argentina and Brazil. This investment was divided into different media channels such as TV (66.3%), newspapers (11%) and radio (10.5%), and digital (21%). The sectors with significant investment in advertising during 2020 were tourism (11.4%), government (10.8%), telecommunication (9.7%), and personal hygiene (8.7%) (EMIS, 2021). According to the Digital Global Overview Report ("We Are Social," 2021), digital advertisement investment in Colombia reached USD$388 million in 2020. Such investment was divided across the categories of social media (45%), digital search (34.2%), banner ads (11.4%), video ads (6.5%), and classified ads (2.9%) (Statista, 2021).

In 2020, the COVID-19 pandemic impacted the advertising industry by decreasing investment and changing its composition. Concerning the composition, lockdowns to prevent the spread of the virus made companies reduce their "out of home" advertisement investment by 90% (e.g., street and shopping mall banners) while increasing digital advertising by 15% during 2020 (Portafolio, 2021b). The shrinkage of the Colombian economy in 2020 reduced the total advertising investment by 15.15%. Further, the employment generated decreased by 12.6% (EMIS, 2021). Despite this temporary stagnation, the Colombian advertising sector remains competitive, and it is expected that investment will rise to 14% in 2022 (IAB, 2021).

Advertisement Consumption in Colombia

Colombians consume advertising through television (74.9%), internet (12%), paper (6%), and radio (2.13%) (Raddar, 2021). For those who consume advertisements through the internet, social media is declared as the first channel to learn about new brands (66,3%), followed by search engines (63%), looking at the brand sites (46.5%), and mobile apps (36.4%) ("We are Social," 2021). The target group index (TGI) shows that 41% of consumers fully agree that advertising influences their purchasing decisions (EMIS, 2021). Studies argue that people in developing countries may still be more receptive than those in more saturated markets, where the consumers have become less responsive to advertising (Pauwels et al., 2013). This consumer openness to advertising suggests great potential for Colombia's growing and dynamic sector.

Digital advertisement consumption comes mainly from social media platforms. There are 39 million social media users that spend 3 hours and 45 Minutes daily on these sites. The most used platform in the country is YouTube (98%), followed by Facebook (95%), WhatsApp (90%), and Instagram (82%). YouTube has a potential audience of 29.9 million users, who use the platform for entertainment (86%). Facebook has a potential audience of 36 million users, who use the platform mainly for social interaction (60%). WhatsApp has a potential audience of 25 million users, who use the platform mainly for social interaction. Instagram has a potential audience of 16 million users, who use the platform mainly for looking at products and services (81%). Concerning digital search, the most used browser in Colombia is Google Chrome, with 85.1% of users.

Advertisement Outcomes in Colombia

A remarkable outcome of Colombia's advertising industry has been its success in creative awards at festivals. Since 2000, Colombian agencies have successfully participated in major international advertising festivals and received around 556 awards over the last ten years. These awards are mainly related to advertising usage for social purposes, by linking a brand or institution to resolving the country's substantial social problems (e.g., violence or poverty). These outcomes posit the following research question: How has the Colombian context shaped agencies' advertising outcomes?

METHODOLOGY

Given that advertising outcomes are heterogeneous, comprising different purposes and scales, we decided to use case study as a methodological approach to respond to our research question. A case study is "an empirical inquiry that investigates a contemporary phenomenon [the case] in depth and within its real-world context" (Yin, 2003, p. 16). The selected cases were two award-winning advertising campaigns that reveal Colombian usage of advertising for social purposes: "Christmas lights", awarded with Titanium at Cannes Lions 2014, and "La tienda Cerca", awarded with Creative eCommerce Cannes Lions 2021. For the case reconstruction, we gathered data from two complementary sources: interviews with leaders of the campaigns (Jose Miguel Sokoloff - Creative Director of MullenLowe SSP3 and Jorge Velásquez - Creative Director of Draftline & Connections Colombia) and archival data related to the campaigns' outcomes. Next, we present each case.

CASE DESCRIPTION

Christmas Lights

In collaboration with the Colombian Ministry of Defence, this campaign was started in 2011 by the MullenLowe agency. The campaign aimed to incite and invite the paramilitary and guerrilla combatants to demobilize from their armed groups and enter the government reintegration program, which offered them physical and psychological support, educational and labour training according to the participants' interests (e.g., agriculture, construction, etc.), and economic resources to develop an independent life project following Colombian laws. The traditional Ministry's communication strategy to motivate combatants' demobilization was very literal: simply spelling out the benefits of demobilizing and joining the reintegration program.

MullenLowe decided to understand combatants' rationale for staying or leaving the illegal groups as a first step. Several interviews with previously demobilized guerrilla members were carried out. The interviews probed for their motivations to join the rebel movement, their dreams related to its future success, trials and tribulations, and their experience within the insurgency ranks. Interviews revealed ex-combatants' humanity, including their joys, fears, motivations, and desire to return home. This view contradicted the typical image of the hardened and fearsome guerrilla individuals present in the Colombian collective consciousness. The interviews' insights were the basis upon which MullenLowe proposed to change the army's communications approach from a threatening one to a more personal one. The communication aim was to show guerrilla members the possibility of a different, better life waiting for them. Jose Miguel said, "The game was not about making them too scared to stay. It was about giving them the courage to leave." To accomplish this objective, the agency developed four advertising pieces.

The first advertising piece took place in 2010 and focused on making ex-combatants aware they are not alone, providing information about ex-combatants who have been in their situation before and who decided to demobilize, living currently in peace. This set of advertisements involved former combatants narrating their personal stories and inviting others to join them. Local radio stations traditionally listened to by guerrilla members transmitted the pieces. The campaign had a substantial impact as 188 guerrilla members, including three commanders, decided to demobilize in a month. This high rate of demobilization was an outstanding achievement as high-rank combatants are harder to replace in the armed groups, and they could provide critical information about the group's military strategy. The guerrillas prohibited their members from listening to radio stations. As a response, the campaign continued by inviting high-rank ex-combatants to participate in the advertisements. Their demobilization became a symbol to motivate others to do so, and their stories were broadcasted by infiltrating the communications of the guerrilla group (Castilo, 2010).

The second advertisement piece focused on using Christmas lights as a symbol of demobilization. In December 2011, nine 75-foot trees were picked along jungle paths the insurgents used across the country. These trees were decorated with Christmas lights and messages encouraging them to come home for the festivities. When a guerrilla member passed nearby, the tree lights activated with a banner next to them that said, "If Christmas can come to the jungle, you can come home too. Demobilize. At Christmas, everything is possible." In December of 2012, the operation "Rivers of Light" took place as the third advertising piece. In this campaign, civilians who live close to the conflict areas and relatives of guerrilla members were encouraged to write a letter inviting them to spend Christmas together. These letters were put into floating LED-illuminated balls and sent through the rivers used by the insurgents. Guerrilla groups usually locate nearby rivers as they provide secure escape paths. In December 2013, the operation "Bethlehem pathways" took place as the last advertising piece. This campaign used the military's intelligence that guerrillas were shuffling their members around the country to avoid desertion, and that guerrilla commanders dictated death as the punishment for those trying to demobilize (Castilo, 2010). The Colombian military dropped thousands of tiny lights along paths commonly travelled by the guerrillas. These lights draw an escape path for deserters toward the nearest town's plaza, where powerful beacon lights with giant glow-in-the-dark billboards with the phrase "Guerrillas, Follow the Light" were located. Together, the beacons and the tiny lights were designed to function as a light pathway to guide defecting FARC rebels' escape. A fleeing guerrilla member would walk 10 kilometres to reach a beacon.

Between 2011 and 2013, more than 18.000 combatants were demobilized. According to the Colombian government, MullenLowe's advertising campaigns played a critical part in this accomplishment. These demobilization campaigns have been the most awarded in Colombia's advertising history, receiving more than 120 awards in the main festivals of creativity, innovation, strategy, and effectiveness globally. This includes the Black Pencil of the decade at D&AD (England) and the Titanium at Cannes Lions (France). In addition, the campaigns have been replicated to fight against the LRA (Lord Resistance Army) guerrilla group in Uganda and Congo (La República, 2014).

Tienda Cerca

The COVID-19 long lockdown period brought economic difficulties and human suffering to mom-and-pop shops. There are 450,000 stores in the country, with 11,000 of them in danger of shutting down due to COVID; social distancing regulations limited consumers' visits to these stores (Analitik, 2021). These stores are part of neighbourhoods' social dynamics, becoming socialization points for people who buy the everyday household items there. These shops are a key actor for the country's food system, and their activities are embedded in the country's culture and economy (Serrano & Brooks, 2019).

This situation motivated Bavaria (an InBev company), along with the advertising agency Draftline, to start thinking beyond their sales to consider the well-being and sustainability of the mom-and-pop stores that are one the most extensive sales channel for the firm's products (e.g., beer, juices, bottled water, etc.) Therefore, Bavaria and Draftline created a digital platform for the mom-and-pop stores within neighbourhoods in Colombia called "Tienda Cerca". The platform enabled stores to sell through digital channels during the extended period of lockdown and closure of physical stores. The challenge was to create a platform simple enough for owners of these stores, with typically low technology literacy, to use. According to Jorge Velasquez, "the platform could be described as a friendly technology that uses information to create synergies between customers and stores."

The platform geo-located the registered mom-and-pop stores across Bogotá and digitalized information such as owner photos, contact information, and products for sale. If a customer wants a product for delivery, she enters the platform, and based on her location, the app provides information on the three closest shops. The customer selects a shop and sends a message through the platform with her request.

The message is sent through WhatsApp, a technology widely diffused in the country, to the shop owners with the product requirements. The message is received by the shop owner and sent accordingly.

The platform was launched in March 2020, accompanied by an advertising campaign. The advertisement campaign focused on provoking the audience's nostalgic feelings about the essential role of the corner store as a gathering point within Colombian neighbourhoods. It also showed how stores are a critical part of the economy and the culture, with a shopkeeper that knows everyone in the neighbourhood. It further reminds the audience that those consumers no longer need to make a trade-off among savings, time optimization, and the closeness they feel to the corner shop and the shopkeeper. According to Jorge Velasquez, "a business model that is simple, personalized, and human. Tienda Cerca: from the corner to your door."

The campaign outcome includes the registration of around 75,000 mom-and-pop shops in Colombia, 10 million visits from customers, and a sales increase of USD$ 1,200,000 during the first year. Due to its success, the e-commerce platform was copied in nine countries in Latin America, with 425,000 stores registered. In June of 2021, the campaign won the 2021 Gran Prix Cannes award in the E-commerce category.

THE EFFECT OF SOCIAL CONTEXT ON COLOMBIAN ADVERTISEMENT OUTCOMES

The literature on the social context effect on advertising has been analysed under a research theme termed the 'place perspective.' Under this perspective, it has been established that macro-level elements (e.g., culture) and meso-level elements (e.g., field composition) interact to facilitate the creative process in advertising (Sasser and Koslow 2012, Roca et al. 2017). Using this framework, we identify some of the macro and meso-level elements that influenced the exemplar advertising campaigns.

The Colombian macro-level elements that influenced our exemplar cases were: A) Long lasting violent conflict. Colombians have learnt about war practices; B) Strong link with traditional celebrations. Colombian population is mainly Christian and related traditions inspire family gatherings: C) High inequality. The high level of inequality has created an informal market system in which mom-and-pop stores are the main source for neighbourhoods' supplies.

The Colombian meso-level elements that influenced our exemplar cases were: A) Mass media concentration. The high cost of advertising in traditional media led advertisers to innovate looking for alternative or less expensive channels to reach audiences; B) Internet penetration. The country high rates on internet penetration became an opportunity for advertisers to reach audiences; C) Social media adoption. Colombian consumers' high use of social media apps (e.g., WhatsApp) facilitated the translation of the physical commercial interaction into a virtual one during the pandemics.

The macro and meso-level variables have influenced advertisement outcomes in terms of using non-traditional channels to communicate contents with concrete messages that evoke emotions, such as nostalgia, which bring closer the audience to the product/service offered.

CONCLUSIONS

At the outset, we posit the research question: How has the Colombian context shaped agencies' advertising outcomes? We respond to this question by analysing the cases of two award-winning advertising campaigns. The analysis of these campaigns shows Colombia macro-level variables (e.g., long lasting violent conflict. strong link with traditional celebrations, and high inequality), linked with meso-level ones (e.g., mass media concentration, internet penetration, and social media adoption) to shape advertising local practices. These results provide essential insights for advertisement actors (e.g., agencies, clients, governing associations) to identify the specific macro and meso-level characteristics that can contribute to the advertising strengths in each country. These strengths are built upon everyday interaction with a particular country context making them difficult to imitate.

FUTURE RESEARCH DIRECTIONS

We expect that scholars interested in the topic develop further research. Some alternatives include: to develop a more systematic analysis of the advertisement campaigns based on other contextual variables, such as legal and organizational incentives. In addition, a comparison between Colombian and similar countries of Latin America could be implemented to assess if similar contextual variables have resulted in similar advertisement outcomes. Finally, we assessed the outcomes using Cannes awards, a festival that focused on creativity, as the key advertisement outcome source. An interesting approach could be to include awards of festivals with other approaches such as Effie, which focus on investment effectivity. We invite academics to develop further research on this topic.

REFERENCES

ACNUR. (2002). *Informe Sobre Derechos Humanos en Colombia.* https://www.acnur.org/t3/uploads/media/COI_53.pdf

Alvino, C. (2021). *Estadísticas de la situación Digital de Colombia.* https://branch.com.co/marketing-digital/estadisticas-de-la-situacion-digital-de-colombia-en-el-2020-2021/

Analitik. (2021). *Por pandemia pueden desaparecer 11.000 tiendas en Colombia.* https://www.valoraanalitik.com/2021/08/18/por-pandemia-pueden-desaparecer-11-000-tiendas-de-barrio-en-colombia/

Ballentine, K., & Heiko, N. (2003). *Beyond Greed and Grievance: Policy Lessons from Studies in the Political Economy of Armed Conflict.* Routledge. doi:10.1515/9781685853402

Brook, T. V. (2013). *Propaganda that works: Christmas decorations.* https://www.usatoday.com/story/nation/2013/08/13/pentagon-propaganda-information-operations/2646243/

Castilo, M. (2010). *Colombian military's new weapon against rebels: Christmas trees.* CNN. http://edition.cnn.com/2010/WORLD/americas/12/20/colombia.operation.christmas/index.html

Consumer Protection Law. (2011). https://www.funcionpublica.gov.co/eva/gestornormativo/norma.php?i=44306

Departamento Administrativo Nacional de Estadística - DANE. (2021). *Indicadores relevantes*. https://www.dane.gov.co/files/ses/Indicadores_Relevantes.pdf

El Espectador. (2021). *Campaña colombiana para promover la desmovilización se ganó el "Nobel" de la publicidad.* https://www.elespectador.com/judicial/campana-colombiana-para-promover-la-desmovilizacion-se-gano-el-nobel-de-la-publicidad-article/

Emerging Markets Information System. (2021). *Sector Publicitario en Colombia Publicidad, Relaciones Públicas y Servicios Relacionados.* https://www.emis.com/

Florez-Morris, M. (2007). Joining Guerilla Groups in Colombia: Individual Motivations and Processes for Entering a Violent Organization. *Studies in Conflict and Terrorism, 30*(7), 615–634. doi:10.1080/10576100701385958

Hackley, C., & Kover, A. (2007). The trouble with creatives: Negotiating creative identity in advertising agencies. *International Journal of Advertising, 26*(1), 63–78. doi:10.1080/02650487.2007.11072996

Human Development Reports of UNDP. (2019). https://hdr.undp.org/en/content/broadening-our-thinking-vulnerability

IAB. (2021). http://www.iabcolombia.com/wp-content/uploads/2021/02/5.-Resumen-Ejecutivo-Inversio%CC%81n-en-Publicidad-Digital-Total-An%CC%83o-2020.pdf, accessed on 14/11/2021.

IMF. (2020b, December). *Policy Responses to COVID19.* https://www.imf.org/en/Topics/imf-and-covid19/Policy-Responses-to-COVID-19#C

La República. (2014). *Por campaña para desmovilizados, Lowe-Ssp3 ganó premio en Reino Unido.* https://www.larepublica.co/empresas/por-campana-para-desmovilizados-lowe-ssp3-gano-premio-en-reino-unido-2187706

Leung, S., & Hui, A. (2014). A recent look: Advertising creatives' perceptions of creativity in Hong Kong/China. *Services Marketing Quarterly, 35*(2), 138–154. doi:10.1080/15332969.2014.885366

Ministerio de Comercio – Mincomercio. (2020). *Contexto Macroeconómico Colombia.* https://www.mincit.gov.co/getattachment/1c8db89b-efed-46ec-b2a1-56513399bd09/Colombia.aspx

Pauwels, K., Erguncu, S., & Yildirim, G. (2013). Winning hearts, minds and sales: How marketing communication enters the purchase process in emerging and mature markets. *International Journal of Research in Marketing, 30*(1), 57–68. doi:10.1016/j.ijresmar.2012.09.006

Portafolio. (2021a). https://www.portafolio.co/economia/infraestructura/conexiones-a-internet-fija-y-movil-que-hay-en-colombia-segun-mintic-554259

Portafolio. (2021b). *Publicidad exterior una de las que más cae por la COVID.* https://www.portafolio.co/economia/publicidad-exterior-una-de-las-que-mas-cae-por-la-covid-543325

Raddar Forecast. (2021). https://raddar.net/wp-content/uploads/2021/09/Base-Memorias-FORECAST-2021-2022-RADDAR.pdf

Roca, D., Wilson, B., Barrios, A., & Muñoz-Sánchez, O. (2017). Creativity identity in Colombia: The advertising creatives' perspective. *International Journal of Advertising, 36*(6), 831–851. doi:10.1080/02650487.2017.1374318

Scopen. (2021). *Agency Scope.* https://scopen.com/sites/default/files/studies/agency_scope_colombia_2020_-_anexo_informe_tendencias.pdf

Serrano, A., & Brooks, A. (2019). Who is left behind in global food systems? Local farmers failed by Colombia's avocado boom. *Environment and Planning E. Nature and Space, 2*(2), 348–367.

Smith, R., & Xang, X. (2004). Toward a general theory of creativity in advertising: Examining the role of divergence. *Marketing Theory, 4*(1–2), 31–58. doi:10.1177/1470593104044086

Sokoloff, J. M. (2019). *Advertising for impact: How Christmas lights helped end a war. In Perspectives on Impact.* Routledge. doi:10.4324/9780429452796-15

Statista. (2021). *Gasto anual en publicidad digital en Colombia.* https://es.statista.com/estadisticas/1178729/gasto-anual-publicidad-digital-colombia/

Ultravioleta. (2019). *Así se hizo Ríos de luz, una invitación a la desmovilización.* https://ultravioleta.co/asi-se-hizo-rios-de-luz-una-invitacion-a-la-desmovilizacion/

UNHCR. (2020). *Venezuela Situation.* https://data2.unhcr.org/es/situations/vensit

Unidad para la Atención y la Reparación Integral a las Víctimas. (2019). *Registro Único de Víctimas (RUV).* https://www.unidadvictimas.gov.co/es/registro-unico-de-victimas-ruv/37394

United Nations Office on Drugs and Crime. (2021). *Global Overview: Drug Demand / Drug Supply.* http://www.odc.gov.co/Portals/1/publicaciones/pdf/WDR21_Booklet_2.pdf

We Are Social & Hootsuite. (2021). *Digital 2021 Colombia.* https://datareportal.com/reports/digital-2021-colombia

WHO. (2021). *Colombia.* https://covid19.who.int/region/amro/country/co

World Bank. (2020). *Colombia | data.* https://data.worldbank.org/country/colombia

Worldometers. (2021). *Colombia.* https://www.worldometers.info/coronavirus/country/colombia/

Chapter 4
The Effects of Different Developments in Advertising:
An Overview of American Advertising

Selçuk Bazarcı

ⓘ https://orcid.org/0000-0003-0816-1362

Ege University, Turkey

ABSTRACT

Advertising has an ancient history in terms of its origins. Advertisements have evolved over time in accordance with the development of societies, and they directly and indirectly affect the cultural processes of communities. This effect of advertising can be seen clearly in different cultures. In this respect, it is essential to make sense of the advertising schools in different cultures and to reveal their social effects. American advertising is one of the crucial schools that both shape the culture in the national sense and shape the world advertising. Almost every technological innovation of humanity has a counterpart in American advertising. In this study, all the periodic transformations that American advertising has experienced over time have been revealed in terms of the meanings they create socially. In addition, three advertisement campaigns produced by the most prominent advertisers of the period and their social impacts are evaluated.

INTRODUCTION

Developments in technology and different alternatives in the way of using media have an essential role in the transformation of advertising. New digital technologies in this field have significantly changed the way of communication of the firms and influence the consumers through digital media (Lee & Cho, 2020, p. 332). Notably, the direct involvement of interactive media platforms such as social media in human life is decisive in transforming the world into a small global village. However, just as every culture has its own dynamics, every country also has characteristic elements that enrich advertising activities in connection with their cultural background.

DOI: 10.4018/978-1-7998-9672-2.ch004

To define all these issues, it is important to make sense of the concept of international advertising. Moriarty, Mitchell, and Wells (2012, p. 566) define global advertising as an advertising effort designed to promote the same product in many countries and different cultures. International advertising campaigns have two basic starting points: (1) success in one country and (2) a centrally conceived strategy.

In order to achieve success on behalf of the brand, it is important to have a good understanding of international advertising dynamics. At the same time, the stages of development must be accurately defined. Regarding this, Taylor (2002) mentions some obstacles. According to him, there are five basic problems that have hindered the development of international advertising research:

1. Too many descriptive studies of advertising content and not enough research on why various executional techniques are effective in specific markets.
2. A preoccupation with questions of whether campaigns should be standardized to the detriment of seeking answers for pragmatic execution across markets.
3. A lack of rigor in establishing an equivalence in studies comparing data from multiple countries, both in terms of study design and data analysis.
4. A disturbing lack of knowledge about whether and when targeting segments that cut across national boundaries (that is, inter-market segmentation) can be effective.
5. Not enough focus on control of international advertising campaigns, both in terms of who makes the decisions and the extent to which they are effectively implemented.

It is possible to talk about the effects of different schools in advertising over the years. Among these schools, one of the countries that direct the world advertising is the USA. American advertising has a structure that reflects its characteristics from past to present. It is possible to trace the advertisements in America to the 17th century. The efforts by English entrepreneurs to attract new settlers to America were "one of the first concerted and sustained advertising campaigns in the history of the modern world," according to historian Richard Hofstadter. Throughout the seventeenth and eighteenth centuries, enterprising Englishmen printed various books, brochures, and posters to promote America to their countrymen (Sivulka, 2012, p. 6).

In the late 19th century and early 1900s, advertisements containing small promotions, similar to newspaper columns, gained momentum by increasing the purchase of space and time from the media in connection with branding with the development of production systems. When brands had come out in the late 1800s in America, advertising started playing a significant role in imbuing commodities with specific meanings. Ivory soap was no longer called "white soap" but had its own name. It had a distinctive appearance, logo, and package design that hasn't changed much over the years (O'Barr, 2005). Along with these developments, advertising agencies have also become stronger and more active in acting as an intermediary between the brand and the media. After the 1920s, the prevalence of the radio increased and then, after the invention of television, it created a visual world, plus, advertising evolved into a different situation. American advertising has been affected by wars, as well as the entire world advertising, and the industry has evolved in connection with economic and social structures. With the effect of the great depression in 1929 and after the Second World War, the decline in the purchasing power of people has also been a factor in the decrease in advertising activities. Another role that advertising took on during the Second World War was promoting patriotism which also supported the war. Some ads which carried notices asking the public to buy war bonds and contributed the war (O'Barr, 2005).

In the post-war period, more creative content seemed to be at the center of the campaigns in order to increase the sales and maximized interest in the products. At the same time, the invention of television that enabled real-time transmission of visual messages, shaped the advertising of the period. In particular, it is also necessary to mention the innovations created by the advertisers who shaped American advertising. Each of them set an important example for other advertisers with their campaigns. With the change of advertising understanding, the campaigns created by these advertisers and their impacts are among the important developments in American advertising.

AN OVERVIEW OF THE USA IN A GEOGRAPHICAL, SOCIO-POLITICAL, AND CULTURAL CONTEXT

The United States of America is the third-largest country in the world based on population and land area. The United States is also the world's largest economy and one of the most influential nations in the world (Briney, 2019). According to the U.S. Census Bureau, the country has a population of more than 332 million. In every 9 seconds a child is born and a person dies every 11 seconds (Zimmermann, K. A., 2021). Due to the high population rate, the fact that people from different cultures live together contributes to the the multi-cultural structure of the US. It is possible to say that the elements that constitute cultural accumulation in the country are in wide variety and variable structures. For most people residing in the United States, English is the only language spoken at home. However, many languages other than English are spoken in homes across the country. Data on non-natives who speak language other than English and their English-speaking ability provide an interesting portrait of the nation. Routinely, these data are used in a wide variety of legislative, political legal, and research applications (Census, 2021). Modernization, has been a leading factor in almost every development. The US economic power is not limited to only a single continent, both also has an impact other on other counties' cultural and social contexts in different continents.

The United States has an organic connection with Europe. The majority of the cultural areas of the United States are originally European. As a result of European colonists' immigration with their different social structures, this fact has led to the formation of new habitats rich in culture (Britannica, 2022). In this context, American culture, which is created and specific to its own dynamics, is directly based on the output points in Europe and is reshaped in itself.

The United States has been a significant force in the world for long years and has had an important role in each field in creating impact. Especially in the sense of technology and innovation, it has a pioneering structure on other states and nations. Advertising is also one of the sectors that is imposed to direct impacts depending on the developments in the US and other countries. Understanding American advertising and identifying its impacts is especially important in the 20th century. For this, we need to look at the evolution of advertising in the US until today. Because the periodical changes and different their reflections are closely related to both socio-political developments and technological innovations. In this respect, the forms of using the media and the changing daily practices in life are determinants in this development process.

THE DEVELOPMENT OF AMERİCAN ADVERTISING FROM PAST TO PRESENT

American advertising has had a significant impact on the evolution of advertising over time. The social changes have also improved advertising. At the same time, advertisements have had a significant impact on American society. In this respect, it is important to consider the changes and their effects on advertising from a periodic point of view. By looking at the history of advertising, it is possible to make sense of the social structure of that period.

It is not possible to separate developments in American advertising from social changes. Although the foundations of modern advertising were laid in America, it is possible to attribute the beginning of advertising as a profession to Europe depending on technological developments and economic structure (Geçit, 2014, p. 213). It is known that 19th-century advertisements adhere to informative content and are mostly used in newspapers as a news source. The period in which advertising has gained an institutional status in the US is the middle of the 19th century. In 1841, America's first advertising agency was established by Volney B. Palmer (Holland, 1974, p. 357). Palmer drew his strength from his large followers at that time. Developing his own network continuously increased the strength and sustainability of his advertising agency. Palmer's work as a consultant is shown as one of the important elements that provide persuasion in the pre-advertising process for brands. The fact that the concept of agency was used for the first time in real terms and that it had a different understanding in terms of operation created some obstacles for companies to adapt. But Palmer, with his strong communication, carried out this process well and became a pioneer in the establishment of subsequent advertising agencies in terms of being a source of inspiration.

Although advertising campaigns made themselves feel better after the 1800s, the studies were mostly conveyed through newspaper advertisements. However, at the beginning of the 20th century, there was a resurgence of American advertising. In order to understand this historical process, it is important to understand how the advertising perceptions of the period changed. First of all, it is necessary to talk about the trend that continued its influence in the early 1900s and is based on rational advertising practices. During this period, advertisers such as Claude Hopkins, Albert Lasker, John E. Kennedy, John E. Powers, and Ernest E. Calkins have given direction to the advertising understanding. Leading copywriters and advertisers of the time, such as John E. Powers, tried to use the news function of advertisements by prioritizing information in their advertisements at the beginning of the last century (Beard, 2005, p. 55). At the same time, a style of expression in which the cause-effect relationship is at the forefront and direct narration which shaped the advertisement content is frequently featured in the advertisemenst. In the early years of 1890s most of the advertising experts emphasized the basically rational, logical and sensible qualities of man without considering whether these abilities were innate or acquired. In other words, without giving reference to the "nature-nurture" controversery (Curti, 1967, p. 338).

As a general feature of the period, the fact that people focused on more information against the risk of being deceived while purchasing a product enabled the advertisements of that period to be created in line with this expectation. The understandings adopted by different advertisers during these years both shaped the advertising content and profoundly affected other advertisers. For example, John E. Kennedy laid the foundations of the basic sales promise strategy with his cause-effect-based advertising approach (Akyol, 2014, p. 7). According to this strategy, it is aimed to create a logical basis over the repetition of the advertisement by highlighting a unique feature of the product, unlike its other competitors, and convince the consumer in this way.

On the other hand, Lasker focused on why one brand of product should be purchased over another which is called as "reason why" advertising (Morello, 2001, p. 15). Lasker, who defined what the advertising agency should do and how its position should be shaped, had a significant impact on the emergence of modern advertising. It has transformed agencies from being just a tool that performs jobs and prints to a structure that works with and directs brands. The change here has enabled agencies to work more effectively and to focus more on scientific data about the campaign. In the early 1900s, Albert Davis Lasker used three advertising techniques: 'reason why,' 'celebrity endorsements,' and 'preemptive claims,' enabling customers such as Lucky Strike cigarettes, Sunkist oranges, and Van Camp pork and beans to create commercial success stories (Morello, 2001, p. 1).

Lasker has shaped his advertising campaigns with supporting arguments in the persuasion process, using the 'reason why' technique a lot. One of the elements that he highlighted in his campaign especially for the Lucky Strike brand, is that smoking helps lose weight and stay in shape by reducing appetite. He tried to eliminate the questions that would arise in the minds of consumers by using evidence supporting the ideas he put forward with this campaign. The fact that Lasker and other advertisers of the period based their campaigns on a specific strategy led to a more comprehensive and coordinated implementation of the studies. At this point, an opportunity had arisen for advertising agencies to prove themselves. Advertising agencies, which have made their own presence very evident, sought answers to the question of how to increase sales in a completely product-oriented manner while producing campaigns independently of brands. At the same time, since this situation brought success in the short and long run, this has been a factor in the establishment of other advertising agencies and the tendency of brands to turn to independent agencies instead of in-house advertising units.

Another important advertiser of the period was John E. Powers. Powers emphasized reality in his advertising campaigns and avoided exaggerated definitions and descriptions. Tungate (2007, p. 15) describes Powers' belief in truth and how he reflects it on his campaigns through the following story:

He was once hired by a Pittsburgh clothing company that was on the verge of bankruptcy. 'There is only one way out,' Powers told his client, 'tell the truth. . . The only way to salvation lies in large and immediate sales.' The resulting ad read: 'We are bankrupt. This announcement will bring our creditors down on our necks. But if you come and buy tomorrow, we shall have the money to meet them. If not, we will go to the wall.' Impressed by the directness of the ad, customers rushed to save the store.

John E. Powers defended the idea of constructing advertising messages over reality by focusing on consumer interest when advertising was not given much importance. This approach not only made him an essential publicist at the beginning of the 20th century but also revealed the importance of copywriting in the advertising campaign. The success of the advertisements made by Powers has also highlighted the need for brands to work more coordinately with advertising organizations. In this respect, John E. Powers had an important influence on the emergence of different dynamics in the advertising understanding of the period.

Claude Hopkins is one of the important advertisers who left their mark on the period with his campaigns. Hopkins, who both undersigned the most effective campaigns of the period and influenced the advertisers came after him in the history of advertising has always kept sales-oriented advertising activities at the forefront. Hopkins' approach to advertising is shaped entirely based on scientific data. For example, when planning the advertising campaign for the Schiltz brand, the company asked its employees why they didn't talk about all the brewing phases. They also said that the process is the same for all competitors. It was then that Hopkins had the idea, as always, that set the brand apart and used the correct arguments. When Hopkins was hired to promote Schlitz, he discovered that the bottles were steam cleaned just like any other brewery. However, no other brewery had considered including this nugget of information in its advertisements (Tungate, 2007, p. 19). Hopkins's understanding of this approach enabled the consumer to look at the evidence in the persuasion process and perform the purchasing behavior accordingly, instead of conveying a direct message. This process, based on logic, resulted in a change in the advertising understanding of the period and the use of similar methods by different advertisers.

Earnest Elmo Calkins is one of the important advertisers of the period who contributed to the transition to modern advertising with the works he made by using scientific advertising practices. According to Calkins, advertising is the fuel running the engines of industry (Heller, 2017). At the same time, thinking that the advertising understanding of the period should be further differentiated, Calkins produced studies supporting the transformation of advertisements into art in directing consumer preferences. In the 1920s, the fact that American products lagged behind European brands, especially in the clothing sector, was an element in doing something different. Although mass production was the foundation on which the modern American economy was built, many cultural critics felt that items coming off the assembly line lacked good taste (www.printmag.com, Date of Access: 29.10.2021). This situation has led to a change of discourse in advertising and the search for different ways to encourage sales. By focusing on the art aspect of the advertisement, Calkins and his friends wanted to improve the typography and provide a visual function for the advertisement to attract the consumer.

After 1925, the changes in the nature of the economy, especially the need for product differentiation, led to the development of advertising in a more instinctive and non-rational way(Curti, 1967, p. 346). The recession experienced in the period from the First World War to the Second World War also gave direction to American advertising.

Over time social developments have had a direct impact on American advertising. For example, Tungate (2007, p. 35) summarizes the discourses of agencies and brands regarding the war during the Second World War as follows:

Advertising went back to war. As well as being deployed for the purposes of boosting morale, advertising agencies rushed to give the impression that brands were in the thick of the fighting. In a manner that seems even more distasteful today than it did at the time, products were linked to the war effort. For instance, Cadillac claimed to be 'in the vanguard of the invasion,' as Cadillac-built parts could be found in the engines of fighter planes. Texaco assured motorists that the gasoline they were forced to do without was 'being turned into war products to speed our forces to victory.' The tasteful accompanying image was the bright flash of a bomb exploding, with Germans running for cover.

Due to the structure of the period, advertisements turned into a communication tool for the government. The fact that the agend was entirely war-oriented is one of the factors in creating advertising campaigns with more nationalistic content. Because the expectation of the consumer is, in a way, was to provide social benefit and to support those who take care of the interests of the people, with the effect of the nationalism trend that has spread beyond the person himself. In this respect, it is a highly anticipated development that the advertising industry, as a reflection of patriotism, is also a resource that provides the support of the state. In a way, in this period of chaos, it has been important for agencies to create jobs that will be supported by people and adapt to them to survive and ensure continuity. The Second

World War and the spread of television after it changed the dimensions of advertising completely. with the spread of television since the middle of the 20th century, advertising has turned into a different structure and practice. Wallace (2019) summarizes the evolution of television advertising in the United States as follows:

1941: The FCC (Federal Communications Commission) issues commercial licenses to 10 US television stations in May. On July 1, the first-ever commercial airs, a spot by the Bulova watch company that cost $9.

1951: TV ad spending reaches $128 million, up from $12.5 million in 1949: a 10X increase.

1953: Commercially broadcast color television launches.

1955: TV ad spending reaches the $1 billion threshold.

1963: TV surpasses newspapers as an information source for the first time.

Television has changed the structure of advertising as it enables the transmission of both visual and auditory messages together. In particular, the fact that the USA is in a good position in terms of technological developments has been decisive in the progress of advertising campaigns in parallel with these developments. The growing structure of television is also a factor in channeling advertising expenditures to this medium. The transition from print advertisements to image-oriented videos over time is also a factor in developing different areas in the form of advertisement preparation. This dominance, which continued until the 2000s and later, has tended to decrease with the spread of the internet. The fact that the internet has an important place in terms of daily usage frequency in American society has brought an alternative in terms of advertising.

The rapid spread of this new communication tool among the masses in the USA, which is one of the countries that used innovative works for the first time in the spread of television, revealed the necessity of rapid change in advertising practices with a focus on harmony. It was seen that television, which was the new media of the period, took the place of radio in time. It is also possible that the advertising investments spent on television reached high amounts in a very short time. Thanks to US advertising, spending on television rose from US $12 million in 1949 to US $158 million just in three years as brands firmly established themselves on television (Tungate, 2007, p. 34).

One of the developments shaping American advertising is the basic sales promise strategy developed by Rosser Reeves. According to this strategy, it is aimed to differentiate the brand from its competitors by highlighting the most important feature of the brand. According to Reeves, the claim or benefit based on the USP should be dominant in the advertisement and should be constantly emphasized through repeated advertisements (Elden, 2013, p. 345). Today, there are some widely accepted rules in order, a USP project to be successful, which are (1) a readiness to sell the product, (2) the popularity of the product for the potential customer, and (3) a statement that the product is not just special but truly unique. (Miller & Henthorne, 2008, p.50) USP, a creative strategy in advertising, is based on presenting informative content combined with creativity in order to establish a stronger communication between the product and the consumer. In this respect, this understanding has an important place in American advertising in terms of trying different ways and giving a new breath in the transition process to the creative revolution.

CHANGING PERCEPTIONS AND THE CREATIVE REVOLUTION IN AMERICAN ADVERTISING

We must develop our own philosophy and not have the advertising philosophy of others imposed on us. Let us blaze new trails. Let us prove to the world that good taste, good art, good writing, can be good selling. —Bill Bernbach

Advertisements are a kind of intermediary element that creates the process of re-creating the product and brand in the mind of the consumer. People will see your ads more than they will see your product. If your ads look like all others, then your product will also too. (Nelson, 2017) Especially the fact that all products produced today are close to each other in terms of many variables makes the role of advertisements in influencing consumer preferences more important. Advertising is based on attracting the consumer's attention to the main target product. Especially today, among many information stacks, the interest of the consumer in advertisements is very low. In 1970s, it was thought that a person could see 500 to 1600 advertisements averagely per day. Today, it is known that an average person can see between 6,000 to 10,000 advertisements everyday (Carr, 2021). At the same time, the acceleration of the speed and consumption of digital media day by day reveals the necessity for creative content to create efficiency in a more effective way. It has become important for brands to impress consumers in about five seconds or less. For this reason, catching attention in advertising is the first step on the way to purchase. One of the most important elements in capturing attention is presenting creative content.

Creativity in advertising is one of the factors that make the agency's job easier in order to differentiate the brand from its competitors and create a positive image in the minds of consumers. The term 'creative' is used to commonly identify a heterogeneous group of advertising professionals-copywriters, art directors, producers and even in the age of the internet-computer programmers (Young, 2000, p. 19). The creative process includes a comprehensive information sharing that is gathered together with different variables during the ad creation process, rather than just one person finding the idea. American advertising, on the other hand, covers a process that has developed since the mid-1900s on producing an alternative to the advertising understanding of the period. This process of change not only changed the face of American advertising but also had a profound effect on different countries.

The fact that scientific advertising can no longer have the desired effect on the consumer and the search for new ways, has been effective in placing creative works in the center of advertising in the USA. William Bill Bernbach is considered to have brought creativity to American advertising and changed the advertising dynamics of the period with his work. The 1960s, when Bernbach radically changed the basic dynamics of advertising, is shown as the golden age of advertising in America. In this period, both the general structure of advertisements and the existence of advertisements in life have undergone a radical change. Advertising, which has ceased to be just a tool to reach consumers, has been positioned as an art form. Beyond the informative function, the advertisements of that period were shaped to change lives and become a part of life with small touches. William Bernbach, created creative teams in 1960s. These teams were consisted of a copy writer and an art director. These creative teams brought a change in the quality of creative work's revolution which was the most lasting improvements of the organizational process of ads (Young, 2000 p. 19). This situation, which changed the functioning of advertising agencies, has been a factor in maximizing the creativity of the people in the team by focusing more on brands and studies.

Advertising campaigns of the period were created without risk and generally reflected scientific understanding. However, advertisers such as Bernbach argued that creativity should be at the center of advertising in order to make the work more interesting. Bernbach, who changed all the rules regarding advertising and rejected all existing formulas, did not hesitate to spread the ideas he believed in for the advertising world he dreamed of and dragged them along as an example to many advertisers (Geçit, 2014, p. 203). Bernbach's understanding of advertising was realized not only in the preparation of the contents but also in all stages related to the advertising process. Defending that advertising writers and art directors should work together, Bernbach brought this innovation to the working principle of his agency.

After the 1950s, the effect of the change in social lifestyles and technology has undoubtedly been effective in realizing the creative revolution in American advertising. Among the reasons for the creative revolution; the efforts of advertisers who went beyond the limits of the period, the widespread use of television at home, and the increase in the demand for quality advertisements with the increase in the ratio of educated masses in the society can be cited (Nemhauser, 2014). Especially in the 1960s, Bernbach and the managers of other big agencies had the opportunity to transfer their changing and successful advertising understanding to other countries. By the arrival of some of the leading New York advertising agencies in London in 1960s, the modes of transmission were complimented. The techniques and idioms of New York advertising arrived in London with the establishment of London subsidiaries by agencies as DDB and PKL (Nixon, 2017, p. 150).

According to the Bernbach understanding, the intelligence, provocativeness, imagination and creativity of the consumer should be based on product knowledge. In order to do this, generate novel and innovative adversiting was the key point (Nixon, 2017, p. 151). One of the most important supporting factors in Bernbach integrating creativity into advertising content is the revolution he has created in the agency system. As mentioned above, when we look at advertising agencies before Bernbach, there is an understanding that departments are separated from each other like a company, and everyone is trying to complete his/her own work. However, with the change Bernbach wanted to make, agencies have turned into art production centers. Bernbach brought writer-art director together and gave them a creative partnership which enabled strong synergies to be captured in creative thinking. This was so important that it quickly became a general practice through out the advertising world and all creative agency departments have developed ideas about advertising (Mallia ve Windel, 2011, p. 31). This change experienced within the agency has been a factor in both the relations with the advertiser and the roles in campaign control.

Another important representative of the creative age in advertising is David Ogilvy. Believing in the power of in-agency dynamics, Ogilvy talks about the necessity of a creative team to achieve success. While defending the importance of advertising's selling power at the beginning, he believed in the power of more comprehensive and long-term studies in his later periods. Ogilvy summarizes this situation as follows (Ogilvy, 1955):

I used to deride advertising men who talked about long-term effect. I used to accuse them of hiding behind long-term effect. I used to say that they used long-term effect as an alibi-to conceal their inability to make any single advertisement profitable. In those intolerant days, I believed that every advertisement must stand on its own two feet and sell goods at a profit on the cost of the pace. This short-range philosophy was being peddled by agencies which had started out in mail-order advertising. Those mail-order agencies knew how to sell-once. That's all they cared about. That was their job. But they made a profound mistake in applying the principles of one-time mail-order advertising to the creation of campaigns which can only be successful if they sell not once, but time after time, year after year.

David Ogilvy says that while preparing the advertising campaign, a strong link should be created between the integrity that creates the idea and the image of the brand. He emphasized that the creative elements here should also be part of long-term work. According to Ogilvy, it is possible to find answers to many daily creative problems, if the long-term approach is adopted (Ogilvy, 1955). Ogilvy has always believed in the importance of consistency in advertising. For this reason, he focused on advertising content in his campaigns. One of the most important features that Ogilvy added to American advertising is that there is meaningfulness between the elements that make up the advertisement, such as visual and verbal content, and the promise revealed. The fact that it adopts a long-term understanding of success demonstrates the importance of all factors that contribute to the brand image. However, his understanding of the big idea also occupies an important place in his advertising system. He argues that there is a deep connection between the idea that surrounds the advertisement and creativity and that the way to influence the consumer is to find this great idea. Here is Ogilvy's definition of the importance of the big idea: "It will pass like a ship in the night, if your advertising is based on a BIG IDEA (Roman, 2009, p. 85).

The fact that Ogilvy's understanding of the big idea, which he is constantly trying to work out in advertising campaigns and brought significant success over time, has been a factor in other advertisers and agencies frequently resorting to this path. Ogilvy has concentrated on the main motivations for the consumer to focus on one of the two brands that has very clear differences and prefer it over the other. According to him, the manufacturers, who dedicate their advertisers to building the most favorable image, the most sharply defined personality for their brand, are the ones who will get the largest share of these markets at the highest profit in the long run (Ogilvy, 1955). Although it takes a long time to achieve results in this respect, creating sharp personalities for brands and spreading this consistently over a wide period of time will provide significant returns for the brand. This view revealed a new approach to American advertising in the 50s and 60s. The brand image based on a strong personality, rather than the benefits of the brand and the features of the product, came to the fore during the period.

Another important representative of creativity in advertising is undoubtedly Leo Burnett. Burnett, one of the most important representatives of the movement called the Chicago advertising school, argued that advertising campaigns to be created by believing in the power of thought of the consumer should have a deep impact on the consumer. His aim was to create an advertisement around the inherent importance or appeal of a product itself, rather than around copy or a catchy slogan. He hated "unnatural" commercials which he thought were typical of New York agencies or "opportunistic" copy from as what he saw in the U.S. West Coast (Britannica, 2022). His advertising concept is based on originality and icons. Believing in the power of indicators, Leo Burnett made determinations about the brand in his campaigns and prioritized building an image through images that would ensure permanence in the minds of the consumer. At the same time, Leo Burnett says that before starting an advertising campaign, the advertiser must have access to sufficient information about a product. According to him, the advertiser should put himself in the place of the consumer, know how they use a product, and find new ways to persuade the consumer to buy the product (Gürel & Bakır, 2014, p. 180). At this point, visuality focused on changing the perception in the foreground.

Leo Burnett's contributions to post-1950 American advertising were realized in this context. It is well accepted that besides the text, the visual elements also have a structure that changes the preferences. According to Leo Burnett, an effective advertisement must not only be a text-based information element but also contain a structure that is engraved in the mind of the consumer. In order to do this and achieve success, it is important for the advertiser to think like a consumer and identify the elements that will excite and activate him. The influence of Leo Burnett on the history of advertising is considered important not only in the success of the campaigns but also in terms of affecting the behavioral practices in daily life. The icons that Burnett created in his campaigns have also found a response in everyday life. Marlboro advertisements, which are long-term campaigns, affect social perceptions in the period they are published.

THE AGE OF TECHNOLOGY IN AMERICAN ADVERTISING

Increasing the advertising campaigns of the brands has enabled the advertisement to be accepted and to grow as a sector. Especially in the eighties, the power of television and cable broadcasting has revealed the importance of advertising campaigns in reaching consumers. The addition of solution-oriented departments such as the strategy department to the agency structuring has been instrumental in the transformation of advertising as a whole into a coordinated sector. In addition, the development and power of American advertising with each passing day has been a factor in the spread of the American advertising movement not only in the continent but also in Europe and other countries. During this period, many American-origin agencies established new agencies in different countries and ensured the spread of the American school in world advertising.

Among the important impacts of the following technological developments, was the developments in advertising. According to Lee and Cho (2020, p. 332), things that used to exist only in analogue form (e.g. music, video and photos) have now been converted to digital form, and there has been a transition to digital in books, shopping and sensory experiences. The fact that all the human-related elements exist in digital form, naturally supported the prominence of advertisements in such media. However, the increase in the similarity of the products has necessitated advertisements that try to differentiate themselves from their competitors and want to convince their consumers for brands. After the 60s, with the opportunities that the TV brings, TV reshaped the advertisements and created a new lifestyle of advertisements. In the 80s and 90s, television, as a sector on its own, was an important mass communication tool in keeping the advertisement alive. In addition to this, the American economy's directing the world has also ensured that the developing advertising is accepted worldwide. The US uses advertisements as a means of transferring its power, just as it does with Hollywood films.

The rapid inclusion of technology in human life in the 90s and later in the millennium has been a factor in the existence of the internet and interactive systems as a part of human life. The concentration of people on web-based channels is also determinant in shaping digital-based expenditures for advertising activities.

As in all other life dynamics, a direct effect of technology can be mentioned in the advertising industry. In particular, the fact that consumers encounter many similar products in the market has made technology-oriented creativity more important. Tracy Wong (Creative Leader Finalish 2007) suggested that the Internet made all media vehicles more classified and pointed which increased the emphasis on its liability. According to Tracy Wong, in that time of screaming technological advances, what was considered old and near death would never be replaced by technology. Actually, that is good old-fashioned creativity. Creativity in all things, cannot be produced through software, if it is an advertising idea or a new product or not. Everyone must think that the future depends on creativity (Ashley & Oliver, 2010, pp. 120-125).

In connection with this view, we can say that the things that are important for the consumer are mainly based on abstract values. The fact that the consumer sees the brand as a living organism has made it necessary for the brand to build its own existence, especially by using digital media tools. In this respect, in order to create a positive brand image, it is important that the brand is constantly active and can meet consumer expectations.

The features of the internet have been a harbinger of being the beginning of a new era in advertising. Both its cheapness over the years and its rapid spread among the masses have increased the power of the internet day by day. The World Wide Web and the increasing reach of the Internet into more American homes proved a powerful new medium for advertisers to get closer to consumers (Sivulka, 2012, p. 336).

In the early years of the Internet, online advertising was mostly prohibited. This was due to the policies of ARPANET and NSFNet, two predecessor networks of the Internet, which stated that the "use for commercial activities by for-profit institutions is generally not acceptable." In the following periods, efforts to advertise on the Internet with banner ads were carried out. The rapid spread of the Internet, especially in American society, necessitated rapid adaptation to alternative advertising efforts. However, the fact that the rate of time spent on interactive digital media platforms such as social media is quite high during the day is a factor in the concentration of brands on digital rather than traditional media platforms.

In the digital era, target audience reach has evolved into a more important and demanding point. Now, advertising practices are mostly based on reaching the brand when the consumer wants, rather than reaching the consumer. Because today's consumer has the ability to use digital communication tools as they wish. At the same time, along with the digital technologies, the consumers have gained a much more free identity and therefore they have the power of resisting against advertisement campaigns. In this respect, it is a necessity for the brand to prefer more sensitive and effective ways in order to enter the field created by the consumer and to establish effective communication. This significant change in technology and the differentiation of consumer preferences increase the expenditures on digital advertising exponentially.

According to Statista 2021 data, the United States is the largest digital advertising market in the world, with an estimated $137 billion, as it had the highest revenue in the digital advertising market in 2020. In addition, approximately 40% of the budget allocated for advertising in the country is spent on digital advertisements. Advertising spending in the USA is expected to reach approximately $153 billion in 2024 (www.statista.com, Access date: 29.11.2021). The increase in investments in digital day by day has caused both the necessity of creating a digital-oriented department in advertising agencies and the emergence of only digital-based advertising agencies in terms of specialization.

METHODOLOGY

Research Design

In this study, a case study was used as a research design. In the case study methodology, factors related to a situation (such as environment, individuals, events, processes) are investigated with a holistic understanding, and processes such as how these factors affect the relevant situation and how they are affected by this situation are examined (Yıldırım & Şimşek, 2018, p. 73). A case study is one that investigates some problems to answer specific research questions (that may be fairly loose, to begin with) and which seeks a range of different kinds of evidence, evidence that is there in the case setting and which has to be abstracted and collated to get the best possible answers to the research questions (Gillham, 2000, p. 2). At the same time, it is not possible to generalize the results obtained because the case study focuses on a specific situation or event.

Woodside (2010, p. 6) argues that any combination of purposes such as explanation, understanding, prediction, and control in case studies can serve the main purpose due to the nature of the study. According to him, a deep understanding of the factors, interactions, emotions, and behaviors that occur during a certain process should be seen as the main goal by the case researcher.

Research Purpose

From the past to the present, American advertising has an important place in shaping advertising as a sector in the world and in shaping the basic understanding of the period. At the same time, the fact that advertisements contain important codes related to the social structure, beyond being a part of the communication activities of the brands, makes the studies conducted for this situation more meaningful. At this point, the main purpose of this study is to focus on the history of American advertising and make sense of the effects of the period advertising.

Research Questions

In this study, advertisements that change the functioning and structure of American advertising are examined visually and textually. In this respect, answers to the following research questions were sought through the studies examined.

1. How are advertisements shaped in terms of expression and text structure?
2. How are the advertisements designed in terms of visual elements?
3. For what purpose were advertisement dynamics created?

Research Sample

Purposive sampling was used in this study. The reason for purposive sampling is the better matching of the sample to the aims and objectives of the research, thus improving the rigour of the study and trustworthiness of the data and results (Campbell et al., 2020, p. 653). The purposive sampling technique, also called judgment sampling, is the deliberate choice of a participant due to the qualities the participant possesses. It is a nonrandom technique that does not need underlying theories or a set number of participants (Etikan et al., 2016). In the research, advertisements from three different periods, have been taken as sample; that examplify scientific advertising, creative advertising and digital advertising. A total of three advertisements, one from each period, were discussed.

Results And Discussion

Advertising Content: This advertisement by Claude Hopkins for the Pepsodent brand was published as a series. Hopkins focused on the necessity of tooth brushing in the advertisement. However, instead of directly emphasizing tooth decay or a negative effect on health, it brought the argument of the whiteness of teeth as a part of beauty to the fore. In order to increase attention, he wanted to show how the teeth lost their whiteness by using a film layer that covers the whiteness in the advertisement images. By making the consumer feel the reality of the film layer, he aimed to make people feel uncomfortable with the yellowing of their teeth. At the same time, highlighting the benefits of the product provides a real experience to the consumers, informing them both to identify the problem and how to develop a solution for this problem. When we look at the general structure of the period, it seems that the habit of brushing teeth was not very common. Realizing this, Hopkins thinks that the way to sell the product and increase sales can be achieved by gaining the habit of brushing the teeth of the consumers. In this respect, the way to solve the problem is based on informing the consumers and giving them some habits.

Figure 1. Pepsodent advertising
(source: https://buildingpharmabrands.wordpress.com/2013/05/27/the-ad-that-created-a-habit/)

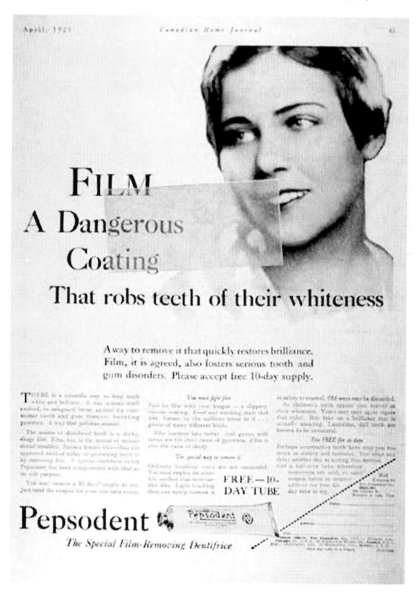

Message Content: "Film: a dangerous coating that robs teeth of their whiteness" was used as the main title in the advertisement. As a subtitle, "A way to remove it that quickly restores brilliance. Film, it is agreed, also fosters serious tooth and gum disorders. Please accept free 10-day supply" text. Then, similar to the column, the importance of brushing teeth and the degree of health for the person were mentioned. In the study in question, informative content is combined with the fear appeal. In addition, it conveys to the consumer that the layer formed on the teeth is similar to a film and that the person can realize it by experiencing it himself with the text of the advertisement.

Visual Content: In the advertisement, the visual content and the text are used in a way that complements each other. With the use of a film-like layer in the middle of the image, it is aimed to create a perception of the general function of the product. At the same time, informative content supports the advertisement image with a heavy text preference. The coupon section in the lower right corner also stands out as a part of period advertising. At the bottom of the image, there is the actual image of the product and the brand name written in large fonts to draw attention to the product.

Figure 2. "Think Small" Volkswagen Beetle advertising
(source: http://trustmarketing.blogspot.com/2005/10/great-commercials-where-theres-beetle.html)

Advertising Content: Bernbach's "Think Small" campaign for the Bettle brand is considered one of the most striking advertisements in both American and world history. With this ad series, which was shaped with the opposite message of the car ads of that period, Bernbach enabled the brand to gain a bold and confident identity.

Bernbach and his agency DDB achieved significant success as a result of this campaign. This radically changed the advertising and understanding of the period. The importance of creativity supported advertising appeals were announced. There were many problems with the brand prior to the campaign. How could DDB sell to the American public, a small, ugly and cheap foreign car which Hitler had played a role in creating it. (Hamilton, 2015)

With this campaign in 1959, Bernbach and his agency DDB revealed important results about how to change the brand perception in the human mind. Namely; the fact that Volkswagen is a brand founded by Hitler had built the existence of a negative brand image in America. At the same time, when we look at the preferences of the period, it is clear that the market shares of small-sized cars such as the Beetle were not very high in America. The dreams of a large, comfortable car, a detached marriage, and a prosperous family, which is called the "American Dream" in the country, were frequently marketed to the American people by advertisers. Contrary to the purchasing understanding of the period, sales increased by 25% after the campaign, an important success that is set as an example not only for that period but also today (Eren, 2013). In this particular study, Bernbach succeeded in attracting the attention of young people by blending consumer demands and expectations with creative work.

A simple structure was preferred in the advertisement content. The space used increases the interest in advertising. At the same time, it is possible to present the advertisement to the consumer in a strong and confident manner by avoiding unnecessary information. In this work, where creativity is at the forefront in general, it seems to be a very ambitious move for the brand to show itself boldly and emphasize its different aspects from its competitors.

Message Content: The advertising message is very short and clear. The slogan *"Think small."* is designed to activate the consumer. At the bottom of the advertisement image, details about the product are indicated in small fonts and presented to the consumer.

Visual Content: As mentioned above, the blank is used extensively in the advertisement image. However, it is seen that the photo of the product is placed in the upper left corner of the advertisement image. In this example, it is aimed to increase the interest in the advertisement by choosing a different understanding from the classical advertisement visual. Editing the advertisement photo in a very small size, on the other hand, makes a reference to the basic promise and features of the product. In this respect, the advertisement image is in a close relationship with the brand structure and identity elements.

Figure 3. "Speak Beautiful" Dove advertising
(source: https://www.instagram.com/p/za82aXPIxv/)

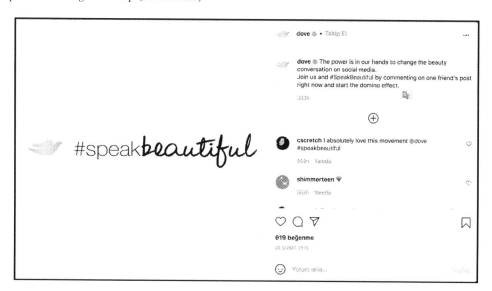

Advertising Content: #speakbeautiful is a campaign created by the brand "Dove" to mobilize consumers through the Instagram platform. Looking at the content of the advertisement, the advertisement was created as a work that wanted to initiate collective action. #speakbeautiful hashtag increases engagement by using the power of social media as part of the Real Beauty campaign that Dove started in 2004 and is still running. It is about actualizing a campaign to provide social benefit by using the power of digital. In this respect, social media and similar digital media platforms facilitate the work of the brand for interaction-oriented studies.

Message Content: Advertising content is completely based on a hashtag and slogan. In the explanation part of the post, a text with a call was used: "The power is in our hands to change the beauty conversation on social media. Join us and #SpeakBeautiful by commenting on one friend's post right now and start the domino effect". The brand aims to provide a direct incentive with this sharing. A simple understanding has been revealed without making too much text crowds in both the advertisement image and the description part. It seems to be a basic output not to bore the consumer and focus their attention on the content of the campaign.

Visual Content: The advertisement image consists only of the dove logo, hashtag, and a short slogan. As with the whole advertisement, it aimed for the user to get general information about the campaign by focusing on the content. It is clear that it is intended to create an attraction through simplicity.

CONCLUSION

Advertising is a cultural element that is produced in the social structure and shaped according to the structure of the society, rather than conveying the communication messages of the brand to the consumers. The concept of advertising, which is formed and transformed within different countries, has not only affected other countries and cultures over time but has also been influenced by other cultures. In this respect, American advertising can be shown as one of the most important advertising schools in the world. Some transformations in technology and social order have deeply affected American advertising. At the same time, American origin advertisements, as a form of media consumption, have important effects both in the national and international context.

There is a direct connection in between technological developments and advertising. This relational structure is decisive in the reproduction of advertisements. At the same time, it is clear that there has been a transformation from a product-oriented structure to a consumer-oriented structure in the advertising studies carried out until today. Especially today, brands that want to reach their consumers tend to turn to alternative advertising channels in order to differentiate themselves from their competitors and persuade their customers to buy. Capturing the difference here is a necessity for brands to survive. Because, with the power created by the internet, it is possible for the consumer to reach many brands among the alternatives. Therefore, in order for the brand to stand out among the alternatives faced by the consumer and to stand out from the others, it is important both shape its work with the right campaigns at the right time and to convey the right messages to them by mapping the appropriate channels for each consumer.

American advertising is one of the schools best adapted to technological transformation. It is a well-known fact that the American media and the advertising industry are pioneers in using the most effective mass media in terms of the media's message transmission forms. It is seen that the USA ranks first in the world in digital advertising expenditures, which have developed in connection with the impact of the internet, especially in the last 25 years (www.statista.com, Access date: 29.11.2021). At this point, it is important to focus on American advertising in order to map the development of world advertising and understand how it has an impact on life.

FUTURE RESEARCH DIRECTIONS

This study is based on understanding the different schools in American advertising. In this context, important campaigns that have left their mark on American advertising have been examined as examples. In order to base the advertising of the period on numerical data and explain it through quantitative data, it may be recommended to conduct an archive study in future studies. At the same time, as a result of comparing the advertisements published on different media platforms with each other in terms of both content and visuality, it can be investigated how the differences between platforms are reflected in American advertising.

REFERENCES

Akyol, Z. (2014). Albert Lasker: Reklamcılıkta "Modern" Zamanlar. In M. Elden & U. Bakır (Eds.), *Reklam Ustaları 1, (1-23)*. Detay.

Ashley, C., & Oliver, J. D. (2010). Creative leaders. *Journal of Advertising, 39*(1), 115–130. doi:10.2753/JOA0091-3367390108

Beard, F. K. (2005). One hundred years of humor in American advertising. *Journal of Macromarketing, 25*(1), 54–65. doi:10.1177/0276146705274965

Briney, A. (2019). *Geography of the United States of America*. https://www.thoughtco.com/geography-the-united-states-of-america-1435745#:~:text=The%20U.S.%20borders%20both%20the,called%20the%20Great%20Plains%20region

Britannica. (2022). *Traditional regions of the United States*. https://www.britannica.com/place/United-States/The-South

Campbell, S., Greenwood, M., Prior, S., Shearer, T., Walkem, K., Young, S., Bywaters, D., & Walker, K. (2020). Purposive sampling: Complex or simple? Research case examples. *Journal of Research in Nursing, 25*(8), 652–661. doi:10.1177/1744987120927206 PMID:34394687

Carr, S. (2021). *How Many Ads Do We See A Day In 2021?* https://ppcprotect.com/blog/strategy/how-many-ads-do-we-see-a-day/

Census. (2021). *About Language Use in the U.S. Population*. https://www.census.gov/topics/population/language-use/about.html

Curti, M. (1967). The changing concept of "human nature" in the literature of American advertising. *Business History Review, 41*(4), 335–357. doi:10.2307/3112645

Elden, M. (2013). Reklam ve Reklamcılık. Say Yayınları.

Eren, E. (2013). *"Think Small" Işığında Volkswagen Beetle Tarihi.* https://pazarlamasyon.com/think-small-isiginda-volkswagen-beetle-tarihi/

Etikan, I., Musa, S. A., & Alkassim, R. S. (2016). Comparison of convenience sampling and purposive sampling. *American Journal of Theoretical and Applied Statistics*, 5(1), 1–4. doi:10.11648/j.ajtas.20160501.11

Geçit, E. (2014). William (Bill) Bernbach: Reklamcılıkta Yaratıcı Devrim. In M. Elden & U. Bakır (Eds.), *Reklam Ustaları 1 (pp. 203-240).* Detay.

Gürel, E., & Bakır, U. (2014). Leo Burnett: İmgeden Zihne Giden Yol. In M. Elden & U. Bakır (Eds.), *Reklam Ustaları 1 (pp. 175-202).* Detay.

Hamilton, M. (2015). *The ad that changed advertising.* https://medium.com/@marathonmilk?p=18291a67488c

Heller, S. (2017). *Earnest Elmo Calkins: Founder of Modern Advertising and a Designer You Probably Don't Know.* https://designobserver.com/feature/earnest-elmo-calkins/39651

Holland, D. R. (1974). Volney B. Palmer: The Nation's First Advertising Agency Man. *The Pennsylvania Magazine of History and Biography*, 98(3), 353–381.

Mallia, K. L., & Windels, K. (2011). Will changing media change the world? An exploratory investigation of the impact of digital advertising on opportunities for creative women. *Journal of Interactive Advertising*, 11(2), 30–44. doi:10.1080/15252019.2011.10722183

Miller, M. M., & Henthorne, T. L. (2007). In search of competitive advantage in Caribbean tourism websites: Revisiting the unique selling proposition. *Journal of Travel & Tourism Marketing*, 21(2-3), 49–62. doi:10.1300/J073v21n02_04

Morello, J. A. (2001). *Selling the President, 1920: Albert D. Lasker, advertising, and the election of Warren G. Harding* (Vol. 1920). Greenwood Publishing Group.

Moriarty, S., Mitchell, N., & Wells, W. (2012). Advertising: Principles and practice (9th ed.). Pearson.

Nelson, K. (2017). *The Greatest Business Secret.* https://swanadvertising.com/blog/greatest-business-secret/

Nemhauser, M. (2014). *The Real Mad Men: The 1960s—A Golden Age of Advertising.* https://www.academia.edu/7288872/The_Real_Mad_Men_The_1960s_A_Golden_Age_of_Advertising

Nixon, S. (2017). Looking westwards and worshipping: The New York 'creative revolution' and British advertising, 1956–1980. *Journal of Consumer Culture*, 17(2), 147–166. doi:10.1177/1469540515571388

O'Barr, W. M. (2005). *A Brief History of Advertising in America.* Advertising Educational Foundation.

Ogilvy, D. (1955). *The image of the brand–a new approach to creative operations.* Academic Press.

Roman, K. (2010). *The king of Madison Avenue: David Ogilvy and the making of modern advertising.* St. Martin's Press.

Sivulka, J. (2012). *Soap, sex, and cigarettes: A cultural history of American advertising.* Wadsworth.

Statista. (2021). *U.S. digital advertising industry - statistics & facts.* https://www.statista.com/topics/1176/online-advertising/#dossierKeyfigures

Tungate, M. (2007). Adland: A global history of advertising (2nd ed.). Kogan Page Publishers.

Wallace, K. (2019, July 11). *The history and future of television advertising.* https://blogs.oracle.com/advertising/post/the-history-and-future-of-television-advertising

Young, C. E. (2000). Creative differences between copywriters and art directors. *Journal of Advertising Research, 40*(3), 19–26. doi:10.2501/JAR-40-3-19-26

Zimmermann, K. A. (2021). *American Culture: Traditions and Customs of the United States.* https://www.livescience.com/28945-american-culture.html

Section 3
International Advertising in Asia

Chapter 5
Advertising in China:
An Analysis of Ads During the COVID–19 Period

Rukiye Gulay Ozturk
ⓘ https://orcid.org/0000-0002-7090-8044
Istanbul Commerce University, Turkey

ABSTRACT

Advertising is a multi-million-dollar industry in China. China's progress in production and technology is highly important in that regard. COVID-19 first broke out in China and took hold of the entire world by the end of 2019, which compelled the attention of every country. In this context, as China is a dominant country in the advertising market across the world and is the place where the pandemic broke out, this study aims to examine the most striking ads of this period by offering a linguistic and visual analysis based on the affect dimension of Martin and White's appraisal theory. It was found that the three most frequently used elements in these ads were security, happiness, and inclination. Employment of these three elements in the advertising communication of the brands in the climate of anxiety and fear during COVID-19 has been considered an appropriate strategic approach.

INTRODUCTION

One of the oldest civilizations in the world, China is one of the fastest-growing and promising markets across the world. China is expected to generate approximately 10.3 billion U.S. dollars of ad spending between 2019 and 2022 as the second largest market in the advertising sector after the United States. (Thomola, 2021). In that regard, it is argued that the advertising industry in China is a dynamic industry that is closely related to China's economic development (Li, 2017:5).

On January 4, 1979, some local ads appeared on Chinese newspaper *Tianjin Daily*. An image of a woman and an informational toothpaste ad are among those examples. Considering the attractive and colorful ads of today, it can be said that the ads of that period did not have the same impact. It was the first commercial ad to appear in the country following the process of reform and opening up initiated

DOI: 10.4018/978-1-7998-9672-2.ch005

by Deng Xiaoping at the Third Plenum of the 11th Central Committee of the Chinese Communist Party (CCP), held on December 18–22,1978. However, this is not the first example of advertising in China. The origins of advertising are commonly dated back to ancient times. Nonetheless, it can be said that the history of advertising in China starts with primitive societies in university coursebooks. In connection with that, in his study, Zhao Chen refers to the clan and tribal totems as the first ads while Ni Ningîn states that these ads dated back to 3000 BCE during the period of slaves and clans. These ads were quite different from the modern ads. Therefore, it has been expressed that the ads as we know today began to appear in the second half of the 19th century in China (Puppin, 2014:178-179).

It is recorded that in the development of advertising, the foreigners who came to the country for spreading these elements for commercial or religious purposes and who employed convincing advertising techniques while doing so had a significant role. However, it was not easy to sell foreign products to Chinese customers during these centuries. The foreign sellers bumped against nationalist boycotts (Puppin, 2014:179). 1920s and 1930s allowed China to live its golden age of advertising prior to the revolution. During this period, the first advertising agencies of the country Carl Crow Inc., Millington's Advertising Co., China Commercial Advertising Agency, and Consolidated National Advertising Co. were born and developed. As a medium, advertising thereby began to appear extensively in various mediums such as newspapers and outdoor spaces. Shanghai became the city where advertising activities were carried out and beautiful Chinese women were put on modern and Western calendar posters. However, this era would not last long due to the outbreak of anti-Japanese resistance (1937–45) and the civil war waged between the nationalists and communists (1945–1949), during which advertising continued to exist even though it gradually lost the crucial role it had played in the previous year (Puppin, 2014:180). When People's Republic of China was founded on October 1, 1949 on the basis of traditional Marxist thought, it led to the decline of advertising, which represented contrary views. It is no coincidence that the advertising agencies, influenced by the socialist movement, merged and founded Shanghai Advertising Corporation (SAC) in 1956 (Hong, 1996:77-78). It is even stated that the advertisements in communist China tried to disseminate their messages through unusual mediums such as railways, lunch boxes, travel magazines, and poker card boxes until 1958 (Jing, 2008: 7).

During the 'Cultural Revolution' that took place between 1966-1976 known as dark years, the advertising sector declined and only political slogans were put on billboards (Hong, 1996:78). During these years, it was observed that the term advertising became a taboo since it was the result of capitalism and it was condemned to disappear like many products and shops. This process continued till the last stage of 1978. With the modernization and reform movements that began after this year, advertising sector gradually began to make a comeback. With the permission of Chinese Government, advertising agencies like Dentsu, Young & Rubicam, McCann Erickson, and Leo Burnett began to operate, create demand, and encourage consumption in the country. During that period, it is not surprising that advertising evolved into a form of information from a giant dumpster and began to acquire a good name for itself. Another striking issue was that while the socialist advertisements were based on accuracy and had no creativity, capitalist advertisements did not require accuracy and included creativity as an important component (Puppin, 2014:181-182).

In 1980s, it was observed that the experts struggled to make sure that advertising had a good reputation and China became one of the important countries in the field of advertising with its economic and technological developments accompanied by the substantial changes in advertisers, mediums that are used, and consumers. By the end of 2019, with the outbreak of COVID-19 in the city of Wuhan in China, the eyes were once again drawn to China. The content of the advertisements produced in China during this period both as an important actor in advertising sector and also as the place where the chaos began is an issue that is worth examining.

The aim of this study is to first examine the geographical, economic, socio-economic, cultural structures in China, and provide a linguistic and visual analysis of the advertisements produced during the pandemic period in China.

BACKGROUND

China is an established civilization dating back 4000 years in the history of Far East. Throughout its history, it reigned in the region under the government of various khanates, at times under a great empire and at times under smaller feodal structures consisting of princedoms or sometimes under the government of small kingdoms when princedoms united, without ever compromising its civilization. The history of China was recorded with the invention of writing, which occurred around 1500 BCE, and it contributed to the illumination of the region's history as well. China has been a source of inspiration for Asia and Europe with its technological breathroughs throughout history. Developments such as the invention of gunpowder and printing press and being the place where silk was originated enabled China to become a commercial center that established commercial ties (Silk Road) with places tens of thousands of kilometers away (SDAM, 2017:1).

China is the largest Asian country and has the largest population across the world. Including 56 different ethnic groups, 93% of Chinese population is composed of the Han and the rest of the 7% is made up of other ethnic groups (SDAM, 2017:3). While Beijing is the country's cultural, economic, and communication capital, Shanghai is the industrial center and Hong Kong is the commercial center as well as being port city. China's climate ranges from extremely dry and desert like conditions in the northwest to tropical monsoons in the southeast. With more than 4,000 years of recorded history, China is one of the few countries in the world that have the traces of the earliest stages of civilization. A multinational country, China has a population composed of diverse ethnic and linguistic groups. Belief systems such as Confucianism and Taoism that formed the basis of Chinese governance are also the foundation of the country's belief system. Starting from 1949, atheism has grown stronger in the country. On the other hand, since the late 1970s, China's interaction with the international economy with regard to world trade has remarkably increased. Especially since the late 1970s, the country has moved away from a Soviet-type economic model. China is among the world's largest producers of industrial and mineral products in addition to rice, wheat, soybean, peanut, and cotton. With the accession of China to the World Trade Organization in 2001, the first steps for economic liberalization were taken.

China celebrates many national holidays such as New Year's Day, the Spring Festival (Lunar New Year), Youth Day (May 4), and National Day (October 1) and many festivals such as Lantern Festival (late winter), Tomb Sweet Day (April 4 or 5), and the Mid-Autumn Festival (October). China has also been an important actor in Winter Olympics and Olympic Games since 1980s (Suzuki, 2021). Accustomed to a life closed to the outside world, China closed itself to the world both in terms of governance and as a society after the revolution. Historical Confucianism was replaced by atheism and a cultural degeneration spread to the society. Undergoing huge technological changes recently, China has tried to rise to its feet against the embargo of the West. In recent years, China has drawn attention as a country that has made a name for itself with its geo-strategic structure, population, and technological production

(SDAM,2017:1-2). However, advertising in the country can be considered as one of the sectors with a long history.

The history of Chinese advertising is dated back to the Song dynasty (Wang, 2008). In the 1920s and 1930s, advertising in Shanghai was a dynamic industry and foreign advertising agencies and brands competed with the local Chinese brands before World War II. During the Cultural Revolution in China, advertising was considered a superfluous instrument (Chen, 1991). Following the Third Plenary Session of the Eleventh Central Committee of the Chinese Communist Party, the period of Deng Xiaoping -the leader of China at the time- turned into a milestone for the resumption of commercial advertising. Since then, advertising has gained strategic and symbolic significance in opening up society to the outside world and developing the economy in China. Especially with the influx of foreign brands into the country in the 1980s, the Chinese consumers began to purchase these brands (like Toshiba, Toyota, and Sony). Similarly, it is stated that Chinese advertising agencies and academics collaborated with Dentsu and a few Japanese advertising agencies. The activities of American advertising agencies in the country since 1990s led to the creation of advertisements based on hard sell techniques while Chinese advertisers later adapted these to soft sell techniques. While salaries were low in Chinese advertising agencies during the first stages, it has been recorded that experts in this field are offered high salaries in 2000s (Li,2017: 2). Nevertheless, it has been expressed that both foreign and Chinese cultural elements and symbols are used heavily in Chinese advertisements, and that the humanitarian values between the East and West are frequently encountered in these advertisements. It is also emphasized that Chinese consumers are more likely to purchase the products that they encounter in their travels abroad (Li, 2017:4). Advertising and marketing industries are globally in a dramatic state of flux, and that situation is mirrored in China (Forbes, 2011:13). Besides, the country's technological development, the increase in the use of mobile media, and the influence of conscious consumers laid the ground for the reduction experienced in traditional marketing channels and the growth observed in outdoor and online ads (https://marketingtochina.com/advertising-china/, 03.07.2021). Thus, it can be seen that more funds are allocated to digital advertising in response to the increasing cost of TV ads and the decreasing readership of print media (Li, 2017: 4). It is also highlighted that digital and mobile will be of critical importance for all the brands in their marketing activities (Forbes, 2011: 13). Despite the stagnation caused by the pandemic in China, the recorded growth in the digital advertising inverstments during this period is remarkable (https://marketingtochina.com/advertisin-china/, 03.07.2021) In accordance with this, with the transition from socialist to capitalist advertising, the Chinese customers' demand for foreign products has increased and thanks to the developments in the digital field in particular, digital platforms have turned into powerful advertisers and unlike many consumers in many countries, Chinese customers have not used adblocks when they have liked the ads. The growth in the digital advertising investments during the pandemic has been considered important. This study will first provide the general characteristics of China, and then address advertising and digital advertising in China, the advertising as a sector during COVID-19 pandemic, and it will lastly provide a linguistic and visual analysis through looking at 10 striking advertisements from China.

Historical Development of Advertising in China

In 1920s and 1930s, advertising was already a dynamic industry in Shanghai. Foreign advertising agencies and brands were competing with their Chinese counterparts before World War II. After the Chinese Communist Party took over China in 1949, the government decided to gradually eliminate commercial advertising thinking that a centralised socialist economy did not need advertising. During the Cultural Revolution (1966-1976), there was almost no commercial advertisements apart from a few advertisements that presented information about export to foreign countries (Chen, 1991).

The first foreign advertisement of China was aired on Shanghai TV Station in 1979 and it was a commercial of Swiss Roda wristwatch. This one-minute commercial providing information about the wristwatch in English was broadcast only twice. However, it had a huge impact on Chinese consumers. Hundreds of consumers went to local stores in the next few days. Interestingly, the product was not sold in China until four years later and it was stated that the advertisers focused more on image advertising rather than selling their products as China had not developed a market yet (Li, 2016: 62) Following the fall of the Iron Curtain in 1980s, the importance and gross output of advertising increased (Cappo, 2003:6). State-controlled economy almost completely eliminated the need for advertising and this system lasted until the mid-1980s (Chan, Wan and Qu, 2003: 458). However, from 1984 to 1990, the number of television stations increased from 93 to 509 (Huang, 1994: 223). By the end of 1995, there were 2740 stations made up of broadcasters, cable stations, and university television channels (Tu, 1997: 4). The World Trade Organization membership had an effect on the internationalization of the advertising sector (Tan, 2002). Outdoor advertising has grown considerably while SMS spam has become a direct marketing trend (Keana and Spurgeon 2004:7). Much of the growth in Chinese advertising during this period has been attributed to transnational foreign companies. In mid-1980s, Ogilvy & Mather advertising agency was established in China (Chang, Wan and Qu, 2003: 466). However, this growth has largely been on a local scale. The joint ventures with foreign agencies have facilitated the transfer of the knowledge-based technologies that are essential for advertising. It has been even recorded that advertising is seen as a dynamo supporting export. According to the China Advertising Association, the number of the advertising agencies in the country rose to 68.935 by 2002 with the government support (CAA, 2003). On the other hand, nationalism and cosmopolitanism are among the themes that stand out among Chinese advertisements. It is particularly observed that Chinese brands draw more on the attraction of nationalism. For instance, Chinese brands such as Li Ning, a sportswear brand, and Haier, a home appliance brand, have been using national pride heavily in marketing their products. In order to reinforce the sense of national pride in nationalistic commercials, the commercials commonly use Chinese rituals, symbols, myths, and cultural elements. Besides, one can also observe that Chinese brands try to balance nationalism and cosmopolitanism. It is stated that the perception of Westerness is made up of product quality and prestige (Li, 2016: 63-64).

Another issue that draws attention in Chinese advertising is the issue of creativity. Advertising practitioners regularly celebrate the value of creativity, so much so that one leading Chinese ad man is compelled to write 'If you don't have creativity, you are dead' (Ye, 2003:IV). Advertising practices are currently reshaped (Keana and Spurgeon, 2004:2). As Gilbert Yang, of the Shanghai Advertising Association points out, advertising is a 'people business' and 'one of the fastest-growing service industries in China' (Yang, 2004). The most renowned advertising agencies in the country are Ogilvy and Mather, J. Walter Thompson, and Saatchi & Saatchi and it is emphasized that first domestic agencies have derived a lot of knowledge and experience from these agencies (Wang, 2005). In accordance with this, with the arrival of foreign agencies and advertisers in China, the foreign effect on advertising has become visible. It has stood out that the concept of creativity has gained weight with the transition from socialist commercials to capitalist advertising and that creativity has become one of the building blocks in encouraging export after the accession to the WTO. In addition to that, the rapid developments in technology have played a role in the development of digital advertising in China. In this regard, it will be beneficial to provide information about digital advertising.

Digital Advertising in China

China is a massive market for every industry. It has transformed Chinese people into the most digitalized consumers in the world (GMA Marketing to China, September 4, 2019). However, China's unique social media ecosystem is a compelling challenge for brands in terms of adapting their marketing strategies and brand messaging while trying to decipher the local narrative (Ang, 2021). When a Chinese consumer sees a product being discussed positively on a social media site, especially by a friend or acquaintance, s/he is far more likely to buy the product than its counterpart in other countries. Peer recommendation has a huge influence on Chinese culture, as formal institutions are less likely to be trusted (GMA Marketing to China, September 4,2019). Advertising and interacting with consumers on social media sites such as Instagram, Facebook, Twitter or even TikTok (the international version of Douyin) has now become the norm for many international brands. However, Chinese consumers use different social media platforms than the Western world such as WeChat, Weibo, Douyin, and QQ (Ang, 2021). In the majority of interactive campaigns, marketing through WeChat and Weibo is important (GMA Marketing to China, September 4, 2019). 'WeChat is China's equivalent of WhatsApp, Facebook, and Paypal all combined into one app. China's digital e-commerce landscape is very different from the rest of the world. As Annemarieke Kostense, the Managing Director of Greater China at Digital Jungle, an Asia-Pacific digital agency put it: "China is fascinating and hard for foreign companies to navigate, because it has no Facebook, no Instagram, and no Twitter." (Kontsevaia and Berger, 2016: 37-38). Besides, WeChat has developed a set of applications within its own app since its launch. For example, it added a payments system connected to JD.com, one of China's biggest online stores. In this way, it has ensured that people shop more on WeChat's own platform, which, in turn, hurt China's e-commerce giant, Alibaba, a dominant actor on the e-commerce scene until then (Rein, 2015). In the successful 'Style Your Life' campaign carried out by Japanese clothing company Uniqlo, consumers were asked to take pictures of the clothes that they tried in the store and post them online. Thanks to the campaign, the company increased their WeChat followers from 400,000 to 1 million and their sales rose by 30% (Doland, 2015). As can be clearly seen from this example, it is possible to accomplish highly positive results without spending any money by using WeChat's advertising platform (Kontsevaia and Berger, 2016: 38).

In their recent China Mobile Internet report, Quest Mobile has illustrated that millennials in China spent most of their free time (46 hours a month) on social media. Short-form video content attracts them like 'a moth to light,' and they thereby find themselves hooked on social media sites for more than 40 hours a month. In the battle for attention, creating entertaining and short videos on platforms like Douyin is an important marketing strategy for businesses in China. In that regard, to many businesses and luxury brands invest in social media. The fact that Chinese millennials are active in social media platforms, official websites, and search engines, that they share brand information and are not hesitant to voice their opinions play an effective role. Generation Z that makes up about 15% of China's population will have a significant role in the growth of consumption in the coming years. Apart from being highly familiar with social media and forms of entertainment, this generation is also attracted by gamification and exclusive offers. It has been observed that platforms such as Bilibili build brand awareness for younger consumers. Another noteworthy issue is that online shopping is considered a way of life for the

Chinese and they spend more through online shopping platforms on special days. It is therefore expected that the e-commerce market is China will exceed 1.5 billion dollars in 2021 and the annual growth rate will be 6.65% by 2025 (Ang, 2021). Key opinion leaders (KOL) also play an important role in Weibo and WeChat marketing. The posts and suggestions of KOLs have an enormous effect on many of their followers/subscribers in convincing them to buy a certain product and establishing brand loyalty (GMA Marketing to China, September 4, 2019). Meanwhile, one can take a look into more specialized platforms (Xueqiu (Snowball), Keep, Mafengwo, Xiao Hong Shu (Little Red Book), which cater for unique niches. Another powerful strategy is to utilize the large and active user groups on Chinese forums (Baidu Tieba, Zhihu, Douban Group etc.). Forums in the West may be outdated but in China they are still significant because forums provide valuable insight about targeted consumer groups and create the chance of sharing brand experience and image. The search engine market in China is made up of various players and the lion share in the market belongs to Baidu (GMA Marketing to China, September 4, 2019). Even though it is predicted that digital advertising will balance the gap emerging in the competition between Chinese and foreign advertisers and agencies working in the digital field, it is thought that China will have a hard time given the networks, knowledge, and experience of the foreign brands and agencies in this field. On the other hand, factors such as the fact that closed societal system in China, a remnant from socialist system, has turned onto social media platforms that are unique to China thereby presenting a continuity and the ban on capitalist social media platforms clearly show that the existing traditional government system has not completely disappeared. Although the currently used social media platforms have unique characteristics, it is obvious that China is a powerful and active country in terms of benefiting from the power of social media platforms, Key Opinion Leaders, gaming and mobile platforms in the functioning of digital advertising just like in the rest of the world. In connection with this, it might be worth looking into what has happened in the advertising sector in China during COVID-19 period.

Advertising in China During COVID-19 Pandemic

Before coronavirus, the advertising market was expected to reach to $865 billion USD by 2024. Coronavirus has made it imperative to reconsider this expectation since the pandemic has led to an immediate decrease in advertising spending. Publicis data belonging to the first quarter showed that year-on-year revenue in China decreased by 15%. Countries in Europe saw an average reduction of 9%; Germany and France fell 7% and 12% respectively (Li and Hall, June 8, 2020). Prior to COVID-19, digital advertising was dominant. While digital advertising accounted for 45% of the e-commerce transactions, mobile payment penetration was three times higher than that of the US. COVID-19 has accelerated the consumption of digital technology in the country. About 55% of the Chinese customers have used online shopping after the crisis reached a peak. In healthcare, interactions among pharmacies, physicians, and patients have inreased (Seong et.all, 2021:12-13). Consumers in their 20s and 30s have begun to save money like they did in the rest of the world and Chinese consumers have begun to show more interest in insurance and purchasing healthier and eco-friendly products in the wake of COVID-19 (Seong et.all, 2021:14). Therefore, the consumers' preference of more cautious, eco-friendly, healthier products, and the inclination to purchase only their primary needs and not to spend money across the world has also been observed in China. Even though a sharp fall has been recorded in Chinese advertising spending, the advertising investments have grown, especially in digital advertising, in the following period as it did in other countries.

In the wake of pandemic, it has been emphasized that outdoor advertising has experienced a fall and the sectors such as restaurants, entertainment, and travel have been adversely affected by this crisis. On the other hand, there have been positive developments in this field as well. For example, the merging of the digital with outdoor advertisements and QR code application has reduced its cost and increased its effectiveness. Besides, people can enjoy 3D technology without using glasses and the power of LED-equipped drones in outdoor commercials (Cheung, 2021). It can therefore be stated that although there has been a significant fall in the outdoor, film, and travel industries at the beginning of the pandemic, a remarkable growth has been recorded in the field of digital advertising in China during the pandemic period with the intense use of QR code, drone, and 3D technology in which the boundary among social media, digital media, and outdoor platforms has been eliminated in 2021.

China's digital ecosystem has the most sophisticated structure in the world, with 850 million internet users. The constant pursuit of innovation by large technology companies and risky investments in important digital technologies have led to a rapid evolution of China's digital landscape before the COVID-19. Meanwhile, the virus outbreak enabled the emergence of new digital solutions necessary for companies and consumers that are forced to practice physical distancing, led to the rapid growth of 'stay-at-home economy', and has transformed the consumer and employee behavior in various ways (Boudet et al., 2020). For example, Nike hosted workouts for consumers who had to stay at home on its mobile apps, rekindling demand and providing 80% increase in engagement, as well as more than 30% increase in first-quarter digital sales in China (Bowman, 2020). During the lockdown period, companies employed a variety of digital tools to stay connected with customers, even in those sectors that traditionally rely on physical interactions. For instance, a leading real estate company launched 'virtual showrooms' and online consultations through a WeChat mini program. (Mengmeng, 2020). During COVID-19 many remote working applications that have fundamentally changed the dynamics of the industry have become increasingly important (Analysys Qianfan, 2020). In connection with this, telecom companies in China have maintained their goal of developing 5G technology for next generation communication and carried on their works in that direction despite the pandemic (Jiwei, 2020).

In a research conducted by the UN revealing the effects of COVID-19, it has been stated that the customers who thought that this process would affect online shopping the most were Chinese customers (United Nations Conference on Trade and Development, 21) and Chinese customers mostly preferred domestic applications for their online shopping, with 92% Alipay and 70% WeChat (United Nations Conference on Trade and Development, 29). In the same research, it has been emphasized that the type of advertisement that the online consumers in China shared the most was the online video ads that were aired on mediums such as YouTube

(United Nations Conference on Trade and Development, 31). Another striking finding from the research is that Chinese customers were enthusiastic about using different mediums while shopping on digital platforms after COVID-19 outbreak (United Nations Conference on Trade and Development, 31). As marketers invested in short video, e-commerce, and social media, digital advertising revenue in China grew 23% in 2020. This growth was demonstrated in R3's latest China Media Inflation Trends report, which also found out that Chinese digital giants Baidu, Alibaba, and Tencent increased their dominance in the market from 65% to 69% in 2020. The following findings were also obtained in the research reports (Lim, 2021):

- Through their commercial activities on social media, key opinion leaders (KOLs) provided engagement and conversion, and they became the fastest-growing media type in terms of media investments in 2020.
- Short videos on platforms like Douyin, Kuaisho, and Bilibili served to specific target audiences and they showed rapid growth. With regard to digital advertising revenue, short video outperformed e-commerce by 39% in 2020.
- It is predicted that mobile internet will grow in 2021.
- It is stated that 2021 will witness a remarkable growth in outdoor advertising with the use of Mega LEDs.
- CCTV and the top four satellite TV companies (Hunan Satellite, Jiangsu Satellite, Zhejiang Satellite, and Dragon TV) will give similar price offers while local television companies will try to attract advertisers with better prices.

On the other hand, it is stated that gaming industry in China has made rapid progress and luxury brands in particular have effectively used this field to attract Generations Y and Z. Luxury brands like Louis Vuitton, Moschino and Prada made investments in the ACG (Anime, Comic, and Games) subculture in China and technology, food & beverage, and sports brands also benefited from this field. Video games, considered an escape route for Chinese consumers, have been among the digital platforms that grew in popularity during the pandemic period. In addition to this, marketing strategies of the brands during this period also drew on the power of the virtual influencers just like in the West. For example, in Tencent's game called QQ Dance, Xing Tong -a virtual idol- became the brand ambassador of Li Ting, a sportswear brand from Beijing. He appeared in a campaign of Levi's during Shanghai Fashion Week and the brand thereby achieved to have millions of fans in real life. While virtual influencers appeared on stage with their first virtual version during Bilibili Macro Link concert in December 2020, in Kuaishou's Spring Festival held in February 2021, real life performance artists like the folk singer Tengger and artists created in computer environment such as AC Niang and digital avatars such as 'Selu' were brought together. Virtual influencers are also becoming a valuable instrument for brands that are interested in drawing advantage from China's e-commerce livestreaming boom (Booker, 2021). In that regard, even though China has experienced a fall in advertising investments in the first phase of COVID-19 process, it has had the chance to become stronger in digital advertising particularly thanks to the innovations on digital platforms and its powerful digital activities in 2020-2021.

Linguistic and Visual Analysis of the Advertisements in China during COVID-19 Period

The Goal, Scope, and Limitations of the Research

In this study, 10 advertisements that were aired and found successful in China during COVID-19 period will be analyzed linguistically and visually and what these brands emphasized in terms of their linguistic and visual attributes will be evaluated. Within the scope of this study, advertisements that can be accessed over internet have been addressed.

The Universe and Sample of the Research

The commercials that were aired and deemed successful in China during the pandemic and that can be accessed through internet constitute the universe of the research. 10 advertisements were chosen through convenience sampling method and they were analysed.

Research Questions

This study attempts to seek answers to the questions indicated below:

1) What is the most frequently used element in the commercials that were aired in China during the pandemic regarding the affect dimension?
2) What is most frequently used expression in the commercials that were aired in China during the pandemic in the linguistic affect dimension?
3) What is the most frequently used visual in the commercials that were aired in China during the pandemic in the visual affect dimension?

Research Methodology

This research provides a linguistic and visual analysis of commercials in accordance with happy/un-happy, in/security, dis/satisfaction, and dis/inclination categories within the affect dimension of Martin and White's appraisal theory that they developed in 2005. For this end, a visual and linguistic analysis of the commercials has been made in consonant with the goal of this study.

The Analysis of the Research and Its Findings

In the study, linguistic and visual analysis has been carried out in the context of affect dimension. You can see these analyses in Table 1 and Table 2.

As can be seen from Table 1, the most frequently used element in linguistic affect dimension is security followed by happiness and inclination. The fact that all the advertisements give the message of security from beverage to food, sportswear to accommodation demonstrates that the brands have chosen the right element for creating linguistic impact against the climate of chaos and incertainty during the pandemic. The second most frequently used element is happiness, which can be attributed to the fact that it was used to provide orientation to people so that they could cling to life in a country where the pandemic started and first great losses were incurred. The third most frequently used element is inclination, which demonstrates that consumer-oriented advertisements were given weight to during this period as well. Even though the pandemic is a worldwide crisis, the fundamental thing is what the consumer wants. For this reason, the positive impact characteristic comes to the fore in the impact dimension.

Table 1. Affect dimension (Linguistic)

Advertisements	Happy/Unhappy	In/Security	Dis/Satisfaction	Dis/inclination
Coca-Cola's Wuhan special edition campaign	-	Security (Sometimes you would come to Henan to eat braised noodles, I would go to Wuhan to eat hot dry noodles. I put my best wishes on this can and hope you understand. Get well soon)	-	-
Levi's International Women's Day campaign	Happy (Wear it for yourself, you are in shape)	Security (Wear it for yourself, you are in shape)	Satisfaction-(Wear it yourself, you are in shape)	Inclination (Wear it yourself, you are in shape)
Nike	Happy ('You Can't Stop Us. We may start from different places, but together we'll rise stronger')	Security ('You Can't Stop Us. We may start from different places, but together we'll rise stronger')	-	-
McDonald's	-	Security (McDonald's 5G. The fast food giant is going to launch a 5G smart product in China, on April 15, 2020.)	-	Inclination (McDonalds 5G. The fast food giant is going to launch a 5G smart product in China, on April 15, 2020.)
Oreo collaborates with Chinese singing star Jay Chou	-	Security (Singing star Chou. Jay Len loves it, so be it! Be fair by eating Oreo with Milk and Tea!)	-	Inclination (Singing star Chou. Jay Len loves it, so be it! Be fair by eating Oreo with Milk and Tea!)
Wieden+Kennedy Advertising Agency	Happy (You can't mask a smile)	Security (You can't mask a smile)	Satisfaction (You can't mask a smile)	Inclination (You can't mask a smile)
Perfect Diary –International Nurses Day	-	Security ('When asked to join the fight against the virus, she did so immediately and she swore not to return home before defeating the virus. It was this conviction that supported us during the fight against the virus.')	-	-
Alibaba X Tmall	-	Security (1-'Please Show your QR Code' 2) 'Keep Healty' 4) Green and Health 5) Wear Good Mask 6) Wash Hands Frequently 7) Health Every Day)	-	-
AirBnb's	Happy (Good luck comes)	Security (Good luck comes)	Satisfaction (Turn your happiness around. The reunion you want, happens at Airbnb)	Inclination (Turn your happiness around. The reunion you want, happens at Airbnb)
Innocent	-	Security (Open Green)	-	-

Table 2. Affect dimension (Visual)

Advertisements	Happy/Unhappy	In/Security	Dis/Satisfaction	Dis/inclination
Coca-Cola's Wuhan special edition campaign	-	There is a noodle figure shaped like a heart on the Coca-Cola can. Because the pandemic broke out in Wuhan, Coca-Cola gave the message 'I am with you.' The heart on the can delivers the message of security more emphatically.	-	-
Levi's International Women's Day campaign	The advertisement features a confident, young, beautiful woman shopping in a supermarket with her kid. The image of the child reflects happiness.	The woman image in the advertisement reflects a confident female character.	In the advertisement, we see an image of a woman wearing a Levi's jean and is satisfied with doing so.	In the advertisement, it is seen that both the woman and child wearing a Levi's jean are content with themselves.
Nike	On the right side of the image, there is a smiling man. He has a happy expression on his face.	In the advertisement, when two different images are brought together, one can see people both on the right and left who raised their hands in the air and created a secure space by uniting their power.	-	-
McDonald's	-	The advertisement features an orbital visual that looks like the corner of smartphones and evoke the presence of technology. It gives a sense of security to the target audience by creating the perception of advanced technology.	-	-
Oreo collaborates with Chinese singing star Jay Chou	-	In the advertisement image, the famous Chinese singer presents Oreo with the milk mixture in his hand and gives a sense of security to the target audience.	In the advertisement image, the famous singer expresses his satisfaction with the product indirectly by recommending Oreo.	In the advertisement, image, the famous singer implies to the target audience that he likes Oreo and that they should try it.
Wieden+Kennedy Advertising Agency	In this advertisement, it is said that 'You can't mask a smile' and we see people with various mimics on their faces making funny faces. They communicate a sense of happiness to people.	Even though the necessity of wearing a mask during the pandemic prevents people from seeing others' facial expressions, this advertisement provides a sense of security both by featuring people wearing masks and also by letting us see these people's facial expressions.	In the advertisement image, it is seen that the people wearing masks are satisfied with doing so.	In the advertisement image, it is seen that the people wearing masks enjoy doing so.
Perfect Diary – International Nurses Day	In the image on the right of the advertisement, there is a nurse who worked for long hours and whose shift just ended. She has deep marks on her face with her mask on. She is seen as having a happy expression on her face after Perfect Diary make-up.	On International Nurses Day during the pandemic, the hard work and sacrifice of the nurses during this process has been conveyed with the image of a nurse whose shift just ended and whose mask led to deep marks on her face. A nurse with a tired face is an image that increases the respect and trust toward the nurses in target audience.	-	-
Alibaba X Tmall	-	The young model wearing a black t-shirt on which many pandemic messages are written and his self confidence gives a sense of security.	-	-
AirBnb's	The advertisement first shows a happy family portrait.	In the advertisement, one can feel the sense of security that the family provides.	The girl, the main character of the advertisement, is depicted as satisfied when together with her family and as dissatisfied when she is not with them.	The advertisement shows the satisfaction of the family when they rent a house in the city close to where their daughter lives and spend their future years together through Airbnb.
Innocent	-	In the advertisement, there are juice bottles filled with the juice produced from the apples, kiwis, and strawberries that are placed in the nature on green grass and there is a signboard on which 'Open Green' is written. The advertisement tries to deliver a sense of security to the target audience with regard to the naturalness of these juices.	-	-

As can be seen in Table 2, the most frequently used element in visual affect dimension of these advertisements is security followed by happiness and inclination. The fact that the security message is also delivered visually demonstrates that brands have chosen the right element to use against the climate of chaos and uncertainty of the pandemic. The second most frequently used element is happiness, which can be attributed to the fact that it was used to provide orientation to people so that they could cling to life in a country where the pandemic started and first great losses were incurred. The third most frequently used element is inclination, which demonstrates that consumer-oriented advertisements were given weight to during this period as well. The parallelism between the visual and linguistic elements is valuable in terms of ensuring the effectiveness of the advertisement communication process in the target audience. It can be said that the brands have become successful in advertisement communication during this process. In the visual analysis, positive features were used as well. In accordance with these findings, the most frequently used element, security, indicates that the brands were aware of the fact that the individuals were in pursuit of security during the pandemic.

SOLUTIONS AND RECOMMENDATIONS

Since this study is limited to the pandemic period, it is no coincidence that the most frequently used element was found to be 'security' in the advertisements. During a time when the negative feelings affecting the entire world such as anxiety and fear were intense, the fact that the brands active in China preferred a communication language based on positive feelings such as 'security' and 'happiness' is a proper strategy and it provides an effective communication method. It is thought that it would be a sound strategy for brands to use this narrative language in their communication language until the pandemic is over.

FUTURE RESEARCH DIRECTIONS

In this study providing a linguistic and visual analysis of 10 advertisements that were aired and found successful during the pandemic period, the sample of this study has remained limited both in terms of language and access to advertisements. In the future, a wider selection of advertisements consisting of advertisements both from traditional and digital mediums could be used for analysis to examine the advertising style of the country. In addition, the attitudes that these advertisements create and the contextual properties of these advertisements can be compared.

CONCLUSION

The advertisement sector in China is a professional and dynamic sector that is directly affected by the developments in the economy (Li, 2016:64). Having made a name for itself with its historical, cultural, and technological developments and its economic power, China has once again made an indelible mark in the world history toward the end of 2019, with the outbreak of COVID-19 virus.

One of the most important dynamos of the country's economy, advertising sector is not limited to Chinese borders. The activities of both local and foreign brands in the country have increased the investments in advertising communication works in this field. In this regard, China has become the country with the greatest share in the advertisement market after the US. Historically, it can be seen that the socialist advertising approach that relied on a controlling state governance and Marxist philosophy slowed down the development of advertising in the country, and even halted it at times. Back then, advertising did not have any positive connotations. With the approval of foreign products in the country after 1970s and the accession of China to the World Trade Organisation, the country shifted to a capitalist way of advertising. Since then, Western products have appeared in advertisements and been on sale in China. It can also be observed that a Westernized language and advertising approach has been gradually embraced and advertising has taken on a positive meaning. During COVID-19 period, as it has been observed across the world, China has been the first country to experience the greatest loss compared to any other country in advertising investments due to being the first country that underwent this process. Although China suffered heavy loses in the beginning of the pandemic, it has entered a stage in 2020-2021 when its digital advertising investments and practices in particular have become stronger. China has produced successful works in many different digital advertisement types such as using e-commerce, artificial intelligence, QR code, and game-oriented advertising, and the popularization of Key Opinion Leaders. The brands' messages such as 'Stay at home', 'Practice social distancing', 'Wash your hands' during the first stages of the pandemic also appeared in China like the rest of the world. As can be seen in this study as well, in the advertisements that have been found successful during the pandemic, the element of security has come to the fore both linguistically and visually in the affect dimension.

Consequently, China is one of the biggest advertisers and markets in the world with its population, growing economy, and technology. Although it landed huge blows during the first phase of the pandemic, it has been continuing to make rapid developments with the implementation of practices that turn the crisis at hand to opportunity. We don't know how long the pandemic will last; however, it is considered important that the brands who will give advertisements in this market focus on studies that are respectful toward the nationalistic values coming from China's socialist advertising tradition and reflect the times we live in and Western modernity, with a focus on digital communication channels, and advertising communication that is based on a reliable and sincere language.

REFERENCES

Advertising in China – The Most Effective Strategies. (2021). Accessed from https://marketingtochina.com/advertising-china/

Analysys Qianfan. (2019, December). *Mobile App Top 1000*. Analysys Qianfan's official post on Zhihu. Accessed from https://zhuanlan.zhihu.com/p/102983491

Analysys Qianfan. (2020, March). *Mobile App Top 1000*. Analysys Qianfan. Accessed from https://qianfan.analysys.cn/refine/view/rankApp/rankApp.html

Booker, A. (2021). *What the World Needs to Learn From Chinese Content Commerce: Part Four*. Accessed from https://jingdaily.com/what-the-world-needs-to-learn-from-chinese-content-commerce-part-four/

Boudet, J., Gordon, J., Gregg, B., Perrey, J., & Robinson, K. (2021). *How marketing leaders can both manage the coronavirus crisis and plan for the future*. McKinsey. Accessed from https://www.mckinsey.com/business-functions/marketing-and-sales/our-insights/how-marketing-leaders-can-both-manage-the-coronavirus-crisis-and-plan-for-the-future

Bowman, J. (2020). *3 Reasons Why Nike Can Overcome the Coronavirus Crisis*. Nasdaq. Accessed from https://www.nasdaq.com/articles/3-reasons-why-nike-can-overcome-the-coronaviruscrisis-2020-03-29

CAA. (2004). *Officer Orations*. China Advertising Association. Accessed from www.iaacongress-china.com/en/about1.htm

Cappo, J. (2003). *The Future of Advertising: New Media, New Clients, New Consumers in The Post-Television Age*. McGraw-Hill.

Chang, J., Wan, I., & Qu, P. (Eds.). (2003). *China's Media and Entertainment Law*. TransAsia, Price Waterhouse Coopers.

Cheung, M.-C. (2021). *OOH Advertising Returns in China, Bearing New Opportunities*. Accessed from https://www.emarketer.com/content/ooh-advertising-returns-china-bearing-new-opportunities

Doland, A. (2015). How Uniqlo doubles its WeChat followers in China: "Style Your Life" push allowed customers to share fun photos in campaign that tapped into China's obsession with all things mobile. *Advertising Age*. Accessed from https://adage.com/article/special-report-women-to-watch-china-2015/uniqlo-doubled-wechat-followers-china/300039

Forbes Insights. (2011). *Marketing to the New Chinese Consumer*. Accessed from https://images.forbes.com/forbesinsights/StudyPDFs/Marketing_to_the_Chinese_Consumer.pdf

GMA Marketing to China. (2019). *Key Marketing Strategies for China Market*. Accessed from https://marketingtochina.com/key-marketing-strategies-for-china-market/

Hong, C. (1996). Advertising in China: a socialist experiment. In K. T. Frith (Ed.), *Advertising in Asia: Communication, Culture and Consumption*. Ames. Iowa State University Press.

Huang, Y. (1994). Peaceful Evolution: The Case of Television Reform in Post-Mao China. *Media Culture & Society*, *16*(2), 217–242. doi:10.1177/016344379401600203

Jing, W. (2008). *Brand New China: Advertising, Media, and Commercial Culture*. Harvard University Press.

Jiwei, L. (2020). *Sector Pulse Under The Epidemic: China's 5G Commercialization Pace is Not Slowing*. Xinhua. Accessed from http://www.xinhuanet.com/tech/2020-03/03/c_1125656066.htm

Keana, M., & Spurgeon, C. (2004). Advertising Industry and Culture in Post-WTO China. *Media International Australia*, *111*(May), 104–117. doi:10.1177/1329878X0411100111

Kontsevaia, D. B., & Berger, P. D. (2016). Mobile Marketing in China: Can WeChat Turn Their New Advertising Strategy into a Sustainable Advantage? *International Journal of Marketing Studies*, *8*(4), 37–43. doi:10.5539/ijms.v8n4p37

Li, H. (2016). *Advertising in China.* Accessed From https://www.chinacenter.net/2017/china_currents/16-1/advertising-in-china/

Lim, S. (2021). *Digital Ad Revenue in China Grew in 2020 – Despite Coronavirus Spending Cuts.* Accessed From https://www.thedrum.com/news/2021/01/14/digital-ad-revenue-china-grew-2020-despite-coronavirus-spending-cuts

Mengmeng, S. (2020). *Evergrande Projects Going Strong in Online Sales, Beike VR Property Sales Reshapes New Property Sales Value Chain.* Xinhua. http://www.xinhuanet.com/house/2020-03-13/c_1125706856.htm

Puppin, G. (2014). Advertising and China: How does a love/hate relationship work? In *The Changing Landscape of China's Consumerism.* Chandos Publishing. Accesses From https://www.researchgate.net/publication/286113045_Advertising_and_China_How_does_a_lovehate_relationship_work doi:10.1533/9781780634425.177

Rein, Sh. (2015). *End of Copycat China: The Rise of Creativity, Innovation, and Individualism in Asia.* Wiley.

SDAM. (2017). *Yeni Dünya Düzeninde Çin Halk Cumhuriyeti.* Accessed From http://sdam.org.tr/image/foto/2017/12/17/Yeni-Dunya-Duzeninde-Cin-Halk-Cumhuriyeti_1513529142.pdf

Seong, J., Ngai, J., Woetzel, J., & Leung, N. (2021). *China Consumer Report. Understanding Chinese Consumers: Growth Engine of the World.* Accesses From https://www.mckinsey.com/~/media/mckinsey/featured%20insights/china/china%20still%20the%20worlds%20growth%20engine%20after%20covid%2019/mckinsey%20china%20consumer%20report%202021.pdf

SuzukiC. (2021). *China.* Accessed from https://www.britannica.com/place/China/The-eastern-region

Tan, Z. (2002). Sports Communication in China. China Media Monitor Intelligence (HK).

Thomola, L. L. (2020). *Advertising in China - statistics & facts.* Accessed From https://www.statista.com/study/14624/advertising-in-china/

Thomola, L. L. (2021). *Advertising in China - statistics & facts.* Accessed From https://www.statista.com/topics/5604/advertising-in-china/#dossierKeyfigures

United Nations Conference on Trade and Development. (n.d.). *Covid 19 and E-Commerce Findings from a Survey of Online Consumers in 9 Countries.* Accessed From https://unctad.org/system/files/official-document/dtlstictinf2020d1_en.pdf

Wang, J. (2005). *From Advertising to Branding: Framing Chinese Consumer Culture.* Routledge Curzon.

Ye, M. (2003). *Creativity is Power (Chuangyi jiushi quanli).* Gongye Publishing.

KEY TERMS AND DEFINITIONS

Capitalist Advertisement: Advertisement based on capitalist philosophy.

China: The world's most crowded country.

Coronavirus Disease (COVID-19): An infectious disease caused by SARS-CoV-2 virus, that broke out in Wuhan, China and rapidly spread to the rest of the world.

Key Opinion Leaders: Institutions or people with powerful social status and whose word is trusted and listened to while making an important decision.

Sina Weibo: Combining Facebook and Twitter, Sina Weibo is a microblog used in China.

Socialist Advertisement: Advertisement based on socialist and Marxist philosophies.

Chapter 6
Research on Social Media Advertising in China:
Advertising Perspective of Social Media Influencers

Poshan Yu
https://orcid.org/0000-0003-1069-3675
Soochow University, China & Krirk University, Thailand

Yuejia Liao
https://orcid.org/0000-0003-0120-5967
Independent Researcher, China

Ramya Mahendran
https://orcid.org/0000-0001-9585-9077
Independent Researcher, India

ABSTRACT

This chapter focuses on the development of social media advertising in China, especially influencer marketing through social media posts. More specifically, this study examines how the personal traits of social media influencers, the characteristics of the content posted by them, the form of advertising, and the users' personal preferences influence the effectiveness of these influencers' advertising. Through this research study, the authors conclude that social media influencers in China act as great assets to advertising and in recent times have gained the attention from many brands. During COVID-19, social media usage increased dramatically and helped influencers increase their followership. In an ever-accelerated pace of this digital and social era, it is worthy for brands to rethink how to collaborate and partner with these influencers. It is also significant for influencers to think about how to maintain long-term relationships and garner meaningful interactions with their fans and fellow influencers.

DOI: 10.4018/978-1-7998-9672-2.ch006

INTRODUCTION

The COVID-19 pandemic has bought in many changes in the way humans interact, it has increased the social distance and isolation, it has reduced the social interaction. While the physical world was undergoing drastic changes, so did the digital world. Now people spend more time online. This has provided opportunities for many online businesses and made traditional businesses reimagine the way they take their offering to the customer and promote their products and services. Online shopping and online commodity recommendation has attracted the attention of businesses. According to the report released by China Internet Network Information Center in April 2020, due to the impact of COVID-19, the time spent on the Internet by Chinese individuals has significantly increased. According to the survey of online consumers in 19 countries done by United Nations Conference on Trade and Development (2020), over 3000 consumers form nine countries were asked if they were shopping more often online than before the outbreak of the COVID-19 pandemic. Amongst 227 respondents from China 31% strongly agreed that their online shopping has increased and 47% of them agreed. That is nearly 8 out of 10 people agree that their online buying behavior has changed or increased after the pandemic. It was stated by Influencer Marketing Benchmark Report (2021) that despite all the uncertainties caused by COVID-19 in 2020, influencer marketing is still a highly popular and effective form of marketing.

Nowadays, most mobile phone users shop online and can be targeted with different formats of online advertisements. According to the 49th Statistical Report on Internet Development in China (2022), by December 2021, China's online shopping users had reached 842 million, accounting for 81.6 percent of the total number of Internet users in China. There is no doubt that, brands are fighting to capture consumers' attention through online advertising.

According to the Forecast of China's Media Industry released by GroupM (2021), in the last five years, when it comes to expenditure for media in China, Internet ranks over all other media formats including TV and radio. Also, the share of Internet advertising spending has reached nearly 90%. 2021 KOL Marketing White Paper proposed that short videos and promotions by key opinion leader (KOL) are the "double focus" of advertisers' social marketing in 2021. Therefore, when we focus on the advertising industry in China, we cannot ignore the marketing role of KOLs and social media influencers.

Brands use social media influencers to create appealing content and advertise their products and services to the appropriate audience base. The volume of sales they bring can be used to measure the effectiveness of the advertisements. According to the return on investment (ROI) of influencer marketing infographic released by GRIN which is a website related to influencer marketing and creator management, the ROI generated by influencer marketing can be 11 or even more times higher than that of banner ads. A worldwide survey by Statista (2020) states that 60% of the marketers involved in the research agreed that influencer marketing has a better ROI. Therefore, we need to measure the effectiveness of the said advertising campaign by observing consumers' engagement and reactions to it, especially their purchasing behavior. Before we dwell into social media influencers and consumers, attention should be paid to the popular social media platform in China. If we were to rank all social media platforms according to daily user activity, WeChat, TikTok and Kuaishou will top the list, followed by Weibo, Bilibili and Xiaohongshu according to the White Paper by a 2021 KOL Marketing. Different types of brands prefer different kinds of social media platforms and formats of advertising. Zhu (2014) claimed that newly emerging social e-commerce platforms such as Xiaohongshu, Mogujie, and Meilishuo employ user-generated content as a key tool to help online shoppers. This paper will focus on said platforms that are leveraged for online advertising and explore their social media influencers and influencer marketing trends.

With the rise of these social media platforms, social media influencers are now recognized as an effective via medias for brands to gain attention from the audience and influence their purchasing behavior. According to Djafarova and Trofimenko (2018), influencers are social media users who have received significant attention from other users and gained a sizable network of followers. Zhu and Chen (2015) also pointed out that in addition to being content creators, these influencers can also act as content strategists. Since they already possess a good understanding of the needs of the consumer given that they are sometimes part of the target audience themselves and also their extensive interactions with their followers, they can provide more attractive advertisement and increase the possibility of consumption. A social media influencer is also known as a social media influencer (SMI). The content sponsored by SMI usually comes in the form of product reviews.

As Evans et al. (2017) reported that a SMI both creates and publishes a post (one that might include pictures, video, audio or text), advertising the product or service through various channels such as Instagram, YouTube (Vlogs), Twitter and Blogs. Additionally, these posts are sponsored (also known as paid-sponsorships) by the brand sponsor, creating a win-win for the brands and influencers. So, more and more brands are beginning to seek out social media influencers (SMIs) for marketing promotions. Direct comparisons of influencers and celebrities have found that online ads featuring influencers elicited more wishful identification, homophily, and trust than celebrities (Schouten, Janssen, & Verspaget, 2020). Generation Z who are the newest generation born between 1995 and early 2010s (Priporas et al., 2019), consumes content more than any other age groups (Adobe, 2018). Generation Z is the largest generation, constituting approximately 32% of the global population (Miller and Lu, 2018) and they appreciate the communication of brands on social media (Vitelar, 2019) particularly through SMI as they find them more authentic (Wolf, 2020). Recommending products and brands through influential people on social media platforms can more effectively convince consumers, rather than using traditional advertising.

On social media platforms, apart from the individualistic influence social media influencers is able to achieve, the contribution of algorithms that run on the background cannot be ignored. With the information provided by users about their likes, dislikes, tastes and preferences, personalized advertisement has become a preferred way for digital advertisers to interact effectively with users (Chung, Wedel, & Rust, 2016), promoting the growth of social commerce. Howard and Kerin (2004) pointed out that users tend to have higher purchase intention for the product recommended in these personalized ads. Researchers found that users perceive personalized ad content as more appealing and more connected to their interests, and have higher purchase intentions for the product recommended in personalized advertisements (Howard & Kerin, 2004; Lambrecht & Tucker, 2013).

According to Chung-Wha (Chloe) Ki et al. (2020), few studies have explored the combined impact of individual traits and content-driven traits of SMIs on followers. Therefore, this paper focuses on the influence of different traits of social media influencers and its impact on consumers' purchasing behaviors. In this paper, hypotheses that are to be tested and the methods of testing are discussed. Through the research, we can establish that influencers should continue creating interesting and attractive content as this is the most popular advertising channel nowadays. They should ensure to be both interactive and considerate when cultivating and growing their network of followers and also exert the same to their extended community, in order to have a stable and loyal consumer base.

ADVERTISEMENT IN CHINA

According to the Annual Insight Report on China's Online Advertising Market conducted by iResearch, the scale of online advertising market in China reached 646.43 billion yuan as of 2019. In the long run, based on the continuous optimization of marketing structure by internal enterprises, the widespread popularization of 5G technology and the growing success of new marketing formats such as live-streaming, stories and short video, the advertising market will enter a stage of upward growth. According to Xia (2020), the advent of social media networking has enabled advertisers to promote their products and services on social media platforms.

According to the Forecast of China's Media Industry released by GroupM (2021), in terms of media spending, compared with different media, the investment of the Internet is currently the highest. Sales and Marketing teams in China regard social media as a critical tool in building relationship with their customers (Niedermeier et al., 2016). Figure 1 shows the share of expenditure on different media platforms. It is worth noting that compared to other media platforms, the value of connection build on social networking platforms will become more important because "trust" plays an increasingly critical role in consumer decision-making. The interpersonal network that is behind the success of the growing social platforms will become a competitive field for advertisers. Advertising expenditure on social media channels is expected to increase by 14.2% year-on-year in 2022.

Figure 1. Share of media expenditure on different media platforms
Source: (GroupM, 2021)

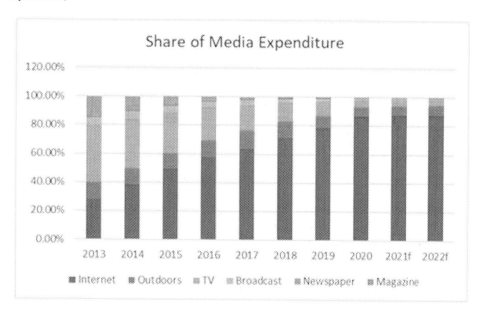

Moreover, it can be observed from the figure 2 that advertisers intend to increase the budget of online media for their future advertising needs. Live-stream shopping is a new method that helps Chinese customers shop online. It has become both a tool for business marketing and a driving force behind the growth of e-commerce sales (Ma, 2021). Compared with other online media marketing methods, video, and live broadcast (live streaming) can not only convey more information in a short time, but also works in real-time and has highly interactive capabilities like live chat. Thus, helping enhance the authenticity of the content and cultivate genuine interest from the followers. At the same time, video content in short videos formats and live streaming easily capture the users' attention and helps manage users' divided interests, non-availability of time and shorter attention spans. According to Cao et al. (2021), short video platforms are more widely used by people of all ages in China. Platforms like TikTok which can target users with topics that they have already expressed an interest in, avoiding advertising abuse. While browsing videos on a platform like TikTok the viewers are made to consecutively scroll the feed and are exposed to short promotional videos in between their watching of videos in their areas of interest. Thereby making social media influencers into undoubtedly important communicators of the short video platforms. These influencers know how to get the viewers' attention in video formats as short as 30 seconds, which could be in form of reels, stories, or videos.

However, it is to be noted that targeting users on topics on expressed interests on social media, might lead to information cocoon. This can affect consumption of the users by exposing them to the same type of content again and again, based on their past impressions and interactions. Information cocoon occurs when users hear only what they want to hear, view what they want to view, and what confirms their own believes and experiences. But the problem starts to occur when the viewer is not very good at expressing their interest area, doesn't know how to follow and react with the brands and use hashtags and other social media markers that starts to establish a user's interest areas. Thereby they become targeted by demographic markers like location, language, gender, age group and so on. This carries forward into social media influencer marketing, especially when targeting through ad preference.

Figure 2. Different module that Chinese advertisers plan to increase marketing budget to
Source: (iResearch, 2020)

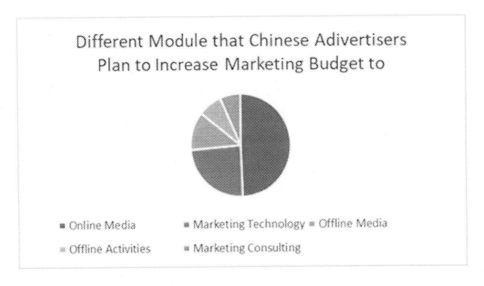

According to the research on marketing strategies being adopted by advertisers conducted by iResearch, as shown in Figure 3, the top 3 focus areas are on developing a digitized consumer community, creating quality content for content marketing and investing in self-owned online platform. A quick

Google search on the phrase "Content is King" will reveal that it is still popular as ever (Müller and Christandl, 2019). The cognition of Chinese Internet companies has gradually moved away from the traditional perspective of purely paying attention to data, resources, and price competition. Instead, they try to consider marketing operation and content marketing as competitive advantages. It is also worth noting that, social media marketing is able to do the above in an effective way, by helping cultivate and grow an online community, and in increasing the quality of content created and interactions fostered.

Figure 3. The distribution of marketing strategies being adopted by Chinese advertisers in 2020
Source: (iResearch, 2020)

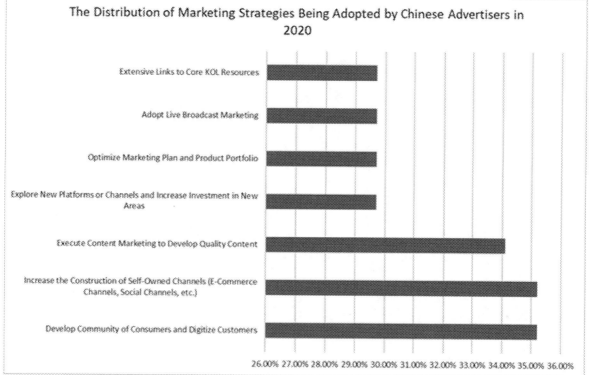

17 years ago, in 2005, YouTube uploaded the first-ever video making video sharing into a viral phenomenon. Almost all online and mobile platforms have made way for digital video content sharing. From short format recorded videos to live streaming, it is the newest by most lasting trend there is, in the visual heavy consumption trend of social media. The Internet world and app world has become a common advertising channel for different industries. According to the market insight on China's internet advertising developed by QuestMobile AD INSIGHT (2021) different industries tend to invest differently on the online advertising. As seen in Figure 4, the beauty industry is the top spender on Internet based advertising, followed by food and beverage companies and e-commerce platforms. The beauty and skin care industry in turn spends different amounts on different media platforms. As seen in figure 5, they invest heavily on TikTok advertising than any other online media platform. As a short video platform in China, TikTok is also one of the most important social media platforms. TikTok attracted 100 million

active users monthly in the US alone as of August 2020 (Sherman, 2020). It is stated by Zhu & Yang (2020) that TikTok's advertisement revenue topped USD 27.2 billion dollars in 2020, thanks to its high levels of user traffic.

Figure 4. Share of online advertising spending of top industry in 2020
Source: (QuestMobile, 2021)

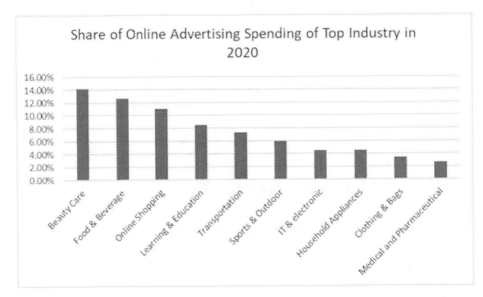

Figure 5. Share of Top 10 advertising media of beauty care industry in 2020
Source: (QuestMobile, 2021)

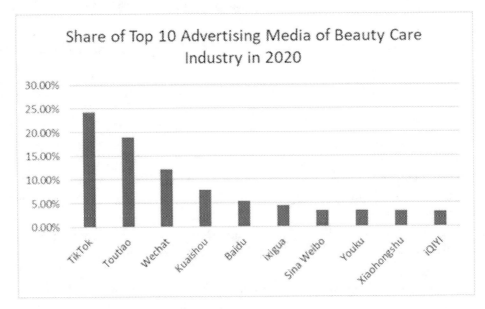

With the boom of new media, people suffer from information overload on social media and other online platforms. Social media advertisements are enabled via page ads, sponsored posts and stories, sponsored direct messages, pop-up ads, celebrity endorsements and recommendations from social media influencers both online and on the app. For Chinese consumers, social media is an important channel to get information of various products. According to Statista Digital Market Outlook (2020), the market size of social media advertising was about USD $97.7 billion in 2020 and accounted for 27.5% of the total digital advertising market, globally. Meanwhile in China,31.8% of the digital advertising revenue comes from social media.

Communicating through social media is now an effective service that most brands use to interact with existing and potential consumers (Wajid et al., 2020). It can be observed from the figure 6 that from 2015 to 2018, China has shown a steady increase in revenue when it comes to social media advertisement, and it is started taking a bigger share when compared to the overall online advertising investment and will continue to increase in the coming years.

Figure 6. Share of Social Media advertisement in the total online advertising revenue in China from 2015-2022
Source: (iResearch, 2020)

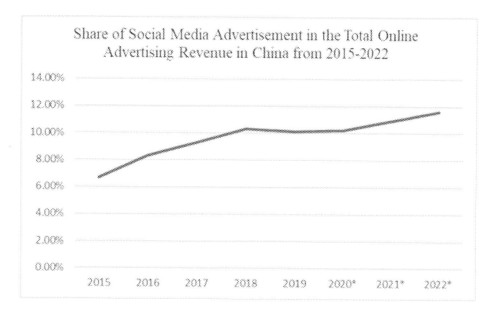

The use of traditional one-way communication to enhance consumer perception and boost favorable attitudes towards product value has been dramatically losing its persuasive influence because of the overwhelming use of social media like Facebook to connect with peers (Akar and Topcu, 2011; Kim and Ko, 2010). It is stated by Mahmud Akhter Shareef et al. (2019) that most of the fastest-growing companies are eagerly striving to promote product awareness and exposure to gain a favorable perception through viral marketing on social networks.

THEORETICAL FRAMEWORK

Social Media Influencers

Given the evolution and rapid development of the Internet, social media platforms have become important via medias for people to interact and connect with others in daily life. People can not only see a variety of posts about the lives and lifestyles of others on social media, but they can also obtain information on the different products and services they need and want. Social media can be used to develop one's own circle of friends, at the same time creates an avenue to follow and connect with celebrities and some users who have attracted a huge followership and fanbase in a specific field. It is reported by Sundermann and Raabe (2019) that the SMIs are different from the rest of the social media users. They can develop a more substantial network of followers and build high quality, dynamic and intimate relationships with their followers. According to Evans et al. (2017), social media influencers become opinion leaders, and their social media statuses lie between being celebrities and being friends, and this new form of users were made possible as social media opportunities have boomed. Jerslev (2016) stated that SMIs also differ from traditional celebrities who seek an accentuated distance from consumers. Celebrities are known for their non–social media activities (e.g., sports, music), influencers are "born" on social media, where they develop the main activity for which they are known for (Schouten, Janssen, & Verspaget, 2019; Tafesse & Wood, 2021). Followers and consumers consider SMIs as more approachable, credible, and similar to them (Schouten, Janssen, & Verspaget, 2020).

At present, with their wide-spread reach, social media influencers can help many businesses advertise their products and services. MCN (Multi-Channel Network) is a new mode of economic operation among social media influencers. It is stated by Jacob and Kevin (2016) that an MCN is any entity or organization which either partners with content creators or directly produces a variety of distinctive content and works to perform business and marketing functions on the platform in which said content is released. This mode combines professionally generated content (PGC) of different types of contents and formats like video, audio, blog posts, images and so on to ensure the continuous content generation with a strong and continued capital support and the stable realization of business. The growth of MCN, as seen in figure 7, shows that the market for social media influencers and the demand for high-quality content is growing.

In the previous discussion, KOL was mentioned and will be introduced in detail in the subsequent discussion. Although the topic in discussion is related to SMI, KOLs are quite similar to them. As stated by the Influencity Blog that the main difference between KOL and SMI is that KOLs do not use blogging as their main via media, and don't identify themselves as bloggers. Some of the products they recommend on the social media are for advertising purposes and some are to share their personal or real-life use experience, while SMIs are full-time bloggers. At present, the line between social media influencers and KOL is blurring because when KOLs reach a certain followership and fanbase, they also collaborate with brands to promote products and become like SMIs. SMI and KOL are actually people of similar nature, and one can become both if intended or move from being one to another.

According to the KOL White Paper (2021) jointly released by China Advertising Association and Miaozhen System, social media influencers on each platform can be divided into five levels. If we create a pyramid structure for influencers, they fall into the super-head level, head level, shoulder level, waist level and tail level based on their number of fans. The KOL who are super-head level on Sina Weibo (a Chinese microblogging platform) have more than 10 million fans. Different kinds of KOL play different role in advertising. For example, KOL who have ten million fans will create a topic and make it popular quickly, establishing them as trend creators, from trending content to trending hashtags to trending online challenges. According to Wang et al. (2020). The KOLs can be categorized into common users, miniature KOLs, medium KOLs and top KOLs based on the number of followers they have, and they get classified as experts in a particular field by having verified accounts, and the information they provide on a homepage. For instance, one can notice words like 'official account' or 'official page' to know if the source of information is authentic. On platforms like Instagram, you will notice a blue color icon with a tick mark next ot the username, that indicates that a particular account is verified. On video sharing platforms when a paid promotion is occurring, the video gets tagged as one that contains a paid promotion, and if the user is promoting a product without any affiliation to the company, they have by themselves started declaring that it is not a paid promotion. This also helps us know if the authenticity of the information the KOL is providing.

Figure 7. Number of MCN institutions in China from 2015-2019
Source: (iResearch, 2020)

Figure 8. KOL classification
Source: (Miaozhen Systems & China Advertising Association, 2021)

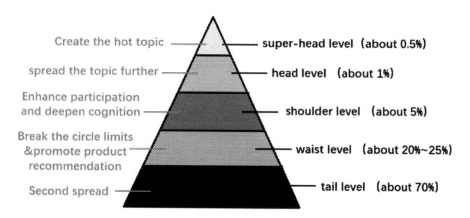

KOL are not just judged by number of followers but also the activity status of the followers. It is proposed by QuestMobile NEW MEDIA in Cross-platform KOL Ecology Research Report (2021) that head-level KOL refer to the people who capture the top 5% of active followers on the platform. It is pointed out by Wang et al. (2020) that top KOLs tend to register a higher average participation frequency and more average interaction when compared to other users. People place higher trust on the information provided by the top KOLs. Head-level KOL in Weibo (a microblogging platform) and Xiaohongshu (also known as RED, is a social media and e-commerce platform) attract more attention from female users, while other platforms have a balanced gender ratio. The majority of active fans of head-level KOL on each platform are young people under the age of 30, among which Bilibili (nicknamed B Site in China, is a Chinese video sharing website). has a prominent feature of youth, while WeChat (a multi-purpose instant messaging and social media platform) public accounts are more attractive to people over the age of 36.

KOL from different social media platforms have different characteristics, thus the content posted by them can be different. Music, dance, film and television entertainment and food are popular on TikTok (a short-video sharing platform) while content about pet, lifestyle and parent-child is more attractive on Kuaishou (video-sharing app). Based on the content system of hot recommendation and forwarding mechanism, Weibo has become the base camp of content for entertainment. Celebrities and KOL of film and television entertainment are the most active. On the WeChat public account platform, users care more about the quality of text. In the fields of education, finance, and economics KOLs are well developing (Cross-platform KOL Ecology Research Report in 2021). Given the scalability of the internet and speed of diffusion, content creators and contributors can rapidly gain an increasing number of engaged followers and increase their popularity in specific fields (Tan, 2017). The more this occurs they start becoming trusted and credible sources of information to their followers and thereby get scouted by brands for partnerships. Social media influencers are becoming more powerful than celebrity endorsements and create much better impact for brands. The KOLs are breaking the traditional marketing barriers like cost and are challenging the formats: which have primarily been TV, magazines, and billboards. Also, KOLs bear higher relatability to the user because they are like the people they are endorsing to; their backgrounds, age, socio-economic statuses, sometimes even looks are similar to that of the consumer.

Influencer Marketing

Social media influencers who can help to develop communities of consumers and influence consumers' buying behavior are important for brands to create content and / or promote their products and services. Influencer marketing also leverages on the power of word of mouth – wherein an individual working with a brand starts to attract other users. If we are to infer from Thomas Smiths book "Successful Advertising" we can see that "more frequency equals more effectiveness", and by using influencer marketing, brands can make sure that their products, and its benefits are repeated again and again. When people around us, similar to us, are talking about a topic, it draws on our attention. Influencers are a league apart because they have heavy followership, drawing even more attention to a message.

It is proposed by InfluencerMarketingHub (2019) that influencer marketing can be defined as marketing communications in which influencers promote a brand's offerings on their own social media pages. It is worth mentioning that in addition to social media influencers who can influence consumers' consumption behaviors, KOC groups can also influence people around them by sharing shopping experiences. According to Duan (2019), the so-called KOC, or "Key Opinion Consumer", expresses true feelings,

Figure 9. The relationship between different subjects (Authors)

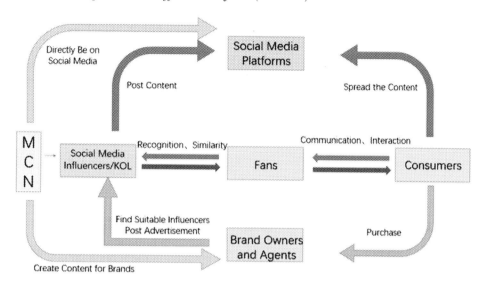

shares life experiences and communicates with other consumers based on their identity as a consumer group. The relationship between consumers and social media influencers is illustrated in the figure 9.

It is pointed out by Kim (2021) that influencer marketing can be viewed as multi-layered relationship marketing involving influencer, consumer, influencer-brand, and brand-consumer relationship. According to Lubna (2021), as the social media influencer's (SMI) power increase, consumers and viewers are likely to transfer the SMI's personal characteristics onto the promoted brand(s). In a related topic, consumers, and viewers (even if not users) can acquire some of the norms, attitudes, motivations and behaviors of the SMI's and can also act favorably towards the products and services promoted by them, thereby making brand affinities. There is a level of blind faith we start developing on the SMIs we follow. So, we can observe a growing connection between brands and social media influencers. Moreover, more and more people have opportunities to become social media influencers with the rapid growth of social media.

The market size for influencer marketing worldwide has been on a rise from 2016 through 2021. According to Statista Research Department, the market size rose from $3 billion to $9.7 billion in just three years (please mention year over here or last three years). In a Chinese consumer survey conducted by Rakuten Insight in October 2020, 81% of respondents who followed at least one influencer on social media said that they have bought products endorsed by influencers. A large number of these respondents were convinced by the promotion of influencers. It can be observed from the research of share of consumers who follow social media influencers in Asia Pacific done by Rakuten Group (2020), China ranked the first, which can show the popularity of social media influencers in China. It is pointed out by Chung-Wha (Chloe) Ki et al. (2020) that influencer marketing has become an integral part of retailers' digital marketing strategies, as they believe that this new marketing method can effectively translate into higher profits. According to the Forecast of Advertiser & KOL Marketing Market Inventory and Trend (2021), in 2020, the market size of influencers reached 67 billion yuan, up 37% year on year. Also, brands use multiple marketing methods to fully stimulate users' enthusiasm and improve marketing efficiency through influencers.

Fertik (2020) said that influencers have been proved to be effective in marketing. Enterprises tend to prefer influencer marketing as their main marketing method on social media. Influencers use the social capital accumulated by their high levels of interactions and long term relationship and trust they have built with their followers to collaborate with enterprises to endorse products, services and brands thus performing influencer marketing in a subtle but effective way.

Yu and Hu (2020) illustrated that in social media marketing, influencer endorsement is a widely used strategy. It is said by Zhou et al. (2021) that SMIs are increasingly involving in influencer marketing to promote products. People often search for product information on traditional e-commerce platforms. They can also gain information through social media, acquaintances' recommendation and so on.

Figure 10 shows the shopping platforms well known to consumers. Among these platforms, in addition to China's largest online shopping platforms like Taobao and JD, social media such as Xiaohongshu, which is popular among the younger generation, also provides purchase services (e-commerce) in the app in addition to being a social media platform. The influencers can recommend a product, then provide a link in the post for consumers to buy with one click.

Figure 10. The shopping platform well known to consumers
Source: (Miaozhen Systems & China Advertising Association, 2021)

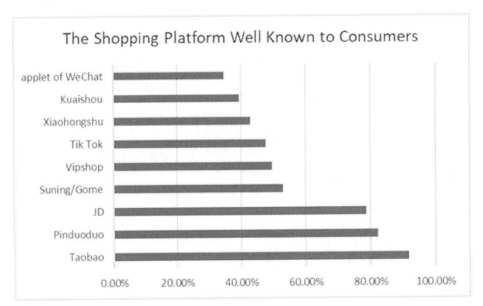

As seen in figure 11, social media is becoming a popular way for consumers to get information about products. A large proportion of influencers of these social media can provide information about the products and services they are promoting on the platform. For example, Li Jiaqi also knows as the "Lipstick King" is a famous Chinese live-streaming influencer who became legendary for selling 1.7 billion in goods under 12 hours. A conservative estimate of Li Jiaqi's livestreaming sales was over one billion RMB (Hua et al., 2021). He is a popular influencer on Sina Weibo in China.

Many influencers on Xiaohongshu have their own online communities and they regularly publish product recommendations based on their use experience, which can help to expand the influence. In this case they are acting as consumers themselves, so followers don't just see a product or service endorsement, but someone using it in real-time and real-life contexts. This increases both the possibility and potential of growth for social media marketing.

Figure 11. The proportion of consumers getting information from different social e-commerce platforms
Source: (DATA100 Insight; Internet Society of China; Sina.com.cn; Various sources (Chuangqi e-commerce research center), 2020)

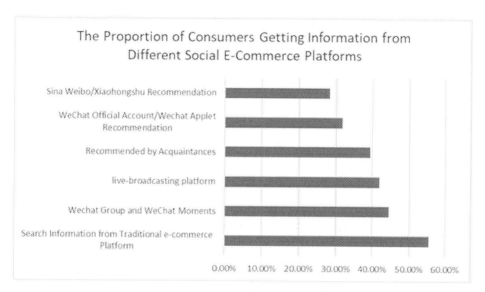

In China, the marketing value of KOL is different in different industries. For the beauty and makeup industry, Li Jiaqi and Wei Ya are very well-known in China. They were not celebrities or popular people in the traditional sense, but they were stars born on the social media platform, so they may not be star or popular people before social media, but now they hold almost celebrity like fame and popularity. Ma (2021) claimed that live-streaming commerce has grown explosively in China, and the extensive lockdowns caused by the COVID-19 pandemic propelled its growth further. Li Jiaqi and Weiya bring considerable sales to beauty makeup brands through live broadcasting. At present, there are also a lot of social media influencers from different fields being seen by beauty brands. From figure 12 we can draw a conclusion that the KOL in beauty makeup industry have the highest value. These influencers promote products by sharing usage experience and analyzing how it works on different people.

Figure 12. Marketing value of KOL in top 10 industries in 2020
Source: (Miaozhen Systems & China Advertising Association, 2021)

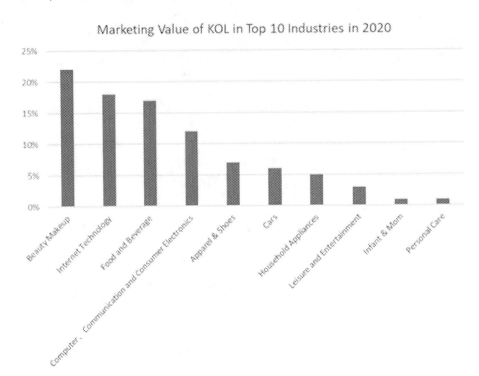

CHARACTERISTICS OF BUSINESS TRANSFORMATION OF CHINESE SOCIAL MEDIA INFLUENCERS SECTOR BEFORE AND AFTER THE COVID-19

The COVID-19 pandemic deeply impacted the economy of different countries. Global events tend to create long-lasting and widespread impact, both positively and negatively. Being one such event, the COVID-19 pandemic could change how we see the world, the ways we think, the way we interact and communicate and possibly even our very lifestyles. In addition, the pandemic might have a profound impact on Corporate Social Responsivity (CSR), consumer ethics, and basic marketing philosophy (He & Lloyd, 2020). There are many critical success factors for a company's CSR initiative, amongst which are companies' involvement with the local community and local government. Companies aim to not only create awareness of their services, but promote responsible and safe consumption, use and disposal of their products and services. That means they need to start influencing both their employees and their consumers and at times society at large. They want to showcase what they stand for and care for, and this is a great premise for engaging social media influencers. This has also significantly changed the CSR activities they chose to involve in and the ways in which social media influencers are promoting the product. For instance, many brands came forward to showcase how they are performing no contact delivery services, how they have vaccinated their employees, how they have sanitized their work environment. During this pandemic, many influencers in China helped farmers who have difficulties selling products during the epidemic through live-streaming platform, thereby creating new ways of reaching the customer, for providers who don't have a formal brand, product or service. But according to Statista

Digital Market Outlook (2020), amongst all digital advertising segments, social media and video sharing platforms are least affected by the pandemic. According to the research done by iResearch (2020), in the first quarter of 2020, China's social advertising revenue reached 16.3 billion yuan, down 14.9% from the previous quarter and up 30.3% compared with the same period last year, reflecting the increased time users spent on social media platforms during the pandemic lockdowns. There was also a sharp increase in advertising exposure and the improvement in advertising delivery efficiency.

Many scholars have studied the psychological changes of consumers under COVID-19. According to Ngo et al. (2020), in the post-COVID-19 pandemic era, empathy, which is putting yourself in someone else's shoes, and the ability and desire to appreciate others' emotions and perspectives, was considered one of the essential elements of NPD (New Product Development). Customer / User Empathy is considered as the primary driving force for Integrated Social Media Interaction (ISMI) strategy and is even more relevant in highly competitive global marketplace where brands suffer both from direct and indirect competition. The research done by He and Lloyd Harris (2020) shows that during the pandemic, there has been a positive impact of social media in the new product development phase. This can be attributed to the rapid online shift that the pandemic has forced many companies to take, pushing even the most traditional ones to do so, in order to survive. When moving online you start getting used to newer research methods, trends, analytical tools, feedback systems and learning curve is much faster. According to Sandip Rakshit et al. (2021), the use of social media networks as a source of knowledge for new ventures (products and services) is a systematic component of the new product development process for existing small and medium sized enterprises (SMEs) during the COVID-19 pandemic.

During the pandemic, the use of social media for information browsing and communication has undoubtedly become a great choice for people to spend time at home. As seen in figure 13 increasing number of people said they have been spending more time on social media during the pandemic.

Figure 13. People in different countries who spending more time on social media during the pandemic
Source: (Miaozhen Systems & China Advertising Association, 2021)

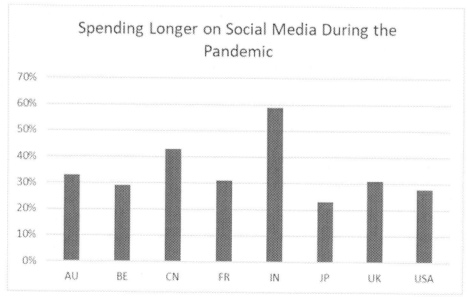

The outbreak of COVID-19 has forced people to stay at home, leaving them with more time to spend on social media due to the prolonged home life and inability to communicate face-to-face during the epidemic. People have increased their social media usage during the outbreak of COVID-19 compared to before COVID-19 (Luo et al., 2021). The growth of influencer marketing accelerated with the outbreak of COVID-19, during which people increasingly turned to social media for entertainment and virtual social experiences (Etzkorn, 2021).

According to iResearch advertisers survey, during the pandemic in 2020, businesses used social e-commerce and other means to better meet consumer needs. The pandemic brought benefits to users by the way of live streaming e-commerce (also known as Live Commerce) which is a business model in which retailers, influencers, or celebrities sell products and services via online video streaming where the broadcaster demonstrates and discusses the offering and answers audience questions in real-time. After the outbreak of the pandemic, the platforms with a significant increase in consumer activity are live broadcasting platforms, followed by short video platforms, which have become the key marketing means adopted by advertisers. It is stated by Ma (2021) that live-stream shopping has witnessed a leap in development since the COVID-19 outbreak in 2019. The occurrence of the pandemic has extremely limited the offline consumption scenario. After the outbreak of the pandemic, most advertisers in China believe that digital marketing upgrades are necessary.

As for followers and consumers, the pandemic had increased the rate of social media exposure. They tend to pay closer attention to social media. According to Business Insider, annual business investment in influencer marketing will reach $15 billion by 2022 (Schomer, 2019). As a supporter of brand advertisement, social media influencers need to pay attention to the needs of the consumers, such as the increasing need to make online purchases for everyday products like groceries and other household supplies during the pandemic. Influencers also need to pay attention to consumers' worldviews. For example, the rise of nationalism in the context of geopolitical tensions caused by the pandemic, made it important for influencers to choose the brands they help to promote.

By comparing figure 14 and figure 15, we can conclude that the advertisements in response to COVID-19 gain more approval from consumers than normal advertisement. We can find the data of China in the graph which shows that Chinese people have a strong sense of social responsibility. In addition, Chinese companies have made considerable efforts to take advantage of the COVID-19 situation for cultivating relationships with their consumers as well as the public, and most of their strategies generated satisfying results. Meituan app, a popular Chinese food delivery platform, offers contactless delivery and payment (Yu et al., 2022). Food delivery personnel on this platform take temperature checks every day and present them to the platform to enhance users' trust. It is not difficult to conclude that in the face of major social events, the positive response and reaction by brand towards these events will increase the appreciation of consumers.

As content producers and advertising channels favored by advertisers, social media influencers should also pay more attention to social responsibilities. In addition, due to COVID-19 pandemic, offline consumption has been limited and people have more time to spend on social media. So influencers need to strategize on how to maintain stable update frequency, maintain high-quality content output and attract continuous attention from fans. Successful Social Media Fashion Influencers (SMFIs) usually post something that their followers wish to have, but do not (Saul, 2016). After the pandemic, with people going back to work and school, how social media influencers can retain their followership and viewership is also a question that needs to be addressed.

Figure 14. Levels of approval for brand activities: running 'normal' advertising campaigns
Source: (GWI, 2020)

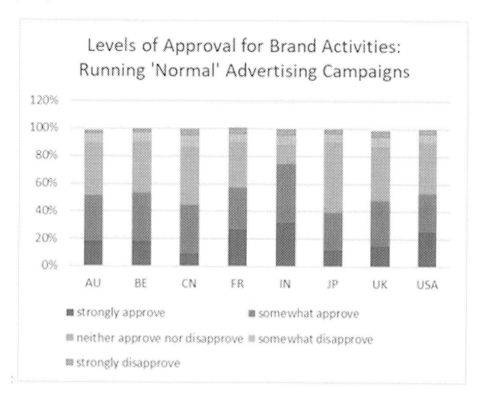

Figure 15. Levels of approval for brand activities: running advertising in response to COVID-19
Source: (GWI, 2020)

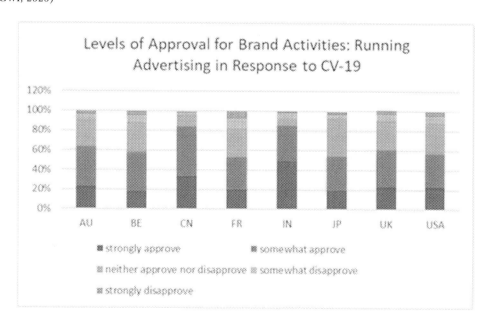

DISCUSSION OF SOCIAL MEDIA INFLUENCERS' IMPACTS ON CONSUMERS' BUYING BEHAVIOR

Social media influencers have now become an important factor affecting consumers' buying behavior. It is stated by Rakuten (2019) that brands can leverage the prior cultivated relationship between consumers and influencers by having the influencer promote their offerings to consumers who already embrace their image or views. As seen in the figure 16, most people who engaged in this research said that their purchase decisions were influenced by what the influencers recommended and promoted. It is also interesting to note that, SMI can become part of the brand identity itself, or some are scouted like ambassadors for a brand, so they end up influencing only one type of product from on field. Just like in celebrity endorsement they are held accountable for not using or promoting use of any competing brands. This is also a cautionary tale as the same SMIs can become negative influence on a brand, when they act as critiques, and reviewers. These are presented as product, version, or feature comparison of products in the same category and is a popular method used in different industries from cars to electronic products, to cosmetics. Even while the influencer seems like a neutral party giving an honest opinion about the subject matter, there is always personal preference and interests that come into the picture, therefore appealing the user to consume certain product or certain brand.

Figure 16. Impact of social media influencers on purchasing in China as of October 2020
Source: (Rakuten Insight, 2020)

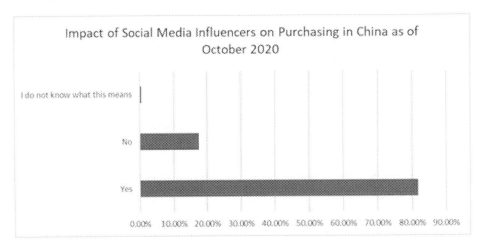

By literature study, we summarize the factors that will affect consumers' purchase behavior. They are mainly divided into the personal traits of the social media influencers, the content they create or promote, their familiarity with the consumers, and the type of community the influencers cultivate. Figure 17 shows the factors that influence consumers' purchasing behavior.

First, let's discuss the personal characteristics of the influencers. Users tend to be attracted to influencers who are similar to themselves. According to Zhang et al. (2018), when users identify an influencer who is similar and relatable to their own personality, they psychologically establish a potential identity foundation. People tend to relate to people who have similar attitude, situation, backgrounds, and context as them. Sometimes it can be related to or irrespective of their age, background, status, gender, and other demographic indicators. When we find someone of similar taste and preferences and interest area, we are more bound to seek them out. This also makes us more predisposed to the content published by these influencers. Similarity between influencers and followers and content consumers is thought to promote interpersonal relationships and strengthen emotional bonds. It is pointed out by Chung-Wha (Chloe) Ki et al. (2020) that a SMI whose persona is similar to the followers will convince the followers to see the SMI as a human brand who fulfills their need for relatedness. Similarity is the first step in getting consumers to pay attention to influencers.

Figure 17. The factors that will influence consumers' purchasing behavior (Authors)

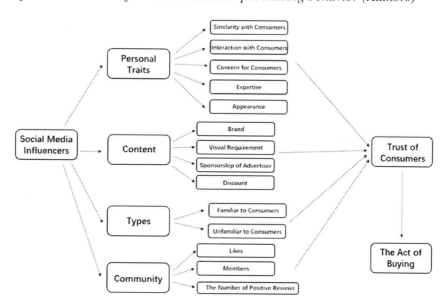

If you consider the Jobs-to-be-done framework, most consumers use or hire a product or service to get a job done. If we are to take being presentable and beautiful as an ultimate goal, then products from cosmetic brands may help us accomplish that goal. There are many ways to get a job done, for instance if one wants to become beautiful, they can eat healthy, dress better, cultivate more healthy habits and so on. So, when there are too many options to get a job done, consumers tend to be confused and over-whelmed – we call this decision paralysis. This applied for products and services, especially in highly competitive industry segments which offers too many choices. This is where influencers make a great impact, they are similar to the user, they have similar needs, and goals. So, when consumers see them using and benefiting from a product usage it makes the choice easier to make. At present, in China's influencer market, the recommendation of beauty products has attracted wide attention, and many consumers tend to choose influencers who have similar skin type and ability of buying that are similar to them. Therefore, similarity can be regarded as a positive factor for consumers' purchasing behavior.

The ability of interacting with fans is important to maintain favorability from users. Regular interaction with fans helps foster a stable community. According to Tan (2017), from the perspective of interaction between social media influencers and consumers, influencers answer questions and collect feedback from fans and participate in brand activities with them, which can enhance their connection. Fans will also tend to trust influencers more, thus promoting their relationship.

The professionalism of social media influencers also affects consumers' trust in them. Social media influencers who have accumulated knowledge in a particular field are generally more persuasive while selling products in that field. At present, social media influencers are divided into beauty bloggers, food bloggers, travel bloggers and car bloggers, who can suggest and recommend accurately to their consumer base. In order to find out whether the professionalism of influencers will affect consumers' purchasing behavior, we will set the indexes that affect professionalism as "the ability to provide new information" and "knowledge reserve" in our survey. Professionalism refers to the ability of the sender to provide accurate information. Ki and Kim (2019) claimed that content created by social media influencers serves as an important source of information for their followers and other social media influencers to make informed product choices or purchase decisions. More importantly, how to choose a brand is important for influencers, which can also show their expertise. Many influencers have become cautious in entering collaborations with brands and deliberately select partners that are consistent with their personal brands (Watson, 2020) to maintain their trustworthiness and coolness in the eyes of their followers. If a brand doesn't deliver what is promises to, it ruins the reputation of the brand as well as everyone who identified with it, which makes the influencers a target of consumer criticism.

In addition to the characteristics of social media influencers mentioned above, we were also curious to see if the appearance of influencers influenced consumers' appreciation of them and thus their purchasing behavior. Based on the characteristics of the social media influencers, the following hypotheses are proposed:

H1. Social media influencers who are more similar to consumers, more interactive with consumers, more concerned about consumers' needs, more professional and better looking can enhance consumers' trust, thus promoting consumption.

As Liu et al. (2019) pointed out that judging from the content posted by the influencers, the visual elements on the Weibo (video over text or pictures) add to the vividness of the experience shared by the vlogger. Video dissemination based on daily life scenes enhances the dissemination effect of product placement marketing.

In the age of social media, which emphasizes information transparency, users value the intrinsic motivation and non-commercial orientation of SMIs. According to Wang (2020), the introduction of marketing based on life scenes effectively alleviates the tension caused by commercial content, so that influencers can complete brand cooperation while avoiding users' aversion to direct advertising, and finally effectively convert existing followers into actual consumers. Coursaris and Van Osch (2016) stated that on social media, beauty brands are increasingly influenced by vloggers. Carolina Stubba and Jonas Colliander (2019) concluded that social media influencers communicate their views on products and brands through social media posts on a near daily basis. While many of these posts are sponsored by a brand, paving ways paid promotions and partnerships, others are personal and sincere suggestions from influencers. Influencers may choose to add a disclosure to a post about a non-sponsored product to highlight their impartiality. The results showed that fair product posts were less likely to be viewed as advertising than posts for sponsored products, and thus generated higher information credibility. It is to be noted that, while influencers can appear to promote their favorite brands and personal usage even without formal brand partnerships, there could be a long-term strategy to gain the brand's attention and prove their worth as an influencer, thereby paving way for financially beneficial partnerships in the future.

In addition, the brands selected by social media influencers will also have an impact on consumers. The choice of high-quality, cost-effective, and well-known brands by social media influencers can enhance consumers' trust, thus weakening consumers' resistance and promoting consumption.

Moreover, discounts are a common marketing tool in consumption, so it is reasonable to speculate that social media influencers will attract consumers' attention more when they provide special discounts and promocodes. Based on the characteristics of the content published by the above social media influencers, we propose the following hypotheses:

H2. Visual effects have an impact on consumers, and content with more design sense can enhance consumers' goodwill, weaken their resistance, and thus promote purchases.

H3. Based on personal experience, that is, posts without advertising goals can enhance consumers' trust, thus promoting consumption.

H4. The choice of high-quality and well-known brands by social media influencers can enhance consumers' trust, thus promoting consumption.

H5. Discounts offered by social media influencers have positive impacts on consumers.

Wang et al. (2021) maintained that from the perspective of community, consumers can interact with others by responding to other consumers' posts, which can develop social relations and support each other's purchasing decisions. When they observe that their peers trust a brand, they are more inclined to build trust in the brand community. According to Kumar and Reinartz (2016), brands can derive value from consumers directly through their purchases, or indirectly through other activities, such as recommendations and goodwill, which will influence others on social media, creating brand identify, and product purchase through word of mouth. These are often sighted to be more powerful and long-lasting for brands. The customer lifetime value also increases with repeated interactions and purchases made with a brand. As the overall trust increases, they become highly likely candidates for cross selling and upselling of products and services from the same brand or products and services endorsed by the influencer as they are brands in themselves. It was reported by Samadrita and Indranil (2020) that a higher volume of likes on Facebook leads to a higher likelihood of purchasing and recommending a product on the linked e-commerce site. However, is it the high number of 'likes' on the post or the high praise of a social media influencers that develops consumer trust is to be verified.

H6. The higher the number of 'likes' of the post and high praise of a social media influencers, the higher the consumer's trust in them, thus increasing the possibility of purchase.

H7. The higher the number of followers a social media blogger has, the larger the number of communities they can establish, which can enhance the trust of consumers and thus increase the possibility of purchase.

In addition, we also believe that different types of social media influencers have different influences on each buyer. People are more likely to trust social media influencers they know well. Therefore, we also put forward the following hypothesis:

H8. Consumers are more likely to trust influencers they are familiar with.

Methodology

By means of random sampling, a corresponding questionnaire survey[1] was carried out on 224 people mainly composed of young people. A total of 224 questionnaires were issued and 224 were returned, of which 172 were valid, with an effective rate of 76.79%, meeting the needs of this survey. 118 of them, who were used as a reference for the study, said in the questionnaire that their purchasing behavior was influenced to some extent by social media influencers. Of the 118 samples, 17 were male and 101 were female. According to the research content and research needs, questionnaires were developed, including questions related to social media influencers and purchasing behaviors. Table 1 shows the basic information of the 118 samples.

Table 1. The sample of the research

Demographic	Categories	Percentage
Gender	Male	14.41%
	Female	85.59%
Age	Under the age of 18	0%
	18 to 25 years old	83.9%
	26 to 30 years old	7.63%
	31 to 40 years old	5.08%
	41 to 50 years old	2.54%
	51 to 60 years old	0.85%
	Over 60 years old	0%
Job	Full-time student	77.12%
	Production staff	2.54%
	Salesman	3.39%
	Marketing/Public relations personnel	3.39%
	The personnel of the service	0.85%
	Administrative/Support staff	1.69%
	The human resource	0%
	Financial/Audit staff	3.39%
	Civilian/Clerical staff	2.54%
	Technical/R&D personnel	0.85%
	Management personnel	4.24%
	Teacher	0%
	Consultant	0%
	Professional (e.g., accountant, lawyer, architect, healthcare professional, journalist, etc.)	0%
	Other	0%

At the beginning of the questionnaire, it mainly investigates the social media platforms that can influence people's purchasing behavior, the channels of online consumption, the frequency of online purchase and whether social media influencers will influence their consumption. Through the first four questions shown in table 2 we have a basic understanding of the current influential social media platforms and online shopping platforms, and those who are not influenced by social media influencers are excluded. Therefore, out of 172 people, 118 ended up completing the follow-up questions because they were influenced by social media influencers.

Table 2. The daily purchasing behavior of the subjects

Behavior	Categories	Percent
Social media platforms that influence consumption	Little Red Book	58.14%
	Taobao	84.88%
	Meituan	58.72%
	Sina microblog	47.67%
	WeChat	63.37%
	Other	11.05%
	The social media platforms don't influence my consumption	1.16%
The frequency of consumption through social media platforms	Every day	9.88%
	At least once a week	34.88%
	At least once a month	42.44%
	At least once every three months	7.56%
	At least once every six months	1.16%
	At least once a year	1.16%
	Almost no	2.91%
Products that are often purchased on social media platforms	Daily necessities	77.84%
	Beauty makeup products	59.28%
	Food	74.25%
	Clothing and footwear	76.05%
	Electronic products	25.15%
	Luxury goods	6.59%
	Other products	1.8%
The impact of social media influencers on purchases	I **pay close attention** to influencers' posts, they can affect my purchase	20.96%
	I **only read** recommendations from influencers **when there is a need to buy**	49.7%
	I will pay attention to the daily posts, but **I don't purchase under the recommendation of influencers**	21.56%
	I **don't pay attention to** the influencers' product recommendations and they have no influence on my consumption.	7.78%
	Other impacts	0%

Results

This questionnaire investigates the influence of social media influencers on consumer trust and recognition based on a five-level scale. We divided the answers into five levels: "strongly agree," "somewhat agree," "indifferent," "disagree," "strongly disagree." Those who choose "strongly agree" count one point, while those who choose "strongly disagree" count five points. Therefore, the higher the score, the negative correlation between this factor and consumers' purchasing behavior, and the lower the score, the promotion of this factor to consumers' consumption.

We use an intelligent online statistical analysis platform called SPSSAU to analyze the reliability of the five-level scale of the questionnaire, and it is concluded that the Cronbach α coefficient is 0.99, and the total correlation of each problem correction item is greater than 0.89, indicating high reliability.

As can be seen from the questionnaire results, when it comes to the similarity between consumers and bloggers, consumers pay more attention to the influencers who have values and personality consumers agree with. Choosing influencers who are similar to consumers is not so necessary. There are about 72% people who engage in this survey agreed that the interaction between influencers and consumers can increase the likelihood of consumption. Moreover, there are about 85% people who engage in this survey agreed that influencers should concern more about consumers' needs, which can increase the possibility of purchasing. Consumers also pay more attention to an influencer's professionalism than their appearance. Influencers with expertise in a particular field are more likely to attract consumers' attention. So H1 can be supported.

When it comes to the content social media influencers post on social media, consumers prefer video more than pictures, about 60% of those surveyed said that the visual aesthetic of an influencer's post influenced their acceptance of a recommendation. Additionally, consumers prefer products recommended by social media bloggers based on user experience rather than advertisement. When an influencer promotes a brand consumers know and trust, it increases consumers' likelihood of consumption. Simultaneously, consumers care more about the number of positive comments from the consumer community than the number of likes on a post. Discounts also have an incentive for consumers to purchase. More than 60 percent people surveyed said that they will increase their desire to buy because of discounts. So H2-H6 can be supported.

It can also be found that the types of social media influencers will influence people's trust on the post. According to the survey, people are more likely to accept products recommended by influencers they know well. There are about 51% of people who engage in this survey agreed that the number of fans of influencers has impact on their buying behavior. H7 and H8 can be supported.

Although our assumptions are all valid, the degree of influence of each factor on consumers' purchasing behavior is different. It can be observed that some factors have stronger positive impact on consumers, while others not so much. Knowing the factors that can have a strong impact on consumers is instructive for businesses.

Table 3. Measurement items of key variables

Construct	Mean	Standard deviation
1. Similarity with Consumers The influencers I follow have similarities with me (such as similar life attitude, brand pursuit, economic conditions, etc.)	2.31 (A score of 1 is a strong agreement)	0.92
The influencers I follow have personalities and values that I agree with	1.72 (A score of 1 is a strong agreement)	0.73
2. Interaction with Consumers The interaction between influencers and me can increase the likelihood of consumption	2.19 (A score of 1 is a strong agreement)	0.81
3. Concern for Consumers Influencer's attention to fan's needs will enhance my trust in bloggers	1.95 (A score of 1 is a strong agreement)	0.78
4. Expertise The influencer's ability to provide new information (product updates, brand recommendations) has an impact on my trust in them	3.58 (A score of 5 means a strong agreement)	0.96
The influence the knowledge of an influencer in their field has on my acceptance and trust of their product recommendations	4.04 (A score of 5 means a strong agreement)	0.84
5. Appearance The influence of the appearance of the influencers on my acceptance of their product recommendation	3.11 (A score of 5 means a strong agreement)	1.10

continues on following page

Table 3. Continued

Construct	Mean	Standard deviation
6. Visual Requirement Vlogs and other video recommendation posts posted by influencers can make me know more about the product and are more attractive than picture posts	2.06 (A score of 1 is a strong agreement)	0.84
The visual beauty of the content (Ad photos, Ad language design, etc.) has an impact on my acceptance of their recommendations	2.40 (A score of 1 is a strong agreement)	0.97
7. Advertisement or Sincere Recommendations Recommendations based on the influencer's own experience are more likely to persuade me to buy than endorsement	1.91 (A score of 1 is a strong agreement)	0.97
8. Brand When an influencer promotes a brand, I know and trust, it increases my likelihood of consumption	1.87 (A score of 1 is a strong agreement)	0.78
9. Discount The influence of discount offered by influencers when recommending products on my purchasing possibility	3.69 (A score of 5 is a strong agreement)	1.01
10. Likes The impact of the number of thumbs-up on content posted by influencers on my purchase likelihood	3.26 (A score of 5 is a strong agreement)	1.14
11. Positive Review The influence of the number of favorable comments on the products on my purchase likelihood	3.9 (A score of 5 is a strong agreement)	1.02
12. The Number of Fans The influence of the number of followers of a blogger on my trust in their recommendation and purchase	3.35 (A score of 5 is a strong agreement)	1.02
13. Types of The Influencers Influencers I know well affect my spending more than influencers I don't know well	1.91 (A score of 1 is a strong agreement)	0.84

OPPORTUNITIES AND CHALLENGES FOR CHINESE SOCIAL MEDIA INFLUENCERS IN ADVERTISING

Social media is becoming a highly competitive market space, with businesses vying for attention of their users. Most of these platforms are multi-sided, with users, brands, advertisers, sellers, and others making up the different kinds of users that leverage them for different purposes. As for the brands their ultimate aim is to establish a social media presence, interact with their consumers, promote their product and services. This they accomplish by having their own pages and profiles. They also navigate this highly competitive space through influencer marketing which is now evolving into long-term partnerships between them and influencers (McNutt, 2021). On Twitter, 49% of respondents rely on product recommendations from KOLs, and 40% of users purchase products recommended by KOLs. According to Eyal (2018), one study reported that 92% of social media users trust influencers more than traditional marketing channels. Therefore, social media has become an important channel for consumers. Social media advertising, as a form of online advertising with interactive features (Tuten and Solomon, 2017), has become the preferred choice for advertisers because it provides a channel through which brands and consumers can engage in mutually beneficial interactions. They can have honest conversations and dialogues about their like, dislikes, preferences. Also, the level of formality involved in interacting with

KOLs is much lesser and highly relatable. It also gives high freedom of choice, for both sides to choose if they want to engage or not, if so to what extend they want to. According to Li et al. (2016), as we are flooded with different kinds of information, consumers need to make complex decisions, using the greatest range of information accessible to them. This means that in order to optimize the decisions they make, consumers must be able to access and collect relevant information from different channels, and decide by making repeated comparisons of the information and insights they have gathered and investing more cognitive resources into their decision making. At present, there are many opportunities for social media influencers in the market, and many young people see their advertising on social media as the main way to make money.

There are some challenges for influencers to face with. By observing the research released by iResearch (2020), with the increasingly saturated development of the first and second-tier cities and the reduction of online dividend, the sinking market appears in the commercial market. In February 2020, the scale of network users in the sinking cities accounted for 48.6%, which increased by nearly 10% compared with that in February 2017. This means that the online catalyst habit of users in the sinking market has been deeply formed. How to increase the number of fans and create better content marketing strategies are questions for merchants and influencers to answer. It is also important to increase user loyalty and prevent user churn. At present, due to the surge of information, people's time is increasingly occupied by various apps, and many people appear to be in a state of information fatigue. How to break through the barrier of homogeneous information and how to bring the new information into user's vision are worth thinking about.

CONCLUSION AND RECOMMENDATIONS

The scale of China's online advertising market is increasing. Social media advertising, with its interactivity, has become a critical site for brand-consumer relationship building. Social media platforms provide challenges as well as opportunities for influencers. It allows ordinary people to gain fans, satisfy their emotional needs in the virtual world, and gain the favor of advertisers. Influencers need to improve their professional competence, produce high-quality content, undertake social responsibilities while pursuing profits, and avoid pan-entertainment.

Moreover, social media influencers' choices of brands are also important because it also reflects their level of professionalism. Advertising based on their own experience is more persuasive than ordinary endorsement advertising. More importantly, it is also significant to pay attention to the needs of consumers and enhance the interaction with them.

There is a long way for influencers to go because it is not easy to develop a large group of followers and maintain the number of fans. It is claimed by Zhou (2020) that China has entered a silent era from the era of advertising disturbance, advertising is content, and content is advertising, good content needs to have spontaneous transmission to break out. Online advertisements are booming these years, which shows that there are still a lot of opportunities for influencers to pursue.

FUTURE RESEARCH DIRECTIONS

Though the rapid development of technologies like machine learning, AI and advanced digital marketing tools bring efficiency into brand management, it also brings many concerns like privacy-related issues where users' personal information gets disclosed intentionally or unintentionally. According to Holmes (2019), as the attention is shifting from familiar public feeds channel to the recent private messaging channel on social media brings major challenges for both brands and advertisers. It was stated by John et al. (2018) that with growing user awareness of the personalization practice, personalized ads could decrease ad performance if it activates concerns about privacy and provokes users' negative responses. In terms of individual privacy, information accuracy, mental health, social media platforms are also bringing lot of ways to monitor the interactions we have with each other. We can unfollow uninterested topics, reduce suggestions of certain kind, block users, restrict comments and sharing and so on. This is beneficial for both influencers and other users. Personalized ad recommendations can help brands reach their potential users; cross sell and upsell to current customers, but this sometimes comes at the cost of user privacy and is worth looking into.

Digital media has made information access quicker, faster, and highly personalized. Users are very keen on selecting the content they want to be shown and recommended. They want their social media feeds to be highly personalized and customizable, so much so, no two feeds in the social media universe are alike, almost akin to a digital DNA. Sunstein (2006) first proposed the term information cocoon and defines it as "communication universes in which we hear only what we choose and only what comforts us and pleases us". However, long-term selective acquisition of specific information may lead to the formation of information cocoon (Jiang & Xu, 2021). From the social media service provider side, you see personalized information recommendations being made by machine learning algorithms that show the user information that are related to their past usage-behavior, search history, location, and topic preferences, this causes a narrowing of information field of vision, again exposing the user to the information cocoon effect. There are other similar concepts like echo chamber (Jamieson & Cappella, 2008), filter bubble (Pariser, 2011), where the users are intellectually isolated from alternative point of views, and opinions. All of the above are caused by selective exposure to like-minded opinions due to personalized content brought by social media. (Borgesius et al., 2016). The user becomes separated from information that disagrees with their viewpoints, thus limiting their exposure to diverse content, and that would likely play into product and service suggestion and ad recommendations. How to find the boundary between personalized information recommendation and concerns like information cocoon on social media is worth discussing.

To conclude, while paying attention to the considerable profits brought to brands by social media advertising, we should also consider issues related to morality, ethics and laws pertaining to the users and their privacy.

ACKNOWLEDGMENT

The authors extend sincere gratitude to:
- Our colleagues from Soochow University, the Australian Studies Centre of Shanghai University and Krirk University as well as the independent research colleagues who provided insight and

expertise that greatly assisted the research, although they may not agree with all of the interpretations/conclusions of this chapter.

- China Knowledge for supporting our research.
- The Editor and the International Editorial Advisory Board (IEAB) of this book who initially desk reviewed, arranged a rigorous double/triple blind review process and conducted a thorough, minute and critical final review before accepting the chapter for publication.
- All anonymous reviewers who provided very constructive feedbacks for thorough revision, improvement, extension, and fine tuning of the chapter.

REFERENCES

Adobe. (2018). *Adobe experience manager 6.4: defining the next wave of content driven experiences.* Retrieved from https://blogs.adobe.com/digitaleurope/digital-marketing/adobe-experience-manager-6-4-defining-the-next-wave-of-content-driven-experiences/

Akar, E., & Topcu, B. (2011). An examination of the factors influencing consumer's attitudes toward social media marketing. *Journal of Internet Commerce, 10*(1), 35–67. doi:10.1080/15332861.2011.558456

Amy, W. (2020). *Ongoing Home Media Consumption and The Coronavirus Worldwide 2020.* Retrieved from https://www.statista.com/statistics/1170493/ongoing-in-home-media-consumption-growth-coronavirus-worldwide-by-country/

Bhattacharyya, S., & Bose, I. (2020). S-commerce: Influence of Facebook likes on purchases and recommendations on a linked e-commerce site. *Decision Support Systems, 138,* 113383. doi:10.1016/j.dss.2020.113383

Cao, X., Qu, Z., Liu, Y., & Hu, J. (2021). How the destination short video affects the customers' attitude: The role of narrative transportation. *Journal of Retailing and Consumer Services, 62,* 102672. Advance online publication. doi:10.1016/j.jretconser.2021.102672

China Internet Network Information Center. (2020). *The 45th China Statistical Report on Internet Development.* Retrieved from http://www.cnnic.net.cn/hlwfzyj/hlwxzbg/

Chuangqi E-Commerce Research Center. (2020). *China's Social Commerce Consumer Shopping Behavior Research Report 2020.* Retrieved from https://www.sohu.com/a/435530596_120250072

Chung, T. S., Wedel, M., & Rust, R. T. (2016). Adaptive personalization using social networks. *Journal of the Academy of Marketing Science, 44*(1), 66–87. doi:10.100711747-015-0441-x

CNNIC. (2022). *The 49th Statistical Report on Internet Development in China.* China Internet Network Information Center (CNNIC).

Colliander, J., & Dahlén, M. (2011). Following the fashionable friend: The power of social media: Weighing publicity effectiveness of blogs versus online magazines. *Journal of Advertising Research, 51*(1), 313–320. doi:10.2501/JAR-51-1-313-320

Collinson, P. (2020). Panic buying on wane as online shopping takes over, says bank. *The Guardian, 30.*

Coursaris, C. K., & Osch, W. V. (2016, July). Exploring the effects of source credibility on information adoption on YouTube. In *International Conference on HCI in Business, Government, and Organizations* (pp. 16-25). Springer. 10.1007/978-3-319-39396-4_2

Djafarova, E., & Trofimenko, O. (2019). 'Instafamous'–credibility and self-presentation of micro-celebrities on social media. *Information Communication and Society*, 22(10), 1432–1446. doi:10.1080/1369118X.2018.1438491

Duan, C. (2019). KOC: New marketing outlet in the era of private domain traffic. *China Advertising*, 11, 115–116.

Etzkorn, K. (2021). *How digital shopping will evolve: Three trends to watch*. Retrieved from https://www.forbes.com/sites/forbestechcouncil/2021/04/09/how-digital-shopping-will-evolve-three-trends-to-watch/?sh=6d43c2e737

Evans, N. J., Phua, J., Lim, J., & Jun, H. (2017). Disclosing Instagram influencer advertising: The effects of disclosure language on advertising recognition, attitudes, and behavioral intent. *Journal of Interactive Advertising*, 17(2), 138–149. doi:10.1080/15252019.2017.1366885

Eyal, G. (2018). *Why influencers fail to disclose commercial relationships and the brands that enable them*. Adweek. Retrieved from https://www.adweek.com/digital/whyinfluencers-fail-to-disclose-commercialrelationships-and-the-brands-that-enablethem/

Farivar, S., Wang, F., & Yuan, Y. (2020). Opinion leadership vs. para-social relationship: Key factors in influencer marketing. *Journal of Retailing and Consumer Services*, 59, 102371. doi:10.1016/j.jretconser.2020.102371

Fertik, M. (2020). *Why is influencer marketing such A big deal right now?* Retrieved from https://www.forbes.com/sites/michaelfertik/2020/07/02/why-is-influencer-marketing-such-a-big-deal-right-now/#5be7c9d375f3

Friestad, M., & Wright, P. (1994). The Persuasion Knowledge Model: How People Cope with Persuasion Attempts. *The Journal of Consumer Research*, 21(1), 1. doi:10.1086/209380

Gao, D., Pan, Q., & Xia, L. (2021). *Forecast of China's Media Industry*. Retrieved from https://mp.weixin.qq.com/s/rWmEKAMgDyTzFaVApAK9iA

Gardner, J., & Lehnert, K. (2016). What's new about new media? How multi-channel networks work with content creators. *Business Horizons*, 59(3), 293–302. doi:10.1016/j.bushor.2016.01.009

Group, M. (2021). *This year, Next year: China media Industry Forecast*. Retrieved from https://mp.weixin.qq.com/s/NqnxyX8ooOjyNSMc_rAFCw

He, H., & Harris, L. (2020). The impact of Covid-19 pandemic on corporate social responsibility and marketing philosophy. *Journal of Business Research*, 116, 176–182. doi:10.1016/j.jbusres.2020.05.030 PMID:32457556

Holmes, R. (2019). *The Rules Of Social Media Just Changed. Here's How To Keep Up*. Retrieved from https://www. forbes. com/sites/ryanholmes/2019/04/17/the-rules-of-social-media-just-changed-heres-how-to-keepup

Howard, D. J., & Kerin, R. A. (2004). The effects of personalized product recommendations on advertisement response rates: The "try this. It works!" technique. *Journal of User Psychology, 14*(3), 271–279. doi:10.120715327663jcp1403_8

Hua, Y., Bao, L., & Wu, X. (2020). The product-selling strategy under direct and indirect value Identification. *Journal of Cleaner Production, 279*, 123591. doi:10.1016/j.jclepro.2020.123591

Huang, Q., Jin, J., Lynn, B. J., & Men, L. R. (2021). Relationship cultivation and public engagement via social media during the covid-19 pandemic in China. *Public Relations Review, 47*(4), 102064. doi:10.1016/j.pubrev.2021.102064

InfluencerMarketingHub. (2019). *The State of Influencer Marketing 2019: Benchmark Report.* Retrieved from bit.ly/2Ge2xUX

InfluencerMarketingHub. (2021). *Influencer Marketing Benchmark Report 2021.* Retrieved from https://influencermarketinghub.com/influencer-marketing-benchmark-report-2021/#toc-6

iResearch. (2020). *2020 China Online Advertising Market Annual Insight Report.* Retrieved from https://report.iresearch.cn/report/202007/3614.shtml

Jamieson, K. H., & Cappella, J. N. (2008). *Echo chamber: Rush Limbaugh and the conservative media establishment.* Oxford University Press.

Jerslev, A. (2016). Media times in the time of the microcelebrity: Celebrification and the YouTuber Zoella. *International Journal of Communication, 10*, 19.

Jiang, T. T., & Xu, Y. R. (2021). Narrowed Information Universe: A Review of Research on Information Cocoons, Selective Exposure, and Echo Chambers. *Intelligence. Information & Sharing, 38*(5), 134–144.

John, L., Kim, T., & Barasz, K. (2018). Ads That Don't Overstep: How to Make Sure You Don't Take Personalization Too Far. *Harvard Business Review, 96*(1), 62–69.

Karp, K. (2016). New research: The value of influencers on Twitter. *Twitter.* Retrieved from https://blog.twitter.com/2016/new-research-the-value-of-influencers-ontwitter

Ki, C. W. C., Cuevas, L. M., Chong, S. M., & Lim, H. (2020). Influencer marketing: Social media influencers as human brands attaching to followers and yielding positive marketing results by fulfilling needs. *Journal of Retailing and Consumer Services, 55*, 102133. doi:10.1016/j.jretconser.2020.102133

Ki, C. W. C., & Kim, Y. K. (2019). The mechanism by which social media influencers persuade consumers: The role of consumers' desire to mimic. *Psychology and Marketing, 36*(10), 905–922.

Kim, A. J., & Ko, E. (2010). Impacts of luxury fashion brand's social media marketing on customer relationship and purchase intention. *Journal of Global Fashion Marketing, 1*(3), 164–171.

Kim, D. Y., & Kim, H. Y. (2021). Trust me, trust me not: A nuanced view of influencer marketing on social media. *Journal of Business Research, 134*, 223–232. doi:10.1016/J.JBUSRES.2021.05.024

Kumar, V., & Reinartz, W. (2016). Creating enduring customer value. *Journal of Marketing, 80*, 36–68. doi:10.1509/jm.15.0414

Ladhari, R., Massa, E., & Skandrani, H. (2020). YouTube vloggers' popularity and influence: The roles of homophily, emotional attachment, and expertise. *Journal of Retailing and Consumer Services, 54,* 102027. doi:10.1016/j.jretconser.2019.102027

Lambrecht, A., & Tucker, C. (2013). When does retargeting work? Information specificity in online advertising. *JMR, Journal of Marketing Research, 50*(5), 561–576. doi:10.1177/002224371305000508

LaVoie, N. R., Quick, B. L., Riles, J. M., & Lambert, N. J. (2017). Are graphic cigarette warning labels an effective message strategy? A test of psychological reactance theory and source appraisal. *Communication Research, 44*(3), 416–436. doi:10.1177/0093650215609669

Liu, M. T., Liu, Y., & Zhang, L. L. (2019). Vlog and brand evaluations: The influence of parasocial interaction. *Asia Pacific Journal of Marketing and Logistics, 31*(2), 419–436. doi:10.1108/APJML-01-2018-0021

Lu, B., Fan, W., & Zhou, M. (2016). Social presence, trust, and social commerce purchase intention: An empirical research. *Computers in Human Behavior, 56,* 225–237. doi:10.1016/j.chb.2015.11.057

Luo, T., Chen, W., & Liao, Y. (2021). Social media use in China before and during COVID-19: Preliminary results from an online retrospective survey. *Journal of Psychiatric Research, 140,* 35–38. doi:10.1016/J. JPSYCHIRES.2021.05.057

Ma, Y. (2021). Elucidating determinants of customer satisfaction with live-stream shopping: An extension of the information systems success model. *Telematics and Informatics, 65,* 101707. doi:10.1016/J. TELE.2021.101707

Marketing, R. (2019). *Influencer marketing global survey consumers.* Rakuten Marketing.

Marketing, R. (2020a). *Impact of social media influencers on purchasing in China as of October 2020.* Rakuten Marketing. Retrieved from https://www.statista.com/statistics/1200644/china-influencers-impact-on-purchasing/

Marketing, R. (2020b). *Share of consumers who follow social media influencers in Asia Pacific in 2020, by country.* Rakuten Marketing. Retrieved from https://www.statista.com/statistics/1181355/apac-share-of-consumers-who-follow-social-media-influencers-by-country-or-region/

McNutt, L. (2021). Influencer marketing predictions for 2021. *PR Daily.* Retrieved from https://www.prdaily.com/5-influencer-marketing-predictions-for-2021/

Miaozhen Systems & China Advertising Association. (2021). *KOL Marketing White Paper.* Retrieved from https://mp.weixin.qq.com/s/Tp_EPqyQG7VMF07Boi_3Yw

Müllerb, J., & Christandl, F. (2019). Content is king – But who is the king of kings? The effect of content marketing, sponsored content & user-generated content on brand responses. *Computers in Human Behavior, 96,* 46–55. doi:10.1016/j.chb.2019.02.006

Nafees, L., Cook, C. M., Nikolov, A. N., & Stoddard, J. E. (2021). Can social media influencer (SMI) power influence consumer brand attitudes? The mediating role of perceived SMI credibility. *Digital Business, 1*(2), 100008. doi:10.1016/J.DIGBUS.2021.100008

Ngo, L. V., Nguyen, T. N. Q., Tran, N. T., & Paramita, W. (2020). It takes two to tango: The role of customer empathy and resources to improve the efficacy of frontline employee empathy. *Journal of Retailing and Consumer Services, 56*, 102141. doi:10.1016/j.jretconser.2020.102141

Niedermeier, K. E., Wang, E., & Zhang, X. (2016). The use of social media among business-to-business sales professionals in China: How social media helps create and solidify guanxi relationships between sales professionals and customers. *Journal of Research in Interactive Marketing, 10*, 33–49. doi:10.1108/JRIM-08-2015-0054

Pariser, E. (2011). *The filter bubble: What the Internet is hiding from you.* Penguin UK.

Phillip, J. (2018). The Commercial Appropriation of Fame: A Cultural Analysis of the Right of Publicity and Passing Off. *European Intellectual Property Review, 1.*

Priporas, C. V., Stylos, N., & Kamenidou, I. E. (2020). City image, city brand personality and generation Z residents' life satisfaction under economic crisis: Predictors of city-related social media engagement. *Journal of Business Research, 119*, 453–463.

QuestMobile. (2021a). *2020 China Internet Advertising Market Insight.* Retrieved from https://mp.weixin.qq.com/s/ikrOOmOiKkxl6ZI1b9UHRQ

QuestMobile. (2021b). *New Media in Cross-platform KOL Ecology Research Report.* Retrieved from https://mp.weixin.qq.com/s/xwsovZlbRA94vxGf7AbsIQ

Saul, H. (2016). Instafamous: Meet the social media influencers redefining celebrity. *The Independent.* Retrieved from https://www.independent.co.uk/news/people/instagram-model-natasha-oakley-iskra-lawrence-kayla-itsines-kendall-jenner-jordyn-woods-a6907551.html

Schomer, A. (2019). Influencer marketing: State of the social media influencer market in 2020. *Business Insider, 18.*

Schouten, A. P., Janssen, L., & Verspaget, M. (2020). Celebrity vs. Influencer endorsements in advertising: The role of identification, credibility, and productendorser fit. *International Journal of Advertising, 39*(2), 258–281. doi:10.1080/02650487.2019.1634898

Shareef, M. A., Mukerji, B., Dwivedi, Y. K., Rana, N. P., & Islam, R. (2019). Social media marketing: Comparative effect of advertisement sources. *Journal of Retailing and Consumer Services, 46*, 58–69. doi:10.1016/j.jretconser.2017.11.001

Sherman, A. (2020). *TikTok reveals detailed user numbers for the first time.* Retrieved from https://www.cnbc.com/2020/08/24/tiktok-reveals-us-global-user-growth-numbers-for-first-time.html

Statista Research Department. (2021a). *Global influencer market Size 2020.* Retrieved from https://www.statista.com/statistics/1092819/global-influencer-market-size/

Statista Research Department. (2021b). *Global Instagram influencer market value 2020.* Retrieved from https://www.statista.com/statistics/748630/global-instagram-influencermarket-value/

Sundermann, G., & Raabe, T. (2019). Strategic communication through social media influencers: Current state of research and desiderata. *International Journal of Strategic Communication, 13*(4), 278–300. doi:10.1080/1553118X.2019.1618306

Sunstein, C. R. (2006). *Infotopia: How many minds produce knowledge*. Oxford University Press.

Tafesse, W., & Wood, B. P. (2021). Followers' engagement with instagram influencers: The role of influencers' content and engagement strategy. *Journal of Retailing and Consumer Services, 58*. .jret-conser.2020.102303 doi:10.1016/j

Tucker, C. E. (2014). Social networks, personalized advertising, and privacy controls. *JMR, Journal of Marketing Research, 51*(5), 546–562. doi:10.1509/jmr.10.0355

Tuten, T. L., & Solomon, M. R. (2017). Social media marketing. *Sage (Atlanta, Ga.).*

United Nations Conference on Trade and Development. (2020). *COVID-19 and Ecommerce: Findings from a survey of online consumers in 19 countries*. Retrieved from https://unctad.org/search?kcys=shopping+more+often+online

Venngage. (2019). *ROI of influencer marketing infographic*. Retrieved from https://venngage.com/gallery/post/roi-influencer-marketing-infographic/

Vitelar, A. (2019). Like me: Generation Z and the use of social media for personal branding. *Management Dynamics in the Knowledge Economy, 7*(2), 257–268. doi:10.25019/mdke/7.2.07

Wajid, A., Raziq, M. M., Ahmed, Q. M., & Ahmad, M. (2021). Observing viewers' self-reported and neurophysiological responses to message appeal in social media advertisements. *Journal of Retailing and Consumer Services, 59*, 102373. doi:10.1016/J.JRETCONSER.2020.102373

Wang, X., Wang, Y., Lin, X., & Abdullat, A. (2021). The dual concept of consumer value in social media brand community: A trust transfer perspective. *International Journal of Information Management, 59*, 102319. doi:10.1016/J.IJINFOMGT.2021.102319

Wang, Y. (2020). From "online communication" to "offline imitation": Video bloggers on the user's virtual interaction and willingness to buy factors. *Journalism and Communications Review, 6*, 73–85.

Wang, Z., Liu, H., Liu, W., & Wang, S. (2020). Understanding the power of opinion leaders' influence on the diffusion process of popular mobile games: Travel Frog on Sina Weibo. *Computers in Human Behavior, 109*, 106354. doi:10.1016/j.chb.2020.106354

Watson, L. (2020). Sustainable influencers: Hypocrites, or catalysts of change. *Sourcing Journal, 20.*

Wolf, A. (2020). *Gen Z & Social Media Influencers: The Generation Wanting a Real Experience*. Academic Press.

Xia, J. (2020). "Loving you": Use of metadiscourse for relational acts in WeChat public account advertisements. *Discourse, Context & Media, 37*, 100416. doi:10.1016/j.dcm.2020.100416

Yu, P., Liu, Z., & Hanes, E. (2022). Supply Chain Resiliency, Efficiency, and Visibility in the Post-Pandemic Era in China: Case Studies of MeiTuan Waimai, and Ele.me. In Y. Ramakrishna (Ed.), Handbook of Research on Supply Chain Resiliency, Efficiency, and Visibility in the Post-Pandemic Era (pp. 195–225). IGI Global. doi.org/10.4018/978-1-7998-9506-0.ch011.

Yu, S., & Hu, Y. (2020). When luxury brands meet China: The effect of localized celebrity endorsements in social media marketing. *Journal of Retailing and Consumer Services*, *54*, 102010. doi:10.1016/j.jretconser.2019.102010

Zhou, S., Blazquez, M., McCormick, H., & Barnes, L. (2021). How social media influencers' narrative strategies benefit cultivating influencer marketing: Tackling issues of cultural barriers, commercialised content, and sponsorship disclosure. *Journal of Business Research*, *134*, 122–142. doi:10.1016/J.JBUSRES.2021.05.011

Zhou, Y. (2020). *IP celebrity Li Ziqi, Interpretation of "KOL map" behind Popular Models*. Retrieved from https://mp.weixin.qq.com/s/yFSoKO1eIBxWDC4Dezfpiw

Zhu, J., & Yang, Y. (2020). Exclusive: TikTok-owner ByteDance to rake in $27 billion ad revenue by year-end: sources. *Retrieved*, *11*(14), 2020.

Zhu, Q. (2014). *Research and Application of User Generated Content in the New Generation of Internet Environment*. Science Press.

Zhu, Y., & Chen, H. (2015). Social media and human need satisfaction: Implications for social media marketing. *Business Horizons*, *58*(3), 335–345. doi:10.1016/j.bushor.2015.01.006

Zuiderveen Borgesius, F., Trilling, D., Möller, J., Bodó, B., De Vreese, C. H., & Helberger, N. (2016). Should we worry about filter bubbles? *Internet Policy Review. Journal on Internet Regulation*, *5*(1).

KEY TERMS AND DEFINITIONS

Echo Chamber: An echo chamber comes into being where a group participants choose to preferentially connect with each other, to the exclusion of outsiders. The more fully formed this network is, the more isolated from the introduction of the outside views is the group, while the views of its members are able to circulate widely within it.

Filter Bubble: A filter bubble emerges when a group of participants, dependent of the underlying networks structures of their connections with others, choose to preferentially communicate with each other, to the exclusion of outsiders. The more consistently they exercise their choice, the more likely it is that participants own views and information will circulate amongst group members, rather than information introduce from the outside.

Information Cocoon: An information cocoon occurs due to a user's active choices and an algorithm passive choice. It is what the platforms chooses to expose you to user to based on expressed interests, tastes, and preferences. It is related to the idea that people see, hear, and seek what they like, pleases and comforts them and are closed to the idea of newness that challenges it. However, the downside of this phenomenon is non-exposure to opposing point of views, and non-awareness towards the things that exist outside our areas of interests.

ENDNOTE

[1]   In the research, the consent of the participants has been received.

Chapter 7
A Study on the Prime Time Television Advertorial in India

Mehmet Sinan Tam
https://orcid.org/0000-0001-9897-0803
Bandirma Onyedi Eylul University, Turkey

Kazım Babacan
https://orcid.org/0000-0002-7668-8601
Karadeniz Technical University, Turkey

ABSTRACT

Because of its dense population and rising economy, many companies in India appeal to their consumers through advertising agencies. In the Indian advertising sector, the agencies that became dominant were British agencies until 1947 and local agencies starting from 1947. When the country gained its independence in the 1990s, foreign advertising agencies again became dominant in the country with the new economic approach adopted. This research aims to explore the advertising practices in the prime-time zone on Indian television channels with a special focus on the prime-time zone advertisements of the ABP News TV channel, which broadcasts continuously on YouTube and has the most followers. In the research, it is concluded that health advertisements are broadcasted more frequently on TV than in other sectors. Performance and quality are frequently emphasized in the advertisement content, and the positioning strategy is more frequently adopted by advertising agencies.

INTRODUCTION

Throughout history, India has had numerous wealthy civilizations, and it continues to host various ethnic, religious, and cultural distinctions that are the remnants of these previous civilizations. Pakistan, Bangladesh, and Sri Lanka, all of which gained independence after 1947, were all located on Indian land. India remained a British colony until 1947 when it gained freedom. The four nations that make up this region speak the same language, eat the same cuisine, have similar traditions, and have similar cultural characteristics (Shankar, 2015, p. 74). This richness may be both an opportunity and a stumbling block

DOI: 10.4018/978-1-7998-9672-2.ch007

for advertising. By 2026, the advertising sector in India is expected to grow by 11%. It is thought that the course of the COVID-19 pandemic will be a significant determinant in the realization of this rate at higher or lower levels (Imarcgroup, 2021). Although the course and duration of the pandemic are decisive here, the strategies used by advertising agencies will also play a vital role.

Under British rule, India's first advertising activity in the modern sense began with newspaper advertisements. For a long time, newspaper advertising has been the most widely used advertising medium in India (Chaudhuri, 2007). Due to the Indian government's prohibitions on international advertising firms, Indian advertising companies dominated the country until the 1990s. However, in just three years, the worldwide advertising business acquired eleven of the country's top twenty advertising companies (Ciochetto, 2010, p. 193).

The advertising industry should not be seen as a marketing strategy that only offers certain products to the consumer. This industry also instills some role models, messages about looking healthy and living in this society (Pradhan, 2021, p. 9). On the other hand, how the agencies, which are the main players of this industry, address the consumers on behalf of the brands and how they try to create an impression have a decisive role in this installation (Koslow et al., 2003). Based on this framework, it can be stated that advertising agencies as a bridge in the creation of a certain attitude or behavior change by transmitting advertising messages to consumers.

Kumar and Gupta (2016, p. 304) emphasize that advertising agencies or companies that produce messages to meet the demands of the customers in the advertising understanding of the future know where to focus, use technology effectively in advertising messages, distribute the advertising messages to the consumers themselves, make the right media choice, and fully grasp the place of the consumer and the product in the life cycle can be successful in their advertising work. China and India have attracted the attention of the world with their economic breakthroughs in recent years. The study aims to bring an up-to-date perspective on the Indian advertising industry and its advertisements. This study examines all advertorials broadcast for a week in the prime time zone of the Indian ABP News TV channel, which broadcasts live on both terrestrial and YouTube channels and aims to reveal the advertising practices of India, which is seen as the greatest economic power in the future. These ads, which were coded by the Maxqda20 program and were analyzed by the content analysis method.

BACKGROUND

The Geo-Geographical, Socio-Political, Economic, and Cultural Structure of India

The name India derives from the Sanskritic language family and is called Bharata or Bharat by the locals to name their sub-cultural diversity. On the other hand Greek historian Megasthenes called the country Indika. Among the Turkish and Afghan dynasties the country was called Hindustan and the locals living there were called Hindu. Throughout history the country has especially been a source of rich advertorial routes and has been at the center of commercial activities (Eck, 2012, pp. 45-46).

The mainland of India is grouped under four headings: Great Plains, Himalayan Mountains, Peninsular Uplands, and the Indian Coasts and Islands. These four titles are classified into 28 states that make up all the mainlands and 192 geographical locations that make up these 28 states (Singh, 1971, pp. 40-44). While the number of people living in all of these regions is approximately one billion 400 million, the population density per square kilometer is 468.66. The most populous city in the country is Delhi (World Population Review, 2021). India is a country bordering Pakistan, Afghanistan, China, Nepal, Myanmar, Bangladesh, Sri Lanka, Bhutan, and the Maldives. It is a neighbor to countries with different political, cultural, geographical, and lifestyle characteristics.

Since more than half of the country is suitable for cultivation, today a very dense part of the country still lives in rural areas. People living in these regions live in makeshift houses with a few rooms or in shelters made of mud called Kacha (Pletcher, 2011, pp. 45-46).

According to the Union Nations report, while there are 4635 ethnic groups living in India, these ethnic groups are divided into 80,000 parts. 655 religions or belief systems, 18 educational languages, and 6661 mother tongues are spoken. There are still many places in the country that civilization has not reached and regions that cannot be accessible even by means of transportation. In addition to different age segments, in the country, disadvantaged segments such as the homeless, nomads, and forest/island inhabitants are quite numerous (Union Nations, 2015, pp. 4-5). In literacy rates, urban residents (80.9%) are also positioned at a higher percentage than rural residents (67.8%). In both urban and rural areas, men (80.9%) had a dramatically higher percentage of literacy than women (64.6%). The general literacy rate of the country is 73.0% (Katiyar, 2016, p. 52).

India is the second-most densely populated country in the Asia continent with many ethnic, religious, and linguistic differences. The social structure in the country has been arranged in a way that will be transferred from family members to future generations through the system called caste. An individual from a caste only marries within his own caste. This system plays a dominant role in all other social life processes of the individual (Beteille, 2020). In ancient sources, it is stated that there are objects like clothing, accessories, etc., which distinguish men and women in the upper classes of the Indian continent from other lower classes. Therefore it can be noticed at first glance who belongs to which class and that such class differences are experienced much more intensely among the lower classes. In addition, it has been stated that those living in the northern part of the country adopt such contradictions more than those in the south (Ward, 1850, pp. 87-88).

The caste system, which is still practiced in rural settlements in India, can contain different functioning mechanisms. For example, a marriage forbidden by one caste can be made free by another caste. Even though each caste has its own characteristics, there are also commonalities among the castes. These are realized under three headings. In heredity, the children of the individuals in the caste are also subject to the castes of their parents from birth. In endogamy, only marriage to members of their own caste is allowed. Eating and receiving food, each caste's rule to eat together and take food from others may be subject to certain conditions. Meals will not be eaten together with the castes who do not meet these conditions, and it is not welcomed for the upper caste to meet at the same table with the lower caste or to receive food from the lower castes (Blunt, 2010, pp. 1-2). Among these three common features, endogamy is studied more intensely than the others (Sekhon, 2000, p. 44). Although the country expresses the caste system as illegal, this social division still continues on the basis of five classes. While Brahmins (priests and teachers) are at the top of the caste system, they are followed by Kshatriyas (warriors and rulers), Vaisyas (farmers, merchants, and artisans), and Sudras (laborers), with Harijansor Dalits at the bottom (Rao, 2010, p. 97). The dynamics that determine the political structure of India also cause internal political problems in the country. The main characters of this cycle are social, economic, and cultural differences (Chakrabarty, 2008, p. 170). Apart from these three issues, it has been observed that gatekeeping in India in recent years has been extremely effective in making decisions on political issues, especially in rural areas (Pattenden, 2011, p. 193). Although it is very difficult to find metaphors to be used in achieving political unity in countries where many races, religions, and languages live, the idea of an independent India can express a common denominator for all segments.

While India adopted the socialist economic model from 1951 until the collapse of Soviet Russia in 1991, it switched to a free market economy with the dissolution of the Soviet Union in 1990. With this new market economy it has adopted, the country has achieved significant increases in annual growth rates in a short time. In addition to industry, there is a very significant number of people who make a living in agriculture, fisheries, and forestry sectors in the country (Pletcher, 2011, pp. 50-52).

Avery important part of the country, especially the middle-aged population, lives below the poverty line in India. In addition, the caste system in the country is still used as a cover for the exploitation of the labor of certain classes *(especially women)* (Mohan, 2016, p. 167). Since gaining independence, India initially followed a self-sufficient policy in agricultural activities, and in the following years, this idea was abandoned in favor of the idea that agricultural products should be exported. However, in recent years, the annual growth in agriculture has developed at a lesser rate compared to other sectors (Siddiqui, 2020, p. 41). In India, where 50 percent of households earn a living directly or indirectly from agricultural activities, economists predicted that not poverty but pandemics would kill people in the COVID-19 era, contributing to the country's dramatic decline (Chaudhary et al., 2020, p. 177). It is thought that India and China, the two hugely populated countries on the Asian continent, will carry the world's industrial sector to this continent in the near future (Yusuf et al., 2007, p. 49). As a matter of fact, after the USA, China and India take first and second places among the innovation centers of the world (Crescenzi & Rodríguez-Pose, 2017, p. 1016). India's economic development in recent years has played an active role in its interest in renewable energy sources (Kakwani & Kalbar, 2020).

The cultural values of India are expressed by the people living outside the Indian subcontinent, especially by the western people, with the motto of the land of contrasts and differences. The differences are not only limited to appearance, life, or religious values but are also emphasized by the dimension of expressing feelings and thoughts (Nussbaum & Sen, 1987, p. 6). The food culture in the country is based on agricultural products, which are also economically dominant. The vegetarian food culture, in which vegetables and fruits are dominant, is generally dominant in the country (Sen, 2004, p. 37).

It is possible to find local cultural items in almost every region of the country. More than two hundred languages are spoken in the country at the same time (Gajrani, 2004, p. 2). In Indian culture, everything symbolized by religion and values or personalities belonging to national identity *(such as Mahatma Gandhi)* usually has an important cultural place (Singh & Singh, 2008, pp. 86-87). The fact that the values adopted by local or regional peoples are different from each other presents a rich cultural mosaic in terms of Indian culture. Although the cultural characteristics in question may appear to be a challenge for advertisers or agencies, it can be said that they have an important opportunity to design messages specific to the characteristics of specific target audiences and to create the desired attitude or behavior patterns in the consumer based on these messages.

The elements of Indian culture, combined with traditional rituals, advertisements, films, and television programs aimed at the country's younger generations, are presented as a modern, cosmopolitan, and globalizing value (Favero, 2021, p. 5). So much so that in recent years, traditional cultural elements, especially dance and music belonging to Indian culture, especially Bollywood, have been used seriously in terms of both adhering to the traditions of the Indian diaspora outside the country and bringing the citizens of other countries to India through tourism (Matusitz & Payano, 2012). This soft power element also helps to break down misconceptions and prejudices about the country by providing a positive image of Indian culture (Athique, 2019, p. 470).

Advertising Industry in India

An advertising agency can be characterized as an outside eye acting on behalf of a firm in the branding of a company in the broadest sense. Advertising agencies carry out their activities by giving various recommendations to companies or by conducting advertising activities on behalf of the companies (Zednik, 2008). The most basic job of advertising agencies is to carry out advertising activities of companies and to convince consumers of the product or service offered by the company (Armstrong, 2011). The success of advertising agencies depends on the specific goals they set for the campaign and the measurability of these goals (Britt, 2000, p. 29). On the other hand, advertising agencies also play a significant role in bringing the advertising work done in a country to a global dimension. The top ten global advertising companies are located in the capitals of industrialized societies (Ciochetto, 2011). This situation has caused the first studies in other countries in the field of advertising to start under the guidance of industrialized societies.

The first professional advertising agency in India was established by the British, who occupied the region. While the first advertising agency, B. Datramand Company started its activities in 1905, it was followed by new ones in the following years (Tandon, 2018, p. 23623). In the 1960s and 1970s, advertising agencies that adopted the principle of localization developed *(JWT Hindustan Thompson Associates)* and had a dominant role in the Indian advertising industry for a certain period (Mazzarella, 2003). Economic reforms and developments in communications in the 1990s led to the growth of the Indian advertising industry. Large advertising budgets, increased market competition, and the growth in the diversity of communication tools leading to high media penetration have contributed significantly to the advertising industry. The entry or re-operation of multinational companies and global advertising agencies into the country was also effective in this growth. On the other hand, collaborations of global advertising companies with local agencies have resulted in the branding of these agencies or their take-over by international advertising industries in the coming years. As a matter of fact, the top 20 agencies in India today maintain their existence either as a part of this alliance or as a result of strategic global partnerships (Patwardhan et al., 2009, p. 108). The developments in the field of advertising in the 90s in the country also played an active role in the country's transition from a socialist state to a free economy. On the other hand, although the advertising sector developed relatively later than in western countries, the economic progress of the country in recent years has brought both the growth of the advertising industry and new opportunities.

In addition to individuals living in urban areas, millions of people also live in rural areas in India. For this reason, advertising agencies write advertisement texts in a language where cultural elements are at the forefront in order to address the people living in these regions (Gupta, 2005). Even if it turns into an international agency, whether it is an advertising agency of Indian or foreign origin, advertising agencies serve as a crucial tool in teaching specific cultural elements to the public. Certain products, brands, and companies originating from different countries include local cultural elements in their advertisements in order to both announce to consumers that they are a local brand and look local. In the transfer of cultural elements, this process is operated by campaigns made through advertising agencies (Mazzarella, 2003, p. 30). Almost all advertising agencies in India apply the concept of 360-degree branding. Within this concept, all advertising agencies implement this branding approach by applying TV advertisements, print advertisements, websites, e-mail marketing, direct marketing, radio advertisements, telemarketing, using web banners, outdoor advertisements, public relations, rural communication, and designing inputs on packaging (Joshi et al., 2010, p. 21).

The majority of agencies that have managed to position themselves within the Indian advertising industry are located in the capital city of India and in densely populated cities (The manifest, 2021). In particular, New Delhi and Mumbai are the two most prominent cities in terms of advertising agencies in India (Faulconbridge et al., 2011, p. 65). The Indian advertising agencies operating internationally, mostly employ men work as well as people with postgraduate degrees as the workforce of these agencies (Patwardhan et al., 2011, p. 677). Media agencies, advertising agencies, the most influential people in the advertising industry, and the companies that have advertised the most in India in recent years are listed in the table below (Emarketer, 2017; ET Brandequity, 2019; Shah, 2014, p. 215).

Table 1. Top 10 of the Indian advertising industry

	Media Agency	Advertising Agency	The Most Influential People in Advertising	Top Ten Advertisers
1	Mindshare	Ogilvy	Piyush Pandey (Ogilvy Group)	Hindustan Unilever
2	Madison World	JWT	Prasoon Joshi (McCann Worldgroup)	Amazon
3	Lodestar Universal	Lowa Lintus	Sam Balsara (Madison World)	Procter & Gamble
4	Lintas Media Group	Mudra India	Agnello Dias (Taproot Dentsu)	Reckitt Benckiser
5	Percept Media	McCann Erickson	Shashi Sinha (IPG Mediabrands)	Flipkart
6	Starcom	DDB Mudra	Ashish Bhasin (Dentsu Aegis Network)	Maruti Suzuki
7	Carat	Le Burnett	Rohit Ohri (FCB Group)	ITC
8	Dentsu Media	Draftfeb Ulka	Nandini Dias (Lodestar UM)	Bharti Airtel
9	Zenith Optimedia	Dentsu	Swati Bhattacharya (FCB Ulka)	Mondelez
10	MudraMax	Taproot	CVL Srinivas (WPP Group)	Godrej Consumer Products Ltd.

Source: (Emarketer, 2017; ET Brandequity, 2019; Shah, 2014, p. 215).

Satellite receivers, the increase in the number of television channels after 1960, the rise in income level, and the new media tools that emerged with the development of digital technologies have been decisive in the transformation of advertising from a local location to a global one (Flew & Smith, 2014, Thomas, 2006). Although the advertising industry tried to achieve success in advertising by instilling admiration for the west in individuals, in the last 20 years, it has been replaced by appealing to the minds and hearts of individuals with a universal or specific cultural value (Ciochetto, 2011).

India, which has the second-largest population in the world, has attracted the attention of both advertisers and advertising agencies in recent years because of its dense population. According to GroupM's mid-year forecast, it is estimated that the global advertising industry will grow by up to 19% and the advertising industry in India by at least 20% by the end of 2021. It was stated in the same report that the main channel that triggered this development would be digital media, and that television advertising would show stable or little development (GroupM, June 14, 2021). In another report by the same institution, it was stated that the majority of Indian consumers have experienced a change in what they consider or think most important in their lives since the pandemic broke out, and this change is also reflected in their purchasing decisions (GroupM, November16, 2020). In 2020, the first year of the pandemic, almost all countries tried to stay at home with various restrictions. These restrictions were gradually lifted, with a downward trend in the number of cases of vaccination. Therefore, it can be stated that the TV watching practices of households have increased, and this has contributed to a burst in TV advertising.

It is assumed that the Covid-19 pandemic will affect significant changes in the Indian advertising industry in the coming years. The most obvious of these changes is undoubtedly seen in advertising. With the pandemic, it is thought that along with traditional media, advertising will shift to the media where the Internet, Over the top (OTT), video games and e-sports competitions are played. On the other hand, it is stated that the percentage of development of the advertising sector by 2025 will gain momentum in India (7.6%), which is more than twice the percentage that will be realized on a global scale (GEMO, July, 2021). In addition to all these changes, the advertisers have continously emphasized the ways to protect the target audiences from the virus in their health-themed advertisements since the outbreak of Covid-19 (Shah & Tomer, 2020, p. 91). It has been found that in Covid-19 themed advertisements, the attitude of consumers towards the brand rather than the advertising content is determinant in buying behavior (Karamchandani et al, 2021, p. 3). It can be stated that during the pandemic period, Indian consumers act by considering which brand offers this product or service instead of the product or service offered.

Advertisements are mostly made for food products in India. Food advertisements are followed by those for drugs and cosmetics, soap, automobiles, tobacco, household appliances, and petroleum products, respectively (Srinivasan, 2001, p. 150). In this advertisements, consumers are intensively confronted with the themes, language, and discourse content that include humor, status/luxury, emotional intimacy, and romantic relationships (Srivastava et al., 2017, p. 57). The glocal advertising strategy, which combines local and global elements, is used more frequently in TV commercials (Dash, 2012). For example, in chocolate advertorials, consumers are confronted with pleasure and happiness, as in Hollywood and American commercials. Likewise, in food products targeting especially children, the product is marketed with a cartoon character favoured or liked by children or popular at that time (Razdan & Arora, 2021).

In India, which is located within the Eastern culture, advertisers address their consumers in a language appropriate to the values of this culture. Presenting unnecessary details about the product and service, giving direct messages to the consumer, and displaying character and messages where individuality is at the forefront are not much preferred (Mooij, 1998). Indian citizens have a positive attitude towards advertisements with local motifs. However, elements of popular culture spread by foreign mass media can also influence individual purchasing behavior (Bansal, 2017). At this point, the product sold by the advertisers or the service itself plays a distinctive role in the question of whether the consumer will be presented with a local or global language. In this context, the question of what strategies have been used in Indian advertisements in recent years comes to the fore.

There are differences between different age and gender groups in adopting a negative or positive attitude towards advertising in India (Singh & Kaur, 2014). However, with the developments in digital advertising, the advertising industry has begun to shape itself according to this medium, and ultimately, the informative and entertaining aspects of advertising have been effective in driving the purchase intention of Indian youth who encounter advertisements in digital media (Jain et al., 2018, p. 97). In addition, the short-term or long-term advertising campaign strategy adopted by the advertisers during the advertising campaign also played a decisive role in the positive effect of the advertisement on the consumer (Baidya et al., 2012).

Television and print media still have a dominant structure in the Indian advertising industry (Mehta et al., 2017). In India, which is the second most populated country in the world, the use of many social media applications is in the first place compared to other countries. For this reason, advertising agencies in India appeal to their consumers not only with traditional media tools but also with social media platforms. In India, social media advertising is not limited to products and services in the classical sense. For example, in the last elections, Narendra Modi spoke to the electorate through social media by practicing many social media applications. His messages through this network were mostly focused on political issues, followed by informative, socio-economic, and cultural values, respectively (Moinuddin, 2021). Various religious organizations hold fundraising campaigns using local newspapers, regional TV channels, and flyers, and social media platforms such as Facebook and YouTube can be given as examples (Saxena & Saxena, 2021, pp. 191-192).

The gender-based language of the advertisement is also used in India as in every other country. From the 1950s until today, words expressing body image, eroticism, and sexual pleasure or desires are frequently used in advertisements (Sur, 2020, pp. 139-140). Although the Indian advertising industry was protected by various laws in certain periods, it also carried out sexist campaigns. For example, in the 1980s, in densely populated cities such as Mumbai *(Bombay)*, Delhi, and Amritsar, gender determination tests were publicly advertised, and advertising agencies mediated especially families who learned that they had girls to take attitudes towards terminating this pregnancy (John, 2021, p. 359).

The advertising industry in India also faces some challenges. These are competition and declining margins, the evolution of new media technologies, expansion in the market regions, advertisers' fight with rate obsession, less consolidation, more fragmentation, and value-added services. Besides these, various difficulties are also seen in the titles of market with advanced technologies, growth of social media and networking, paradigm shift in rural strategies, match fit of media mix with customers' expectations, advertising associations and laws (Joshi et al., 2010). Apart from these titles, the fact that the country has very different cultural characteristics also limits the ability of advertisers to produce messages that affect everyone on a national scale.

In India, where there are thousands of channels, there are three leading organizations that protect the rights of viewers and the interests of these channels. While the Indian Broadcasting Foundation (IBF) plays an important role in protecting the interests of more than 250 broadcasting traditional and electronic media members, the Advertising Standards Council of India, which is an independent organization, takes an active role in audits related to advertising (Kumar, 2011, p. 33). The most basic rule set for advertising is legal, decent, honest, and truthful (Srinivasan, 2001, p. 151). Apart from these two unofficial institutions, the Ministry of Information and Broadcasting also legally operates in various fields such as TV, radio, printing, and cinema broadcasting. It is an official government agency responsible for making and enforcing rules, laws, and regulations.

TV COMMERCIALS IN INDIA: ABP NEWS TV

Academic studies on the advertising sector in India, which is the world's second-fastest-growing economy and the fastest-growing advertising sector, are quite limited (Patwardhan et al., 2011, p. 668). As a matter of fact, as stated above, the studies on India were mostly written on specific technical and structural issues. They have been handled more frequently, especially with the culture and the Covid-19 pandemic, which has affected the whole world in recent times. A weekly ad generation of a TV channel broadcasting online 24/7 on both TV and YouTube has been discussed in detail in this study, as well as which products and services are most frequently offered to consumers in the advertisement content, and which sector is most frequently addressed to consumers under which advertising strategy. In this sense, the research differs in terms of revealing the issues and what it emphasizes in these advertisements.

On the other hand, this chapter distinguishes itself from other studies, as it reveals the media agencies, advertising companies, the most influential personalities, and advertising agencies in the advertising industry in India in recent years.

This study, which is suitable for the content analysis case pattern (Yin, 2018), aims to explore the advertising practices in the prime time advertorials on Indian televisions. It has attempted to answer questions about the advertising industry in India in general, the advertising strategies used in Indian TV advertorials, the value emphasized in the advertisement, and which sectors frequently advertise to the prime time commercials. A purposive sampling approach was adopted in the research due to its suitability for qualitative research designs (Etikan et al., 2016). The prerequisite of uninterrupted live streaming on YouTube India was sought for the channel included in the research sample.

The ABP News TV channel, which meets this condition and has the highest number of followers, was determined as the research sample. While the related channel has 31 million subscribers on You-Tube, the content of the channel has been watched over nine billion times (Socialblade, 2021). With this aspect, the channel allows Indian citizens living outside India to access and watch TV content for free.

In the study, data was collected by determining the limitations in the titles of time, channel, and advertising content. In the research, the advertisement contents of the ABP News TV channel between 1-7 September were taken as the data pattern. Advertising content published in prime time, which is seen as the most-watched TV channel, is only taken. Semiotic analysis was not applied to the received advertisement contents. Codings were made about the language, discourse, music, and communication style in the advertisement content, as well as the advertised products and services. The code table for advertising content was developed based on previous studies (Axinn & Krishna, 1993, Khairullah & Khairullah, 2013, Srikandath, 1991, Rodrigues & Singhal, 2017).

Before the coding of the dataset was started, the dataset was translated into English by a master student living in India who knew Indian culture and language. The coding process was done in two stages. The data set collected in the first stage was coded separately by both authors. After the coding, comparisons were made, and the different categories were reviewed. In the second stage, the data set was coded by an expert in the field of advertising, and the coding process was completed. Afterward, the index level increased from 0.84 to 0.93 with the inter-coder reliability analysis made with the Maxqda program (Kassarjian, 1977).

In the research, five questions were determined to explore Indian prime time TV advertising practices.

Research question 1: What are the key findings in the ads in the prime time zone in India?
Research question 2: Are there any similar and divergent aspects in weekday and weekend advertisements?
Research question 3: What characteristics do industries frequently market to consumers in their products or services?
Research question 4: Which advertising strategy do advertisers use more in the sectoral context?
Research question 5: What do advertising agencies emphasize more often in their advertising strategies?

Findings and Analysis

A total of 75 brands were advertised in the prime-time advertorial on the Indian ABP NewTV channel between September 1 and 7, 2021. The most advertised sector in the relevant date range was health (19.09%). Here, herbal medicines, medical supplies, and pharmacy services have been the branches that advertise very frequently within the health sector. The health sector was followed by building and building materials, cosmetics, mobile apps, food, vehicles, banking and insurance, clothing, electronics, kitchen stuff, education, and baby care sectors, respectively. The fact that the epidemic is still ongoing can be said to be effective. Health-related products and services were followed by construction materials. Cement and iron were the most frequently advertised products in this sector. In the cosmetics sector, which ranks third, companies producing hair and oral care products were more frequently advertised to the prime time advertorial. Indian advertising agencies used 14 advertising strategies in the prime time advertorial.

Among these advertising strategies, the most frequently used strategies are as follows: positioning, soft sell, celebrity or expert, humor, and utilitarianism/rationality, unique selling proposition/USP, hyperbole, hard sell, storytelling, brand image, fear, global, glocal, and sexuality. Advertisements are mostly in Indian-English (40.48%), Indian (36.9%) and English (22.62%) languages. Brands that appeal to their consumers mostly in terms of emotion (46.46%) have constructed their advertisements with local music (73%) and voice-over (46.85%) intensely.

There were also topics that the advertisers emphasized on the products and services that they produced. While quality, performance and safety were the aspects that were emphasized very closely within these headings, these three were followed by price value, naturalness, status, availability, special offers, comfort, taste, beauty, components and contents, family, nutrition, cleanness and hygiene, national identity, new ideas, independent research and guarantees (See: Table 2).

According to Figure 1, where the differences and similarities between the advertisements published on weekdays and weekends were given, no difference was observed in the language and type of music used in the advertisement, nor in emotional and rational intonation. However, there were differences in the titles of the sector, the advertising strategy, the form of communication established in the advertisement, and the quality of the product and service (red line).

While almost every advertisement peculiar to each sector was broadcasted in the prime time zone both on weekends and weekdays, kitchen supplies and clothing companies broadcasted their advertisement content focused only on weekdays in the prime time zone. In the context of advertising strategies, the glocal strategy was used on weekdays, and the global strategy was used only on the weekend. There was no difference in all remaining advertising strategies (blue line).

While no difference was observed regarding the weekend in the title of the highlighted quality of the product, there was a difference in the emphasis of guarantee and sexuality during the week. On the other hand, the situation of asking questions in the communication title constructed within the advertisement remained only for a week.

Advertisers marketed the products or services they provide to the consumers by emphasizing different qualities in the sectoral context. The quality of the product and service offered to the consumer in the advertisement and the advertising strategy with which this is done are also expressed in figure 2. According to the figure 2, price value of vehicles, building materials, electronics, beauty, cosmetics, and clothing, clothing and mobile apps, baby care, taste, naturalness, and nutrition, food, comfort, and new ideas, electronics, safety, health, and family, building materials, statues, clothing, quality, availability, mobile apps, guarantees, kitchen supplies, cleanliness, and hygiene, cosmetics and special offers, processed more intensively in the banking and insurance sectors.

Tablo 2. Basic findings

Emphasis	%	Adv Strategy	%	Sector	%
Quality	9.91	Positioning	16.91	Health	19.09
Performance	9.91	Soft Sell	14.98	Building Materials	16.36
Safety	9.46	Celebrity/Expert	12.08	Cosmetics	10.91
Price Value	7.66	Humor	12.08	Mobile App	10.91
Naturalness	7.66	Utilitarianism/Rationality	11.59	Food	8.18
Status	7.66	Unique Selling Proposition/USP	10.14	Vehicles	7.27
Availability	5.86	Hyperbole	6.28	Banking & Insurance	5.45
Special Offers	5.41	Hard Sell	4.35	Clothing	5.45
Comfort	5.41	Storytelling	3.86	Electronics	5.45
Taste	5.41	Brand image	3.38	Kitchen stuff	5.45
Beauty	5.41	Fear	1.45	Education	2.73
Component & Contents	4.50	Global	1.45	Baby Care	2.73
Family	4.05	Glocal	0.97	**Communication**	**%**
Nutrition	2.70	Sexuality	0.48	Voice-over	46.85
Cleanness/Hygiene	2.70	**Emotional Rational**	**%**	Dialogue	27.03
National Identity	2.25	Emotional	46.46	Monologue	19.82
New Ideas	1.80	Rational	32.32	Question	6.31
Independent Resarch	1.35	Mixed (E/R)	21.21	**Language**	**%**
Guarantees	0.90	India-English			40.48
Music	**%**	Indian			36.90
Local	73.0	English			22.62
West	27.0				

In the sectoral context, each brand implemented different advertising strategies in its advertising campaigns. However, there are also advertising strategies that each sector uses more frequently in advertising campaigns. According to Figure 2, where the findings about which sector uses which advertising strategy more frequently, vehicles, positioning, soft sell and brand image, banking and insurance, soft sell, utilitarian/rational, humorous, health, storytelling, brand image, hard sell, glocal, positioning and fear, building materials, hyperbole and positioning, clothing, celebrity/expert has frequently applied positioning and sexuality in advertising practices. On the other hand, there were also companies that addressed their consumers within the framework of a single strategy in their advertising content. These sectors are baby care, global, cosmetics, USP, electronics, soft sell, kitchen stuff and food, celebrity and expert, education, positioning and mobile app and they have practiced utilitarian/rational advertising strategies more predominantly in advertising campaigns.

Figure 1. Differences and similarities in advertising content on weekdays and weekends

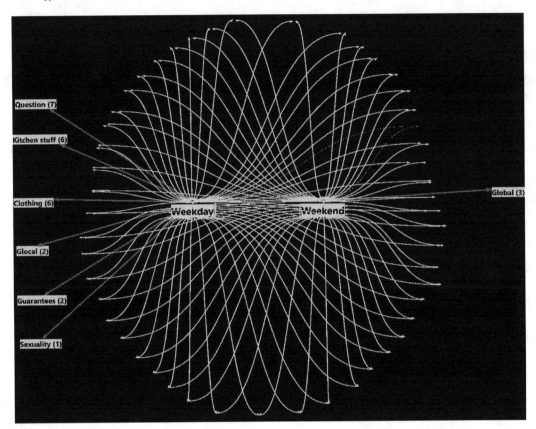

Figure 2. Intense relationships between industries, advertising strategy, and emphasis themes

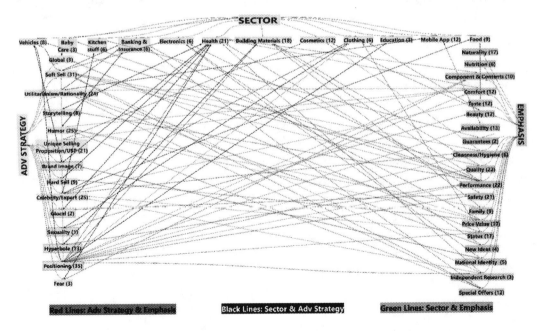

Firms also emphasized many aspects of their products or services with the advertising strategies they use. In the context of advertising strategies, the strategy most frequently used by companies and which attributes were used more frequently in these strategies are given in Figure 2. Advertisers emphasized themselves more frequently with the advertising strategies they used in the titles of *"positioning"*, component & contents, comfort, availability, clean/hygiene, quality, performance, safety, status and independent research, *"soft sell"*, clean/hygiene, quality, performance, independent research and special offers, *"utilitarian/rational"*, comfort, price value, new ideas and special offers, *"celebrity/expert"*, taste, clean/hygiene, status, and independent research, *"humor"*, comfort, family, price value and special offers. In addition, advertising agencies have realized their advertising strategies by emphasizing only one aspect of products and services. The intense relationships that take place under a single title are also global, status, storytelling, performance, USP, comfort, brand image, national identity, hard sell, price value, glocal, safe, sexuality, beauty, fear, component or contents, and hyperbole. They used performance attributes in their prime time advertising strategies.

CONCLUSION

India is the second-most populous country in the world with different geographical, cultural, and socio-political structures. In addition to traditional media, social media tools are also experienced by individuals in the country. At this point, advertisers who experience many media tools use print media and TV more dominantly, especially in advertising campaigns. The advertising sector, which developed rapidly in the 90s in the country, carried out their work with advertising campaigns focused on personal products under the leadership of national and international advertising companies. In the contents of this campaign, target audiences in urban and rural areas were addressed more frequently with local folkloric elements (Ciochetto, 2004, p. 157).

TV advertising in India generally follows a western origin with folkloric features. Until 2000s, advertisements in the country frequently appeared with standardization or localization strategies (Sengupta & Frith, 1997). Celebrity advertising with famous faces of Bollywood is very common in India, where brand loyalty is tried to be achieved in this way. It is seen that the same situation is also observed with various cartoon characters among children (Prakash at el., 2012; Singh & Kaur, 2014). On the other hand, advertisement activities in the country are shaped according to the market, culture and environmental factors in which the product or service is targeted (Khairullah & Khairullah, 2003). The major financial value increase of the best of all time of Indian TV advertising was in 2020 (262 billion Indian rupees), and it is expected that 2022 will be completed with 258 billion Indian rupees (Statista, 2022).

In this research, in which the prime time ads of the ABP News TV channel, which broadcasts 24/7 on YouTube, between September 1-7, 2021, were examined, important findings were obtained for Indian advertising. Advertisers often addressed the target audience in Indian-English and Indian languages in the ads they published in the prime time advertorial, while very often they addressed their target audience accompanied by background music and voice-overs belonging to Indian culture. Apart from the voice-overs, the sections in which the actors spoke as a dialogue or monologue in the advertisement were also included in the advertisement setups. A strategy has been followed in such a way that appeals to the feelings of consumers in the aforementioned fiction.

The COVID-19 pandemic, which has continued to affect the world, has played a dominant role in all advertising campaigns in the Indian advertising industry in recent years. So much so that about a fifth of the ads in the prime time created content related to health products. These contents were followed by building and construction materials, which had a rate of approximately one-fifth. The remaining three-fifths were followed by products and services from cosmetics and mobile apps, food and vehicles, and other sectors, respectively. On a sectoral basis, the advertisements of companies engaged in product-based production took up more space in the lineup.

Positioning, soft sell, celebrity/expert, and humorous strategies were the most used advertising strategies *(Total: 56.05%)*. At the same time, these four strategies were used very frequently together with other strategies. While a language is often built on rational criteria in the positioning, soft-sell strategy, the audience is intensely emotionally addressed in celebrity/expert and humorous situations. Indicators and discourses in which family, national identity and cultural elements are deployed in advertisements play a driving force in getting Indian consumers to adopt a positive attitude towards advertisements (Mukherji, 2005). As a matter of fact, it has been determined in the study that such elements are included in the advertising content and the consumer is tried to be persuaded by presenting a sub-message of "one of you."

In a study on pre-millennium prime time Indian advertisements, it was found that advertisements were mostly prepared with informative content for the consumer in terms of performance and quality (Axinn & Krishna, 1993, p. 171). This result is in line with the findings of the research, but additional new dimensions were identified in addition to these variables. In the research, it was found that, apart from quality and performance, advertising agencies frequently emphasize the titles of safety, price value, naturalness and status in their advertising campaigns and inform consumers. The word "safety" was emphasized in products and services for health, price value for banking and insurance, naturalness for food, and status for clothing brands.

Marketing of natural products through the use of religious identities in advertisements is frequently used to persuade consumers, especially in Asian countries where belief systems such as Buddhism, which emphasize the role of herbal medicines in health, are widely adopted (Kala, 2005). In the research, it was observed that the emphasis on naturalness in TV advertorial is practiced not only by celebrities or experts, but also by making use of religious identities and personalities.

Considering the economic situation of the people in Indian advertisements, TV advertising campaigns are generally made at the point of basic needs. Three headings come to the fore here: food, clothing, and shelter (Vilanilam, 1989, p. 488). In the study, in addition to the aforementioned titles, health is also included. Therefore, it can be stated that the income status of the consumer or the level of development of the country and the issues that are unusual on a global scale have a decisive role in the campaigns in TV advertisements. On the other hand, in the Indian TV advertorial, the thesis that modern and traditional elements blend eastern and western values (Khairullah & Khairullah, 2013, pp. 278-279) can also be expressed for this research.

In summary, Indian advertising agencies employ many advertising strategies together, and it has been found in the research that brands try to convince consumers by concentrating on various messages in the fields in which they operate. In addition, Indian advertising practices included more advertising differences on weekdays than on weekends. The world's second-most densely populated country still has a market where both local and international advertising agencies can compete. India has many opportunities for advertising agencies and brands that are not currently expanding into the Indian market. In other words, the biggest problem that will force advertising companies to adapt is cultural diversity.

For agencies that assimilate the target audience well and can craft more specific advertising messages, this issue may present an opportunity for them to deal with their competitors.

FUTURE RESEARCH DIRECTIONS

Only prime-time television ads were investigated in the research. It is suggested that scholars perform research on other TV broadcasting besides this one. Researchers' investigation of alternative advertising channels in terms of both content and semiotics is regarded as valuable in comprehending Indian advertising practices.

REFERENCES

Armstrong, J. S. (2011). How should firms select advertising agencies? *Journal of Marketing, 60*, 131–133.

Athique, A. (2019). Soft power, culture and modernity: Responses to Bollywood films in Thailand and the Philippines. *The International Communication Gazette, 81*(5), 470–489. doi:10.1177/1748048518802234

Axinn, C. N., & Krishna, V. (1993). How informative are the prime time television commercials in India? *Media Asia, 20*(3), 168–172. doi:10.1080/01296612.1993.11727101

Baidya, M., Maity, B., & Ghose, K. (2012). Measuring dynamic effects of advertising: A case study in India. *Journal of Indian Business Research, 4*(3), 158–169. doi:10.1108/17554191211252671

Bansal, D. (2017). Globalization of consumer culture: An empirical survey of consumers in Delhi. *Business Analyst, 38*(1), 213–239.

Beteille, A. (2020). *Society and politics in India: Essays in a comparative perspective*. Routledge. doi:10.4324/9781003136262

Blunt, E. (2010). *The caste system of northern India*. Isha Books.

Britt, S. H. (2000). Are so-called successful advertising campaigns really successful? *Journal of Advertising Research, 40*(6), 25–31. doi:10.2501/JAR-40-6-25-31

Chakrabarty, B. (2008). *Indian politics and society since independence: Events, Processes and ideology*. Routledge. doi:10.4324/9780203927670

Chaudhary, M., Sodani, P. R., & Das, S. (2020). Effect of COVID-19 on economy in India: Some reflections for policy and programme. *Journal of Health Management, 22*(2), 169–180. doi:10.1177/0972063420935541

Chaudhuri, A. (2007). *Indian advertising: 1780 to 1950 A.D.* Tata McGraw-Hill Publishing.

Ciochetto, L. (2004). Advertising and globalization in India. *Media Asia, 31*(3), 157–169. doi:10.1080/01296612.2004.11726750

Ciochetto, L. (2010). Advertising in a globalized India. In K. M. Gokulsing & W. Dissanayake (Eds.), *Popular culture in a globalized India* (pp. 192–204). Routledge.

Ciochetto, L. (2011). *Globalization and advertising in emerging economies: Brazil, Russia, India and China*. Routledge.

Crescenzi, R., & Rodríguez-Pose, A. (2017). The geography of innovation in China and India. *International Journal of Urban and Regional Research, 41*(6), 1010–1027. doi:10.1111/1468-2427.12554

Dash, A. K. (2012). *Advertising strategy and cultural blend: Glocal identities in Indian TV commercials* [Doctoral dissertation, IIT Kharagpur]. DSpace. Retrieved 12/20/21 from: https://www.idr.iitkgp.ac.in/xmlui/handle/123456789/1699

Eck, D. L. (2012). *India: A sacred geography*. Harmony Books.

Emarketer. (2017, February 17). *Top 10 advertisers in India, ranked by total media ad spending*. Retrieved 12/26/21 from: https://www.emarketer.com/chart/205233/top-10-advertisers-india-ranked-by-total-media-ad-spending-2016

ETBrandequity. (2019, August 7). *Agency reckoner 2018-19: Top 50 most influential people in advertising*. Retrieved 11/30/21 from: https://brandequity.economictimes.indiatimes.com/news/advertising/agency-reckoner-2018-19-top-50-most-influential-people

Etikan, İ., Musa, S. A., & Alkassim, R. S. (2016). Comparison of convenience sampling and purposive sampling. *American Journal of Theoretical and Applied Statistics, 5*(1), 1–4. doi:10.11648/j.ajtas.20160501.11

Faulconbridge, J. R., Beaverstock, J. V., Nativel, C., & Taylor, P. J. (2011). *Cities and advertising globalization New York, Los Angeles and Detroit in a global perspective*. Routledge.

Favero, P. (2021). *Image-Making-India visual culture, technology, politics*. Routledge.

Flew, T., & Smith, R. (2014). *New media: An introduction*. Oxford University Press.

Gajrani, S. (2004). *History, religion and culture of India*. Gyan Publishing House.

GEMO. (2021). *Segment review – Spotlight on India*. Retrieved 10/28/21 from: https://images.assettype.com/afaqs/2021-07/d2232870-68ae-4238-9e7f-71aece3d3033/GEMO_2021___India_Cut_Report___Final.pdf

Group, M. (2020, November 16). *Covid-19: A game-changer for media and purchasing*. Retrieved 10/22/21 from: https://www.groupm.com/covid-19-a-game-changer-for-media-and-purchasing/

Group, M. (2021, June 14). *Global advertising to grow by 19%*. Retrieved 12/10/21 from: https://www.groupm.com/this-year-next-year-global-2021-mid-year-forecast/

Gupta, O. (2005). *Advertising in India: Trends and impact*. Kalpa Publishing House.

Imarcgroup. (2021). *Indian advertising market: Industry trends, share, size, growth, opportunity and competitive analysis forecast 2021-2026*. Retrieved 11/09/21 from: https://www.imarcgroup.com/advertising-industry-india

Jain, G., Rakesh, S., & Chaturvedi, K. R. (2018). Online video advertisements' effect on purchase intention: An exploratory study on youth. *International Journal of E-Business Research, 14*(2), 87–101. doi:10.4018/IJEBR.2018040106

John, M. E. (2021). Sex selection, family building strategies and the political economy of gender. In S. Mani & C. G. Iyer (Eds.), *India's economy and society lateral explorations* (pp. 355–367). Springer. doi:10.1007/978-981-16-0869-8_13

Joshi, M., Joshi, S., Singh, V. K., & Nagar, S. (2010). Challenges of Indian advertising agencies. *Pragya: Journal of Information Management, 9*(1), 20–28.

Kakwani, N. S., & Kalbar, P. P. (2020). Review of Circular Economy in urban water sector: Challenges and opportunities in India. *Journal of Environmental Management, 271*, 1–15. doi:10.1016/j.jenvman.2020.111010 PMID:32778294

Kala, C. P. (2005). Health traditions of Buddhist community and role of amchis in trans-Himalayan region of India. *Current Science Association, 89*(8), 1331–1338.

Karamchandani, S., Karani, A., & Jayswal, M. (2021). Linkages between advertising value perception, context awareness value, brand attitude and purchase intention of hygiene products during COVID-19: A two-wave study. *Vision: The Journal of Business Perspective*, 1-14. doi:10.1177/09722629211043954

Kassarjian, H. H. (1977). Content analysis in consumer research. *The Journal of Consumer Research, 4*(1), 8–18. doi:10.1086/208674

Katiyar, S. P. (2016). Gender disparity in literacy in India. *Social Change, 46*(1), 46-69. doi:10.1177/0049085715618558

Khairullah, D. H. Z., & Khairullah, Z. Y. (2003). Dominant cultural values: Content analysis of the US and Indian print advertisements. *Journal of Global Marketing, 16*(1-2), 47–70. doi:10.1300/J042v16n01_03

Khairullah, D. H. Z., & Khairullah, Z. Y. (2013). Cultural values in Indian television advertising. *Journal of Promotion Management, 19*(2), 265–281. doi:10.1080/10496491.2013.769477

Koslow, S., Sasser, S. L., & Riordan, E. A. (2003). What is creative to whom and why? Perceptions in advertising agencies. *Journal of Advertising Research, 43*(1), 96–110. doi:10.2501/JAR-43-1-96-110

Kumar, S. (2011). Role of Indian broadcasting federation in preventing inappropriate content in TV programmes. *International Journal of Engineering and Management Research, 1*(1), 33–35.

Kumar, V., & Gupta, S. (2016). Conceptualizing the evolution and future of advertising. *Journal of Advertising, 45*(3), 302–317. doi:10.1080/00913367.2016.1199335

Matusitz, J., & Payano, P. (2012). Globalization of popular culture: From Hollywood to Bollywood. *Sage: South Asia Research, 32*(2), 123–138. doi:10.1177/0262728012453977

Mazzarella, W. (2003). *Shoveling smoke: Advertising and globalization in contemporary India.* Duke University Press.

Mehta, D., Mehta, N. K., & Jain, S. (2017). Advertising industry of India: Problems and prospects. *Asian Journal Management, 8*(3), 491–493. doi:10.5958/2321-5763.2017.00079.8

Mohan, K. (2016). Rural and regional development. In R. B. Singh (Ed.), *Progress in Indian geography* (pp. 161-170). Indian National Science Academy.

Moinuddin, S. (2021). *Digital shutdowns and social media: Spatiality, political economy and internet shutdowns in India.* Springer. doi:10.1007/978-3-030-67888-3

Mooij, M. (1998). *Global marketing and advertising - Understanding cultural paradoxes.* Sage Publications.

Mukherji, J. (2005). Maternal communication patterns, advertising attitudes and mediation behaviours in urban India. *Journal of Marketing Communications, 11*(4), 247-262. doi:10.1080/13527260500167223

Nussbaum, M., & Sen, A. (1987). *Internal criticism and Indian rationalist traditions.* World Institute for Development Economics Research of the United Nations University.

Pattenden, J. (2011). Gatekeeping as accumulation and domination: Decentralization and class relations in rural South India. *Journal of Agrarian Change, 11*(2), 164–194. doi:10.1111/j.1471-0366.2010.00300.x

Patwardhan, P., Patwardhan, H., & Vasavada-Oza, F. (2009). Insights on account planning: A view from the Indian ad industry. *Journal of Current Issues and Research in Advertising, 31*(2), 105–121. doi:10.1080/10641734.2009.10505269

Patwardhan, P., Patwardhan, H., & Vasavada-Oza, F. (2011). Diffusion of account planning in Indian ad agencies. *International Journal of Advertising, 30*(4), 665–692. doi:10.2501/IJA-30-4-665-692

Pletcher, K. (2011). *The geography of India: Sacred and historic places.* Britannica Educational Publishing.

Pradhan, A. (2021). Food substitutes, health supplements and the geist of fitness. In S. Malhotra, K. Sharma, & S. Dogra (Eds.), *Food culture studies in India consumption, representation and mediation* (pp. 3–10). Springer Nature. doi:10.1007/978-981-15-5254-0_1

Rao, J. (2010). The caste system: Effects on poverty in India, Nepal and Sri Lanka. *Global Majority E-Journal, 1*(2), 97–106.

Razdan, D., & Arora, J. (2021). Chocolate and the holly factory: Analyzing the "role" of chocolate in select films from Hollywood. In S. Malhotra, K. Sharma, & S. Dogra (Eds.), *Food culture studies in India consumption, representation and mediation* (pp. 85–96). Springer Nature. doi:10.1007/978-981-15-5254-0_9

Rodrigues, S. B., & Singhal, D. (2017). Music placement in Indian television advertisements. *International Journal of Advanced Research in Management and Social Sciences, 6*(3), 116–129.

Saxena, A., & Saxena, V. (2021). Religiosity, ritual practices, and folk deity worship: Bawa Jitto shrine in March Block of Jammu Region. In A. Chauhan (Ed.), *Understanding culture and society in India: A study of Sufis, saints and deities in Jammu Region* (pp. 177–194). Springer. doi:10.1007/978-981-16-1598-6_9

Sekhon, J. (2000). *Modern India.* McGraw-Hill.

Sen, C. T. (2004). *Food culture in India.* Greenwood.

Sengupta, S., & Frith, K. T. (1997). Multinational corporation advertising and cultural imperialism: A content analysis of Indian television commercials. *Asian Journal of Communication, 7*(1), 1–18. doi:10.1080/01292989709388295

Shah, K. (2014). *Advertising and integrated marketing communications.* Tata McGraw Hill Education.

Shah, M. K., & Tomer, S. (2020). How brands in India connected with the audience amid Covid-19. *International Journal of Scientific and Research Publications, 10*(8), 91–95. doi:10.29322/IJSRP.10.08.2020. p10414

Shankar, S. (2015). *Advertising diversity: Ad agencies and the creation of Asian American consumers.* Duke University Press.

Siddiqui, K. (2020). A comparative political economy of China and India: A critical review. In Y. C. Kim (Ed.), *China-India relations: Geo-political competition, economic cooperation, cultural exchange and business ties* (pp. 31–58). Springer Nature. doi:10.1007/978-3-030-44425-9_3

Singh, R., & Kaur, P. (2014). Maternal Attitude towards TV Advertising in India. *Management and Labour Studies, 39*(2), 160–173. doi:10.1177/0258042X14558182

Singh, R., & Singh, R. S. (2008). Cultural Geography. In D. K. Nayak (Ed.), *Progress in Indian Geography* (pp. 81-88). Indian National Science Academy. Retrieved 12/15/21 from: http://citeseerx.ist.psu.edu/

Singh, R. L. (1971). *India: A regional geography.* Silver Jubilee Publication.

Socialblade. (2021). *Top 100 youtubers in India sorted by subscribed.* Retrieved 11/30/21 from: https://socialblade.com/youtube/top/country/in/mostsubscribed

Srikandath, S. (1991). Cultural values depicted in Indian television advertising. *The International Communication Gazette, 48*(3), 165–176. doi:10.1177/001654929104800302

Srinivasan, R. (2001). Advertising in India. In I. Kloss (Ed.), *Advertising worldwide* (pp. 149–168). Springer. doi:10.1007/978-3-642-56811-4_7

Srivastava, E., Maheswarappa, S. S., & Sivakumaran, B. (2017). Nostalgic advertising in India: A content analysis of Indian TV advertisements. *Asia Pacific Journal of Marketing and Logistics, 29*(1), 47–69. doi:10.1108/APJML-10-2015-0152

Statista. (2021, March 14). *Revenue from television advertisements across India.* Retrieved 10/15/21 from: https://www.statista.com/statistics/233489/tv-advertising-revenue-in-india/

Sur, S. (2020). Family planning and the masculinity of nirodh condoms in India. In S. Sur, R. Kumaramkandath, & S. Srivastava (Eds.), *Stories of desire sexualities and culture in modern India* (pp. 134–151). Cambridge University Press. doi:10.1017/9781108637770.009

Tandon, N. (2018). Growth of advertising industry in India. *International Journal of Recent Scientific Research, 9*(1), 23622–23625. doi:10.24327/ijrsr.2018.0901.1502

Themanifest. (2021, November). *Top 100 advertising agencies in India.* Retrieved 09/09/21 from: https://themanifest.com/in/advertising/agencies

Thomas, A. (2006). *Transnational media and contoured markets*. Sage.

Union Nations. (2015, October 5-6). *Census of India: Lessons learnt and the way ahead.* Retrieved 11/06/21 from: https://www.un.org/en/development/desa/population/events/pdf/expert/23/Presentations/EGM-S2-Chandramouli%20presentation.pdf

Vilanilam, J. (1989). Television advertising and the Indian poor. *Media Culture & Society, 11*(4), 485–497. doi:10.1177/016344389011004009

Ward, F. W. (1850). *India and the Hindoos: being a popular view of the geography, history, government, manners, customs, literature and religion of that ancient people, with an account of Christian missions among them.* Baker and Scribner.

World Population Review. (2021). *India population 2021 (Live)*. Retrieved 10/10/21 from: https://world-populationreview.com/countries/india-population

Yin, R. K. (2018). *Case study research and applications*. Sage.

Yusuf, S., Nabeshima, K., & Perkins, D. (2007). China and India reshape global industrial geography. In A. L. Winters & S. Yusuf (Eds.), *Dancing with Giants: China, India, and the global economy* (pp. 35–66). The World Bank.

Zednik, A., & Strebinger, A. (2008). Brand management models of major consulting firms, advertising agencies and market research companies: A categorization and positioning analysis of models offered in Germany, Switzerland and Austria. *Brand Management, 15*(5), 301–311. doi:10.1057/palgrave.bm.2550096

KEY TERMS AND DEFINITIONS

ABP News TV: It is a Hindi-language television channel owned by the ABP broadcasting group. ABP News TV broadcasts 24/7 both on its own website and on YouTube.

Advertising: In the most general terms, it is the promotion, transfer and persuasion of anything to the relevant target audience through mass media. The ultimate goal of the advertisement, is to persuade the consumer to buy something or to create a positive image or perception about the institution.

Advertising Strategy: It refers to the methods and techniques used in advertising to reach and persuade the consumer. The advertising strategy is determined by seeking answers to the questions of how the advertised product or service will be presented to the target audience in the most effective way, how the content will be shaped, and how the advertisement will be prepared in the general framework. In determining the advertising strategy, the product or service itself, whether the institution has a national or international structure, and the profile of the target audience has an important place.

India: Located in the Asian continent, it is the second-most populous country in the world. People with many ethnic and cultural characteristics live in India, whose official name is the Republic of India.

Prime Time: It is the qualification given to the time period in which the content broadcast on television is watched the most. In general, it is used to express the broadcast zone that corresponds to the local time range of 19:00 - 23:00 of each country.

Chapter 8
Adaptation Strategy in International Brands:
An Examination in Iranian Advertising

Meltem Özel
 https://orcid.org/0000-0002-4037-7393
Istanbul Esenyurt University, Turkey

Onur Karakaş
 https://orcid.org/0000-0001-8437-4671
Kocaeli University, Turkey

ABSTRACT

In this chapter, the adaptation strategy, which is one of the global advertising strategies, is used in the analysis of advertisement. The adaptation approach is based on the fact that nations located in different geographies in the world are structurally and culturally separate from each other, and advertising messages are reshaped according to these differences. The approach aims to cooperate with the country's local agency and adapt the advertisement to the country's cultural characteristics. The study aims to determine how cultural differences are emphasized in global advertising strategies and how these differences are adapted in ads.

INTRODUCTION

Advertisement is a communication idea that alter the way people think and/or behave about a certain product, service or organization. Advertisement requires disparate ways of looking at managing. Advertising management has four broad elements. These elements are the 4Ps of advertisement. These are people, process, planning and profit (Kelly & Sheehan, 2021, p.10). Advertisement is outlined as 'a paid, mediated format of communication from a describable resource, designed to convince the target to take some action, in the future or now (Richards & Catharine, 2002). Advertising is the most popular and most extensively discussed form of marketing communication, undoubtedly because of its prevalence.

DOI: 10.4018/978-1-7998-9672-2.ch008

Advertisement is also a very important integrated marketing communication tool especially for corporations such as car manufacturers whose products and services are targeted at mass consumer marketplaces, as it is very cost-efficient at reaching out large audiences. Advertisement's other main strength is its capacity to create a brand image or identities, speedily and convincingly (Belch et al, 2020, p.40). The authors aim to determine how cultural differences are emphasized in global advertising strategies and how these differences are adapted in ads.

In this research, the geographic, socio-politic, economic and cultural country profile, media and advertising sector in Iran is examined. Next global advertisementing strategies are explored and the adaptation strategy for global advertisements is evaluated in the context of Hofstede's theory of cultural dimensions and cultural onion model (Hofsede & Bond, 1984; Hofstede et al, 1990). In the study, Iranian advertisements were determined as the universe of the research and the advertisement produced by Lipton for Iran was chosen as the sample of the research by random sampling method. Iran has a unique social structure with its historical, cultural, political and socio-economical state. Considering the problems Iran has especially with Western countries and the image of the Western world in the country, the study becomes significant in in terms of how international companies can overcome the important adaptation problems.

Among other studies that use Hofstede's cultural onion and/or cultural dimensions model in the literate are Eryiğit's (2020) study, in which the glocal approaches of BMW, Volkswagen and Mercedes-Benz brands that adopt the glocal marketing approach through examining their Instagram posts as well as Onurlu & Zulfugarova's (2016) research, in which they examine five global brands' television advertisements in Turkey regarding whether global brands take cultural differences into account while applying their advertising strategies in local markets.

In this study, it was observed that, Lipton attaches importance to global advertising strategies in order to reach target audiences with different characteristics and in different markets. Furthermore, it is clear in the study that, Lipton aims to give messages appropriate to Iran's eating habits, geographical and cultural characteristics, gender roles, religious values and various social rituals. On the other hand, when Lipton's advertisement is evaluated in terms of Hofstede's theory of cultural dimensions and cultural onion model, it can be understood that "collectivism" dimension is intensively at the forefront in the advertisement. It is striking that people of different status are in communication in advertising. This reflects the low power gap in power distance. Cultural dimensions like femininity and low uncertainty avoidance are at the forefront in the advertisement. Although there are many restrictions in Iran, Iran has a tolerant society. For this reason, the theme of happiness seems to be the leading advertisement theme and this fact reflects tolerance.

IRAN COUNTRY PROFILE

The Islamic Republic of Iran is a Southwest Asian country with deserts and mountains located on an area of 1,648,000 km^2. Eastern Iran is located on a high plateau with vast sand deserts and wide salt plains. The plateau is surrounded by higher mountains such as Elburz to the north and Zagros to the west. Afghanistan and Pakistan are its neighbors on the east, Turkmenistan, Azerbaijan and Armenia are its neighbors on the north, Turkey and Iraq are its neighbors on the west. Iran's population is 82 million. The capital of the country is Tehran, the country's largest city and the country's political, cultural, commercial and industrial center. Iranian Rial is the currency of the country. Ayetullah Seyid Ali Hamaney is the Religious Leader and Hasan Ruhani is the President of the country. The official language is Persian. The name of the modern Persian language is sometimes referred to as Persian in English texts. Azeri, Turkmen, Halac, Afshar and Kashgai dialects of Turkish, as well as Kurdish, Arabic, Baloch languages are also spoken in Iran. Persians and Azeris constitute the ethnic majority, respectively, while Turkmens, Kashgais, Afshars, Khalajs, Kurds, Lors, Arabs and Balochs are other important ethnic groups living in Iran (Republic of Turkey Ministry of Foreign Affairs, Identification Bracelet of Country, 2021; Islamic Republic of Iran Ministry of Foreign Affairs, General Information, 2021).

The literacy rate in the country is 87.6%. Iranian society is divided into two main parts: traditional and modern. The classes in the traditional part are those who support the Islamic Government, have family businesses in the "bazar" or business. The sections in the modern segment are close to the Western lifestyle and culture (Republic of Turkey Tehran Embassy Commercial Consultancy, 2019, p.1).

The Iranian official calendar is arranged according to the solar year and the Iranian months. March 21, equal to 1 Ferverdin, is the beginning of the Iranian New Year. Lunar calendar in Iran is also announced officially. Lunar year is 10 days less than Solar year. Therefore, the days of religious rites, which are set according to the lunar calendar, are different every year from the next and previous years. Especially during Ramadan and also in Muharram, Muslim Iranians are fasting. Threfore these rituals influence daily and routine life. Some days in these two months are public holidays. Friday is public holiday. Iranian culture has been a dominant culture of the Middle East and Central Asia for many years. Persian was considered the language of intellectuals for much of the 2nd millennium BC, and before this period Persian was the language of religion and people. Sassanid influence also carried over to the Islamic world. Much of what later became known as Islamic sciences, such as literature, philology, philosophy, medicine, jurisprudence, architecture and sciences were acquired by the wider Muslim countries from the Sassanid Persians. (Islamic Republic of Iran Ministry of Foreign Affairs, General Information, 2021). No Ruz is Iran's most important national celebration of spring Equinox that the origin back into Iran's early history (Bradley, 2007, p.75).

The political structure of Iran in the last century is divided into two separate periods: The "Period of the Pahlavi dynasty" and the "Islamic Republic" (Niray & Deniz, 2010, p.2). In Period of the Pahlavi dynasty, Iran mainteined policy of modernisation and centralization (Lewis, 2006, p.432). Reza Shah focused modernization on education and the army. And he also gave importance to technology. Reza Shah aimed to establish thoughts of patriotism and nationalism in the education system. Reza Shah wanted to modernize the country, inspired by Turkish leader Mustafa Kemal Atatürk. He aimed to build up Western thoughts in the education system as well. Furthermore, he canceled capitulations and supported statist economy. After the death of Reza Shah, his son Mohammad Reza Pahlavi started to rule the country. Reza Pahlavi, gave importance to relations with Western countries. Pahlavi's focus only on economic liberalization caused the democratization process to be incomplete (Çitlioğlu, 2009, p.29-30; Bradley, 2007, p.4). Pahlavi favored authoritarian models of modernization and failed to adapt their political institutions to the social and economic changes it brought (Arif, 2012, p.5). Pahlavi's modernisation attempts did not match Iran's economic growth. During the Pahlavi Period, large portions of the population, especially middle class, had no voice in politically. Every opposite thought was supressed by state controlled secret police service SAVAK. During mid 1970s, the economy began to deteriorate. High inflations, cuts in real wages and falling real income caused major disappointment in the public. All these factors laid the basis for the Islamic revolution in 1979 (Clowson & Rubin, 2005, p.69-90).

Rajaee divided the political structure in Iran into four different generations such as The Politics of Revival between 1920s–1960s, The Politics of Revolution between 1963–1991, The Politics of Islamism between 1989–1997 and The Politics of Restoration between 1997–2005 (2007).

After a series of events in 1979, Shah was collapsed and his replacement with an Islamic Republic under Ayatollah Khomeini. The revolution was highly important for the speed at which a pro-Western authoritarian monarchy was replaced with an anti-Western totalitarian theocracy (McCarthy, 2019). The success of the 1978–79 revolution was followed by the relatively speedy institutionalization and conservatism. Consolidation of political power by an increasingly narrow circle of revolutionaries led by Ayatollah Khomeini, not surprisingly, the official discourse became one of Shi'a traditionalism and political conservatism (Kamrava, 2008, p.12). Unlike Rezah Shah, Ayatollah Khomeini denied the secular politicians over the Islamic state (Bradley, 2007, p.5). After the 1979 revolution, the concept of the glory of Islam gained importance. The glory of Islam meant that people's dress code should be controlled, men and women should not swim together, women should not go to football matches, Iranian should wear scarf from the age of nine, music should be censored, card games should be banned. There are serious restrictions on the entertainment industry and the media (Bradley, 2007, p.2-67).

Today, Iran is one of the most democratic countries in the Middle East. People select the president and Majlis (parliament). Both men and women have the right to vote in president and Majlis elections. Founded on April 1st 1979, the Islamic Republic of Iran has a unique form of government. The Constitution states that sovereignty will be exercised by the legislative, executive and judicial organs under the auspices of the Revolution Guide. According to the Constitution, the President is the head of the executive. Nonetheless, determining the priorities of the foreign and domestic policy agenda or the administration and management of the security forces and armed forces is the responsibility of the Revolution Guide. The President is elected by the people for a period of four years and for a maximum of two consecutive terms, among candidates who have received the approval of the Guardian Council of the Constitution. If any of the candidates does not receive more than 50% of the votes in the first round, the two candidates with the most votes compete in the second round (Republic of Turkey Ministry of Foreign Affairs, Political Outlook of Iran, 2021; Crane et al, 2008, p.7).

Ayatollah Khomeini wanted to spread his wayof pan-Islamism to the world. He encouraged the Shi'a majority in Iraq to establish an Islamic Republic against Saddam. Iraq invaded Iran in September 1980. Iran protected its homeland with the support of hundreds of thousands of volunteers. In May 1982, it drove the Iraqis from their lands. Khomeini did not accept Saddam Hussein's offer of a ceasefire and thousands of Iranians died on Iraqi soil over the course of 6 years (Bradley, 2007, p.46-47).

Half a million people by connections with Mojahadeen, demonstrated against the regime on June 20, 1981, thousands were arrested and some were executed instantly. The internal war end by the 1983 summer with the Khomeini's victory (Bradley, 2007, p.54-56).

After Homeini's death in 1989, Ali Akbar Hashemi Rafsanjani became the new president and remained in power until 1997. Rafsanjani, who promised to open Iran to the West, was expected to keep the "second republic" alive, but the period of elation lasted in three years. Mohammad Khatami, came to power in 1997 elections. The fourth generation, called politics of restoration, refers to the years 1997 to 2005. In 2005 Mahmoud Ahmadinejad was elected as predident of Iran (Rajaee, 2007, p.151-237).

The last Presidential elections were held on 19 May 2017. President Rouhani was elected President for the second time, taking 57.1% in the first round. The Islamic Consultative Assembly is the main legislative body of the Islamic Republic of Iran and has 290 elected members. Members of Parliament serve for 4 years. Parliament has duties such as making laws and ratifying international documents.

The approved bills are submitted to the Guardian Council of the Constitution for approval and become law after approval. The last Islamic Consultative Assembly elections were held on 21 February 2020 (Republic of Turkey Ministry of Foreign Affairs, Political Outlook of Iran, 2021).

The Iranian economy, which was developing in the 1960s and 1970s, began to deteriorate after the revolution and the middle class was most affected by this situation. Following the Islamic Revolution in 1979, Iran had siginificant problems. The Khomeini controlled the all political and economic power. Khomeini regime had significant economic power. The country used at least 20 percent of its income to subsidize transportation and food, and to motivate its dark supporters. Especially in the 1980s, significant economic problems were experienced. The US has severely restricted Iran's exports by imposing strict sanctions, and has also disrupted the country's industrial infrastructure, which is dependent on US spare parts. Iraq has damaged many of Iran's economic assets, especially the oil refinery in Abadan. In the mid-1880s, the state implemented a normalization regime. The wrong and volatile economic policies implemented by the state caused intense inflation in the country. People had serious difficulties in accessing basic necessities. After the oil crisis of 1998-1999, Iran's economy grew rapidly. Between 1999 and 2006, GDP increased by an average of 49 percent annually due to a 13.3% increase in oil production and an increase in oil prices in the world market. Data from the World Bank and other sources show that inflation fell after the Shah period, but remained at a high of 10.5 percent in 2017. (Bradley, 2007, p.57-59; McCarthy, 2019, Crane et al, 2008, p.8).

Because of its large reserves of petroleum and natural gas, Iran holds an important position in world economy and security of international energy. GDP is $452 billion (2018). The important industries are oil, petrochemical, textile, cement, food derivatives (especially extracting edible oil and refining sugar) and other materials for building construction. Country imports machineries, industrial metals, medicines and chemical derivatives. Carpet, petrochemical products, oil, fruits, dry fruits (dates, raisins and pistachios), caviar, leather, dresses and apparels and foodstuffs are the exports of the country (Islamic Republic of Iran Ministry of Foreign Affairs, General Information, 2021). According to the data of the Central Bank of Iran, 37% of household expenditures are housing, electricity, water, natural gas and gasoline, 24% food and beverage, 11% transportation, 9% other goods and services, 6% health. services, 5% clothing and clothing, 4% household appliances, 2% communication, restaurant and hotel, 2% entertainment and cultural activities (Republic of Turkey Tehran Embassy Commercial Consultancy, 2019, p.1).

Iranian culture is deep rooted in history. Three types of cultural identities predominate in Iran (Karimifard, 2012). The first of these is the National Identity, which comes from the pre-Islamic Iranian civilization. The second is the Post-Islamic Islamic Identity. The third is the Modern Identity, which was formed after the entry of modernity into Iran. These cultural identities form the basis of Iranian identity. On the other hand, it is also claimed that the heterogeneity of these elements led to many social and political conflicts in the country, leading to an identity crisis in the country. (Zahed, 2004). The dominant authoritarian discourse in Iran tries to dominate western identity elements by promoting national/ Islamic identity. (Mohammadpur, Karimi, & Mahmoodi, 2013).

Nation state, history and geography mind have always been respected and supported in Iranian culture. The folklore and customs, rituals, and works of prose and poetry of many Iranian cultures have been presented to the world, all known as Iranian cultural heritage. Iran's cultural heritage has survived from the ancient period of Iranian history and is an integral part of Iran's national culture and identity. Some rituals such as Nowruz are performed not only in Iran but also outside the borders of Iran. This reveals that Iranian culture is an ancient civilization. The whole world sees it as a sign of Iranian culture. Some of the Iranian traditions were continued after Islam. Some of these rituals, such as the recently celebrated Centennial and Mehregan celebrations, are still part of Iran's cultural heritage. (Ahmadi, 2004, p.54-55).

in line with the GLOBE (Global Leadership and Organizational Behavior Activity) study (House et al., 2004), which conducted a study on 62 countries, including Iran, Iran's cultural practices can be explained as follows:

- High power distance,
- Individualism,
- High performance orientation
- Strong-in group collectivism,
- High male orientation

The most basic distinguishing characteristic of Iranian culture is family and in-group orientation, which propounds loyalty and commitment to small groups such as family and close friends (Javidan & Dastmalchian, 2003). Javidan and Dastmalchian (2003) state that Iran is not an Arab cultural group but a part of the South Asian cultural group consisting of countries such as Thailand, Malaysia and India. Corporate collectivism or social is not a strong suit of Iranians. People in positions of power and authority are given extreme privileges and status. The culture of the country is distinguished by a mixture of strong family ties and a high level of individuality. Iranian culture is patriarchal, legally and culturally, men have more privileges and rights than women. Gender discrimination and gender discrimination have created different codes of behavior and roles for both genders. These codes and roles are still valid today. There are more restrictions on individual freedoms, dress codes, and relationships with the opposite sex for girls than for males.

According to Khajehpour, Namazie and Honari (2013), there are some certain characteristics of Iranian culture listed below:

- Friendly and Hospitable (significance of face and honor),
- Dualism in public and private behaviour (dishonesty, survival, indirect communication),
- Proud and nationalistic people with ancient history (Xenophobia and sense of superiority)
- Collectivist / Family orianted (Low level trust for out-group / Nepotism)
- Short term thinkers (Lack of long term planning)
- Negative and conspiracy minded (lack of accountability, not taking responsibility)

ADVERTISING

When it comes to international advertising or multi-country advertising, advertisers need to consider the different phases of the two types of advertising strategies; adaptation and standardization. Circulation of the identical advertising messages across various countries without adapting relating to the customer group is named International Advertising Standardization. By utlizing this strategy, the same advertising message might be used in dissimilar geographical spaces or countries. Due to the idea of globalization, nowadays the world is seen as a common market place. As a result, the world market has become increasingly homogeneous, making it possible for international companies to offer standardized products or services all over the world. Circulation of the well-known advertising messages in different areas or countries on an international base is called as the standardization of international strategy. In different countries or geographical areas, standardization of international advertising strategy has become probable in consequence of the influences of internet, television and movies. Although the people in different countries have different cultures, language, values, religions, rules and regulations their wants and needs are almost identical. This logical background lies at the basis of the standardization of international advertising strategies. Insomuch as consumers with the same or similar demands and needs might be motivated by standardized advertising applications. (Levitt, 1983). In the concept of advertising standardization strategy emerges when the execution tactics of advertising components, such as visuals and copy, are kept the same across advertisements in several countries (Nelson & Paek, 2007, p.65).

The second key approach to international advertising is adaptation (harmonization). Within the scope of advertising industy, adaptation is described as usage of different advertising messages in different market places (Wang & Yang, 2011, p.25). Localization or adaptation of an international advertising strategy accepts that each market for the advertising campaigns are clearly different from each other because of the distinctions in languages, cultures, rules, regulations, religions and foreign media (Pratt, 1956). Papavassiliou and Stathakopoulos (1997) imply that international advertising determinations might be viewed on a continuity with bipolar ends of the continuity being standardization of creative advertising tactics and strategy, and adaptation of creative advertising strategy and tactics.

Along with globalization, international market competition has increased. Brands operating in global markets emphasize cultural characteristics rather than economic variables in the markets in which they operate. For this reason, international brands need to develop advertising strategies following the culture and values of the local markets they target. The study aims to determine how cultural differences are emphasized in global advertising strategies and how these differences are adapted in ads. Within the scope of the study, the advertising film produced by Lipton, a global brand, for Iran was analyzed. Iran is a Muslim Middle Eastern country with a population of 82 million. Most of the household expenditures in Iran consist of expenditures such as housing, electricity, water, natural gas and gasoline. The food and beverage sector, on the other hand, constitutes the second most spent area in the country with a rate of 24%. Advertising industry in Iran has scientific and professional deficiencies. A limited budget of 750 million dollars is allocated to the advertising and promotion sector in Iran. Reasons such as the lack of advertising discipline in universities and the inadequacy of advertising professionals stand as other obstacles to the development of the advertising industry in Iran. In the last 10 years, there has been an increase in the number of advertising companies in Iran, but this factor has not yet had a sufficient impact on the advertising sector in terms of creativity. Due to the embargoes applied in Iran, there are not many international companies in the country. Embargoes applied to international brands also negatively affect the development of the international advertising industry. Advertisements in Iran are generally evaluated in two different categories, before and after the 1979 revolution. After the 1979 revolution, the rules and restrictions in the advertising industry increased and serious differences were experienced in advertisements. Among the most widely used media tools in Iran, TV comes first with a rate of 93%. Outdoor advertising is accepted as the most effective advertising medium in the country. In outdoor advertising, the most effective tools are roadside billboards, digital billboards and advertising spaces in public transportation vehicles (Republic of Turkey Tehran Embassy Commercial Consultancy, 2019, p.3). Influencer advertising, which has been applied in the social media environment in the country in recent years, has been increasing remarkably. When the distribution of expenditures in TV advertisements is analyzed, it is seen that the food and beverage sector ranks first with 22%.

Media in Iran

In the Mass Media Communication Article of the Constitution, it is mentioned that the mass media, television and radio should follow the requirements of the Islamic Revolution and serve to spread the Islamic culture. For this reason, the media should be used as a forum for the healthy expression of different ideas, but the propaganda and spread of anti-Islamic and destructive practices should be strictly avoided. (Islamic Republic of Iran Ministry of Foreign Affairs, Constitution, 2021).

The first written press in Iran started in the middle of the seventeenth century and initially rhe newspapers were published. The beginning of continuous broadcasting found the middle of the nineteenth century. Radio broadcasts began in Iran in 1926, and television began to be watched in homes in 1958 (Shasavandi, 2016, p.41-44).

The major daily newspapers for Iran are printed in Tehran. The top-line newspapers comprise Jumhori-yı Islami, Resalat, Kayhan, Abrar, and Ettelaat (countrydata.com). There are more than 50 newspapers in Iran. Some of dailies are printed in English. For example Tehran Times is one of the most popular newspapers printed in English (BBC, 2017).

There are six national channels, six international channels and 30 local channels, all of which are state-owned, in the TV sector in Iran. When the main radio stations in Iran are examined, it is seen that Sarasari, which makes family programs, Payam, which makes traffic programs, Vaerzesh, which makes sports programs, Farhang, which makes cultural programs, are the leading commercial channels. There are no private TV channels in Iran. Existing channels broadcast in line with official approaches. Channels 1, 2, 3 and 4 have a general broadcast. Channel 4 focuses on art and cultural broadcast. News Channel "Haber TV", education channel "Amuzeş TV", shopping channels "Bazar" and "Borsa TV", documentary channel "Nemayiş TV" and a broadcaster on local issues "Şoma TV" are comprised of the broadcasting channels in Iran. Futhermore, each states have their own broadcasting channels (Yegin, 2013, p.75).

In 1993, the Iranian government decided to establish a national data network and introduced the internet. This was done by Data Communication of Iran (DCI), which was the representative of the Telecommunication Company of Iran (TCI) (Shoraka&Omidi, 2002, p.28). There are 72 million internet users in the country and the internet penetration is 89%. Looking at the purposes of internet usage, it is seen that the internet is used mostly for content search with 59%, followed by social media use with 50%. It is stated that 35% of people use the Internet for entertainment, 48% for business purposes, 35% for reading news, 30% for online banking, 40% for messaging applications, and 10% for blogs. Instagram is the most popular social media tool in the country. Facebook and other social media channels are losing their popularity due to government restrictions. In addition, telegram, a popular instant messaging application, is also on the decline in the country (Republic of Turkey Tehran Embassy Commercial Consultancy, 2019, p.4).

It is possible to claim that the media and mass media in Iran are under the serious control of the state. Serious restrictions are imposed on internet access in Iran. Watching satellite broadcasts and using satellites are also prohibited. With these prohibitions, the regime aims to prevent access to alleged inappropriate content. However, it cannot be said that the regime was very successful in this regard. Because almost every home has satellite dishes and people mostly watch television channels broadcasting from abroad. Also, filter breakers are very widely used in Iran for internet censorship. Thus, the censorship mechanism can be forced somewhat. Media environments, on the other hand, are more easily and strictly controlled. Many newspapers in Iran were sentenced to be closed temporarily or permanently for publishing against to regime (Yegin, 2013, p.75).

Advertising Industry in Iran

In 1980, the new revolutionary government took over ownership of banks, insurance companies, dams and irrigation facilities, large-scale manufacturers, radio and television stations, communications and transportation companies, and companies in other sectors in Iran under nationalization (Crane et al quoted from Alizadeh, 2008, p.79).

The size of the Iranian advertising and promotion sector is 750 million dollars and Iran spends 9 dollars in advertising expenditure per capita. In Iran's advertising market, the share of TV and radio is 60%, the share of outdoor advertisements is 28%, the share of digital advertisements is 9%, and the share of newspapers and magazines is 3% (Republic of Turkey Tehran Embassy Commercial Consultancy, 2019, p.2).

Due to international sanctions against Iran, foreign capital inflows into the country are very low. It is seen that the efforts to create a self-sufficient economic model applied in the country make it difficult for international companies to take place in the country (Republic of Turkey Tehran Embassy Commercial Consultancy, 2019, p.2).

Rules and Regulations

There are some important laws regarding television and radio advertisements, print advertisements and social media advertisements in Iran. Atheist publications that are biased against Islamic rules or the promotion of topics that appear to harm any aspect of the Islamic Republic are strictly not allowed. Any propaganda regarding obscene or prohibited religious acts, inappropriate images or subjects that violate public morals are not allowed. It is forbidden to associate with groups or individuals that may be against Iran's interests, dignity or security. It is forbidden to insult the leader of the revolution, the relevant religious authorities and the religion of Islam in any way. Both men and women have to abide by the Islamic headscarf. Before advertisements, products and services must be formally verified by well-known research centers in Iran. E-commerce suppliers should be informed about products and services in an accurate, complete and transparent manner. The name of the business should be clearly shared with the target audience. Before all advertisements, permission must be obtained from the relevant institutions, especially the Ministry of Culture and Islamic Guidance (Zigma8, 2018).

Strict Islamic rules have a deep influence in advertising in Iran and have led to the emergence of some rules for international advertising in Iran. Advertising that promotes corruption and superstition or goes against the country's official religions is prohibited. Advertising of a particular good or service should in no way threaten another similar product or service. Ads must not offend people with certain disabilities or illnesses. It is forbidden to advertise goods and services in religious, scientific and educational centers. Advertisements should not insult the country's official religions, customs, traditions, ethnicities, accents and dialects. The use of tobacco and similar scenes that are harmful to human health or addictive and that explicitly or implicitly encourage their consumption are not allowed. Advertisements that promote the destruction of the human environment, forests, pastures, natural resources and natural habitats of animals are prohibited. Advertising should not incite fear or violence. Materials and images showing harassment of animals cannot be used in advertisements. Authors in advertisements must comply with all laws and relevant regulations regarding the protection of the material and intellectual property of authors and artists. There is no place for female abuse in advertisements. The appearance of the characters used in the advertisement should be in accordance with the national and religious traditions of the society. Advertisements should not be associated with women and men gender preference. It is forbidden to promote goods and services that are not suitable for consumption, use or purchase by children in advertisements. Foreign language promotion, typos and mispronunciations are not allowed in advertisements. If it is necessary to use a foreign text while editing the ads, the size of the Persian text should be larger than the size of the foreign language text. If the subject of the advertisement requires it, it is necessary to bring the official flag and full map of the country in the advertisement in order to use the map and the flag of the Islamic Republic. Advertising should not devalue domestic goods. Advertising of foreign country goods, services and products is permitted, unless their domestic supply and sale is prohibited by law. Advertising on the facilities, walls, buildings and structures of foreign embassies and political representatives is prohibited. Advertising on the facilities, walls, buildings and structures of official and civil natural and legal persons can be done with the prior permission of their owners and officials. In accordance with the Note 4 of Article 6 of the Law on Amending the Laws and Regulations of the Iranian Institute of Standards and Industrial Research and Industry, the advertisement of goods and products for which the application of the standard is obligatory depends on having a license to use Iran's standard brand and industrial research. Advertisers and advertisers must have the necessary, credible and legal documents for claims and claims regarding the subject of advertisement (Zigma8, 2021a).

Three institutions are responsible for the publication of advertisements in Iran. The first is Iran's official TV and radio channel, IRIB, and is responsible for TV and radio advertisements. The Ministry of Culture and Enlightenment and Municipalities are responsible for outdoor advertisements. Those who want to advertise in the country must obtain preliminary permission from these organizations. There is no clear legislation regarding the broadcast status of advertisements. Iranian producers have the right to advertise free on the state channel, and foreigners who have invested in Iran do not have this right. Advertising of foreign products on state TV, radio and printed publications is prohibited. Foreign investors in the country are expected to advertise on state channels. Ads suggestions have to be in accordance with one of the 4 ad formats determined by IRIB, which is a major obstacle to creative advertising (Republic of Turkey Tehran Embassy Commercial Consultancy, 2019, p.3). The IRIB has an influential position in shaping national identity, ideas, values and gender stereotypes (Ghandeharion & Yazdanjoo, 2017, p.3).

Advertising Tools

Advertising plays a fundamental role in both reflecting and shaping culture (Shasavandi, 2016, p.32). Following the 1979 Iranian revolution, Khomeini banned advertisements on the grounds that they led the people to Western civilization. However, after a few years, especially after the Iran-Iraq war in 1988, the advertising industry became active again (Amouzadeh & Tavangar, 2008, p.133).

In Iran, the department of advertising is only available at the associate degree and undergraduate level in scientific and applied universities. There is no advertising department in the country at the masters and doctorate level. There are deficiencies in terms of resources, such as advertising models and advertising strategies. Foreign sources have not been translated into Persian and have not been brought into the literature. Since there are deficiencies in advertising education, the needs of the market in the field of advertising cannot be fully met (Ahmadi, 2016).

When we look at the advertising medium in Iran, it is seen that TV has a share of 93%, internet 85%, outdoor advertising 58%, cinema 36%, newspaper 34%, magazines 32% and radio 22%. The most effective advertisement medium is outdoor advertisements. When the distribution of expenditures in TV advertisements is examined, it is seen that 22% of the food and beverage sector, 21% of GSM operators, internet service providers, banks and financial institutions, 11% of cosmetics and personal care products, 10% of hygiene and detergent products, 8% of kitchen appliances, 6% of governmental institutions, 6% of products like computer, 6% of building construction materials, 4% of carpets and furniture, 2% of transportation, 2% of office tools and equipment and 1% of jewelry sector. In outdoor advertising, the most effective tools are roadside billboards, digital billboards and advertising spaces in public transportation vehicles (Republic of Turkey Tehran Embassy Commercial Consultancy, 2019, p.3).

When the distribution of advertising expenditures in printed publications is examined, it is seen that 28% of the food and beverage sector, 16% of GSM operators, internet service providers, banks and financial institutions, 13% of cosmetics and personal care products, 13% of hygiene and detergent products, 9% of kitchen appliances, and governmental institutions. 6%, computer etc. products are 5%, building construction materials are 5%, carpets and furniture are 2%, transportation is 1%, office tools and equipment are 1%, and the jewelery sector is 1%. Due to the problems experienced in money transfer in the country, it is not possible to advertise on accounts such as Google, Youtube, Instagram from within the country. Banner advertisements are preferred through websites with high number of clicks in the country, but it is seen that current applications are not used in banner applications because these sites do not make the necessary technological innovation investment. Influencers are preferred for promotion on Instagram, and these people can issue invoices through agencies (Republic of Turkey Tehran Embassy Commercial Consultancy, 2019, p.4). Influencer marketing is very popular in Iran and is becoming more and more viral every day. Anyone with a large following can become a social media influencer, such as a prominent fashion photographer, a widely read web development blogger, or a valuable marketing executive on LinkedIn (Zigma8, 2021b).

ADAPTATION STRATEGY IN INTERNATIONAL BRANDS: AN EXAMINATION IN IRANIAN ADVERTISING

Lipton is a tea brand owned by Unilever which is between six largest international brands in Iran. It was founded by Thomas Lipton in 1800s in Glasgow, Scotland. It is now available in over 110 countries. Lipton is particularly popular in parts of Europe, North America, the Middle East, Asia and Australia. Lipton states that around the world, drinking tea means friendship, hospitality and sharing moments together. According to Lipton, tea represents a short break, taking five minutes to yourself, and recharge your batteries. Lipton defines nature as its tea factories and positions its brand as a natural brand. It emphasizes on its website and in most of its advertisements that teas are grown using natural rain, wind and sunlight (Lipton, 2021).

A commercial for Lipton, one of Unilever's brands, was produced by Kanoon Iran Novin production company in 2017. Turkish advertising agency Fikr'et acted as the idea and concept consultant of the commercial. For the advertisement Lipton worked with an International agency because of its global strategies. The shooting of the Iranian commercial started on January 26, 2017 and was completed in 2 weeks. The advertisement was shown on the official Iranian TV channel. The agency took care to shoot in accordance with the rules of the IRIB. The agency conducted a research on Iran's local tea drinking habits (what they drink next to tea, in which occasions they drink it, with whom they drink) before the commercial. Iran, which is in a close geography with Turkey, has cultural similarities with Turkey in terms of breakfast habits, tea drinking habits with friends and family. For this reason, Fikr'et, the idea and concept agency of the commercial, adapted the commercial film "Lipton - Çayın Yeri Başka", which

153

was published in Turkey and achieved great success, for the Iranian market. The famous actor did not take part in the commercial; however Famous actor Changiz Jalilvand voiced the commercial (Yücel, 2021).

METHODOLOGY

Along with the globalization, the international market competition has increased. Brands operating in global markets emphasize cultural characteristics rather than economic variables in the markets in which they operate. For this reason, international brands need to develop advertising strategies following the culture and values of the local markets they target. The study aims to determine how cultural differences are emphasized in global advertising strategies and how these differences are adapted in ads. Random sampling method was used in the study. In random sampling, participants are chosen from the universe of that each member of the universe has an equal probability for selection to participate in the study (Kazdin, 1992). Within the scope of the study, the advertising film prepared by Lipton, a global brand, for Iran was analyzed. The adaptattion strategy, which is one of the global advertising strategies, was used in the analysis of the advertisement. The adaptation approach is based on the fact that nations located in different geographies in the world are structurally and culturally separate from each other, and advertising messages are reshaped according to these differences. The approach aims to cooperate with the country's local agency and adapt the advertisements to the country's cultural characteristics (Aktuğlu & Eğinli, 2010, p.169). At the end of the analysis, the results are discussed and suggestions for more comprehensive future studies are also made.

Hofstede's Cultural Onion Model

Geert Hofstede and Gert Jan Hofstede (2010) developed the "Cultural Onion Model" to define and compare different cultures. A culture is like an onion with different layers. A viewer of culture from the outside must progress slowly, understanding each layer to get to the core of the culture. Cultural dissimilarities can be represented in different ways as symbols, rituals, heroes and values. Symbols are images, gestures, words or objects that have specific meanings and are recognized only by those who share the culture. Elements such as words in a language, clothing and hair style can also be evaluated under this category. Heroes, dead or alive, imaginary or real, are people who have extremely important characteristics in a culture and are therefore seen as role models for behavior. For instance, Asterix in France and Snoopy in the USA. Rituals are collective activities. Rituals are not essentially needed to accomplish a goal, but the rituals are considered absolutely essential and necessary by the members of a culture. Because of that, they are performed for their own sake. Ways of greeting and paying respect to others, social and religious ceremonies are related to rituals. There are various examples which related to rituals: It is the way you shake hands, the way you serve tea, how you invite people, how you give a present and how you visit those who invited you.

Values form the core of culture. Values are opinions that describes what in life is noted significant, and they are among the primary things children learn. Because the values are learned so early in peoples' lives, people are often insensible of their values. Defining or discussing the values could be arduous, and outsiders cannot directly see them. They can only see the symbols, heroes and rituals of a culture and try to assume what the values – the inner core – are.

One of the key concepts of Hofstede's theory is that culture is the influence of society on the thinking and acting of individuals, a so-called "mental programming". This means that the common consciousness of individuals living in different cultural ensembles is created by the mental programming of cultures. (Kiss Ildikó, 2014, p.305)

Hofstede's Cultural Dimensions Theory

Many researchers in the second half of the twentieth century have hypothesized about the nature of the primary issues of societies that would present distinct dimensions of culture. In the 1970s, Hofstede got accession to a grand survey database about related sentiments and values of people in over 50 countries around the world (Hofstede, 1980). Since modern cultures are too complicated and subculturally heterogeneous, the strategy used in original study was a limited-sample strategy based on syllogism of the alike subcultures in distinct countries. The standard of matching limited samples often can only be evidenced ex post-facto: If the differentiations we discovered between cultures in one sample set, are approved by those found by others in other matched samples, our matching was sufficient (Hofstede, 1980).

As a result of a series of studies, Hofstede claimed that there are 5 different cultural dimensions. The five dimensions are classified:

1) **Power Distance,** connected to the different resolutions to the basic problem of human inequality. This dimension measures "the extent to which less powerful members of organizations and institutions within a country expect and adopt that power is distributed unequally" (Hofstede, 2001). Individuals in large power distance countries like Brazil, Venezuela and France etc. admit the inequality of power in their society while USA, Austria, Denmark and Scandinavian countries symbolize the opposite pole of power distance dimension (Hofstede, 2001)

2) **Uncertainty/Avoidance,** connected to the grade of stress in a society in the face of an unknown situations. UAI specifies the extent to which a community feels jeopardized by unclear situations and the extent to which a community attempts to beware these situations by taking up seriously rigid codes of behavior, a belief in the certainty, establishing formal rules, and not withstanding abnormal ideas and actions. People with high uncertainty avoidance are perturbed with security in life, feel a major need for written rules and consensus, less willing to take risks while people in low uncertainty avoidance communities are less perturbed with security, rules and these people are more risk indulgent (Hofstede, 1980). Lifetime employment is more widespread in high/strong uncertainty avoidance countries such as Greece, Japan and Portugal etc. whereas high job variability more commonly emerges in low/weak uncertainty avoidance communities such as Ireland, USA and Great Britain. etc. (Hofstede, 2001).

3) **Individualism/Collectivism,** connected to the concretion of individuals into basic groups. Individualism claims that "a society in which the connections between individuals are unstable – everybody is hoped to look after him/herself and his/her close family only". However, collectivism stands for "a society in which people from birth onwards are combined into powerfull, coherent in-groups, which throughout people's lifetime continue to keep them in exchange for absolute loyalty" (Hofstede, 2001). Individualists value personal independence, individual expression, pleasure, personal time and collectivists value interrelation of favours, a sensation of affinity and respect for tradition. Individualistic societies such as Australia, Canada and USA etc. assume that

democracy should ideally be shared by everyone, which is difficult to understand in collectivistic societies such as Pakistan, Indonesia and Chile etc. (Hofstede, 2001)

4) **Masculinity/Femininity,** describes the fourth dimension where masculinity stands for a community in which social gender roles are absolutely dissimiliar: men are supposed to be pretentious, rigid and focused on material accomplishments; women are supposed to be tender, humble and concerned with the quality of life. While femininity stands for a community in which social gender roles overlap, both women and men are expected to be tender, humble and concerned with the quality of life (Hofstede, 2001). Masculine individuals' choices are accomplishment, bravery, and material achievements in opposition to feminine individuals, who identify success in terms of intimate human relationships and quality of life. Typical masculine countries are Mexico, Japan and Italy etc. On the other hand, there are Scandinavian societies, which are considered as feminine societies, at the opposite pole. (Hofstede, 2001).

5) **Indulgence/Restraint,** dimension was added to the model in 2010 in order to synchronize with the new studies on happiness themes. This dimension was partially embedded in the research led by Michael Minkov, a Bulgarian sociologist and the creator of the comprehensive World Values Survey. A indulgent community is one that values the pleasure of human needs and desires; A measured community regards the value of hiding pleasures and curbing ones' desires in order to regulate more with its social norms.

"Indulgent societies will tend to concentrare more on individual happiness and well-being, leisure time is very important, and there is greater personal control and freedom. This is in contrast with restrained societies where positive emotions are less freely explained and freedom, happiness and leisure are not given the same significance" (Maclachlan, 2013).

In the research, within the scope of the adaptation strategy of global advertisements and Hofstede's theory of cultural dimensions and Cultural Onion model, answers were seeked for the following questions:

1) Is the advertisement designed according to the cultural characteristics of the target audience? Are the given messages in Lipton Iran advertisement appropriate to Iran's culture, traditions and daily life?

2) In the Lipton Iran advertisement, what are the symbols, heroes, rituels, values observed in the Lipton Iran advertisement?

3) In the Lipton Iran advertisement, what are the key messages and metaphors that make emphasis on power distance in the advertisement?

4) In the Lipton Iran advertisement what are the key messages and metaphors that make emphasis on individualism/collectivism?

5) In the Lipton Iran advertisement what are the key messages and metaphors that make emphasis on masculinity/femininty?

6) In the Lipton Iran advertisement what are the key messages and metaphors that make emphasis on indulgence/restraint?

7) In the Lipton Iran advertisement what are the key messages and metaphors that make emphasis on uncertainty avoidance?

SOLUTIONS AND RECOMMENDATIONS

The Lipton Iran commercial lasts 50 seconds. The commercial begins with "Hi Iran". At that time, the Farça "Hi Iran" lettering in black letters on a yellow background and Lipton's logo in Persian alphabet are on the screen. Selam is used as hello in Iran. It is also used as an abbreviation of "Selamun Aleykum". Among Muslims, "Selamun Aleykum " is used to mean may Allah's peace be upon you. The Lipton company uses a salutation specific to Iranian culture in this ad. The commercial continues with the demonstration of people picking tea in nature. And right behind it, the world map with the Lipton logo appears on the countries where the Lipton company is located, and Iran is zoomed in. Then, images from the "Spice Bazaar" are displayed on the screen. Meanwhile, the voice-over said, "As Lipton, we have been operating in the tea industry for 125 years and we have observed the unique use of the tea you are used to in different cultures. We understand that you are the only one. You are at the center of delicious tastes." says. A man sips his tea, then is shown various varieties of dried rose. Then there is a tea serving tray, and while the tea brewed with lipton is served in the teapot, it is seen that there are dried roses in the glass bowl. After the tea is poured into the glasses, rose petals are thrown into the glass. On the screen, three hijab dressed women women, chatting over tea, and two men playing chess while drinking tea are seen on the screen. Meanwhile, the voice over says "Tea is an important part of your life". As the footage progresses, the voice-over says "Tea is friendship, tea is family, tea is life itself, its color is the color of positivity. Its taste is the warm taste of conversations. Its scent is the fresh scent of nature. New Lipton Tb range, for you as you wanted." says. A moment when the extended family drinks tea, a birthday celebration with friends and tea is served, a couple watching the sunset on the bench while drinking tea, a moment when women chat and drink tea in a restaurant, a moment when mountaineers drink tea while relaxing on the mountain appear on the screen in sequence.

Table 1. Analysis of Lipton Iran in context with Hofstede UI Model

COMPONENTS OF UI MODEL	LIPTON IRAN
Symbols	*Dried Rose *Logo of Lipton with Persian alphabet *Hijab dressed women *Casual dressed men *Language of the advertising is Persian (Supported by English subtitles).
Heroes	-
Rituels	*Saluting at the beginning of the advertising (Salam Iran!) *Servicing of the tea (Emphasizing of the tea as a part of the rituels of the society) *Conversations and tea drinking (Kind of group routine)
Values	*"Tea is family" (emphasizing the importance of the family.) *"Tea is friendship (Emphasizing the importance of friendship). *No men in womens' groups and no women in mens'groups. The moments when men and women are together are often depicted as family. (There is a construction of social relations in accordance with the Islamic regime and Islamic values.) *Tea usually served by women

When the Lipton Iran advertisement is analyzed according to Hofstede's UI model, it is observed that the advertisement contains messages and metaphors which are compatible for Iran's tradition, culture and value elements. From dressing styles to gender roles and religious values, it is clearly observed that Lipton Iran advertisement has images and symbols in order to correspond the cultural characteristics of the target audience.

Table 2. Analysis of Lipton Iran in context of Hofstede's Cultural Dimensions

CULTURAL DIMENSIONS	LIPTON IRAN
Power Distance	The prevalence of interpersonal dialogue indicates a low power gap.
Individualism/Collectivism	Collectivism is at the forefront in advertising. Family and friend groups are usually in the foreground in the advertisement.
Masculinity/Femininity	Femininity is at the forefront in the advertising. Because femininity is related to equality, solidarity etc. In the ad emphasizing the positivity ("Tea is color of positivity"), ("Its color is color of positivity"), ("Its scent is the fresh scent of nature").
Indulgence/Restraint	Indulgence is at the forefront in the advertising. The usage of friendship, positivity and family themes in the advertisement and the presence of happy people in the images bring the dimension of tolerance to the fore.
Uncertainty Avoidance	Relationship models based on mutual trust, consistency and stability, such as family and friendship, were highlighted in the advertisement. Thus, low uncertainty avoidance is at the forefront in the advertising.

When the Lipton Iran advertisement is analysed in the context of Hoftede's Cultural Dimensions, it is possible to say that the advertisement reflects low power gap dimension. Because, groups of people take in place in the advertisement frequently and people appear in informal enviroments in a friendly manner. Although culture of Iran has both individual and collectivist characteristics, collectivistic charactericties of Iran is foreground in the advertisement. Making emphasis on communities such as friend groups and family, reflects collectivism dimension. Femininity is at the forefront in the advertising. A reason for this is because femininity is related to equality, solidarity etc. In the advertisement, there are various messages and metaphors emphasizing positivity and this is compatible with the femininity dimension in the advertisement. On the other hand, messages and metaphors which are related to positivity, friendship and happy people also reflects dimension of tolerance. Also, it can be stated that indulgence is at the forefront in the advertising. The people in the footage use informality in interaction with others. Therefore, it is safe to say that low uncertainty avoidance is at the forefront in the advertising. Because informality is completely foreground in the advertisement.

In this study, the adaptation strategy of global advertisements is evaluated in the context of Hofstede's theory of cultural dimensions and cultural onion model, and it will be a guide for studies aiming to analyze the advertising strategies of global brands. In addition, a comparative analysis can be made by examining the advertising strategies of the Lipton brand in other countries.

CONCLUSION

Advertising as a communication process is implemented in an environment that includes different value judgments, beliefs, customs and habits. Along with globalization, businesses have begun to use localized creative strategies accepting that each culture has different consumption habits and communication styles. Therefore, the global businesses implement various advertising strategies in order to reach their target audiences. Global brands take into account the cultural structure of the market in which the advertising message is transmitted in their advertising practices and try to show sensitivity to the cultural structure of the society. Because the cultural structure and value variables of a society affect the perception of the message by the target audience and are important in the behavior of the targeted audience. This study aims to determine how cultural differences are emphasized in global advertising strategies and how these differences are adapted in ads. Within the scope of the study, the advertising film prepared by Lipton, a global brand, for Iran was analyzed.

When Lipton's advertisement is analyzed, it is seen that the brand attaches importance to global advertising strategies in order to reach target audiences with different characteristics in different markets. When the messages given in the analyzed advertisement are analyzed in the context of the adaptation strategy, it is determined that Lipton aims to give messages appropriate to Iran's eating habits, geographical and cultural characteristics, gender roles, religious values and various social rituals. The inclusion of familiar images or expressions in advertisements designed according to the cultural characteristics of the target audience facilitates the interpretation of advertising messages and creates a feeling of intimacy between the brand and the target audience. The use of images and symbols that correspond to the cultural characteristics of the target audience in ads makes it easier for the target audience to make sense of the messages given. For this reason, in advertisements where the adaptation strategy is used, close connections can be established between the target audience and the brand. Thus, the emergence of negative consequences such as inability to perceive, misunderstanding, and development of negative reactions arising from cultural differences in the country where the advertisement is broadcasted are prevented.

The symbols, rituals and values used in the advertisement reflect the Iranian culture. While it is possible to see collectivism and individualism together in Iranian culture, collectivism, which is seen more intensely, was preferred in Lipton advertisement. It is striking that people of all levels are in communication in the advertisement. This reflects the low power gap in power distance. Femininity is at the forefront in the advertising. And also, low uncertainty avoidance is at the forefront in the advertising. Although there are many restrictions in Iran, Iran has a tolerant society. For this reason, the theme of happiness seems to be at the forefront in the advertisement and reflects tolerance.

REFERENCES

Ahmadi, H. (2004). Iranian national identity: Foundations, challenges and requirements. *Cultural Research Journal*, *1*(6), 5–55.

Ahmadi, S. (2016). *On Professionalism and Specialized Training in Iranian Advertising Industry.* https://www.academia.edu/34280136/On_Professionalism_and_Specialized_Training_in_Iranian_advertising_industry_pdf

Aktuğlu, I., & Eğinli, A. (2010). Küresel Reklam Stratejilerinin Belirlenmesinde Kültürel Farklılıkların Önemi. *Selçuk İletişim Dergisi, 6*(3), 167–183.

Allwood, J. (1985). Intercultural Communication. *Papers in Anthropological Linguistics, 12,* 1-25.

Amouzadeh, M., & Manoochehr, T. (2008). Sociolinguistic aspects of Persian advertising in post-revolutionary Iran. In M. Semati (Ed.), *Media, culture, and society: Living with globalization and the Islamic state* (pp. 130–151). Routledge.

Arif, M. (2012). *The Iranian Revolution: The Role and Contribution of Ayatollah Ruhollah Khomeini.* https://www.researchgate.net/publication/283580147_THE_IRANIAN_REVOLUTION_The_Role_and_Contribution_of_Ayatollah_Ruhollah_Khomeini

BBC News. (2017). *Iran Profile – Media.* https://www.bbc.com/news/world-middle-east-14542234

Belch, E. G., Belch, M. A., Kerr, G., Powell, I., & Waller, D. (2020). *Advertising: An Integrated Marketing Communication Perspective.* McGraw-Hill Education.

Bernard, L. (2006). *Ortadoğu* (S. Y. Kölay, Trans.). Arkadaş.

Bradley, M. (2007). *Iran Open Hearts in a Closed Land.* Authentic.

Carey, J. W. (1988). *Communication as Culture: Essays on Media and Society.* Routledge.

Çitlioğlu, E. (2009). İran'ı Anlamak. In *Uluslararası Güvenlik ve Stratejik Araştırmalar Merkezi, Araştırma, Analiz ve Projeksiyon Çalışması.* https://www.academia.edu/2460213/%C4%B0RANI_ANLAMAK

Clawson, P., & Rubin, M. (2005*). Eternal Iran Continuity and Chaos.* Palgrave Macmillan Country Data. https://www.countrydata.com/cgi-bin/query/r-6508.html

Crane, K., Lal, R., & Martini, J. (2008). Iran's Political, Demographic, and Economic Vulnerabilities. Rand Corporation.

De Mooij, M. (2010). *Global marketing advertising: Understanding cultural paradoxes.* SAGE publications.

Eryiğit, M. (2020). Instagram'da Glokal Yaklaşım Örneği Olarak "Bmw, Volkswagen Ve Mercedes-Benz" Analizi. *Kocaeli Üniversitesi İletişim Fakültesi Araştırma Dergisi,* (15), 140-163. Retrieved from https://dergipark.org.tr/en/pub/kilad/issue/53856/732150

Ghandeharion, A. & Yazdanjoo, M. (2017). Governmental Discourses in Advertising on Iran's State Television. *CLCWeb: Comparative Literature and Culture, 19*(3).

Hofstede, G. (1980). *Culture's Consequences: Comparing Values, Behaviours, Institutions and Organizations Across Nations* (2nd ed.). Sage Publications.

Hofstede, G., & Bond, M. H. (1984). Hofstede's culture dimensions: An independent validation using Rokeach's value survey. *Journal of Cross-Cultural Psychology, 15*(4), 417–433. doi:10.1177/0022002184015004003

Hofstede, G., & Hofstede, J. (2010). *Culture And Organizations-Software of the Mind.* McGraw- Hill International London.

Hofstede, G., Neuijen, B., Ohayav, D. D., & Sanders, G. (1990). Measuring organizational cultures: A Qualitative and quantitative study across twenty cases. *Administrative Science Quarterly*, *35*(2), 286–316. doi:10.2307/2393392

House, J. R., Hange, J. P., Javidan, M., Dorfman, W. P., & Gupta, V. (2004). *Culture, Leadership, and Organizations*. https://en.mfa.ir/

Javidan, M., & Dastmalchian, A. (2003). Culture and leadership in Iran: The land of individual achievers, strong family ties, and powerful Elite. *The Academy of Management Perspectives*, *17*(4), 127–142. doi:10.5465/ame.2003.11851896

Kamrava, M. (2008). *Iran's Intellectual Revolution*. Cambridge University Press. doi:10.1017/CBO9780511756146

Karimifard, H. (2012). Constructivism, national identity and foreign policy of the Islamic Republic of Iran. *Asian Social Science*, *8*(2), 239–246. doi:10.5539/ass.v8n2p239

Kazdin, A. E. (1992). *Research design in clinical psychology* (2nd ed.). Allyn & Bacon.

Kelly, L. D., & Sheehan, K. B. (2021). *Advertising Management in a Digital Environment*. Routledge. doi:10.4324/9781003107828

Kertai-Kiss, I. (2014). The Fit of National and Organisational Cultures in International ScientificLiterature. In Management, Enterprise and Benchmarking – In the 21St Century. Óbudai Egyetem.

Khajehpour, B., Namazie, P., & Honari, A. (2013). *A Study on Iranian Values*. NIAC Leadership Conference. Washington DC: The Simorgh Foundation.

Levitt, T. (1983). The Globalization of Markets. *Harvard Business Review*, *61*(3), 92–102.

Lipton. (2021). https://www.lipton.com/us/en/home.html

Majid, A. (2013). *Cultural influence in Advertising A Comparative analysis between Telenor TV: Advertisements in Sweden and Pakistan* [Master Thesis]. University of Gothenburg.

Massoume, P. (2001). *Culture of Iran: Codes of behavior, Iranian Experience*. https://www.iranchamber.com/culture/articles/codes_behavior.php

McCarthy, N. (2019). *40 Years On: Iran Before And After The Revolution*. https://www.statista.com/chart/16900/key-economic-social-data-about-iran/

Mohammadpur, A., Karimi, J., & Mahmoodi, K. (2013). Predicament of identity in Iran: A qualitative meta-analysis of theoretical and empirical studies on identity. *Quality & Quantity*, *48*(4), 1973–1994. doi:10.100711135-013-9875-8

Nelson, M., & Paek, H. (2007). A Content Analysis of Advertising in a Global Magazine Across Seven Countries: Implications for Global Advertising Strategies. *International Marketing Review*, *24*(1), 64–86. doi:10.1108/02651330710727196

Niray, N. & Deniz, D. (2010). İran İslam Cumhuriyeti: Tarihi, Siyaseti ve Demokrasisi. *Fırat Üniversitesi Orta Doğu Araştırmaları Dergisi*, *6*(2).

Onurlu, Ö., & Zulfugarova, N. (2016). Küresel Markaların Yerel Pazarlardaki Reklam Stratejileri İle Kültürel Farklılıklar Arasındaki İlgi Üzerine Bir Uygulama. *Öneri Dergisi, 12*(45), 491-513. Retrieved from https://dergipark.org.tr/en/pub/maruoneri/issue/17906/187980?publisher=e-dergi-marmara?publisher=e-dergi-marmara

Papavassiliou, N., & Stathakopoulos, V. (1997). Standardization Versus Adaptation of International Advertising Strategies: Towards a Framework. *European Journal of Marketing, 31*(7), 504–527. doi:10.1108/03090569710176646

Pratt, E. E. (1956). *Building export sales-advertising. In Modern International Commerce*. Allyn and Bacon.

Rajaee, F. (2007). *Islamism and Modernism The Changing Discourse in Iran*. University of Texas Press Republic of Turkey Tehran Embassy Commercial Consultancy.

Republic of Turkey Ministry of Foreign Affairs. (2021). https://www.mfa.gov.tr/iran-kunyesi.tr.mfa

Retnowati, Y. (2015). Challenges in Cross Cultural Advertising. *Humaniora. Volume, 27*, 340–349.

Richards, J., & Curran, C. (2002, Summer). Oracles On "Advertising": Searching for a Definition. *Journal of Advertising, 31*(2), 63–77. doi:10.1080/00913367.2002.10673667

Shasavandi, L. (2016). *Gender Representation in Iranian Lifestyle Magazine, Green Family: A Semiological Analysis* [Master Thesis]. Eastern Mediterranean University.

Shoraka, M. & Omidi, M. R. (2002, Spring). The Internet in Iran. *EEE Technology and Society Magazine*, 28-32.

Wang, X., & Yang, Z. (2011). Standardization or Adaptation in International Advertising Strategies: The Roles of Brand Personality and Country-of-Origin Image. *Asian Journal of Business Research, 1*(2), 25–36. doi:10.14707/ajbr.110009

Yegin, A. (2013). *İran Siyasetini Anlama Klavuzu*. Seta.

Zahed, S. (2004). Iranian national identity in the context of globalization: Dialogue or resistance? *CSGR Working Paper, 162*(5).

Zigma8. (2018). *Legal Insights On Marketing And Advertising Laws in Iran*. https://zigma8.com/legal-insights-on-marketing-and-advertising-in-iran/

Zigma8. (2021a). *Rules and Regulations of Out of Home Advertising in Iran*. https://zigma8.com/rules-and-regulations-of-out-of-home-advertising-in-iran/

Zigma8. (2021b). *Why Influencer Marketing in Iran is so popular?* https://zigma8.com/why-influencer-marketing-in-iran-is-so-popular/

KEY TERMS AND DEFINITIONS

Adaptation Strategy: Integrated marketing and advertising strategies for global brands based on cultural and local dimensions.

Harmonization Strategy: Integrated marketing and advertising strategies for global brands based on cultural and local dimensions.

Standardization Strategy: Establishing common strategies for the entire world as a single market with little meaningful variation.

Chapter 9
The Use of Celebrity Endorsement Strategy and American Impact in Japanese Advertising:
The Case of American Celebrities

Ipek Krom

https://orcid.org/0000-0002-9420-0913
Istanbul Esenyurt University, Turkey

ABSTRACT

This research aims to analyze the American impact on Japanese advertising through the use of celebrity endorsement strategy. In order to reach this aim, at first the geo-politics, economy, history, and culture of Japan is analyzed. In the research, three soft cell Japanese advertisements are chosen, in which American Hollywood and pop music icons are starring. According to the results of the research, the use of American celebrities adds popularity, attractiveness, likability, sympathy, and sexual appeal to the products as well as humor appeal to the advertisements in order to draw attention. Although Japanese cultural elements can be found in the advertisements like the masculine culture, samurai heroism, and the appreciation of the Japanese working class, the advertisements are generally under the consumption imposition of American culture with higher-status symbols, upward capitalist social comparison, and sexual objectification of women.

INTRODUCTION

In the second half of the 20th century, among Western societies, Japan and other regions in Southern Eastern Asia, goods and services were becoming more and more available. Together with a consumption ideology, the notion of consumption enabled capitalism to gain a valid and reputable position for millions of people along with a series of social, cultural and economic practices. Furthermore, the development

DOI: 10.4018/978-1-7998-9672-2.ch009

of structuralism approach by Claude Levi-Strauss, the use of signs and symbols gained importance. In such societies, the use of these signs and symbols especially gained extensive use in advertisements and became an important part of consumption culture. Consumption was becoming based on desires rather than on basic needs more and more (Bocock, 2009, pp. 12-13). On the other hand, today's postmodernist society has a consumption-based perspective over production. The sign economy has gained a global dimension and it can be stated that consumption has gained more social importance. Furthermore, since the products have similar properties the differences between products can be drawn with their connection values or through their images (Odabasi, 2004, p. 40). According to Cashmore (2006):

Consumer culture was originally built on the avarice, envy, and possessiveness that flourished in the postwar years. But it became ordinary, common, and everyday so that we eventually came to understand ourselves as the kind of creatures that had spending in our DNA. Consuming was, to use Schor's word, naturalized. Some writers have pointed out the ways in which celebrities, perhaps inadvertently, promote aspirational consumption by becoming mobile advertisements. In this sense, celebrity culture is at one with commodification – the process whereby everything, including public figures, can be converted into an article of trade to be exchanged in the marketplace (p. 12).

In order to gain competitively differential advantages, it is vital for the firms to use certain advertising strategies. These advertising strategies create positive images in the minds of the consumers while supporting the remaining elements in the marketing mix such as branding, pricing, product design and place decisions. Celebrity endorsement strategy is one of these commonly used creative advertising strategies, which help to attain this result (Erdogan, 1999). One of the reasons for the use of celebrity endorsement strategy is that we are living in a highly competitive era and the consumers are exposed to a large volume of advertisements. Celebrity endorsers enable the brands to stand out from the existing media clutter in the process of communicating the advertising messages to the consumers (Tanjung & Hudrasyah, 2016). The celebrity endorsement strategy in advertising identifies the brand with celebrities and this fact enables the brand to gain fame in a short period (Kocabas & Elden, 1997, p 129).

Japanese soft cell advertising strategy relies on celebrities extensively and is accepted as one of the most effective advertising strategies in Japan (Olafsonn, 2014; Park, 2018). The brands consider celebrity image as an important tool to communicate their messages to the public since the celebrities have a positive image in the eyes of the public (Olaffson, 2014). Aware of the fact that this trend has become phenomenal, other Asian countries have begun to follow the same marketing strategy Armielia, 2018).

In order to examine Japanese advertising from a global perspective, this research includes a literature review of Japanese country profile, Japanese advertising industry as well as the use of celebrity endorsement strategy in Japan. In the article case study method is used to examine American celebrities' appearance in Japanese advertisements, which is one of the signs of the American impact on Japanese advertising. Through studying the use of American celebrities in Japanese advertisements, the meanings that are transferred to the products and the possible impacts on the Japanese consumers are examined.

GEOGRAPHY, HISTORY, SOCIO-POLITICS, ECONOMY AND CULTURE OF JAPAN

Situated in the east coast of Asia, Japan is an island country starting from northeast stretching towards northwest for about 1500 miles (2400 km) towards the Western North Pacific Ocean. Four main islands of the country including Hokkaido, Honshu, Shikoku and Kyushu together with many smaller islands take up nearly the entire land area of Japan (Hurst, 2021). The total land area of Japan is approximately 145, 856 square miles (378,000 square kilometers) (Ministry of Foreign Affairs of Japan, Japan act Sheet, Geography & Climate).

According to the 2021 estimates, the population of Japan is 125,497.000. On the other hand, the capital city Tokyo in east-central Honshu, is one of the most populated cities in the world (Hurst, 2021). When we consider Japan in terms of land area and population, Japan is in fact a relatively small country located in Far East. Furthermore, many imperative elements that boost the economic development, doesn't exist in Japan such as raw materials like iron, coal, oil and others unlike other Western European Countries and North America. Foreign trade is vital for Japanese economy for its economic survival and development (Akgun & Calis, 2003). Therefore, through the past century, this basic fact has led the country into imperialism, war, devastation and global trade. From this point of view, economic globalization is critical in protecting Japanese well-fare (Andressen, 2002, pp. 3-4).

It is during the Heian period that Japanese system of government appeared, in which the emperor was the leading figure along with powerful families from behind the scenes. This system also laid the foundation of feudalism in Japan, which have endured for almost 700 years. Japan isolated itself from the rest of the world for centuries only to appear in the world scene reluctantly in the middle of nineteenth century (Andressen, 2002, pp. 40-8) In 1854, Commodore Matthew Perry's war treats forced the country to sign a treaty with the United States. Soon other Western powers forced treaties of their own, which opened Japan to Western disruption (Howell, 2008). Meiji Era had begun, with the imperialist signals of Japanese capitulation. However, emperor Meiji appointed a delegation the mission of examining Western countries political, commercial, economic and educational systems. After this mission the Western- Style modernization of Japan began: the constitution was changed to include an appointed parliament; the government was centralized; education system was improved; the country was industrialized and a powerful army and navy was formed (Seval, 2017). After 1931, the Japanese army had more control over politics. After the coup attempt of the army and in between 1937 and 1945, Japan was directed by military governments. The imperialist aims of the military-government first lead the county into a multifaceted war with China and then the country entered into the Second World War against the United States and its allies. The war ended with devastating results for Japan and the country was occupied for the first time in its history (Akkemik, 2019, p. 485). Hiroshima and Nagazaki was bombed by the U.S. army and the result was a social, economy-political and cultural devastation. However, one result of the post war arrangements was that the U.S. guaranteed Japan's national security for five decades (Akgun & Calis, 2003). Japan rose from its ashes and managed to become the world's third largest economy through industrialization and international trade in the following decades. Until 1970, it doubled its industrial capital and became one of the main exporters of consumer electronics, steel, optical goods and ships (Patrick & Rosovsky, 1976). During the war, there was a general hatred in between Japanese and American societies. On the other hand, according to the more recent public opinion polls, seventy-four percent of Japanese public and ninety-one percent of the American opinion leaders see each country as a reliable ally. Together with the U.S., Japan were the two largest contributors to promote economic growth and stability in the postwar era and they funded major institutions like World Bank, the International Monetary Fund and the United Nations. After the close alliance of the U.S. and Japan Soviet expansion in East Asia was blocked and this fact prepared the end of the Cold War (Green, 2007). Another important reason for Japan to build good relations with the U.S. was that the U.S. was an important market for Japanese goods and Japan developed its international relations with other countries over the U.S. Therefore, after the Cold War period Japan tried to maintain its close relationship with the U.S. and European Union (Akgun & Calis, 2003). In 1895 the Bank of Japan pursued an expansionary monetary policy due to the pressure from the U.S. to correct its trade surplus by increasing the value of Yen. The result of this was a speculative boom in real estate and equities giving rise to a severe competition in banking with reckless lending practices. This situation prepared the era of the "bubble economy" and caused a "Great Recession" in the economy. However, with the new millennium a series of market-oriented reforms were made in commerce and finance through government regulations. As these reforms stated to show their result in 2003, the rise of China as a global industrial force became a major reason for economic recovery since Japan benefited greatly from China's economic growth. After the millennium the Liberal Democratic Party (LDP) gained political dominance in Japan (Tsutsui, n. d.) and this dominance still prevails.

The indigenous religion Shinto has been a part of the lives of the Japanese society starting from the foundation of Japan up to the modern times. However, there has been a mutual influence between Shinto and Buddhist believes after the introduction of Buddhism to Japanese society in the 6th Century (Ministry of Foreign Affairs of Japan, Japan act Sheet, Religion, n.d.). Japanese school year for most elementary, junior high and high schools starts in April 1st and ends in March of the following year (Ministry of Foreign Affairs of Japan, Japan act Sheet, Education, n.d.). The percentage of Japanese high school graduates going to four-year universities was 57.9% in 2018.

Japan's political system, which dates back to 1947 is constitutional democracy with the principal of "separation of powers," in which the national government is formally divided into legislative, judicial and executive organs. The emperor, who acts as the symbol of State as well as the unity of the people, appoints the prime minister according to the nomination of the Diet and takes role only in matters of state such as declaration of amendments of the constitution, laws, treaties and cabinet orders and convention of the Diet (Ministry of Foreign Affairs of Japan, Japan Fact Sheet, Governmental Structure, n.d.). The current prime minister of Japan Fumio Kishida, who was elected to the presidency of the LDP acts as the head of the government of Japan. He has replaced Yoshihide Suga, who has resigned after one year in office. Kishida is now leading the LDP as the prime minister to succeed in the elections that will be held in November (BBC, 2021).

Suffering from a widespread deconstruction during World War II, Japan was considered as a "less developed country" during the postwar era. Two decades later, averaging an annual growth rate of 8%, Japan became the first country to gain the "developed" status during the postwar era. Japan managed this through high rates of personal savings & investment in private sector facilities, a labor force with high ethical criteria in working, an abundant supply of low-priced oil, innovative technology as well as government interference private sector industries. Due to being a major beneficiary of swift growth advanced by the International Monetary Fund and General Agreement on Tariffs and Trade based on free trade principles, in 1968 Japan became the second largest economy of the world, following the United States (Ministry of Foreign Affairs of Japan, Japan act Sheet, Economy, n.d.). During the 1970s and 80s, exports were a major reason in Japan's economic growth. Today, Japan is the world's third largest economy, and it has a considerable role in the international community as a major aid donor, source of global capital as well as credit (BBC, 2020).

Due to the fact that Japan does not have a great deal of inhabitable land, living in harmony, has become an important characteristic of Japanese culture. The reason to this is because people have had to live in close distance within communities. In addition, the climate has had an important role on the collectivist nature of Japanese society since people couldn't grow rice without the help of others in order to achieve high production in a limited amount of space. Another characteristic of Japanese culture is that they are generally tolerant of ambiguity in order to maintain harmony and increase compromise. For instance, people do not refuse each other, or say no directly even if they are in disagreement. Especially after World War II and the opening up of Japan in the 19th Century after many years of seclusion, Japanese people have become quite Westernized in order to keep up with them and as a result Western Culture lifestyles have been accepted and adopted increasingly such as wearing blue jeans, sleeping in a bed, listening to rock music and eating with knife and fork. For over a long period the Japanese have regarded silence as a virtue similar to "truthfulness." Silence in Japanese culture means implicit mutual understanding or the fact that what is true in Japan will actually exist in silence. Historically, Japan was a matrilineal society where men and women seem to have had equal relations in social, political and economic terms in their daily lives. During the medieval times, which is known as Kamakura and Muromachi periods in Japan, social and political priority was appointed to men. In comparison to most Western countries, the position of Japanese women in society is still lower than men although the relationships in between the two genders are changing rapidly nowadays since women are working outside the home as well as a new consciousness has been formed towards marriage. Following the Meiji Restoration in 1868 and after World War II, Japan promptly went through a modernization period and rebuilt the ruined country in order to become a powerful economic nation. Still today the Japanese are often regarded as diligent or sometimes to the point of workaholic (Davies & Ikeno, 2002, pp. 1-75).

JAPANESE ADVERTISING INDUSTRY AND THE JAPANESE CONSUMER

Japanese advertising market ranks as the third largest advertising market in the world, following United States and China (Statista Research Department, 2021). The literacy rate in Japan is %99 and with regard to per capita circulation of newspapers, Japan ranks as the first in the world (Ramanathan, 2011). Not long ago, television was traditionally the leading medium considering the advertising expenditures in Japan. However, after 2019 internet became the leading medium due to the increasing advertising expenditures in online and event advertising. The major reason for the growth of the internet medium was due to performance-based advertising. Until the rise in the spread of the coronavirus (COVID-19) in 2020, the total advertising expenditures saw a stable growth in Japan. However, after the spread of coronavirus the market size shrank by about 780 billion Japanese Yen up to a total of 6.2 trillion Yen. However, Japan's advertising market still accounts for more than one percent of Japan's nominal gross domestic product (GDP), which proves that advertising market holds a strong position in Japan.

The leading advertising agencies in Japan are Dentsu and Hakuhodo, both of which are headquartered in Tokyo and are active in television, marketing and promotion and internet medium fields. Dentsu, is especially a top shareholder in some television companies and therefore holds a strong position on television advertising slots. In the recent years, both agencies have become active in overseas markets along with internet advertising and acquired several foreign companies overseas (Statista Research Department, 2021).

Japan is among the few countries in the world where advertising agencies receive their payments from the clients through commissions of advertisements placed in the media. Meanwhile, major agencies give full service which is comprised of creative production functions, media purchases and marketing research. This form of media payments was abandoned at first in UK in the 1980s and later in the US in the 90s since it caused a differentiation between creative agencies as well as media buying agencies and proliferated the creative agencies in terms of creativity (Nixon, 2003 as cited in Kawashima, 2006).

As a result of the rise of globalization and the dissemination of transnational consumption practices, new socio-economic and cultural dynamics have begun to have an impact on different geographies including Japan. Global chains are one of the most prominent manifestations of this process. As a result, a new urban consumption culture has begun to transform. In Japan global branded chains are viewed as flows of commodities, images and cultural representations that connect them to the rest of the world (Grinshpun, 2012).

Japanese society is among the most consumption oriented and urbanized societies in the world. While image and style are major market commodities, the consumption patterns in Japanese cities are shaped through transnational practices and trends, primarily via the transmission of global brands and products (Grinshpun, 2012). In 2011 Japanese consumers' expenditure on the global luxury branded goods market accounted for one quarter of worldwide expenditure in this market according to Japan Market Resource Network's estimates. Although a downtown has been recorded in comparison to the 40 percent expenditure recorded in 2007 by JMRN, this rate is still a quite high number in comparison to Europe's and North America's 20 percent (JMRN, 2011 as cited in Grinshpun, 2012).

THE USE OF CELEBRITY ENDORSEMENT STRATEGY IN JAPAN

As members of people surrounded with popular culture in a globalized world, we often encounter celebrities in our daily lives in mass media. These celebrities are from any field such as sports, journalism, politics, arts and entertainment industry. According to Boorstin (1971, p. 58), who has made one of the most widely known definitions of celebrity: "the celebrity is a person who is well-known for their well-knownness." Turner (2013), on the other hand, makes a more role defining and socio-cultural description of celebrity:

Celebrity is a genre of representation and a discursive effect; it is a commodity traded by the promotions, publicity, and media industries that produce these representations and their effects; and it is a cultural formation that has a social function we can better understand (p. 10).

The use of celebrities in advertisements is called celebrity endorsement strategy and is often encountered in advertising industry worldwide. Celebrities add credibility to the endorsed products, which results in the increase of brand awareness due to factors such as the attractiveness, trustworthiness, expertise and brand-fit of the celebrity (Ugwuanyi et al., 2018). The reason firms use celebrity endorsement and invest significant amounts of payments to represent brands and organizations is due to the fact that the endorser qualities such as attractiveness, likeability and trustworthiness will be transferred to the represented product and generate successful outcomes for the advertisement campaigns. Furthermore, according to researchers, in comparison to advertisements that use non celebrities, advertisements that use celebrity endorsers attain more positive attitudes towards advertising and have a greater increase in purchase intentions (Atkin & Block, 1983; Petty et al., 1983). However, in order to avoid potential pitfalls, there needs to be a brand-fit in between the celebrity and the brand meaning the celebrity qualities should be appropriate, relevant and desirable (Erdogan, 1999). According to researchers, if the consumers consider that the celebrity is involved in unethical activities, this fact discourages them to purchase the endorsed product (Ogunsiji, 2012; Chapman & Leask, 2001).

Celebrity endorsement is a characteristics of Japanese advertisement industry (Olaffson, 2014; Park, 2018; Armiela, 2018). According to Kilborn (1998, as cited in Praet, 2001) more than %70 percent of Japanese TV advertisements make use of celebrity endorsement strategy. One of the most important reasons for the frequent use of this strategy is that %90 percent of the consumers find such advertisements more likable, popular or memorable in comparison to other advertisements as stated by Video Research. Another reason for the frequent use of celebrity endorsement in Japanese advertising is that Japanese consumers find these messages more trustworthy (Melville, 1999). According to Praet (2001)'s research findings in Japanese TV advertising celebrities are featured much more often than countries like France and U.S. Since most of the Japanese advertisements last for as long as 15 seconds, having a strong dynamic in order to draw attention is a critical factor and celebrities are a highly important feature to provide this impact (Asahina, 1997, as cited in Yamada, 2005).

Furthermore, foreignness and the use of foreign celebrities is a common strategy for Japanese advertisers. According to Yasutake (1983, as cited in Yamada, 2005) foreign elements are used in Japanese advertisements, because this strategy draws interest and enables the marketers to differentiate their products from others. According to this research around %46,2 of Japanese advertisements includes foreign elements such as celebrities, phrases, scenery and messages. Another important point is that around two thirds of these foreign elements employed in these advertisements indicate American or European influence.

THE CASE ANALYSIS OF THE USE OF CELEBRITY ENDORSEMENT STRATEGY AND AMERICAN IMPACT ON JAPANESE ADVERTISEMENT INDUSTRY

Aim and Methodology

The aim of this study is to research the cultural characteristics of Japanese advertising and to find out the impact of American influence on Japanese advertising through use of celebrity endorsement strategy. The methodology of this research is case study analysis. According to Yin case study is a research method that is used in order to interpret various situations like phenomena related to individuals, groups, organizations, society, politics and others. Yin classifies case studies into three groups including explanatory, exploratory and descriptive. Explanatory case studies are preferred when research questions include "how" and "why" questions to analyze situations that have operational links over a time period rather than frequencies (Yin, 2003, pp. 1-7). In order to reach this aim, the explanatory case study method is used in this research. In the study three Japanese advertisement in which well-known American Hollywood and Pop Music Celebrities star in are taken as multiple case studies. The universe of the study is Japanese originated products' advertisements in which American celebrities are used in some way such as starring artist, voiceover and etc. In the research the purposive sampling method is used and all selected advertisements are broadcasted in 2021 in order to give a recent perspective. Two of the selected advertisements portray the celebrities as unusual characters which is a typical part of Japanese soft sell advertising. This fact in fact originates from the notion of "hen na gaijin", which can be translated as strange foreigner. Japanese actors traditionally never engage in such unusual behavior unless they are professional comedians. Through this unusual performance of foreign actors, comic relief is tried to be achieved in Japanese advertising (Olaffson, 2014, p. 19). The first advertisement chosen is the Laudrin' Home ad of Nature Lab, in which American pop icon Katy Perry is shown fantastically as a Dalmatian dog. The second advertisement is the 2021 version of Boss Coffee Alien Jones Investigating Earth series in which Tommy Lee Jones acts as an alien. Finally, in other to give a holistic perspective Shiseido 2021 advertisement in which American pop icon Lady Gaga acts as herself is chosen. In the study the answers of the following research questions are explored:

Research Question 1: What are the Japanese cultural characteristics portrayed in the advertisements?
Research Question 2: How is Japanese culture influenced by American subculture as its portrayed in the advertisements?
Research Question 3: How is the celebrity endorsement strategy used in the advertisements?

Evaluation of the Research Data

Laudrin' Home and Katy Perry: Japanese Soft-Cell Advertisement

This Japanese advertisement of Laudrin' Home brand of Nature Lab is starring Katy Perry and is produced in 2021 (Katy Perry Fanatics, 2021). Laudrin' Home is a Japanese home scented products brand which includes products like laundry detergents, laundry softeners, fabric refreshers and room diffusers (Laudrin' Home, 2021). The advertisement is produced in a luxury mansion in California, U.S.A. (Japan News, 2021). In the advertisement as soon as the landlord leaves the house- as we realize this fact from the closing of the door from the inside and the male raincoat hanging on the raincoat stand- the Dalmatian dog of the house that is inside fantastically transforms into Katy Perry wearing white and polka-dot clothes holding a Laudrin' fabric refresher in her hand. She sprays the refresher towards the raincoat and the hat. Immediately the raincoat and the hat come alive and start dancing. Next, we see the cuckoo clock bird come out and sing and meanwhile Katy Perry is singing her song 'Smile'. As she continues walking and dancing in the mansion singing her song, she sprays the fabric refresher to the armchair. Together with this the armchair comes alive as it starts dancing and moving around the house together with her. Later on, we see the room diffuser joining the tempo of the song and the coffee table under it starts dancing. Then, the Dalmatian Lady adds Laudrin' fabric softener to the washing machine and later on we see the Dalmatian Lady moving and dancing in the house with Laudrin' fabric refresher in her hand together with the dancing armchair, raincoat hanger and washing machine. In the next scene we see Laudrin' products with the subtitles of "My Sweet Home" and the female voiceover says, "My sweet home, Laudrin' at home." Then, we hear the sound effect of a car door locking with remote control and the Dalmatian Lady looks at the audience in a panic. Then she transforms herself again as the Dalmatian dog of the house and we see the door opening. As the advertisement is produced in a Californian style luxury mansion, we see that the setting that the advertisement takes place is entirely American and symbolizes a high status. The furnishing of the house is entirely American style as well. However, the painting on the wall showing Napoleon together with a ball-room dressed lady reminds us of French aristocracy origin. The strongest American symbol in the advertisement is the world-famous American pop star Katy Perry. However, in the advertisement she is portrayed as a Dalmatian dog. Dalmatian dog is also of American Hollywood Culture from the famous film 101 Dalmatians. These symbols portray the high-status life pointed in the advertisements and reveal that the product is intended to appear as a high-status brand. The Japanese elements presented in the in the advertisement is the fantastic transfiguration of the Dalmatian dog into a Dalmatian Lady taking care of the house. The Dalmatian Lady in fact symbolizes the Geisha culture with her singing as well as dancing performance and caretaking to please the landlord. The fact that Perry is indeed a transfigured dog is also an emotional connection to draw the attention of the audience and adds humor appeal to the advertisement. Another important factor that draws attention, adds popularity as well as likability to the advertisement is the use of celebrity endorsement strategy. The fact that fantastic Dalmatian Lady is Katy Perry adds humor to the advertisement and adds a higher status brand image to the Laudrin' brand. Furthermore, the singing and dancing of the Dalmatian Lady to the audience like a geisha makes the target audience feel that the celebrity is one of them and they feel sympathy.

Iron Boss Coffee and Tommy Lee Jones: Japanese Soft-Cell Advertisement

The 2021 version of the Iron Boss Coffee advertisement (Yorkie, 2020) is one of the recent advertisements of Alien Jones investigating earth series, in which Tommy Lee Jones stars as an alien examining the world disguised as the Hollywood actor Tommy Lee Jones. In the series he undertakes working class jobs and enjoys drinking Boss Coffee. In the advertisements he performs in Hollywood action films like scenes. He is indeed the humorous version of the Japanese hard-working workers, whose extreme efforts had important roles in handling with the economic crisis (Burkett and Hart-Landsberg, 2010). Japanese society can be considered as workaholic and extreme pressures and expectations lies on the shoulders of the working class According to Ono, in order not to disrupt the group harmony or because their bosses do not take holidays, workers refrain from taking holiday leaves. The reason to this is because in comparison to the individualistic and non-hierarchical nature of the Western societies, Japanese society is collectivist and hierarchical. (Demetriou, 2020). In the advertisement we first see Alien Jones placing documents in his briefcase and a colleague warning him not to be late for the meeting with top customers and to take a taxi. Jones replies as "Got it" and running towards the skyscraper window he jumps down from the window of the skyscraper breaking the glass window. We start hearing the soundtrack of the Hollywood film Mission Impossible. Falling down from the skyscraper, he lands on the floor breaking the stone tile ground. To the surprise of the people around falling down with the immense power, next he jumps on the top of a taxi. He holds on to the taxi's roof sign and breaks it. Next, he starts sliding on the taxi roof sign holding on to the taxi from behind. Both the lady in the taxi and his colleague looking down from the broken skyscraper window looks surprised. His colleague says, "He's surprisingly energetic today". Then he starts running up the wall of another skyscraper. Talking on the mobile phone, Jones says, "I will be there in one minute," while still running up the wall of the skyscraper. His colleague looks in a wondering manner at the Iron Boss Coffee can on the copying machine and says, "Is it because he drank this?" Next, we see Jones breaking through two walls and entering the meeting room with cement wall pieces shattering around. He stands before the people in the room with his briefcase in his hand and says, "Sorry to keep you waiting," while covered in cement wall dust. To the surprise of the staff in the meeting room, Jones says, "Here are the documents," and starts distributing a copy of the documents to each person in the meeting room. Then the male voiceover makes the interpretation of

Jones saying, "On this planet sometimes one is unusually brimming with energy." Then we see an Iron Boss Coffee can dropping down to the shelf of the beverage vending machine. In the following scene we see his colleague holding the Iron Boss Coffee can. He says, "Maybe I will try, too" and as soon as he drinks the coffee, he looks amazed as Mission Impossible soundtrack starts playing again. Then, it writes "For When Coffee Isn't Enough," on the yellow screen and next we see an Iron Boss Coffee can with splashing yellow liquid. The voiceover says "Boss Coffee Energy drink," as we hear another voiceover saying, "Iron Boss" in a accentuated tone. The Iron Boss Coffee is a new energy drink from Boss Coffee Brand and in the advertisement, we see many scenes similar to Hollywood action films like Matrix, Back to the Future and Captain America. For instance, the jumping down from the window scene is similar to that of the film Captain America in which Steve jumps down from one building window breaking inside from the window of another building. However, this scene is more of original although its similar as Alien Jones directly jumps down from the window of the skyscraper towards the floor. His landing down scene with scattered cement tile pieces is similar to that of the film Matrix Reloaded in which Morpheus jumps from one skyscraper to another breaking the ground. Still in the advertisement Jones lands down in an immense power. Neo also jumps from the skyscraper in this film; however he falls down to the ground as the ground swallows him and then throws him out. Jones' sliding on the taxi cab roof sign is similar to that of Marty McFly escaping from Biff's gang riding on a skateboard he made out of a child's soapbox. Running up the wall scene is similar to Trinity running up and across two walls and breaking wall scene is similar to that of Steve's unsuccessful attempt to break the wall in Captain America. Although they have similarities the scenes in the advertisement are different than the ones in the Hollywood films, are more exaggerated and successful portraying Alien Jones like a super hero. Indeed with his super heroic character in the films after drinking Iron Boss Coffee, Jones portrays a humor added version of the struggle of the hardworking Japanese working class. In the advertisement an appreciation can be examined for the working-class efforts in the Japanese culture. The Hollywood action scenes on the other hand represent the extreme conditions due to capitalism. In the advertisement Jones is more successful in his action scenes and this represents the Japanese working class victory against capitalism from a capitalist Japanese point of view under American influence. The celebrity endorsement strategy use in the advertisement with Tommy Lee Jones as an alien imitating Hollywood scenes, draws the target audience's attention to the advertisement making it popular and adds on to the humor and likability impact.

Shiseido and Lady Gaga: Japanese Soft-Cell Advertisement

Shiseido is a Japanese originated luxury cosmetics brand which is world widely known. The 2021 advertisement of Shiseido with Lady Gaga features the popular American pop singer as herself (AngieRazzi, 2015). The advertisement starts with the text Shiseido with Lady Gaga introducing the celebrity endorsement strategy use of the brand and to create brand awareness. In the first scene Lady Gaga opens the white door of a hotel room from the inside with a light make up in an everyday routine. As the door opens the song Cheek to Cheek sang by Lady Gaga begins. Next, we see her opening bathroom curtains wearing a velvet hair bonnet, funky glasses and hair curler preparing for an occasion. She opens the bathroom curtain several times hiding behind it as if starting a performance and then looks behind a wall to the target holding a flower. Next, we see Lady Gaga sitting before a dressing table, receiving a cup of tea from someone and later putting make up on. Meanwhile the voiceover we hear Lady Gaga saying, "Everyone shines in their own unique way. But only you know what your beauty is". Meanwhile she is playing with her dog, which is wearing the same purple color velvet hook as her bonnet while she imitates applying make-up on the dog. Next, we see her dressed in a white night gown lying on the bed playing with her dog. Then we see her closing a closet before the eyes of the target audience. In the next scene in black and white we see Lady Gaga walking out a premier. She starts giving poses to the media walking on the red carpet. As soon as she gets inside her Limousine the scene gains color again. Inside the Limousine Lady Gaga takes of her blonde wig and starts dressing up in her own different style. Meanwhile the voiceover of Lady Gaga says, "Don't let anyone tell you what makes you beautiful." Then she attends an after party in a joyful manner and gets excitedly welcomed by her friends. Then she starts enjoying the after party and at last as she closes a red velvet curtain the voiceover Lady Gaga says, "Be yourself. That is what make you beautiful." In the final scene we see the red logo of Shiseido and the voiceover Lady Gaga says, "Shiseido." In the entire advertisement we see the opening of the doors, the curtains as well as the closing of closets and curtains giving the message that the life of a celebrity is a show. The textual and visual argument of the advertisement is that beauty should be defined by personal standards, not by expectations. However, there are important conflicts regarding beauty understanding in the advertisement. When Lady Gaga opens the door and welcomes the target audience to her daily life, although she is wearing a light make up, she is dressed and prepared as if she is going out for an occasion in comparison to a normal woman's standards. The day especially chosen to reveal the life of Lady Gaga is not an ordinary day. She is about to attend a premiere and getting ready for it. Furthermore, even though half of the advertisement is about her getting ready for the occasion, she looks stylish in all the scenes although she should be without make up with wet and tangled hair. The premiere scene is intentionally shown in black and white as if to give the message that Shiseido doesn't define beauty from social standards and expectations. The following scenes in which Lady Gaga is dressed up to her own personal standards are shown in color and a lively manner to underline this message. However, the during the entire advertisement the celebrity is under a beauty imposition, which conflicts with the given message since the definition of beauty in the advertisement is made from the outside looks rather than giving importance to inner beauty. The advertisement reveals the emphasis Japanese culture imposes regarding the beauty of a women, which accordingly is defined from outside looks rather than inside. In the advertisement scenes Lady Gaga is constantly is opposed to scopophilia that is male gaze in which the female face and body objectified is a source of pleasure. According to this term reversibly being looked at is also a source of pleasure (Mulvey, 1975, p. 8), which turns the woman into a sexual object. The advertisement also reveals the consumption culture of America under the imposition of beauty. According to these masculine standards a woman has to look beautiful in all occasions turning her into a sexual object who is gender role is always to arise desire even though she can be famous, well-known, working or self-made. On the other hand, the use of celebrity image strategy adds a high status to the brand. The star seems to be shown in daily routine to create sympathy and an American pop icon is used to give attractiveness and add popularity to the brand.

CONCLUSION

Japan has long been under American political, cultural and economic imperialism and impact throughout history. Once economically devastated in the Second World War, the military protection and the trade support of America have opened up Japanese economy to the world. On the other hand, through intelligent economic development policies including manufacture of high-technology and process industry trade as well as the existence of a productive working class, Japan has managed to overcome the economic turbulences caused by United States like the Second World War and bubble economy becoming the third economic power in the world. Consumption and the dissemination of consumption culture are the important elements of American capitalism ideology and globalization. Through the adaptation of capitalism ideology with the American impact, Japan has also become a culturally materialistic society in which status signs and brands play an important role. As we can see from the advertisements status symbols play an important role in Japanese society. In all the advertisements analyzed we can see the use of brand image strategy through celebrity endorsement strategy. The fact that these celebrities are of American origin and world-wide famous add power to the high-status sign image of the products. The use of these American celebrities adds popularity, likability and attractiveness to the products. Furthermore, as Katy Perry stars as a dog and Tommy Lee Jones stars as an alien add humor appeal to the advertisements, since both Perry and Jones are world famous celebrities. This factor draws the attention of the target audience to the advertisements. Using world famous celebrities for all brands, also gives strength to the brand identities and positions the products in the target audience's mind as prominent, popular, attractive, likable Japanese originated international brands. Katy Perry's dancing and singing performance like a Geisha and Tommy Lee Jones' super-heroic performance representing the well appreciated working class are among the examined Japanese cultural elements in the advertisements. In this way, the target audience can feel sympathy towards the celebrities and this factor enables the target audience to develop positive attitude for the products as well as emotional connections. The advertisements also reveal a masculine Japanese culture as Japan rates at 95 percent in masculinity being among the most masculine societies in the world. Workaholism, excellence and perfectionism in material production, hard-working are among the signs of masculine organizational culture (Hofstede Insights, n.d.) we can see in Iron Boss Coffee Advertisements. This fact is also an upward social comparison of the capitalist Japan and a sign of American impact. Furthermore, Katy Perry's role as a Dalmatian Dog symbolizing the female companion and Lady Gaga's presentation in sexually objectified terms for the male gaze taking pleasure in exhibition through the use of scopophilic terms are also signs of a masculine culture both in Japanese culture and American culture. Especially the beauty imposition in Shiseido advertisement is an objectification of woman imposed by the American image culture. Although the advertisements preserve their Japanese cultural origin, we can state that they are generally under American consumption influence with higher-status symbols, upward capitalist social comparison and sexual objectification of women.

FUTURE RESEARCH DIRECTIONS

This research analyses celebrity endorsement strategy used Japanese advertisements from the scope of American impact using case study method. Celebrity endorsement strategy is a highly used advertisement strategy in Japanese advertising. On the other hand, this study is a first with its focus on American impact. For future research other Japanese advertisements can be analyzed using semiotics, content analysis and other methods. Furthermore, the impact of globalization on Japanese advertisements can be studied for future directions.

ACKNOWLEDGMENT

I would like to thank to Prof. Dr. Celal Oktay Yalın and Associate Prof. Dr. Selda Ene for their valuable insights.

REFERENCES

Akgun, B., & Calis, S. (2003). Reluctant giant: The rise of Japan and its role in the post-cold war era, *Perceptions. Journal of International Affairs*, *8*(1), 1–13.

Akkemik, K. A. (2019). *Japonya'nin iktisadi ve sosyal tarihi Cilt:1 Savas oncesi donem (-1945)* [The economic and social history of Japan Vol: I Pre-War period (-1945)]. Bilgi Universitesi Yayinlari.

Andressen, C. (2002). *A short history of Japan: From samurai to sony*. Allen & Unwin.

AngieRazzi. (2015). YouTube, Lady Gaga Shiseido (campaign) commercial full official HD, https://www.youtube.com/watch?v=irD-NJ27Y7k

Armiela, A. A. (2018). Celebrity endorsement in Japan tourism based on consumer celebrity worship. *Ultima Management*, *10*(2), 65–80. doi:10.31937/manajemen.v10i2.982

Atkin, C., & Block, M. (1983). Effectiveness of celebrity endorsers. *Journal of Advertising Research*, *23*(March), 57–6I.

BBC News. (2020, September 16). *Japan country profile*. https://www.bbc.com/news/world-asia-pacific-14918801

BBC News. (2021, 4 October). *Japan's parliament elects former diplomat Fumio Kishida as new prime minister.* https://www.bbc.com/news/world-asia-58784635

Bocock, R. (2009). *Tuketim* [Consumption]. Dost Kitabevi Yayinlari.

Boorstin, D. (1971). *The image: A guide to pseudo-events in America*. Atheneum.

Burkett, P., & Hart-Landsberg, M. (2003). The economic crisis in Japan: Mainstream perspective and an alternative view. *Critical Asian Studies*, *35*(3), 339–372. doi:10.1080/14672710320000109881

Cashmore, E. (2006). *Celebrity/ culture*. Taylor & Francis e-library.

Chapman, S., & Leask, J. A. (2001). Paid celebrity endorsement in health promotion: A case study from Australia. *Health Promotion International*, *16*(4), 333–338. doi:10.1093/heapro/16.4.333 PMID:11733452

Davies, R. G., & Ikeno, O. (2002). *The Japanese mind: Understanding contemporary Japanese culture*. Tuttle Publishing.

Demetriou, D. (2020). Employees in the country whose brutal office culture has led to several deaths are beginning to rethink the tradition. *BBC Worklife*. https://www.bbc.com/worklife/article/20200114-how-the-japanese-are-putting-an-end-to-death-from-overwork

Erdogan, Z. (1999). Celebrity endorsement: A literature review. *Journal of Marketing Management, 15*(4), 291–314. doi:10.1362/026725799784870379

Fanatics, K. P. (2021). YouTube, Katy Perry x Laudrin Home (Ad), https://www.youtube.com/watch?v=SDtc-SpV92Y

Green, M. J. (2007). The U.S.-Japan alliance: A brief strategic history. *Education about Asia, 12*(3), 25-30.

Grinshpun, H. (2012). The city and the chain: Conceptualizing globalization and consumption in Japan. *Japan Review, 24*, 169–195.

Hurst, G. C. (2021). Japan. In *Britannica*. https://www.britannica.com/place/Japan

Insights, H. (n.d.). *Country comparison*. https://www.hofstede-insights.com/country-comparison/japan/

Japan News. (2021). *World famous star Katy Perry is reappointed as Randolin's new muse! Appeared in a cute Dalmatian.* Nature Lab. Co. Ltd. https://re-how.net/all/1349144/

Kawashima. (2006). Advertising agencies, media and consumer market: the changing quality of TV advertising in Japan. *Media, Culture & Society, 28*(3), 393-410.

Kocabas, M., & Elden, M. (1997). *Reklam ve yaratici strateji: Konumlandirma ve star stratejisinin analizi* [Advertising and creative strategy: Positioning and the analysis of celebrity endorsement strategy]. Yayinevi Yayincilik.

Laudrin' Home. (2021). https://www.laundrin.jp/?_ga=2.147118195.593313241.1638015063-448976400.1637432911

Melville, I. (1999). *Marketing in Japan*. Butterworth Heinemann.

Ministry of Foreign Affairs of Japan. (n.d.a). *Web Japan, Japan fact sheet, Economy*. https://web-japan.org/factsheet/en/pdf/e04_economy.pdf

Ministry of Foreign Affairs of Japan. (n.d.b). *Web Japan, Japan fact sheet, Geography & climate*. https://web-japan.org/factsheet/en/pdf/e01_geography.pdf

Ministry of Foreign Affairs of Japan. (n.d.c). *Web Japan, Japan fact sheet, Governmental structure*. https://web-japan.org/factsheet/en/pdf/e08_governmental.pdf

Mulvey, L. (1975). Visual pleasure and narrative cinema. *Screen, 16*(3), 6–18. doi:10.1093creen/16.3.6

Odabasi, Y. (2004). *Postmodern pazarlama: tuketim ve tuketici* [Postmodern marketing: Consumption and consumer]. Kapital Medya.

Ogunsiji, A. S. (2012). The impact of celebrity endorsement on strategic brand management. *International Journal of Business and Social Science, 3*(6), 141–145.

Olaffson, J. B. (2014). *Advertising to the Japanese consumer: Japanese advertising culture examined* [Bacholor's Thesis]. Sigillum University.

Park, J. (2018). Celebrity advertising in Japan: Tommy Lee Jones as alien investor in Suntory TV commercials. *Journal of Global Media Studies, 22*, 51–57.

Patrick, H., & Rosovsky, H. (1976). Understanding the Japanese economic miracle [Review of Asia's new giant: How the Japanese economy works]. *Brookings Bulletin (Washington, D.C.), 13*(1), 4–7.

Petty, R. E., Cacioppo, J. T., & Schuman, D. (1983). Central and peripheral routes to advertising effectiveness: The moderating role of involvement. *The Journal of Consumer Research, 10*(December), 135–146. doi:10.1086/208954

Praet, C. L. C. (2001). Japanese advertising, The world's number one celebrity showcase? A cross-cultural comparison of the frequency of celebrity appearances in TV advertising. *Proceedings of the 2001 Special Asia-Pacific Conference of the American Academy of Advertising*, 6-13.

Ramanathan, S. (2011). *Advertising self regulation in Asia and Australiasia.* Asian Federation of Advertising Associations. https://icas.global/wp-content/uploads/2011_04_Ad_SR_Asia_Australia.pdf

Seval, H. F. (2017). Japon kalkınmasının temel taşı: Meiji restorasyonu ve Iwakura heyeti [The basic stone of Japan's development: Meiji restoration and Iwakura construction]. *Is ve Hayat, 3*(5), 101–118.

Skov, L., & Moeran, B. (1995). Introduction: Hiding in the light: from Oshin to Yoshimoto Banana. In L. Skov & B. Moeran (Eds.), Women, media and consumption in Japan. University of Hawaii Press.

Statista Research Department. (2021). *Major ad agencies Japan 2019: Based on sales revenue.* https://www.statista.com/statistics/1009998/japan-leading-advertising-agencies-by-sales/

Tanjung, S., & Hudrasyah, H. (2016). The impact of celebrity and non-celebrity endorser credibility in the advertisement on attitude towards advertisement: Attitude towards brand and purchase intention, *International Conference on Ethics of Business, Economics, and Social Science Proceeding*, 231-45.

Tsutsui, W. M. (n.d.). *Late Twentieth Century Japan: An introductory essay, Imagining Japanese History.* Program for Teaching East Asia, University of Colorado. https://www.colorado.edu/ptea-curriculum/sites/default/files/attached-files/20-essay.pdf

Turner, G. (2013). *Understanding Celebrity.* Sage Publications.

Ugwuanyi, C. C., Okeke, C., & Emezue, L. (2018). Celebrity advertising, brand awareness and brand recognition: A structural equation modelling approach. *European Journal of Business and Management, 10*(28), 17–24.

Yamada, M. (2005). *An analysis of Japanese TV commercials that feature foreign celebrities: A content analytic and interview approach* [Graduate Thesis]. University of Oklahoma.

Yin, R. K. (2003). *Case study research: Design and method* (3rd ed.). Sage Publications.

Yorkie, (2020). YouTube, Spaceman Jones Iron Boss-Japanese AD-Tommy Lee Jones, https://www.youtube.com/watch?v=xHugeSZcJSI

Chapter 10
TV Commercial Space in the UAE:
A Regional Hub for Advertisement Production

Suzana Dzamtoska Zdravkovska
American University of Ras Al Khaimah, UAE

Sabir Haque
American University of Ras Al Khaimah, UAE

ABSTRACT

A thriving media ecosystem today requires a vibrant content production ecosystem. The MENA region today boasts several established and emerging media ecosystems. Key criteria essential for establishing a healthy media production workflow are location, production, infrastructure and support, incentives and investment returns, city infrastructure and safety, as well as access to talent. This chapter aims to establish UAE as a hotspot for film and TV production, making it a regional hub for television advertising production. The study includes the new framework of UAE media strategy, looking close into the media regulations which have revolutionized the media-free zones in all the emirates of the UAE. The research approach is of an exploratory and descriptive nature involving a problem-centered interview (PCI) that offers a structured interview procedure investigating individual perspectives on the UAE film and TV advertising industry.

INTRODUCTION

The growth of the media ecosystem worldwide since the birth of film and television is unprecedented. Content production is at the core of this growth story. It can take any shape, but what remains at the center of this progress story is a thriving global media ecosystem. The MENA (Middle East and North Africa) region has several established media ecosystems, many competing to be the best in the region.

DOI: 10.4018/978-1-7998-9672-2.ch010

UAE has claimed among the top spots, establishing itself as a regional center for film, television, and social media. The success can be attributed to UAE's world-class infrastructure and its ideal geographical location. It offers excellent incentives to producers seeking to produce films and other content in the country.

Dubai shot into prominence with the launch of Dubai Media City in 2001. The city has, over time, become a growth story, and so has the media city, attracting talents from all over the world with its foray into filmmaking, advertising, and television broadcasting. Abu Dhabi too joined media production with the creation of Twofour54 in the year 2008. Since then, it has grown manifold by offering some attractive ownership possibilities and ease in registration and licensing. The facility houses a campus-like collaborative space, including a studio of 300,000 sq km. The area also has an advanced post-production facility. Within a decade of its setup, Abu Dhabi announced a new offer of waiving license and registration for new companies and freelancers for two years. Some of the major blockbusters shot in the UAE recently are Star Wars: The Force Awakens, 6 Underground, and Mission Impossible - Ghost Protocol. More than 90 productions from the Hollywood and Indian film industry have been shot in the UAE.

Suppose we investigate the essential requirements for creating a healthy media production ecosystem. The following areas can be identified as key to its success: location, production support with the proper infrastructure, incentives and return to investment, city infrastructure, safety, and access to talent.

The most effective way to create awareness of a brand is through TV Advertising. But that's changing as TV AD spending moves towards the digital realm as the TV advertising business model is seeing a dramatic shift. This chapter focuses on the TV commercial space in the UAE, which has become a regional hub for Television Advertising production. The region's challenging economic state, mainly due to the Covid 19 pandemic, has disrupted the economy, but the shift was already underway. Even though ad spending has declined since 2015, UAE is still among the region's leading advertising markets.

The over-the-top (OTT) media services are forecasted to drive the growth of the reinvented TV advertising business model. The reason for such a reach and retention offered by OTT services is due to its 100% video advertising viewable and non-skippable features. These are included in all the leading OTT platforms such as Netflix, Amazon Prime Video, and the newly commissioned Disney Plus. These types of advertisements are called Subscription Supported Video-on-Demand Services. As the audience views such ads, it reinforces the brand's image. As per Magna Global (2021), OTT video ad spending is expected to reach $5 billion globally in a year. UAE's own homegrown OTT streaming service, such as Starzplay, has added anime content, a Turkish TV channel, and an exclusive sports partnership over the last year. The service has seen a sharp growth in its subscription base through sign-ups, conversions, and consumption in the TV streaming industry.

Meanwhile, Digital advertising has been appealing to a growing number of advertisers since it creates opportunities for smaller budgets, often on a fully automatized ecosystem, for all sorts of ad formats. Ad expenditures in the digital environment already surpassed the amounts spent on traditional TV screens in the UAE. TV advertising remains by far the most efficient medium in terms of brand image safety and viewers' conversion into actual consumers, the industry seems to have reached a turning point with last year's crisis. However, with new capabilities brought onto TV screens by the deployment of IP based receptions and digital OTT services, the growing proportion of households equipped with connected screens, and the integration of advanced features in traditional linear broadcast streams, new opportunities are flourishing for advanced advertising products bridging the gap between TV and digital. This study will closely follow the transition and provide an outlook for the future.

COUNTRY PROFILE OF UAE

UAE is strategically placed on the southern side of the Strait of Hormuz, which overlooks the vital port for crude oil. UAE shares a border with Oman and Saudi Arabia and comprises seven self-governed states. The seven emirates are Abu Dhabi, Dubai, Sharjah, Ras Al Khaimah, Ajman, Umm Al-Qaiwain, and Fujairah. The emirates bring four ecosystems to the country: desert, maritime, freshwater, and mountains. On 2nd December 1971, the country was declared a federal state.

Abu Dhabi is believed to have more than one-tenth of the world's proven oil reserves, making it a key contributor to the national budget. Its first ruler and President of the union, Sheikh Zayed Bin Sultan Al Nahyan, used the oil reserves to usher in a new era by investing heavily in education, health care, and the country's infrastructure. The commercialization of oil reserves meant an increase in the income level of the Emirati population. The government soon adopted a policy for a large influx of expat laborers into the country's infrastructure projects. In the last three decades, the UAE has become a multicultural, multiethnic society, with over two-thirds of the population being expats, mainly from India, Pakistan, Bangladesh, and the Philippines.

Historically, traditional Emiratis were nomads, called Bedouins, living a lifestyle of a small oasis farming. The oil economy made spectacular changes to the country's desert environment, leading to massive forestation projects with the spread of desert farms in Al Ain, then moving to the rest of the country. It was broadly a desert economy and sea-oriented culture, including parling and sea trading due to the vicinity of operational ports.

UAE's leadership has embarked on an ambitious plan to diversify the economy from heavy hydrocarbon reliance to lead the country into new economic sectors. The power distribution within the country was an equitable federal and individual emirate distributed equally between the seven emirates. It was the vision of the nation's founder, Sheikh Zayed Bin Sultan Al Nahyan, to modernize the country. He was instrumental in bringing the emirates together into the union, making him the natural choice for the inaugural president of the country. He remained president until he died in 2004.

On the other hand, Dubai holds for itself a unique position among the emirates by facilitating international financial flows. In 1991, Dubai's oil production peaked at 410,000 barrels per day. Today, It can be called a post-oil state, sharing a symbiotic relationship with Abu Dhabi. Over the years, it has become a global commercial center, from a regional trading center to a smart global city. Dubai has led the country towards economic diversification, driven by construction and real estate. Abu Dhabi soon followed suit.

But the economic crises in 2008-09 led by the real estate crash exposed Dubai to more than 120 billion dollars in debt. Abu Dhabi came in to bail out Dubai, met all its immediate financial obligations, and brought the country's economy towards stability. The federal government and Dubai's authorities have taken concrete steps toward stabilizing the economy and restoring investor confidence after the crisis. Despite the enormous financial and social impact of the credit crisis, it is widely seen as having been a catalyst for essential sector reforms that will help sustain economic growth in the future. Over the years, the local authorities have responded to the economic downturn with various measures to narrow the deficit by reining in spending. The creation of free zones is central to Dubai's development strategy as it has become an essential vehicle for the government to attract foreign investments. Today, Dubai has significant stakes in several large companies operating in the country as they are often referred to as government-related entities (GREs). The government has created an eclectic diversification strategy through the GREs with a portfolio of business and services that includes seaports, real estate, hotels, airports, and other companies across the globe.

After the economic crisis and bailout by Abu Dhabi, the rule of Abu Dhabi and the President of the UAE, Sheikh Khalifa bin Zayed gradually withdrew from public life due to his ill health. Continuing the economic leverage over Dubai, Crown Prince Mohammed Bin Zayed Al Nahyan became the country's de-facto leader, starting a new chapter in the country's history. He also introduced a new foreign policy with his unique focus on the country's internal and external security in response to the 2011 Arab Spring. Together with the ruler of Dubai and prime minister of the country, Mohammed Bin Rashid Al Maktoum, they are known as the pioneers of the country's modern development.

In May 2022, the official WAM news agency announced the death of the ailing President Sheikh Khalifa bin Zayed. Sheikh Mohammed bin Zayed Al Nahyan was elected as the third president of UAE, continuing the unity and stability of the nation.

Post pandemic, the most prominent spectacle of EXPO 2020 Dubai, ran from October 2021 until March 2022. The theme of Connecting Minds and Creating the future coincided with UAE's 50th-anniversary celebration and defined the country's economic and geopolitical position in the world. It also helped cement the country's status as a sound financial center despite the regional tension as manifested in the conflict in Yemen aided by Iran.

UAE MEDIA LANDSCAPE

Satellite Television and Growth of the Media Industry

In 1969, Abu Dhabi Television became the first TV channel in the UAE. Many more stations and channels began their operation soon after. Dubai joined ranks in 1972 with a television channel, and in 1977, it launched a television exclusively for its expat population: Dubai 33. Between 1972 and 1980, the Ministry of Culture rolled out a comprehensive territorial network for TV and Radio. It catered to the country's emerging news outlets until today (UAE's Media Landscape: An Overview, 2017).

Satellite television revolutionized the industry in the 1990s. The growth spurred Dubai and Abu Dhabi broadcasters to air their content to an international audience. The growth in the industry led to the launch of the country's first media-free zone (MFZ) in Dubai. Since its launch in 2002, various foreign media outlets have been operating in Dubai. The opportunity to produce content for a foreign audience in a tax-free environment appealed to the leading broadcasters from the world and opened offices in the media-free zone. They had to still abide by the local laws and MFZ's guidelines (UAE's Media Landscape: An Overview, 2017). The most popular networks that opened their offices were the BBC, CNN, AFP, and Al-Arabiya.

For the Arab region to thrive in the creative business and cater to the entire region, it needs to have an integrated capability of local expertise and a stable economy (Dubai SME & An Agency of the Department of Economic Development – Government of Dubai, 2010). The report looks into the opportunities available in the media industry in the region and points toward why the UAE is the best possible location to build a world-class content creation zone in the world at large. Noting that the industry has been a focus area of development since 2001, with government investment in infrastructure in the form of Dubai Media City (DMC), the report highlights:

Additionally, DMC also paved way for Television broadcasters in the Gulf and multinational advertising agencies to cater to the growing base of large companies in free zones like JAFZA[1] and DAFZA[2]". The industry has been completely led by government initiatives like DMC and the new free zones: International Media Production Zone and Dubai Studio City. In the 10 years since its inception the industry has grown into a cluster of large and small media companies catering to the media requirements of not only the domestic market but the entire Arab world (Mauritania to Oman) (p. 8).

The report further illustrates the benefits of creating a Dubai Media City, a free zone allowing up to 100% foreign ownership. It also points toward the state-of-the-art infrastructure providing confidence to every media organization to come to the emirate and grow alongside the country.

The Dubai Media City has emerged as a region's most vibrant media community that fashions the most prominent global and local media brands in the last two decades. It showcases how freelancers, startups, and SMEs can co-exist with large enterprises. Dubai was named 'The capital of Arab Media' in 2020'.

According to the Economic and Social Commission for Western Asia (ESCWA) (2015), due to the positive growth of the publishing market, the Dubai Production City was launched in July 2003. Initially christened as an international media production zone, it has become a specialized media production hub for innovators. Today, it offers widespread content production, printing, publishing, and packaging services. It has one of the best infrastructures for art production and vast retail and residential complexes. Dubai Studio City followed the media production zone in 2005. It uniquely positions itself as a facility provider for companies with access to broadcast, film, television, music, and entertainment.

Parallelly, Abu Dhabi was taking giant strides with the launch of Twofour54, named after the geographic coordinates of Abu Dhabi. It was launched in 2008 and quickly cemented the reputation of Abu Dhabi's media industry. Like its contemporaries, Dubai houses some of the most sophisticated studios and world-class facilities and services. It has launched many talent development initiatives to train the next generation of content creators and film production professionals.

Media Free Zones

As stated in the Quadrennial Periodic Report United Arab Emirates 2020, "The United Arab Emirates has the region's highest concentration of media free zones, which are business communities for the media sector. Each Emirate has a media city/zone where startups, established media enterprises and talented professionals can work in close proximity, creating a hub for innovation and creativity" (UNESCO 2020).

In addition to the most developed Emirates, Abu Dhabi and Dubai, free media zones have been established in the other five Emirates: Umm Al Quwain, Fujairah, Sharjah, Ras Al Khaimah, Ajman.

The Umm Al Quwain Free Trade Zone (FTZ) was established in 1987. This progressive and investor-friendly FTZ has been established to favor small and medium-sized enterprises and micro-businesses, which will benefit from favorable set-up costs, 100% company ownership along-with zero currency restrictions (Umm Al Quwain Free Zone - UAQ, n.d.).

The Emirate of Fujairah has an authority called Creative City Fujairah Free Zone, launched in 2007 as an alternative to Dubai Media City, which focuses on professional service activities. It does not have any trading activities (Ovchinnikov, 2020). This Creative City Free Zone specializes in Media, Events, Consulting, Education, Communication, Marketing, Music and Entertainment, Design and Technology, complements existing media clusters in the region and facilitates further creativity in these fields (Creative City Free Zone Authority, 2021).

Launched in February 2017 with the goal of being a world-class media hub for innovative facilities and services, Sharjah Media City (Shams) covers a broad range of business activities available to those wishing to start an entrepreneurial business in the UAE (Business Setup in Sharjah, UAE | Company Registration in Free Zone - Sharjah Media City (Shams), 2021).

The RAKEZ Media Zone was established in the Emirate of Ras Al Khaimah (RAK) where there is a great demand for inventive media providers in number of areas including Media production, TV and Radio Broadcasting, Event Management, Animation, Music, Entertainment, and Publishing. This media zone, which is part of the Ras Al Khaimah Economic Zone, was established in April 2017. It has a nurturing and synergistic environment intending to encourage the establishment of media firms or the expansion of existing media companies in Ras Al Khaimah (RAK). "RAKEZ Media Zone also brings media-related businesses close to their peers, creating a neighborhood of media suppliers and vendors that embrace B2B collaboration for the growth of their respective businesses" (RAKEZ MEDIA ZONE, n.d.).

Ajman Media City Free Zone, launched in 2018 in the city of Ajman, is the newly established free zone in the United Arab Emirates with a focus on creating a reliable, harmonious, and professional business environment (Ajman Media City Free Zone. n.d.).

According to the report from UNESCO (2020):

The free zones provide a strong regulatory environment and streamlined services for obtaining permits and visas, thereby allowing media startups and established businesses to plan growth and innovation strategies. Media companies established in the free zones can be 100% foreign owned, and are exempt from personal, income and corporate taxes as well as customs duties for goods and services.

Emphasizing that "free zones offer a variety of office space, as well as production and business facilities, talent development initiatives, business training and support services, business training and support services", the report states:

As a result of the protection and freedom offered in the free zones, and the stability, security and infrastructure in the country, the UAE has attracted media enterprises and talent from across the world. This has created an environment where diverse voices and rich media content are produced, consumed, and distributed in the country, region, and the world (UNESCO, 2020).

The data below show the enormous potential of the media space in the UAE, as the largest business community in the region committed to creating a media space with all the modern conditions for creating media content.

- Twofour54, Abu Dhabi's Media Free Zone is home to 600+ media companies, 1000+ freelancers, 130+ entrepreneurs, and 5000+ media professionals (About Twofour54 Abu Dhabi, 2021).
- Dubai Media City Free Zone is home to 1,500+ companies, 25,000+ professionals from 142+ nationalities, (https://dmc.ae/). It produces publications in 5 languages and broadcasting in 11 languages (UNESCO (2020), including Arabic, English, Chinese, German, Tagalog, Hindi, and Urdu (Khaleej Times, 2020).
- Dubai Production City has more than 220 companies and 6,800 professionals (Leading Media Production Zone | Dubai Production City. n.d.).

- Dubai Studio City is the region's leading business community for film and television production, home to more than 275 companies and 2,800+ professionals (About Us | Dubai Studio City, n.d.).
- Over the last five years, Dubai Media City, Dubai Production City and Dubai Studio City have offered roughly 55 free workshops to over 2,000 participants. In 2020, they offered 10 virtual sessions tailored to the media, film, and music industry (UNESCO, 2020).

Dubai as "Arabian Hollywood"

Asking the question "Could Dubai also become the Arabian Hollywood?", John Vivian (2013) points out:

It was California sunshine, after all, that drew the infant U.S. filmmaking industry from the East Coast to Hollywood early in the 1900s. The more sunshine, the more days for outdoor shooting. With movie-making could come a host of related media industries—particularly television. The brainstorming that began with a tourist oriented Dubailand complex mushroomed (pp. 411-412).

According to the European Broadcasting Union (EBU), "Dubai Media Incorporated (DMI), one of the largest media organizations in the Middle East, houses a group of media channels (press, radio and TV) that has achieved remarkable success throughout the Arab world and is renowned for its creativity, integrity and professionalism as a media conglomerate" (European Broadcasting Union, 2017). The EBU information About Dubai Media Incorporated states:

Through a clear vision that focuses on innovation and quality and working in line with the strategic objectives of the Government of Dubai, DMI seeks to lead with the organization's distinctive Arabic and English media resources that represent original content while speaking to the social, cultural, and family values of the UAE. DMI has embarked on new forms of media with continuous development of new media services that are paralleled with relevant developments in the country and are aimed to create dialogue and connections between citizens of the UAE. DMI is committed to create a new Emirati media generation able to depict, portray and demonstrate the image of Dubai, and the UAE, by continuing to contribute to the formulation of media (European Broadcasting Union, 2017).

This pioneering media organization of the government of Dubai (established in 2003) focused on innovation, quality and working in line with the strategic objectives of the Government of Dubai, comprises a number of print, radio and TV channels including: Dubai TV, Al Bayan newspaper, Sama Dubai, Dubai One, Dubai Sports, Dubai Racing, Noor Dubai Radio & TV, Emarat Al Youm, Emirates 24|7, and Masar Printing Press (Dubai Media Incorporated, n.d.).

Media Regulation

UAE laws and regulations related to media and media content are clearly stated and explained on the official government portal dedicated to media and media regulations in the UAE. From the numerous laws and regulations related to the media, we single out those that are related to the topic of this research.

Table 1.

General Framework of the UAE Media Strategy

"In January 2021, the UAE Cabinet approved the general framework of UAE Media Strategy which is overseen by the UAE Government Media Office. The approval was done with an aim to strengthen the UAE's position and reputation at the regional and global levels. The strategy will:

- *intensify the role of government communication within the federal authorities*
- *reinforce the concept of partnership, cooperation and integration between national media authorities*
- *establish partnerships with global media entities*
- *manage the country's reputation and its achievements within local and international media coverage*
- *create a digital media environment capable of keeping pace with rapid changes and interacting with the world.*

The strategy will also focus on several areas of national priority while:

- *relying on the efficient and influential presence of the government in all media outlets*
- *promoting national culture and identity through all communication channels*
- *utilising modern technologies and digital media to interact with the public"*

(Media Regulation n.d.).

According to the UAE regulatory framework for media activities:

All media institutions creating audio, visual, print, and digital content in the UAE's mainland and free zones must comply with the standards for media content contained in the Federal Law No. 15 of 1980 Concerning Press and Publications and other laws and regulations in force (Media Regulation n.d.).

Table 2.

Federal Law No.15 for 1980 Concerning Press and Publications

"Federal Law No.15 for 1980 Concerning Press and Publications regulates printing and publishing licensing and activities in the UAE and it applies to traditional media content such as newspapers, magazines and television broadcasting, as well as digital media content. The law sets outs guidelines on materials which are prohibited from publication and penalties imposed on the publishing company and associated staff if found in violation of the Publications Law.

This law covers provisions for:

- *publishing houses and publications*
- *circulation of publications*
- *newspapers, periodic publications and new agencies*
- *importing and exporting publications, newspapers and newsletters*
- *films and other related work*
- *content prohibited from publication*
- *penalties*
- *others"*

(Media Regulation n.d.).

At the federal level, regulator of media in the UAE is the Media Regulatory Office (MRO) that manages and regulates media activities and free media-related zones in the UAE. This office operates under the Ministry of Culture and Youth, renamed from Ministry of Culture and Knowledge Development after the merger of National Media Council with Federal Youth Authority. Accordingly, the Ministry of Culture and Youth takes over the responsibilities of National Media Council (Media Regulation n.d.).

Media Regulatory Office includes two main departments: The Media Regulation Department and The Department of Media Licenses and Media Content Follow up. The Media Regulation Department "is responsible for preparing research and foresight studies related to the media, formulating legislation, regulations, standards, and foundations for organizing and licensing media and media activities" (Media

Regulatory Office, n.d.). The Department of Media Licenses and Media Content Follow up "is responsible for issuing licenses and following up on media content. It also implements legislations, regulations, and standards related to media services and media content" (Media Regulatory Office, n.d.).

In 2018, the UAE National Media Council implements a new system for managing all electronic and digital media activities on land and in free zones, covering all means of expression: writing, painting, music, photography, or others that are transferable to individuals in any form whether print, audio, visual, electronic, and digital or any other technological means. Under the new system, as highlighted by the Media regulation, prior approval is required for the following media activities:

- "trading, showcasing, selling, and printing video and audio materials on websites and social media,
- electronic publishing and on-call printing,
- electronic advertisements,
- publishing news,
- any electronic activity that the council deems appropriate to be added" (Media Regulation n.d.).

In the direction of this research, particular attention is paid to the advertising content policies and the official guide for advertisers. Namely, in October 2018, the National Media Council (NMC) issued an Official Advertising Guide in order to clarify the standards for the advertising industry in the UAE and at the same time protect the public from marketing promotions that do not comply with applicable standards. The document specifies the terms of licensing for advertising activities for individuals, companies, and institutions (Media Regulation n.d.).

The provisions of the Advertising Guide (2018) apply to the advertising content of any media activity practiced within the UAE, including the media activities of the printed, audio and visual media and organizations that print, publish, broadcast, circulate or distribute advertising content; institutions, companies and persons licensed to engage in advertising activities; any person who prints advertising content within the UAE or trading advertising content, including from the one that is imported from abroad; any person, company, institution or entity that publishes paid or for any financial consideration or otherwise on websites and social media; and any other persons or entities that the Council deems appropriate to be added (Advertising Guide, 2018, p.5).

The following definition of *Advertisement* is outlined in the Advertising Guide: Any means intended to inform all people about a certain commodity or purpose, whether by presentation or publication in writing, drawing, image, symbol, sound, or other means of expression. The definition of an *Advertiser*, according to this guide is: Any individual, organization or company that publishes advertisements on various media, whether tangible or intangible (Advertising Guide, 2018, p.4).

The Advertising Guide in separate sections covers the laws and decisions that regulate advertising; advertising content standards (*Table 1*); conditions for advertisements for all print, audio and visual media organizations (*Table 2*); conditions for electronic advertising on social media; advertising activities on social media exempt from licensing; the terms of licensing for advertising activities for individuals, companies and institutions; advertising activities licensing, advertising activities fees, as well as the penalties for violating the stated rules for advertising content.

Table 3.

Advertising Content Standards:
  1. "Refrain from offending God and Islamic beliefs and show respect for other heavenly religions.
  2. Show respect for the United Arab Emirates government and its emblems and political institutions.
  3. Show respect for the cultural and cultural heritage of the State.
  4. Avoid harming national unity and social cohesion, and provoking sectarian, doctrinal and tribal strife.
  5. Show respect the UAE's systems and policies at the internal level and its relations with other countries.
  6. Refrain from harming the economic system in the UAE and spreading rumors and misleading news.
  7. Show respect for the UAE's policies to promote its national identity.
  8. Avoid disseminating information that harms or abuses children and women, or any other social groups, or incites hatred and violence.
  9. Avoid publishing images or words that could violate public morality.
  10. Any advertising for witchcraft, sorcery and astrology shall not be allowed.
  11. Respect the intellectual property rights.
  12. Comply with codes of conduct and standards of honesty, including compliance with the rules governing business, especially in regard to consumer protection and fair competition controls, prohibition of commercial fraud and illegal monopoly.
  13. Advertising for alcoholic beverages or narcotics is not permitted in any form, whether directly or indirectly.
  14. Tobacco advertising, smoking of all kinds and methods of using them, or any other services or products that are prohibited from advertising, shall not be permitted.
  15. Comply with the rules of health advertisements contained in Cabinet Resolution No. 4 of 2007 and its amendments, on health advertisements.
  16. Avoid publishing advertisements that contain false, malicious, and misleading information.
  17. Respect the national identity of the UAE.
  18. Observe the conditions and terms concerning the use of the flag, emblem and national anthem of the UAE.
  19. Obtain the prior approval of the concerned authorities for advertisements requiring prior approvals, such as those related to health, education, real estate, Hajj and Umrah campaigns and others"

(Part 5, Advertising Guide 2018).

Table 4.

Conditions for Advertisements:
  1. "The advertisement should not be vague, ambiguous, or not clear.
  2. The advertisement should not include or contain false or misleading claims, or is intended to exaggerate, claim exclusiveness, despise competitors and all that involve fraud and deception.
  3. The advertisement should not include any false, fake or unrightfully formulated mark, sign or image.
  4. The advertisement should be real and unexaggerated and must not create any confusion by any means with any other brand names, products or activities.
  5. Obtain the prior approval of the competent authorities in regard to specialized advertisements, such as those related to medicine, medicine, energy drinks, promotions and special offers, as well as real estate, universities, educational institutions, nurseries, Hajj and Umrah promotion campaigns and the like.
  6. The media should not publish any advertisement that involves a crime or violates the principles and standards of the media content and the age rating applicable in this regard, or it may harm the public interest directly or indirectly.
  7. The advertisement must be clearly identified, appear distinct and independent from other editorial and information materials, and set boundaries that separate advertising from any other material, and intervals in broadcast situations.
  8. In the case of advertisements that contain, directly or indirectly, the promotion, advertising or endorsement of the person or the advertiser of a particular product or service, the advertiser must clearly disclose whether there is any financial gain in a business relationship with the person or the owner of the advertised product or service"

(Part 6, Advertising Guide 2018).

Media Production

Due to the robust media infrastructure, the emirate of Dubai and Abu Dhabi has been able to provide an ecosystem that is home to leading content creators in the region and globally. "Since 2005, Dubai Studio City, alongside Dubai Media City and Dubai Production City, has been home to 3,000 companies, including StarzPlay, MBC, Dubai Media Incorporated, Discovery Networks Central & Eastern Europe, Middle East, and Africa – employing 34,000 professionals" (Anupa Kurian-Murshed, 2018).

Dubai Studio City has been instrumental in realizing more than 4,000 productions between 2017 and 2020. The total worth of the projects is up to AED 400 million.

Some of the renowned global productions include "Star Trek Beyond", Tom Cruise's "Mission Impossible", Jackie Chan's "Vanguard" and "Kung Fu Yoga", and several popular TV productions such as "Master Chef Arabia" and "The Cube". The result of filmmaking activity is beneficial to various components of the media industry and ancillary industries such as food and hospitality.

Star Trek spend a little over Dh 110 million in Dubai within three months of the production.

The crew hired more than 1,500 staff which included 150 overseas workers from Canada and the US. The team discovered new working personnel in the country, and by the time the production wrapped up, the producers registered three new companies in the country (Business, 2020).

The industry also needs to provide specialized infrastructure for such a big scale Hollywood production. The production house Kemps Film TV Video shipped a special camera, available only in the US to Dubai. The infrastructure allows the producers to be in their comfort zones. Flying in the crew from all over the world was easy due to Dubai's air connectivity. Today, the country is well connected, with multiple flights available from South Africa, India, Australia, the USA, and Canada. Coupled with the ease of good transportation, major productions like Star Trek moved their set designs from Canada to Dubai with efficient coordination with the Dubai Customs.

Dubai's success story holds many lessons. Over the years, Abu Dhabi's media sector has emulated many such successes. As per the Oxford Business Group (2021), Abu Dhabi has emerged as a regional center for film and television production in the last decade. Abu Dhabi has come up with some attractive offers, such as a 30% rebate that adds up to 5 million dollars on expenses paid for international production. Some of the recent major film productions in Abu Dhabi are box office hits like "Sonic The Hedgehog" and "Bunty Aur Babli 2."

As demonstrated with the Star Trek example, the local production industry profits and benefits employment and business for ancillary entrepreneurs and SMEs. These include catering, transport, storage, and shipping companies. Abu Dhabi's economy has benefited from such overtures toward the production companies. It is estimated that for every Dh1 ($.027) spent by ADFC on incentives, Dh 31.0 ($0.84) is returned to Abu Dhabi's economy due to such economic measures. As mentioned before, Twofour54 finds itself in the heart of the infrastructure and the project base.

As per James Hartt, director of business development and strategy at Twofour54, waiving the fees has added a significant impetus to the strategy,

By waiving these fees, we have significantly reduced the financial barrier for some businesses. We have since seen twice as many small businesses set themselves up at twofour54. Any company with its paperwork in order can set itself up here in twofour54's media zone in less than 24 hours (Digital Studio ME, 2019).

Today, the Abu Dhabi media zone is favored by more than 550 media firms and 700 freelancers. Some of the prominent international names based on the site are National Geographic, Cable News Network (CNNN), Sky News Arabia, and Fox International Channels Middle East.

Fostering the Local Talent

To meet the demands of media firms, a steady flow of qualified media professionals is a critical element of this success. The industry draws on a growing pool of graduates from media and film programs offered by media programs in Abu Dhabi and Dubai. CNN is committed to encouraging the country's youth to take up journalism by offering educational and training programs. The programs aim to equip the youth with the latest skillset used in journalism and broadcast.

Since the day CNN began its broadcast from Abu Dhabi, the network has worked continually to expand its multilingual content for greater audience outreach. It has changed its programming to fuel the expanse. A team of experienced journalists led the CNN Academy to train content creators and production specialists with essential industry skills, including broadcast technologies, field production, and interview techniques. The participants get a closer view of how CNN gathers information, verifies sources, and creates content across all platforms (WAM, 2021). The program's syllabus also includes insights from the local media industry and new media courses such as digital storytelling and mobile journalism.

Twofour54 has a training hub, which houses the creative lab and Image Nation's film studios. Both the initiatives have provided facilities and infrastructure for training and learning.

Since 2017, Abu Dhabi has invested more than AED 30 billion into the creative and cultural industries. As the pandemic nears its end, the emirate is back in strength with the vibrancy of its cultural ecosystem. The emirate has worked towards revitalizing heritage architecture such as Qasr Al Hosn, creating awareness among the local population. The city now hosts the renowned Louvre Abu Dhabi (Mubarak, 2021). As the latest installment of the Dune Franchise hits the theatre, the CGI investment by Abu Dhabi is bearing fruits. The Creative Media Authority is entrusted with overseeing the Yas Creative space launched in 2020. The new area will be home to new businesses and is expected to encourage entrepreneurs to bring their businesses to the island.

Since 2016, the ADFZ has invested over Dh 1.5 bn ($408.3m), which has resulted in significant job creation and upskilling. Until the end of 2018, the zone has created over 4000 jobs playing a pivotal role in creating the local talent, which is integral to the media zone's success.

The investment and development of the local talent have led to the latest local blockbuster film release titled "Al Kameen" (The Ambush) in November 2021. The film was produced by Image Nation Abu Dhabi and AGC International. AGC is a subsidiary of AGC Studio, US (BroadcastPro ME, 2021). The movie was screened across the country, and Vox Cinemas distributed it. The film is one of the largest Arabic language film production ever produced in the Gulf Region. The film production team had over 400 casts and crew, out of which a majority were Emiratis led by an all-Emirati cast. As pointed out by Hana Kazim, it was a proud moment for the talented local team. Hana Kazim, Manager – Film production, Image Nation Abu Dhabi says:

Demonstrating the epic bravery of a group of Emirati soldiers, Al Kameen is a unique production for the UAE. As the largest ever Arabic-language production in the GCC regarding cast and crew numbers, we are incredibly proud of this inspirational film. It is a true testament to the talented crew in Abu Dhabi and the Emirates' ability to draw in world-renowned industry names (BroadcastPro ME, 2021).

Abu Dhabi University (ADU) joined hands with Twofour54 in December 2020 to develop talents through programs supported by gaming giant Unity Technologies (WAM, 2021b). The partnership will use gaming to drive the youngster's imagination and creativity. The objective is to provide the students with technical know-how in the training course material. It will help students grapple with the most complex issues providing a space for conversation and social integration. The topics covered in the course include climate change and the future economy.

Another educational platform created by Image Nation Abu Dhabi is the Arab Film Studio. It aims to position the emirate of Abu Dhabi to be a creative hotspot and help make the next generation of Arab filmmakers empowered to tell their stories. Image Nation has successfully enabled the trainees to upskill their film production workflow. Today's film school has four streams - documentary filmmaking, fiction narrative, scriptwriting, and a summer program for high school students. So far, the studio has celebrated screenings of 200 films produced by its graduates in film festivals across the world and has helped the professional careers of its students.

An example of students working in a live production was Image Nation courtroom drama titled 'Justice.' It became the first local Netflix drama series, shot in Abu Dhabi. The Arabic show bought together Emmy award-winning writer and Academy award-winning producer, and it went on to become the region's most expensive TV show.

The country certainly needs more TV programming, and Image Nation Abu Dhabi is slated to fill that gap. Traditionally the middle east broadcasters have focused primarily on producing shows for the Ramadan period. Most of the program is telecasted during the holy month, without investing in original programming for the rest of the year. This needs to change to make the industry sustainable. So, it is clear Image Nation needs to produce for television as well. Image Nation turned broadcaster with the launch of its Pan-Arabic TV channel Quest Arabiya in 2015 (BroadcastPro ME, 2015). It partnered with the Discovery Network to offer 22 countries its channel broadcast and is on its way to becoming a true pan-Arabic market in the middle east.

TV Commercial and Advertising Agencies

The advertising industry in the middle east was in a nascent stage until the 1980s. Small, independently owned agencies dominated the industry. Everything changed in the 1990s as the countries saw a sharp rise in investment, leading to large multinational agencies joining the fray.

According to Hiorns (2014) "today's advertising industry is rolled up into five major holding companies, mainly WPP, Omnicom, IPG, Dentsu, and Publicis."

The global network Publicis Group is structured around four hubs, with headquarters in Dubai: Publicis Health, Publicis Sapient (for digital solutions), Publicis Media (includes Starcom, Zenith, and Digitas among others), and Publicis Communications (includes Publicis Worldwide, Leo Burnett and Saatchi & Saatchi among others). In 2002, Publicis bought Leo Burnett Group of Companies Middle East and North Africa. The latter first opened its doors in 1981 as the first multinational agency based in the region (Hiorns, 2014).

Similar examples and patterns of restructuring materialized in other global networks, including WPP, Young & Rubicam, JWT, and Omnicom.

The early development of media has impacted the emergence and development of advertising. Toward the mid-to-late-1990s, an additional factor accelerated this development further. A wave of media liberalization through the region changed media consumption patterns and rendered television the medium of choice for viewers and advertisers alike.

The Arab Media Outlook report (2009–2013) defines the pan-Arab market as follows: "Pan-regional advertising expenditure refers to advertising spend by regional media outlets that cover multiple countries in the Arab region" (Dubai Press Club, 2010). In a footnote, the definition continues and identifies the countries as follows, "Pan-Arab refers to advertising across Bahrain, Jordan, Kuwait, Oman, Qatar, Saudi Arabia, UAE, Lebanon, Syria, and North Africa" (Dubai Press Club, 2010). As mentioned in the Introduction, the authors will focus primarily on the landscape of UAE Television Advertising.

The Arab media market, in terms of television viewership, was a flourishing side of the business (Hamilton, 2007). Among advertisements, the placement rate was high in entertainment and leisure programming. The report concluded with the forecast much higher in the middle east than in developed countries for TV consumption. Due to the proliferation of TV stations in the country, advertisement opportunities grew.

A limited news bulletin was introduced in 1992 by the MBC Group in the region. As the US-led invasion of Iraq began in 1991, the climate for satellite news and distribution got a shot in the arm. As per a report by AME Info (2006), the total number of free to air satellite channels rose by 163 percent since January 2004, reaching 263 channels. The free-to-air channels were broadcasting on Arabsat and Nilesat.

As internet advertisement was introduced into the market, the middle east proved to be a significant draw. Studies from 2000 until 2007 show that the increase in Internet usage in the middle east has eclipsed the world average over the same period (Internet World Stats, 2008).

UAE is home today to the leading international advertising firms such as Viola, M&C Saatchi, and JCDecaux. Even local companies make a decent advertising expenditure.

Media zones like Twofour54 are home to dozens of local and international advertising firms, such as Viola, M&C Saatchi, and JCDecaux. Local companies, too, make considerable advertising expenditure. For example, UAE flagship carrier, Etihad Airways, spends around $ 30 million a year on marketing and advertising.

Focusing on the television sector, the GCC video industry, including free TV, pay-TV, and online video, was estimated to generate revenue of $1.6 bn in 2020. The data shows a depression of 13% year on year, particularly in the TV advertisement & subscriptions. The growth in online video spending offset it (Advanced Television, 2020). The COVID crisis was going to make it worse. And it did across the TV sector. But a rebound is expected in 2022, while the TV industry still faces new challenges. As per the same report, Pay-TV and Free TV will decline by 2025. The trend of pre-covid will continue in the same direction, with online video surpassing TV to account for more than 60% of the market by 2025. The cost prospects will be driven by low-cost pricing and partnership bringing in premium local and global content online. This opens the space for the OTT platforms to come in.

METHODOLOGY

The research is based on descriptive interview method and secondary data collection, in an effort to obtain an appropriate evaluation of the social dimensions of the covered issue.

A methodological triangulation was performed through the review of literature related to the changing TV commercial and advertising landscape, its move towards digital and the creation of new synergies in the industry.

Interviews, as a qualitative method of research, were a useful mechanism in this study in order to obtain primary data through the perceptions and attitudes of selected media experts and to gain a more in-depth insight.

Media organization working in the sector of advertising & film production were identified and the researchers got in touch with media professionals over 15 years of experience in the UAE industry. An intentional purposive sample was chosen, incorporating three experts from the field of advertising, film & TV production houses.

According to the Annual Economic Report 2019, the total labor force in the UAE in 2018 was 7.384 million. The UAE's workforce's wages during 2017 and 2018 in the Arts, Entertainment, and Creative sciences sector stood at 1.1%. A report by PwC expects entertainment and media revenues to increase by 3% in the region between 2019 and 2024, exceeding the 2% rise forecast. According to Mena Cinema Forum, the UAE is set to join the world's top 10 leading markets for global box office revenues by 2030. The UAE makes up 25% of the total OTT subscriptions in the MENA region, the second highest percentage. The growth of the media industry relies heavily on its experienced leadership. The creative personnel employed in the UAE media industry has a wide gamut of sectors: advertising, media production, community arts, design, event management, filmmaking and animation, and others. For the purpose of this study, the focus remained on advertising agencies and media production houses.

These experts were heads of relevant associations in the sector and companies that stand out for their work with TV commercials in the field of advertising, as well as experts linked to film production services in the UAE:

1. **Mark Fiddes, International Creative Director - Advertising, PR, Digital Media & Marketing**
   (Date of the Interview: 12 October, 2021)

Figure 1.

International creative director Mark Fiddes has worked across the globe to grow some of the world's most successful brands. From the Reckitt Benckiser portfolio – including Durex, Finish, Dettol and Vanish – to Nivea, Jaguar and Bel Cheeses – he has pioneered integration of digital marketing, social media and traditional advertising through all channels to build consumer and stakeholder engagement. He has over 100 international awards and has been a judge twice at the Cannes Festival. Over several decades, he has worked for the Havas and FCB networks to achieve some of their most significant new business wins and awards. Most recently, he has helped double the size of Havas in MENA winning over 50% of pitches. He currently works from Dubai directly with clients and agencies on brand breakthroughs

2.   **Ashish Varghese, Filmmaker** *(Date of the Interview: 12 October, 2021)*

Figure 2.

Ashish Varghese is a filmmaker based out of Dubai, UAE, known for his short films "Aram Ghar" (2014), "L'attente: The Wait" (2016) and "Aai: Mother" (2018). He is the Head of Production for DDB Dubai and also Executive producer and Director at a Boutique Production House "The Farm". Ashish has produced commercials for various brands and has been a director for projects associated with Lipton, Neutrogena, Jonshson's Baby, Johnson's Handwash, Arial, Tide, Porsche etc. His real passion lies in directing and producing fiction films. His work entails short films such as "Aram Ghar" (2014), "L'attente: The Wait" (2016) and "Aai: Mother" (2018). His short films have won multiple awards locally and globally. In 2013, he was also Local assistant director to Farah Khan in her successful Bollywood movie "Happy New Year" shot in Dubai. He won Best Director Award in 2017 at UAE Short Film Festival (UAESFF) for his work on "L'attente: The Wait".

3.   **Guy Sinclair, Executive Producer, Phoenix Film** (Date of the Interview: 10 October, 2021)

Figure 3.

Guy started his career at Elstree studios in the UK and is one of the most respected, multi-awarded producers in the Middle East, with over 30 years in film and television industry. Guy has worked on many memorable and ground-breaking brands and government campaigns across the MENA region (Brands Emirates airlines, Etihad airways, Caltex, Shell, Bentley, Ford, Honda, Toyota, Mercedes, HSBC, Cadbury's, Kiri fromage Kraft, GSK, Pepsi, P&G Reckette Benkiser, Unilever, Dubai Tourism, Saudi Tourism) and with celebrities such as Nicole Kidman, Kylie Minogue, Robbie Williams, Roger Federer, Cristiano Ronaldo, Tiger Woods, Son Heung Min, Sebastian Vettel, Charles Leclerc, Grant Imahara, Amr Diab, Myriam Fares.

Structured interview questions were drafted specific to the industry, the experts belonged to. The key structure of the interview included:

- Impact of Pandemic to their industry
- Transition to digitalization
- Changes in the business model due to new media technologies
- Influence of the demography to the media industry in the UAE
- Information on the key clientele from the industry they represent
- Growth of the local market and the key influences
- Censorship or Self-Censorship
- Relationship between the Advertising agencies and the film production houses
- Crew and Talent requirement and availability in the UAE
- Future trends in the industry

Given the complexity of the UAE media landscape, descriptive analysis of interviews provided a tropical guide, focusing on expert knowledge, which is widely characterized as specific knowledge in a particular field of action, wherever the expert's hails from be it advertising specific or broadly television broadcasting.

The expert interview has helped to emphasize the importance of investigating experiences and perspectives of the interviewees for developing a better understanding of the industry.

The study was collecting secondary data through search on the history, growth, and regulatory mechanism of the UAE media industry. For this purpose, the authors were using government publications, as well as available information on the websites of individual Emirates. Also, industry newsletters and magazines were used as secondary sources for industry updates related to the field of advertising and media production. Analytical and descriptive approach were employed based on primary and secondary data collection.

Key Research Questions

The study aims to investigate vibrant content production ecosystem in the UAE media sector making it a regional center for film, television, and social media. The key research questions include:

1. Establish UAE as a hotspot for Film and TV production, making it a regional hub for television advertising production
2. Transformations in the TV Commercials and advertising sector as a knock-on effect due to the pandemic
3. Challenges for the advertising agencies which includes media regulation, cultural sensitivities, and transition to digitization.

FINDINGS

The influence of streaming on Television and video has been phenomenal. The industry requires a new ecosystem to fix the inefficiencies inherent in its market practices. As a headline in a report noted, 'TV isn't going anywhere – it's going everywhere.'

TV advertising used to be a traditional bastion of large brands with big budgets, but the digital platforms are changing the game. Now, the industry is faced with millions of advertisers, big and small, using sophisticated digital advertising and social media to reach out to their customer base. Media production also has seen an influx of small production houses, stiffening the competition further.

The researchers began the interview with the experts by focusing on some of the fundamental changes the TV commercial advertising industry in the UAE has seen over the last decade, particularly addressing the pandemic's impact on the sector and nuances of the local industry.

Impact of the Pandemic on Advertising Expenditure

Surprisingly, viewership was not a problem during the pandemic; millions of homebound people had limited entertainment options. But the economic fallout of the pandemic has caused companies to slash TV ad budgets. As global data come in, more than 40 percent cut in budgets by leading brands, and at the same time, networks offered commercial time at double-digit discounts. Providing a local perspective, Asish Verghese says the lockdowns were particularly difficult for freelancers in Dubai, as no shoots were taking place. The pandemic introduced a new mode of working from home. Ashish was one of the three producers globally who did the first shoot in a lockdown in Australia. The crew from two countries used the latest communication technologies, with a 12 men crew supervising the shoot from home using their laptops while the live feed was coming in through zoom. Although the technology can get better, streaming technology has evolved and improved with every update over the last few months.

Guy Sinclair, a film producer, provides a broad perspective of the UAE TV commercial industry. According to him, UAE has emerged to be a very competitive location for international feature film production & local television production, comparable to Eastern Europe and South Africa. He feels the technology has become cheaper, and he expects the production cost also to go down, which he feels is a problem.

We will still need to respect the creative process to create a good quality product in whatever genre we work in - film, TV content or social media. Consumers are getting very sophisticated and as an industry we must maintain traditional standards of production although be mindful and competitive in delivering entertainment that is engaging. So there lies the challenge for the production industry in the UAE - Post-Covid-19 to increase production volume, while maintaining creative excellence at a competitive but correct price. (Guy Sinclair)

Post-Pandemic, the industry has slowly adapted to the new normal. Big studios have the scale and budget efficiencies to accommodate the evolving landscape. However, many industry standards for health and safety will likely remain permanent, and shoots will continue to take more time and cost more money than before the pandemic. However, due to the market pressure, the production houses need to keep the cost down, putting more pressure on their bottom line. We are entering the new future of television advertising: fast, cheap, and minimalist.

Social media has cut into the TV expenditure. The pandemic has boosted digital literacy by six years in its first six months. But it is also the e-commerce platform that has found its way into social media and made it the first and the nearest platform for advertisers.

When I arrived in MENA to head up Havas creativity five years ago, the split of work streams in the agencies was around 70% TV to 30% social media. I can safely say that has turned around to 70% social to 30% TV. (Mark Fiddes)

Changes in the Business Model

The agency model is struggling for a whole number of reasons. The traditional process of months and months of planning and research followed by months in production is sped up to a week by digitization. Indeed, clients are going direct to production houses for their content instead of waiting for the agency to catch up. As Mark puts it, in 2021 alone, 70% of clients have also looked at bringing projects in-house to creative departments run internally. He provides the example of the Oliver model that actively insources creative services to giants like P&G and Unilever. Talking about challenges, Mark further elaborates how the critical challenge for agency holding companies like WPP and Omnicom is to find a new operating model that allows them to attract and retain top strategic and creative talent while being able to deliver fast.

Many clients have woken up to the new choices enabled by digital working and digital distribution. Whether this is insourcing talent or going straight to production companies or working with small social media start-ups and then repurposing that content for advertising, the range of options for clients is much greater than ever before. Add to this the availability to clients of senior advertising talent that has been cost cut from agencies in the past few years – in order that they can preserve their very slim margins – and the future looks very challenging. One option is that the media arms of the holding companies will simply sweep the creative parts into their own remit. (Mark Fiddes)

The trends show that the traditional processes of creating and getting advertising to market didn't translate well with the modern social media sphere. It was expensive and slow. The modes for finding content have multiplied, and marketers have to meet consumers where they are. Is Mobile the medium of today? A question posed by Ashish, who feels, the transition to digitization is a challenging evolution for everyone, for marketeers and for content creators,

During the days of TV and as all the legends state it "The golden era" of advertising, films could be shot in cinemascope 23:9 and still play on TV. With the digital era we are lucky if we get to frame for a 16:9 because, unlike yesterday, the director now needs to think about how the film would look on a 1:1 & a 9:16 ratio and how well will it be consumed by the mobile audience. This limits creativity and freedom on what we can do with actors, but then these formats have created a new generation of communication, which is successful and absorbed well. (Ashish Verghese)

The shift from film format (analog) to digital has been relentless in the last decade. Film format has remained a novelty to be used for a TV commercial shoot. It used to be a norm, but today we see a relentless drip-feed of new digital film formats. The 35 mm reel is no longer the standard today. Yesteryear giant Technicolor shut down its last film lab; Fujifilm is no longer in the business of producing the film. Kodak, the last remaining producer, filed for bankruptcy protection in 2012, exited legacy businesses, and sold off its patents before re-emerging as a sharply smaller company later. Historically UAE was never keen on shooting in film format due to a lack of available resources. Guy describes that the emergence of digital has done good for the local film industry, and with the setup of media zones, locally grown companies have mushroomed,

The production industry of shooting local and international productions has grown exponentially and that was helped by the creation of Dubai Studio City and Twofour54, Abu Dhabi. Many international and local grown production companies have seen an opportunity to invest and develop their business locally in the UAE. So, although we are not comparable to Europe or the USA in terms of volume of companies, we do have every facility available to us here in the UAE, from sound stages, camera equipment, grip equipment, lighting equipment, generators, trucks, tracking vehicles, helicopters, drones, mobile vanity, and green caravans. There is every production support facility available in the UAE. (Guy Sinclair)

Media Regulation in the UAE

The visuals that naturally come to mind when one thinks of the middle east and TV commercials are:

- Beautiful desert landscape sequences.
- Off-road automotive advertisements.
- Luxurious tourism pieces in some of the world's most iconic resorts.

But the process that leads to such a shoot may seem arduous for a newcomer to the industry. However, achieving it as desired by visual directors and TV commercial producers isn't as tricky. Guy runs a production house in Dubai, and he outlines the process of filming permission.

Filming permissions are easy to source through the Dubai Film & TV Commission and the Abu Dhabi Film Commission, open for all registered local production houses. They can apply online for the permit, which usually takes three to five days to be authorized. International production companies need to contract with a local registered production house to film in the UAE, and sometimes they can obtain rebates from the commissions on serviced productions. (Guy Sinclair)

The permissions on a production level begin from Cast permits, Government permits for the shoot (DFTC) until private location permits. Getting approval is one thing, but one of the significant aspects of location permits for international production could be scripts or visual portrayals, which can conflict with the country's laws. All the media councils within the region take this as a serious note. However, unlike the question of media censorship often raised about the region, there is nothing exceptional to observe that you would not apply in any other progressive Western society. Guy feels very strongly that production houses should respect the culture of the local indigenous community, respect the religious beliefs, and respect the laws of the country.

Mark echoes the same sentiment and adds that 'one size fits all' has never, as some global brands may insist on it vehemently. One has to remember,

They are your market, and the best ideas will be ones that springboard from deep insights into society and its beliefs and behaviors. For example, how did we manage to make Durex the most talked about brand on Saudi Twitter during the last World Cup – we listened to what Saudi men (and women) were saying. We did not force the global solution upon them. There was no need. (Mark Fiddes)

Kingdom of Saudi Arabia (KSA) has been a massive market for all the brands leading Guy's production house to shoot two versions of the commercial or print, one which caters specifically to the KSA market and the second generic to all the other regions. The content coming out of GCC is brand specific. It communicates mechanics very clearly, leaving the creative with a challenge to put this together creatively with limited room due to the multiple nationalities they need to address. The commercials and communication that pop out regardless are the best and set a standard globally.

Collaboration between Production House and Advertising Agency

The traditional relationship between production companies and advertising agencies is that they manage a client's marketing strategy, develop the creatives, and collaborate with a director and the production house they represent. However, with the expansion and fragmentation of the market with digital content and social media, the relationship has changed. Today, some producers work alongside agency creatives, while others are often directly commissioned by the client. Guy Sinclair outlines the process as such: AD agencies create the concepts aligned with the client and then brief production houses to propose directors and budgets for the project. The best director, budget, and the production house execute the job. The selection is made based on a treatment note written by directors on how they envision the script written by the creative department in an agency. If they align with the creative vision and the brand guideline, they catapult to the top position to win the job. With the agency's help, the production house then sets a schedule to which they adhere and have the films delivered in their desired formats for the media.

Guy explains further how big agencies operate in Dubai. Guy further describes a scenario where some clients approach production companies directly with projects outside of agency contracts that would be anything below the line. This means anything that is not positioned on traditional above-the-line media such as TV, Print & Outdoor.

To maintain the lion's share of a client's business, big agencies have set up their own in-house Production departments to service clients' production needs, thus cutting out the traditional production service & facility companies. In Dubai, large advertising agencies such as Hogarth (WPP), Prodigious (Publicis), The farm (DDB), The Village (Havas), Hug (AKQA), Media Monks, and Tag follow such practices. (Guy Sinclair)

Mark Fiddes feels that the relationship is changing. Due to budgetary constraints, most big agencies have set up their own production companies internally, primarily to handle the low-budget social media content they don't want to see going elsewhere. At the same time, several production companies work directly with clients – like Prime Productions, on the new Emirates Burj Khalifa film. Indeed, Emirates SVP Brand Marketing Richard Billington has made a point of not working with agencies. Mark also adds that Drugs, sex, and alcohol shouldn't make it to any communication in this region,

These are the three elements that generally spice up mediums and keep audiences entertained. They also expand your horizon of creativity, but in this region, we also avoid wardrobes that are above knees and elbows. KSA commercials initially and strictly had Veils, but with the recent developments the veils are either not there or are loose. (Mark Fiddes)

The changes in UAE's freedom of expression are fueling many international production companies to set up satellite offices here in the UAE. The freelance production talent from Europe, Asia, and South Africa started to trickle in and has grown to a healthy level of skill available to producers. These, in turn, have been a catalyst for bringing on and teaching local talent to join the industry. Key film-making talents come from worldwide on a contract basis, but now they come to live and work here in the UAE, a testament to the growing opportunities. As a new fledging industry, we will always need to grow the talent pool, and with new media and digital content, we should start to give more opportunities for the talent pool to grow faster.

SOLUTIONS AND RECOMMENDATIONS

The evolution of the tight-knit TV industry meant a limited selection of production houses were producing content for TV or movie theatres. The media industry in the UAE follows a simple windowing process that usually involves movie theatres followed by pay-TV and then free TV. As discussed previously, the month of Ramadan was the only month of the significant monetization cycle. Whatever content would end up in YouTube would be for residual revenues, a cheat, and a convenient catch-up solution. This content flow lasted until late 2017. That's when the OTT platforms started appearing in the MENA region at almost the same rate way it seemed for Linear TV back in 1997.

A sharp rise followed this in demand from new buyers coming to the Arabic content marketplace. However, the industry is almost entirely funded by ad spend rather than subscriber-based revenues. The budget was too small for new digital newcomers to ramp up production value leaving the monetization life cycle in a predicament. A quick-based solution offered by content distributors was to split the rights of video assets by catering to the small budgets of the OTT platforms. Still, YouTube had a sharp decline of 92% in video assets uploaded, witnessed in Ramadan 2019.

This marks the beginning of the OTTs in the MENA region, a race for services for the linear channels and a slightly more money-making device than YouTube. But again, this lasted for only another year, as OTT platforms struggled to make enough money from a region used to receiving free Arabic content. So, the only way forward was for the OTT coming forward by getting into productions themselves with Originals. Netflix announced its expansion in the MENA region back in 2016. It was great news for regional production houses, as it meant new content commissioning. The first Emirati Drama on Netflix, 'Justice,' went on the floor in 2017. It should be noted that the first regional OTT platform ICFlix released its own original production in 2014 with Egyptian movies.

Both International and regional OTTs are setting aside budget now for exclusive Arabic Originals. This is very encouraging for every producer in the region as it means originals will be privately funded to increase the valuation of the OTT Platforms, if not for immediate profitability.

Netflix being a solid competitor in the region, all OTT providers in the market need to focus on originals and work towards creating a delicate balance between subscription video on demand (SVOD) models and ad-supported monetization, whether digital or linear. Knowing that Drama always does well in the MENA region, OTT's new releases are 56% drama series while 40% focus on societal stories/ relationships. The OTT platforms have chosen a safer ground for now when it comes to selecting the genres of their productions. However, looking at the global success of thrillers, suspense, crime, and mystery genres globally, it would be interesting to see if new genres are introduced for the Arabic viewers in the region.

For the production houses, the transition to digitization was a difficult but necessary change for the industry. Today, the smartphone is the medium of choice for the majority. The 'golden era' of advertising saw productions shot on cinemascope ratio of 23:9, and it would still play on Linear TV. As the digital era began, the requirement was not limited to shooting for 16:9. Still, the client also demands a 1:1 & 9:16 aspect ratio due to the popularity of social media platforms such as Instagram, Snapchat, and TikTok. This limits the creativity and freedom of the content creators, but in return, these new formats have created a whole new generation of communicators with a broad appeal and followers. Digitization has also speed things up beyond control. The production timelines and budgets are squeezed because the cameras are getting smaller & accessible. Today, it is difficult to convince a client to ramp up the production cost when freelancers can execute it in a fraction of a fee with cheap consumer-grade recording equipment.

FUTURE RESEARCH DIRECTIONS

In the future, after the end of the Covid 19 pandemic, it is desirable that this study continue in the direction of a comparative study of the circumstances in which TV production and advertising activity will take place in the Emirates and other countries in the MENA region.

It will be especially challenging and useful for media researchers to conduct a broader comparative study of the forecasts of Global Entertainment & Media Outlook 2021–2025 (PricewaterhouseCoopers, n.d.), according to which in the coming period there will be an exceptional increase in digital formats - virtual reality, according to which in the coming period there will be an exceptional rise of digital formats - virtual reality, Cinema, Data consumption, Out-of-home advertising and OTT video.

CONCLUSION

The media sphere in the Emirates is full of challenges for local and international workers in the film, TV, and advertising industry. Rarely in any country globally, the UAE simultaneously corresponds to the essential prerequisites for one of the most creative and demanding professions related to television, film, and advertising production. The media production houses and advertising agencies operating from the UAE have great potential in the Saudi market. The kingdom is going ahead with its plan to open around 350 cinemas by 2030. The big media players in the UAE are already seizing on the opportunity to invest in quality productions but also developing skills and talent in a region to meet the increasing demands from Saudi Arabia.

The country offers an excellent infrastructure with all the necessary settings (external and internal), with significant spatial locations for the specific media activity related to production and advertising.

What deserves special mention is the country's safety - the UAE achieved first place in the roaming of the population at night alone, and second in the world for the safest countries according to the results of the Gallup Report for Security and Order 2021 (Ray, 2021), as well as the clear unequivocal government regulations and procedures for the media business.

Government support is seen through the various types of licenses available to locals and foreigners, especially creative activities. The Media Zones opened in the Free Economic Zones in the UAE provide all the necessary support for starting a business, with the constant availability of their contact services (by phone or online). The creation of media zones by the UAE Government and the emirates of Abu Dhabi, Dubai & Sharjah has created their own niche when it comes to media and film production pushing the country to the global map.

The sensitivity of culture deserves attention, especially by foreigners who get involved in the media business in the UAE, but this is not something new for film, television, and advertising representatives. Market research and culture in a country is a common practice followed by experienced professionals in this field.

The pandemic has expedited the industry changes that were in the offing for the next decade. For example, the split of workstreams between social media and television has dramatically shifted towards the former. It also has accelerated solutions that today allow productions to work simultaneously on one project across the continent.

The spurred introduction of Out-of-Home digital content & social media has changed the landscape of media production. Media professionals feel that even though technology has progressed at breakneck speed, film shoots supervised entirely in-person augur better for the end-product. The pandemic has not dented UAE's position as a destination for an international film production site. The critical challenge for the industry is to increase production volume while maintaining creative expression and excellence.

REFERENCES

A Small and Medium Enterprises Development Perspective of the Media Industry in Dubai. (2010). Retrieved October 21, 2021, from https://sme.ae/SME_File/Files/DUBAI_SME_Media_Industry_Report.pdf

About twofour54 Abu Dhabi. (2021, February 3). Retrieved August 30, 2021, from Twofour54. https://www.twofour54.com/en/who-we-are/about-twofour54/

About Us. (n.d.). *Dubai Studio City*. Retrieved September 21, 2021, from https://dubaistudiocity.ae/discover/about-us

Advanced Television. (2020, December 7). *Report: GCC video industry sees revenues of $1.6bn in 2020.* etrieved September 20, 2021, from https://advanced-television.com/2020/12/07/report-gcc-video-industry-sees-revenues-of-1-6bn-in-2020/

Advertising Guide. (2018). *National Media Council*. Retrieved August 29, 2021, from https://u.ae/-/media/Media/Media-In-UAE/NMC-AD-Guide-EN-PDF-presntation.ashx

Ajman Media City Free Zone. (n.d.). Retrieved September 20, 2021, from https://www.amcfz.ae/en/

Al Arabiya English. (2021, November 18). *UAE named world's safest country to walk at night: Gallup report*. Retrieved September 25, 2021, from https://english.alarabiya.net/News/gulf/2021/11/18/UAE-named-world-s-safest-country-to-walk-at-night-Gallup-report

Anupa Kurian-Murshed. (2018, November 7). *Big budgets, exotic locales, infrastructure: Dubai's movie business*. UAE – Gulf News. Retrieved October 25, 2021 from https://gulfnews.com/uae/big-budgets-exotic-locales-infrastructure-dubais-movie-business-1.2222348

BroadcastPro ME. (2015, June 9). *Image Nation and Discovery to launch new Arabic channel*. Retrieved October 25, 2021 from https://www.broadcastprome.com/news/image-nation-and-discovery-to-launch-new-arabic-channel/

BroadcastPro ME. (2021, November 25). *Emirati action film 'Al Kameen' releases today in Vox Cinemas*. Retrieved October 25, 2021 from https://www.broadcastprome.com/news/emirati-action-film-al-kameen-releases-today-in-vox-cinemas/

Business, A. (2020, December 15). *15 years on, how Dubai Studio City has put the emirate on global movie map*. Arabian Business. Retrieved September 28, 2021, from https://www.arabianbusiness.com/industries/media/455930-15-years-on-how-dubai-studio-city-has-put-the-emirate-on-global-movie-map

Business Setup in Sharjah, UAE | Company Registration in Free Zone - Sharjah Media City (Shams). (2021). *Shams.Ae*. Retrieved September 21, 2021, from https://www.shams.ae/

Creative City Free Zone Authority. (2021, October 17). *Creative City Free Zone Authority - Business License Registration!* Creative City. Retrieved September 25, 2021, from https://creativecity.ae/

Danesi, M. (2009). *Dictionary of Media and Communications*. Routledge.

Digital Studio, M. E. (2019, January 9). *Production houses must train next generation of GCC film-makers, says Image Nation.* Retrieved September 15, 2021, from https://www.digitalstudiome.com/production/31106-production-houses-must-train-next-generation-of-gcc-filmmakers-says-image-nation

Dubai Media Incorporated. (n.d.). Retrieved October 10, 2021, from https://web.archive.org/web/20111108173917/http://www.dmi.gov.ae/default_En.asp

Dubai Press Club. (2010). *Arab Media Outlook.* Author.

Dubai SME & An Agency of the Department of Economic Development – Government of Dubai. (2010). *A small and medium enterprises development perspective of the Media industry in Dubai.* Dubai SME. https://bit.ly/3wAOAbt

Dubai Studio City. (n.d.). *Global production, broadcasting and entertainment hub.* Retrieved September 21, 2021, from https://dubaistudiocity.ae/

Economic and Social Commission for Western Asia (ESCWA). (2015, November 11). *International Media Production Zone.* United Nations Economic and Social Commission for Western Asia. Retrieved September 15, 2021, from https://archive.unescwa.org/international-media-production-zone

European Broadcasting Union. (2017). *About Dubai Media Incorporated.* Retrieved September 20, 2021, from https://www.ebu.ch/files/live/sites/ebu/files/News/2017/02/ABOUT%20DUBAI%20MEDIA%20INCORPORATED.pdf

Fanack.com. (2021, September 6). *Media in the United Arab Emirates - Chronicle.* Retrieved September 11, 2021, from https://fanack.com/united-arab-emirates/media-in-uae/

Freezone Company Setup | Dubai Media City. (n.d.). *Media Hub in Dubai.* Retrieved August 30, 2021, from https://dmc.ae

Gallier, E. G. (2021, January 6). *SVOD vs TVOD vs AVOD: What's the Best Content Delivery System?* Retrieved January 10, 2021, from https://www.harmonicinc.com/insights/blog/svod-vs-tvod-vs-avod-whats-the-best-content-delivery-system/

Hamilton, B. A. (2007). *Booz Allen Hamilton Finds Television Programming Improving in the Arab World.* Booz Allen Hamilton. Retrieved September 13, 2021, from https://www.boozallen.com/markets/international/middle-east-north-africa.html

Hiorns, B. (2014, April 2). *Leo Burnett focuses on driving regional growth in the Middle East and North Africa with new appointment.* Creative Pool. Retrieved September 21, 2021, from https://creativepool.com/magazine/inspiration/leo-burnett-focuses-on-driving-regionalgrowth-in-the-middle-east-and-north-africa-with-new-appointment.2765

Internet World Stats. (2008). *Internet World Stats Blog for 2008.* Retrieved November 10, 2021, from https://www.internetworldstats.com/blog.htm#:%7E:text=1%2C574%20Million%20Internet%20Users!&text=A%20new%20year%20and%20new,persons%20for%20year%2Dend%202008

Leading Media Production Zone. (n.d.). *Dubai Production City.* https://dpc.ae/

Magna Global. (2021, December 13). *Magna Global advertising forecast.* Mediabrands. Retrieved December 21, 2021, from https://cn.ipgmediabrands.com/magna-global-advertising-forecast-global-advertising-market-reaches-new-heights-and-exceeds-pre-covid-levels/

Media Regulation. (n.d.). *The Official Portal of the UAE Government.* Retrieved September 20, 2021, from https://u.ae/en/media/media-in-the-uae/media-regulation

Media Regulatory Office. (n.d.). *Media Regulatory Office. UAE Ministry of Culture and Youth.* Retrieved September 12, 2021, from https://mcy.gov.ae/en/mro/

Meyer, D. M. (2017, September 15). *What Is TV Production?* Retrieved December 24, 2021, from https://ourpastimes.com/what-is-tv-production-12190691.html

Middle East and North Africa (MENA). (n.d.). Retrieved December 28, 2021, from https://www.investopedia.com/terms/m/middle-east-and-north-africa-mena.asp

Mubarak, M. K. A. (2021, November 25). *50 years since its founding, the UAE is a more creative place than ever.* The National. Retrieved September 10, 2021 from https://www.thenationalnews.com/opinion/comment/2021/11/25/50-years-since-its-founding-the-uae-is-a-more-creative-place-than-ever/

OTT/Over The Top | Definition. (n.d.). Retrieved January 5, 2022, from https://www.adjust.com/glossary/ott-over-the-top/

Ovchinnikov, A. (2020, June 15). *Fujairah Creative City Free Zone Company Formation.* Emirabiz. Retrieved November 21, 2021, from https://emirabiz.com/creative-city-fujairah/

Oxford Business Group. (2021, February 8). *Why have media producers flocked to Abu Dhabi?* Retrieved August 29, 2021, from https://oxfordbusinessgroup.com/overview/ready-prime-time-calculated-investments-and-incentives-aimed-developing-local-production-capacity

Pay-TV. (n.d.). Retrieved December 25, 2021, from https://www.merriam-webster.com/dictionary/pay-TV

PricewaterhouseCoopers. (n.d.). *Global Entertainment & Media Outlook 2021–2025.* PwC. Retrieved October 21, 2021, from https://www.pwc.com/outlook

RAKEZ Media Zone. (n.d.). Retrieved August 27, 2021, from https://rakez.com/ar/About/Zones/Zone-Detail/rakez-media-zone

Ray, B. J. (2021, November 20). *Law and Order Survives the Pandemic.* Gallup.Com. Retrieved August 20, 2021, from https://news.gallup.com/poll/357311/law-order-survives-pandemic.aspx

Turan, M. (2020, June 19). *Business Setup in Dubai | Company Formation in Dubai, UAE.* Emirabiz. https://emirabiz.com

Twofour54 Abu Dhabi media zone | Business Setup & Freelance Visa UAE. (2021, June 2). *Twofour54.* Retrieved September 20, 2021, from https://www.twofour54.com/en/

UAE's Media Landscape: An Overview. (2017, March 9). *ICFUAE | International Campaign For Freedom in the UAE.* Retrieved October 20, 2021, from http://icfuae.org.uk/research-and-publications/uae%E2%80%99s-media-landscape-overview

Umm Al Quwain Free Zone - UAQ. (n.d.). *UAE Free Zones*. Retrieved September 21, 2021, from https://www.uaefreezones.com/uaq_umm_al_quwain_free_zone.html

UNESCO. (2020). *Quadrennial Periodic Report United Arab Emirates 2020 UNESCO Diversity of Cultural Expressions*. Retrieved October 10, 2021, from https://en.unesco.org/creativity/governance/periodic-reports/submission/6975

Vivian, J. (2012). *Media of Mass Communication* (11th ed.). Pearson.

W. (2020, November 5). Dubai Media City celebrates 20-year anniversary. *Khaleej Times*. Retrieved August 21, 2021, from https://www.khaleejtimes.com/uae/dubai-media-city-celebrates-20-year-anniversary

WAM. (2021a, April 10). *CNN Academy launches in Abu Dhabi to train region's next generation of journalists*. Retrieved August 21, 2021, from https://www.wam.ae/en/details/1395302871508

WAM. (2021b, April 11). *ADU, twofour54 to train next generation of Abu Dhabi game developers*. Retrieved August 11, 2021, from https://www.wam.ae/en/details/1395302896894

Welcome to UAE Free Zones. (n.d.). *UAE Free Zones*. Retrieved September 21, 2021, from https://www.uaefreezones.com

What Are Media Productions? (n.d.). Retrieved December 10, 2021, from https://fonktown.es/what-is-media-productions/

ENDNOTES

[1]   Jebel Ali Free Zone.
[2]   Dubai Airport Free Zone Authority.

Section 4
International Advertising in Europe

Chapter 11
Tourism Advertising and Destination Image Building Through Cultural Heritage in Croatia:
A Comparative Study of Dubrovnik and Split

Ceren Gül Artuner Özder
https://orcid.org/0000-0003-1496-2772
Beykent University, Turkey

ABSTRACT

Through this research, an attempt is made to understand how Croatian coastal cities Dubrovnik and Split, with rich historical and cultural heritage, promote, market, and advertise this heritage through the official websites of local tourism organizations. In this context, after examining the general discourses on the homepage of the official websites of these cities, the discourses they adopt to promote their historical and cultural wealth in order to create a destination image are analyzed using content analysis. To do this, key concepts are discovered, and themes are determined, under which these concepts are collected inductively. The coding process is performed based on the concepts extracted from the data. Then, the two destinations, the official sites, and the sites to which they link are analyzed on the basis of the themes and concepts, discussing their weaknesses and strengths, identifying gaps, and making improvement proposals.

DOI: 10.4018/978-1-7998-9672-2.ch011

INTRODUCTION

In this chapter, Croatia is evaluated historically, geographically, ethnically, religiously, culturally and linguistically by way of introduction. Then, the importance of tourism for Croatia is discussed, looking at the reasons for its popularity as a tourist destination throughout its history characterized by wars and conflicts that resulted in several changes of government, due to its strategic position at the intersection of cultures and centers of power between the Near East and the West. According to the reports of the European Commission, the Croatian Ministry of Tourism and other researchers, the importance and contribution of tourism phenomena to the Croatian economy are evaluated quantitatively and qualitatively. Focusing on the cities of Dubrovnik and Split, information such as the number of visitors and overnight stays, etc. is provided. The strengths and weaknesses of Croatia as a tourist destination are discussed and proposals are made to attract the target tourist profile.

Next, the general structure of the advertising industry in Croatia is presented. The market share of different media and their relative effectiveness in reaching audiences are analyzed, with a focus on internet advertising. Since the main focus of the study is to examine the discourse on the official websites of Croatia's tourist destinations, the following part of the study focused on advertising, promotional and marketing content on the official website of the Croatian Tourism Board and the official websites of Dubrovnik and Split.

Since the pros of Croatia's focus on cultural tourism as an alternative to mass tourism are emphasized, it is aimed to examine the elements on the websites of Dubrovnik and Split in the context of cultural tourism and briefly inform about cultural heritage tourism in Croatia in the next section. Subsequently, the importance of running effective advertising campaigns and promotions in creating the image of a destination is mentioned and the possible current and future consequences for Dubrovnik and Split of adopting such strategies are discussed.

In the following section, the reader is introduced to the main objective and structure of the research, i.e. the form in which it is constructed and executed. The data obtained from the content analysis applied to the discourses discovered by examining the official websites of the cities of Dubrovnik and Split have been subjected to analysis, the results have been shared, the deficiencies and strengths have been discussed and the emphasis has been placed on the aspects that need to be improved in the discussion section.

In the last part of the study, solutions are developed that would allow Dubrovnik and Split to appeal more to the target tourist profile by paying attention to certain points in the discourses on their websites and to generate more tourism revenue by putting less effort and resources into it. After making recommendations for future research on the same topic, the concluding section mentions the importance of effectively managing all media on the web, especially with a holistic approach to building, protecting and enhancing a tourism destination's reputation in this day and age. Furthermore, it states that a destination's advertising and marketing strategies should be based on an effective image and reputation analysis on internet platforms. The chapter ends by mentioning the importance for Croatia, as a tourist country, to use the possibilities offered by the web as effectively as possible in the creation and development of advertising and marketing strategies for the country's economy and its future.

BACKGROUND

Brief History, Geography, Ethnic and Religious Composition, Culture and Language

Thanks to its particular geographical position, Croatia is like a bridge uniting East and West, i.e. Central Europe and the Southern Mediterranean. Through its history, a vast artistic, literary and musical tradition has been built up in the country. The cultural heritage is certainly not limited to those recognized by UNESCO (whc.unesco.org) and goes beyond museums, monuments, churches, synagogues, mosques and cathedrals (croatia,hr, n.d.). Located at the north-west of the Balkan Peninsula, Croatia is a small country with an area of 56,594 km^2, but its geography is diverse with high mountains, islands and islets numbering up to a thousand, a long coastline, caves, lakes, rivers and waterfalls. Accordingly, the country is characterized by different types of climate, including continental, Mediterranean and mountainous in different regions (David-Barrett et al., 2022). Croatia is mainly composed of three regions, namely Slavonia (in the northeast), Istria (on the northern Adriatic coast) and Dalmatia (covering the coastal strip). Croatia's cultural orientation could be defined as Western because of the Roman impact in law, literature, and its adoption of European institutions and economic system for a long time. 89.6% of the population is Croatian, with about 20 minorities, the largest of which are Serbs (4.5%), while the others (Bosniaks, Slovenes, Hungarians, Italians, Austrians, Bulgarians, Albanians, Czechs, Germans, etc.) have less than 0.5% each. Catholicism (87.8%) is the main religion in the country. Orthodox Christians make up 4.4% and Muslims 1.3% of the total population. The official language is Croatian, a South Slavic language, which uses the Latin alphabet extended by some diacritical marks, while Serbian is written in the Cyrillic. Although they are generally considered to be the same language, in terms of grammar, pronunciation and vocabulary, there are some differences between Serbian and Croatian. This is due to the different periods of foreign domination: While the Croatian language is influenced by German, Italian and Hungarian, the Serbian language bears traces of Turkish and Russian, regardless of the dialects for both languages (David-Barrett et al., 2022; larousse.fr, n.d.).

Croatia, which has shared the fate of any country with natural wealth, favorable climate, long coastlines and an important strategic position, has lived under many governments throughout its turbulent history, full of wars, regime and power changes, conquests and reconquests. If we are to proceed in chronological order, the Croatian people were subjected to the Byzantine Empire during the 7th century A.D., to the Duchy of Croatia from 7th century to 925, to the Kingdom of Croatia from 925 to 1102, to the Kingdom of Croatia and Dalmatia (united with Hungary) from 1102 to 1526, to the Kingdom of Croatia (Habsburg) from 1526 to 1868, to the Kingdom of Croatia and Slavonia from 1868 to 1918, to the State of Slovenes, Croats and Serbs from 29 October 1918 to 1 December 1918, to the Kingdom of Slovenes, Croats and Serbs from 1918 to 1929, to the Kingdom of Yugoslavia from 1929 to 1941, to the Independent State of Croatia from 1941 to 1945, to the Federal People's Republic of Croatia from 1945 to 1963, to the Socialist Federal Republic of Yugoslavia (SFRJ) from 1963 to 1991, and to the Republic of Croatia from 1991 to the present (larousse.fr, n.d.).

The cultural and historical heritage of the country has been forged by the strong influences of European Catholicism, Orthodox Christianity, Ottoman culture and especially Venetian culture. The proof is that Croatian cuisine is strongly influenced by Turkish, Central European and Italian cuisine. The Adriatic coast of the country was long under Venetian rule and the influence of Venetian architecture and art on the architectural heritage is remarkable. On the territory of Croatia, there are numerous remains of ancient Greek and Roman civilizations. Among them are the palace of the Roman emperor Diocletian (4th century) in Split, the ancient city of Salona in the vicinity Split, the ancient city of Narona around Metković, and the arena in Pula (1st century). A very characteristic remnant of Byzantine art in Croatia is the Euphrasius Basilica in Porec (6th century). The country is characterized by numerous traces of much older civilizations spread throughout its territory. In particular, the Vučedol culture from the Early Bronze Age, 3000-2200 BC, discovered in the Vukovar region, is a source of curiosity and enchantment. It is considered to be contemporary with Ancient Egypt (the Old Kingdom), the Sumerian civilization and ancient Troy. Another prominent archaeological site is "Bribirska Glavica" located in the vicinity of the town of Skradin, where the Croatian dignitaries Šubić-Bribirski had their seat. Also, archaeological excavations have been undertaken in this place known as Varvaria, a municipality that had already been settled by Illyrians, in the early Roman period. In the 14th century it was a fortress of strategic importance. Among the oldest Croatian cultural heritages, the baptismal font of Prince Višeslav of Nin (around 800) could be mentioned. In Croatia, there are about 150 pre-Romanesque churches, mainly on the coast, built between the 9th and 11th centuries. About fifteen of them are well preserved, including the church of St. Donat in Zadar, built in the 9th century, one of the most impressive monuments of pre-Romanesque architecture in whole Europe. The construction of the Church of St. Krševan in Zadar, which is recognized as the predecessor of all great Roman and Gothic cathedrals built in Europe, began in the early 10th century and was completed in 975. Monolithic stone funerary monuments, called *stechak*, are another type of characteristic monument of the region and some of them weigh about 30 tons. The oldest of these monuments date from the 13th century. Similarly, in present-day Bosnia and Herzegovina and on the Croatian island of Brač, there are stone inscriptions that are believed to be the first documents written in the Croatian Cyrillic alphabet, dating from the 10th to 12th centuries. The researchers discovered that these documents also contain Glagolitic letters. In general, it is said that a good number of written documents from medieval Croatia contain three types of writing at the same time: Glagolitic, Cyrillic and Latin in particular, which shows the non-exclusivity and coexistence, which is quite unique in the history of European culture. Besides the simultaneous use of three scripts, the use of three languages at the same time - Croatian, Latin and Church Slavonic - is also exceptional (Zubrinić, 1995).

Under the SFRJ, the country underwent significant cultural changes following the Western modernism and post-modernism movements, which had effects on the architecture, arts and lifestyle of the population, affecting the formation and accumulation of tangible and intangible cultural heritage (David-Barrett et al., 2022; Graham, 2021, Katunarić, 2007; Kordej-De Villa, & Šulc, 2021; larousse.fr, n.d., Matan, 2020). At the time of SFRJ, it can be claimed that Yugoslavia invented another "version of communism" after throwing away its ties with the Soviet Union and Cominform in 1948 and following the league of "non-aligned movement", which allowed it freedom of expression and a certain autonomy in the cultural, economic and other spheres of life, if compared to other socialist countries. This resulted in the flowering of Croatian culture along the lines of the Western heritage (David-Barrett et al., 2022). It can be said that modernism took off in Yugoslavia with the arrival of artists from European countries, especially from Berlin, Prague and Vienna, following the independence of the South Slavic state. These artists, who brought a new breath of fresh air by interpreting traditionalism in a different way, had a particular influence on the trends and lifestyles in the largest cities of the Kingdom, namely Belgrade, Zagreb and Ljubljana. After World War II, with the foundation of SFRJ, Tito adopted the movement of realistic socialism during his alliance with Stalin, from 1945 to 1948. This movement essentially diverged from the modernism of Western countries, and aimed primarily to integrate art and revolution. In the works of art, revolutionary heroes were chosen as main figures: Revolution, soldier figures and working class were given a special emphasis. The Batina monument, an expression of the importance attached to the alliance with Stalin, is considered the most representative symbol of this period, as is the use of posters and signs with communist iconography as a means of propaganda in public places. The tendency of socialist realism was to integrate historical and folkloric elements into art, but many Yugoslav architects opposed this phenomenon and continued their work following the modernist approach adopted after the First World War. After breaking ties with the Soviet Union in 1948 due to general dissatisfaction with the centralized system established by Stalin, Tito created his own socialist regime, following the non-aligned, totally independent of both the Western and Eastern blocs. Under this regime, he considered it important to preserve the ethnic harmony of the country composed of several peoples. These economic and political changes led to the creation and interpretation of an art and architecture characteristic of Yugoslavia (Kerkezi, 2018, p.29).

After 1948, the links between the Yugoslav identity and modern architecture are visibly established and under the effort of industrialization and modernization of the country devastated during World War II, the modernist movement is extended beyond the borders of the large cities to the four corners of the country. Tito aimed to establish his ideal of "brotherhood, equality, unity" in the ideology of governance and local and regional equilibrium (Kerkezi, 2018, pp.29-30). The detachment of Yugoslavia from the Soviet Union resulted in an opening to the West and exhibitions were held in the capitals of the republics constituting the Yugoslav federation. With the arrival of the 1950's, one encounters buildings that resemble the works of Le Corbusier, as well as cubic buildings with whitewashed facades, adopting a simple and uncluttered style, expressionist and sometimes crude structures that make up the large glazed office buildings, representative of this post-war era in Yugoslavia. During this period, it could be advanced that the construction of villas and individual residences decelerated at the expense of the construction of common and public buildings with an accentuated approach of expressionism and grotesque. Between the two periods that Yugoslavia went through, we must mention that the industry, the educational system, the social and cultural relations and the economy of the country underwent major transformations as well as the policies adopted. A certain form of freedom was established through self-management and the unity of the working class, which had its consequences on the field of art as well (Kerkezi, 2018, p.30), that had visible consequences on Croatian art and cultural heritage accumulation too.

Croatian artists have given numerous works of art in the field of photography, painting as well as traditional arts like fine textiles, embroidery and lace. In the mid to late 20th century, Croatian naive painting became famous beyond the country's borders. Cinema and music have a special place in contemporary Croatian culture. Since 1972, Zagreb, known worldwide with its school of animation and which won an Oscar in 1961, periodically hosts an international festival of animated films. As for music, Croatia reflects its rich culture through many forms such as folklore, opera, jazz, rock among others. Traditional music is characterized by the *tamburitza*, a stringed instrument similar to a mandolin, also known by its Turkish name "*tanbur*". The traditional dance is called Kolo, played at weddings and festivals and also appreciated in other countries of the former Yugoslavia such as Montenegro, Kosovo, Northern Macedonia and Serbia (David-Barrett et al., 2022).

World heritage sites designated by UNESCO in Croatia are Diocletan Palace and medieval Split, Dubrovnik old town, early-Christian Euphrasius basilica complex in Poreč, historical core of Trogir, national park Plitvice lakes, St. James cathedral in Šibenik, Stari Grad plain, Stećci - mediaeval tombstones, the Venetian works of defence between the 16th and 17th centuries, and the ancient and primeval beech forests of the Carpathians and other regions of Europe. UNESCO also named the Croatian intangible cultural heritage items as Ojkanje singing, two-part singing and playing in the Istrian scale, Klapa multipart singing of Dalmatia, southern Croatia, Bećarac singing and playing from Eastern Croatia, annual carnival bell ringers' pageant from the Kastav area, Nijemo Kolo, silent circle dance of the Dalmatian hinterland, The Sinjska Alka, a knights' tournament in Sinj, lacemaking in Croatia, traditional manufacturing of children's wooden toys in Hrvatsko Zagorje, procession "Za Križen" (following the cross) on the island of Hvar, festivity of St. Blaise, patron saint of Dubrovnik, spring procession of Ljelje/Kraljice (Queens) from Gorjani, gingerbread craft from Northern Croatia, Mediterranean diet, the Batana eco-museum, Međimurska popevka, a folksong from Međimurje, and art of dry stone walling, knowledge and techniques (croatia.hr, n.d.)

Importance of Tourism to Croatia

According to the report of the European Commission (Orsini & Ostojić, 2018, p. 4), Croatia has always been a very popular tourist destination due to its geographical position connecting the West and the East and the beauty of its nature with a very special character. This popularity increased with the acceleration of international tourist activities in the region after the collapse of the Eastern bloc. Despite significant losses due to the unfortunate war in the 1990s, it has recovered significantly. Since 2002, tourism activity has been following an increasing trend in Croatia and its share in GDP increased between 2012- 2016 from 3.8% to 4.7%. In 2017, 80 million foreign tourists stayed overnight in the country, and the total registered overnight stays were 86.2 million. As 19.4% of GDP, tourism brought in EUR 9.5 billion to the country and the sector employed 99,467 people, representing the 7.2% of total employment in Croatia. In terms of total exports, the share of tourism was 38%. Thus, the contribution of the tourism sector to the Croatian economy cannot be underestimated (Kordej-De Villa & Šulc, 2021, pp. 346-347). Certainly, the coronavirus outbreak caused a drop in tourist arrivals to hotels and other accommodation facilities in Croatia but it can be stated that this drop remained limited to 7 million of tourist arrivals in 2020. In the pre-pandemic period, tourism had peaked at 19.6 million arrivals in 2019 (including residents and non-residents) (Luty, 2021). About one fifth of the Croatian economy is driven by the tourism sector. Even in 2020, tourist arrivals in the country were 40 percent of 2019, the period before the Covid-19 pandemic. Ilić (2021) predicted that in 2021, Croatia expected five percent economic growth with the surge in the tourism sector. Recently, the Croatian Ministry of Tourism announced in a press release via the state agency Hina that in August 2021, the country received 46 percent more tourists than in August 2020, making a total of 30.7 million. If this figure is compared to August 2019, when the number of tourists peaked, it is only 7% lower. In August 2021, the percentage of tourist visits increased by 59% compared to August 2020 with a total of 4.3 million and decreased only by 14% compared to August 2019. It was also announced that domestic tourists generated 4 million bed nights, while foreign tourists generated 26.7 million bed nights. Istria County recorded 8.6 million, Split-Dalmatia County 5.8 million, Primorje-Gorski Kotar County 5.7 million, Zadar County 4.8 million, Šibenik-Knin County 2.8 million, and Dubrovnik-Neretva County 1.9 million overnight stays respectively. However, it is important to note that all of these counties are located on the Adriatic coast of Croatia. Not surprisingly, Dubrovnik and Split were the two most popular cities with 164,000 and 160,000 visitors staying overnight. Dubrovnik and Split have a particular importance in Croatian tourism since Dubrovnik is the most prestigious tourist destination in Croatia, which is also a UNESCO World Heritage Site, and Split, the second largest city in the country after Zagreb, founded within the monumental ancient Roman walls of the famous Diocletian's Palace. By country of origin, 1.1 million German, 338,000 Pole, 317,000 Austrian, 250,000 Czech, 239,000 Slovenian and 205,000 Italian tourists have visited Croatia in August 2021 (HINA, 2021).

It is also important to note that of the more than 5.5 million international tourists who visited Croatia in 2020, 1,081,000 were under 14 years of age, 682,710 were 15-24 years of age, 945,580 were 25-34 years of age, 1,131,000 were 35-44 years of age, 939,940 were 45-54 years of age, 522,240 were 55-64 years of age, and 242,510 were 65 years of age (and older) (Luty, 2021).

Regarding the two destinations that will be analyzed in this text, in August 2021, Dubrovnik welcomed 159,066 tourists and 638,601 overnight stays were recorded. The numbers have reached again those of the period before the pandemic and during August 2021 it was almost impossible to find a free bed, and restaurants and bars were full. Compared to last August, the number of visitors has increased by 120% in Dubrovnik according to the figures provided by the eVisitor system. It is also noted that in August 2021, Dubrovnik has seen 67% (about 2/3) of the numbers of 2019, when the number of tourists had broken records. For the most part, tourists from the United Kingdom, France, Germany, the United States, Croatia, Russia, Poland, the Netherlands, Spain and Italy preferred to stay in Dubrovnik in August 2021. The number of overnight stays in hotels and in private villas, apartments and rooms in Dubrovnik in August was about the same, which shows that private accommodation is as popular as hotels. Hotels recorded 275,619 overnight stays and 64,680 arrivals and private accommodation recorded 279,873 overnight stays and 72,480 arrivals. Thomas (2021) who provided the above information added that in September 2021, when he wrote this article, 14,174 visitors were still staying in Dubrovnik, most of them being English, German, American, French and Russian and he announced that soon Dubrovnik would be linked to 50 destinations if the circumstances of the pandemic allowed it.

As for Split, Rogulj (2021) reports that in July 2021, more than 14,000 tourists were staying here, according to the eVisitor system. Since the beginning of July, 254,000 overnight stays and 67,600 tourist arrivals have been recorded and she notes that arrivals have increased by 94% and overnight stays, 80% compared to July 2020. Tina Ćurković, from the Split Tourist Board, reported that most tourists came from Poland, Germany, France, the United States, and Croatia itself (Rogulj, 2021).

Although Croatia is the most important country in the European Union in terms of international tourism spending, which accounts for almost 20% of GDP, the adoption of a 3S model (sun, sea, sand) that is limited to coastal tourism activities in the high season, rather than diversifying the tourism product with special interest types of tourism and extending it to all seasons, leads to an underutilization of the country's valuable assets (Kordej-De Villa & Šulc, 2021, pp. 344-345; Krstinić Nižić & Drpić, 2013, pp. 160-161; L. Christou, 2012, pp. 21-23). Another important problem is the low spending of tourists compared to other tourist destinations in Europe (Ivanović, Bogdan, & Bareša, 2018, pp. 152-153; Jelušić, 2017, p. 89). It is observed that cheap types of accommodation are offered and therefore preferred by most visitors, which may well be a habit dating back to the socialist era. The researchers state that income elasticity is a more significant determinant than other Mediterranean tourist destinations in Croatia, although tourists visiting Croatia are less price sensitive compared to other countries the researchers examined. No increase is observed in the average tourist expenditure while there is a considerable increase in international tourist arrivals and overnight stays, which should increase the country's tourism revenues (Bellulo & Križman, 2000, pp. 91-92). Apparently, the engine of the Croatian economy is the tourism sector, but the model that the country adopted after the disintegration of Yugoslavia, namely mass tourism, is not proving to be sustainable in the long run. The establishment of a tourism strategy based on sustainability by differentiating the tourism product (e.g. with special interest tourism) and spreading it over all seasons could revive tourism in Croatia (Gamberožić & Tonković, 2015, pp. 85-87; Jelinčić & Žuvela, 2012, pp. 80-81; Urošević, 2012, pp. 69-70). The spillover effect on other sectors could be strengthened, and the damage to the environment as well as the congestion and crowding of people in certain places could be avoided. Despite the awareness of Croatian authorities on the issue, the practice does not always seem to be easy because of the difficulty of breaking the habits once established. Without the coordinated effort and determination of those responsible for the sector and politicians, the hoped-for development in terms of scope and quality could be difficult to achieve (Logar, 2010, p. 134).

General Structure of Advertising Sector in Croatia

In terms of advertising, television remains the most important medium in Croatia, reaching about 90% of the market. Another flourishing medium is outdoor advertising. In terms of market share, television carries 60% of advertising, newspapers 15%, magazines 10% and outdoor billboards 5%. Radio, which is growing rapidly, receives 10% of total advertising expenditure. There are 4 public and 5 private TV channels in Croatia. In addition, there are 6 local and 5 regional channels. Cable and satellite TV give access to dozens more channels. The largest number of advertisements are on telecommunications, financial institutions, soft drinks, newspapers and transport vehicles. However, advertising of tobacco products, alcoholic beverages and spirits are prohibited on TV according to regulations. The three main channels are Croatian Radio-TV (public) and RTL and Nova TV (private). 60% of advertising expenses are related to print advertisements in the 6 national daily newspapers. There are also 6,000 billboards with prices ranging from USD 140 to USD 265 per month. Optima, Iskon, A1 and T-Com are the main internet service providers. Apart from that, there are offices of several international advertising agencies in Croatia, as well as offices of Croatian agencies and several public relations agencies (U.S. International Trade Administration, n.d.).

Bilić and Primorac (2018) argue that internet advertising increased up to eight times between 2008 and 2017. They report that in 2015, the total net investment in internet advertising was 168 million Croatian kuna and the gross commercial revenue of about 261 registered websites was about 109.94 Croatian kuna. (1 Croatian kuna (HRK) = 0.15 USD in Jan. 2022). They estimate that Facebook and Google got 52% of internet advertising in the country in 2015. Due to the social, political, legal and economic problems faced by journalist, they argue that citizens evaluate the main disadvantages of digital news in "advertising overload, sensationalist reporting, substantial news without deep analysis and unreliable information."

Tourism Advertising in Croatia on Tourist Board's Official Websites

The different types of advertising activities conducted in the tourism sector are considered a crucial factor nowadays to attract targeted visitor groups to a particular destination that would best meet their expectations. Kronenberg et al. (2016, pp. 353; 369-370) argue that advertising is a much more important factor shaping international tourism demand than income levels or price levels of tourism products in a destination. Another important issue is the need for an effective "online customer orientation", which involves good market segmentation, raising awareness of the target visitors to the products and services using online channels, and customizing the tourism product according to the personal attributes of the visitor using online sales promotions, considering that online communication is a key success factor in destination marketing (E. Christou, 2011, p. 818; Inversini et al., 2011, p. 10). The success of a destination in being competitive and attracting more tourists is increasingly linked to the image it provides to users on the Internet. The official websites of a tourist destination play an indispensable role nowadays to achieve this objective. As part of her research, El Maazouzi (2020) highlights the value-added strategy used by

Morocco's official tourist sites, which consists of an effective combination of services and products in the creation of diversified and extensive service packages to better meet the demands of tourists. To be more attractive, this strategy aims to provide accurate information and high-quality content to impress potential tourists in the decision phase to buy products and services. El Maazouzi (2020) refers to Wang and Strong's (1996) "information quality's conceptual framework" in the context of tourism websites. According to them, five factors, namely "relevancy, amount of information, completeness, value-added, and timeliness" constitute the backbone of a high quality destination official website that would shape the buying behavior of a potential visitor in the searching and decision-making process. Although different social media platforms play a crucial role in the decision-making process of the contemporary visitors (Liu et al., 2020), the official tourism websites of destinations are still important, being a source of reliable information and reference for various review sites like TripAdvisor or OTAs.

One could also establish some complementarity between the different advertising channels and claim that they generally work together to achieve communication-related goals (Morosan, 2015, p. 49). The digital and online promotion, advertising, and marketing activities of HTZ, the Croatian Tourist Board, involve advertising on search engines, advertising on online portals, and using social networks for communication and advertising. It has a website (www.croatia.hr) available in 16 languages and updated regularly with new content and media (Turkalj, Biloš, & Deželjin, 2019, p. 724). Indeed, the working plan of HTZ shows that significant amounts of money were allocated to internet advertising under the heading of online communication (Lekić, Franjić, & Mencer Salluzzo, 2015, p. 155).

Accordingly, HTZ selected on January 2021 five marketing and PR agencies operating in international markets for advertising Croatia's tourism destinations and products on ten selected markets and promised to launch in February 2021 safety labels to guarantee safe stay in Croatia. Nikolina Brnjac, Minister of Tourism and Sports and President of HTZ, claimed that their main goal was to create a good image of Croatia as a popular tourist destination through an effective promotional campaign on international markets. HTZ director Kristjan Staničić added that choosing the right agencies to conduct marketing and PR campaigns abroad is crucial for the success of Croatian tourism policies and building an image of Croatia as a safe destination that sets high standards, fully prepared to welcome guests with a wide range of diversified services and products. The marketing agencies MediaCom, Real Group, Pro Media Group, Check-in PR and Aviareps have been chosen by HTZ to develop a media plan and shape the advertising strategy as well as to carry out the marketing activities for Croatia in the ten selected markets. In this context, media relations will be established by Aviareps, while activities concerning social media and communication on online and digital channels will be under the responsibility of Hills Balfour. Considering the importance of advertising on social networks to attract and retain visitors, HTZ has made important decisions to exist effectively on platforms such as Instagram, YouTube, the search engine Google and Facebook and has chosen some strategic partners to promote the Croatian tourism product on international markets. For 2021, they decided to cooperate with 43 partners legally, including 32 tour operators and tourist agencies and 11 carriers (CroatiaWeek, 2021a; HTZ, 2020).

Additionally, during the Covid-19 pandemic, for the summer of 2021, in order to convince foreign tourists to spend their vacations in Croatia, the Croatian National Tourist Board has prepared an advertising campaign aimed at Central and Western European countries as well as Russia. The slogan for this campaign, which is scheduled to be actively implemented through the end of July, was designed as follows: "Trust me, I've been there" (CroatiaWeek, 2021b). It is intended to gain the trust of potential visitors and is accompanied by beautiful photos of Croatia.

Another important detail for the effectiveness of this campaign is the diversity of media types that are used in its execution. In addition to the most popular TV channels, social networks, the most visited internet portals, billboards, digital panels and public transport were widely used in the campaign. The effort to promote Croatia as a safe and attractive destination, which has taken all the necessary measures to fight against Covid-19 ("Safe Stay in Croatia" campaign launched by the government), is an aspect that is highlighted in these advertisements, beyond the efforts to attract tourists here for vacation. Using the "safe stay label" in Croatia, the Croatian Tourist Board has designed a new, highly customized campaign, different from previous ones in that it is shaped - and then adjusted - according to the expectations and tastes of each market it focuses on. In order to succeed, they use satisfied customers from different countries who have already visited Croatia as campaign figures and try to attract new customers from these countries through their positive feedback and word of mouth (CroatiaWeek, 2021b; Ilić, 2021). An important point of criticism is that the campaign again emphasizes "summer vacations".

The diversification of tourism products and the promotion of particular types of tourism (such as cultural heritage, wine and food, nature, water sports, etc.) is achieved through twelve specially prepared videos of fifteen to thirty seconds, for different tourist profiles. These ads are used frequently on digital platforms and television channels (CroatiaWeek, 2021b).

Likewise, HTZ launched a new and very striking advertising spot, namely "Croatia Full of Life" (youtube.com). Supported by an interesting promotional video filmed in world famous places of Croatia and available on the official YouTube channel of HTZ (released in 2017) and in which features famous Croatian sportsman and artists, HTZ aims to position Croatia as an important sporting events destination as well as an enology, gastronomy, boating and sailing, nature, cultural heritage tourism, and other diverse types of special interest tourism (Denor Travel, n.d.).

CULTURAL HERITAGE TOURISM IN CROATIA

Willis (2014) defines cultural heritage as "the legacy of physical artifacts and intangible attributes of society inherited from past generations". According to him, "physical artifacts include works of art, literature, music, archaeological and historical artifacts, as well as buildings, monuments, and historic places, whilst intangible attributes comprise social customs, traditions, and practices often grounded in aesthetic and spiritual beliefs and oral traditions". He adds "intangible attributes along with physical artifacts characterize and identify the distinctiveness of a society". In its turn, historical heritage is defined in IGI Global's dictionary (n. d.) as "consisting of buildings having historic and artistic values, usually with a high seismic vulnerability". Although these two terms seem to refer to different things at first glance, it can be maintained that cultural heritage is rather a generic and inclusive term that also covers historical heritage. For this purpose, the term "cultural heritage" is used in this text as an umbrella term covering also the historical heritage.

In a common way, many scholars admit the existence of a "complex, intricate and symbiotic" relationship between the terms tourism and heritage (Light, 2014, p. 472). Reisinger (1994) defines cultural tourism as "the specific interest based on seeking and participating in new and meaningful cultural experiences, whether aesthetic, intellectual, emotional or psychological" (p. 25), where the primary motive for visiting a given destination is a cultural attraction. Similarly, the National Trust for Historic Preservation defines cultural heritage tourism as "travel to experience the places, artifacts and activities that authentically represent the stories and people of the past and present, including cultural, historic and natural resources" (Partners for Livable Communities, 2014).

Cultural heritage, as a driving force for tourism development, offers at the same time many opportunities for cultural, social and economic reconstruction. As an important asset of cities and regions, cultural and heritage objects bring benefits and contribute to economic development. They also serve to improve the social conditions of a country by solving the problems of seasonality of tourist movements and carrying capacity due to the density created by visitors in certain tourist hotspots or regions and by creating new jobs. Similarly, local cultural values are revived, national creativity is strengthened and traditions are preserved, giving the local population pride in having such valuable and unique assets to offer as a differentiated tourism product. It cannot be denied that knowledge of cultural heritage is a strong motivation for visitors and that it contributes to the building of a brand image for the city or region by allowing the valorization of these heritage-related assets and by offering a competitive advantage over other tourist destinations (Ismagilova, Safiullin & Gafurov, 2015, p. 158).

In the case of Croatia, there is a great potential of cultural heritage tourism for the optimization of the tourist offer. 84% of foreign tourists believe that Croatia is a country with a rich cultural heritage and the majority (71%) link it to the rich Croatian museums and art galleries. Similarly, Croatia is defined as a land of festivals and cultural events by 50-60% of visitors. With the interaction of all stakeholders, it would be possible to adopt a precise policy of heritage protection in order to exploit such a large cultural capital that still remains under the surface. For instance, although Dubrovnik and Split are the most visited cities on the Croatian coast, the historical monuments are not visited as frequently as other attractions in Split. Thus, in order to establish a sustainable cultural tourism strategy, local people and tourism coordinators need to be trained and educated in the management of cultural and historical assets, and government agencies and policy makers need to be agile during the planning and implementation processes (Kordej-De Villa & Šulc, 2021, pp. 355-356). Croatia has adopted the hybrid model for the protection of cultural heritage, using public funds and monument rental for financing, which leads to disadvantages in this area compared to countries with a long-established tradition of heritage preservation, all with the lack of sufficient promotion of cultural resources in the supply of tourism products and the near inaccessibility of some localities for visitors (Poljanec-Borić, 2017, pp. 18-21).

THE ROLE OF EFFECTIVE ADVERTISING IN DESTINATION IMAGE BUILDING AND ITS IMPLICATIONS FOR DUBROVNIK AND SPLIT

The image of a destination plays a crucial role in the selection process of tourists and it goes without saying that a destination with a positive and solid image convinces them much more easily. Due to the intangible nature of the tourism product, the destination image is the only way to help potential tourists evaluate the pros and cons of a destination, as they mostly decide based on their perceptions rather than objective facts. Since destination image has a significant effect on the level of satisfaction during and after a visit, it becomes an imperative factor in gaining a competitive advantage in international markets (Puh, 2014: 543). In particular, cognitive (knowledge and beliefs) and affective (feelings) evaluations of a destination directly affect the building of the image in the tourism field (Baloğlu & McCleary, 1999; Stern & Krakover, 1993 in Llodrà-Riera et al., 2015, pp. 320-321).

The findings of the research conducted by Kronenberg et al. (2016, pp. 352; 369-370) point that advertising is a significant factor in shaping international tourism demand at the destination level. While

Inversini et al. (2011, p. 10) contend that technology provided by internet infrastructure and an effective use of online communication means are strong marketing tools and key to success of a destination marketing organization's communication strategy, Lai and Vinh (2013, pp. 18-25) establish a sound relationship between effective online promotion and destination loyalty of visitors. Similarly, E. Christou (2011, pp. 821-825) highlights the importance of online customer awareness in tourism marketing activities. Effective promotional activity including marketing and advertising campaigns at the national, regional, and local levels designed to build destination identity as an important element of the destination image (Hunt, 1975, pp. 1-2) is key to success and is important to the sustainability of a long-term destination management policy.

Hence, HTZ launches a major tourism advertising campaign four times a year, two of them taking place before and after the high tourist season in order to increase demand in the low season, and the other two, which are brand campaigns designed to boost the country's image, create a brand, and increase brand awareness (Turkalj, Biloš, & Deželjin, 2019, p. 718). In the case of Dubrovnik and Split, it is clear that a good image is a crucial factor for the competitiveness of the destination, especially in terms of cultural heritage tourism, which must be promoted in order to overcome the problem of seasonality and to allow a substantial increase in tourist spending while reducing the duration of overnight stays. According to the SEM results obtained by Puh's (2014, pp. 540-543) research, the quality of the natural environment, the availability of leisure and recreational activities, the existence of favorable economic and social conditions and the friendly atmosphere of the place have a positive impact on the image of the destination, which in turn has a significant positive effect on tourist satisfaction. She argues that taking these results into account could serve as a guide for the design of marketing and advertising policies to improve the image of the destination. To this end, cultural heritage must be managed both as part of the natural environment and as a leisure element in the image-building process. Since advertising messages tend to attract tourists mainly during the high season, the discourse needs to be reconstructed in order to attract tourists motivated by special interest tourism who would visit these destinations during the low season as well. In this case, the perception of the advertising messages of tourists and readers in general should be explored to build a more accurate identity and undertake more targeted promotional efforts in the advertising campaigns of Dubrovnik and Split (Bait, Baldigara, & Komšić, 2019, pp. 32-33).

RESEARCH'S OBJECTIVES, STRUCTURE, ANALYSIS, FINDINGS AND DISCUSSION

The principal aim of this research could be defined as exploring the main themes that surge in tourism advertising and marketing in two of the most popular touristic destinations of the Dalmatian coast of Croatia, namely Dubrovnik and Split, carrying out a detailed analysis of terms frequently used in official websites of tourist boards of these cities. Through this analysis, the author will attempt to present the strengths and weaknesses of the discourse adopted and make recommendations for improving the content of the web pages in question and the sub-pages to which they link.

Within the framework of this research, after examining the general discourses on the homepage of the official websites of Dubrovnik and Split Tourist Boards, the discourses they adopt to promote their historical and cultural wealth to create a destination image, and the elements that emerge from these discourses were analyzed. Official tourism boards' websites are preferable to other sources because they are easy to access, provide reliable, legal, and up-to-date information, and do not involve direct advertising for the products or services of a particular establishment or business. In addition, they are a better source for researching elements of cultural heritage and reflect the institutional viewpoint of the state.

Since it is considered the most suitable method for the structure of this research among the qualitative methods, it was decided to use content analysis. To do this, key concepts were first discovered through the content analysis method, and themes were determined under which these concepts were collected inductively after being edited logically (Bengtsson, 2016, pp. 8-17; Dinçer, 2018, pp. 178-179; Erlingsson & Brysiewicz, 2017, pp. 93-99; Luo, 2019). The coding process were carried out according to the concepts extracted from the data. Then, the two destinations, the official websites and the websites they link to (subpages) were analyzed based on the themes and concepts, discussing their weaknesses and strengths, identifying the gaps, and making development proposals. The concepts are collected from the English version of the websites concerned. The umbrella (or main) terms are created by using an inductive method, identifying open codes and combining them with other open codes including same contents to create some sub-concepts, categories and themes that are organized in their turn as main concepts, categories and themes as described by Kyngäs (2020). The main themes are named according to the connotations that the group of concepts gathered brings out in the author.

In this context, the concepts and the umbrella themes under which they are gathered under two separate tables for Dubrovnik and Split (Due to the space restrictions in this book section, the author cannot publish these voluminous tables here. However, upon request, the author can send them to those interested). For this analysis, the websites of Dubrovnik and Neretva County Tourist Board (visitdubrovnik.hr) and Tourist Board of Split (visitsplit.com), as well as the websites they give a link were used.

Za sva vremena, Dubrovnik[1] (For all time, Dubrovnik)

After a detailed analysis of the web page "visitdubrovnik.hr> explore>attractions>culture" (Dubrovnik and Neretva County Tourist Board, n.d.) and the websites it links to, the important concepts encountered were noted according to the purpose for which they are used in the sentence and gathered under the main themes determined. In the tables prepared by the author, the frequency of use of each specified concept in all the texts examined is numerically stated in the column to the right of the concepts. According to their intended use, some concepts are included under multiple themes. These concepts are written in italic characters. Superlatives and adjectives used to emphasize the importance of a concept or the intensity of a feeling or experience are also included in this analysis. The research was conducted by the induction method. Concepts used at least five or more times are given special attention in the analysis.

According to the data, the most frequently used concepts under the "Religion & Mysticism" term are monastery(ies) (27), Franciscan (8), cathedral (6), church(es) (6) and symbol(s) (6). In the case of Dubrovnik, it is observed that the element of religion is mostly referred to in cultural heritage tourism using religious architecture and subsequently, religious sects and abstract concepts in the history of religion.

Under the heading of "War, Independence, Heroism, Patriotism, Disasters & History", concepts like earthquake (17), Dubrovnik Republic (16), for centuries (15), 15th century (14), historical (13), fort (13), church(es) (12), fortress (12), history (12), defence (11), 14th century (11), old (10), 16th century, councils (8), freedom (8), great (8), legend/s/ary (8), Venetian(s) (8), destroyed (7), port (5) and protected (5) are often encountered. Thus, it can be stated that the devastation of the city and its historical heritage by earthquakes and its reconstruction efforts, the battles fought especially against the Venetians, the destruction and reconstruction of the city after the wars and periods of occupation, the main defense points such as forts, fortresses and harbors, the supernatural and heroic strength of the defenders, the importance of an independent state, democracy and republic for the people living there and the important periods in time (centuries) as well as the long history of the city are highlighted.

Under the term "Architecture", the most often used concepts reveal to be city (74), palace (53), built (27), building(s) (17), constructed (17), tower (16), construction (14), gate (city gate) (12), Gothic (12), stone (12), bell (11), structure (11), works (11), adapted (10), architecture (10), city wall (10), column(s) (10), great (10), house (10), master(s) (10), most (10), Renaissance (10), fountain (9), town (9), beautiful/ly (8), large/st (8), monumental (8), old (8), ambient (7), Baroque (7), builder(s) (7), church(es) (7), fortress (7), lovely (7), cloister (6), erected (6), appearance (5), beauty (5), build (5), convent (5), gold (5), luxurious (5), magnificent (5), and material(s) (5). Accordingly, it is observed that by focusing on settlements such as cities and towns, the level of development in the region is emphasized within the historical flow. In this context, special buildings like palaces, towers, fountains, churches, fortresses etc. are widely mentioned and depicted in detail. By using nouns and adjectives relative to the construction, re-construction and adaptation processes of these buildings, the works done by the local and foreign builders and architects are reminded. Correspondingly, different architectural styles which marked the buildings like Gothic, Baroque and Renaissance are mentioned. The materials used like stone, gold etc. are equally noted. Finally, many adjectives, superlatives and adverbs such as "great", "large/st", "monumental", "beautiful/ly", "magnificent", "luxurious", etc. are frequently used to reinforce the feeling of preciousness and uniqueness of Dubrovnik's architectural assets.

Concepts like archive(s) (13), cultural (13), great (13), church(es) (11), collection (11), old (10), master(s) (9), most (9), statue (9), summer festival (8), valuable (8), work(s) (8), item(s) (7), painter (7), painting(s) (7), exceptional/ly (6), art(s) (5), artistic (5), heritage (5), library (5), manuscript(s) (5), museum (5), preserved (5), treasure (5), and wealth (5) are classified under the term "Science, Arts & Cultural Wealth". When talking about science, art and cultural life in Dubrovnik, sculpture art, painting, poetry and literature, valuable archives, collections, objects, paintings, libraries, sculptures and manuscripts are often mentioned. In this context, buildings such as churches and museums were cited, the importance of the Dubrovnik Summer Festival was evoked, various adjectives, superlatives, adverbs and nouns such as "precious, exceptional/perfect, treasure, wealth" were used to emphasize the importance of the works and cultural elements found there, references were made to masters and painters, and efforts to preserve the cultural heritage were emphasized.

Nima Splita do Splita[2] (There is no other place like Split)

The research for Split is conducted in the same way as for Dubrovnik, by undertaking a detailed analysis of the web page "visitsplit.com>experiences>city of culture" (Tourist Board of Split, n.d.) and the websites it links to.

According to the data, "dedicated" (5) is the most widely used concept under the theme "Religion & Mysticism" in expressions like "dedicated to the chief deity of the Roman pantheon, Jupiter", "dedicated to the Assumption of Mary", "dedicated to St. Lucia of Syracuse", "dedicated to St. John the Baptist" and "dedicated to St. Theodor". Considering this, it may have been thought that identifying historic monuments and structures with Roman gods and important clerics in the history of Christianity would further increase their value to visitors and attract more attention.

Under the heading of "War, Independence, Heroism, Patriotism, & History", fortress (19), Middle Ages (10), Military (9), Ivan Meštrović (8), 19th Century (7), 20th Century (7), Venetian(s) (7), Emperor (6), Roman (6), and Illyrian (5) are the most frequently used concepts. The detailed description of the life, works and philosophy of Ivan Meštrović, a great architect, sculptor and painter who lived in Split and an artist of national value for the whole of Yugoslavia, is important in order to emphasize the city's deep ties with architecture, art and culture. Accordingly, the references to the developments of certain periods such as the Middle Ages, the nineteenth and twentieth centuries, and the years when the city was ruled by the Illyrians, the Romans and the Venetians, are intended to certify that the multicultural structure and the rich historical heritage of the city rest on the foundations of great civilizations. The frequent use of concepts such as fortress and military is perhaps intended to salute the spirit of initiative and sacrifice of its inhabitants by recalling that this rich city located on the most attractive coasts of Europe was constantly threatened with attack and was forced to develop a defense mechanism, and that it managed to protect all these historical and cultural assets under these harsh conditions.

Under the theme of "Architecture", the most commonly used concepts are: building (43), palace (34), construction (31), church (29), city (24), monument(s) (24), architectural (19), stone (14), fortress (11), monumental (11), cathedral (9), walls (9), Adriatic (8), atrium (8), marble (8), architecture (7), bronze (7), courtyard (7), original/ly (7), preserved (7), villa (7), erected (6), Ivan Meštrović (6), architect (5), reconstruction (5), and representative/ness (5).

Numerous references have been made to buildings such as palaces, churches, castles, cathedrals, and the components of these structures such as the atrium, courtyard, wall, which form the rich and diverse architectural structure of Split shaped under different administrations and cultures. In order to draw attention to the importance of the conservation and sustainability of the city's architectural tradition, concepts such as "preserved", "re/construction", "architect/ure" are frequently used and emphasis is placed on the mental strength and artistic abilities of the human resources qualified in this field as well as the effort they have put into building this city. The frequency of use of these words allows to understand that materials such as stone, marble and bronze occupy an important place in these structures. There have also been numerous references to Meštrović, the great master of architecture. Monumental" is often used to describe the grandeur of Split's buildings, "representative/ness" to show the spirit of the era they represent, the internalized values, the love of art and culture, and "original/ly" to emphasize the originality.

The most widely used terms under the heading of "Science, Arts, & Cultural Wealth" are: museum (163), exhibition (44), collection (38), remains (22), archaeological (22), sculpture (21), gallery/ies (19), illusions (19), exhibited (17), permanent exhibition (14), special/ly (e-) (13), experience(s) (13), display/ed (12), heritage (12), maritime (12), exhibit(s) (11), Ivan Meštrović (10), valuable (10), present (to) (10), cultural/ly (10), ship(s) (10), historic/al –pre (9), oldest (8), Adriatic (8), geological (8), objects (8), wooden (8), unique (7), drawings (7), institutional (7), media (7), relief(s) (7), studio (7), dedicated (7), character (6), tradition(s)/al (6), events (6), painter (6), theme (6), works of art (6), medieval (6), preserved (5), artefacts (5), collect/ing/ed (5), furniture (5), independent (5), plaster (5), portraits (5), research (5), sculptor (5), stylistic (5), and zoological (5).

Reflecting the support for all types of fine arts and the desire to protect, develop and maintain them, concepts such as "museum", "exhibition", "collection", "sculpture", "gallery/systems", "drawings", "reliefs" are frequently used and detailed information about them is provided, trying to make the art assets and the arrangements for their management in the city the focus of the visitors' attention. It is emphasized that the originality of art and culture in Split originates from the element of independence, and that original and comprehensive studies in all fields of science are produced as a result of the great effort, dedication and conscious research of scientists. A particular language and style is used that draws attention to the institutional and traditional structure of this city that makes all these features unique, where institutions such as the Museum of Natural Sciences and the Museum of Marine Sciences have been created, difficult to find elsewhere in the region and in the world.

When talking about the Museum of Illusion in Split, one of the most successful examples of contemporary museality, which attracts visitors from all over the world, one cannot but notice the use of the "figure of speech" and the presentation of the institution with the help of successful advertising language. What is crucial is to be able to use this style to promote other historical and cultural facilities and attractions and to adapt them accordingly. Adverbs, adjectives and superlatives such as "unique", "special", "valuable", "oldest" emphasize the uniqueness of the cultural heritage in the city. It is understood that materials such as wood and plaster are used in the works of art, and many references are made to the painters and sculptors who contributed to the creation of the unique tangible artistic assets of the city, such as the great master Mestrovic, and the qualities of the works they created.

SOLUTIONS AND RECOMMENDATIONS: AN OVERALL ASSESSMENT ABOUT DUBROVNIK'S AND SPLIT'S TOURIST BOARDS' OFFICIAL WEBSITES

Welcome messages, slogans, images and videos on official websites of the tourist boards of both cities (visitdubrovnik.hr; visitsplit.com) are of high quality and engaging nature. In particular, the official website of the Croatian National Tourist Board (croatia.hr), with its welcome message "Trust me, I've been there" and its slogan "Croatia full of life", serves the purpose of destination advertising perfectly in terms of high quality visuals and videos, which constitute a successful example of advertising with short and concise, yet striking and engaging descriptions of destinations. With the section "Full of world heritage", it provides the visitors with valuable information about events and cultural heritage assets in Croatia too. However, some of the pages to which Dubrovnik and Split Tourist Board's official websites link (subpages) do not have an English version. In some, partial English is also used. For example, although English is used on the homepage, the subtitles and descriptions are not in English. This is especially the case for some pages to which the official Split website links. It is also observed that linked pages contain long stories about the institution or facility in question. It is important to shorten them and make them easy to understand.

Therefore, the pages of the institutions and organizations that the official websites of these destinations link to should be organized with a more professional understanding. In this context, consistency and integrity should be ensured in the discourses between the homepage and the linked page, and they should be designed and processed in a coordinated manner. It is therefore necessary to eliminate this discontinuity between the web pages of the two tourist cities and the pages to which they refer, as well as the confusion of linked pages, and to write summary texts in English, enriched with significant and striking titles that will immediately inform the tourist, as on the official website of the Croatian Tourist Board.

Whatever is intended to be emphasized at the regional or national level, those elements should be determined and agreed upon by a committee formed with the contributions of lexicists, rhetoricians, literary figures, communicators, sociologists, psychologists, advertisers, political scientists, economists and academics from many branches, and catchy, memorable, powerful discourses and slogans should be developed. For example, when a particular museum is mentioned, three keywords depicting that museum should come to mind. In doing so, the web pages of other destinations around the world, which are successful in cultural heritage tourism and attract a significant number of tourists, can be examined and retraced.

Briefly, it can be maintained that the official websites of the two tourist cities and the web pages to which they link are inadequate to promote and advertise tourism effectively and remain weak for the promotion of such historically and culturally important destination assets. Since there are many valuable academics in Croatian universities who are experts in tourism, it is believed that the inclusion of their opinions in the design of these websites would make a valuable contribution.

In addition, instead of bringing the religious element to the forefront, it is needed to develop a more scientific and impartial discourse that embraces all civilizations. This should pave the way for appealing to groups of high-income tourists who are not of the same religion as Croats (in the Far East, etc.). A tourism policy that focuses too much on European tourists, arguing that they are geographically, traditionally and religiously close, has had a limiting effect on the development of Croatian tourism in some respects. It is understood that Croatia wants to attract high-income tourist groups, but it needs to diversify the countries it targets to ensure the long-term sustainability of tourism. It must always be kept in mind that emphasizing religious elements to attract some will deter others, and the potential dangers of such rhetoric should not be ignored. Emphasis on the religiosity of the population should not outweigh the region's tourism product and expressions that that have no place in professional advertising and marketing should be avoided.

Another important deficiency identified in terms of cultural tourism promotion is that the nature, characteristics and quality of the existing human resources of the region are not adequately mentioned. The people of Croatia are highly educated and composed of individuals with different skills, but the emphasis on these characteristics is inadequate in both destination's websites. Links to the websites of contemporary Croatian artists should be provided, and contemporary professionals working on cultural heritage should be introduced. In a common framework with universities and research organizations, all these pages should be reviewed and integrated into the discourses of official tourist boards' websites. For those who want to learn more in depth, English versions of scientific articles and books written about cultural heritage should be created and reached from tourist boards' official websites with a single click. In this context, Krajnović, Bosna and Jasić (2012) propose the development of a "4-D brand model" for Dalmatian tourist destinations, which would involve "a unique set of fundamental characteristics that cannot be copied" (pp. 4-7), from the region's rich UNESCO-protected historical monuments and cultural phenomena, as well as the region's lifestyle, including art and artists. They claim that by integrating these properties into an attractive tourist product that would be effectively promoted, the demands of contemporary tourists would be fully met.

Pages about festivals and events should be more interactive, comprehensive and impressive. The history of all these festivals and events must be presented in simple but effective language in a comprehensive manner. For most events, only dates and frequency of occurrences are mentioned, and the information provided is not satisfactory all the time. In fact, Wu (2018) argues that an effective tourism website "should establish common ground with readers by inviting them into the text" (p. 170) by using more persuasive phrases to engage in an efficient dialogue with the reader. Furthermore, he argues that in order to shape the perceived image of a destination in the minds of tourists, organizations should give primacy to the affective and evaluative dimensions of the destination image.

The language used on the official websites of Tourist Boards should be more advertorial and attractive, and those who wish to do so should be able to read in-depth didactic text by clicking on the links provided, but long and complex information should be avoided on the home pages. Therefore, the texts to be included in these sites should be short, clear and intriguing, and figures of speech should be used at times. These texts, which should also be supported by high resolution and quality images and videos, should be prepared with the care they deserve as they will serve as a golden key to show the world the importance of these unique cities on the Croatian Riviera in terms of history and culture and to develop these important types of tourism. In fact, the growing interest of foreign visitors in Croatian tourism products could be related to HTZ's increased promotional efforts, especially on digital platforms, and it can be observed that online advertising efforts are the most substantial part of HTZ's activities. In the meantime, the latest forms of digital advertising and promotion have the capacity to make potential visitors more aware of the various tourist offers in Croatian destinations and should be used on a widespread basis (Turkalj, Biloš, & Deželjin, 2019, pp. 726-727).

CONCLUSION

It is a fact that destination managers are sacrificing considerable time, money and resources to make their destinations more visible on the web and to make it up to compete for a larger share of the global tourism market by using various online marketing techniques and strategies. Also, it should be noted that search engines index all kinds of websites such as reviews, blogs, wikis, evaluation sites as well as official websites. As Inversini et al. (2009) have mentioned, the organization of the official website of a destination is very important to build a decent image and reputation. However, one should not underestimate the role played by unofficial information sources that contribute to the construction of a destination's image in a dramatic way. As a result, destinations need to manage and organize their online reputation and brand image in a holistic way, i.e. by gathering and coordinating all actors and providers of information and services about the destination on any kind of platform intended to create tourism experiences, what Croatia needs the most. Inversini and Cantoni (2011) and Inversini et al. (2010) also found that managing a destination's online reputation in a holistic way requires leveraging users' online contributions to reshape marketing strategies and the destination's image reputation.

Similarly, Micera and Crispino (2017) point out that the systematic use of web reputation analysis of a certain destination would greatly help in developing effective promotional strategies to persuade the targeted type of tourist to visit that destination. In this way, it would be easier to co-create tourism products and services with local providers and to shape these products and services according to the needs and demands of the targeted clientele, which proves to be a wise formula for Croatian destinations.

While confirming that reputation is an essential component of a destination's competitiveness, Minghetti and Celotto (2015) point out that the analysis of user-generated content, which turns out to be explicit popularity, and the resulting engagement, called implicit popularity, is conducted separately from each other. However, they argue that monitoring the online performance of a destination deserves a more comprehensive and holistic approach with the ability to encourage tourists to comment while improving the engagement of potential tourists. To this end, the authors propose the prototype of an integrated tracking system called PlaceRank, designed to analyze the explicit and implicit reputation of a destination at the same time. The authors confirm the validity of the methodology, showing that the most popular cities are those about which a good number of people share their opinions on the web. They also found that the contents of less popular or less appreciated cities did not manage to go viral on the web, which is one more reason for Croatian destinations to effectively manage their websites and find ways to insert interactive platforms to encourage visitors to make more comments.

Furthermore, Iglesias-Sánchez et al. (2019) tried to find out the influence of the conversations that take place on web 2.0 on the reputation of tourism destinations, especially in different social media platforms and also investigated the role of co-creation practices in this process. Their research findings show that while social media monitoring is a challenge for tourism, it can also be used as a strategic tool in the decision-making process and in creating a sustainable destination brand. In particular, they emphasize the central role played by tourists in reinvigorating a destination's competitiveness with respect to others through their support of online posts about their experiences and opinions. With this in mind, Croatia needs to adopt some key strategies to effectively manage social media throughout the destinations' official web pages, such as monitoring online conversations on their own web 2.0 and other platforms, or using an "innovative social listening method" to facilitate the potential visitor's decision process and as a strategic tool for building the destination's image and reputation in a sustainable way.

Although Croatia has a plethora of cultural, historical, and natural resources, research findings show that some elements of the tourism offer should be improved, with particular emphasis on advertising and marketing activities with the help of advanced technologies and the power of the web to build a profile for Croatia as a high-quality destination with widely diversified tourism products (Alkier, Stilin, & Milojica, 2015, pp. 204-205). In this context, reviewing and reshaping the discourse on Croatia's official tourism websites plays a key role in achieving the goal of the country's marketing strategies. Considering the digitized world and changing tourist profiles, it is obvious that all these initiatives, which are vital for achieving sustainability goals in the long term, will be repaid in the next decade. Therefore, the calculation of the labor, overtime, resources to be allocated and budget to be spent for this purpose should be made with all these elements in mind. It should be noted that in a country like Croatia, where the tourism industry is the engine power in the development of the country, investing in the future of the tourism industry is equivalent to investing in the country's future.

FUTURE RESEARCH DIRECTIONS

One of the most important weaknesses of this research is that its sample is limited. The sample can include more cities and tourist regions, the same research model can be repeated not only in terms of cultural tourism, but also in terms of gastronomy, nature tourism, urban tourism, etc. Furthermore, this research can be enriched by using a quantitative research method such as survey. Employees of governmental institutions, locals and tourists can be interviewed to find out their opinions about the content of websites of certain destinations and the obtained data can be analyzed by quantitative methods. Relationships between specified arguments and dependent variables can be revealed. In addition, with different qualitative analysis techniques such as interviews, focus group interviews, phenomenology, ethnography, situational study (embedded theory), action research, new dimensions can be added to the research and the cultural, psychological and sociological dimensions underlying the discourses in the messages on the websites can be investigated. This research model can be repeated by examining the official websites of different countries and the findings can be compared with those of this research.

REFERENCES

Alkier, R., Stilin, Ž., & Milojica, V. (2015). Strategic and marketing aspects of tourism offer development of the republic of Croatia. In *4th Biennial International Scientific Congress ICONBEST - Economic Analysis of Global Trends in Tourism, Finance, Education & Management* (pp. 196-207). Retrieved 2021, August 06 from https://www.researchgate.net/ publication/ 304023578 _ STRATEGIC _AND_ MARKETING _ ASPECTS _OF_ TOURISM _ OFFER _ DEVELOPMENT _OF_THE_ REPUBLIC _OF_ CROATIA

Bait, M., Baldigara, T., & Komšić, J. (2019). Web advertising messages in Croatian tourism: Exploring qualitative and quantitative perspectives. *TOSEE - Tourism in Southern and Eastern Europe, 5*, 31-45. doi:10.20867/tosee.26

Baloğlu, S., & McCleary, K. W. (1999). A Model of Destination Image Formation. *Annals of Tourism Research, 26*(4), 868–897. doi:10.1016/S0160-7383(99)00030-4

Bellulo, V., & Križman, D. (2000). Utjecaj promjena u dohocima glavnih emitivnih zemalja na turistički promet u Hrvatskoj. *Ekonomski Pregled, 51*(7-8), 681–700.

Bengtsson, M. (2016). How to plan and perform a qualitative study using content analysis. *NursingPlus Open, 2*, 8–14. doi:10.1016/j.npls.2016.01.001

Bilić, P., & Primorac, J. (2018). The digital advertising gap and the online news industry in Croatia. *Medijske Studije, 9*(18), 62–80. doi:10.20901/ms.9.18.4

Christou, E. (2011). Exploring online sales promotions in the hospitality industry. *Journal of Hospitality Marketing & Management, 20*(7), 814–829. doi:10.1080/19368623.2011.605038

Christou, L. (2012). Is it possible to combine mass tourism with alternative forms of tourism: The case of Spain, Greece, Slovenia and Croatia. *Journal of Business Administration Online*, 21-23. https://www.atu.edu/jbao/spring2012/is_it_possible_to_combine.pdf

Croatian National Tourist Board. (n.d.). *Trust me, I've been there*. Retrieved 2021, June 15 from https://www.croatia.hr/en-GB

CroatiaWeek. (2021a, January 22). *Croatian Tourist Board selects five international agencies for advertising activities in 2021*. Travel. Retrieved 2021, June 16 from https://www.croatiaweek.com/ croatian – tourist – board – selects – five – international – agencies -for- advertising – activities -in-2021/

CroatiaWeek. (2021b, May 19). *Croatia launches 'Trust me I've been there' tourism campaign*. Travel. Retrieved 2021, June 16 from https://www.croatiaweek.com/ croatia – launches – trust – me – ive – been – there – tourism - campaign/

David-Barrett, L., Bracewell, C. W., Lampe, J. R., & Pleština, D. (2022). Croatia. *Encyclopedia Britannica*. Retrieved 2022, January 28 from https://www.britannica.com/place/Croatia

Denor Travel. (n.d.). *New advertising spot of the Croatian Tourist Board – Croatia full of life*. Retrieved 2021, July 20 from https://www.orebic-korcula.com/ new – advertising – spot -of-the- croatian – tourist – board – croatia – full -of-life/

Dinçer, S. (2018). Content analysis in for educational science research: Meta-analysis, meta-synthesis, and descriptive content analysis. *Bartın University Journal of Faculty of Education*, *7*(1), 176–190. doi:10.14686/buefad.363159

Dubrovnik and Neretva County Tourist Board. (n.d.). *Culture*. Retrieved 2021, June 15 from https://visitdubrovnik.hr/attractions/culture/

El Maazouzi, A. (2020). *The impact of official tourism websites on the destination image: The case of Morocco*. Uppsala University. Retrieved 2022, January 29 from https://www.diva-portal.org/smash/get/diva2:1474902/FULLTEXT01.pdf

Erlingsson, C., & Brysiewicz, P. (2017). A hands-on guide to doing content analysis. *African Journal of Emergency Medicine*, *7*(3), 93–99. doi:10.1016/j.afjem.2017.08.001 PMID:30456117

Gamberožić, J. Z., & Tonković, Ž. (2015). From mass tourism to sustainable tourism: A comparative case study of the island of Brač. *Socijalna Ekologija: Časopis za Ekološku Misao i Sociologijska Istraživanja Okoline*, *24*(2-3). Advance online publication. doi:10.17234/SocEkol.24.2.1

Graham, A. H. (2021). *New Design on Croatia's Coast*. Retrieved 2022, January 28 from New York Times webpage, https://www.nytimes.com/2011/10/23/travel/new-design-on-croatias-coast.html

HINA - State Agency. (2021). *Croatia's tourism industry boasts 2021 figures nearly matching 2019 levels*. Retrieved 2022, January 29 from https://hr.n1info.com/english/news/croatias-tourism-industry-boasts-2021-figures-nearly-matching-2019-levels/

HTZ - The Croatian National Tourist Board. (2020). *Call for expression of interest in the implementation of promotional campaigns with strategic partners in international markets in 2021*. Retrieved 2021, August 05 from https://www.htz.hr/sites/default/files/2020-10/Call%20for%20strategic%20partners%202021.pdf

Hunt, J. D. (1975). Image as a factor in tourism development. *Journal of Travel Research*, *13*(3), 1–7. doi:10.1177/004728757501300301

IGI Global Dictionary. (n. d.) *What is Historical Heritage*. Retrieved 2022, January 29 from https://www.igi-global.com/dictionary/historical-heritage/48689

Iglesias-Sánchez, P. P., Correia, M. B., & Jambrino-Maldonado, C. (2019). Challenges in linking destinations' online reputation with competitiveness. *Tourism & Management Studies*, *15*(1), 35–43. doi:10.18089/tms.2019.150103

Ilić, I. (2021). *Croatia puts safety at heart of 2021 tourism campaign*. Reuters. https://www.reuters.com/article/health-coronavirus-croatia-tourism-idUSL8N2LJ0A1

Inversini, A., Brülhart, C., & Cantoni, L. (2011). MySwitzerland.com: Analysis of online communication and promotion. *Information Technology & Tourism*, *13*(1), 39–49. doi:10.3727/109830511X13167968595741

Inversini, A., & Cantoni, L. (2011). Towards online content classification in understanding tourism destinations' information competition and reputation. *International Journal of Internet Marketing and Advertising*, *6*(3), 282–299. doi:10.1504/IJIMA.2011.038240

Inversini, A., Cantoni, L., & Buhalis, D. (2009). Destinations' information competition and web reputation. *Information Technology & Tourism*, *11*(3), 221–234. doi:10.3727/109830509X12596187863991

Inversini, A., Marchiori, E., Dedekind, C., & Cantoni, L. (2010). Applying a conceptual framework to analyze online reputation of tourism destinations. In U. Gretzel, R. Law, & M. Fuchs (Eds.), *Information and Communication Technologies in Tourism 2010* (pp. 321–332). Springer. doi:10.1007/978-3-211-99407-8_27

Ismagilova, G., Safiullin, L., & Gafurov, I. (2015). Using historical heritage as a factor in tourism development. *Procedia: Social and Behavioral Sciences*, *188*, 157–162. doi:10.1016/j.sbspro.2015.03.355

Ivanović, Z., Bogdan, S., & Bareša, S. (2018). Portfolio analysis of foreign tourist demand in Croatia. *Ekonomski Vjesnik*, *31*(1), 149–162. https://www.proquest.com/scholarly-journals/portfolio-analysis-foreign-tourist-demand-croatia/docview/2066619719/se-2?accountid=15454

Jelinčić, D. A., & Žuvela, A. (2012). Facing the challenge? Creative tourism in Croatia. *Journal of Tourism Consumption and Practice*, *4*(2), 78–90. http://hdl.handle.net/10026.1/11694

Jelušić, A. (2017). Modelling tourist consumption to achieve economic growth and external balance: Case of Croatia. *Tourism and Hospitality Management*, *23*(1), 87–104. doi:10.20867/thm.23.1.5

Katunarić, V. (2007). Traditionalism, Modernism, Utopianism: A Review of Recent Works on Transition in Croatia. *Politička misao, 44*(5), 3-27. Retrieved 2022, January 28 from https://hrcak.srce.hr/26397

Kerkezi, R. (2018). Transformation of Modernism in Socialist Yugoslavia Architecture. *Prizren Social Science Journal*, *2*(3), 18–31. doi:10.32936/pssj.v2i3.61

Kordej-De Villa, Ž., & Šulc, I. (2021). Cultural heritage, tourism and the UN sustainable development goals: The case of Croatia. In M. B. Andreucci, A. Marvuglia, M. Baltov, & P. Hansen (Eds.), Rethinking sustainability towards a regenerative economy (pp. 341-358). Springer. doi:10.1007/978-3-030-71819-0_19

Krajnović, A., Bosna, J., & Jasić, D. (2012). Possibilities and constraints of region branding in tourism: The case of Dalmatia. *Tranzicija, 14*(30), 1-14. Retrieved 2021, August 06 from https://hrcak.srce.hr/94569

Kronenberg, K., Fuchs, M., Salman, K., Lexhagen, M., & Höpken, W. (2016). Economic effects of advertising expenditures–a Swedish destination study of international tourists. *Scandinavian Journal of Hospitality and Tourism*, *16*(4), 352–374. doi:10.1080/15022250.2015.1101013

Krstinić NižićM.DrpićD. (2013). Model for sustainable tourism development in Croatia. *Tourism in Southern and Eastern Europe, 2nd International Scientific Conference Tourism in South East Europe 2013*, 159-173. https://ssrn.com/abstract=2289408

Kyngäs, H. (2020). Inductive Content Analysis. In H. Kyngäs, K. Mikkonen, & M. Kääriäinen (Eds.), *The Application of Content Analysis in Nursing Science Research* (pp. 13–21). Springer. doi:10.1007/978-3-030-30199-6_2

Lai, W. H., & Vinh, N. Q. (2013). Online promotion and its influence on destination awareness and loyalty in the tourism industry. *Advances in Management and Applied Economics, 3*(3), 15-30. https://www.semanticscholar.org/ paper/ Online – Promotion -and-Its- Influence -on- Destination -Lai- Vinh/ 821d7 0f1f29 7892 aa 7e277 8d634 73be 52c75 8334

Larousse. (n.d.). *Croatie*. Retrieved 2021, September 9 from https://www.larousse.fr/encyclopedie/pays/Croatie/115207

LekićR.FranjićT.Mencer SalluzzoM. (2015). Relation between media and tourism – Example of Croatia as a tourist destination. *3ʳᵈ International Scientific Conference Tourism in Southern and Eastern Europe*. https://ssrn.com/abstract=2637285

Light, D. (2014). Heritage tourism (Book review). *Tourism Planning & Development*, *11*(4), 472–473. doi:10.1080/21568316.2014.900287

Liu, X., Mehraliyev, F., Liu, C., & Schuckert, M. (2020). The roles of social media in tourists' choices of travel components. *Tourist Studies*, *20*(1), 27–48. doi:10.1177/1468797619873107

Llodrà-Riera, I., Martínez-Ruiz, M. P., Jiménez-Zarco, A. I., & Izquierdo-Yusta, A. (2015). A multidimensional analysis of the information sources construct and its relevance for destination image. *Tourism Management*, *48*, 319–328. doi:10.1016/j.tourman.2014.11.012

Logar, I. (2010). Sustainable tourism management in Crikvenica, Croatia: An assessment of policy instruments. *Tourism Management*, *31*(1), 125–135. doi:10.1016/j.tourman.2009.02.005

Luo, A. (2019). *Content analysis: A step by step guide with examples*. Retrieved 2021, May 11 from https://www.scribbr.com/methodology/content-analysis/

Luty, J. (2021). *Number of foreign tourist arrivals in Croatia in 2020, by age*. Retrieved 2022, January 29 from https://www.statista.com/statistics/1275897/croatia-international-tourist-arrivals-by-age/

Matan, C. (2020). Construction methods and materials in modernist Croatia during the 1930s. *Construction History*, *35*, 113–134.

Micera, R., & Crispino, R. (2017). Destination Web reputation as "smart tool" for image building: The case analysis of Naples city-destination. *International Journal of Tourism Cities*, *3*(4), 406–423. doi:10.1108/IJTC-11-2016-0048

Minghetti, V., & Celotto, E. (2015). Destination Web reputation: Combining explicit and implicit popularity to build an integrated monitoring system. *Ereview of Tourism Research*, *6*, 1–5. Retrieved April 20, 2022, from https://agrilifecdn.tamu.edu/ertr/files/2015/02/SP01_RecommenderSession_Minghetti.pdf

Morosan, C. (2015). The influence of DMO advertising on specific destination visitation behaviors. *Journal of Hospitality Marketing & Management*, *24*(1), 47–75. doi:10.1080/19368623.2014.891962

Orsini, K., & Ostojić, V. (2018). *Croatia's tourism industry: Beyond the sun and sea*. Economic Brief of European Commission, No.036. https://ec.europa.eu/info/publications/economy-finance/croatias-tourism-industry-beyond-sun-and-sea_en

Partners for Livable Communities. (2014). *Cultural heritage tourism*. Retrieved 2021, July 20 from https://www.americansforthearts.org/sites/default/files/culturalheritagetourism.pdf

Poljanec-Borić, S. (2017). Prikladni modeli razvojnog korištenja kulturne baštine. In M. O. Šćitaroci (Ed.), *Znanstveni kolokvij Modeli revitalizacije kulturnoga naslijeđa - zbornik radova* (pp. 18–22). HERU. https://www.bib.irb.hr/912433

Puh, B. (2014). Destination image and tourism satisfaction: The case of a Mediterranean destination. *Mediterranean Journal of Social Sciences*, *5*(13), 538–544. doi:10.5901/mjss.2014.v5n13p0538

Reisinger, Y. (1994). Tourist-host contact as a part of cultural tourism. *World Leisure & Recreation*, *36*(2), 24–28. doi:10.1080/10261133.1994.9673910

Rogulj, D. (2021). *Faithful Czech, German, and Polish Tourists Saving the 2021 Tourist Season in Split.* Retrieved 2022, January 30 from https://www.total-croatia-news.com/travel/54825-2021-tourist-season-in-split

Stern, E., & Krakower, S. (1993). The Formation of a Composite Urban Image. *Geographical Analysis*, *25*(2), 130–146. doi:10.1111/j.1538-4632.1993.tb00285.x

Thomas, M. (2021). *Dubrovnik records impressive tourism figures in August.* Retrieved 2022, January 30, from https://www.thedubrovniktimes.com/news/dubrovnik/item/12078-dubrovnik-records-impressive-tourism-figures-in-august

Tourist Board of Split. (n.d.). *City of culture.* Central Dalmatia: Split-Dalmatia County Tourist Board. Retrieved 2021, June 16 from https://visitsplit.com/en/184/city-of-culture

Turkalj, D., Biloš, A., & Deželjin, R. (2019). The effects of digital promotion investment in Croatia's Tourism Product. In *5th International Scientific Conference ToSEE - Tourism in Southern and Eastern Europe 2019 "Creating Innovative Tourism Experiences: The Way to Extend the Tourist Season"* (pp. 715-728). 10.20867/tosee.05.3

UNESCO World Heritage Centre. (n.d.). *Properties inscribed on the World Heritage List.* United Nations. Retrieved 2021, July 22 from https://whc.unesco.org/en/statesparties/hr

Urošević, N. (2012). Kulturni identitet i kulturni turizam - između lokalnog i globalnog (primer Pule u Hrvatskoj). *Singidunum Journal of Applied Sciences, 9*(1), 67-76. http://scindeks.ceon.rs/article.aspx?artid=2217-80901201067U

U.S. International Trade Administration. (n.d.). *Croatia - Country Commercial Guide.* Retrieved 2022, January 30 from https://www.trade.gov/country-commercial-guides/croatia-selling-factors-and-techniques

Wang, R. Y., & Strong, D. M. (1996). Beyond accuracy: What data quality means to data consumers. *Journal of Management Information Systems*, *12*(4), 5–33. doi:10.1080/07421222.1996.11518099

Willis, K. G. (2014). The use of stated preference methods to value cultural herʂtage. In V. A. Ginsburgh & B. Throsby (Eds.), *Handbook of the Economics of Art and Culture* (Vol. 2, pp. 145–181). Elsevier. doi:10.1016/B978-0-444-53776-8.00007-6

Wu, G. Q. (2018). Official websites as a tourism marketing medium: A contrastive analysis from the perspective of appraisal theory. *Journal of Destination Marketing & Management*, *10*, 164–171. doi:10.1016/j.jdmm.2018.09.004

YouTube. (2017). *Croatia full of life - new promotional video 2018.* HTZ. Retrieved 2021, June 20 from https://www.youtube.com/watch?v=0XbIR7e9PYM

Zubrinić, D. (1995). *Croatian Art.* Retrieved 2022, January 28 from https://www.croatianhistory.net/etf/art.html

ADDITIONAL READING

Grzinić, J. (2007). Strategy of tourism in Croatia for competing on the European tourism market. *Revista Tinerilor Economisti, 1*(9), 51-58. https://ideas.repec.org/a/aio/rteyej/v1y2007i9p51-58.html

Kelić, I., Erceg, A., & Čandrlić Dankoš, I. (2020). Increasing tourism competitiveness: Connecting Blue and Green Croatia. *Journal of Tourism and Services*, *20*(11), 132–149. doi:10.29036/jots.v11i20.138

ENDNOTES

[1]   Song performed by Tereza Kesovija in the album "Samo Malo Intime", 1999, Croatia Records©.
[2]   Song performed by Tereza Kesovija, in the album "Moja Splitska Ljeta", 1980, Jugoton©; Croatia Records©.

Chapter 12
The Hungarian Advertising Market and an Award-Winning Effie Case Study as Good Practice

Árpád Ferenc Papp-Váry
https://orcid.org/0000-0002-0395-4315
Budapest Metropolitan University, Hungary

Réka Kerti
Budapest Metropolitan University, Hungary

ABSTRACT

The advertising industry is an essential part of the Hungarian economy, which had an important role in rebuilding it after the COVID-19 pandemic. The industry is quick to adopt online and technological innovations. Digital media spend was the highest in 2020, and global partners such as Google and Facebook took the biggest slice. The case study introduces a recent EFFIE Hungary award-winning campaign with an unusual consumer review driving idea that relied on digital channels. The chapter fills gaps in the literature as well as provides essential information for global advertising teams.

INTRODUCTION

Advertising is a profitable business tool (Ebiquity, 2018). It belongs under the Promotion activities in the marketing mix by McCarthy (1960). Promotion, or marketing communication, includes advertising, public relations, sales, and direct marketing. According to the American Marketing Association (n.d.), advertising *"is a business practice where a company pays to place its messaging or branding in a particular location"*. A study estimated that on average Americans are exposed to 4,000 - 10,000 ads a day, and although there is no report to support it, the number in Hungary is likely similarly in the thousands (Simpson, 2017). Therefore, to be noticed by customers, brands need to stand out (Godin, 2020).

DOI: 10.4018/978-1-7998-9672-2.ch012

However, standing out is not enough. Campaigns with multiple channels are more effective than those that only use one channel, because channels amplify each other's effectiveness, thus creating a whole that is greater than the sum of its parts (Cox, Crowther, Hubbard & Turner, 2011). Ideally, the different channels have different roles in a campaign. Two distinct roles are differentiated: brand building and activation. Brand building works primarily on an emotional level and aims to build a relationship with the customer. In contrast, activation works on a rational level and aims to nudge customers to take action. Sales activation activities should be targeted, but brand building campaigns should have a wide reach to communicate with as many prospective customers are possible (Binet & Field, 2012).

The number of channels that are available for advertisers has grown significantly since the release of the first iPhone in 2007. Hungarians are tethered to their screens, the majority of them cannot spend an hour without them, and 38 percent of respondents check their phone at least every 10 minutes (Birkás, 2018). Likewise, during the Covid-19 pandemic (from now on referred to as "the pandemic") people spent even more time in front of screens. Sports events, including the Olympics, did not allow viewers in the stadium, everyone had to follow these events from home. Instead of in-person office time, work meetings happened online. Social interactions also moved online to a wide range of platforms from social media to emerging gaming communities. Moreover, Facebook's recent announcement on their metaverse predicts that this phenomenon will persist, even after the pandemic ends (BBC, 2021). Advertising is following changing customer behaviour.

Advertisers like to use digital media channels for multiple reasons, these channels generate a huge amount of data that fuels personalisation, as well as enabling a new level of communication between the brand and the customer. Digital media allows for highly precise targeting and measurement practices, thanks to the vast amount of data in the system (Katz, 2019). Furthermore, The Economist (2017) claimed that the most valuable resource is no longer oil, but data. Data allows brands to adjust their advertising dynamically, to test and learn in real-time, to identify the most effective activities (Katz, 2019). Digital media also brought a revolution to communication models. Before digital media, brands communicated with customers as a one-way method, however, now brands can also receive communication from customers, thus creating a feedback loop (McKinsey, 2016). Instead of brands trying to convince customers, brands can now include customers in the decision making, for example, Lego fans can share their ideas and interact on a dedicated website, and these ideas may even be launched as actual Lego sets (Fagerstrøm, Bendheim Sigurdsson, Foxall, & Pawar, 2020). This is a new decentralised and agile way of working, one that encourages active listening and gives more power to the customers. This in turn results in a better response to customer needs, increased trust, and brand loyalty (Shrivastava, 2016).

Media planning has also evolved in the 2010s, from the classic paid, owned, and earned (POE) model to adding an extra element, shared content, and to creating the PESO model. Within this model by Dietrich (2014), paid media is everything that the advertiser pays to promote (for example, advertising on TV, radio, digital, or social media), owned media is all the content on the brand's own platforms (for example, content on the brand website or social media pages). The model differentiates earned and shared media. Earned media in this model encompasses the classic public relations activities (for example, relationship building with investors or news outlets), in contrast, shared media includes all the content that is shared by the customer. Shared media includes all the likes, shares, comments, and reviews created by the customers. Customer reviews are crucial for brands because these are one of the top places for brand research online. Only using search engines and looking on social networks are more popular ways to research brands online (Hootsuite, 2021a). Consequently, when customers seek information, the sources they trust are shifting. According to Kartajaya, Kotler, and Hooi (2019), people are much more likely to believe in the "f-factor" that is the opinion of other people, for example, what their friends, families, other fans, or followers are saying, rather than the message in traditional marketing communications. This gave rise to rating platforms such as Google Reviews and Tripadvisor. Therefore, the traditional purchase funnel shifted, which ended at the moment of purchase and added an additional step of recommendations, thus creating a step where fans advocate the brand to potential customers. Trustpilot (2020) reported that people often need a little nudge to write a review, however, the key reasons to write one are to help the decision making of others, to share their experience, and to reward the company. Online reviews are important in tourism, these help tourists make informed decisions about their plans (Filieri & McLeay, 2014).

This book chapter aims to present an award-winning case study and the latest advertising context. This case study with its high level of detail cannot be found publicly anywhere else. Additionally, there is no other publicly available academic paper that compares advertising and its context in Hungary before and after the pandemic. The chapter starts a little broader, establishing the essential big picture factors that affect Hungarian advertising, including social, economic, political, and technological factors. Then after a brief summary of the history of advertising in Hungary, the second part of the chapter draws attention to the economic impact of the industry and the latest media spend data of 2020. The third and final part of the chapter introduces the Effie Awards Hungary award-winning case study, called the Double Shot Coffee Review Boost campaign. This final part begins with an overview of the Effie Awards Hungary but focuses on the in-depth details of the campaign and its success factors.

THE BIG PICTURE FACTORS AFFECTING ADVERTISING IN HUNGARY: A DISCUSSION ABOUT SOCIAL, ECONOMIC, POLITICAL, AND TECHNOLOGICAL FACTORS

This section begins with a general overview of the Hungarian society and economy, with a particular focus on the pandemic and its impact on people's lifestyles and the wider economy. Then the country's unique foreign relationships are discussed as well as the state of tourism in the country. Finally, the section analyses Hungarian's online presence, technology adoption, and online shopping behaviour, again while highlighting key changes since the pandemic began.

The Hungarian Society is Battling Some Challenges

Hungary is situated in Central Europe, along with Poland, the Czech Republic, Slovakia, and Austria, etc. Slightly less than 10 million people live here (Eurostat, 2021a). Hungary's population is slowly declining (KSH, 2021a). 14.5 percent of the population is under 14 years old, 65.6 percent of the population is 15-64 years old, and 19.9 percent are over 65 (Eurostat, 2021b). In other words, Hungary is an aging society, just like most of the European countries (Eurostat, 2021b). Furthermore, according to KSH (n.d.), in 2018 Hungarians were less likely to experience happiness than the EU-27 (i.e. the 27 countries that are part of the European Union as of 2021) average.

Although these are the latest statistics, it is likely that this happiness index only decreased in 2020 because of the lifestyle changes concerning the pandemic. These changes impacted most of the world: home education and home office became the norm, People fulfilled their entertainment needs at home and practiced living in smaller quarters. They had limited social connections that had a particularly significant effect on the elderly. As a result, Hungarians battled with psychological stress, anxiety, or depression (Osváth, 2021). As difficult as these lifestyle changes were in 2020, a non-representative study of internet users found that more than three-quarters of those working with computers would prefer not to go back to the office full-time, instead, they would like to work in some form of hybrid arrangement (Telenor, 2021). This makes people's reliance on digital solutions even greater than before.

The Economy is Developing but the Pandemic Set the Country Back Temporarily

After the overview of the society, the economic overview will be discussed next. Recently, the country's economy has been developing dynamically, and EU funds have also helped it to gain momentum. Overall, however, GDP per capita in 2020 was far from the EU-27 average, with less than 13 thousand Euros in Hungary versus over 26 thousand Euros in the EU and especially far from Western Europe (Eurostat, 2021c). In terms of the Hungarian people's financial status in 2019, the adjusted gross disposable household income per capita in Hungary (over 16 thousand Euros) was again far from the EU-27 average (over 23 thousand Euros) (Eurostat, 2021d). In 2020 the employment rate was 69.7 percent with an unemployment rate of 4.3 percent, this is better than the EU-27 average of 67.6 percent and 7.1 percent (Eurostat, 2021d; Eurostat, 2021f). Additionally, these statistics reveal a year-on-year decline between 2019 and 2020, corresponding with the time of the pandemic and the above-mentioned lockdowns (Eurostat, 2021c; Eurostat, 2021e; Eurostat, 2021f). For several months, the Hungarian borders were closed and non-essential retail outlets (for example, fashion, furniture, electronics stores, shopping malls, and restaurants) were operating with limited store hours or had to stay completely closed, only offering pick-up services. As a result, several companies went bust (Pénzcentrum, 2020a).

An Appealing Meeting Point between the East and West

Before discussing further, the chapter will briefly describe the historical context of the country concerning its ties to the East and West. After the First World War, Hungary lost two-thirds of its territory in the Treaty of Trianon in 1920. Then, after losing in the Second World War, it was occupied by the Soviet Union until its collapse. Although Hungary was never part of the Soviet Union, like Estonia or Ukraine was, it belonged to the so-called Eastern bloc with Poland and Bulgaria. Soviet troops began to withdraw in 1989, and after 40 years of socialism, the first free elections took place in 1990. Symbolising divorce from the Soviet past, on 16 March 1999 Hungary joined NATO. Then on 1 May 2004, along with the other Visegrád countries and altogether 10 formerly Eastern bloc countries, Hungary joined the EU. This was a clear attempt to strengthen its ties with Western Europe. During the 2010s, Viktor Orbán achieved much stronger relationships with emerging BRICs and MINT countries, Russia, China, and Turkey.

When discussing the international relations of Hungary it is essential to discuss more in-depth the capital city of Budapest and in particular tourism in Budapest next as the Hungarian political and economic power is disproportionately located here (KSH, 2021c). In terms of the population, 1.7 million people and almost half of the immigrants (45 percent) out of the 200 thousand in Hungary live here (KSH, 2021b; KSH, 2021d; KSH, 2021e). Compared to the population of the city, Budapest is a popular tourist destination, over 4.6 million tourists visited Budapest in 2019 (Statista, 2021a). Tourism is very important in Hungary, according to the National Tourism Development Strategy ("Nemzeti Turizmusfejlesztési Stratégia"), it generates 12.1 percent of the nation's GDP, and the plan is to increase this to

16 percent by 2030 (Magyar Turisztikai Ügynökség, 2021). Interestingly, Budapest provides favourable economic conditions for the film industry, therefore it has appeared in many Hollywood movies. Sometimes Budapest appeared as itself, for example, in the Gemini Man (2019), Dune (2021), and Black Widow (2021) movies. However, most often Budapest plays the role of another city, like Paris, London, and Rome in the movie Munich (2005). During the filming of these movies, celebrities often post about Hungary, e.g., when Will Smith did the 'Shiggy Challenge' from the Chain Bridge (Papp-Váry & Tóth, 2021) it was covered by the biggest news outlets. Budapest is famous for many things, its baths, Danube panorama, and architecture, as well as its coffee culture. This inspired the "Some Like it Hot" Hungarian country branding advert in which Tony Curtis is sipping coffee in the famous Café Gerbeaud. Hungarian tourism, like in all countries, was severely hit by the pandemic, yet tourism still exceeded expectations in 2021, the summer delivered 25 percent more guest nights than in 2020. Guest nights from foreign tourists also increased by 40 percent year-on-year (Marketing & Media, 2021a). However, the total number of guest nights was still 57 percent lower than in the same month of the pre-pandemic year of 2019 (Marketing & Media, 2021b).

This uplift in tourism was supported by the Hungarian Tourism Agency ("Magyar Turisztikai Ügynökség) that, besides organising several international events, maintained a strong online presence on key social platforms (including Facebook, Instagram, Twitter, YouTube, and even a podcast on SoundCloud).

Online Presence is Growing Quickly, and Technology Adoption is also Healthy

Next, to discuss the Hungarian people's online presence the paper analysed the state of technology and internet usage in Hungary. First, the number of mobile connections, internet users, and social media users is established. These numbers are compared to the global numbers and Hungary is above average on all three metrics. Then Hungarian technology adoption is discussed, both before and after the pandemic. Multiscreening, an important technology adoption phenomenon completes this section.

In terms of the number of mobile connections in Hungary, Hootsuite (2021b) reported that for a total population of 9.65 million, there are 11.35 million mobile connections, which is 117.7 percent of the total population. This is slightly higher than the global 102.4 percent. As mentioned above, Hungary also has a healthy number of internet users. There are 8.1 million internet users, which is 83 percent of the population (Hootsuite, 2021b). This is significantly higher than the global 59.5 percent results (Hootsuite, 2021a). If the Hungarian internet usage data is broken down per device, 51.6 percent of internet access came from a laptop or desktop, 46.3 percent from a mobile, 2 percent from a tablet, and 0.15 percent from other devices, for example, from video game consoles (Hootsuite, 2021b). Finally, there are 7.09 million active social media users, which is 73.5 percent of the population, this is a year-on-year growth of 8.3 percent (Hootsuite, 2021b). This is again significantly higher than the global 53.6 percent results (Hootsuite, 2021a). Almost every social media usage is done on a mobile device (94.7 percent) (Hootsuite, 2021b).

In terms of technology adoption before the pandemic, research by Gemius Hungary (2019) found that three-quarters of the 15+ years old owned a smartphone, almost all (95 percent) of these people connected to the internet on their smartphones, and on average spent 13.5 hours weekly with mobile browsing. In terms of Internet of Things (IoT) products penetration, smart TVs were becoming more popular, over one-third of the respondents owned one. Smartwatch penetration was also slowly growing, reaching 10 percent of the internet population. Smartwatches are most attractive to the younger target audience (15-20 years old) as well as to those with higher education (Gemius, 2019). In 2020, during the pandemic and its above-mentioned lifestyle changes, one of the leading electronics retail stores, Extreme Digital, reported that TVs, WiFi routers, tablets, headphones, gamer products, and laptops were very popular (Pénzcentrum, 2020b). These were often necessary because the home became the main location for entertainment, education, as well as for remote working.

An important phenomenon to highlight when talking about technology adoption is multiscreening. Multiscreening is prevalent in Hungary as well. According to Kurucz (2019), more than 80 percent of internet users with a smartphone have been on their smartphones while watching TV. When analysing a specific TV program, they spend approximately 20 percent of their time on a second screen, while this increases to almost 50 percent during the ad break. In terms of content on the second screen, audiovisual content is uncommon, they are most likely to be on social media, looking for information on the internet, or communicating with others. More than half of the respondents said that they immediately followed it up online after seeing a brand on TV (for example, they searched for more information or visited the brand's website), and 27 percent even purchased online as a result of seeing an ad on TV.

The Rise of E-Commerce and Cashless Payment

After analysing the state of technology and internet usage in Hungary, this final section of the environmental context will discuss another topic that is related to online presence: the evolution of commerce and payment methods, particularly the difference before and after the pandemic. Before the pandemic, the in-store experience was an essential part of the customer experience, this offered extra services (for example, highly visual "instagrammable" environment and products), it was an opportunity to collect valuable customer information, as well as these carefully composed retail outlets motivated customers to share the experience. For example, at the time of writing this book chapter on the global scale of Instagram, there were over 270 million posts with the hashtag #foodporn and over 140 million posts with the hashtag #coffee. However, in Hungary, the closure of retail outlets due to the pandemic accelerated the rise of e-commerce, 96 percent of the adult population that owns a credit card have now shopped online (Szepesi, 2021). This makes the online shopping journey important, considering that the number of retail stores per capita is only half of Poland's and a fifth of Western European countries (Portfolio, 2021). In terms of the total Hungarian population, 4.86 million people purchased a product on the internet in 2020 that is a 35.6 percent year-on-year increase (Hootsuite, 2021b). This is faster growth than the global average that is a 25.7 percent increase (Hootsuite, 2021a). However, the average annual spend on consumer goods online per person is more than double globally (703 US Dollars or 603 Euros) than the 301 US Dollars (258 Euros) in Hungary (Hootsuite, 2021a; Hootsuite, 2021b). Hungarians also increased their spending on online food delivery with a 37.7 percent year-on-year increase with an average annual spend of 36 US Dollars (31 euros) (Hootsuite, 2021b). This is again faster growth than the global 27 percent year-on-year growth, however average annual spent lags behind the global 112 US Dollars (96 Euros) (Hootsuite, 2021a). The pandemic made a big impact on payment methods as well. While before the pandemic Hungarians' preferred payment method for online shopping was an even spread between cash, card or they did not have a preference, after the pandemic cash purchasing fell and contactless payment became popular (Molnár, 2021). A study by Ipsos (2021) found that Hungarians are shopping online in multiple contexts such as while lying in bed (57 percent), while watching TV (52 percent), even during working hours (45 percent). Other online shopping environments include on public transport, in the bathroom, in-store, and some even during dangerous situations like driving or cycling.

ADVERTISING IN HUNGARY

After the analysis of the big picture factors impacting advertising in Hungary, the second part of the chapter presents the Hungarian advertising industry itself. Looking at the advertising industry, many tend to believe that advertising only existed after the break with socialism, in the 1990s. This is, in a sense, logical, since before that, during the socialist era the market was centrally planned without true market competition. Even if brands existed, there was much more advertising for the product categories themselves. In this chapter, however, the authors will focus on the recent past. The section will study the economic impact of the industry as well as the latest media spend data. As digital, similarly to other countries, is the leading media in terms of media spend, the section will deep-dive into this further.

The Brief History of the Hungarian Advertising Sector since the 1920s, through the Socialist Era to the Present

Hungarian advertising existed a long time ago, its history is more than a hundred years old. Hungarian advertising and Hungarian advertising science were already hot topics in the 1910s and 1920s. Several writings were published that laid the foundations of advertising, although these works later were forgotten (Szabó-Kákonyi & Papp-Váry, 2013). The first definition of admen was published in 1922, by Blockner Izidor: "They find their reasons to exist in the financial growth of their client. [...] They have many years of experience, they have economic qualifications, know the business market, and especially the psychology of the audience, [...] They lay down their advertising plan with certainty and determination [...], they take into account all possible options, so [...] they cannot be surprised [...] they complete their paths with great precision and careful foresight." What is even more interesting, the notion of brands, segmentation, or integrated marketing communication already appeared in works almost a hundred years ago, even if the professional terminology was different at the time (Szabó-Kákonyi & Papp-Váry, 2013).

In the next main chapter in the history of advertising in Hungary, i.e. during the socialist era, advertising was quite different as there was no market economy. The market was under state control. As there was no real market competition, the role of advertising was to improve a company's general image and to inform consumers about its latest products. As a result of this environment, advertisement content was often cheerful or funny (Bettina, 2020). Understandably, these ads have a notable fan base, for example, at the time of writing this book chapter, the video called "Retro advertisements" ("Retró reklámok") had 800 thousand views on YouTube (2014). The pioneer of this socialist era was István Sas, who won several awards at the Cannes Advertising Festival in the 1970s and 1980s. He was the subject matter expert on advertising psychology that is an interdisciplinary between social sciences and marketing. He popularised theories in cognitive processing, the impact of psychological factors, and motivation theories in Hungary (Sas, 2007).

Since 1989, the country has had both international and national brand advertising, and multinational agencies have also established themselves in the country, for example, Young and Rubicam or DDB. Additionally, many international brands choose to develop and produce their advertising locally. For example, Coca-Cola produced a bespoke spot featuring Lake Balaton, the largest lake in Central Europe that is also nicknamed "The Hungarian Sea".

The Marketing Sector Contributed to the Production of Over One Billion Euros Gross Value Added (GVA)

After the brief recount of advertising history, this section will discuss the economic impact of the sector. An important organisation, the Hungarian Marketing Association ("Magyar Marketing Szövetség" or "MMSZ"), carried out comprehensive research in 2020, based on their findings, *„Marketing and the creative industry are the driving forces of the economy"* (MMSZ, 2020). Marketing Indikátor presents the economic role and weight of the marketing sector, including GVA, jobs, and the tax generated by the sector. The results are compared to the other countries within the EU. This section then ends with an outlook into the role of marketing in the future and a note about the potential admen of the future.

The marketing sector is characteristically dominated by small- and medium-enterprises (SMEs). The research found that in 2019 there were 17.3 thousand companies in the sector and out of this number only 61.4 percent showed economic activity in the past, additionally, there is no big corporate with over 250 employees in the sector (MMSZ, 2020).

The impact of marketing is relevant for advertising because marketing is often thought of interchangeably with advertising, even though marketing encompasses a broader sector, including market research, PR and communication, direct marketing, and of course, advertising (MMSZ, 2020). Taking into account the spill-over effects, the study found that the marketing sector contributed to the production of 402.4 billion Forints (1,113.7 million Euros) GVA in 2018 that is 1.1 percent of the total GVA of Hungary. Every 1,000 Forints (2.77 Euros) GVA in the sector contributed an additional 860 Forints (2.38 Euros) to the total Hungarian economy (MMSZ, 2020). In 2019, the sector provided 27,800 jobs and the work of every 100 workers in the sector created further 111 job opportunities (MMSZ, 2020). In terms of indirect effects, the marketing sector contributed 137.4 billion Forints (380.4 million Euros) to the national income in terms of tax revenue. This is a higher amount than the tax revenue generated from small businesses or the duty tax of alcoholic beverages and other products (MMSZ, 2020). The Marketing Indikátor also compared these results on an international scale. In terms of GVA per employee, the effectiveness of the marketing sector in Hungary is in line with the European Union (EU-28, including the United Kingdom). In comparison with other countries in the region, GVA per employee is lower in Slovakia but significantly higher in Poland and the Czech Republic. Marketing has an important role in innovation, however, in 2016, only 12,9 percent of Hungarian companies had marketing innovation initiatives. This is below the EU-28 average. Out of the EU countries, only Romania, Poland, and Bulgaria had a lower number of companies that carried out marketing innovation than those in Hungary (MMSZ, 2020).

The marketing sector predicts a strong future. First, MMSZ (2020) in the Marketing Indikátor highlighted four areas in which the marketing industry can be of particular help in re-energising the Hungarian post-pandemic economy. The following will stimulate the growth and development of a sustainable, circular economy: 1) Build strong Hungarian brands on the international market, promote them, drive sales, and develop brand loyalty, for example, through the Hungarian Multi Programme ("Magyar Multi Program"). 2) Development of locked down sectors, for example in terms of digital services, and as a specific area, support the relaunch of tourism and the development of product tourism. 3) Develop customer awareness through specific programmes from school age. 4) Encourage innovation through developing training programmes for businesses. Second, the talent pool to support these plans is growing, as marketing is very popular among prospective university students. It is consistently one of the top university subjects to apply for, for example, in 2021 it was the second BSc programme, only preceded by business and management (Eduline, 2019).

The Biggest Budget within the Total Media Spend was Allocated to Digital Channels

The total communications spending of Hungary in 2020 was 401.9 billion Forints (1,112.8 million Euros), this is a year-on-year decrease of 15.8 percent that is likely due to the pandemic. The biggest portion of this was spent on media (59.6 percent), the second-biggest portion was the cost of the creative and media services (MRSZ, 2021a). Next, the chapter analyses media spend and in particular digital media spend.

According to The Hungarian Advertising Association ("Magyar Marketing Szövetség" or MRSZ), total media spending in 2020 was 240 billion Forints (664.6 million Euros). It is important to note, however, that 2020 is the first year of the Covid-19 pandemic and its associated restrictions, therefore spending on media declined by 2.8 percent. Industry experts are forecasting that it will take until 2024 for the industry to exceed the results of 2019 (MRSZ, 2021b). The only exception to the declining trend was seen in digital channels that were able to grow by 5.5 percent (MRSZ, 2021a). Additionally, digital was also the media that received the highest spend of 44.7 percent (with Facebook and Google as the leading digital media owners), followed by television with 26.7 percent, and press with 15.4 percent. Outdoor media spend significantly decreased to 8.5 percent and radio media spend decreased to 4.2 percent. The mandatory closure of cinemas meant that they were the hardest hit media: in 2020 it only received 0.5 percent of the total media spend. Similar to the global trends, digital spending is growing year on year MRSZ, 2021c; Jandó, 2020). However, if this is compared with the international data of Statista.com, then Hungary is still lagging behind, it has not reached the international average of over 60 percent (Statista, 2021b).

In terms of top companies, over-the-counter medicine companies Sanofi-Aventis and GlaxoSmithKline and FMCG companies Procter & Gamble and Ferrero continued to dominate media spend charts (Marketing & Media, 2021c). Media spend on tourism was not as drastically cut, as it was earlier expected, there was only 29 percent spend difference year-on-year (Marketing & Media, 2021d)

Within Digital Spend, Global Partners are Taking the Biggest Volume of Spend

As digital was the only media that grew in 2020, the chapter deep-dived into it further. The year 2020 ended on a more positive note than industry experts predicted in Q2, there was a small growth in digital, in contrast to the decline seen in other media. Industry experts are even forecasting a 6 percent growth in digital advertising spending for 2021 (IAB Hungary, 2021a). This section first discusses the reasons why global online platforms are popular in Hungary. Afterward, it discusses the key future challenges, adblocking, and Google's decision to stop supporting third party cookies.

Despite concerns about brand safety and the platforms' negative impact on people's mental health media, spending on global online platforms increased. The Hungarian department of the Interactive Advertising Bureau (IAB Hungary) (2021b), the European industry body for digital marketing and advertising, reported a 59 percent spend out of the total digital spend. This number is so high because target audiences are on these platforms at scale and brands follow them (Kreatív, 2021). Google and Facebook own the most popular websites by traffic in Hungary and these platforms allow for exceptional targeting and measuring capabilities (Hootsuite, 2021b; Fülöp, 2021). These global online platforms are particularly interesting for SMEs because it is possible to advertise with a few thousand Forints, compared to local online media owners, where the minimum budget threshold could be around 100,000 Forints (around 280 Euros) (KPMG, 2021). Perhaps due to this, Facebook is the most popular advertising platform choice for SMEs since 2016 (KPMG, 2021). Although there is no lower limit to the amount a brand can spend on Facebook, experts agree that this budget needs to be big enough to make an impact on business and not just communications objectives (Fülöp, 2021).

In terms of the future of digital advertising, adblocking is a good predictor as it provides a good measure of the level of online ad dislike on the market. The top reasons globally for using an ad blocker are that they see too many ads (22.3 percent), that they are irrelevant (22.3 percent), or that the ads they see are intrusive (19.9 percent) (Hootsuite, 2021a). There are different statistics for the state of adblocking in Hungary (see PageFair, 2017; IAB Hungary, 2017; Hootsuite, 2021a). However, it is certain that in response to ad blocking and the rising number of browsers with built-in ad blockers on offer, Google announced in 2020 that they will stop supporting third party cookies from 2022 onwards (Google Blog, 2020). This is important for Hungary because the majority (70.1 percent) of Hungarians access the internet via a Google Chrome browser (Hootsuite, 2021b). Since then, the original 2022 deadline has been pushed back until 2023 but this will make a significant impact on advertising in Hungary (Google Blog, 2021).

THE CASE STUDY OF THE LATEST PLATINA EFFIE HUNGARY WINNER: THE DOUBLE SHOT COFFEE REVIEW BOOST CAMPAIGN

The final part of this book chapter will discuss the Double Shot Coffee Review Boost campaign, including an overview of the award, followed by a thorough introduction of the campaign itself. This includes first a brief summary, background, target audience, objectives. Afterward, this will be followed by the key insights, the strategy, the activation of the idea, and the section finishes with the discussion of the results and any other factors that may have contributed to the success.

Judging of the Prestigious Effie Awards Hungary Awards

This section gives a brief overview of the award. Double Shot Coffee, the coffee shop, and its agency, DOT Creative's campaign won the famous Platina Effie at the Effie Awards Hungary 2020 as well as the „low budget economic campaigns" category. The organisers of Effie Awards Hungary awarded this year's effectiveness awards based on the evaluation of a jury of 120 people (Effie, 2021b). They highlighted the „*exemplary and creative approach that used simple but excellent tools that were able to achieve and even exceed the goals of the small business run by young people in an integrated way, and at the same time achieving long-term effectiveness*" (Effie, 2021b). The campaign, which cost less than 5 million Forints (approx. 14 thousand Euros) and ran between 1st April – 28th June 2019, quadrupled the business' revenue with a ~1000 percent growth in online reviews. The Effie Awards Hungary is one of the prestigious local advertising awards, this has been awarded for 20 years and it is judged based on the proven effectiveness of marketing communications activities. In particular, scoring is based on weighted criteria of 1) challenge, background, and objectives (23.3 percent), 2) insight, strategy, and idea (23.3 percent), 3) activation (23.3 percent), 4) results (30 percent) (Effie, 2021a). Ipsos analysed what made a campaign more likely to be successful on this award than the rest. The Effie Awards Hungary Analysis by Ipsos (Takó, 2020) claimed that the best practice recommendations to win an award are the following: 1) Focus the objectives 2) Do research upfront 3) Campaigns with lower budgets (less than 500k Forints or 1.4 thousand Euros) are more likely to win 4) Measure hard business metric (e.g. revenue gain or new customer acquisition) rather than communications objectives (e.g. awareness).

Summary of the Double Shot Coffee Campaign

To briefly summarise the campaign, Double Shot opened a new location in one of Budapest's most popular touristic areas. However, this was not enough for success, the shop struggled to make a profit. Instead of launching a simple awareness campaign, the team focused all its efforts on maximising positive online reviews. They conducted primary research, developed staff training, upgraded the brand's online presence, then spent the limited paid media budget on ads that were asking customers to submit reviews. In just 3 months the campaign delivered ten times growth in positive reviews, the business revenue has tripled, and the campaign had to end much sooner than the planned end date.

The rest of this section will go through the background to the campaign, the target audience, and the objectives, followed by the key insights, the strategy, the activation of the idea, and it will finish with the discussion of the results and any other factors that may have contributed to the success.

Background

The coffee shop opened a new unit in 2019 in one of the busier areas of Budapest. The owner initially believed that the excellent location, the quality of the service, and the expected growth of the category were going to be enough to achieve success. However, the coffee shop ended up operating at approximately only 35 percent capacity. Competition was fierce from a constant flow of new coffee shops and bistros, in an area that was already full of gastronomic offerings. The year 2019 was a particularly competitive one in the gastronomy sector in Budapest. The biggest challenge, however, was that people had very little knowledge about truly quality coffee. Recently, McDonald's, Costa Coffee, Starbucks, and MOL, one of the biggest gas stations in Hungary, – with their large distribution capabilities and marketing budgets – have achieved the perception that they sell quality coffee. Small brands could only break through this existing perception by getting people to try their products and experience the difference themselves. After these initial challenges, the owner of the shop realised that his business could only grow with the help of communication.

The Target Audience

The team working on the campaign needed to find a more sophisticated target audience than the classic socio-demographic targeting. The strategy defined and simplified the targeting: in addition to an interest in 'coffee', the team specifically targeted foreign tourists as well as local foreigners. The rationale behind putting a foreign audience in focus is two-fold: 1) the aim is to influence the decision making of foreigners 2) the category of specialty coffee is less developed in Hungary, so the team wanted to also validate the quality of the coffee shop towards the locals. In addition, foreigners are much more likely to rate places than locals. This is due to A) they have more time as they are visiting during their holidays or travels B) they are happy to provide information that will help other tourists C) they use this information as a reminder that – if they visit again – can be used as a guide D) they are in the right mindset, tourists read plenty of information ahead of their trip, so it is more likely that they will remember to share their opinion; this behaviour is lost in everyday life. In addition, those interested in quality coffee and foreigners are considered to be the most homogenous target group, which has also made effective targeting much easier.

Objectives

The primary objective was a business objective, to achieve a minimum 50 percent traffic increase to ensure the future of the coffee shop. This amount was essential to cover the basic costs of operating the coffee shop, to make a profit and also generate some savings. However, long-term growth required more to be done, so the agency instead aimed to double the traffic. Behaviour change is the basis of delivering the desired business results. The goal was to get more online reviews, however, the exact number of reviews required was not quantified in the brief. The agency estimated that they needed hundreds of online reviews to succeed, at a conversion rate of 15 percent. This means that they had to reach existing and previous customers as efficiently as possible.

Insight

Online reviews have a significant impact on purchase decisions. Research shows that 93 percent of customers say that reviews make an impact on their decision making, as well as these reviews contribute to every part of the customer journey, so reviews have longer-term effects (Podium, 2017).

There were supporting insights that refined the strategy. First, the fact that if you do not ask, you will not get much feedback. Second, all touchpoints need to be optimised (from server to end customer) for the campaign to be a success. Smaller budgets are common in the SME sector. And if a campaign has a smaller budget, cost effectiveness is key. Therefore, thirdly, the key insight for the strategy was that foreigners are more likely to post reviews, they are a more cost-effective audience to target.

Strategy in a Sentence

Maximise the number of customer reviews achieved instead of spending the available budget on classic ads; thus creating and validating the quality perception of the coffee shop and positively influencing customer decision making.

Activating the Idea

Restaurants, coffee shops, and other gastronomic service providers need to have an appropriate visual presence and adequate information online to be successful. Customers consider recommendations and reviews as essential sources of information online. Besides the brand's online pages, these recommendations and reviews on independent platforms are seen to be the most reliable information.

Therefore, the team's hypothesis was that if the communication touchpoints of Double Shot coffee shop (including the website, social pages, Tripadvisor page, 4quare, Google Business page) are made visually appealing and informative and the customers are reached on these independent social platforms, then the coffee shop will be successful despite the limited media budget.

The task started with research, every guest in the shop was asked to complete a brief survey. This was rewarded with a coffee voucher. Additionally, the agency conducted in-depth interviews with their most loyal fans and foreign customers that were willing to participate. Materials were placed in-store and the staff were trained to encourage participation in the research. The staff training included a protocol of conversation specifically to reassure foreign customers that their honest opinion matters. The owner set out to try to incorporate all the feedback into the future of the coffee shop. As a result of this feedback, the website was adjusted, and the team was ready to launch the advertising campaign.

Additionally, the survey results indicated that the majority of foreigners came to the coffee shop using Google or Tripadvisor. Therefore, the team chose Google as their primary advertising platform because of its superior targeting capabilities. The ads targeted foreigners (both tourists and locals), in English. In terms of the landing page, some drove to the Double Shot website, some drove to the review platforms. Customers in-store were also encouraged visit the coffee shop's website, this resulted in a sizeable remarketing list. This list was then used to create look-a-like audiences, people who are similar to those who have visited the website. The messaging of the campaign included three phases. The initial messages in programmatic, Google Display Network (GDN), and Facebook did not claim that Double Shot makes the best coffee, neither did it include a discount or a prize. Instead, these ads asked people to try and then review the place because Double Shot's aim is to serve the best coffee in town. In the second phase the message became more confident and claimed that if people tried the coffee, they would definitely give it a five stars review. The third phase of the campaign expanded its focus to other products besides coffee to include breakfast and lunch menu items.

Shortly after the start of the campaign, the team's insights were confirmed. First, until they did not ask for a review, they barely received any. However, during the campaign, the number of reviews increased by several hundred percent. Second, foreigners were really more willing to give feedback, and also when they did, this feedback tended to be more objective. Traffic also increased in-store.

In terms of media strategy, the team spent less than 1 million Forints (less than 2,800 Euros) on paid media, this is lower than what was spent by their competitors, and it is roughly the same budget year-on-year. This budget was spent on geolocated advertising on programmatic platforms, GDN, and Facebook. Additionally, the campaign used two owned media touchpoints: 1) the brand website that was designed by the agency (https://doubleshot.hu/) and the Facebook page (https://www.facebook.com/doubleshot-budapest). The campaign also used PR outreach to coffee blogs but what truly cemented their success is their focus on customers and getting them to share their honest reviews on independent platforms.

Results

The ultimate indicator of success was that the campaign had to end prematurely. The campaign was set to run for half a year (between 1st April – 30th September 2019) but instead it was stopped after three months (1st April – 28th June 2019) as per the client's request. This is because the coffee shop has reached an average of 90 percent capacity and any further increase would have endangered the quality of service. As a result, the business objective was fulfilled ahead of time. The average gross monthly sales in Q1 2019 were 3.4 million Dorints (9.4 thousand Euros) and in Q2 2019, when the campaign was live, the average gross monthly sales increased to 8.7 million Forints (24 thousand Euros). Furthermore, record sales were reported in June 2019 with a gross monthly sale of 12.1 million Forints (33.5 thousand Euros). At the same time, the unquestionable success of the campaign is best demonstrated by the fact that after the campaign ended, the level of revenue did not decline. Therefore, the campaign managed to achieve longer-term results with a modest budget.

Other Factors

Other factors besides the campaign contributed to the success of the campaign, for example, the brand identity, the design and interior of the store, and the brand website. In addition, the staff training ahead of the research and the incorporation of the feedback from the research into the service were also important factors. The coffee shop appeared in some international coffee blogs with non-paid content. The location and growth of the gastronomic market and solvent customer base also supported the success of the campaign. However, these factors – as seen in the past –on their own would not have been enough to achieve success.

CONCLUSION

The book chapter opens with an introduction that establishes the necessary theory for the paper, including the definition of advertising, rules of success, the trend of digital and its impact on advertising, and the latest rise in how important customer reviews became. The core of the chapter is split into three parts. First, the big picture factors that affect advertising are discussed. Second, it is established that the industry plays an important role in the Hungarian economy. Additionally, media spend in 2020 year-on-year declined, however, digital spend still managed to increase a little. Within digital, global partners (such as Facebook and Google) received the biggest portion of this spend. The third and final part of the chapter introduced the Platina Effie winner Double Shot Coffee Review Boost campaign. The Effie Awards Hungary was chosen as this local award is one of the most prestigious awards in Hungary and it is single-mindedly focused on delivering business results. As an exceptional example of this rigorous criteria, the campaign from Double Shot Coffee and DOT Creative Agency achieved a 10 times growth in positive reviews and tripled the business revenue. The campaign was such a success that they had to stop it before the scheduled end date.

LIMITATIONS AND FUTURE RESEARCH

As any other paper, this chapter also has its limitations. First, the analysis only focused on one campaign. Even though it was the single Platina Effie award-winning campaign from the latest awards, it would still be useful to add to the analysis case studies from other categories. Additionally, several books and articles have been written about advertising in Hungary, therefore this chapter only included topics that were deemed the most relevant for the case study. The addition of more case studies would mean that further advertising context could be added. Second, in terms of the selection of another award-winning campaign, it is recommended that one with a bigger budget and/or one that uses a different channel mix is encouraged. Last but not least, although this campaign was from the final awards of the Effie Awards Hungary, it was still about a campaign that ran before the pandemic. Therefore, a follow-up interview would be beneficial with the winning team to discuss the latest developments following the end of the campaign.

This chapter has both theoretical and practical applications. It fills some literature gaps about the latest developments in advertising in Hungary and it provides a framework for further analysis. In terms of practical applications, this book chapter will act as an essential guide for global advertising teams that are looking for the latest insight on the Hungarian advertising market.

ACKNOWLEDGMENT

The authors would like to thank Adrienne Kaminszky, executive director at IAA Hungary, Ilona Pócsik president at IAA Hungary, the main organizers of Effie Awards Hungary, and Attila Kassitzky, managing director of Dot Creative Agency, who let us present their case study in this book chapter.

REFERENCES

American Marketing Association. (n.d.). *Discover the differences between marketing and advertising and how each relates to modern business.* Retrieved 22 October 2021, from https://www.ama.org/pages/marketing-vs-advertising/

BBC. (2021). *Facebook to hire 10,000 in EU to work on metaverse.* Retrieved 22 October 2021, from https://www.bbc.com/news/world-europe-58949867

Bettina. (2020). *Reklámok a szocializmus idejéből! Neked melyik volt a kedvenced?* Retrieved 29 October 2021, from https://www.magyarorszagom.hu/reklamok-a-szocializmus-idejebol-nekem-melyik-volt-a-kedvenced.html

Binet, L., & Field, P. (2012). *The Long and the Short of It: Balancing Short and Long-Term Marketing Strategies.* IPA.

Birkas, P. (2018). *A magyarok közel harmada mobilfüggő.* Retrieved 28 October 2021, from https://24.hu/tech/2018/02/06/a-magyarok-kozel-harmada-tartja-magat-mobilfuggonek/

Cox, K., Crowther, J., Hubbard, T., & Turner, D. (2011). *Datamine 3. New Models of Marketing Effectiveness From Integration to Orchestration.* WARC.

Dietrich, G. (2014). *PR is More than Media Relations.* Spinsucks. Retrieved 23 October 2021, from https://spinsucks.com/communication/pr-media-relations/

Ebiquity. (2018). *Profit Ability: the business case for advertising.* Thinkbox. Retrieved on 28 October 2021, from https://www.thinkbox.tv/Research/Thinkbox-research/Profit-Ability-the-business-case-for-advertising

Eduline. (2021). *Ez a tíz legnépszerűbb alapszak a 2021-es felvételin: vezet a gazdálkodási és menedzsment.* Retrieved 23 October 2021, from https://eduline.hu/erettsegi_felveteli/20210319_legnepszerubb_szakok_a_felvetelin

Effie. (2021a). *Hatékony aktivitásból sikeres pályamű! Effie Awards Hungary 2021. A díj, ami számít.* Retrieved 22 October 2021, from https://effie.hu/2021/downloads/effie2021_hatekony-aktivitasbo-sikeres-palyamu.pdf

Effie. (2021b). Retrieved 19 October 2021, from https://effie.hu/2021/

Eurostat. (2021a). *Population on 1 January by age and sex*. Retrieved 29 October 2021, from https://ec.europa.eu/eurostat/databrowser/view/demo_pjan/default/table?lang=en

Eurostat. (2021b). *Population by age group*. Retrieved 29 October 2021, from https://ec.europa.eu/eurostat/databrowser/view/tps00010/default/table?lang=en

Eurostat. (2021c). *Real GDP per capita*. Retrieved 28 October 2021, from https://ec.europa.eu/eurostat/databrowser/view/sdg_08_10/default/table?lang=en

Eurostat. (2021d). *Adjusted gross disposable income of households per capita*. Retrieved 29 October 2021, from https://ec.europa.eu/eurostat/databrowser/view/sdg_10_20/default/table?lang=en

Eurostat. (2021e). *Employment rates by sex, age and citizenship (%)*. Retrieved 29 October 2021, from https://ec.europa.eu/eurostat/databrowser/view/lfsa_ergan/default/table?lang=en

Eurostat. (2021f). *Unemployment rates by sex, age and citizenship (%)*. Retrieved 29 October 2021, from https://ec.europa.eu/eurostat/databrowser/view/lfsa_urgan/default/table?lang=en

Fagerstrøm, A., Bendheim, L. M., Sigurdsson, V., Foxall, G. R., & Pawar, S. (2020). The marketing firm and co-creation: The case of co-creation by LEGO. *Managerial and Decision Economics*, *41*(2), 226–233. doi:10.1002/mde.3077

Filieri, R., & McLeay, F. (2014). E-WOM and accommodation: An analysis of the factors that influence travelers' adoption of information from online reviews. *Journal of Travel Research*, *53*(1), 44–57. doi:10.1177/0047287513481274

Fülöp, I. (2021). *Mennyi teret kell engedni a Facebook-hirdetéseknek?* Retrieved 21 October 2021, from https://kreativ.hu/cikk/mennyi-teret-kell-engedni-a-facebook-hirdeteseknek

Gemius Hungary. (2019). *Trendek az okoseszközök piacán 2019*. Retrieved 13 October 2021, from http://www.gemius.hu/all-reader-news/trendek-az-okoseszkoezoek-piacan.html

Godin, S. (2020). *Purple cow*. Penguin Books Limited.

Google Blog. (2020). *Building a more private web: A path towards making third party cookies obsolete*. Retrieved 21 October 2021, from https://blog.chromium.org/2020/01/building-more-private-web-path-towards.html

Google Blog. (2021). *An updated timeline for Privacy Sandbox milestones*. Retrieved 21 October 2021, from https://blog.google/products/chrome/updated-timeline-privacy-sandbox-milestones/

Hootsuite. (2021a). *Digital 2021. Global Overview Report*. Retrieved 21 October 2021, from https://hootsuite.widen.net/s/zcdrtxwczn/digital2021_globalreport_en

Hootsuite. (2021b). *Digital 2021: Hungary*. Retrieved 21 October 2021, from https://datareportal.com/reports/digital-2021-hungary

Hungary, I. A. B. (2017). *Hol tart a reklámblokkolás hazánkban?* Retrieved 21 October 2021, from https://blog.iab.hu/wp-content/uploads/sites/3/2017/03/evolution_iab_lfmcs_ag-2.pdf

Hungary, I. A. B. (2021a). *AdExpect 2021*. Retrieved 14 October 2021, https://iab.hu/dokumentum/iab-hungary-adexpect-2021/

Hungary, I. A. B. (2021b). *AdEx IAB Hungary. Digitális reklámköltési adatok*. Retrieved 14 October 2021, from https://iab.hu/wp-content/uploads/2021/04/IAB_HU_Adex_2020.pdf

Ipsos. (2021). *Fizetési Élmény Riport 2021*. Author.

Jandó, Z. (2020). *Kormányközeli cégeknél landol a magyar reklámpénzek harmada*. Retrieved 17 August 2021, from https://g7.hu/vallalat/20201015/kormanykozeli-cegeknel-landol-a-magyar-reklampenzek-harmada/

Kartajaya, H., Kotler, P., & Hooi, D. H. (2019). *Marketing 4.0: moving from traditional to digital*. World Scientific.

Katz, H. (2019). *The media handbook: A complete guide to advertising media selection, planning, research, and buying*. Routledge. doi:10.4324/9780429434655

KPMG. (2021). *Globális platformok hatása a magyar kommunikációs iparra*. KPMG.

KSH. (2021a). *Népesség és népmozgalom*. Retrieved 29 October 2021, from https://www.ksh.hu/nepesseg-es-nepmozgalom

KSH. (2021b). *Az adott évben be-, illetve kivándorló külföldi állampolgárok, valamint az adott év január 1-jén Magyarországon engedéllyel tartózkodó külföldi állampolgárok adatai*. Retrieved 29 October 2021, from https://statinfo.ksh.hu/Statinfo/haViewer.jsp

KSH. (2021c). *Egy főre jutó bruttó hazai termék megye és régió szerint*. Retrieved 14 October 2021, from https://www.ksh.hu/stadat_files/gdp/hu/gdp0078.html

KSH. (2021d). *A lakónépesség nem, megye és régió szerint, január 1*. Retrieved 14 October 2021, from https://www.ksh.hu/stadat_files/nep/hu/nep0034.html

KSH. (2021e). *A Magyarországon tartózkodó külföldi állampolgárok megye és régió szerint, január 1*. Retrieved 29 October 2021, from https://www.ksh.hu/stadat_files/nep/hu/nep0050.html

KSH. (n.d.). *A boldog érzelmi állapotok megélésének gyakorisága ország, országcsoport szerint [%]*. Retrieved 30 October 2021, from https://www.ksh.hu/stadat_files/ele/hu/ele0032.html

Kurucz, I. (2021). *Megkedveltük a home office-t*. NRC. Retrieved 13 October 2021, from https://nrc.hu/nrc-hirek/nrc-kutatas-homeoffice_1/

Magyar Turisztikai Ügynökség. (2021). *Nemzeti Turizmusfejlesztési Stratégia 2030*. Retrieved 9 August 2021, from https://mtu.gov.hu/documents/prod/NTS2030_Turizmus2.0-Strategia.pdf

Marketing & Media. (2021a). *Rekordot döntött a belföldi turizmus*. Retrieved 22 October 2021, from https://mmonline.hu/cikk/rekordot-dontott-a-belfoldi-turizmus/

Marketing & Media. (2021b). *Turizmus: 2020-at már leköröztük, 2019-hez képest hatalmas a lemaradás*. Retrieved 22 October 2021, from https://mmonline.hu/cikk/turizmus-2020-at-mar-lekoroztuk-2019-hez-kepest-hatalmas-a-lemaradas/

Marketing & Media. (2021c). *Jól hajrázott a reklámpiac*. Retrieved 21 October 2021, from https:// mmonline.hu/cikk/jol-hajrazott-a-reklampiac/

Marketing & Media. (2021d). Retrieved 21 October 2021, from https://mmonline.hu/cikk/reklampiac-szebb-kepet-festenek-az-adatok/

McCarthy, E. J. (1960). *Basic Marketing:A Managerial Approach*. Irwin.

McKinsey. (2016). *Are you really listening to what your customers are saying?* Retrieved 29 October 2021, from https://www.mckinsey.com/business-functions/operations/our-insights/are-you-really-listening-to-what-your-customers-are-saying

MMSZ. (2020). *Marketing Indikátor, Ágazati tanulmány*. Retrieved 17 August 2021, from https://market-ingindikator.hu/uploads/documentitem/0/marketing-indikator-tanulmany-final-20201207-1607354412. pdf

Molnár, Cs. (2021). *Őrületes, mi megy az online boltokban - lecserélték a magyarok a karácsonyt*. Retrieved 13 October 2021, from https://www.napi.hu/magyar-vallalatok/jarvany-vasarlas-kiskereskedelem-online-fizetes-utanvet-karacsony.727230.html

MRSZ. (2021a). *Media and Total Communications pending Hungary 2020*. MRSZ.

MRSZ. (2021b). *MRSZ Barométer – A válság hatásai a reklámiparban. Harmadik lekérdezés*. MRSZ.

MRSZ. (2021c). *Press Release. Figures show an obvious decline for the communications market in 2020: media spending shrank nearly 3 percent, while total communications spending plunged a very significant 16 percent (2021)*. Retrieved 17 August 2021, from https://mrsz.hu/cmsfiles/9f/ef/MRSZ_press-release_2020_media-communication-spending_20210414_ENG.pdf

Osváth, P. (2021). A COVID–19-pandémia mentálhigiénés következményei. Hogyan tudunk felkészülni a pszichodémiás krízisre? *Orvosi Hetilap*, *162*(10), 366–374. doi:10.1556/650.2021.31141 PMID:33683216

PageFair. (2017). *The state of the blocked web*. 2017 Global Adblock Report. Retrieved 21 October 2021, from https://blockthrough.com/blog/adblockreport/

Papp-Váry, Á., & Tóth, T. Zs. (2021). Analysis of Budapest as a Film Tourism Destination In Global Perspectives on Literary Tourism and Film-Induced Tourism. IGI Global.

Pénzcentrum. (2020a). *Rengeteg céget számolt fel a járvány: ezek az ágazatok buktak a legnagyobbat*. Retrieved 25 October 2021, from https://www.penzcentrum.hu/egeszseg/20200807/rengeteg-ceget-szamolt-fel-a-jarvany-ezek-az-agazatok-buktak-a-legnagyobbat-1100546

Pénzcentrum. (2020b). *Elképesztő, mennyi kütyüt vettek idén a magyarok: ezeket keresték legtöbben*. Retrieved 13 October 2021, from https://www.penzcentrum.hu/vasarlas/20201229/elkepeszto-mennyi-kutyut-vettek-iden-a-magyarok-ezeket-kerestek-legtobben-1108444

Podium. (2017). *State of Online Reviews*. Retrieved 23 October 2021, from https://www.podium.com/ resources/podium-state-of-online-reviews/

Portfolio. (2021). *Még mindig kevés pláza van Magyarországon, de ez nem biztos, hogy baj.* Retrieved 13 October 2021, from https://www.portfolio.hu/ingatlan/20210917/meg-mindig-keves-plaza-van-magyarorszagon-de-ez-nem-biztos-hogy-baj-501026# Sas

Shrivastava, P. (2016). Effect of co-creation on customer experience, trust and brand loyalty. *International Journal of Sales & Marketing Management Research and Development.*, 6(6), 1–14.

Simpson, J. (2017). Finding Brand Success In The Digital World. *Forbes.* Retrieved 22 October 2021, from https://www.forbes.com/sites/forbesagencycouncil/2017/08/25/finding-brand-success-in-the-digital-world/?sh=17a3b5a626e2

Statista. (2021a). *Number of tourist arrivals in accommodation establishments in Budapest, Hungary from 2000 to 2020.* Retrieved 29 October 2021, from https://www.statista.com/statistics/986072/budapest-tourist-arrivals-in-accommodation/

Statista. (2021b). *Distribution of advertising spending worldwide in 2023, by medium.* Retrieved 18 August 2021, from https://www.statista.com/statistics/269333/distribution-of-global-advertising-expenditure/

Szabó-Kákonyi, A. & Papp-Váry, Á. (2013). *A magyar reklámtudomány kezdetei az 1910-es, 1920-as években és mai napig tartó hatásuk.* A SJE Nemzetközi Tudományos Konferenciája. Komárom.

Szepesi, A. (2021). *Online fizetés: a magyarok megszokták az új rendszert.* https://www.napi.hu/magyar-vallalatok/felmeres-online-fizetes-eros-ugyfel-hitelesites.736849.html

Takó, A. (2020). *Effie Awards Analysis by Ipsos.* Retrieved 21 October 2021, from https://effie.hu/2021/downloads/ipsos-pres-effie.pdf

Telenor. (2021). *Velünk marad a home office egy friss kutatás szerint.* Retrieved 14 October 2021, from https://www.telenor.hu/sajto/kozlemeny/velunk-marad-a-home-office-egy-friss-kutatas-szerint

The Economist. (2017). *The world's most valuable resource is no longer oil, but data.* https://www.economist.com/leaders/2017/05/06/the-worlds-most-valuable-resource-is-no-longer-oil-but-data

Trustpilot. (2020). *Why do people write reviews? What our research revealed.* Retrieved 22 October 2021, from https://business.trustpilot.com/reviews/learn-from-customers/why-do-people-write-reviews-what-our-research-revealed

YouTube. (2014). *Retró reklámok.* Retrieved 29 October 2021, from https://www.youtube.com/watch?v=T7cYHrspUQY&t=284s&ab_channel=KrisztinaFeh%C3%A9rv%C3%A1ri

KEY TERMS AND DEFINITIONS

Advertising: One of the tools in the marketing mix, it includes all paid-for communication with customers.

Case Study: In this book chapter a case study is an in-depth analysis of a real-life advertising campaign.

Customer Review: An opinion about a company/brand/product/service shared by the customer.

Digital Media: It includes all online media channels, for example, display, search, or social media.

Effie Hungary: The Hungarian sister award of the global Effie Awards, it is one of the most prestigious advertising awards in Hungary, it judges campaigns based on their effectiveness results.

European Union (EU): An economic and political union of 27 member states as of 2021, including Austria, Belgium, Bulgaria, Croatia, Republic of Cyprus, Czech Republic, Denmark, Estonia, Finland, France, Germany, Greece, Hungary, Ireland, Italy, Latvia, Lithuania, Luxembourg, Malta, Netherlands, Poland, Portugal, Romania, Slovakia, Slovenia, Spain and Sweden. Statistics that refer to 28 member states were created before the United Kingdom left the European Union.

Hungary: A country in Central Europe that is part of the European Union.

Interactive Advertising Bureau (IAB) Hungary: The Hungarian department of IAB that is the European industry body for digital marketing and advertising,

Magyar Marketing Szövetség (MMSZ): The Hungarian Marketing Association or MMSZ is the Hungarian industry body for marketing.

Magyar Reklámszövetség (MRSZ): The Hungarian Advertising Association or MRSZ is the Hungarian industry body for advertising.

Chapter 13
Research on the March 8th Women's Day–Themed Advertisement in Russia

İlkay Erarslan
https://orcid.org/0000-0002-1550-3693
Beykent University, Turkey

ABSTRACT

Social advertising is an important element that influences attitudes, beliefs, and behaviors. It also aims to make an impact by drawing attention to the fundamental social problems of different countries. In international digital marketing campaigns, International Women's Day is one of the contents used in advertisements with the corporate support of brands. The present research aims to examine what expressions were used to describe the admiration for the March 8th Women's Day-themed social advertisement in the Russian advertisement of Nike and whether the advertisement was perceived as feminist in the audience's verbal expressions. Considering the resource and time constraints, a YouTube sample was included. In the study, the content analysis technique was used and the main female characters as well as the expressions expressing admiration for the advertisement were analyzed.

INTRODUCTION

Russia is a country that has spread to Europe and Asia in the historical process. Due to this spread, it has lived together with Eastern cultures and civilizations and Western culture along with value judgments. After accepting the orthodoxy of Christianity, Russia has shaped its domestic and foreign policy accordingly (Yılmaz, 2015: 113). Russia, which surrounds the Arctic Ocean in the north of Asia, stretches from Europe to the North Pacific Ocean and spreads over an area of 17,098,242 km². Russia is surrounded by four geopolitical regions: Northern Europe, Western Asia, Central Asia, and the Far East. According to the 2010 census, the languages spoken in Russia are Russian (85.7%), Tatar (3.2%), and Chechen (1%). The other languages spoken in Russia make up 10.1%. The officially recognized religions in Russia are

DOI: 10.4018/978-1-7998-9672-2.ch013

Orthodox Christianity, Judaism, Islam, and Buddhism (Eser, 2017, 5). Since the geopolitical split in the Union of Soviet Socialist Republics (USSR), Russia has regarded organizational mechanisms aimed at keeping the countries in the region together under its leadership as a solution (Alım&Aksu, 2019: 2). After the dissolution of the USSR, Russia's regional policy was shaped by determining the former Soviet geography as the country's area of interest. After the close relations with the West between 1991-1993, the Yeltsin administration in Russia began to give more weight to developments in its region (Sakwa, 2008: 369). For Russia, thinking that the center of gravity of global politics is moving away from the West and that different power centers are being formed, compared to the 1990s, the center of gravity of its foreign policy is no longer limited to the country's western side, oriented toward NATO and the EU, but also the whole of Eurasia, especially with the rise of China (Alım&Aksu, 2019: 16). After Vladimir Putin came to power, he has continued Yeltsin's foreign policy in recent years. In the first decade of the 21st century, Russia has again shown itself as a strong player. Russia's presidency of the UN Security Council and the G-8 in 2006 further increased its role in the international arena (Kemaloğlu, 2016: 8-10). In line with the Eurasian Union's policy, in which Putin set priorities, the Presidents of Russia, Belarus, and Kazakhstan signed an agreement on November 18, 2011, to establish the Eurasian Union by 2015. With the agreement, the Eurasian Commission and Eurasian Economic Area were established within the scope of the European Union Commission model (Yılmaz, 2015: 118).

Russia continues to hold the title of the country with the largest territory in the world. Russia has borders with 16 countries (Kemaloğlu, 2016: 3). With a population of 146 million, the Russian Federation is the most populous country on the European continent and the largest country in the world in terms of surface area. It has the 9th largest economy in the world in terms of nominal GDP and the 6th largest economy in terms of purchasing power parity. Nowadays, while private enterprises carry out a significant part of commercial and economic activities and production, the public sector assumes effective control over natural resources (especially oil and natural gas) and financial markets (Bulut, 2018: 346). Russia, which has ranked fifth in the world with its population and land size, has also become the country with the largest economic potential among the former Soviet Republics with its rich natural resources (Güler, 2012: 100). Russia has experienced significant economic transformations since the early 1990s. During the relevant period, the country became open to the outside world by switching to a free market economy (Yüksel, 2016: 44).

The Russian Federation, which had a fluctuating economic structure until 2000 under the effect of the transition to a market economy, has caught a good economic trend with the formation of political stability after the 2000s (İşcan and Hatipoğlu, 2010: 28). The currency of Russia is the Russian ruble. While 1 dollar was 34 rubles in 2014, the Russian ruble depreciated due to the embargo imposed on Russia and the decrease in energy prices and rose to around 1 dollar being equal to 60 rubles as of the beginning of 2017. According to the gross domestic product per capita in 2014, Russia ranks 49th in the world with $24,805 (Kemaloğlu, 2016: 3).

Russia has the largest advertising market in Central and Eastern Europe. It is projected to have the 13th highest-ranking ad spend worldwide, with US$ eight billion in 2022. More than 473 billion Russian rubles were spent on advertising in 2020. Due to the coronavirus (COVID-19) pandemic, there was a decrease compared to 2019. However, digital advertising has increased in Russia, with the online advertising budget increasing more than nine times between 2010 and 2020. Internet advertising surpassed television in 2018, the first year it had the highest spending (Elegina, 2021).

Every country has to develop its foreign policy to be effective on international platforms and protect its own interests. In the years following the disintegration in Russia, especially in 1993, it entered a recovery process and adopted a new strategy in its foreign policy in order to establish new relations with the countries that left the Soviet Union and gained their independence (Hacıtahiroğlu, 2014: 270-271). Central Asia is important for Russia. Therefore, it has taken steps to become the dominant power in Central Asia with the impact of the cultural bond inherited from the Soviet Union, and it is clear that it will continue to do so. The transportation and control of energy resources take an important place for Russia. In the global struggle, it has always been trying to ensure stability in Central Asia, increase border security, and sign common policies with regional states (Aydın, 2015: 7).

Before the Russian Revolution, women's lives were diverse. Rich women were educated from the opening of higher education courses in the 1870s, while peasant women were mostly illiterate. In the patriarchal society, until 1917, women did not have the right to vote and could not hold public office (British Library, 2021). Women who held a demonstration demanding suffrage in St. Petersburg in 1913 staged another demonstration on March 8th, 1917 (Timeanddate, 2021). The present research aims to examine the female characters in the March 8 Women's Day-themed advertisement of the Nike brand in Russia and determine the harmony and effectiveness between the advertisement theme and the advertisement. To this end, the audience comments for the brand's advertisement on YouTube and the comments used to express admiration for the Nike advertisement in Russia were examined.

To achieve this goal, the study will be carried out by discussing the following topics: Russian Economy and Politics, History of the Russian Advertising Industry, March 8 Women's Day-themed Advertisement in Russia, Methodology, and Conclusions.

BACKGROUND

Russian Economy and Politics

The Union of Soviet Socialist Republics (USSR) was formed in December 1922 as a union of sovereign republics to give political form to the diversity of peoples and nations of the new republic, which later took legal form when the Soviet Union was adopted in the first constitution in January 1924 (White, Sakwa and Hale, 2010: 1). Due to economic problems in the 1950s and many false reasons, the Stalinist system was under pressure to change. There was pressure to continue in line with the demands and needs of a society based on culture and technology politically and economically. However, by the 1980s, the system previously designed for services ceased to be useful (Waller, 2005: 5-6). The Soviet Union began to experience economic stagnation since 1979. Military spending was on the rise. According to the CIA assessment, Soviet military spending was increasing at an annual rate of 3% (Dongak, 2011:3). Apart from the Second World War, the event that had the strongest impact on the country's collective memory in Russia's recent history was the collapse of the Soviet Union in 1991 and the ensuing decade of political and economic chaos (Belmonte and Rochlitz, 20019: 233). There was an 80% turnout in the referendum held in March 1991 to continue as a renewed federation of sovereign republics where the rights and freedoms of people of all nationalities are recognized (White, 2010: 2).

Twenty years after the collapse of communism in Russia and the establishment of an independent Russia in 1991, the new political system and the political reflection of this situation continue (White, Sakwa and Hale, 2010: 1). In the 1980s and 1990s, financial crises occurred in developing economies worldwide. Since such countries could not pay their debts, they faced crises similar to those experienced by the global economy in 2008-2009. The financial aid from the IMF and the World Bank led to the implementation of policies that would reorganize their economic structures. During this period, Russia was also affected by the BRIC economies (Ciochetto, 2011: 4). The transformation processes in the USSR and post-communist Russia between 1985-1990 exhibited two main features. First, these processes formed part of the crisis of industrial society and signaled change. Second, these processes resulted in a major revolution (Mau and Drobyshevskaya, 2012: 22). In the late 1980s, Western institutions such as the IMF and the World Bank developed a standard recipe for transition economies. In late 1991, Yeltsin sought the advice of Western institutions (Eser, 2017: 43). In the late 1990s, Yeltsin was unable to fix the deteriorating economy. The government's problems were exacerbated by the escalating international economic crisis. Since the Asian economic crisis in 1997 affected oil prices, the Russian economy was more severely damaged (NTI, 2021). With advice from Western economists and institutions, Yeltsin set up his program for Russia's independent economic policy just days after the collapse of the Soviet Union. He then presented the program to the parliament on September 28, 1991. The program included the following:

- Economic stability based on the tight monetary and credit policy of the ruble until a separate Russian currency was created for strengthening.
- Price liberalization.
- With privatization and the growing private sector, the mixed economy establishment and acceleration of the land reform.
- Reorganization of the financial system, tight budgetary expenditure reforms in the control, banking, and taxation systems (Eser, 2017: 43-44).

Yeltsin's decisions to implement economic reforms in 1992 caused controversy within the scope of these reforms. Scholars have called their co-main component, economic reforms, "shock therapy" (Weiler, 2004: 10). Although Yeltsin's policies in the 1990s affected the duration of the economic downturn, the contraction in the economy continued. This shows that all Eastern European countries and the former Soviet Union experienced a significant economic decline after communism (Treisman, 2019: 4). Privatization was a rapidly advancing aspect of the Russian economic reform. In 1996, Russia carried out privatization in 80 percent of its state institutions. This rate was much higher than those in Poland and China, which are considered two of the most successful examples of capitalist reform (Weiler, 2004: 12).

During the privatization period between 1992 and 2000, large private finance-industry-media groups were established in Russia. Large enterprises in most sectors of Russian industry were generally independent until 2000, except for the fuel and energy sectors. If they joined larger groups, this was subject to the principle of mutual autonomy. Large cross-regional companies covering many industry sectors began to actively merge in 2001 (Paszyc and Wisniewska, 2002: 46-47). After the 1998 financial crisis, Russian Aluminum, Severstal, Alfa Group, and other large companies increased their acquiring key businesses in regions far from the basis of their original activities. With the crisis in 1998, the ruble's depreciation made investments in Russia more profitable. After the ruble depreciated by 75 percent after the 1998 crisis, reinvesting some assets in Russia became profitable. Despite their decreasing role in politics after the election of Vladimir Putin in 2000, oligarchs take an important position in Russia's political and economic life. Business is regarded as a powerful new player in Russian politics, which can work with both the federal and regional governments. Despite Putin's federal reforms, Russia's largest companies consider it important to maintain good relations (Orttung, 2004: 51-58). Between 1990 and 2000, the Russian Federation faced major problems while contributing to the construction of democracy and economy like other countries in the region. In international politics, it has lost its reputation and prestige in Central Asia and the Caucasus (Elma: 131).

The so-called Color Revolutions of the 2000s challenge Russia's ideals of liberalization and democratization and its interests abroad and at home. The Russian administration followed the Color Revolutions in the former Soviet republics between 2003 and 2005 with concern. The Russian administration regarded the Rose Revolution in Georgia (2003), the Orange Revolution in Ukraine (2004), and the Tulip Revolution in Kyrgyzstan (2005) as an effort of Western actors and the USA to initiate regime change in the region. The color revolution was regarded as an ambitious attempt of the post-Soviet states to reach Russia. The Kremlin prevented the Color Revolutions from affecting Russia and enabled Putin to effectively manage the 2007-2008 elections (Wilson, 2010: 21). Despite the leaders' hopes that Russia would provide stability in the 2008-2009 international financial crisis, the country succumbed to the effects of the global crisis (Treisman, 2009: 19). Although Russia does not approach its cooperation with Western political institutions moderately, integration into the global economy has been one of its priorities (Mankoff, 2009: 35).

When Putin became president in 2012, the economic development model of the country that had experienced the crisis in 2008 lost its effect (NTI, 2021). Vladimir Putin, who became the President of Russia for the third time, approved the New Foreign Policy Doctrine of Russia on February 18, 2013, and revealed his country's foreign policy understanding in the new period with a new concept. In the document, it is emphasized that the international system is evolving toward a multipolar system and the economic and political possibilities of dominating the global system have weakened (İsmayılov, 2013: 89). Political and economic crises occurred in Russia in 2014. Putin continued to distract attention from the weak economy by promoting the 2014 Winter Olympics, which cost more than $50 billion (NTI, 2021).

The global recession causes the need for a radical transformation of markets and businesses. The goal of the economic and growth crisis to create a post-industrial society, playing a dominant role both in Russia and developed countries, disappears. The Ministry of Economic Development announced that Russia's estimated GDP growth rate could be 3.0 percent in 2014, 3.1 percent in 2015, and 3.3 percent in 2016. This means that it is one of the leading ways to overcome difficulties in economic development (Silka, 2014: 310). B. Santo, who was one of the first to evaluate innovation as a tool of economic development, showed that the result of implementing innovations appears as a development variant (Gurieva and Dzhioev, 2016: 6). In the development process of the Russian economy, economic instability is observed, e.g., the decline in oil prices, the lack of external financing, the devaluation of the ruble, and economic sanctions against the Russian Federation. The environment for the operation of the innovation sector has not been created yet, and there is no high demand for innovation (Morkovkin et al., 2017: 10). 2019 was an important year for Russian business. The Russian stock market was one of the top performers, gaining more than 40% in dollar terms. Russia is not the only country with economic and social status differences, and this problem bothers many countries. As Vladimir Putin's last term as president ends in 2024, an approaching period of political uncertainty may complicate the situation for Russia (NTI, 2021).

Women's Rights in Russia

International Women's Day, defined by the United Nations, is an international day celebrated on March 8th each year. It is devoted to developing political and social awareness of women based on human rights and celebrating their economic, political, and social achievements. International Women's Day is a focal point in the women's rights movement. Women in Russia have a rich and varied history over centuries in different regimes. Since Russia is a multicultural society, there are significant differences in the ethnic, religious, and social status of women in Russia (Wikipedia, 2021). Class differences have been observed in the participation of women in social life in Russia since the 18th century. During this period, the Russian aristocratic women, who had large lands, had the right to travel to Europe, to trade, and to manage property. The situation of rural women in Russia in the 19th century was much more difficult than that of urban women. Peasant women were oppressed by their husbands. The fact that men saw women as people of a lower level played a role in this (Dalyan et al., 2018: 476-481). In Russia, women took the first steps in social life during the time of Peter I, and with his urging, noble women and men came together in ball-like organizations (Hosking, 2011: 371-372). In the late 1880s, women in rural areas had various forms of freedom from the tutelage of their husbands, such as succession and equal treatment with men. They took the initiative and achieved some gains in certain areas. However, women's rights in Russia on these dates were very few compared to European states, which led to women's rebellion movements (Dalyan et al., 2018: 484). Women who held a demonstration demanding suffrage in St. Petersburg in 1913 staged another demonstration on March 8th, 1917. Creating an equal society in every aspect was one of the main goals of the Russian Revolution. Creating a gender-equal society via giving women's rights was a part of that plan. Therefore, the Marxist-Socialist women's movement was born in Russia and spread to Europe and other parts of the world. Many historians state that this demonstration marked the beginning of the Russian Revolution. Four days after the performance, the Russian Emperor Nicholas II abdicated, and the provisional government gave Russian women the right to vote (Timeanddate, 2021). Marxists followed the Communist Manifesto. Their basic thesis was that all economic, sexual, personal, and political areas of society should change (Göçeri, 2004. 73). From the Stalin era to the late 1960s, the Communist Party declared that the "women's problem" had been resolved. Since Russia and the USSR were patriarchal societies and constituted the rise of male-female-dominated societies for a significant part of the Soviet era, women's history was not considered an important subject of study. Foreign historians and social scientists studying Russia formed an important discipline until the second half of the twentieth century, focusing on economic forces and studying previously neglected groups in the USSR such as women and the working class (Marsh, 1996: 1).

In the late 1980s, women made up 51% of the working class in the Soviet Union. However, the conditions of many women's workplaces were poor. People who did not accept to work in poor conditions were generally left to perdition. Some were forced to stay in dormitories (Karakuş, 2019: 1585-1586). Under Gorbachev and Yeltsin, women did not have political power compared to previous periods in Soviet history. The reforms of the Gorbachev era in 1988 reduced the proportion of women at the top of the government (Marsh, 1996: 11). In July 1989, miners went on strike to improve women's working conditions. While they wanted a 60 percent increase in their wages, they also wanted maternity leave with an additional 6-day leave. With perestroika[1], women partially lost their job security (Karakuş, 2019: 1594). The 1993 Constitution of Russia guarantees the equality of women and men. Nevertheless, women struggle with inequality in many sectors. People in Russia expect women to prioritize motherhood. The government stated that heavy work posed a threat to women's safety and reproductive health and banned women from occupations such as aircraft repair, construction, and firefighting. The country adopted reforms in 2019 to reduce the number of curtailed jobs from 456 to 100 (Borgen Project, 2021). Women now work outside the home, and the employment rate of men and women in Russia is 66.1% and 76.2%, respectively (in the age range of 15-64 years as of 2018) (Wikipedia, 2021).

A Brief History of the Russian Advertising Industry

Russian advertising is based on ancient traditions. The beginning of advertising in Russia differs from that in Europe due to the culture and history of Russia (Tsetsura and Kruckeberg, 2021).

Russia was affected by the following transitions in the last two centuries:

- Agrarian society and imperial monarchy by the nineteenth century,
- In the second half of the 19th century, the growth of capitalism and the rise of another party system under authoritarian rule,
- The short era of multi-party democracy in 1917,
- The socialist revolution at the beginning of the twentieth century and the economic recession,
- Restructuring as a policy of the Communist Party reforms that resulted in the collapse of the USSR,
- Establishment of Russia as an independent state and being influenced by "Western" liberal democracy (Hallin and Mancini, 2012: 119-120).

Historical changes in Russia have seriously affected the media and journalism model. In 1878, the first advertising organization was opened in Moscow, and the famous slogan "Advertising is an engine of commerce" was launched. At that time, Russian advertising was quite developed. In 1917, a legitimate reason was needed to end the Bolshevik crackdown on the opposition press since the balance of political forces in Russia could change. Hence, the Press Decree was issued by the Council of People's Commissars on 27 October (Sheresheva and Antonov-Ovseenko, 2015: 178). After the 1917 Bolshevik Revolution, the private sector was abolished, and the commercial advertising industry drastically shrunk. In the 1960s, the Soviet Export magazine was published, in which products manufactured in the USSR were advertised for customers abroad (Ustinova, 2006: 267). Historically, up to the early days of socialism, most advertisements in Russia contained direct messages. Very few advertisements used persuasive communication elements. Advertising has often been defined as promotional communications sponsored by the Soviet government to transport surplus or faulty goods in planned economic inventories. From 1994, Russia's advertising professionals have drawn on the marketing and advertising expertise of the West to develop their advertising content (Wells and Auken, 2006: 34).

Since the collapse of the Soviet Union, Russia has revised its economic activities between 1991 and 1998. Privatization and the integration of global capital markets into the economy were among them. Furthemore, Russia transitioned from a centralized economy to a market-oriented economy with the "shock therapy" reform. With the ruble crisis in August 1998, Russian consumers were shaken by the decline in the ruble's value, economic instability, and price increases due to the fall of the local currency. The first period in the history of Russian advertising covers the years 1991-1996 when the commercial crisis was experienced. Most advertisements were aimed at the Russian male audience, businessmen, and wealthy people (Chadraba and Springer, 2008: 205). From 1990 onward, the economy and advertising began to improve in Russia. Advertising has become one of the main factors affecting and shaping the media since the 2000s (Iepuri, 2017: 58). During the last 15 years, the advertising industry made a giant step forward in Russia, reflecting radical changes in social and economic relations, technologies, and mass media (Repiev, 2004). With the opening of the Russian market after the BRIC economies, an opportunity was provided to foreign investments. With the increased advertising expenditures, foreign advertising agencies began to dominate this market (Ciochetto, 2011: 13).

Types of Products in Different Advertising Genres

The majority of TV commercials for dairy products and national food are in Russian since they target citizens of the Russian Federation. In the TV advertisement for the Russian national dish pelmeni (a type of dumplings), advertisers use the language, music, and images of Russian folklore tales. Non-Russian brands such as Panasonic, Land Rover, or Kodak often use English brand names written in Roman script. Sometimes, Russian TV commercials simply "borrow" and dub Western clips but promote a different product because "Copywriting is still an almost unheard of craft in most Russian agencies" (Ustinova, 2006: 273-274). Historical themes are often used in TV commercials, such as video clips advertising Russian beer and lottery commercials. Images of Russian national heroes are used in logos and labels and political advertisements, symbolizing respect for traditional Russian products, their high quality, and originality. Advertising of national products is used for positive connotations as representations of the Soviet past (Iepuri, 2017: 65). Nostalgic products are becoming popular in Russia and the former Eastern Bloc. Production rights are sought for Soviet era brands, including Zhigulyovskoye beer and Prima cigarettes. Since the collapse of the Soviet Union, Russian marketers have introduced new products to appeal to the nostalgic feelings of Russian consumers. Russian Anniversary Cookies are an example of a product that reminds many Russians of their past and has been familiar to many generations. This product has recently been reproduced with new marketing techniques (Holak et al., 2007: 650-654). For example, a television commercial for a Russian juice brand (My Family) shows a happy Russian family in an apartment furnished in a Soviet era style like in Soviet movies of the 1960-1970s. The images presented in the advertisement evoke nostalgic feelings by reminding them of Soviet times (Iepuri, 2017: 65). In Russia, the number of charitable and non-profit organizations increases in implementing socially prepared projects. Such institutions may engage in social advertising to support their activities. Cooperation of the state, society, advertising industry, business, and non-profit organizations is important for the development of social advertising in Russia (Popkova et al., 2018: 13).

Western technology in Russian advertising is emphasized in advertisements. Direct translations from English to Russian were done. During the first period of advertising in Russia, advertisements that appealed to "Western" or "pre-revolutionary nostalgic native Russian" values rather than marketing communications were prepared (Chadraba and Springer, 2008: 206). The perception of Western advertising in the former Soviet Union prevents Western companies from using mass information media to reach potential customers in the former Soviet republics. The study by Wells (1994) states that many people adopt Western advertising terminology by interviewing professionals, academics, and university students (Wells, 1994: 83-85). When Western commercials first appeared on Russian television, the foreign products advertised were a novelty for the Russians because they were popular (Iepuri, 2017: 60). Since 1990, television has become the first mass communication tool (Hallin and Mancini, 2012: 125). According to Mediascope, TV is still the largest mass media in Russia. The older viewers are, the longer time they watch TV. In 2019, viewers aged 54+ spent 359 minutes watching TV every day, viewers aged 35-54 spent 221 minutes, children aged 4-17 spent 102 minutes, and people aged 18-34 spent 132 minutes on average (RMAA Agency, 2020). Radio is another rapidly growing segment of Russian commercial media (Hallin and Mancini, 2012: 125).

With approximately 150 million users, Russia's internet audience is the largest in Europe and the seventh largest in the world. The internet advertising budget in Russia in 2018 was higher than spending on television advertising in 2017. Internet advertising in Russia appears to be growing faster than any other type of advertising (Croud.com, 2018). It shows significant growth since television and the internet are among the driving forces of the Russian advertising market. According to VTB Capital's forecasts, with the economic development following the financial crisis, the value of the advertising industry would appreciate by 2014 (Warc, 2010). The internet in Russia remains the most developing segment, and the volume of the internet advertising market increased by 20%, which is equal to 244 billion rubles. According to the Russian Association of Communication Agencies (RACA), the advertising market development in 2019, the volume of the Russian advertising market was approximately 493.8 billion rubles. The growth of the Russian market in 2019 was provided by internet advertising (RMAA Agency, 2020). The English language and American values influence advertisements in Russia as part of global advertising. In Russian advertisements, English may be used for products, company names, and logos not to personalize the message of multinational companies. The presence of English and Western allusions in advertisements that appeal to middle-class and young people seems to indicate the expensiveness, selectivity, and prestige of the product (Ustinova, 2008: 96).

March 8 Women's Day-Themed Advertisements in Russia

International Women's Day began to be celebrated in Russia on March 2, 1913. Women held a demonstration in St. Petersburg demanding the right to vote (Timeanddate, 2021). The founder of the Russian Communist Party, Vladimir Lenin, declared Women's Day a public holiday in 1917 (History.com, 2021). In Russia, International Women's Day is celebrated with food and drinks with family or friends. Many women receive gifts such as flowers on March 8th. Women's Day has become a national holiday in Russia since 1918. It became a non-working day in 1965. International Women's Day remained a public holiday in Russia after the dissolution of the former Soviet Union. Nowadays, March 8th is a holiday to honor motherhood, beauty, and spring (Timeanddate, 2021).

March advertisements are considered social advertising to influence attitudes, beliefs, and behaviors. Social advertising aims to make an impact by drawing attention to the main social problems faced by different countries (Popkova et al., 2018). International digital marketing campaigns have recently used the International Women's Day holiday with less political content in advertisements with the corporate support of brands (History.com, 2021). Some studies state that brand popularity is not important in Russia. However, if a firm aims to reach audiences rather than just trendsetters, it should consider applying brand popularity (Whang et al., 2015: 807). The Russian-based YouTube advertisement of the Nike brand with the theme of March 8th International Women's Day was published with the slogan "You're made of what you do." In the 2-minute commercial by the Wieden Kennedy Dutch advertising agency, a little girl begins to sing a children's song in Russian on stage in front of a large crowd (Erbaş, 2018: 368). Different themes are used to raise awareness of International Women's Day. Themes against gender discrimination and inequality are used. Messages celebrating women's achievements are given. It delivers inspiring messages from famous and successful women. We can give a few examples of these;

"I raise up my voice—not so I can shout but so that those without a voice can be heard… We cannot succeed when half of us are held back." – Malala Yousafzai

"When women are held back, our country is held back. When women get ahead, everyone gets ahead." – Hilary Clinton

"The success of every woman should be the inspiration to another. We should raise each other up. Make sure you're very courageous: be strong, be extremely kind, and above all be humble." – Serena Williams

"There's power in allowing yourself to be known and heard, in owning your unique story, in using your authentic voice." – Michelle Obama (Edinburgnews, 2021).

In the advertisement analyzed within the scope of the study, it has been determined that the idealized "strong woman" representations are the "empowered" woman, the self-confident woman, the active woman in the working life, the combative woman who destroys prejudices, the individual activist woman, and the woman figures who reverse gender roles. In the advertisement, the girl says that girls are made of accomplishments and achievements, passion, bravery, dignity, will that is harder than stone, strength, fire, and freedom from other people's opinions.

METHODOLOGY

The study aims to reveal the depiction of the female characters in the March 8th Women's Day-themed advertisement in the Russian advertisement of the Nike brand and determine the harmony and effectiveness between the meaning of the theme and the advertisement. To this end, the audience comments on the brand's advertisement on YouTube were examined, and it was revealed what expressions were used to describe the admiration for the Nike advertisement in Russia. Considering the resource and time constraints, it was included in the YouTube sample where the advertisement was published.

Research Model

In the study, the content analysis technique was used, and the general evaluation of the Women's Day advertisement on YouTube, where the advertisement was broadcast, was analyzed with the code table created for the analysis of the main female characters and the expressions used to define the admiration for the advertisement.

Content analysis is basically a coding process. Communication studies are grouped and coded by placing them in a certain conceptual framework. Coding in the content analysis includes conceptualization and operationalization. What is meant by conceptualization is to explain what is meant by the concepts used in the study (Öztürk et al., 2016: 366). With the content analysis, data are defined, and similar data are brought together within the framework of predetermined concepts and themes so that the facts hidden in the data can be presented to the reader in a more understandable way (Ük, 2019: 6). The content analysis, which is used to measure and define the content dimensions of message groups in a text sample, is a research method used to clearly reveal and explain in detail the content of communication in an objective, systematic, and non-qualitative manner (Yurttaş, 2018: 1179). The coding criteria for which content analysis was carried out in the study are as follows: the theme of the advertisement, the number of characters in the advertisement, the gender of the character, the place, the role, the basic behavior, the occupation category, the outfit, the age, the body part that appears in the advertisement, the use of voice-over and gender, whether the character is a speaker, and gender identity (Ük, 2019: 6). The coding framework, adapted from the studies by Erbaş (2018) and Ük (2019), was created to examine advertising components and evaluate the research questions.

In the study, the codes in the audience's verbal expressions were determined as the themes included in the advertisement, and the codes were created. In the absence of different researchers, Mackey and Gass (2005) state that reliability can be evaluated based on the researcher's judgment of the data in the same way at different times. For example, at the first or second time, it can be based on a re-evaluation of a slice of the dataset or the entire dataset (Mackey and Gass, 2005: 243). For the study's reliability, 500 audience verbal expressions were checked again one month later, and the same results were obtained.

While creating the codes, the "wow," "amazing," and "love" comments were coded as "love and beautiful." The "cry" in the comments was coded as "emotional" in the depictions.

Examining the theme of Women's Day in a brand and across a country constitutes the study's limitation. The following basic research questions were determined for the examined advertisement.

- What expressions were used to describe the admiration for the Nike advertisement in Russia?
- Was the advertisement perceived as feminist in the audience's verbal expressions?
- What are the distribution ratios of female characters, and how are they defined?

Sampling

'You're made of What You Do,' a YouTube advertisement with the theme of March 8th, International Women's Day, of the Nike brand published in Russia, was examined. The YouTube advertisement was chosen due to the ease of access to the advertisement on the web and the accessibility and updateability of viewer comments. The most recent 500 user verbal expressions out of 3097 comments were examined. These verbal expressions were randomly addressed and interpreted to examine the verbal expressions of users with regard to the advertisement, the impressions of how the Women's Day theme in the advertisement affected commentators were discussed, and it was revealed whether the advertisement was perceived as feminist in the audience's verbal expressions. Furthermore, the content of the advertisement was analyzed, and it was interpreted whether the female characters in the advertisement were presented as feminist. The YouTube address used for the advertisement review: https://www.youtube.com/watch?v=Y_iCIISngdI. Researchers can access the advertisement from this address.

Findings and Results

In the advertisement, the door to the concert hall opens, and an ice skater enters. Afterward, a little girl continues to sing the song's lyrics, "Girls are made of iron, striving, self-dedication, and battles." In the continuation of the song, she says that girls are made of perseverance and grace that gives pride to the entire nation. Meanwhile, a woman performing ballet appears in the hall among the audience. Power is emphasized in the rest of the song, while two women are shown skateboarding and running. Afterward, the song ends with the words indicating that girls are made of passion, bravery, dignity, will that is harder than stone, strength, fire, freedom from other people's opinions, accomplishments and achievements. In the final scene of the adversisement, the girl singing the song is shown on a soccer field preparing for a penalty kick. The slogan "You're made of what you do" and the brand's logo appear on the screen.

Due to the theme of March 8th Women's Day, the analysis in Table 1 was performed to assess whether the female characters in the advertisement were sufficiently weighted, and the distribution ratios of the female characters and how they were defined were revealed. The commercial film, which constitutes the sample, was coded by considering the criteria defined according to the general theme of the advertisement, the number of characters in the advertisement, the use of voice-over in the advertisement, the gender of the voice-over, and whether the characters were speakers, and the results in Table 1 were obtained. Thirteen professional female athletes and 1 girl are the main characters. Ten women, 21 girls, and 20 men are featured in the advertisement as side characters. It is observed that female characters predominate in the advertisement. However, it is seen that the number of men is higher in the characters. The weight is equalized in this area, and it is observed that there is no gender-based advertisement. The advertising theme includes "Support for Women's Business Life and Entrepreneurship," "Challenging Gender Roles," "Power of Women," and "Value and Importance of Women."

Table 1. Content analysis results regarding the general evaluation of the women's day advertisement

Coding Criteria	Frequency (n)	Percentage (%)
Number of Characters in the Advertisement		
Main Female Character	13	20
Side Female Character	10	15.39
Main Male Character	0	0
Side Male Character	20	30.8
Main Girl Character	1	0.65
Side Girl Character	21	32.4
Main Boy Character	0	0
Side Boy Character	0	0
Total	**65**	**100**
Number of Characters Talking		
Female Speaker	1	0.23
Male Speaker	0	0
Child	22	95.7
Total	**23**	**100**
Voice-Over Use		
Yes	1	100
No	0	0
Total	**1**	**100**

To assess whether the advertisement's content was feminist, the location of the female characters, their behavior in the advertisement, their age range, the body parts appearing in the advertisement, their roles in the advertisement, the preferred clothes, and their feminine-masculine appearance were examined. Table 2 shows frequency values regarding the analysis of main female characters in the advertisement. The basic behaviors exhibited by the female characters in the advertisement consist of different sports branches. In the advertisement, 13 female athletes appear in the clothes of the sports they do. It is seen that the female athletes in the advertisement are professionals. The 13 women in the advertisement have a masculine style. It is seen that the young and middle-aged category of women was selected for the advertisement. Twenty-two children are featured in the advertisement. The advertisement was shot indoors and outdoors. The full body of 35 female characters in the advertisement is visible, and 22 of them wear casual clothes. The main characters are athletes and have a masculine style. It is determined that the idealized representations of "strong women" in the advertisement analyzed within the scope of the study are "strong" women, self-confident women, active women in working life, and combative women who destroy prejudices of society with a feminist perspective, individual activist women, and female figures who reverse gender roles. In the advertisement, the girl says that girls are made of accomplishments and achievements, passion, bravery, dignity, will that is harder than stone, strength, fire, and freedom from other people's opinions. Considering their behavior in the advertisement, the distribution ratios of female characters and how they are defined are determined.

Table 2. Frequency values regarding the analysis of main female characters in the advertisement

Coding Criteria	Frequency (n)	Percentage (%)
The Main Place of the Female Characters in the Advertisement		
Workplace	0	0
House	0	0
Outdoors	0	0
Both Indoors and Outdoors	1	100
Other Interiors	0	0
Total	1	100
Basic Behavior Exhibited by the Female Characters in the Advertisement		
Business	0	0
Housework	0	0
Sport	13	28.9
Leisure Activity	0	0
Other	32	71.1
Total	**45**	**100**
Occupational Role Category of the Female Characters in the Advertisement		
Expert	13	28.9
Non-Expert	0	0
Unemployed, No Visible Job	32	71.1
Total	**45**	**100**
Age of the Female Characters in the Advertisement		
Young	22	48.9
Middle-aged	13	28.9
Old	10	22.2
Total	**45**	**100**
The Visible Part of the Female Character's Body in the Advertisement		
Face	0	0
Upper Part of the Shoulder	0	0
Upper Part of the Waist	10	22.2
Whole Body	35	77.8
Total	**45**	**100**
The Role of the Female Characters in the Advertisement		
Housewife, Mother, Wife	0	0
Artist	0	0

continues on following page

Table 2. Continued

Coding Criteria	Frequency (n)	Percentage (%)
Sportswoman	13	100
Career-Oriented Employee	0	0
Convenience-loving	0	0
Beautiful, attractive	0	0
Entertainment, Shopper	0	0
Sexual Object	0	0
A Decorative Object	0	0
Total	**13**	**100**
The Clothes of the Female Characters in the Advertisement		
Workwear, Uniform	0	0
Suit, Formal Look	10	22.2
Casual clothes	22	48.9
Sportswear	13	28.9
Total	**45**	**100**
Gender Identity of the Female Characters in the Advertisement		
Feminine	10	41.6
Masculine	13	54.17
Unidentified	1	4.17
Total	**24**	**100**

In Table 3, it was examined what expressions were used to describe the admiration for the Nike advertisement in Russia and whether the advertisement was perceived as feminist in the audience's verbal expressions. It was concluded that the advertisement was feminist in 21.80% of the verbal expressions. In the verbal expressions, apart from the word "feminist," expressions such as "Encourage, Emotional, Proud to be a woman" were also considered feminist. It was indicated that the advertisement was successful in 20.60% of the verbal expressions. In 17.20% of the verbal expressions, the audience stated that they liked the advertisement and found it beautiful. In 7.40% of the verbal expressions, the audience indicated that the advertisement was inspiring. While 6.60% of the verbal expressions expressed the audience's appreciation of the advertisement as showing the power of women, the advertisement was found efficient in 6.80% of them.

Upon examining the verbal expressions, it is seen that the advertisement was liked since it was feminist. Due to the strong image of women in the foreground and the inspiration it creates for the audience for the future, it is observed that Nike makes an effective advertisement in line with its brand image with a feminist perspective.

It seems that Russian commenters were touched by the fact that an old Russian song was used in the advertisement, and they were surprised that the song was not in English. Commenters from other countries stated that the video was prepared with love and beautiful energy, and it was visually good and meaningful. Some commenters emphasized the advertisement's effectiveness by emphasizing the success of the Nike brand in changing the minds. Female commenters expressing their pride in being a woman show the appeal for the March 8 Women's Day-themed advertisement of the Nike brand.

Table 3. Frequency values of the expressions used to describe admiration

Coding Criteria	Frequency (n)	Percentage (%)
Feminist	109	21.80
Change the world	6	1.20
Love and beautiful	86	17.20
Visually good	25	5.00
Advertisement successful	103	20.60
Efficient	34	6.80
Emphasizing women's success	3	0.60
The brand that changes minds	3	0.60
Attractive	7	1.40
Importance given to women	3	0.60
Pride	1	0.20
Power of women	33	6.60
Respect for women	17	3.40
Inspiration	37	7.40
Happiness	1	0.20
Value	1	0.20
National Value	31	6.20
Total	**500**	**100**

People expressed their appreciation for the commercial in the following way;

"I love the message, You're made of what you do."

"Doesn't matter how many times I watch this, I always cry."

"Every time I watch this video - tears appear in my eyes! Brilliantly filmed."

"This literally got me goosebumps. That is how good it is."

"It's so great that the brand tries to change the minds around the world; I love this publicity, and I want to include more people who are in a different condition."

"This made me cry and feel strong at the same time. Thanks for this."

"Nike has such good inclusive commercials."

"This makes me feel proud of being a girl."

"This is so powerful! Thank you, Nike."

"This video has inspired me so so much."

"Thanks for giving such importance to girls."

"Nike: what are women made of?

I: bravery, independence, strength, beauty, uniqueness."

"Everyone should watch this and be respectful. We can do this all, not like boys. Like a girl."

"This is great - thanks, Nike."

"I can't believe I even started crying."

"This girl has got such a powerful and strong voice, u go girl!"

"This is probably one of the best advertisements I've ever seen in my life."

"It's so great that the brand tries to change the minds around the world; I love this publicity, and I want to include more people who are in a different condition."

"This is so inspiring!"

"At first, I thought it would be an English version of the song, and then I freaked out."

"I cried watching it; it's so beautiful. Thanks for it, Russia."

"It's incredibly cool."

"You can always do more to make the world a better place, Nike, but I love this spot and how you are standing my Serena and Kap!"

"I usually don't write comments for stuff like this, but this video has inspired me so so much."

"It makes me so happy to see companies supporting young women!"

"We must always value women; they are our future."

"This is exactly what women are made of, and never forget that. Great commercial!"

"I thought it was a NIKE advertisement, but it turned out to be a great message to the World."

"This is the best ad campaign about female empowerment. Honestly, people need to start paying more attention to female athletes instead of just ignoring them; girls are also good at sports."

"Women were made to do hard things...so believe in yourself."

"Good attempt to promote women's empowerment."

"I agree with you. Girls made of all of the world."

"This is very heartwarming; I love the atmosphere and all the sentiments. The message is very powerful and very well executed."

"I am proud to be a woman." (YouTube, 2021)

The verbal expressions examined showed that the advertisement was generally liked. Some commenters stated that Nike's advertisement made them want to go out and change the world. Commenters thanked women for being given importance. They stated that everyone should watch the video and respect it and said that women could do anything.

CONCLUSION

International Women's Day, defined by the United Nations, is an international day celebrated on March 8 every year. It is devoted to developing political and social awareness of women based on human rights and celebrating their economic, political, and social achievements. International Women's Day is a focal point in the women's rights movement (Wikipedia, 2021). With the widespread and intense feeling of consumer culture, the functions of advertisements in daily life also change and transform. Advertising, which in its traditional form only aims to convey messages about businesses and brands, has gained a function beyond this nowadays and has started to become relevant to the agenda of the consumer's daily life, apart from the organization's agenda (Ük, 2019: 2). Russian advertising differs from European or American advertising due to sociocultural differences. The post-Soviet period enabled Russian society to be influenced by the West. Although Western ideas have influenced Russian society very rapidly, old Russian traditions and patriotism are experiencing a renaissance. Western advertising in Russia is affected by Russian culture (Iepuri, 2017: 59). Many public issues related to various topics are the focus of social advertising. Social advertising is used to influence attitudes, beliefs, and behaviors. Social advertising aims to make an impact by drawing attention to the main social problems of different countries (Popkova et al., 2018). Social problems encountered in different subjects are included in the target of social advertising. Social advertising is an important element influencing attitudes, beliefs, and behaviors. It also aims to make an impact by drawing attention to the fundamental social problems of different countries. In international digital marketing campaigns, International Women's Day is one of the contents used in advertisements with the corporate support of brands. International digital marketing campaigns have recently used the International Women's Day holiday with less political content in advertisements with the corporate support of brands (History.com, 2021). Upon examining the "strong woman" discourse in the advertisement content with the theme of March 8, it is observed that the representations of "strong women" in many advertisements aim to strengthen the brand image rather than women (Şener, 2020: 146).

In this study, the Russian-based YouTube advertisement of the Nike brand with the theme of March 8th International Women's Day was published with the slogan "You're made of what you do." In the 2-minute commercial by the Wieden Kennedy Dutch advertising agency, a little girl begins to sing a children's song in Russian on stage in front of a large crowd (Erbaş, 2018: 368). In the advertisement, the door to the concert hall opens, and an ice skater enters. Afterward, the little girl continues to sing the song's lyrics, "Girls are made of iron, striving, self-dedication and battles." In the continuation of the song, she says that girls are made of perseverance and grace that gives pride to the entire nation, and meanwhile, a woman performing ballet appears in the hall among the audience. Power is emphasized in the rest of the song, while two women are shown skateboarding and running. Afterward, the song ends with the words that girls are made of passion, heart, dignity and will that is harder than stone, strength, fire, and freedom from other people's opinions, accomplishments and achievements. In the final scene of the advertisement, the girl singing the song is shown on a soccer field preparing for a penalty kick. The slogan "You're made of what you do" and the brand's logo appear on the screen.

To assess the advertisement content, whether the female characters in the advertisement were sufficiently weighted and the distribution ratios of female characters and how they were defined were determined. It is seen that female characters predominate in the advertisement.

To reveal whether the advertisement content is feminist, the location of the female characters, their behavior in the advertisement, their age range, the body parts appearing in the advertisement, their roles in the advertisement, the preferred clothes, and their feminine-masculine appearance were examined. In the advertisement analyzed within the scope of the study, it was determined that the idealized representations of "strong women" in the advertisement were "strong" women, self-confident women, active women in working life, and combative women who destroy prejudices of society with a feminist perspective, individual activist women, and female figures who reverse gender roles. In the advertisement, the girl says that girls are made of accomplishments and achievements, passion, bravery, dignity, will that is harder than stone, strength, fire, and freedom from other people's opinions. Considering the behavior of female characters, their roles and attitudes in the advertisement, it is observed that there is a feminist weight.

In the verbal expressions, apart from the word "feminist," the words "Encourage, Emotional, Proud to be a woman" were also considered feminist. According to these results, the advertisement is feminist, and the verbal expressions show that commenters liked it. It is revealed that Nike made an effective advertisement in line with the brand's image with a feminist perspective since the advertisement prioritizes the image of strong women and inspires the audience for the future.

The verbal explanations examined demonstrated that the advertisement was generally liked. Some of the commenters stated that Nike's advertisement made them want to go out and change the world. Upon examining the verbal explanations, it is seen that the advertisement was liked because it was feminist. Due to the strong image of women in the foreground and the inspiration it creates for the audience for the future, it is seen that Nike makes an effective advertisement in line with its brand image with a feminist perspective.

FUTURE RESEARCH DIRECTIONS

Recommendations for future academic studies are presented below:

a. The study examined a single brand advertisement containing the subject of March 8. Future research can examine March 8 Women's Day-themed advertisements of different brands.
b. Research can be done in the context of cultural characteristics of two countries by analyzing women-themed advertisements prepared by the brand in two different countries.
c. The study assessed whether the advertisement was perceived as feminist in the verbal expressions of the audience. The presence of a sexist approach in these expressions can be determined by expanding the sample volume for the verbal expressions used in the analysis.

REFERENCES

Alım, E., & Aksu, F. (2019). Eurasian Economic Union as a Power Centre Under the Leadership of Russia. *International Journal of Political Science & Urban Studies, 7*, 1-22. doi:10.14782/ipsus.594377

Aydın, A. (2015). Küresel Müdacele Politikaları: Orta Asya'da Rusya, ABD ve Çin [Politics of Global Campaign: Russia, USA and China in Central Asia]. *Suleyman Demirel University The Journal of Visionary, 6*(13), 1-11.

Belmonte, A., & Rochlitz, M. (2019). The political economy of collective memories: Evidence from Russian politics. *Journal of Economic Behavior & Organization, 168*, 229–250. doi:10.1016/j.jebo.2019.10.009

BorgenProject. (n.d.). https://borgenproject.org/womens-rights-in-russia/

British Library. (n.d.). https://www.bl.uk/russian-revolution/articles/women-and-the-russian-revolution

Bulut, R. (2018). Russian Federation Economy, Opportunities Offered to Foreign and Turkish Entrepreneurs. *Journal of Social Research and Behavioral Sciences, Vol, 4*(6), 345–357.

Chadraba, P. G., & Springer, R. (2008). Business Strategies For Economies in Transition Book of Readings on CEE Countries. Cambridge Scholars Publishing.

Ciochetto, L. (2011). Globalisation and Advertising in Emerging Economies Brazil, Russia, India and China. Routledge.

Croud.com. (2018). https://croud.com/blog/a-guide-to-advertising-in-russia/

Dalyan, M. G., Bayır, Ö. Ö., & Ceyhan, M. Ş. (2018). Understanding Contemporary Woman on Trail of The Past: A Comparative Study on Socio-cultural Statuses of Russian and Armenian Women (Geçmişin izinden Bugünün Toplumsal Kadınını Anlamak). *Tarih Okulu Dergisi, 11*(37), 463–494.

Dongak, E. (2011). *The Role of SMEs in Russian Economy After Transition: The Study of Russian Printing Industry* [Master's thesis]. Yıldız Teknik University Social Science Institute.

EdinburgNews. (n.d.). https://www.edinburghnews.scotsman.com/news/people/international-womens-day-2021-inspirational-quotes-theme-and-why-google-is-celebrating-with-a-doodle-3156358

Elegina, D. (2021). *Advertising in Russia - statistics & facts*. https://www.statista.com/topics/7836/advertising-in-russia/#dossierKeyfigures

Elma, F. (n.d.). Post-Soviet Russia and Central Asia [Sovyet Sonrası Rusya ve Orta Asya]. *Journal of Azerbaijani Studies*, 129-143.

Erbaş, S. (2018, March-April). Kültürlerarası Reklam Araştırmaları: Nike 8 Mart Dünya Kadınlar Günü Reklam Kampanyası Örneği. *Akademik Bakış Dergisi*, (66), 357–375.

Eser, M. (2017). *Place Of Oligarchs in The Foreign Trade and Politics Of The Russian Federation* [Master's thesis]. Manisa Celal Bayar University, Social Science Institute.

Göçeri, N. (2004). Ideas Affecting the Women's Movement [Kadın Hareketini Etkileyen Fikir Akımları]. *Ç. Ü. İlahiyat Fakültesi Dergisi, 4*(2), 61-76.

Güler. (2012). Russia in the Transition Process from Socialism to Capitalism: What Kind of Capitalism? [Sosyalizmden Kapitalizme Geçiş Sürecinde Rusya: Nasıl Bir Kapitalizm?]. *Business and Economics Research Journal, 3*(3), 93–120.

Gurieva, L. K., & Dzhioev, A. V. (2016). *Sustainable development of the Russian economy*. http://science-almanac.ru/documents/77/2016-02-02-Gurieva-Dzhioev.pdf

Hacıtahiroğlu, K. (2014). Küreselleşmenin Siyasal Etkileri, Göç ve Ukrayna-Rusya Krizi [Political Effects of Globalization, Migration and Ukraine-Russia Crisis]. *Trakya Üniversitesi Sosyal Bilimler Dergisi, 16*(2), 259-284.

Hallin, D. C., & Mancini, P. (2012). Comparing Media Systems Beyond the Western World. Cambridge University Press.

History.com. (n.d.). https://www.history.com/news/the-surprising-history-of-international-womens-day

Holak, S. L., Matveev, A. V., & Havlena, W. J. (2007). Nostalgia in post-socialist Russia: Exploring applications to advertising strategy. *Journal of Business Research, 60*(6), 649–655. doi:10.1016/j.jbusres.2006.06.016

Hosking, G. (2011). *Russia and the Russians, from the Early to the 21st Century [Rusya ve Ruslar, Erken Dönemden 21. Yüzyıla]* (K. Acar, Trans.). İletişim Yayınları.

Iepuri, V. (2017). What Makes Russian Advertisements Russian? Contemporary Russian Advertising as a Sociocultural Phenomenon. *Russian Language Journal, 67*, 55–76.

İşcan, İ., & Hatipoğlu, Y.Z. (2011). Transition to Free Market Economy in Russia and 2008 Global Crisis. *İstanbul Üniversitesi İktisat Fakültesi Dergisi, 61*(1), 177-237.

İsmayılov, E. (2013). An Evaluation of South Caucasus and Central Asia in 21st Century Russian Foreign Policy Doctrines [Yüzyıl Rusya Dış Politika Doktrinleri'nde Güney Kafkasya ve Orta Asya Değerlendirmesi]. *Marmara Üniversitesi Siyasi Bilimler Dergisi, Vol, 1*(1), 87–105.

Karakuş, G. (2019). USSR's Overview of the Women [Sovyetler Birliği'nde Kadının Konumuna Genel Bakış]. *Akademik tarih ve Düşünce Dergisi, 6*(3), 1580-1598.

Kemaloğlu, İ. (2016). Yüzyılın Başında Rusya Federasyonu. *Marmara Türkiyat Araştırmaları Dergisi, 3*(2), 1-14. DOI: doi:10.16985/MTAD.2016227938

Mackey, A., & Gass, S. M. (2005). *Second Language Research: Methodology and Design*. Routledge.

Mankoff, J. (2009). Russian Foreign Policy: The Return of Great Power Politics. Rowman & Littlefield Publishers.

Marsh, R. (1996). Women in Russia and Ukraine. Cambridge University Press.

Mau, V., & Drobyshevskaya, T. (2012). Modernization and the Russian Economy: Three Hundred Years of Catching Up. SSRN *Electronic Journal*. https://www.iep.ru/files/RePEc/gai/wpaper/0032Mau.pdf doi:10.2139/ssrn.2135459

Morkovkin, D., Shmanev, S., & Shmaneva, L. (2017). Problems and Trends in Innovative Transformation of Russian Economy and Infrastructure Development. *Advances in Economics, Business and Management Research*, volume 32, *3rd International Conference on Economics, Management, Law and Education (EMLE 2017)*, 10-13.

NTI. (2021). *The State of the Russian Economy: Balancing Political and Economic Priorities*. https://www.nti.org/analysis/articles/state-russian-economy-balancing-political-and-economic-priorities/, (08.10.2021)

Orttung, R. W. (2004, March/April). Business and Politics in the Russian Regions. *Problems of Post-Communism, 51*(2), 48–60. doi:10.1080/10758216.2004.11052162

Öztürk, E., & Şener, G. (2016). Product Placement in The Social Media Era: A Content Analysis on Instagram and Instabloggers [Sosyal Medya Çağında Ürün Yerleştirme: Instagram ve Instabloggerlar Üzerine Bir İçerik Analizi]. *Global Media Journal TR Edition, 6*(12), 355–386.

Paszyc, E., & Wisniewska, I. (2002). Big business in the Russian economy and politics under Putin's rule. *CES Studies*, 45-57. http://pdc.ceu.hu/archive/00002224/01/big_business.pdf

Popkova, E. G., Litvinova, T., Mitina, M. A., & French, J. (2018). Social Advertising: A Russian Perspective. *Management, 39*, 17. https://www.revistaespacios.com/a18v39n01/a18v39n01p17.pdf

Repiev, A. (2004). *A Glimpse of Russia's advertising and marketing*. Retrieved from http://www.-repiev.ru/articles/ghlimps_en.htm

RMAA Agency. (2020). https://russia-promo.com/blog/advertising-market-of-russia-2019-results

Sakwa, R. (2008). *Russian Politics and Society*. Routledge. doi:10.4324/9780203931257

Şener, G. (2020). Can Commodified Feminism Empower Women? Feminist Critical Discourse Analysis of International Working Women's Day Advertisements [Metalaşmış Feminizm Kadınları Güçlendirir mi? 8 Mart Dünya Emekçi Kadınlar Günü Reklamlarının Feminist Eleştirel Söylem Analizi]. *Kültür ve İletişim, 22*(2), 146-172.

Sheresheva, M. Y., & Antonov-Ovseenko, A. A. (2015). Advertising in Russian periodicals at the turn of the communist era. *Journal of Historical Research in Marketing*, 7(2), 165–18. doi:10.1108/JHRM-09-2013-0055

Silka, D. N. (2014). On priority measures for creating the basis for the development of the Russian economy. *Life Science Journal*, 11(7s), 310–313.

Timeanddate. (n.d.). https://www.timeanddate.com/holidays/russia/women-day

Treisman, D. (2009). *Russian politics in a time of economic turmoil*. https://www.sscnet.ucla.edu/polisci/faculty/treisman/Papers/RBS%20Final%20Decmeber%2026,%202009%20with%20figures.pdf

Tsetsura, K., & Kruckeberg, D. (2021). *Strategic Communications in Russia Public Relations and Advertising*. https://books.google.com.tr/books?hl=tr&lr=&id=efz0DwAAQBAJ&oi=fnd&pg=PT118&dq=History+of+The+Russian+Advertising+Industry&ots=ZtHGatj2FH&sig=KKukAbTxKhS-HnQD268bIDOU8wI&redir_esc=y#v=onepage&q=History%20of%20The%20Russian%20Advertising%20Industry&f=false

Ük, Z. Ç. (2019). Evaluation of Gender Stereotypes through Women's Day Advertisements [Toplumsal Cinsiyet Stereotiplerinin Kadınlar Günü Reklamları Üzerinden Değerlendirilmesi]. *UİİİD-IJEAS*, 2019(24), 1-16.

Ustinova, I. P. (2006). English and American Culture Appeal in Russian Advertising. *Journal of Creative Communications*, 3(1), 77–98.

Ustinova, I. P. (2008). *English and emerging advertising in Russia*. Academic Press.

Waller, M. (2005). Russian Politics Today. Manchester University Press.

Warc. (2010). https://www.warc.com/newsandopinion/news/russian-advertising-market-set-for-growth/26448

Weiler, J. (2004). *Human Rights in Russia: A Darker Side of Reform*. Lynne Rienner Publisher.

Wells, G. L., & Auken, S. V. (2006). A Comparison of Associational and Claimless-Informational Advertising in Russia. *Journal of East-West Business*, 12(1), 29–48. doi:10.1300/J097v12n01_03

Wells, L.G. (1994). Western Concepts, Russian Perspectives: Meanings of Advertising in the Former Soviet Union. *Journal of Advertising*, 23(1), 83-95.

Whang, H., Ko, E., Zhang, T., & Mattila, P. (2015). Brand popularity as an advertising cue affecting consumer evaluation on sustainable brands: A comparison study of Korea, China, and Russia. *International Journal of Advertising*, 34(5), 789811. doi:10.1080/02650487.2015.1057381

White, S. (2010). Soviet nostalgia and Russian politics. *Journal of Eurasian Studies*, 1(1), 1–9. doi:10.1016/j.euras.2009.11.003

White, S., Sakwa, R., & Hale, H. E. (2010). Developments In Russian Politics. Palgrave Macmillan.

Wikipedia. (2021). *Women in Russia*. https://en.wikipedia.org/wiki/Women_in_Russia

Wikipedia. (n.d.b). https://en.wikipedia.org/wiki/Perestroika

Wikipedia.(n.d.a).https://tr.wikipedia.org/wiki/D%C3%BCnya_Kad%C4%B1nlar_G%C3%BCn%C3%BC

Wilson, J. L. (2010). The Legacy of the Color Revolutions for Russian Politics and Foreign Policy. *Problems of Post-Communism, 57*(2), 21–36. doi:10.2753/PPC1075-8216570202

Yılmaz, S. (2015). New Eurasianism and Russia [Yeni Avrasyacılık ve Rusya]. *Sosyal ve Beşeri Bilimler Araştırmaları Dergisi, 2015*(34), 111-120.

Youtube. (n.d.). https://www.youtube.com/watch?v=Y_iCIISngdI

Yüksel, S. (2016). Causal Relationships Between Growth, Unemployment and Inflation in the Russian Economy [Rusya Ekonomisinde Büyüme, İşsizlik ve Enflasyon Arasındaki Nedensellik İlişkileri]. *Finans Politik & Ekonomik Yorumlar, 53*(614), 43-57.

Yurttaş, Ö. U. (2018). Content Anslysis of Political Ads: 2018 General Elections in Turkey [Siyasal Reklamlara Yönelik İçerik Analizi: 2018 Türkiye Genel Seçimleri]. *Turkish Studies, 13(26)*, 1171–1186.

ENDNOTE

[1] Perestroika is a political reform movement within the Communist Party of the Soviet Union in the 1980s. It means restructuring in the Soviet political and economic systems (https://en.wikipedia.org/wiki/Perestroika).

Chapter 14
A Scenario Integration Study in Brand Communication:
"Let's Turn Off the Taps" Advertising Case

Merve Çelik-Varol
https://orcid.org/0000-0002-0698-929X
Beykent University, Turkey

Nazlım Tüzel-Uraltaş
https://orcid.org/0000-0001-7682-2164
Marmara University, Turkey

Erdem Varol
https://orcid.org/0000-0003-3940-2122
Marmara University, Turkey

ABSTRACT

In this study, the commercial film titled Let's Turn Off the Taps of the Finish brand, which has been awarded the Silver Award in Crystal Apple in the category of Media Use–Television Section in 2020 will be analyzed. One of the advertisements of the "Tomorrow's Water" campaign, which is an awareness movement led by Finish Turkey and supported by National Geographic Turkey, Let's Turn Off the Taps draws attention to the risk of Turkey becoming water-poor soon and aims to raise awareness about this problem. In addition, Taner Ölmez, the leading actor of the The Miracle Doctor series, took part in this commercial, and the commercial was shot in Lake Kuyucuk. The commercial, which draws attention with the slogan "The end of the water is seen" broke a new ground in Turkey and brought a different dimension to the scenario integration work by bringing together the TV series The Woman and The Miracle Doctor broadcast on Fox TV.

DOI: 10.4018/978-1-7998-9672-2.ch014

INTRODUCTION

The advertising industry in Turkey emerged in the middle of the 19th century. In the aforementioned years, which coincided with the last periods of the Ottoman Empire, the newspapers that emerged after the widespread use of the printing press began to receive advertisements to meet their costs and the first advertisement examples emerged. From that period to the present day, the advertising sector has continued to develop and has emerged as one of the cornerstones of the cultural economy. In other words, the Turkish advertising industry has developed depending on the social, political, and economic dynamics of Turkey and has become one of the main structures of the country. In this context, the advertising industry is a global industry that is growing day by day for Turkey, which has been changing and transforming sectors. When the development process of advertising in Turkey is examined, it is possible to say that printed media organs have developed primarily. The development of printed publications led to the expansion of the readership of newspapers and contributed to the development of press advertising. The development of press advertising has also enabled the advertising sector to develop. The period between 1957 and 1961 is called the "dark years" for the Turkish advertising industry because of only the "Official Announcements Company" has the right to place advertisements in newspapers and magazines. But the 1980s are considered decidedly important for the history of the Turkish advertising. In the 1980s, advertising agencies with foreign partners were established; advertising discourses changed and the advertising industry underwent a major transformation. The concepts of "creativity", "authenticity", "success in advertising" gained importance in the mentioned years, and competitions involving "different" and "original ideas" gained momentum during this period. It can be said that the 1980s was one of the most intense periods of globalization for the advertising industry in Turkey. Each developing and changing technology has brought different and new channels, and the 1990s has become a period in which advertising measurements were made and advertising types developed and changed. In the 2000s, advertisements that benefit from the innovations offered by internet technology are not only used as paid messages to promote goods and services, to create changes in consumers' attitudes and behaviors, to direct them to a certain thought, to increase sales figures, but also appeared to draw attention to social problems and raise awareness. In this context, there have been more complex communication campaigns in which various media are integrated, rather than advertisements in which a single medium is used. These communication campaigns, which are more effective, faster, and more attractive, are an effort that brands use quite a lot today.

In the digital consumption era that we live in, advertisements are also frequently used to inform, raise awareness and mobilize the public. The reasons such as the increase in the awareness of the consumers, the importance of the concept of sustainability, the increase in the number of environmentally sensitive consumers, the ability to give rapid feedback to advertisements through social media, the existence of advertisements that repeat the same messages, and the increase in global competition have led to the change and transformation of concepts such as brand communication and advertising communication. For instance, nowadays, similar advertising messages make ads ordinary, reduce the attractiveness of advertising messages, and cause consumers to be insensitive to the same advertising content. In today's competitive conditions, where products and brands are so similar to each other, it is considered very important to call out to consumers by producing different strategies in postmodern marketing communication studies.

"Postmodern brand communication", where different strategies are blended with the right messages, new approaches are in question, and differing from traditional communication studies, aims to raise awareness by considering the attitudes, behaviors, and also values of the society. In this context, it is necessary to evaluate the concept of "brand communication" as a concept that aims to convey the right messages to the right target audience at the right time and use the right strategies. Due to its nature, the postmodern period we live in decidedly allows for the coexistence of differences. For this reason, advertising messages in postmodern brand communication strategies can consist of content that brings different subjects, people, and positions together.

Advertising with scenario integration and environmentalist discourse, which can be evaluated in postmodern brand communication, attracts a lot of attention. The increasing awareness and sensitivity towards concepts such as "sustainability", "environmental awareness", and "unnecessary consumption", which have increased in recent years, encourages consumers to evaluate brands and products with these aspects. In today's world where limited resources have become even more limited, it is possible to say that "environmentally sensitive", "high ecological concerns", "sustainable" and "recyclable" brands or advertisements are more in demand as well as the quality, nature, and pricing of products and brands. In this context, the advertisement messages in question not only increase the reputation of the brand but also aim to raise the awareness of the consumers against the social problem highlighted in the advertisement. "Social advertisements" aim to raise awareness and mobilize the masses against any social problem, by revealing any social problem, protecting the benefit of society.

As one of the types of advertisements, advertisements with social content contribute to social awareness within the framework of the principle of social benefit by positively changing the attitudes and behaviors of the masses. Aiming at positive changes in the attitudes and behaviors of society, advertisements with social content reach the masses quickly and affect the behavior of individuals. These advertisements, which are sensitive to social problems, address themes such as environmental problems, climate changes, and unconscious consumption of resources, earthquakes, and erosion. It can be said that nowadays advertisements are prepared not only with commercial concerns but also by considering the social benefit. In this context, advertisements with social content should be prepared with remarkable communication strategies by knowing the target audience very well and also taking into account the habits of the target audience. In other words, for ads with social content to be effective, it is crucial to determine a target audience that can take action quickly, address the audience with the right messages at the right time, support the message with different communication tools when necessary, and be measurable.

In this study, the commercial film titled "Let's Turn off the Taps" of the Finish brand, which was awarded the Silver Award in Crystal Apple in the category of Media Use –Television Section- in 2020 will be analyzed. One of the advertisements of the "Tomorrow's Water" campaign, which is an awareness movement led by Finish Turkey and supported by National Geographic Turkey, "Let's Turn Off the Taps" draws attention to the risk of Turkey becoming water-poor soon and aims to raise awareness about this problem. In addition, Taner Ölmez, the leading actor of the "The Miracle Doctor" series, played in this commercial, and the commercial was shot in Lake Kuyucuk. The commercial, which draws attention with the slogan "The End of the Water is Seen", broke new ground in Turkey and brought a different dimension to the scenario integration work by bringing together the TV series "The Woman" and "The Miracle Doctor" broadcast on Fox TV. In addition, the advertisement of Finish - "Let's Turn Off the Taps", which can be evaluated in the context of today's postmodern brand communication and social advertising, is very important in terms of understanding and making sense of today's changing and transforming communication works by giving a holistic message.

Turkey: The Country Connecting Asia and Europe

Turkey, officially the Republic of Turkey, is located in Anatolia, a point where Asia and Europe converge. In this context, due to its geographical location, Anatolia has also witnessed the passage of different masses of people. Turkey, which hosts many different civilizations, has also allowed different cultures to come together (tbb, 2021). The country, which has 81 administrative units, consists of 7 regions: the Black Sea Region, the Marmara Region, the Aegean Region, the Mediterranean Region, the Central Anatolia Region, the Eastern Region, and the Southeastern Region. It is possible to mention the unique climatic conditions, geographical features, and cultural structure of each region. In addition to this, it is known that the fertile soil of Anatolia, where Turkey is located, has hosted many civilizations due to its many microclimates.

As a country that has spread over a wide area geographically, encountered and dominated various cultures, Turkey has succeeded in influencing many civilizations in the political, social, and cultural fields (Türkiye Kültür Portalı, 2021). These riches in the cultural structure have also influenced the traditional arts, culinary culture, language and dialects, and music culture. Cultural heritages transferred from the past to the present have also been registered by UNESCO, and the number of elements registered in the National Inventory of Intangible Cultural Heritage of the Ministry of Culture and Tourism of Turkey has reached 294. In addition, 20 of these cultural elements are registered on the UNESCO Intangible Cultural Heritage List. In this respect, Turkey is among the 5 countries that registered the most intangible cultural elements with UNESCO (Çiftci, 2021).

Turkey is in a very important position not only with its unique cultural heritage but also with its economic income sources, agriculture, animal husbandry, industry, tourism, and underground treasure. Considering its environmental characteristics such as climate, landforms, water resources, seas, and vegetation, it appears as a very important country especially in the fields of agriculture and tourism. In this context, tourism activities in Turkey occupy a substantial place among the growth elements of the economy. Considering the Mediterranean and Aegean coasts, historical and cultural heritage of Turkey, it is inevitable fact that it is a famous touristic country (Özdemir and Öksüzler, 2006).

When Turkey's geographical, economic, social, and political structure is evaluated, it can be said that it is a country that is open to development. In addition, it is one of the notable countries of the world with its historical and cultural heritage, rich water resources, and underground treasure. It is an important country not only with its geopolitical location, geographical and economic characteristics, historical and cultural heritage but also in terms of its success in different industries.

In addition to all its geographical and cultural richness, Turkey has favorable conditions for major brands to invest in. For example, with its young and dynamic population, Turkey can react quickly to technological developments. Today, a young and technology-friendly target audience is seen as a remarkable market for brands, as the most important economic activities are in parallel with technology. Advertisements, which are the most important tool of brands in terms of promotion and consumption, appeal to the young population, the young population can quickly respond to these advertisements.

Turkey as a Productive Country for the Global Advertising Industry

The concept of advertising, which can be defined as the whole of written, audio and visual works carried out to direct consumers to a good or service, to attract attention, to increase sales figures, to protect and increase brand value, has started to be seen frequently in newspapers, which have become an important communication tool after the spread of the printing press. Advertising in mass media in Turkey first appeared in 1840 with the publication of the newspaper, Ceride-i Havadis. The first of the illustrated advertisements in commercial terms was published in 1864, in the newspaper, Tercüman-ı Ahval (Koloğlu, 1999).

The Turkish advertising industry, which was revived with press advertisements given by foreign institutions in the Republican Period, increased the newspaper circulation with the alphabet reform and the increase in literacy rate, and press advertisements became a very important source of income (Töre, 2011: 35). Audio technologies, which are actively used after the development and widespread use of written media, have contributed to the development of advertising to a great extent. The 1950s appear as the years when the radio was used as an effective medium. The development of electronic media brought television broadcasting to the agenda, and the use of television was a milestone for the Turkish advertising industry. The 1970s were the years when television was first used as an advertising medium by the Turkish advertising industry. In 1961, the "Press Advertising Agency", which is very important for the Turkish advertising industry, was established. This development is considered as one of the breaking points of the Turkish advertising industry due to reasons such as the increase in the value given to advertising agencies and advertising, and the rise in advertising expenditures of institutions (Töre, 2011: 35).

Due to the liberal economic policies that came to the fore in Turkey in the 1980s, foreign investors showed interest in Turkey and foreign partners began to come to advertising agencies. It can be said that the Turkish advertising industry has achieved successful productions as the number of advertising agencies has increased and institutions have started to carry out long-term advertising activities. Additionally, the increase in foreign partnerships brought professionalism to the Turkish advertising industry and contributed to the development of creative strategies (Elden, 2016: 156).

In the 1990s, the increase in the number of television channels, the increase in the trust in print media, the widespread use of them, and their reach to large masses contributed to the development of advertising strategies and the increase in advertising and marketing activities.

In the early 1990s, the monopoly of the Turkish Radio and Television Corporation (TRT), which was the only channel in Turkey, came to an end, and private channels broadcasting from outside Turkey started broadcasting from within the country after the permission and their number increased. This situation brought up the issue of viewing rates increased the number of channels to be advertised, and the Broadcasters Audience Research Board (TIAK) was established with the participation of the Advertisers Association, Association of Advertising Agencies, International Advertisers Association, and broadcasting organizations. In addition, the Press Audiences Research Board (BIAK) was established in 1996 to control issues such as press monitoring and measurement (Çağlak, 2016). It can be said that the main task of these important institutions such as TIAK, BIAK, RIAK (Radio Monitoring and Research Board), which are used to measure the effectiveness of the media, is to measure whether the right communication messages reach the right target audience at the right time.

With the proliferation of private television channels, the increase in competition among channels, and the understanding of the importance of effective advertising and marketing activities for institutions, the value attributed to measurement increased, and the Radio and Television Supreme Council (RTÜK) became operational in 1994 to ensure the control of private channels so that the said value does not lead to unfair competition (Elden, 2016: 157).

In addition, the importance of outdoor advertising was noticed in the said period and billboard advertisements came to the fore in 1997 (Hızal, 2005: 118). Also, advertising agencies have brought a different perspective to the sector by including the said advertisements in the media planning of the institutions.

In the 2000s, innovations in information and communication technologies allowed the emergence and realization of different channels and offered wide opportunities to the advertising sector. Today, reasons such as smartphones, artificial intelligence, and the increase in social media have affected not only the global advertising industry but also the Turkish advertising industry and contributed to the emergence of new advertising models. Integrated advertising campaigns have come to the fore for reasons such as the fact that conventional media, especially television, still maintains its power, and that it is possible to reach a more specific target audience in digital media, it is more economical, and it is measured faster. Today, the main reasons for the increase in the number of brands that benefit from the effects of digital media and add social media to their traditional advertising efforts are making more precise measurements, reaching more people, providing ease of sharing on social media, and providing a viral effect very quickly and very easily.

World-renowned brands paid more attention to these advertising activities and tried to achieve the success they achieved in conventional advertising in digital media as well. For example, Bing collaborated with world-famous artist Jay-Z for Bing Maps, placing 320 pages of Jay-Z's autobiographical book in 15 separate cities in traditional and social media. Among the places where the pages of the book in question were placed were t-shirts, coats, billiard tables, and pool floors. Afterward, users were asked to photograph these places and upload them to their addresses. As a result, the average of visits per user was 11 minutes. Moreover, there was an 11.7 increase in the number of people visiting Bing. At the end of the campaign, 1.1 billion dollars of media exposure was achieved (Erkut, b.t.).

Similarly, at the 14th Felis Awards in 2019, advertising campaigns such as "Turkey's Water-Finish", "Women To Admire - Fox Networks Group", "Dear Brother-LÖSEV", "Be the Lantern - Fenerbahçe", "What a Beautiful Thing To Read - Idefix" were awarded for their achievements in Turkey (Kocasu, 2019).

It can be said that integrated advertising campaigns, in which digital and conventional channels are blended with different communication messages, were evaluated within the scope of "postmodern brand communication" as a remarkable and effective strategy, and the 2000s became a turning point for the Turkish advertising industry. In this context, postmodern brand communication has also brought up the use of different advertising discourses and different media on social problems together. In our age, advertising has become not only a method of persuasion that tries to increase product promotion and sales, but also a tool aimed at drawing attention to the points where society is sensitive. Interactive and fast media used in the digital age we live in have made it easier to draw attention to different social problems, and distinct and remarkable advertising contents shared have spread rapidly. Advertisements that include scenario integration work and environmental discourse, which can be evaluated within the scope of postmodern brand communication, are in an indispensable position for the Turkish advertising industry. In today's world, where consumers have become more conscious of goods and services, eco-consciousness has risen, and the concepts of "sustainability" have gained importance, brands have attached great importance to "advertisements with social content". In this context, it is considered important to use accessible channels together, to reach the right target audience at the right time with the right messages, to call and mobilize consumers through interactive channels when necessary, and to raise awareness for these communication efforts to be effective.

FINISH - "LET'S TURN OFF THE TAPS" ADVERTISING CASE

In this section, the commercial film of the Finish brand named "Let's Turn Off the Taps", which was awarded the Silver Award in the "Crystal Apple" competition, which is a very important competition for the Turkish advertising industry in the Television Category in 2020, will be analyzed and then the scenario integration work using the TV series "The Woman" and "The Miracle Doctor" broadcast on Fox TV will also be mentioned.

Significance

Today, the rapid change in the production-consumption balance creates differences in brand communication. In the postmodern consumption era, concepts such as brand communication and advertising are also undergoing change and transformation due to reasons such as the increase in the education level of consumers and being more sensitive to social problems.

The commercial film of the Finish brand, *"Let's Turn Off the Taps"*, which comes across as a postmodern communication work and has a scenario integration work by breaking new ground in Turkey, is important in terms of both containing the concept of social advertising and being a brand communication work. The examination of the said commercial is important both in terms of revealing the changing and transforming brand communication concept and making sense of the advertisement with social content. In addition, considering that this study will contribute to the relevant literature, it will be possible to contribute to the emergence of new approaches in the next generation advertising studies of brands.

Purpose

This study aims to analyze the commercial film Finish - *"Let's Turn Off the Taps"* with a social content themed "careful consumption of resources", which is one of the problems that exist in social life. Another aim of the study is to examine the scenario integration work carried out in parallel with the two domestic TV series broadcast on Fox TV and the commercial film in question. In this study, which will be carried out in line with these purposes, this brand communication study, which gives social advertising and holistic messages, will be analyzed and interpreted.

Universe and Sample

The universe of this study is the list of winners of the Crystal Apple competition in 2020, one of the most important "Advertising Awards" competitions in Turkey, organized every year by the "Advertising Association". The sample of the study is the commercial film *"Let's Turn Off the Taps"*, which is included in the list and received the Silver Award in the best media use-Television category. The advertising film in question was considered important and selected in terms of being Turkey's first scenario integration work and drawing attention to excess water consumption, which is a social topic.

Method

This study aims to analyze the advertisement work called Finish - "Let's Turn Off the Taps", which is a scenario integration study that is also a social advertisement, which is realized for the first time. This advertising campaign, which provides a holistic advertising message, will be examined using the content analysis method.

As An Environmentally Responsible and Sustainable Campaign: Finish - "Let's Turn Off The Taps" Case

Today, consumers' being more sensitive about decreasing resources, the increase in environmentalist discourses, the importance of the concept of "sustainability" in every sector, and the emphasis on eco-consciousness have led brands to prepare "advertisements with social content". Currently, advertisements not only focus on commercial activities but also aim to raise awareness of social problems by taking the public interest into account. Many brands in Turkey adopt these advertising campaigns, draw attention to any problem and work to improve the quality of life.

Today, one of the issues that need attention and precautions is the reduction of water resources. According to the reports of organizations such as the United Nations and UNESCO, water resources are decreasing and drought is being experienced in Turkey and the world due to reasons such as global warming, increased drought, and increasing population (austrotherm, 2020). It is crucial to use water resources carefully and consciously, which are necessary for the continuation of the ecosystem. In this context, the advertisement campaign called Finish -"Let's Turn Off the Taps", which was carried out to draw attention to the environmental problem in question, received great attention and received many awards. The commercial film in question was shot at Lake Kuyucuk in Kars Province of Turkey, and Taner Ölmez played in the commercial. Created by Havas Istanbul, the commercial begins with Taner Ölmez's vocalization of the musical track "Suyun Sonu Görünüyor (The End of Water is Seen)". The second part of the commercial meets the audience with the disappearance of Taner Ölmez, who sang the song on the cracked, arid lands of Lake Kuyucuk, and the screen showing the dry areas with a wider angle. In the second part of the commercial, the mother and child who place the dishes in the dishwasher in a kitchen meet with the audience. After the rhetoric "Turkey is at risk of being water-poor", the plates that are washed with excessive water consumption and put in the dishwasher attract attention. Right after, the message, "We can save 57 liters of water in every wash, 40 times the water of Kuyucuk every year, by simply stopping swilling out the dishes" is given in the commercial film. It can be said that the main purpose of the commercial film, which uses the slogan "Let's turn off the taps, don't let the water end", is to create behavior changes by convincing or motivating the target audience to a specific topic or a specific problem. In this context, the commercial film, which highlights the fact that water resources are decreasing and Lake Kuyucuk is facing drought, invites individuals to be careful about water consumption.

It is known that advertisements with social content, which address social and environmental problems through mass media, also offer ideas for solutions to these problems. In this context, in the commercial titled Finish - "Let's Turn Off the Taps", recommendations were presented to solve problems such as drought, the decrease in water resources and the drying up of Lake Kuyucuk, and how much savings could be saved by not swilling out the dishes were shared with the audience. In addition, it can be said that the presence of an actor like Taner Ölmez, who has recently become popular, has appeared in various public service ads, and is known for his social awareness, is quite effective. As a result, it is aimed to change the individual behaviors towards global and environmental benefits, in other words, to direct them to the positive, in the commercial film that appeals to the emotions of individuals by using both visual and auditory elements.

Figure 1.
Source: "Let's Turn Off the Taps So That the Water Doesn't End"- Finish Pazarlamasyon.com, 2021.

A First in Turkey: Scenario Integration Study

The commercial titled Finish -"Let's Turn Off the Taps" involves the "scenario integration work" that can be evaluated within the context of postmodern brand communication and is a first in Turkey. Drawing attention to the risk of Turkey becoming water-poor shortly and successfully raising awareness, the Finish -"Let's Turn Off Taps" campaign gives a holistic message and shares a common scenario by bringing together two of Fox TV's most popular TV series, "The Woman" and "The Miracle Doctor".

The work in question, performed by Havas Istanbul and featuring the crossover of two series of the same concept on the same channel in a common scenario adds a different dimension to brand communication. Turkey's two most popular and watched TV series were selected for the integrated advertising campaign, which supports each other in both channels, gives holistic messages, and aims to reach a wider target audience.

When Bahar (Özge Özpirinççi), whom we see in the role of "mother" in the TV series "The Woman" broadcasted on Fox TV on Tuesday evening, November 19, takes her ill son Doruk (Ali Sami Sefil) to the emergency room, they encounter Ali Vefa (Taner Ölmez). This situation constitutes the first step of the scenario integration study. The story, which was left unfinished with the aforementioned encounter scene, continues on Thursday, November 21, in the TV series "The Miracle Doctor". Doctor Ali Vefa, who focuses on Bahar and Doruk standing at the door of the emergency room in the said series and takes care of them, draws attention to the issue by telling Bahar that Turkey is a country that suffers from water shortages. In the sequence where Bahar is observed to be quite confused, it is seen that she exhibits a different behavior with the words "the flowing water stops for children".

Doctor Ali Vefa's statement that Bahar cannot understand the subject and that his patient, Doruk, is dehydrated, appears as a remarkable scene.

In this scenario integration work, which is quite effective and gives striking messages, Doruk's illness due to dehydration and the messages given in the commercial named Finish -"Let's Turn Off the Taps" constitute a complementary feature. According to the scenario, a small child who becomes sick by being dehydrated symbolizes the risk of future drought, while the words of Dr. Ali Vefa are a precaution on this issue.

Considering the integration of the scenario and the messages given by the commercial, it is seen that a very important issue is highlighted, solutions are offered and the public is motivated to take action. The aforementioned successful campaign also spread rapidly with the hashtags "#akansulardurur" (flowing water stops) and "#birdamlamucize" (a drop of miracle) supported by the audience on social media. In this context, the integrated advertising campaign, which was also supported on social media, succeeded in conveying the message that Turkey is at risk of becoming water-poor shortly, to a wider audience.

Collaborating with the North Nature Association to protect Lake Kuyucuk, which contains 232 different bird species, and to keep the water resources of the future under control, Finish has achieved a new success with the said integrated campaign. Finish won not only the Crystal Apple Silver Award but also the Grand Prize in the field of "Transforming Marketing Effect" at Felis, another important competition that triggers creativity for the Turkish advertising industry. Finish, which is also an award winner from the Integrated Campaign Department and the Media Department, was also "Brand of The Year" (DigitalAge, 2020).

When the motto "Let's Turn Off the Taps" of Finish brand and the conducted scenario integration work are evaluated as a whole, it can be seen that in today's increasing competitive conditions, it effectively captures consumers who avoid similar content, offers solutions to an environmental problem that concerns Turkey and needs to be taken, and protects individuals against the said problem. results have been achieved. In addition, it is an inevitable fact that more individuals or consumers are reached with the viral effect provided by the support of social advertisements in interactive media.

In addition, the brand creates a sense of trust in the consumer by creating advertising films on the same theme in a series and publishing the same problem decisively with different slogans, and thus, this situation gives the brand a reputation. Nowadays, with the increase in environmentalist discourses and the increase in awareness with social media, consumers show more sensitivity and draw a conscious profile on issues such as "wellness", "sustainability" and "natural life". In this context, as the number of environmentally sensitive brands increases, it will be easier to become a reputable brand in the eyes of consumers, as well as to adopt an environmentally friendly lifestyle.

FUTURE RESEARCH DIRECTIONS

In addition, in recent years, due to reasons such as increasing awareness of today's consumers with digitalization, increasing sensitivity towards "environmental" and "green" products, giving more importance to "health" and "naturalness", and increasing awareness of "natural life" it is seen that brands focus on commercials with social content. In this context, the Finish brand has drawn attention to a very important problem for Turkey, created awareness, and made a long-term investment in corporate identity studies. In other words, it supported the messages it gave on an important issue concerning society with integrated communication campaigns and maintained a successful advertising campaign by communicating with consumers through different channels.

The integrated communication campaign in question, aimed at informing and raising awareness of the society, has a multifaceted effect and creates a behavioral change in the society. In this context, it can be said that Finish - "Let's Turn Off the Taps" advertisement, which can be considered within postmodern brand communication concept, involves social responsibility, public service advertising, and advertisement with social content, scenario integration study, and public relations advertising.

CONCLUSION

In this study, information about the geographical, economic, and cultural characteristics of Turkey, one of the most important countries in the world, was given, the Turkish advertising industry was explained, and then the commercial film Finish - "Let's Turn Off the Taps" and its integration study, which is a first in Turkey, received the Silver Award in Crystal Apple and can be evaluated within the scope of postmodern brand communication, was examined.

It is known that Turkey has a high potential among the countries of the world with its geopolitical position and economic resources. Turkey is a cosmopolitan country that has been greatly influenced by different cultures by hosting many civilizations with its geographical features. It has attracted attention with its underground and aboveground treasures and has managed to become a strong tourism country with its historical texture.

It can be said that Turkey stands out not only with its geographical features and cultural background but also with its success in different sectors. The advertising sector, which developed and enriched with the increase in the number of advertising agencies in Turkey in the 1970s and 1980s, has become an industry where technological developments are followed very closely and easily. Currently, the sector in question, which operates in categories such as newspapers, radio, television, outdoor, is developing and transforming with new and interactive media offered by Internet technology. In this context, the Turkish advertising industry is in an exciting position with successful efforts that adapt to innovations on a global scale.

The Turkish advertising industry, which has become an industry that triggers creativity with different advertising competitions, also draws attention with its openness to innovations and firsts. The changing and transforming world order, diminishing natural resources, and sustainable living policies cause advertising activities to be carried out not only for promotion or sales but also to draw attention to any social or environmental problem and to raise awareness.

On the other hand, environmental problems such as the increase in the consumption rate of individuals, destruction of natural resources, and increase in air-water and soil pollution, climate changes, and decrease in water resources have a negative impact on Turkey as well on a global scale. In this context, it is obvious that successful communication studies on this subject achieve their goals in the long run and instill awareness on the subject to consumers.

The commercial film titled Finish -"Let's Turn Off the Taps", which was examined in this study, both drew attention to the drought problem in Lake Kuyucuk and brought a different perspective to the Turkish advertising industry by bringing solutions to the issue. The long-term advertising campaign has had wide repercussions not only in conventional media but also on social media. In this respect, it has succeeded in reaching large audiences as a remarkable, interactive, and resounding advertising campaign. At the same time, by blazing a trail, it carried out a scenario integration work and reinforced the message in question by repeating the message it gave in the commercial differently.

REFERENCES

Austrotherm. (2021). *Dünya'da ve Türkiye'de Su Kaynakları Azalıyor!* https://www.austrotherm.com.tr/bilgi-servisi/haberler/duenyada-ve-tuerkiyede-su-kaynaklari-azaliyor

Çağlak, E. (2016). Bu toprakların iletişim tarihi. Nobel Yayınları.

Çiftci, M. (2021). *Türkiye UNESCO'ya En Çok Kültürel Unsur Kaydettiren 5 Ülkeden Biri.* https://www.trthaber.com/haber/kultur-sanat/turkiye-unescoya-en-cok-kulturel-unsur-kaydettiren-5-ulkeden-biri-556718.html

DigitalAge. (2020). *Felis Ödülleri'nde İlk Gecenin Kazananları Açıklandı.* https://digitalage.com.tr/felis-odullerinde-ilk-gecenin-kazananlari-aciklandi/

Elden, M. (2016). Reklam ve reklamcılık. Say Yayınları.

Erkut, A. (n.d.). *Reklam Kampanyasına Dijital Entegre Edilince...* https://www.campaigntr.com/reklam-kampanyasina-dijital-entegre-edilince/

Finish 'Yarının Suyu' Hareketi için Türkiye'de İlk Kez İki Diziyi Bir Araya Getirdi. (n.d.). https://pazarlamasyon.com/finish-yarinin-suyu-hareketi-icin-turkiyede-ilk-kez-iki-diziyi-bir-araya-getirdi/

Hızal, S. G. (2005). *Reklam endüstrisinin topografyası: Türkiye örneği.* İletişim Araştırmaları.

Hızal, S.G. (2005). Topography of the advertising industry: an example of Turkey. *Journal of Communication Research, 3*(1-2), 105-131.

Kocasu, N. A. (2019). *Felis'e Göre Entegre Kampanyaların En İyileri.* mediacat.com/felis-2020-entegre-kampanyalar-bolumu-felis-kazanan-tum-isler/

Koloğlu, O. (1999). Reklamcılığımızın ilk yüzyılı: 1840-1940. Reklamcılar Derneği.

Özdemir, A., & Öksüzler, O. (2006). *Türkiye'de turizm bir ekonomik büyüme politikası aracı olabilir mi? Bir granger nedensellik analizi.* Balıkesir Üniversitesi Sosyal Bilimler Enstitüsü.

Özdemir, A., & Öksüzler, O. (2006). Tourism in Turkey is an economic growth policy toolcould it be? A granger causality analysis. *Balikesir University Institute of Social Sciences Journal, 9*(16), 107-126.

Özgür, A. Z. (1994). Televizyon reklamcılığı. Der Yayınları.

TBB. (2021). *Türkiye'nin Coğrafi Yapısı.* http://www.tbb.gen.tr/turkce/cografya/index.html

Töre, E. (2011). Türkiye'de reklam endüstrisi değer zinciri ve temel göstergeler. *The Turkish Online Journal of Design, Art and Communication, 1*(2), 34-42.

Türkiye Kültür Portalı. (2021). *Türk Tarihine Genel Bakış.* https://www.kulturportali.gov.tr/portal/turk-tarihine-genel-bakis

Chapter 15

From an Empire to Brexit:
Globalization and Glocalization in British Advertising

Onur Serdan Çarboğa
Istanbul Bilgi University, Turkey

Ece Nur Kaya Yıldırım
ⓘ https://orcid.org/0000-0002-4253-5279
Ege University, Turkey

ABSTRACT

To comprehend how British advertising gained its unique identity, this study reviews historical events and phenomena such as imperialism and Brexit, discusses the cultural structure of British society, and considers the advertising industry's political-economic structure. It utilises a modern branch of critical discourse analysis called multimodal discourse analysis and extensively studies the HSBC TV commercial titled 'Home To So Much More', focusing on how its visuals create and represent Britishness and the British way of making advertisements.

INTRODUCTION

In today's world, shaped and understood through the lens of globalization (especially since the 1980s), common features and similarities between markets, target audiences, products, and marketing messages increasingly attract attention and celebration. However, despite the similarities increasing in global scale caused by technological developments and communicational convenience (Levitt, 1983), culture remains the dominant factor in communication (Singh & Appiah-Adu, 2008, p. 133). This means that although global trade and commerce would prefer a target audience with homogenised tastes, 'desires and behaviour are not converging' (De Mooij, 2014, p. 22); therefore, how to address and influence these desires and behaviour remains culturally specific. Douglas and Isherwood (1978) argue that products and culture have a reciprocal relationship in which they shape and carry meaning through each other. On this

DOI: 10.4018/978-1-7998-9672-2.ch015

basis, advertisements act as a front for a culturally established world of consumers and consumer goods (McCracken, 1986). This close connection between culture and, specifically, marketing communication inspires different schools of advertising across several countries and regions.

The United States (US), being the origin country for the theory and thinking of advertising, is considered the benchmark of marketing communication (De Mooij, 2014, p. 273). Comparison between the US and the United Kingdom of Great Britain and Northern Ireland (UK) reveals the highly constitutive role of culture in advertising, as well as the American impact on British advertising during much of the 20th century. Although these two countries seem superficially alike, sharing a common language, similar political and commercial systems, and Anglo-Saxon history, they are distinguished by their approaches to advertising, resulting from their socioeconomic, geographical, cultural, ideological, and communicational differences (Pigott, 1996, p. 248). To better explain, this chapter follows the early history and development of British advertising and the relations between marketing communication practices in the US and UK. The chapter also unfolds the nature of ownership in British advertising and how US dominance was overcome, aiming to understand what forces shaped the unique characteristics of British advertising such as humour, the soft-sell approach, entertainment value, and class division (Nevett, 1992, p. 65).

To take a snapshot of British advertising, this chapter reviews historical events and phenomena such as colonisation, world wars and the Industrial Revolution that directly affected the British advertising field. The UK's colonial past, its international relations during and following the First and Second World War, its ability to translate its past to continue to be a powerful player in the modern globalised world, and finally its re-emerging localization through Brexit will be debated. Moreover, to comprehend how British advertising gained its unique identity, the cultural structure of British society and the advertising industry's political-economic structure are discussed. Through these discussions, this chapter establishes a historical and cultural outline against which to analyse HSBC's '*Home To So Much More*' TV commercial.

'*Home To So Much More*' was deemed appropriate for this study because of its close affinity to the Brexit phenomenon and post-Brexit social climate. Its precursor in 2019, the '*We Are Not An Island*' campaign, was perceived as a direct response to Brexit by the British public. Concerned by being perceived as a strictly global bank for wealthy foreigners, and thus lacking relevance to the British public, HSBC UK has been focusing on what it means to be British and how this naturally entails being international and multicultural too since December 2018, when it first published the commercial titled '*The Global Citizen*'. Therefore, the latest instalment of these efforts provides a unique post-Brexit viewpoint and offers an opportunity to consider what makes an advertising campaign quintessentially British. '*Home To So Much More*' encompasses complex features of British advertising that can be traced back to the field's roots, such as geographical, political, local, and multicultural features, along with the use of humour and soft-sell strategies, all in one single ad.

This chapter utilises a modern branch of critical discourse analysis (CDA) termed multimodal discourse analysis (MMDA) to examine the commercial. CDA is primarily used to explore such concepts as the communication patterns used by large institutions, latent discourses in media texts, and the creation of individual and group identities conveying ideological attitudes, power, and status (Fairclough & Wodak, 1997, p. 272). Therefore, it is useful for examining advertising texts to understand how power relations are established and used and how ideology has been reproduced and transmitted in discourse through the periods of imperialism, globalization, and localization. This study uses MMDA because TV commercials include several different modes of communication, such as sound, visuals, framing, and music. Therefore, a holistic approach is required to fully uncover the power relations and identity politics in several different communication channels.

COUNTRY PROFILE OF THE UNITED KINGDOM

The United Kingdom of Great Britain and Northern Ireland, commonly referred as United Kingdom (UK) is located on an archipelago containing the British Isles, the island of Ireland, and accompanying smaller islands such as the Isle of Man and Isle of Wight. With a surface area of 242,900 km² and a population of 67 million people in 2020 (Office for National Statistics, n.d.), the UK may not be the biggest European country but contributes significantly to the global economic and cultural scape. The UK contains England, Scotland, Wales, and Northern Ireland, among which tensions and rebellions have caused lasting controversies. At the end of the 20th century, Ireland, Wales, and Scotland gained their own parliaments, with the UK government devolving some power and responsibility (BBC, 2017). Although civil tensions between England and the other UK constituents thus diminished, the people remain motivated to preserve their regional identities. Therefore, even though a common British experience and culture is obvious, regional differences, identity anchors, and cultural symbols such as the Welsh language, strong accents, and traditional cuisine and artefacts like kilts all remain prevalent (Briggs, 2022).

The UK suffered from two world wars (despite being on the winning side) and the loss of its imperial reach in the 20th century, and yet remains among the world's biggest economic, military, and cultural powers because of its position as the first industrialised country and home to modern parliamentary democracy (BBC, 2017, 2020). Conversely, British industry was hurt by the First and Second World War and needed almost 40 years to recover. This was helped by the UK joining the European Economic Community, which later became the European Union, in 1973.

As explained by the Encyclopaedia Britannica, even though the UK's head of state is the reigning monarch, sovereignty rests with the parliament, comprising the appointed House of Lords and elected House of Commons. Since the late 1600s The UK has a two-party system in which the electorate prefers to vote largely for one of two certain parties. Conservative Party and the Labour Party are the two major groups since the second decade of the 20th century. The socio-political scape of the country, therefore, had been characterised by strong labour unions, working-class citizens, and a substantial conservative tendency although this has been changing for a time (Briggs, 2022). The rivalry between the two biggest parties even echoed in one of the most influential examples of political advertising, created by one of the most successful British advertising agencies (see Figure 1). However, since the 1990s, the proportion of working-class people among Labour Party voters has been decreasing, while the proportion of university-educated, middle-class people voting Labour has been rising. This has resulted in a 'left-behind' group of voters who are older, working class, and white, and do not necessarily share the inclusive sentiments of the New Labour movement on concepts such as diversity and mobility. This group of voters has also been neglected by the Conservative Party, which has traditionally focused on university-educated, middle-class, white-collar citizens too. Another relevant development was the ever-growing number of immigrants coming first from Central and Eastern Europe, due to free movement of EU citizens, and later from Syria, thus fuelling the Eurosceptic sentiments of conservative people (Goodwin & Ford, 2017; Hobolt, 2016).

In the referendum held on 23 June 2016, 52% voted for the UK to leave the European Union. This caused a shock even among leaders of the 'Leave' campaigns, who had not formulated any viable plans for the actual separation (Blagden, 2017). Economic and political consequences surfaced immediately, such as the British pound losing value, Scottish officials signalling their intention to break away from the UK, and uncertainty about the Irish border (Hobolt, 2016, p. 2). Subsequent developments are neatly summarised by Briggs (2022):

Figure 1. A well-known example of political advertising portraying the rivalry between the UK's two biggest parties

After much negotiation, several deadline extensions, prolonged domestic political discord, and two changes of prime minister, an agreement on 'Brexit' (British exit from the EU) was reached that satisfied both the EU and the majority of Parliament. Thus, on January 31, 2020, the UK became the first country to withdraw from the EU.

Considering the multicultural nature of the UK from the start, as well as its vast reach during the imperial era and ongoing links to Commonwealth nations, this can be considered a rare selfward step by the country.

BRIEF HISTORY OF ADVERTISING IN THE UK

Although the US is believed to be the homeland of advertising, the UK was not unaware of the power of marketing, as the country where mass production of consumer goods originated. In her study of the marketing side of the Industrial Revolution, Elizabeth W. Gilboy (1932) showed that demand was promoted by rising incomes and newly acquired social mobility in the second half of the 18th century; in turn, numerous advertisements began appearing in newspapers, magazines, and on the walls of big towns. This was also encouraged by the establishment of fixed-premises shops in towns, which increasingly replaced open-air markets. The development of waterway networks connecting centres of commerce led to the proliferation of retailers and manufacturers of branded products and the emergence of modern advertising agencies. In the 19th century, British advertisers were spending an annual average of £500,000 on penny presses, which were welcoming to ads, mass-circulated media of the Edwardian era (Corley, 1988, pp. 158–161; Pope, 1983, p. 453). Advertising only grew more and more popular then on. 'After the mid-century, soap manufacturers began to pioneer the use of pictorial advertising as a central part of business policy' (McClintock, 2005, p. 271).

Figure 2. The first British print ad, promoting 'The Pyes of Salisbury'

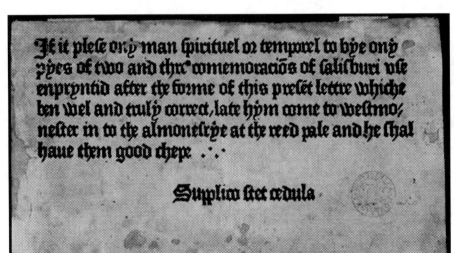

Similarly, to the global trend, British advertising began through the act of buying ad spots in media. Aiming to offer their customers the best possible media buying opportunities, the agents began creating advertisements in the 1800s (Fletcher, 2008). In the 19th century, basic marketing communication techniques such as merchandising with celebrities or product tie-ins had already emerged. This early emergence of basic advertising techniques in the UK can be attributed to the development of the printing press, the high literacy rate, and the country's pioneering position in industrialisation. In this early period, flyers were used as an important advertising medium. It has been estimated that around 1.15 billion flyers were distributed in 1861. The first known print advertisement in the UK promoted a book called *The Pyes of Salisbury* in 1477 (see Figure 2); the first magazine advertisement was published in the 17th century; and the first video advertisement was broadcast on a cinema screen in 1900 (Fletcher, 2008).

Despite the UK's pioneering position on industrialisation and early advertising efforts, advertising professionals initially faced a difficult environment. Sales efforts were viewed as culturally negative in the UK, in stark contrast to their reception in the US (Nevett, 1992). 'As a commercial form, advertising was generally regarded as a confession of weakness, a rather shabby last resort. Most advertising was limited to small newspaper advertisements, cheap handbills and posters' (McClintock, 2005, p. 271). Negative sentiments towards the advertising profession were created by the conflict between the nobles, who derived their income from land, and the bourgeoisie, who derived their income from commerce. Nobles' dislike about all things related to commerce, together with the perception that income from sales efforts was menial and banal, fuelled the anti-advertisement discourse of the time. Through the nuances of British democracy, negative attitudes among members of the House of Lords played a decisive role in the fate of British advertising. Besides the nobles' negative perspective, advertising was also considered immoral because of puffery and deceptiveness. Endeavouring to create an alternative to advertising, lists containing only factual information about products were prepared, but this approach was unsuccessful and short-lived (Fletcher, 2008, p.11). Moreover, the political establishment was concerned by newspapers becoming cheaper as a result of advertising funding, potentially putting even kings in a difficult position. As a way of reducing the accessibility of the press, a one-shilling duty for every advertisement published in newspapers was imposed in 1712 (Fletcher, 2008).

Advertising in the colonial era conveyed a political stance by reflecting the socioeconomic circumstances of the time, especially through the ads of products produced in the colonies. The UK took on the role of civilising the perceived 'primitive' people of the non-western world. The subjugation of indigenous people was legitimised by rendering them as subhuman, and the discourses of this ideology circulated through media and advertising (Bonsu, 2009, pp. 1–4). According to Ramamurthy (2017), tea advertisements represent black workers as born to labour, thus supporting vertical control both politically and economically. As Figure 3 shows, ads for Plantol Soap in 1893 and 1905 (respectively) reflect the era's political perception and discourse surrounding race: the black woman is shown fully dressed and serving the product, whereas the white woman is depicted using it. Moreover, the black woman does not touch the product directly but holds it on a plate, conveying that it is not for her to use. The two women are also portrayed extremely differently: the black woman was intentionally made to look unkempt and envious, and stands before a plain background, whereas the white woman appears sensual and delicate in a scene evoking a fairy tale.

Figure 3. Plantol Soap advertisements

The First World War helped advertising and government propaganda to gain cultural prominence. According to Aulich (2012), it led to the mass production of certain products in a way never before possible and provided a sense of identity for the working class:

Through advertising and publicity, the War brought 'government' and 'high' affairs of state to 'low' commerce. [...] the popularity of the picture of the ordinary serviceman [...] that was intended to exploit the public commercially effectively granted under-represented communities a form of recognition and autonomy that ultimately eclipsed the needs of the market. The War gave wide recognition to people as consumers and challenged the traditional notions of duty and service to the state, as well as the more progressive discourses of organized labour and the women's movement (Aulich, 2012, pp. 110–114).

This means that although the First World War generated an unpleasant environment for commerce and, thus, advertisements, it increased cultural acceptance and recognition of people who had never before seen individuals like them depicted in public imagery (see Figure 4). Besides legitimising the colonial discourse abroad, advertising was also directing the average Joe to develop a consumer identity through depictions of servicemen consuming ready-to-use products, ranging from tobacco to clothes.

Figure 4. Example of common people in war-time British advertising

After 1920, British and American publishing embraced conflicting paradigms. While American broadcasting was always a commercial medium, British broadcasting was monopolised by the BBC and advertising was prohibited. The BBC defined American commercial broadcasting as chaos, while American broadcasters accused the Brits of elitism (Wiener & Hampton, 2007). By the 1930s, radio advertising was on the rise, despite BBC Radio's advertising ban: commercial broadcasters were broadcasting to the UK from Normandy, Luxembourg, Paris, and many other locations. Although 2% of total advertising expenditure was spent on radio during in the 30s, it would take another 40 years for commercial radio to be legalised in the UK (Fletcher, 2008).

Despite the late 1930s and early 1940s being characterised by intense use of propaganda, it is understandable that advertising in the UK stagnated during the Second World War, with shortages of raw materials and limited production. Access to paper was restricted until 1956, yet print media gained momentum after the restriction on its sale was lifted in 1946. In 1948, the *News of the World* broke the world record by selling 8 million weekly copies and *London Evening Standard* became the world's largest evening paper with 1.5 million daily sales (Fletcher, 2008).

With the blooming of post-war open-market economies, marketing communication also rose as consumption increased, and expenditure on advertising peaked in the mid-1950s (Clayton, 2010). Although the Americans were perceived as having advertising know-how in this period, British advertisers also made an assertive start to the 1950s. The Advertising Association organised an assembly titled 'The Duties of Advertising in a Free World', attended by 2,824 delegates from 38 countries (Fletcher, 2008). Some participating countries were former territories of the British Empire. Advertising in this era could thus be interpreted as a governmental effort to transform colonisation into modernisation by showing how corporations bring the necessary experience to teach welfare to developing countries (Ramamurthy, 2017 p. 212). The lifting of the ban on TV advertising in 1954 was another important milestone for British advertising. Although the BBC remained ad-free, ITV was soon established as a commercial broadcaster televising ads (Fletcher, 2008).

British TV advertising was limited by regulation to spot advertisements. When the ban on TV advertising was lifted in the UK, many London agencies already had American partners. However, American TV advertising differed fundamentally, as American TV is open to much more non-programme content and most advertising takes the form of sponsorship. Therefore, the US offered no ready-made solutions, and it took several years for British TV advertising to find its own style and gain international recognition. A breakthrough came in 1961 when the TV commercial for Schweppes Tomato Juice, directed by David Paltenghi and produced by Anglo-Scottish Pictures, won the 1961 Cannes Grand Prix (see Figure 5). Following this success, the British era of creativity began (Fletcher, 2008).

For years, the advertising field in the UK was dominated by big agencies of US origin, which had followed US brands into the UK market and established British branches to serve their international clients (Nevett, 1992, p. 61). Following the First and Second World War, 'British advertising expenditures were curtailed by consumer rationing, price controls, and shortages of newsprint and paper for posters. Potential international advertising by exporters was restricted by sterling controls' (West, 1988, p. 473). These conditions proved challenging for British agencies at home and prevented them from venturing abroad, whereas American agencies enjoyed economic and organisational advantages. These advantages led to US-based agencies dominating the British advertising field. This dominance could be seen in both the billing charts and daily practices of advertising professionals. J. Walter Thompson, the iconic agency representing the American style in London, popularised the usage of strategic briefing in the UK in the second half of the 20th century. Collett Dickenson Pearce imported from Doyle Dane Bernbach (DDB) the collective style of art and copy working together. Art directors gained more responsibility in British advertising, even becoming creative directors (Fletcher, 2008). The Unique Selling Proposition strategy, formulated by Reeves in the US, also gained worldwide recognition in this period (Feldwick, 2007).

Figure 5. Schweppes Tomato Juice ad – 1961 Cannes Grand Prix Winner

In 1960, 12 American agencies collectively accounted for 30% of all advertising agency billing in the UK; in 1970, 24 US-based agencies accounted for 42% of the billing in the UK. However, this dominance began to decline in the 1980s, as illustrated by US-based agencies' proportion of advertising billing dropping to 22% in 1987 (West, 1988, p. 471). UK-based big communication network Saatchi & Saatchi became the second biggest on the billing list of communication networks globally by producing globally famous campaigns (see Figures 1 and 6). In the late 1980s, UK-based advertising companies were able to buy some American advertising legends like J. Walter Thompson and Ogilvy & Mather (Pigott, 1996, p. 247). This shift in dominance within British advertising could be explained by several factors, such as changes in media and communication technologies, rising global competition, and the local tactics, strategies, and tone employed by UK-based agencies. While cultural differences require localized strategies, the invention of account planning and economic changes led to UK-based agencies regaining market dominance and establishing networks with and local branches in 'nearby countries or territories under, or linked to, British rule and law' (West, 1988, p. 488).

Although US-based agencies remained dominant until the 1980s, the transformations that eventually tipped the scales started in the late 1960s. The account planning department was first invented in the UK, from where it spread to the US and beyond. Despite being separate agencies Massimi Pollitt and J. Walter Thompson concurrently used the term 'account planning' for similar but different purposes. Simultaneously, after the emergence of inhouse research departments, the account planning department ensured that information sharing reached a better harmony between agency and client. Researchers also gained a more central role in determining the message of the campaign (Feldwick, 2007). In the 1970s, boutique companies emerged to provide more specialised marketing communications compared to the full-service advertising agencies. The rise of specialised agencies continued in the 1980s, and in 1988 Saatchi & Saatchi founded Zenith Media Buying Services, which became the largest media buying agency in the world (Fletcher, 2008).

Figure 6. D&AD Yellow Pencil winning ad, created by Cramer Saatchi (later known as Saatchi & Saatchi)

Because of the crash of 1989, the beginning of the 1990s was a difficult period for advertising. Between 1989 and 1993, the employment rate in the British advertising industry fell by one-third (Fletcher, 2008). When it comes to ownership of the largest agencies, ten largest agencies in the UK, five were of British origin in 1968 whereas all ten were internationally owned in the 1990s. To satisfy the needs of globalised clients, advertising agencies needed to operate more internationally. Another noteworthy development was the faster narrative form adopted by TV advertising in the UK, representing a shift from the much slower storytelling used in the 1970s and 1980s (Fletcher, 2008).

THE BRITISH WAY

The idea of globalization in advertising raises the question of whether standardisation is possible. With the US considered the homeland of advertising and its apparent cultural closeness to the UK, these two countries have offered distinctively fertile ground for standardisation and globalization research. Numerous academics have studied the similarities and differences of American and British advertising and of their target audiences (e.g. Caillat & Mueller, 1996; Frith & Wesson, 1991; Nevett, 1992; Piggot, 1996). As the two countries share similar historical and cultural values, communication styles, and economic structure, it has been assumed that there must be little cultural distance between them (Piggot, 1996), and many other products of the mediascape have been treated as the same. This is illustrated by the decision of the Academy of Motion Picture Arts and Sciences (organisers of the Oscars) to treat British films as a domestic product (Wiener & Hampton, 2007). To understand the unique aspects of British advertising, it is useful to review studies comparing it with American advertising.

Caillat and Mueller (1996) identified affiliation, tradition/history, and eccentricity as the characteristic values of British advertising in their study comparing British and American beer advertisements. Affiliation refers to belonging and the representation of individuals as part of a group; tradition/history concerns the product and brand's past performance, including details of the founder and year of establishment; and eccentricity describes the inclusion of surprising and often humorous elements. Collectivistic values were prevalent in 85% of the British beer ads examined, compared to only 29.2% of the American ads. Eccentricity was also more prevalent in British beer ads than American beer ads (81.6% vs 4.2%), as was tradition/history (44.7% vs 4.2%). Moreover, humour appeal was found to be used in 91.9% of British ads, compared to only 21.1% of American ads.

In their comparative study of British and American print ads, Frith and Wesson (1991) found less individualism, higher social-class awareness, more indirect expression, and a higher rate of humour in British ads. Specifically, the proportion of ads including more than one person was 55% for British ads and 43% for American ads; the working class was represented by 24% of British ads but merely 1% in American ads; headlines were more likely to use indirect speech in British ads (79% vs 61%); and humour was also more common in British ads (37% vs 18%). Nevett (1992) analysed the differences between British and American TV advertising and explained differences between ads of the two cultures under three main dimensions: the "socio-cultural context", "advertising industry environment", "philosophy, and execution".

Socio-culturally, TV advertisements came to the UK 20 years after the advent of TV, whereas there was no such delay in the US. British advertising is considered to have a soft-sell approach, as it is more indirect and has lower information content (Pigott, 1996). It is also highly entertainment oriented (Bernstein, 1986). British advertisers have historically tried to convince the public that their work is somehow beneficial, thereby overcoming constant attacks (Fletcher, 2008 p. 24) rooted in a societal dislike of advertising (Nevett, 1992). The disapproval of pushy sales leads advertisers to take a more indirect approach, rather than making a direct sales proposition. Arguably, British advertisers use the positivity of humour and entertainment to defend their occupation against constant criticism. Schofield's (1991) comparison of ads from 15 countries revealed that ad campaigns in the UK were less synchronised with sales promotions, TV usage was more widespread, and slice-of-life ads were used more intensively in television compared to other 14 countries. Moreover when British and American print ads are compared, it was seen that British advertisers used humorous headlines more often (37% vs 18%) (Frith & Wesson, 1991).

Another important distinction between British and American advertising lies in the volume of local and national advertisers. The US has a relatively high proportion of local and regional advertisers (Nevett, 1992). Local advertisers tend to have short-term advertising strategies, such as informing the target audience of their presence and announcing seasonal promotional sales campaigns. For this reason, they need argumentative and information-laden advertising setups. By contrast, a significant proportion of British clients are national advertisers (Nevett, 1992). Compared to local advertisers, national advertisers tend to have longer-term advertising strategies, for example focused on strengthening brand positioning and investing in brand perception. For this reason, they are more inclined to use slice-of-life advertisements with less information and more emotional content.

Moreover, the British social perspective on advertising is often reflected in regulation. In particular, only 6 minutes of TV commercials are allowed per hour of broadcasting, whereas up to 27% of total broadcast content is devoted to TV commercials in the US. In addition, TV advertisements in the UK were allowed in natural breaks, which are generally between programmes. Once again, the aim is to disturb the audience as little as possible. This may be reflected in the work of British advertisers, who have tended to create more entertaining content than American advertisers, whose starting assumption is that advertisements will disrupt the viewing experience.

Another original aspect of British commercials is their strong cinematographic structure. When commercial TV was first allowed in 1954, regulation only permitted spot advertisements. Unable to draw on know-how from their American counterparts, British TV advertisers produced 30-second TV ads with cinematic production values, shot by talented directors (Rothenberg, 1989 as cited in Pigott, 1996). British TV advertising used longer, uncut scenes, whereas American TV commercials were shot and edited with many scene changes and two-second cuts (Pigott, 1996).

METHODOLOGY

Douglas and Isherwood (1978) argue that products and culture have a reciprocal relationship in which they shape and carry meaning through each other. On this basis, advertisements act as a front for a culturally established world of consumers and consumer goods (McCracken, 1986). Marketing communication, as part of a larger mediascape, has the power to influence systems of thought in a particular place and a certain time period. In this sense, discourse—the way humans see and make sense of their reality—can be altered by media in general and by marketing communication in particular.

Discourse refers to the processes and phenomena that make certain things thinkable and sayable and regulate who can say them in a particular place and time. Similar to advertising, discourse is shaped by and cannot be separated from its social and cultural context. Discourse, as a social practice, represents, expresses, and mirrors the values and norms that constitute and are dominant within a social and cultural context (Kress & van Leeuwen, 2020). This makes discourse analysis an appropriate approach for analysing advertising practices.

Advertising has always exploited multiple modes of communication, yet postmodernity and digital technology have introduced multiplicity, diversity, and complexity to media and to daily lives. As just one of multiple modes of expression, language cannot be the only vehicle of discourse nor the only way to communicate, represent, and perform identities in today's world (Çoşkun, 2015). Therefore, when analysing 21st century advertising and trying to understand how it develops and reproduces a discourse, one cannot solely focus on written or spoken language but must also consider other communicational tools, such as images, sounds, and colour. Therefore, the classical method of discourse analysis will not be sufficient for advertisements in this digital era of visual saturation.

Although CDA originally focused on language and meaning making through linguistic grammar, multimodality has also been considered since the 1990s. Multimodality is the systematic process of combining and arranging different modes of discourse to convey a certain meaning and motivate a certain action. Accordingly, MMDA focuses on how different modes, such as text, sounds, music, colour, and images, are put together and interact to create effects on audiences (Kress, 2012) in the process of meaning-making (Paltridge, 2012).

Visuals are the dominant mode of overall communication processes, including advertising. People living in the USA today see six to ten thousand advertising images daily (Carr, 2020). According to Kress and van Leeuwen (2020), two of the forefathers of MMDA, these visuals can also act as discursive tools and contribute to creating meaning and knowledge: 'Visual structures do not simply reproduce the structures of "reality". They are the products of social dispositions and of semiotic work. As such they interpret reality, and they can do so in different ways' (p. 47). Drawing from Halliday's (1994) social semiotics and systemic functional linguistics theory, Kress and van Leeuwen focus on how visual components and compositions create meaning.

Halliday (1994) explains that languages make meaning through three metafunctions: ideational, interpersonal, and textual. Ideational metafunction refers to what the text is about, and it details how several semiotic resources are presented and related to one another. Interpersonal metafunction refers to the interaction between text and viewer. Finally, textual metafunction refers to the structure of the text and describes how plural semiotic resources form cohesive multimodal meanings. Kress and van Leeuwen (2020) adapt Halliday's theory to visuals, utilising the metafunctions of visual representation, interaction, and composition.

Using Kress and van Leeuwen's visual semiotics theory, this study seeks to understand how a British TV commercial represents and reproduces both the British way of making ads and the cultural codes of British society. It specifically tackles two research questions:

1. What British cultural codes are represented in HSBC's *'Home To So Much More'* TV commercial?
2. Does that commercial typify British advertising?

To answer the first research question, the analysis will focus on symbolic and tangible elements derived from geographical, political, historical, and social factors. Before answering the second research question, the core values of British advertising need to be defined. The literature review identifies eight core values: affiliation, tradition, humour, high social-class awareness indirect expression, long uncut scenes, soft-sell approach, and long-term advertising strategies. This chapter studies the TV commercial for the *'Home To So Much More'* campaign, focusing on how its visuals represent Britishness and the British way of making ads. To understand the post-Brexit era of British advertising, whether certain elements of British advertising still prevail in modern-day commercials, and (if so) how different layers of meaning are carried, this study uses MMDA.

Analysis

HSBC is among the world's largest financial services companies. Having been established in Hong Kong, the bank has always been perceived as global or at least international. However, in 2019 this perception became a burden for the brand and damaged its relations with customers. In response, HSBC UK introduced the *'We Are Not An Island'* campaign in January 2019, emphasising the qualities that represent Brits and Britishness (see Figure 7).

Figure 7. HSBC's 'We Are Not An Island' campaign poster

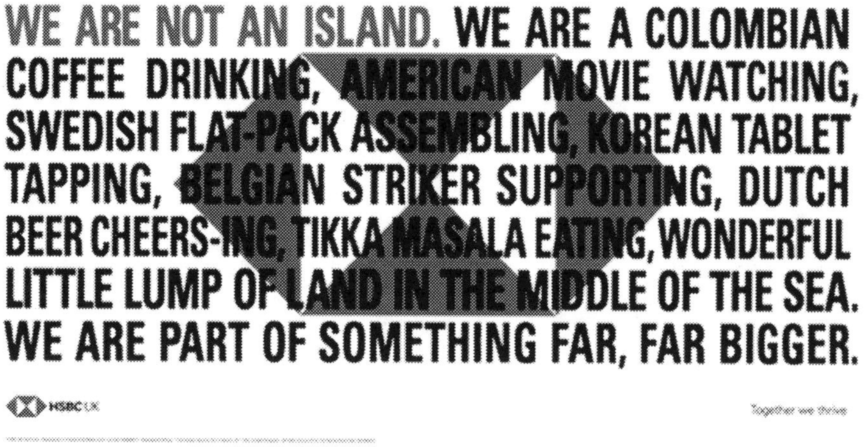

WE ARE NOT AN ISLAND. WE ARE A COLOMBIAN COFFEE DRINKING, AMERICAN MOVIE WATCHING, SWEDISH FLAT-PACK ASSEMBLING, KOREAN TABLET TAPPING, BELGIAN STRIKER SUPPORTING, DUTCH BEER CHEERS-ING, TIKKA MASALA EATING, WONDERFUL LITTLE LUMP OF LAND IN THE MIDDLE OF THE SEA. WE ARE PART OF SOMETHING FAR, FAR BIGGER.

HSBC UK

Together we thrive

Wunderman Thompson, the agency responsible for this campaign, described the brand's position and the idea of reminding British people that HSBC understands what it means to be British:

After years of international heritage as a global bank, HSBC had arguably lost its relevance in the UK. Britons had lost sight of what HSBC stood for, allowing the majority of potential customers to believe it was largely a bank for wealthy foreigners. We set out to re-establish the brand's point of view and purpose in a changing Britain, revitalizing the brand and inspiring audiences to reconsider HSBC UK as a brand with values they share. […] HSBC's daring campaign We Are Not An Island reminded Britain that no matter what your politics are and no matter what happens, the things that make us quintessentially British are inescapably international. (Wunderman Thompson, n.d.)

HSBC UK's *'Home To So Much More'* campaign was published in January 2020. Having initially denied any connection between the *'We Are Not An Island'* campaign and Brexit, the bank accepted the connection and its connotations in its successor campaign, *'Home To So Much More'*:

In this post Brexit climate, the Home To So Much More campaign builds on HSBC UK's brand values of being open and connected, examining the concept of home and what it really means at a time when many people and communities in the United Kingdom were questioning whether they belong here at all. The campaign explores the topic of national identity and questions the question 'Where are you from?' (Wunderman Thompson, n.d.).

The TV commercial *'Home To So Much More'* features British comedian Richard Ayoade asking the question *'Where are you from?'* and offering several possible answers, accompanied by a range of images: grainy footage of a British hospital in what appears to be the 1970s, black-and-white footage of an Indian hospital setting, a museum exhibit featuring a primitive couple, a passport control desk, a 1980s British suburban setting, a backpacking trip, a gay wedding, and footage of a couple moving to a classical Victorian home. As these images passes by, the actor poses various questions to the audience 'Where are you from?'; 'Is it where you were born?'; 'Or where were your parents born?'; 'Or where your great great great…grandparents were born?'; 'Is the answer in your passport?'; 'Is it where you grew up?'; 'Could it be where you found yourself?'; 'Or is it where your heart is?'; 'Perhaps the question is not where are you from but where do you feel at home?'

Figure 8.

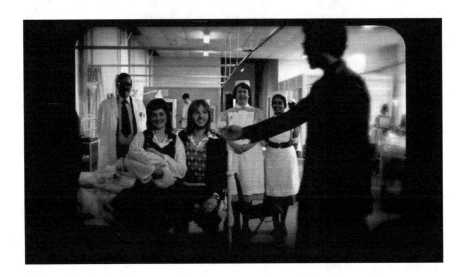

Kress and van Leeuwen's first metafunction, visual representation (or ideation), refers to how the visual elements and the relationship between them are represented. Kress and van Leeuwen, (2020, p. 47) call these visual elements *participants* and the ways they relate to each other *processes*. In a visual composition entailing a transaction, participants play the role of either *actor* or *goal;* an *actor* is the participant who does something to other participants, the *goals*. However, there can also be non-transactional *actors* who feature in a composition without directing their actions towards a *goal*.

Richard Ayoade is the *actor* in every scene of the TV commercial, posing the question *'Where are you from?'* and offering possible answers by moving across time and space. However, he does not interact with other participants except when congratulating couples in the second sequence of the commercial. Omitting goals from the scenes implies that the TV audience is the goal of the composition and the target of all the questions posed. The commercial is thus designed to make the audience question themselves and evaluate their own stance. Other participants, such as the British and Indian families, react to these questions with puzzled faces. They are *reacters* in the composition. Unlike *actors*, *reacters* have *phenomena* instead of *goals*. In the commercial the *actor,* Ayoede asks the questions to the audiences, the *goals*. Then this process, *actor* asking questions, becomes the *phenomenon* the reactional structure in which the families are the *reacters*.

Similar to actions, reactions can also be transactional or non-transactional, according to whether the composition includes another party to relate to with them. In the TV commercial, both kinds of reactions are present: families react to the strange man passing through and asking questions (transactional), and they also turn their gaze to the audience reacting an imaginary response from them. This latter type of non-transactional reaction 'can create a powerful sense of empathy and identification with represented participants' (Kress & van Leeuwen, 2020, p. 62). In this instance, the audience is encouraged to feel a connection with the families in their quizzical state: their role is not to ask or answer the question themselves but to reinforce it.

Ideational metafunction also concerns the interaction processes between *actors*, *goals*, *reacters*, and *phenomena*. Several different processes are present in the commercial. Ayoade's presence as an *actor* and the quick cuts between sequences and frames signal the overall narrative process, which refers to the unfolding of events and change. Besides narrative processes, commercials also include conceptual processes, which can be analytical or symbolic. In an analytical process, the participants have a part-whole relationship and relate to one another in terms of hierarchy or equality. Conversely, symbolic processes concern the meaning or identity of a represented participant. According to Kress and van Leeuwen (2020, pp. 49–55), conceptual processes, unlike transactional structures, focus not on the action but on how the participants fit together to form a composition and what the participants symbolise.

Figure 9.

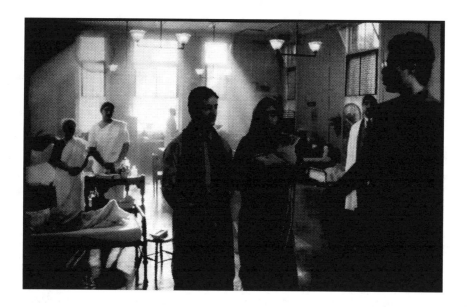

Figure 10.

Figure 8, 9 and 10 depicts four frames juxtaposed in the commercial. In the conceptual structures shown, the depicted roles are not *actor* and *goal* but *carrier* and *attribute*. Here, the British and Indian families who recently welcomed a baby are carriers of many attributes. First, they carry the attributes of their nationality and of being middle-class British and Indian citizens. Because they have clean but non-flashy clothes, we can presume that they are working-class citizens but not extremely wealthy or poor. They exhibit common features of the group or class to which they belong. They also carry attributes related to living in their respective time periods—1970s for the British couple and a time before colour film for the Indian couple. Besides such symbolism, the composition and juxtaposition of the two frames suggests that the participants belong to the same category. This is an example of covert taxonomy, which refers to where 'A set of participants…are distributed symmetrically across the visual space, at equal distance from each other, equal in size, and oriented towards the vertical and horizontal axes in the same way' (Kress & van Leeuwen, 2020, p. 82). This functions to create similarity and equality between the represented participants. Both frames include two parents in the foreground with the woman holding the baby, closely watched by one doctor and two nurses in the background. Therefore, in addition to emphasising that the viewer should seriously consider the *actor*'s question, the two scenes symbolise equality, sameness, and inclusion through their juxtaposition and positions in the composition.

This becomes more obvious when the next frame is introduced in the commercial. Because the *actor* has so far travelled back in time and visited two couples in their natural environment, the audience might expect him to travel even further back to visit the third couple in their own time and living space. However, he instead visits life-size models of a primitive couple in a museum (see Figure 11). The couple are not positioned similarly to the previous two couples and the camera angle differs. This means that while the first and second couples are real, similar people with whom the commercial encourages the audience to identify, the third couple is included just to make the point that when traced back enough we all might have a common ancestor. This is used to show the absurdity of essentialist identity politics and provide comic relief. This is achieved by the framing and camera angles, and by the time the camera spends on the couple. This frame is shot from a different angle point and the camera does not linger on the faces of the cave couple which is something it does for the first two. It is also composed differently than the previous two frames which is almost exact copy of each other signalling similarity.

The second metafunction in Kress and van Leeuwen's work, interactional (or interpersonal), concerns how the producer of an image encodes meaning into it. Kress and van Leeuwen (2020, pp. 113–149) suggest there are several ways to achieve this: contact, social distance, angle, and modality. Contact means whether the image demands or offers interaction through eye contact, which establishes a social relationship between image and viewer. The participant in a composition can look directly into the camera or away. When looking straight at the camera lens, participants can evoke an emotional response from the viewer, such as sympathy, pity, curiosity, avoidance, or anger. In the commercial, both the *actor* Ayoade and the people we are encouraged to feel associated or identified with look at us and demand answers to the questions. Ayoade does this literally by posing the questions, while the families do it with their inquisitive faces. However, some other participants in the commercial serve to offer us a view of what it can be like to live in the UK.

As seen in Figure 12, the commercial presents two men on their wedding day and a serious passport control officer as examples of British life: tolerant, open, and free but without surrendering the British stiff upper lip. These two scenes combine the inclusivity of British culture with light teasing over the 'strict' treatment a non-white Brit might endure at the border.

Figure 11.

Figure 12.

Different relations between text and viewer can also be created through social distance, camera angle, and modality. Social distance refers to the implied closeness of a participant in the text and the audience; different shot distances suggest degrees of importance, involvement, and intimacy. For instance, while a wide shot implies a formal or distanced relationship between two parties, a medium shot suggests a personal relationship and a close shot implies an intimate acquaintance. Moreover, while an eye-level camera angle can suggest equality, a high-level camera angle gives power to the viewer and vice versa. Finally, modality refers to what is deemed realistic in a society and how realism or unrealism is depicted in the text. It can be achieved through distortion, black-and-white effect, grain, colour, illumination, and brightness.

Throughout the commercial, most of the shots are at waist length, implying that we know the people depicted in the frame and should feel equal and similar to them. Only the opening and closing scenes are wide shots, which are designed to give an idea of standard British society. Figure 13 shows these shots, depicting working-class English towns of identical houses. Although not inherently personal or intimate, these shots are designed to show the audience British society and welcome them into the community. In the opening shot, the *actor* with whom we are supposed to have the most connection is standing on a rooftop removed from everyone else; in the closing shot, he is among members of the community, passing by a couple moving house and finally himself entering a house that is quintessentially British, working class, and exactly like its neighbours. This feeling of familiarity and similarity is also enhanced by the camera angles. Most of the shots in the commercial are at eye level. The museum and passport-control scenes are the only times the angle shifts: the primitive man looks slightly downward at us while the passport control officer looks up. These angles might respectively imply the ancient historical value of the primitive man statue. It can also mean and that passport officers can sometimes be testing but are ultimately here to serve you. Finally, modality makes the narrative dynamic and helps the viewer understand how things have progressed in British society. The grainy shots from the 1970s and 1980s depicting the British family and cycling boys show the UK back then, whereas shots depicting the present day are much brighter and smoother. Also, as Figure 14 shows, the commercial features a bright red door in one of the last frames, thus using colour to suggest that the brand, HSBC, represents the answer.

Figure 13.

Figure 14.

Turning to Kress and van Leeuwen's third metafunction, compositional (or textual) metafunction focuses on how elements in the text relate to one another and create a meaningful whole. Kress and van Leeuwen (2020, p. 216) analysed compositional meaning in three dimensions: informational value, framing, and salience.

According to the informational value dimension, left-to-right visual composition is used to convey that what is on the left is given and what is on the right is new. The *actor* Ayoade walks from left to right in each frame, and while he travels through time he always addresses other participants by turning from the right of the frame towards the left as he passes them (see Figures 8 and 9). However, when he is in the present time, the commercial uses centre-margin configuration, drawing focus on the *actor* by placing him in the centre. In only one scene does he stand on the left and point to the right: this occurs when Ayoade refers to the brand that wants to be associated with this progressive and inclusive British society and place itself as the enabler. The red door towards which he points symbolises the world that HSBC opens for its customers.

The non-visual components of the ad are the background music and the monologue the *actor* delivers. As stated above, the monologue mostly consists of questions and some witty, funny remarks. The questions, like the visuals they accompany, demand attention, consideration, and answers from the audience. Moreover, remarks such as 'It is a tricky one', referring to the main question, and 'It's definitely him', referring to the man in the photo that the passport officer is carefully checking, continue the tradition of humorous British advertisements. The background music is a piece from *Oliver!*, a musical adaptation of Charles Dickens' novel *Oliver Twist*. Although the advertising uses only the tune, the film Oliver, its story and soundtracks are expected to be known by the British public. They reinforce the inclusive, accepting, and welcoming tone of the advertising. The lyrics of the first verse are as follows:

Consider yourself at home

Consider yourself one of the family

We've taken to you so strong

It's clear we're going to get along

Consider yourself well in

Consider yourself part of the furniture

There isn't a lot to spare

Who cares?

What ever we've got we share! (Bart, 1960)

DISCUSSION

In answer to the first research question, MMDA revealed three different aspects of British culture conveyed in the TV commercial: globalization, multiculturality, and class consciousness. As the UK is an ex-European Union member, ex-colonial power, and victor in two world wars, globalization and internationalisation were expected to be key elements of British culture. This study's analysis reveals that the global dimension of British culture is represented in the commercial through individuals from different backgrounds and a trip to Mount Everest. Multiculturality is also a very well-known aspect of British culture: as a result of its geographical position and history, the UK contains diverse ethnic clusters that form the multicultural British society and cultural scape. Besides combining four once-separate countries, the UK has received and continues to welcome large numbers of immigrants. These facets of British society are reflected in the commercial through the tartan-wearing groom, who is also gay, and the Indian family. Finally, because the UK's pioneering role in industrialisation caused many labourers to gain and sustain a high level of class consciousness, most British advertisements portray working-class citizens or at least include working-class environments. The *'Home To So Much More'* commercial is no exception, representing working-class people and environments through architectural and individual elements, such as typical British houses, hospitals, and clothing.

The literature review identified eight core values as observable characteristics of British advertising. Although the uniqueness of managerial values and pre-testing approaches are also mentioned in the literature (Fletcher, 2008; Nevet, 1992), those factors are not considered in the study as it is hard to conclusively determine their use in a single advert. The eight core values are affiliation, tradition/history, and eccentricity/humour (Caillat & Mueller, 1996); high social-class awareness (representation of the working class) and indirect expression (Frith and Wesson, 1991); long uncut scenes (Pigott, 1996); a soft-sell approach and long-term advertising strategies (Nevett, 1992). The values found in the reviewed TV commercial are compatible with what previous literature attributes to British advertising, thus affirmatively answering the second research question.

First, affiliation value can be defined by the keywords 'to join, unite, companionship, to be accepted, community' (Pollay, 1983 p. 83). The *'Home To So Much More'* commercial conveys a strong sense of community. It presents the main character and the side characters as a part of a larger group through framing, editing, and movement, such as juxtaposing families from different ethnic backgrounds with very British-looking families, and showing scenes such as cycling children, people attending a wedding ceremony, and walking through a busy neighbourhood. The ad's central message is that whatever an individual's background, they are part of the UK and have a sense of belonging.

Second, the HSBC ad also strongly refers to living and creating traditions. Using past performance as proof of future performance is the main idea behind the 'traditional value, and classic, historical, nostalgic, and long-standing are keywords' to better understand its meaning (Pollay, 1983 p. 80). Besides linking identity with personal history by asking whether home is where one's family is, the ad also refers to creating tradition by searching for oneself. In other words, in addition to referring traditional, historical, and nostalgic symbols, such as family, visual cues of 1970s/80s and mount Everest and traditional clothing, such as tartan to refer the idea of searching oneself it also provides new traditions, such as a gay wedding and a modern couple moving to a Victorian terraced house (see Figures 8, 9, 11, 13, and 14).

As mentioned before eccentricity can be summarised as surprising scenes or humorous intent. In the ad eccentricity is crucial as Richard Ayoade is known as one of the most eccentric comedians in the UK. The ad also presents several humorous scenes: Ayoade's character visiting life-size models of a primitive couple in a museum, after creating the expectation he would visit another real couple from more recent history; the winking model of a prehistoric man; a talking photo in the passport-control scene; Ayoade losing his footing while pretending to trek in the Himalayas; and him talking to 'Bernard' the pigeon.

Moreover, as the main aim of the ongoing HSBC campaign is to challenge the perception of being a foreign bank for wealthy foreigners, the ad features working- and middle-class environments. Cultural indicators throughout the ad hint at the main character being from the working or middle class. The neighbourhood where he lives is depicted as working class (see Figure 13); the new parents in the UK and India are shown as neither poor nor very rich (see Figures 8 to 10); the wedding is small (see Figure 12); and the 1980s neighbourhood with biking kids looks like a middle-class, suburban residential area.

The ad's overall message is that regardless of one's social, ethnic, or sexual characteristics, British society is welcoming and can be home for all these different types of people, and HSBC can be the enabler of this accepting society. Therefore, instead of directly expressing its message about cultural unity, the HSBC ad tries to communicate it indirectly by questioning the meaning of 'home' and asking 'Where are you from?' Posing a question, applying a philosophical perspective, and using humour are typical examples of indirect speech (Frith & Wesson, 1991). They are also in line with prominent characteristics of British advertising, which is generally considered to have a soft-sell approach, as it is more indirect and has low information content (Pigott, 1996). The HSBC ad should be categorised as soft sell as it conveys very little information about a product or service. Instead, it aims to create a feeling of empathy with its audience. The ad's strategic aim is forming and strengthening long-term relationships with customers and enhancing brand perception, rather than drawing attention to a seasonal promotion or specific product.

British advertising also has a long connection to identity politics, internationalisation, localization, nationality, and globalization. The *'Home To So Much More'* campaign preserves the core values of British advertising in the post-Brexit era. The commercial tries to associate internationalism with Britishness, addressing a need that at least partially emerged as a result of Brexit. On a more sociological level, advertising of products like tea or cocoa once symbolised British colonisation and vertical control over production in the imperial era. During that era, advertisements portrayed minorities as second-class people or even subhuman and born to labour. The present HSBC campaign, which has been ongoing for three years, uses similar products like coffee but in a different manner to those historical ads (see Figure 7): whereas imperial minorities were people to be subjugated and made to work, minorities in the post-Brexit era represent globalization and acceptance.

CONCLUSION

From the Industrial Revolution to mass production, and from imperial reach to being a modern global power, the UK has always been a prominent player in the commercial world. The UK's powerful, over-reaching status provided the necessary resources and connections to create an influential advertising field. Although national politics, the devastating economic effects of two world wars, and bans on several branches of advertising have posed significant historical challenges to the British advertising sector, it has still managed to become a distinct school with unique features.

One renowned trait of British advertisers is their unique understanding and usage of humour appeal. British advertising is seen as less informative than its US counterpart, which makes it more entertaining for and acceptable to the target audience. It also has more of a soft-sell approach, combining limited use of calls to action with greater reliance on humorous content. British advertising also tends to use long uncut scenes with traditional and historical cues, group representation, and strong class awareness. In addition to these technical features, British advertising has been largely shaped by political and economic factors. Disapproval of advertising among the British upper class led to several defining measures such as bans and regulations, leading to the emergence of 30-second spot advertising. In addition, the public's negative attitude towards advertising pressured British advertisers to create content that was more humorous and entertaining while less forceful and obnoxious than that used in the US. From the imperial era to post-Brexit society, British advertising has maintained its distinctive values and attributes. This study has summarised these distinctive features of British advertising and showcased them using a current example.

In conclusion, this study demonstrates that the typical features of British advertising, as detailed in the literature, are still present in post-Brexit advertising. Moreover, the *'Home To So Much More'* TV commercial evidently conveys British cultural codes through the individuals and artefacts it represents. While the commercial, which is associated with Brexit, presents an innovative story, it strongly carries the typical features of British culture and advertising.

FUTURE RESEARCH DIRECTIONS

The authors plan to conduct a comparative study. Comparative analysis of a sample of representative ads in the selected medium is viewed to be influential. Such a study could investigate to what extent the typical features of British advertising are actually unique. Moreover, investigating the difference between advertisements of multinational brands pursuing global advertising strategies could provide useful insights for the international advertising field. Studying adaptations of the same strategy in different countries may provide the opportunity for more in-depth analysis of how British cultural codes are reflected in advertisements. Finally, period-specific analysis of advertising could elucidate the perception and experience of a certain period in a particular culture. Globalism encourages traditions to travel between cultures, as well as commercial products. However, the globalised traditional practices of each different culture might reveal significantly diverging experiences.

REFERENCES

Aulich, J. (2012). Advertising and the public in Britain during the First World War. In D. Welch & J. Fox (Eds.), *Justifying war: Propaganda, politics and the modern age* (pp. 109–128). Palgrave Macmillan. doi:10.1057/9780230393295_6

Bart, L. (1960). Consider Yourself [Song]. On *Soundtrack of Oliver!*.

BBC. (2017). *United Kingdom profile - Overview*. Retrieved March 1, 2022 from https://www.bbc.com/news/world-europe-18027954

BBC. (2020). *United Kingdom country profile*. Retrieved from https://www.bbc.com/news/world-europe-18023389

Bernstein, D. (1986). The television commercial: An essay. In B. Henry (Ed.), *British television advertising: The first 30 years* (pp. 251–286). Century Benham.

Blagden, D. (2017). Britain and the world after Brexit. *International Politics, 51*(1), 1–25. doi:10.105741311-017-0015-2

Bonsu, S. K. (2009). Colonial images in global times: Consumer interpretations of Africa and Africans in advertising. *Consumption Markets & Culture, 12*(1), 1–25. doi:10.1080/10253860802560789

Briggs, A. (2022). United Kingdom. In *Encyclopaedia Britannica*. Retrieved March 1, 2022, from https://www.britannica.com/place/United-Kingdom

Caillat, Z., & Mueller, B. (1996). The influence of culture on American and British advertising: An exploratory comparison of beer advertising. *Journal of Advertising Research*, *36*(3), 79–89.

Clayton, D. (2010). Advertising expenditure in 1950s Britain. *Business History*, *52*(4), 651–665. doi:10.1080/00076791003753194

Corley, T. (1988). Competition and the growth of advertising in the U.S. and Britain, 1800–1914. *Business and Economic History*, *17*, 155–167.

Çoşkun, G. E. (2015). Use of multimodal critical discourse analysis in media studies. *The Online Journal of Communication and Media*, *1*(3), 40–43.

De Mooij, M. (2014). Global marketing and advertising: Understanding cultural paradoxes. *Sage (Atlanta, Ga.)*.

Douglas, M., & Isherwood, B. (1978). *The world of goods: Towards an anthropology of consumption*. W. N. Norton.

Fairclough, N., & Wodak, R. (1997). Critical discourse analysis. In T. van Dijk (Ed.), *Discourse as social interaction: Discourse studies* (Vol. 2, pp. 258–284). Sage.

Feldwick, P. (2007). *Account planning: Its history, and its significance for ad agencies. In The Sage handbook of advertising*. Sage Publications.

Fletcher, W. (2008). *Powers of persuasion: The inside story of British advertising: 1951–2000*. Oxford University Press.

Frith, K. T., & Wesson, D. (1991). A comparison of cultural values in British and American print advertising: A study of magazines. *The Journalism Quarterly*, *68*(1–2), 216–223.

Gilboy, E. W. (1932). Demand as a factor in the Industrial Revolution. In Facts and factors in economic history (pp. 620–639). Harvard University Press.

Goodwin, M. J., & Ford, R. (2017). Britain After Brexit: A nation divided. *Journal of Democracy*, *28*(1), 17–30. doi:10.1353/jod.2017.0002

Halliday, M. A. (1994). *An introduction to functional grammar*. Edward Arnold.

Hobolt, S. (2016). The Brexit vote: A divided nation, a divided continent. *Journal of European Public Policy*, *23*(9), 1259–1277. doi:10.1080/13501763.2016.1225785

Kress, G. (2012). Multimodal discourse analysis. In J. P. Gee & M. Handford (Eds.), *The Routledge handbook of discourse analysis* (pp. 35–50). Routledge.

Kress, G., & Van Leeuwen, T. (2020). *Reading images: The grammar of visual design* (3rd ed.). Routledge. doi:10.4324/9781003099857

Levitt, T. (1983). Globalization of Markets. *Harvard Business Review*, *61*(3), 92–102.

McClintock, A. (2005). Soft-soaping empire: Commodity racism and imperial advertising. In M. Fraser & M. Greco (Eds.), *The body: A reader* (pp. 271–276). Routledge.

McCracken, G. (1986). Culture and consumption: A theoretical account of the structure and movement of the cultural meaning of consumer goods. *The Journal of Consumer Research, 13,* 71–84.

Nevett, T. (1992). Differences between American and British television advertising: Explanations and implications. *Journal of Advertising, 21*(4), 61–71.

Office for National Statistics. (n.d.). *Main Figures.* Retrieved from: https://www.ons.gov.uk/

Paltridge, B. (2012). *Discourse analysis: An introduction* (2nd ed.). Bloomsbury Academic.

Payne, A. (2017). 'The growing practice of calling in continental film groups': The European influence on production of early British TV advertising. *VIEW Journal of European Television History and Culture, 6*(11), 70–80.

Pigott, M. B. (1996). The English of advertising: Differences in the British and American languages of television advertising. *Revista de Lenguas para Fines Específicos, 3,* 245–254.

Pollay, R. W. (1983). Measuring the cultural values manifest in advertising. *Current Issues and Research in Advertising, 1,* 71–92.

Pope, D. (1983). *Advertising in Britain: A history* by T. R. Nevett; *Dictionary of trade name origins* by Adrian Room. *Business History Review, 57*(3), 452–454.

Ramamurthy, A. (2003). *Imperial persuaders: Images of Africa and Asia in British advertising.* Manchester University Press.

Schofield, A. (1991). International differences in advertising practices: Britain compared with other countries. *International Journal of Advertising, 10*(4), 299–308.

Singh, S., & Appiah-Adu, K. (2008). Culture, creativity, and Advertising. In M. Vernengo, E. Perez Caldentey, & B. J. Rosser Jr (Eds.), *Business practices in emerging and re-emerging markets* (pp. 133–150). Palgrave Macmillan.

West, D. (1988). Multinational competition in the British advertising agency business, 1936–1987. *Business History Review, 62*(3), 467–501.

Wiener, J. H., & Hampton, M. (2007). *Anglo-American media interactions, 1850–2000.* Springer.

Wunderman Thompson. (n.d.a). *We are not an island.* Retrieved October 2, 2021, from https://www.wundermanthompson.com/work/we-are-not-an-island

Wunderman Thompson. (n.d.b). *Home to so much more.* Retrieved October 2, 2021, from https://www.wundermanthompson.com/work/home-to-so-much-more

ADDITIONAL READING

Briggs, P. M. (1994). "News from the little World": A Critical Glance at Eighteenth-Century British Advertising. *Studies in Eighteenth-Century Culture, 23*(1), 29–45. doi:10.1353ec.2010.0081

Clampin, D. (2009). 'To guide, help and hearten millions': The place of commercial advertising in wartime Britain, 1939–1945. *Journal of Macromarketing, 29*(1), 58–73. doi:10.1177/0276146708328054

Fairclough, N., & Wodak, R. (1997). Critical discourse analysis. In T. van Dijk (Ed.), *Discourse as social interaction: Discourse studies* (Vol. 2, pp. 258–284). Sage.

Fletcher, W. (2008). *Powers of persuasion: The inside story of British advertising: 1951–2000.* Oxford University Press.

Kress, G. (2012). Multimodal discourse analysis. In J. P. Gee & M. Handford (Eds.), *The Routledge handbook of discourse analysis* (pp. 35–50). Routledge.

Kress, G., & Van Leeuwen, T. (2020). *Reading images: The grammar of visual design* (3rd ed.). Routledge.

McLeod, C., O'Donohoe, S., & Townley, B. (2009). The elephant in the room? Class and creative careers in British advertising agencies. *Human Relations, 62*(7), 1011–1039. doi:10.1177/0018726709335551

O'Donohoe, S. (1995). Attitudes to Advertising: A Review of British and American Research. *International Journal of Advertising, 14*(3), 245–261. doi:10.1080/02650487.1995.11104615

Schwarzkopf, S. (2020). Consumer Communication as Commodity: British Advertising Agencies and the Global Market for Advertising, 1780–1980. In Consuming Behaviours (pp. 121-138). Routledge.

Sturgess, B. T., & Wilson, N. (1984). Advertising expenditure and aggregate consumption in Britain and West Germany: An analysis of causality. *Managerial and Decision Economics, 5*(4), 219–227. doi:10.1002/mde.4090050406

KEY TERMS AND DEFINITIONS

Anglo-Saxon: An ethnic name originally used for Germanic tribes that inhabited England, the term generically used for describing English speaking countries.

Glocalization: The process of synchronous universalisation and indigenisation of concepts, systems, and conditions.

Mode: Material resources used in order to create meaning, e.g., language, images, music, etc.

Penny Press: Cheap and sensational mass circulated news papers.

Post-Modernity: The era that comes after modernity that is characterized by changing media sphere, digital representations, conflicting truths and lack of metanarratives and conclusiveness.

Social Semiotics: An approach to human communication studying meaning making as a social practice.

Sterling Controls: A form of economic regulation which was started during war as a financial defense mechanism, restrict exchange of sterling to foreign currencies.

Systemic Functional Linguistics: Michael Halliday's approach to linguistics which regards language as a social semiotic system.

Section 5
International Advertising in Oceania

Chapter 16
Political Advertising in Australia:
Marketing of "Who/What to Vote for"

Mehmet Cihan Toker
https://orcid.org/0000-0003-4099-5957
Istanbul Esenyurt University, Turkey

ABSTRACT

Settled at the crossroads of politics and advertising, political advertising has an idiosyncratic nature that makes it both an embraced and criticized phenomenon. On the one hand, it is considered an integral part of democracies because it enables voters to make their political choices more consciously; on the other hand, it is thought that voters gradually lose their faith in the political process and in politicians, especially due to negative advertising in political campaigns. This chapter aims to explain the paradoxical character of political advertising in the context of Australia. In this route, firstly, Australia's historical development and political and socio-cultural structure are examined. Then, legislative regulation of political advertising in Australia is examined in the context of compatibility with democratic ideals. Lastly, political advertisements featured by the Australian Labor Party and Liberal Party of Australia towards the 2022 federal elections are examined through quantitative content analysis.

INTRODUCTION

Political advertising has become an inherent component of political processes and the advertisement industry, especially in countries where competitive elections take place. Its role in the political process made an increasingly significant ground in parallel with the widening of the electorate base (political market), the augmentation in the need of political actors to convince the voters, and the development of the means of communication. This trend has also brought along a tendency of professionalization for both political agents and the media/advertisement industry. The professionalization trend manifests itself in various aspects such as an increase in the number of surveys and marketing companies specialized in

DOI: 10.4018/978-1-7998-9672-2.ch016

political matters, and expanding funds of political parties for advertising expenses. Today it presents a quite complicated phenomenon that remains to evolve by introducing new partners and communication techniques.

The leading reason that causes this complexity is its connection with politics because the outcome of the exchange originating from political advertising has serious consequences in terms of the political functioning of the states. Legislative regulations, for instance, in this advertising sector is subject to special consideration, some of which can be pretty contentious such as the 'truth in political advertising. In parallel, political advertising is contextual with the states' political structure and political culture. In this chapter, the Commonwealth of Australia, which represents a fertile case to observe the dynamics of political advertising in consolidated democracies, will be examined.

POLITICAL ADVERTISING AUSTRALIA

Country Profile: Brief History, Geography, Ethnic and Religious Composition, Culture, and Language

Located on the largest island and the smallest continent in the world, Australia has a distinct geographical characteristic. It lies between the Indian and Pacific oceans in the southern hemisphere and occupies an entire continent by itself. It has maritime boundaries with Indonesia, East Timor, Papua New Guinea, the Solomon Islands, Vanuatu, New Caledonia, and New Zealand. In addition to the mainland, it comprises the island of Tasmania and some other small islands. It is the sixth-largest country with more than 2.9 million square miles.

The first humans of the island, the ancestors of Aboriginal Australians, are believed to have arrived there almost sixty thousand years ago. Another indigenous people of the island, Torres Strait Islanders, arrived from the northern island, shared by Indonesia and Papua New Guinea today, around 2,500 years ago. The first documented European landing in Australia was recorded by The Dutch East India Company in 1606. Yet, the main transformation began with the colonization of the island by Great Britain in the late 18th century. The establishment of the colony of New South Wales in Port Jackson on 26 January 1788 under the command of Captain Arthur Phillip is considered the beginning of Australia. This date later began to be celebrated as the national day. In the following periods, five new colonies (Van Diemen's Land, Victoria, Queensland, Western Australia, South Australia) were established. Between 1855 and 1890, these six colonies obtained the right to form an autonomous government on their own and laid the foundations of today's Australian political system. By the enactment of the Commonwealth of Australia Constitution Act on January 1, 1901, Australia became an independent country under the umbrella of the Commonwealth (West & Murphy, 2010). However, most of the constitutional links with the United Kingdom break with the enactment of The Statute of Westminster passed on December 1, 1931.

Demographics of Australia is a story about people from other lands coming to make the island their home since the British arrival in 1788. The large majority of settlers came from the British Isles until World War II. Besides, there was significant migration from China and Germany as well during the nineteenth century. In the decades after the War, Australia received a large wave of immigration from across Europe. Exclusivist White Australia policy accompanied all these migrations between 1901-1973 and shaped the ethnic composition (Elder, 2005). Today, immigrants account for 30% of the population, of which immigrants from major Western nations constitute the highest proportion. According to the data of the 2016 census, the most common ancestries in Australia are English by 25.0%, Australian (23.3%), Irish (7.6%), Scottish (6.4%), and Chinese (3.9%). Aboriginal Australians and Torres Strait Islanders make up 2.8% of the population. Australia has no official language, yet 72.7% of people speak English. Other languages spoken by people in daily life include Mandarin (2.5%), Arabic(1.4%), Cantonese (1.2%), Vietnamese (1.2%), and Italian (1.2%). Looking at the religious composition, the most common responses given in the census are No Religion (29.6%), Catholic (22.6%), Anglican (13.3%), and Uniting Church (3.7%) (2016 Census QuickStats, 2017).

Australian culture is shaped significantly by its immigration history. Until the mid-twentieth century, Australian culture was almost exclusively Anglo-Celtic thanks to the exclusivist White Australia policy of the government. The punitive policies pursued against the indigenous people of the island during the colonization and subsequent nation-building process under the guise of the 'civilizing mission' caused their cultural value almost to be lost. After the relaxation of immigration rules, immigrants and refugees from different geographies like the Middle East, Europe, and East Asia left significant traces on Australian culture. Similarly, positive government action to rectify past wrongs has brought about a striking increase in the Aboriginal population and revitalization of Aboriginal arts. It can be said that Australia is home to a diversity of cultures today.

Political Structure

In constitutional terms, Australia, one of the world's oldest continuous democracies, is a federal-state consisting of six states, together with two self-governing territories, and ruled by constitutional monarchy designed according to the Westminster system of separation of powers. Since it is a commonwealth member, the head of state is the governor-general formally appointed by the queen of the United Kingdom of Great Britain and Northern Ireland. Yet, literal reading of the Constitution can be misleading. The queen and the governor-general have a symbolic place and are neutral in the political process. In reality, it is ruled by a parliamentary system in which the prime minister and cabinet possess executive power. The legislation duty is held by the Parliament which is composed of three elements: Since the country is a Commonwealth member, the Queen, represented by the Governor-General, is considered a natural partner of legislation but it is a symbolic office. The Senate and the House of Representatives, on the other hand, are the main branches of the legislative body. Despite some restrictions on the power of the Senate related to the introduction (or directly amending) of some financial issues, the two chambers of the parliament have equal powers. The proposed laws have to be agreed upon by both chambers.

Free and fair elections are the core component of the political system, and they are held under the administration of the Australian Electoral Commission (AEC). The Electoral Act 1918 enforces compulsory voting for all eligible Australians. Parliamentarian elections are held with two different election systems. For the House of Representatives, a full-preference instant-runoff voting system is employed. For, the Senate, on the other hand, an optional preferential single transferable voting system is applied. The federal election is conducted approximately once every three years. In addition, elections for local government and parliaments for each of the six states are held every 3 to 4 years. Since 1901, there have been 47 federal elections. The frequency of elections significantly increases the role of advertising in the political process. Another aspect of election culture that increases the importance of political advertising is that Australia has an unusually high voter turnout ratio compared with consolidated democracies in Europe where the turnout rate is in a consistent decline trend (Solijonov, 2016, pp. 25,26). Approximately 97% of the eligible Australians enrolled in the elections and 91.9% voted in the 2019 federal election.

The high turnout rate can be considered a determinant that signs the high number of citizens interested in political issues and eager to consume political content.

Although there are more than 40 registered political parties at the federal level, the political structure of Australia manifests the characteristics of the mild two-party system. The Australian Labor Party and the conservative coalition of Liberal and National Parties dominate the political structure. The coalition government of Liberal and National Parties won a third three-year term by gaining 77 seats in the House of Representatives in 2019. Scott Morrison, leader of the Liberal Party of Australia, leads the coalition government as the Prime Minister. The Australian Labor Party, led by Bill Shorten, could win 68 seats. The other six seats were shared by the Australian Greens, Centre Alliance, Katter's Australian Party, and three independents.

The voting behavior of the electorate stands out as another important issue that increases the importance of political advertising in Australia. Evidence from the Australian Election Study carried out by Cameron and McAllister (2019a, p. 23) reveals that the electoral volatility rate has been on a rising trend since 1987. Fewer people stay loyal to their party, which also means fewer guaranteed voters for political parties. In another study, conducted to examine the electoral choice of voters in the 2019 federal elections, Cameron and McAllister (2019b) revealed that 66 percent of voters gave decisions by taking political issues into consideration.

Advertising Industry and Media

The history of advertising in Australia can be traced back to the beginning of the 19th century but turning it into a professional occupation took almost a century. By the early 1990s, the advertising industry developed enough that agencies began to form associations to protect their interests such as demanding commission from the media. The first one was founded in Melbourne in 1912. In 1946, the national Australian Association of Advertising Agencies which would be the main advertising agency body with the title Communication Council in the future was founded. Today, the Council has 175 company members coming from different segments ranging from international networks to local independents. (Advertising Council Australia). The top ten advertising agencies and advertisers are listed in table 1.

The advertising industry in Australia experienced a significant transformation during the late 1980s and the early 1990s. Big agencies merged with other agencies and supported forming large advertising associations. These new actors in the advertising market could present more qualified and diversifying services to their clients. This consolidation trend went through another phase which can be marked with emerging of large marketing communication organizations such as Interpublic Group of companies or Omnicom Group. The acceleration of globalization with digitalization and the change in customer demands and needs have inevitably affected the advertising market. Joint-size companies increasingly felt compelled to merge with other agencies. Agencies like Fallon Worldwide, Leo Burnett, Saatchi & Saatchi, and even Mojo, for example, have been acquired by the giant French holding company Publicis Groupe. Despite this giant transformation, however, the concentration level remained low; such that the four largest actors' market shares account for less than thirty percent of total industry revenue. (Belch, Belch, Kerr, Powell, & Waller, 2020, p. 434).

In Australia, total advertising spending is estimated to grow by 9.1 percent in 2021 and counts five percent below the investment level of 2019. According to Zenith, Australia's market was worth A\$16.43bn in 2019, A\$14.29 bn in 2020, and will be worth A\$15.59 bn in 2021 (Buchkingham-Jones, 2021).

Table 1. Top ten advertising agencies and advertisers

Rank	Ad agency	Advertiser group/advertiser
1	Clemenger BBDO, Melbourne	Wesfarmers Ltd
2	The Monkeys, Sydney	Harvey Norman Holdings
3	Che Proximity, Melbourne	Woolworths Ltd
4	R/GA, Sydney	Telstra Corporation Ltd
5	Leo Burnett, Melbourne	Reckitt Benckiser
6	BMF, Sydney	Toyota Motor Corporation
7	McCann, Melbourne	Australian Commonwealth Government
8	MediaCom, Melbourne	My Chemist
9	Leo Burnett, Sydney	NSW Government
10	TBWA\Melbourne	McDonald's Family Restaurants

Source: (Belch at all, 2020)

Sure, the sophistication of political advertising is directly proportional to the structure and the development of the media as well. Australia has a free media system organized with an extensive regulatory framework to provide diversity, independence, and reliability. According to the 2021 World Press Freedom Index (2021) released by Reporters Without Borders, the Australian media ranked 17th and accounted as free media. However, despite restrictive regulations, Australia has one of the highest concentrations of commercial media ownership in the world. The industry's four most prominent players (News Australia, Fairfax Media, Seven West Media, and APN News & Media) are estimated to account for over 90 percent of industry revenue in 2015-16 (Papandrea & Tiffen, 2016, p. 705). Although two public service broadcasters and social media help counter the lack of media diversity, a high concentration level is still a severe problem for the functioning of the democracy, which alerted political elites. On November 11, 2020, the Senate referred to an inquiry about media diversity, independence, and reliability. In the inquiry report, released by the Senate Environment and Communications References Committee, it is revealed that high concentration in media also affects the share of advertising revenues in negative term (Media Diversity in Australia, 2021). This provides a financial dependency that may conceal some hidden relationship between political agents and media or put some pressure on acting objectively, such as publishing criticism of high spending on government advertising (Young, 2006).

It seems that the media environment for political advertising has been in a changing trend for the side of digital media. As seen in Figure 1, voters have begun to prefer digital media more in terms of accessing political content. While television broadcasting market, despite the downward trend, remains a major platform for the political, radio and newspapers seem to be outmoded. According to the Australian Media and Entertainment Outlook 2019-2025 (2021, p. 47) market report of PricewaterhouseCoopers, the compound annual growth rate (CAGR) of the newspaper print circulation market is expected to decline by 5.1 percent between 2019-2025. However, this image can be somewhat misleading for newspapers. If the rates of accessed websites during the election campaigns are analyzed (Figure 2), it is seen that mainstream news media, also including websites of the newspapers and television channels, is the leading platform for the consumption of political content. The CAGR of the newspaper digital circulation market is expected to increase by 11.4 percent and the digital news display advertising market is expected to increase by 3.8 percent between 2019-2025 (Australian Media and Entertainment Outlook 2019-2025, 2021, p. 48).

Figure 1. Following the election in the mass media
Source: (Cameron & McAllister, 2019a)

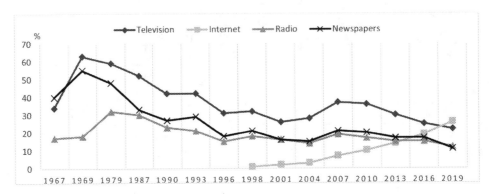

Despite more than two decades of experience and transformation in the voters' praxis towards reaching political content, the shift from traditional media medium (TV, radio, newspapers, and magazines) to the digital in political advertising is a very recent case in Australia. Since there is no legislative obligation for political parties to disclose their advertising expenditure by media in the campaigning period, it is not possible to measure the trend with full accuracy. However, the media market share of campaign advertising of government departments and agencies, released by the Department of Finance annually, present an overview to estimate the tendency. As seen in Figure 3, the market share of digital media for government campaign advertising came close to traditional media in the 2015-2016 fiscal year and passed in the 2019-2020 period. Andrew Huges (2019) also had a similar observation and stated that the campaign period of the 2019 Federal Elections seems to be the first in Australia where the parties advertised more on social and digital platforms than traditional media. In its self-evaluation report on the 2019 federal election result, Australian Labor Party regarded the reluctance to carry out the 'digital-first' campaign strategy as one of the leading causes behind the failure in the election (Australian Labor Party, 2019).

Figure 2. Websites accessed during the election campaign
Source: (Cameron & McAllister, 2019a)

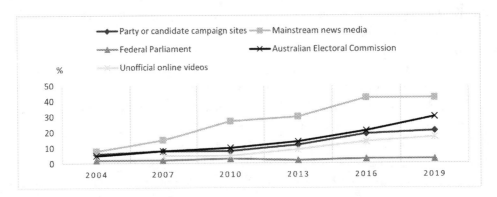

Figure 3. Government campaign advertising expenditure by medium
Source: The data is collected from the Campaign Advertising by Australian Government Departments and Agencies Reports of the Department of Finance (from 2011-2012 fiscal year to 2019-2020 fiscal year).

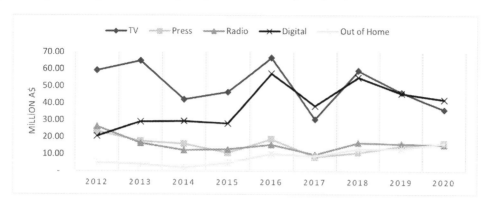

Pandemic has provided significant momentum to people's use of the internet. Total internet access revenue showed marginal growth, reaching A$30.1 billion, in Australia in 2020 and 3,1 percent CAGR is expected between 2019-2025 (Australian Entertainment & Media Outlook:2021-2025, 2021, pp. 21,22). In that regard, it is possible to argue that digital advertising will be the main direction of political campaign in further election periods. However, the change in consumer habits is not the only reason. Digital methods of political marketing provide more effective, more accurate, and more interactively message delivery at a micro-target level. As social media by its nature matches up perfectly to an engaging mass market in a more personalized and market-driven way, it allows for more effective integration of grassroots-style campaigning. The algorithms make us visible when we participate in the political communication process and move us from involuntary receivers to active information seekers (Hughes, 2018, p. 2). Digital campaigning enables political parties to get around the legal restrictions and continue to advertise until the last seconds of the polling time, because advertisings can also be shared or even created by users themselves and, technically, they are not political advertisings since no party is paying for them to be shared on people's feeds.

Regulation of Political Advertising and Some Ethical Considerations

Political Advertising is regulated mainly by the Electoral Act of 1918 and Broadcasting Services of 1992. The provisions defined under these laws have a flexible structure that enables political actors to make maximum use of advertising in their campaigns. For example, there are no limits at all on the amount spent and no requirement to file election expenditure disclosure. What is more, parties and candidates that receive more than four percent of the primary vote are entitled to public election funding. In the 2019 Federal Elections, political parties were paid more than A$68 million, independent candidates and senate groups were paid around A$1 million (Australian Electoral Commission, 2020, pp. 10,11). Similarly, the volume of political advertising is not limited but all political advertisings must contain the name and address of the producer. One more restriction is that a blackout is commenced three days before the election day.

Governments' use of advertising for various purposes such as public service announcements or raising awareness of citizens in publicly important issues (climate change, pandemic, etc.) is a routine part of their administrative activities. However, the use of these publicly funded advertisings in a way that will provide an electoral advantage to the political party in power such as the marketing of government policies is criticized by opposition groups as it undermines the principle of equal competition and misuse of the public budget for partisan purposes. The problem arises especially in countries where the legislative regulations related to the distinction in the use of legitimate government advertising for partisan goals or public policy is blurred.

Table 2. Government campaign advertising expenditure by year

Years	2012	2013	2014	2015	2016	2017	2018	2019	2020
Expenditure (million $)	146,6	148,5	116,4	113,6	186	105,5	169,4	151,4	137,6

Source: The data is collected from the Campaign Advertising by Australian Government Departments and Agencies Reports of the Department of Finance (from 2011-2012 fiscal year to 2019-2020 fiscal year).

As seen from Table 2, Australian governments spent over 100 million $ per year on advertising. It is such a high amount that if compared to the other federal countries, Australia (considering both the State and federal governments) spends more than double on government advertising per capita (Young & Tham, 2006, p. 80). As a result, Australian governments are naturally criticized by opposition parties and the public because of the burden that advertisements place on the budget (Karp, 2020; Young, 2007c). One aspect of these criticisms is about the necessity or quality of the advertisements in terms of graphics and messages. The 'Australian Made' campaign, for instance, which had launched first in 1986 and was maintained by other governments to encourage people to buy domestic goods, subjected to some criticisms as motivating people to go against their common sense and acting financially irrational for the sake of the country. The use of symbols and content that appeal to nationalist feelings in campaign advertisings has been one of the main motivations behind the emergence of such criticisms (Young, 2007a, p. 192). Similarly, Government's anti-terrorism advertisements (like the 'Let's Look Out for Australia' and 'Help Protect Australia from Terrorism') campaigns are also open to ethical questioning since they insinuatingly present Arabs and Muslims as potential terrorists (Younane, 2006). More recently, the government's 'Arm Yourself Against COVID-19' campaign, aimed at increasing the rates of vaccination in Australia, became the subjectof discussions. In a video advertising released in the scope of the vaccine campaign, a young woman connected to a ventilator in the hospital struggling to survive against the disease was displayed. The fact that the video was broadcasted at a time when the under 40-year-old had only recently had access to the vaccine was considered a mistake, supporting the arguments that the government failed to take the necessary steps during the pandemic and failed to supply enough vaccines on time (Jaspan, 2021).[1]

Governments' use of advertising campaigns for partisan purposes, on the other hand, causes more serious debates. The 'Working Nation' advertisements of the Labor government in 1995 which were advertising the government's employment policies at a time, when the unemployment rate was high and the elections were so close, is one of the most salient examples. Similarly, the Howard coalition government's 'Unchain my Heart' in 1998 and 2000, 'Strengthening Medicare' in 2004, and 'WorkChoices' in 2005 campaign advertisings also were accused of being used by partisan sense as they were released just before elections or/and designed for advertising governments policies instead of publicizing (Young, 2007a, pp. 194-201). Despite debates and criticisms, legislative regulations attempt to audit governments' campaign advertisings remained successful for a long time. The Guidelines for Australian Government Information Activities (GIGIA- created in 1983, updated in 1992, and then amended again in February 1995), the basic legal document regularizing government advertising, was so permissive compared to the versions in similar countries such as the UK and New Zealand. The possibility of misuse of government advertising for partisan purposes was not even mentioned let alone prohibited this. The reports submitted by institutions such as the Auditor General, the Senate Finance and Public Administration Committee, which drew attention to the lack of legal regulations and suggested the introduction of various regulations, were rejected or ignored by the governments (Young, 2007b, s. 438-440).

A new phase has begun with the Rudd Government's release of new 'Guidelines on Campaign Advertising by Australian Government Departments and Agencies' in 2008. The new guidelines introduce five new principles providing that the entity's chief executive (known as the accountable authority under the Public Governance, Performance, and Accountability (PGPA) Act 2013 Act) was responsible for certifying the compatibility of the advertising campaigns with the guidelines. According to the third principle, the material used in the advertisings should be presented with objective language and in a style free from the promotion of government argument and policy. Besides, the publication of information funded by the public budget should not be aimed at providing political interest or a positive impression for a particular political party (Asset Management Group, 2009). The Third-party review of a campaign's compliance, which had been undertaken by the Auditor-General according to 2008 guidelines, based on a limited assurance approach, was replaced in 2010 by the Independent Communications Committee, appointed by the government. In 2015, new guidelines were put into service under the title of 'Guidelines on Information and Advertising Campaigns by non-corporate Commonwealth' entities and took the latest form by updates in 2020.

The overarching aim of the guidelines can be described as providing the confidence that public funds are used to meet the genuine information needs of the community in the most effective way and without political purposes of any party. In that regard, paragraphs 34 to 36 of the last version of the government advertising framework explain how being 'objective and not directed at promoting party political interests' principle will be fulfilled: Language should be objective and free of political argument. impression or promote the political interest of a particular political party. In campaigns, the name, slogan, or images of the party in the government must not be mentioned, and the website link of politicians or political parties must not be referred to. Campaigns must not be designed to affect public opinion toward a political party, any member of government or parliament, or a candidate for election. With the same purpose, views, policies, or actions of other actors such as the opposition parties or groups must not be directly attacked or scorned (Australian Government, 2020). Yet, there is a significant point that needs to be highlighted. This framework, in a sense, is a government policy and forces government entities to obey the principles in their campaign ads activities, but lacks legal sanction determined with concrete terms to be applied in the case of violation. Today, government campaign advertisings valued at more than $250,000 or where requested are subject to monitoring of the Independent Communications Committee but only in an advisory sense. In its report on Government Advertising between 2015 and 2019, the Australian National Audit Office, similarly, emphasis to lack of obligation in the implication of the principles. In parallel, it is stated that while the campaign ads generally comply with the stated principles, the compliance with the third principle can be damaged with the statements made by the government members during the campaign process. For instance, the ministerial media release that launched Phase 4 of the 'Powering Forward' campaign contained an overt political argument. In the media release, while the Liberal and Nationals Government is promoted by stating that it is continuing to take action so more Australians pay less for their electricity, the Labor party is disgraced by claiming that it sides with the big energy companies. There was also a similarity in tone and content between statements used in the campaign advertisings and ministerial media releases that can be treated containing overt political argument. In a similar vein, the report also attracts attention to density in the number of the campaign advertisings in election times which implies the use of publicly funded advertisings for the benefit of the party political interests in a roundabout way (Australian National Audit Office, 2019). The overall picture indicates that government advertising in Australia is still vulnerable to be used for political gains especially in election times despite the regulations enacted that strengthen the scrutiny mechanism.

Another issue of public concern like the monitoring of government advertisings is the demand for truth in political advertising. The use of misleading or false statements made in the course of electioneering has been a serious problem. It has an abrasive effect on the trust towards politicians and democracy. It plays a more devastating role in highly polarized societies where people are prone to keep their political stance against the others. The side effect of technology, unfortunately, is seen in this case as well. Much more misleading, deceptive or false political information has gotten in circulation on popular social media platforms such as Twitter, Facebook, and Instagram, as well as in more traditional media outlets. Deployment of bots and algorithms facilitating micro-targeting techniques make people much more vulnerable to this information. These digital technologies produce and disseminate necessary information that makes false statements seen at least possibly true with minimal cost. The need for legislative regulation of truth in political advertising, therefore, has begun to be felt much more.

Legislative regulation attempts on truth in political advertising have been a case in Australia for more than a century. Section 180(e) of the Commonwealth Electoral Act 1911 (Cth) adopted a content-based regulation that prohibited advertising which contained "any untrue or incorrect statement intended or likely to mislead or improperly interfere with any elector in or in relation to the casting of his vote". These provisions were retained with minor additions until 1983 (Pender). Upon the report of the Joint Select Committee on Electoral Reform, established by the Hawke government, Parliament passed amendments to the 1918 Act including a section on truth in pollical advertising. Section 161 (2) of the Commonwealth Electoral Legislation Amendment Act 1983 (Cth) provided:

A person shall not, during the relevant period in relation to an election under this Act, print, publish, or distribute, or cause, permit or authorize to be printed, published or distributed, any electoral advertisement containing a statement –
   a.   that is untrue; and
   b.   *that is, or is likely to be, misleading or deceptive* (p. 68).

Besides defining penalties of a fine (not exceeding $1000 in case of a natural person, $5000 in case of body corporate) or imprisonment (not more than 6 months) or both for breaching this section, the amendment introduced also the right of seeking an injunction from the Supreme Court of the relevant state to prevent breaching. Yet, this regulation was repealed upon the second report of the Committee, published in 1984. Committee's concerns were clustered around the difficulty of establishing the criteria which would determine the trueness of a statement by a Court, the possibility of candidates' tactical use of injunctions to hamper opposing political party's campaign, limited time in the campaign process to finalize the allegations and possible disturbing consequences of this situation on the political process. The Committee suggested that the decision regarding the 'truth' would be better left to the voters. (Joint Select Committee on Electoral Reform, 1984, pp. 21-26). On the other hand, in his dissenting report which was given a place in the Committee's report, Senator Michael Macklin (1984), argued that 'it is surely a small price to pay for a better-informed democracy that politicians are required to tell the truth' (p. 47). Over time, legislative regulation of the truth in political advertising continued to be subjected to parliamentary considerations frequently in various forms because of the complaints about alleged false electoral matters that came into question in election times.[2] The views expressed in the second report, however, have continued to be a dominant approach on this issue and, as a result, there is no legislative regulation in force on truth in political advertising at the federal level.

Despite unresolved attempts at the federal level, South Australia (SA) and the Australian Capital Territory (ACT) have managed to compose a political culture supported by laws. South Australia put its legislative regulation in force by enacting the electoral act (SA) in 1985. Section 113 makes it an offense to authorize or cause electoral advertisements that are inaccurate and misleading in the material sense to be published. The provision authorizes the SA Electoral Commissioner to request such advertisements be withdrawn and publication of a retraction. The Commissioner can also apply to the Supreme Court to enforce that decision. Besides, the law introduces punishments up to $5,000 for individuals or $25,000 for a body corporate. In fact South Australia is such determined to secure political communication against inaccurate and misleading information that the law empowers the Court of Disputed Returns to invalidate the results of an election if advertising affect the election result as well. In 2020, Australian Capital Territory also introduced a similar provision in electoral law which empowers the Commission to seek a retraction and, if necessary, apply to the Supreme Court. Under the new provision, an individual can be fined up to $8,000 and a corporation up to $40,500.

The discussions and expectations on legislative regulation at the federal level have been heightened in the last years in parallel with the increase in social media's capacity of affecting the political land-scape. The Australia Institute, a think-tank organization, has initiated an online campaign demanding a legislative regulation for the truth in political advertising law (We Need Truth in Political Advertising Laws, 2020). The survey conducted by the institute revealed that 87% of Australians supported the introduction of such laws (Browne, 2020). The Joint Standing Committee on Electoral Matters (JSCEM) discussed the possibility of enacting a federal law regulating truth in political advertising in its report on the 2019 federal election. Although the majority in the JSCEM, which consisted of the coalition government representatives, did not support the regulation, dissenting reports from Labor and Greens members stated a strong aspiration for reform. A serious step, however, has been taken by Independent federal MP Zali Steggall's introduction of the Commonwealth Electoral Amendment (Stop the Lies) Bill into the House of Representatives on 25 October 2021. Addressing to the assembly in the second read stage of the bill, Dr. Helen Mary Haines (2021) stated that it's perfectly legal for politicians to lie in their ads, to spin any old tale for the sake of a vote, however, people hate this kind of grubby, low, deceptive politics. Then, she argued that the bill proposed has been tried and tested in legislation that's been in place in South Australia for over 20 years, therefore, it will bring political advertising up to the standards that businesses are held to.

The bill, on the one hand, is organized with the sense of satisfying some earlier concerns like the abuse of the law to hamper the opposite party campaigns. In that regard, the competent court is empowered to refuse an application that is frivolous, vexatious, misconceived, or lacking in substance, or revealing no reasonable prospect for success, which can be considered as an abuse of the process of the court. On the other hand, it has the potential to pave the way for further discussions by enlarging the scope of the law from concrete to likelihood. Section 321K (1) provides that:

A person must not print, publish or distribute, or cause, permit or authorize to be printed, published or distributed, electoral matter if the electoral matter contains a statement in relation to a matter of fact (including an implied statement) that is:

    a.   misleading or deceptive to a material extent; or

    b.   likely to mislead or deceive to a material extent.

Another characteristic of the bill is that it brings a new phase to the issue which is related to the development of technology in the digital world. Section 321K (2) prohibits parties, candidates, and campaigners from impersonating or passing off material as being from another candidate. In the explanatory memorandum of the bill, the drafters emphasized that advances in technology make it easier to fraudulently impersonate a candidate such as deep fakes (Electoral Legislation Amanedment (Stop The Lies) Bill 2021: Explanatory Memorandum). For the time being, when this study is accomplished, this step has not been concluded yet.

An interesting study, conducted by Waller (2002), provides a new reason for enhancing the need for truth regulation in political advertising. Examining the advertising agency-client attitudes towards ethical issues in political advertising in Australia, Waller highlights cognitive differences, particularly in the area of 'accountability', between advertising agency executives and politicians. He found that advertising agency executives appear to feel more strongly in their views on whether political advertising should be accountable to the public and liable for prosecution if found deceptive. The executives also feel more strongly in their views that statements in political advertisements are frequently misleading. On the other hand, while there is general agreement that political accounts are potentially somewhat 'problematic' (Dickenson, 2014), some agencies are still willing to take on political accounts (Waller & Polonsky, 1996). As there appears to be a number of advertising agencies, taking the possible financial and non-financial benefits that can compensate for these problems into account, it is possible to say that politicians can continue to find partners accompany with their having no boundaries campaigning.

Political Advertising in Australia Towards 2022 Federal Elections

Although the elections are six months away, it seems that the campaign race of Australian political parties and candidates for the 2022 Federal Election has already begun. According to the Google transparency report, political parties and third-party groups in Australia have already spent close to $3.5 million for more than 3300 advertisements (Google Transparency Report Australia, 2021). In addition, about $2 million has been spent on Facebook ads by political parties only (Facebook Ad Library Report Australia, 2021). Also, it should be underlined that Liberal-National Coalition has the advantage of government campaign advertising. Sure, it provides a critical opportunity for opposition parties as well. With the 'Liberals Spend $1b On Ads' ad, Labor accused Liberals and Morrison of spending $1b for government ads and using this source for patronage by sending $1m to the market research company of a Liberal politician.

Digital platforms have also become a significant media medium for minor parties and candidates. Clive Palmer's United Australia Party is the most prominent ad payer of Google, with more than $3 million. Similarly, the Greens, Australian Citizen Party, Liberals for Climate have also launched digital campaigns via Google ads and other social platforms such as Facebook. When the advertising strategies of the parties are examined through Google data, it is seen that there is a differentiation in the target audience selection. Major parties set specific cities as the target audience of their advertisements, while minor parties (United Australia and Australian Citizen Parties) set the whole country as their target. Here, it can be argued the choice of this strategy, which causes high expenditure amount for a small number of advertisements by minor parties, is related to the limited party grassroots. Major parties, which have a larger voter base, may have foreseen that the advertisements they publish in the digital environment will reach large masses by the voters' sharing these advertisements on their own social networks.

Google transparency report data show that third-party groups continue to play an active role in this election period as well. United Workers Union has already spent nearly half as much on political advertising through Google as the Labor Party National Secretariat. Some advertisements published by organizations such as GetUp, Class Action Australia, Australian Council of Trade Unions go beyond the purpose of creating public opinion in line with the mission of the organization and acquire a quality that can directly affect voter behavior. Some of these ads, such as GetUp's 'Murdoch & Morrison vs. the ABC' or Class Action Australia's 'Keep Corporations Honest', directly attack Morrison government by name.

Even a cursory glance at the spots and video ads presented to the voters is enough to realize that the 2022 federal election campaign will be overwhelmingly negative. To put the trend in numbers, of the 500 documentary ads posted on the Labor party's Facebook page in the last six months, only 168 were in the positive ad category, while 305 were in the negative ad category, and approximately half of them were harsh ads targeting Prime Minister Morrison personally.[3]

Designing Political Ads

Researchers have examined political ads from different perspectives, such as video styles, types of arguments, language and verbal styles, and emotional dimensions to determine the common characteristics of political ads. Despite some significant findings towards common characteristics, such as appealing to emotions (Weber, 2013; Brader, 2006), it is still not so possible to speak of a common formula for the construction of successful political advertising. It can be argued that one of the leading factors behind not being able to produce a common model is the fact that political ads are quite contextual with the political structure and culture of the countries. In that regard, examining the common characteristics of political ads in a country and attempting to construct common rules for that country can be an appropriate approach. Such kind of an attempt was held by Sally Young (2013) for the Australian context. She mentioned some common characteristics of Australian negative political ads based on her observations. This study also aimed at revealing some common characteristics of Australian political ads.

Methodology

For this purpose, the video ads featured by the Labor Party, the main opposition party, and the Liberal party, which is the big partner of the incumbent coalition government, in their campaign for the 2022 Federal Election, are examined with quantitative content analysis methodology via Maxqda. The dataset is collected from the official social media accounts (Facebook and Youtube) of the two political parties. The scope of the study is limited to the video ads featured between July 2021 and January 2022 and documentary ads are excluded. In that context, 62 video ads (Liberal: 23, Labor: 39) are employed in the analysis.

In the construction of the coding framework, besides the model presented by Young (2013), the typology formed by Johnson-Cartee & Copeland (2010) on the axis of negative political ads in the USA was utilized. In that context, firstly, nine main categories (subject, Theme, Material, production style, emotion, temporality, Music, style, attack style in negative ads) were determined. Then, fifty subcategories, identifying the main categories, were formed (see Table 3). The coding process was held in two stages. In the first phase, the data set was coded by two different coders. In the second phase, the codings were compared and different categories were discussed. At the end of the coding phase, the inter-coder reliability index is found 91,2%.

In the research, four research questions were determined and code co-occurrence analysis was conducted to explore the main characteristics of political advertising in Australia. The research questions are as follows:

RQ 1: What are the common features of political ads featured by the Liberal and Labor Parties?
RQ 2: What are the distinctive differences between styles of the ads used by the parties?
RQ 3: What are subjects emphasized more frequently in the ads?
RQ 4: Which advertising strategy is more preferred?

Table 3. Code table

Subject	%	Material	freq	Production Style	%
Pandemic	40,0	Statistical Information	17	Visual Documentary	20,3
Employment	17,1	Global Comparison	15	Graphic	37,5
Coalition with the Greens	1,4	Cynical Looking of Opponent	23	News Style	3,1
Home Loan Deposit Scheme	1,4	Past Promises-Pitiful Performance	4	Candidate Confrontation	4,7
Childcare	2,8	Political Gaffles	8	Candidate Interactional	14,1
Renewables	11,4	Other	3	Public Figure	6,3
Medicare	14,2	**Temporality**	**%**	Flip-Flops	14,1
Corruption	2,8	Retrospektive	27,4	**Emotion**	**%**
Taxes and Funds	4,3	Prospective	12,9	Fear and Hope	1,6
Sexual Harresment	1,4	Present	59,7	Hope	17,7
Anti-Scam Policy	2,8	**Music**	**%**	Fear	9,6
Inparty Division	5,7	Focusing Music	12,9	Anger	35,4
Economy	14,2	Funny Music	1,6	Fear-Anxiety	20,9
Theme	**freq**	Thriller Music-Sound	17,7	Neutral	14,8
Political Character	14	No Music	67,8	**Style**	**%**
Political Experience-Incompetence	7	**Attack Style in Negative Ads**	**%**	Negative	67,7
Disparagement Humor	15	Direct Attack	88,3	Pozitive	30,2
Mentality	1	Direct Comparison	2,3	Negative and Pozitive	2,1
Political Performance	34	Implied Comparison	9,4		

FINDINGS AND ANALYSIS

Acccording to the findings obtained after the code co-occurrence analysis, Negativity (67.7%) stands out as the main characteristics (see Figure 4). As a matter of fact, it is possible to talk about the continuation of a tradition. Researchers seem to have a consensus on the view that aggressivity and negative style campaigning has been an ingrained character of political advertising in Australia (Braund, 1978; Miskin & Grant, 2004; Plasser & Plasser, 2002, p. 268; Young, 2003). The widespread use of negative advertisements in campaigns has led to discussions about its effect on voters and the functioning of democracy. An important aspect of criticism is that negative advertisements cause people to feel distrust and alienation towards political actors and the political process (Joint Standing Committee on Electoral Matters, 2020).

Figure 4. Code co-occurrence map

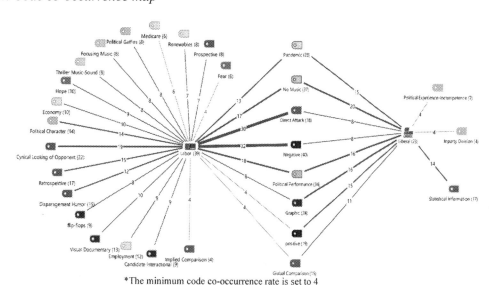

*The minimum code co-occurrence rate is set to 4

In the literature on political advertising, there has been a hot debate related to the effects of negative (attacking) advertisement on electoral behavior. The researchers have different considerations on its pros and cons. For instance, the findings of Meritt (1984) and Garramone (1984) refer to a boomerang effect that negative political advertising evokes a negative impact toward both the targeted opponent and the sponsor. On the other hand, Johnson-Cartee and Copeland (2010, p. 10) argued that expectation for a boomerang effect as the natural outcome of negative ads is quite simplistic. A similar controversy is a case for the pros and cons of negative ads in terms of democracy. Some studies argue that exposure to negative ads has a reducing effect, even at a low level, on voter turnout (Franz, Freedman, Goldstein, & Ridout, 2008; Ansolabehere & Iyengar, 1995). The studies also place emphasis on increase levels of political cynicism and alienation. For instance, Yoon, Pinkleton, and Ko (2007) suggest that high-credibility candidates' use of negative political advertising causes greater cynicism for highly involved participants. This means, in turn, more dissatisfaction with democracy for politically highly engaged citizens. However, some other researchers argue that there is no significant correlation between negative ads and turnout preferences (Krasno & Green, 2008; Wattenberg & Brians, 1999) or participants' cynicism, efficacy, or apathy (Pinkleton, Um, & Austin, 2013). For Pinkleton (1997), negative advertising even may have greater educative benefits than more virulent forms of negative political advertising.

As the number of different arguments offered in the research related to negative political advertising increases, researchers have begun to apply metanalysis techniques to achieve some general findings. In their meta-analytic study covering 52 studies, Lau et all (Lau, Lee, Heldman, & Paul, 1999) find that negative political ads do not appear to be more effective than positive ones. Also, despite the general comprehension, negative political ads do not seem to have abrasive effects. Similary, Allen & Burrell (2002) also find no net benefit to negative versus positive ads. These studies, however, are found reductive by Kaid (2004, p. 175) and Benoit, Leshner, and Chattopadhya (2007) since they are interested only in the question of whether negative ads are more effective than positive ads. Benoit at all (2007) found in their meta-analysis that messages can enhance issue learning and influence attitudes toward candidates. In the reassessment of the earlier study (Lau et all, 1999), covering 111 studies this time, Lau, Sigelman, and Rovner (2007) insist on the conclusion that negative political ads are not more effective than positive ads while acknowledging that they have a more catchy and information-promoting nature. According to them, though negative political ads tend to be more memorable and stimulate knowledge about the campaign, they are not an effective means of winning votes. Besides they do not depress voter turnout. It is only possible to refer to lower feelings of political effectiveness and lower trust in government..

Australian political culture seems to display characteristics that approve the findings of Lau and his colleagues. Although the turnout at election rates is high, the satisfaction with democracy rate is in a downward trend, as seen in Table 4.

Table 4. Satisfaction with democracy

Satisfaction with Democracy	1969	1979	1996	1998	2001	2004	2007	2010	2013	2016	2019
Satisfied	77	56	78	71	74	82	86	72	72	60	59
Not Satisfied	23	45	22	29	26	18	14	29	28	40	41

Source: Australian Election Study (Cameron & McAllister, 2019a, p. 98)

Another significant finding acquired through the analysis is that ratio of using negative style ads is asymmetrical between the two parties. While 80% of the Labor Party's ads are negative, only 37.8% of the Liberal Party's ads are negative. Benoit (2001) explains this asymmetrical ratio in applying negative ads between the incumbent party and the opposition by referring to the opportunity of the incumbent party to reveal a political performance. To him, only the incumbent party has a record in the office, and that record is a resource for incumbents to acclaim and challengers to attack. In other words, as the incumbent parties have the opportunity of revealing a success story in concrete terms, they use positive ads, generally supported with statistical and official information, to convince people. The findings acquired in this study provide evidence supporting this proposition. Almost 83% of the statistical information used ads are preferred by the incumbent Liberal Party, and 83% present of its political ads are in the positive category.

Researchers observe an Americanization trend that employs all-encompassing globalized consumer culture and marketing techniques in political advertising. The widespread use of "KEVIN07" t-shirts by the Labor Party in the 2007 federal election, for instance, can be considered as the meeting of a number of global trends fuzzing the line between the official politics and the neoliberal marketplace (Penney, 2011). The use of flip-flop ads in political campaigns, which become much easier to produce with the developments in digital editing technologies, also provides evidence of the Americanization trend (Young, 2004). The findings acquired in the analysis indicate that this trend continues to be a significant characteristic of political advertising in Australia. It is seen that flip-flop ads are still an important advertising technique. Besides, digital editing technologies are used very effectively in advertisements. Graphic (37,5%) and visual documentary (20,3%), produced by digital techniques, stand out as the most used production styles. Thanks to digital production techniques, images that can have an effective impact on political consumers are brought together in appropriate forms. For instance, Labor frequently uses Scott Morrison's smiling appearance to associate him and his government with disregard and mocking on the issues that are important to the public, such as medicare cuts. In this way, the message 'Morrison does not care about your problems' is tried to be given to the public. Liberal Party, on the other hand, frequently used Albanese's appearance that shows up him stuck in a difficult situation to create an incompetent leader image.

Examination of political advertisements based on topics shows that the conventional issues of politics (such as economy, employment, democracy, taxes) become of secondary importance against the Covid-19 pandemic (40%). In addition, 40% of the economy-related and 25% of employment-related ads are also associated with the pandemic. Vaccination rates, case numbers, economic cost, therefore, become one of the core components of the political ads, such that 82,3% of the statistical information used in the ads are about pandemics. After the pandemic, mostly employed subjects are employment (17.1%), economy (14.2%), renewable energy (11.4%), medicare (8.5%), corruption (2.8%), and childcare (2.8).

Figure 5. Code co-occurrence map for negative ads

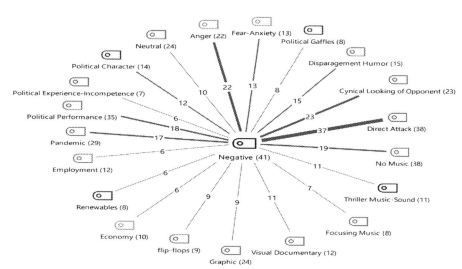

*The minimum code co-occurrence rate is set to 5

Since it is the most frequently used style in political campaigning, focusing on negative ads may provide significant contributions to understanding the dynamics of political ads in Australia. As seen in Figure 5, the 'direct attack' strategy, which mainly targets the party or candidate directly, has been adopted. It is seen that the political performance and political character of the opponent are targeted most frequently in advertisements. Another distinctive feature is the use of derogatory humor, with frequent use of the opponent's cynical appearance and political gaffes. In order to increase the effectiveness of the transferred negative image on the political consumer, tension and focus music were also used to a large extent. From an emotional point of view, we see that negative emotions are processed more. This can be accepted as one of the reasons behind the negative impact of voters' belief in the political system.

CONCLUSION

The Australian experience of political advertising provides important lessons for many countries, especially about the ethical dimension of political advertising. The debates about government campaigning ads and the truth principle in political advertising reveal how complicated the ethical dimension of political advertising is. It is seen that some fundamental issues of democratic regimes, such as the limits of freedom of expression and how the balance will be achieved in the inter-power control system, occur as significant matters in the legislative regulations of political advertisements. Australia prefers an audition mechanism the sanction side of which is left to voters to avoid preventing the use of government advertisements for partisan purposes. The campaigning ads of the government agencies are audited by the Department of Finance in terms of suitability and content. The findings obtained via the audit are reported annually together with the expenditure amounts. With these reports, which are open to access, it is aimed to inform the public and to carry out the sanction phase by the voters during the election period. It can be thought that the effectiveness of the sanction mechanism increases by the political parties' bringing these expenditures to the agenda in their campaigns. However, increasing expenditures during election periods implies that governments continue to benefit from this publicly funded advertising opportunity for partisan purposes.

Australian experience also shows that there is a significant transformation towards the digitalization of political advertising. It can be said that the change in people's internet usage habits during the pandemic has an accelerating effect. Besides, it is observed that the asymmetrical balance that emerged due to the concentration in media ownership has an additional effect on the opposition parties' orientation towards the digital media medium. On the other hand, although digitalization contributes to media diversity and the voice of minor parties to be heard, it is necessary not to make premature predictions about its impact on the quality of democracy. As the examination of the advertisings used by political parties in their campaigns for the 2022 Federal Elections shows that people are exposed to a great number of negative ads aimed at discrediting politicians. The radical increase in the rate of interaction with negative advertisements makes it necessary to conduct new researches on the political attitudes of the people.

FUTURE RESEARCH DIRECTIONS

As the digitalization of political advertising increased in Australia, computer-assisted methodologies earned much more importance. Although the elections are six months away, the parties have already released hundreds of spot ads and tens of video ads both at the state and federal levels. Besides, each item brings along a cluster of data containing interaction components (such as view, like, dislike counts), location, and time. The grand data emerged by digitalization have the potential of providing a clearer view for issues on which a general consensus cannot be reached, such as voters' attitudes towards negative advertising.

REFERENCES

Census QuickStats. (2017, October 23). Retrieved January 17, 2022, from Australian Bureau of Statistics: https://quickstats.censusdata.abs.gov.au/census_services/getproduct/census/2016/quickstat/036

World Press Freedom Index. (2021). Retrieved November 5, 2021, from Reporters Without Borders: https://rsf.org/en/ranking

Advertising Council Australia. (n.d.). Retrieved January 23, 2022, from Advertising Council Australia: https://advertisingcouncil.org.au/about-us/why-we-exist/

Allen, M., & Burrell, N. (2002). The negativity effect in political advertising: A meta-analysis. In J. P. Dillard & M. Pfau (Eds.), *The persuasion handbook: Developments in theory and practice* (pp. 83–96). Sage Publications.

AMEO. (2021). The Australian entertainment & media outlook: 2021-2025. London: PricewaterhouseCoopers (pwc).

ANAO. (2019). *Audit-General Report No: 7 of 2019-2020: Government advertising: June 2015 to April 2019.* Retrieved November 2, 2021, from https://www.anao.gov.au/work/performance-audit/government-advertising-june-2015-to-april-2019

Ansolabehere, S., & Iyengar, S. (1994). Riding the wave and claiming ownership over issues: The joint effects of advertising and news coverage in campaigns. *Public Opinion Quarterly, 58*(3), 335–357.

Ansolabehere, S., & Iyengar, S. (1995). *Going negative: How political advertisements shrink and polarize the electorate.* Free Press.

Asset Management Group. (2009). *Campaign advertising by Australian government departments and agencies: half year report 1 July to 31 December 208.* Canberra: Australian Government Department of Finance and Dergulation. Retrieved September 5, 2021, from https://apo.org.au/sites/default/files/resource-files/2009-03/apo-nid1233.pdf

Australian Electoral Commission. (2020). Election funding and disclosure report: Federal election 2019. Author.

Australian Government. (2020, October). *Australian government guidelines on information and advertising campaigns by non-corporate commonwealth entities.* Retrieved from Australian Government: https://www.finance.gov.au/sites/default/files/2020-10/Australian-Government-Guidelines-Information-Advertising-Campaigns-October2020.pdf

Australian Labor Party. (2019). *Review of labor's 2019 federal election campaign.* Australian Labor Party.

Belch, G. E., Belch, M. A., Kerr, G., Powell, I., & Waller, D. (2020). *Advertising: An integrated marketing communication perspective*. McGraw-Hill Education.

Benoit, W. L. (2001). The functional approach to presidential television spots: Acclaiming, attacking, defending 1952-2000. *Communication Studies, 52*(2).

Benoit, W. L., & Hansen, G. J. (2002). Issue adaptation of presidential television spots and debates to primary and general audiences. *Communication Research Reports, 19*(2), 138–145.

Benoit, W. L., Leshner, G. M., & Chattopadhyay, S. (2007). A meta-analysis of political advertising. *Human Communication, 10*(4), 507–522.

Brader, T. (2006). *Campaigning for hearts and minds: How emotional appeals in political ads work*. University of Chicago Press.

Braund, V. (1978). *Themes in political advertising: australian federal election campaigns 1949-1972*. University of Sydney Department of Government.

Brder, T. (2005). Striking a responsive chord: How political ads motivate and persuade voters by appealing to emotions. *American Journal of Political Science, 49*(2), 388–405.

Browne, B. (2020). *Possible, practical, and popular: opprtunities for truth in poliitical advertising laws in australia*. Retrieved November 2, 2021, from The Australia Institute: https://australiainstitute.org.au/wp-content/uploads/2021/10/211025-Truth-in-Political-Advertising-WEB.pdf

Buchkingham-Jones, S. (2021, July 26). *Australian advertising market to grow 9.1% in 2021 to $15.6bn*. Zenith

Buss, T. F., & Hofstetter, C. R. (1976). An analysis of the logic of televised campaign advertisements: The 1972 presidential campaign. *Communication Research, 3*(4), 367–392.

Cameron, S., & McAllister, L. (2019a). *Trends in australian political opinion: Results from the australian election study 1987–2019*. Canberra: Australian Natinal University. Retrieved December 23, 2021, from https://australianelectionstudy.org/wp-content/uploads/Trends-in-Australian-Political-Opinion-1987-2019.pdf

Cameron, S., & McAllister, L. (2019b). *The 2019 Australian federal election: Results from the Australian election study*. Canberra: Australian National University. Retrieved December 12, 2021, from https://australianelectionstudy.org/wp-content/uploads/The-2019-Australian-Federal-Election-Results-from-the-Australian-Election-Study.pdf

Chang, C. (2001). The impacts of emotion elicited by print political advertising on candidate evaluation. *Media Psychology, 3*(1), 91–118.

Coppock, A., Hill, S. J., & Vavreck, L. (2020). The small effects of political advertising are small regardless of context, message, sender, or receiver: Evidence from 59 real-time randomized experiments. *Science Advances, 6*(36), 1–6.

Cwalina, W. F., & Newman, B. I. (2015). *Political marketing: Theoretical and strategic foundations*. Routledge.

Day, G. S. (1998). What does it to be market-driven? *Business Strategy Review*, *9*(1), 1–14.

Dickenson, J. (2014). "The politics of political advertising" in Australia and Britain, 1970-1989. *The Australian Journal of Politics and History*, *60*(2), 241–256.

Elder, C. (2005). Immigration history. In M. Lyons & P. Russell (Eds.), *Australia's history: Themes and debates* (pp. 98–115). UNSW Press.

Electoral legislation amendment (stop the lies) bill 2021: Explanatory memorandum. (n.d.). The Parliament of the Commonwealth of Australia.

Electoral Matters Committee. (2010). *Inquiry into the Provisions of the electoral act 2002 (Vic) relating to misleading or deceptive political advertising* (Parliamentary Paper No 282). Melbourne: Parliament of Victoria.

Facebook Ad Library Report Australia. (2021, December 10). Retrieved December 12, 2021, from Facebook: https://www.facebook.com/ads/library/report/?source=archive-landing-page&country=AU

Fowler, E. F., Franz, M. M., Martin, G. J., Peskowitz, Z., & Ridout, T. N. (2021). Political advertising online and offline. *The American Political Science Review*, *115*(1), 130–149.

Franz, M. M., Freedman, P., Goldstein, K., & Ridout, T. N. (2008). Understanding the effect of political advertising on voter turnout: A response to krasno and green. *The Journal of Politics*, *70*(1), 262–268.

Garramone, G. M. (1984). Effects of negative political advertising: The roles of sponsor and rebuttal. *Journal of Broadcasting & Electronic Media*, *29*(2), 147–159.

Google Transparency Report Australia. (2021, December 12). Retrieved December 12, 2021, from Google: https://transparencyreport.google.com/political-ads/region/AU

Gunsch, M. A., Brownlow, S., Haynes, S. E., & Mabe, Z. (2000). Differential forms linguistic content of various of political advertising. *Journal of Broadcasting & Electronic Media*, *44*(1), 27–42.

Haines, H. M. (2021, October 25). *Commonwealth electoral amendment (stop the lies) bill 2021*. Retrieved from Parliament of Australia: https://parlinfo.aph.gov.au/parlInfo/genpdf/chamber/hansardr/25166/0067/hansard_frag.pdf;fileType=application%2Fpdf

Henneberg, S. C., & O'shaughnessy, N. J. (2007). Theory and concept development in political marketing. *Journal of Political Marketing*, *6*(2-3), 5–31.

Holtz-Bacha, C., & Kaid, L. L. (2006). Political advertising in international comparison. In L. L. Kaid, & C. Holtz-Bacha (Eds.), The Sage handbook of political advertising (pp. 3-15). Sage Publications.

Hughes, A. (2018). *Market driven political advertising: Social, digital, and mobile marketing*. Palgrave Macmillan.

Hughes, A. (2019, May 6). How digital advertising is shaping this election campaign. *Adnews*. Retrieved November 5, 2021, from https://www.adnews.com.au/opinion/how-digital-advertising-is-shaping-this-election-campaign

Jaspan, C. (2021, July 12). *Australian government vaccine campaign attracts wide criticism on launch.* September 4, 2021 tarihinde Mumberalla: https://mumbrella.com.au/australian-government-vaccine-campaign-attracts-wide-criticism-on-launch-692346

Johnson-Cartee, K. S., & Copeland, G. A. (2010). *Negative political advertising: Coming of age.* Roudledge.

Johnston, A., & Kaid, L. L. (2002). Image ads and issue ads in us presidential advertising: Using videostyle to explore stylistic differences in televised political ads from 1952 to 2000. *Journal of Communication*, 281–300.

Joint Select Committee on Electoral Reform. (1984). *Second report.* Canberra: Parliament of the Commonwealth of Australia.

Joint Standing Committee on Electoral Matters. (2020). *Report on the conduct of the 2019 federal election and matters related thereto.* Canberra: Parliament of the Commonwealth of Australia. Retrieved November 16, 2021, from https://parlinfo.aph.gov.au/parlInfo/download/committees/reportjnt/024439/toc_pdf/Reportontheconductofthe2019federalelectionandmattersrelatedthereto.pdf;fileType=application%2Fpdf

Joseph, S. (2001). *Political advertising and the constitution. In Big Makeover: A New Australian Constitution: Labor Essays 2002.* Pluto Press.

Kaid, L. K., & Holtz-Bacha, C. (1995). *Political advertising in western democracies: Parties and candidates on television.* Sage Publishing.

Kaid, L. L. (2004). Political advertising. In L. L. Kaid (Ed.), *Handbook of Political Communication Research* (pp. 155–202). Lawrence Erlbaum Associates, Inc., Publishers.

Kaid, L. L., & Johnston, A. (2001). *Videostyle in presidential campaigns: Style and content of televised political advertising.* Praeger Publishers.

Karp, P. (2020, December 20). Morrison government spent $128m on advertising in 2019-20, figures reveal. *The Guardian.* Retrieved September 23, 2021, from https://www.theguardian.com/australia-news/2020/dec/25/morrison-government-spent-128m-on-advertising-in-2019-20-figures-reveal

Kerr, G., Johnston, K., & Beatson, A. (2008). A framework of aorporate social responsibility for advertising accountability: The case of australian government advertising campaign. *Journal of Marketing Communications*, *14*(2), 155–169.

Krasno, J. S., & Green, D. P. (2008). Do televised presidential ads increase voter turnout? Evidence from a natural experiment. *The Journal of Politics*, *70*(1), 245–261.

Lau, R. R., Lee, S., Heldman, C., & Paul, B. (1999). The effects of negative political advertisements: A meta-analytic assessment. *The American Political Science Review*, *93*(4), 851–875.

Lau, R. R., Sigelman, L., & Rovner, I. B. (2007). The effects of negative political campaigns: A meta-analytic reassessment. *The Journal of Politics*, *69*(4), 1176–1209.

Lloyd, J. (2005). Square peg, round hole? Can marketing-based concepts such as "product" and the "marketing mix" have a useful role in the political arena? In *Current issues in political marketing* (pp. 24–46). Haworth Press.

Lock, A., & Harris, P. (1996). Political marketing: Vive la diifférence! *European Journal of Marketing*, *30*(10/11), 14–24.

Macklin, M. (1984). Dissenting report. In Second Report (pp. 44-50). Canberra: Parliament of the Commonwealth of Australia.

Maier, J., & Nai, A. (2020). Roaring candidates in the spotlight: Campaign negativity, emotions, and media coverage in 107 national elections. *The International Journal of Press/Politics*, *25*(4), 576–606.

Media Diversity in Australia. (2021, March 31). Retrieved September 17, 2021, from Parliament of Austalia: https://www.aph.gov.au/Parliamentary_Business/Committees/Senate/Environment_and_Communications/Mediadiversity

Merritt, S. (1984). Negative political advertising: Some empirical findings. *Journal of Advertising*, *13*(3), 27–38.

Miskin, S., & Grant, R. (2004, November 24). *Political advertising in Australia* (Research Brief No. 5). Retrieved November 12, 2021, from Parliament of Australia Parliamentary Library: https://apo.org.au/sites/default/files/resource-files/2004-11/apo-nid504.pdf

Ndimele, R. (2015). Language use in political advertising: A rhetorical discourse on "see who wants to be president of Nigeria". *Global Journal of Arts, Humanities and Social Sciences*, *3*(8), 19–31.

Newman, B. I. (1994). *The marketing of the president: Political marketing as campaign*. Sage Publications.

Newman, B. I. (2002). The role of marketing in politics. *Journal of Political Marketing*, *1*(1), 1–5.

Noelle-Neumann, E. (1974). The spirial of slience: A theory of public opinion. *Journal of Communication*, *24*(2), 43–51.

Oates, S., Kaid, L. L., & Berry, M. (2010). *Terrorism, elections, and democracy: Political campaigns in United States, Great Britain, and Russia*. Palgrave Macmillan.

Papandrea, F., & Tiffen, R. (2016). Media ownership and concentration in Australia. In E. M. Noam (Ed.), *Who owns the world's media?* (pp. 703–739). Oxford University Press.

Pender, K. (n.d.). *Regulating truth and lies in political advertising: Implied freedom considerations*. Retrieved November 15, 2021, from Australian National University: https://law.anu.edu.au/sites/all/files/pender_-_tpal_paper.pdf

Penney, J. (2011). KEVIN07: Cool politics, consumer citizenship, and the specter of "Americanization" in Australia. *Communication, Culture & Critique*, *4*(1), 78–96.

Pinkleton, B. (1997). The effects of negative comparative political advertising on candidate evaluations and advertising evaluations: An exploration. *Journal of Advertising*, *26*(1), 19–29.

Pinkleton, B. E., Um, N.-H., & Austin, E. W. (2013). An exploration of the effects of negative political advertising on political decision making. *Journal of Advertising*, *31*(1), 13–25.

Plasser, F., & Plasser, G. (2002). *Global political campaigning: A worldwide analysis of campaign professionals and their practices*. Praeger.

Sheth, J. N., Sisodia, R. S., & Sharma, A. (2000). The antecedents and consequences of customer-centric marketing. *Journal of the Academy of Marketing Science, 28*(1), 55–66.

Sinclair, J., & Younane, S. (2007). Government advertising as public communication: Cases, issues and effects. In S. Young (Ed.), *Government Communication in Australia* (pp. 204–226). Cambridge University Press.

Solijonov, A. (2016). *Voter turnout trends around the world.* International Institute for Democracy and Electoral Assistance.

Valentino, N. A., Hutchings, V. L., & Williams, D. (2004). The impact of political advertising on knowledge, internet information seeking, and candidate preference. *Journal of Communication, 54*(2), 37–354.

Vargo, S. L., & Lusch, R. F. (2004). Evolving to a new dominant logic for marketing. *Journal of Marketing, 68*(1), 1–17.

Waller, D. S. (2002). Advertising agency-client attitudes towards ethical issues in political advertising. *Journal of Business Ethics,* (36), 347–354.

Waller, D. S., & Polonsky, M. J. (1996). 'Everybody hide, an election is coming!' An examination why some Australian advertising agencies refuse political accounts. *International Journal of Advertising, 15*(1), 61–74.

Wattenberg, M. P., & Brians, C. L. (1999). Negative campaign advertising: Demobilizer or mobilizer? *The American Political Science Review, 93*(4), 891–899.

We need truth in political advertising laws. (2020). Retrieved November 2, 2021, from The Australia Institute: https://nb.australiainstitute.org.au/truth_in_political_ads

Weber, C. (2013). Emotions, campaigns, and political participation. *Political Research Quarterly, 66*(2), 414–428.

Weissglass, K. (2005). *Image manipulation in political advertisements: How color and music influence viewer attitudes and emotions.* Haverford College.

West, B. A., & Murphy, F. (2010). *A Brief history of Australia.* Facts on File Publication.

Yoon, K., Pinkleton, B. E., & Ko, W. (2007). Effects of negative political advertising on voting intention: An exploration of the roles of involvement and source credibility in the development of voter cynicism. *Journal of Marketing Communications, 11*(2), 95–112.

Younane, S. (2006). Protecting 'our way of life': Constructions of national identity in government anti-terrorism advertising. *Australasian Political Studies Association Conference,* 1-19.

Young, S. (2003). A century of political communication in Australia, 1901–2001. *Journal of Australian Studies, 27*(78), 97–110.

Young, S. (2004). *The persuaders: Inside the hidden machine of political advertising.* Pluto Press.

Young, S. (2006). Not bitting the hand that feeds? Media reporting of government advertising in Australia. *Journalism Studies, 7*(4), 554–574.

Young, S. (2007a). A history of government advertising in Australia. In S. Young (Ed.), *Government communication in Australia* (pp. 181–203). Cambridge University Press.

Young, S. (2007b). The regulation of government advertising in australia: The politicisation of a public policy issue. *Australian Journal of Public Administration, 66*(4), 438–452.

Young, S. (2007c). Following the money trail: Government advertising, the missing millions and the unknown effects. *Public Policy, 2*(2), 104–118.

Young, S. (2007d). Policy-making in a 'Cold Climate' of ruling party benefit: Party government and the regulation of government advertising in Australia. *Australian Journal of Political Science, 47*(3), 489–502.

Young, S. (2013, August 20). *Here come the negative ads.* Retrieved November 6, 2021, from The University of Melbourne Election Watch Australia: http://past.electionwatch.edu.au/australia-2013/campaign-ads/here-come-negative-ads

Young, S., & Tham, J.-C. (2006). *Political finance in Australia: A skewed and secret system.* Canberra: Democratic Audit of Australia, Australian National University. Retrieved December 3, 2021, from https://apo.org.au/sites/default/files/resource-files/2006-11/apo-nid3933.pdf

ADDITIONAL READING

Hughes, A. (2018). *Market driven political advertising: social, digital, and mobile marketing.* Palgrave Macmillan.

Kaid, L. L. (2004). *Handbook of political communication research.* Lawrence Erlbaum Associates, Inc., Publishers.

Lees-Marshment, J., Rudd, C., & Stromback, J. (2009). *Global Political Marketing.* Routledge.

Cwalina, W., Falkowski, A., & Newman, B. I. (2011). *Political Marketing: Theoretical and Strategic Foundations.* Routledge.

Sinclair, J., & Younane, S. (2007). Government Advertising as Public Communication: Cases, Issues and Effects. In S. Young (Ed.), *Government Communication in Australia* (pp. 204–226). Cambridge University Press.

KEY TERMS AND DEFINITIONS

Flip-Flop Advertisement: An advertisement style which is used to show politicians in opposing parties inconsistent and contradicting themselves.

Government Advertising: Publicly funded ads that are used by governments to inform the public about new initiatives, policies, or programs. They help to advise people on how they might benefit or be affected by or what they need to do to comply with new requirements.

Negative Advertising: A political advertising form that serves as an attack on an opponent's personality, record, or opinion.

Third-Party Groups: A definition that refers to actors operating in the political arena, except political parties and candidates. These actors can be non-governmental organizations, business and labor unions, individuals, and companies.

ENDNOTES

[1]   For more controversial cases in government campaign advertising issue, see (Sinclair & Younane, 2007).

[2]   For detailed information on parliamentary considerations of truth in political advertising, see (Electoral Matters Committee, 2010).

[3]   Repeats were not taken into account and 27 spots, such as daylight saving time reminder, were categorized as irrelevant.

Compilation of References

A Small and Medium Enterprises Development Perspective of the Media Industry in Dubai. (2010). Retrieved October 21, 2021, from https://sme.ae/SME_File/Files/DUBAI_SME_Media_Industry_Report.pdf

Abboud, D. G. (2020). Exploring evolving trends of gender representation in digital advertising in Egypt. *Journal of Architecture, Arts and Humanities*, 5(21), 594–610.

Abdalla, N. (2012). Social protests in Egypt before and after the 25 January revolution: Perspectives on the evolution of their forms and features. In L. A. Secat & H. Gallego (Eds.), *IEMed Mediterranean Yearbook: Med.2012* (pp. 86–92). European Institute of the Mediterranean.

Abdelmoula, E. (2015). *Al Jazeera and democratization: The rise of the Arab public sphere*. Routledge. doi:10.4324/9781315720272

About twofour54 Abu Dhabi. (2021, February 3). Retrieved August 30, 2021, from Twofour54. https://www.twofour54.com/en/who-we-are/about-twofour54/

About Us. (n.d.). *Dubai Studio City*. Retrieved September 21, 2021, from https://dubaistudiocity.ae/discover/about-us

ACNUR. (2002). *Informe Sobre Derechos Humanos en Colombia*. https://www.acnur.org/t3/uploads/media/COI_53.pdf

Adobe. (2018). *Adobe experience manager 6.4: defining the next wave of content driven experiences*. Retrieved from https://blogs.adobe.com/digitaleurope/digital-marketing/adobe-experience-manager-6-4-defining-the-next-wave-of-content-driven-experiences/

Adorno, T. W., & Horkheimer, M. (2014). *Aydınlanmanın diyalektiği*. Kabalcı Yayıncılık.

Adorno, T., Frenkel-Brunswick, E. L., & Sanford, N. H. (1950). *The authoritarian personality*. Harper and Brothers.

Advanced Television. (2020, December 7). *Report: GCC video industry sees revenues of $1.6bn in 2020.* etrieved September 20, 2021, from https://advanced-television.com/2020/12/07/report-gcc-video-industry-sees-revenues-of-1-6bn-in-2020/

Advertising Council Australia. (n.d.). Retrieved January 23, 2022, from Advertising Council Australia: https://advertisingcouncil.org.au/about-us/why-we-exist/

Advertising Guide. (2018). *National Media Council*. Retrieved August 29, 2021, from https://u.ae/-/media/Media/Media-In-UAE/NMC-AD-Guide-EN-PDF-presntation.ashx

Advertising in China – The Most Effective Strategies. (2021). Accessed from https://marketingtochina.com/advertising-china/

Afolayan, F. (2004). *Culture and customs of South Africa*. Greenwood Press.

African National Congress. (2019). *MyANC Youtube channel*. Retrieved 04/28/22 from: https://www.youtube.com/c/MyANC/videos

Ahmadi, S. (2016). *On Professionalism and Specialized Training in Iranian Advertising Industry*. https://www.academia.edu/34280136/On_Professionalism_and_Specialized_Training_in_Iranian_advertising_industry_pdf

Ahmadi, H. (2004). Iranian national identity: Foundations, challenges and requirements. *Cultural Research Journal*, *1*(6), 5–55.

Ajman Media City Free Zone. (n.d.). Retrieved September 20, 2021, from https://www.amcfz.ae/en/

Akar, E., & Topcu, B. (2011). An examination of the factors influencing consumer's attitudes toward social media marketing. *Journal of Internet Commerce*, *10*(1), 35–67. doi:10.1080/15332861.2011.558456

Akgun, B., & Calis, S. (2003). Reluctant giant: The rise of Japan and its role in the post-cold war era, *Perceptions. Journal of International Affairs*, *8*(1), 1–13.

Akkemik, K. A. (2019). *Japonya'nin iktisadi ve sosyal tarihi Cilt:1 Savas oncesi donem (-1945)* [The economic and social history of Japan Vol: I Pre-War period (-1945)]. Bilgi Universitesi Yayinlari.

Aktuğlu, I., & Eğinli, A. (2010). Küresel Reklam Stratejilerinin Belirlenmesinde Kültürel Farklılıkların Önemi. *Selçuk İletişim Dergisi*, *6*(3), 167–183.

Akyol, Z. (2014). Albert Lasker: Reklamcılıkta "Modern" Zamanlar. In M. Elden & U. Bakır (Eds.), *Reklam Ustaları 1, (1-23)*. Detay.

Al Arabiya English. (2021, November 18). *UAE named world's safest country to walk at night: Gallup report*. Retrieved September 25, 2021, from https://english.alarabiya.net/News/gulf/2021/11/18/UAE-named-world-s-safest-country-to-walk-at-night-Gallup-report

Alım, E., & Aksu, F. (2019). Eurasian Economic Union as a Power Centre Under the Leadership of Russia. *International Journal of Political Science & Urban Studies*, *7*, 1-22. doi:10.14782/ipsus.594377

Alkier, R., Stilin, Ž., & Milojica, V. (2015). Strategic and marketing aspects of tourism offer development of the republic of Croatia. In *4th Biennial International Scientific Congress ICONBEST - Economic Analysis of Global Trends in Tourism, Finance, Education & Management* (pp. 196-207). Retrieved 2021, August 06 from https://www.researchgate.net/publication/ 304023578 _ STRATEGIC _AND_ MARKETING _ ASPECTS _OF_ TOURISM _ OFFER _ DEVELOPMENT _OF_THE_ REPUBLIC _OF_ CROATIA

Allen, M., & Burrell, N. (2002). The negativity effect in political advertising: A meta-analysis. In J. P. Dillard & M. Pfau (Eds.), *The persuasion handbook: Developments in theory and practice* (pp. 83–96). Sage Publications.

Allwood, J. (1985). Intercultural Communication. *Papers in Anthropological Linguistics*, *12*, 1-25.

Alvino, C. (2021). *Estadísticas de la situación Digital de Colombia*. https://branch.com.co/marketing-digital/estadisticas-de-la-situacion-digital-de-colombia-en-el-2020-2021/

AMEO. (2021). The Australian entertainment & media outlook: 2021-2025. London: PricewaterhouseCoopers (pwc).

American Marketing Association. (n.d.). *Discover the differences between marketing and advertising and how each relates to modern business*. Retrieved 22 October 2021, from https://www.ama.org/pages/marketing-vs-advertising/

Amouzadeh, M., & Manoochehr, T. (2008). Sociolinguistic aspects of Persian advertising in post-revolutionary Iran. In M. Semati (Ed.), *Media, culture, and society: Living with globalization and the Islamic state* (pp. 130–151). Routledge.

Amy, W. (2020). *Ongoing Home Media Consumption and The Coronavirus Worldwide 2020.* Retrieved from https://www.statista.com/statistics/1170493/ongoing-in-home-media-consumption-growth-coronavirus-worldwide-by-country/

Analitik. (2021). *Por pandemia pueden desaparecer 11.000 tiendas en Colombia.* https://www.valoraanalitik.com/2021/08/18/por-pandemia-pueden-desaparecer-11-000-tiendas-de-barrio-en-colombia/

Analysys Qianfan. (2019, December). *Mobile App Top 1000.* Analysys Qianfan's official post on Zhihu. Accessed from https://zhuanlan.zhihu.com/p/102983491

Analysys Qianfan. (2020, March). *Mobile App Top 1000.* Analysys Qianfan. Accessed from https://qianfan.analysys.cn/refine/view/rankApp/rankApp.html

ANAO. (2019). *Audit-General Report No: 7 of 2019-2020: Government advertising: June 2015 to April 2019.* Retrieved November 2, 2021, from https://www.anao.gov.au/work/performance-audit/government-advertising-june-2015-to-april-2019

Andressen, C. (2002). *A short history of Japan: From samurai to sony.* Allen & Unwin.

AngieRazzi. (2015). YouTube, Lady Gaga Shiseido (campaign) commercial full official HD, https://www.youtube.com/watch?v=irD-NJ27Y7k

Ansolabehere, S., & Iyengar, S. (1994). Riding the wave and claiming ownership over issues: The joint effects of advertising and news coverage in campaigns. *Public Opinion Quarterly, 58*(3), 335–357.

Ansolabehere, S., & Iyengar, S. (1995). *Going negative: How political advertisements shrink and polarize the electorate.* Free Press.

Anupa Kurian-Murshed. (2018, November 7). *Big budgets, exotic locales, infrastructure: Dubai's movie business.* UAE – Gulf News. Retrieved October 25, 2021 from https://gulfnews.com/uae/big-budgets-exotic-locales-infrastructure-dubais-movie-business-1.2222348

Arif, M. (2012). *The Iranian Revolution: The Role and Contribution of Ayatollah Ruhollah Khomeini.* https://www.researchgate.net/publication/283580147_THE_IRANIAN_REVOLUTION_The_Role_and_Contribution_of_Ayatollah_Ruhollah_Khomeini

Armiela, A. A. (2018). Celebrity endorsement in Japan tourism based on consumer celebrity worship. *Ultima Management, 10*(2), 65–80. doi:10.31937/manajemen.v10i2.982

Armstrong, J. S. (2011). How should firms select advertising agencies? *Journal of Marketing, 60,* 131–133.

Ashley, C., & Oliver, J. D. (2010). Creative leaders. *Journal of Advertising, 39*(1), 115–130. doi:10.2753/JOA0091-3367390108

Asset Management Group. (2009). *Campaign advertising by Australian government departments and agencies: half year report 1 July to 31 December 208.* Canberra: Australian Government Department of Finance and Dergulation. Retrieved September 5, 2021, from https://apo.org.au/sites/default/files/resource-files/2009-03/apo-nid1233.pdf

Athique, A. (2019). Soft power, culture and modernity: Responses to Bollywood films in Thailand and the Philippines. *The International Communication Gazette, 81*(5), 470–489. doi:10.1177/1748048518802234

Atkin, C., & Block, M. (1983). Effectiveness of celebrity endorsers. *Journal of Advertising Research, 23*(March), 57–61.

Aulich, J. (2012). Advertising and the public in Britain during the First World War. In D. Welch & J. Fox (Eds.), *Justifying war: Propaganda, politics and the modern age* (pp. 109–128). Palgrave Macmillan. doi:10.1057/9780230393295_6

Australian Electoral Commission. (2020). Election funding and disclosure report: Federal election 2019. Author.

Australian Government. (2020, October). *Australian government guidelines on information and advertising campaigns by non-corporate commonwealth entities.* Retrieved from Australian Government: https://www.finance.gov.au/sites/default/files/2020-10/Australian-Government-Guidelines-Information-Advertising-Campaigns-October2020.pdf

Australian Labor Party. (2019). *Review of labor's 2019 federalelection campaign.* Australian Labor Party.

Austrotherm. (2021). *Dünya'da ve Türkiye'de Su Kaynakları Azalıyor!* https://www.austrotherm.com.tr/bilgi-servisi/haberler/duenyada-ve-tuerkiyede-su-kaynaklari-azaliyor

Axinn, C. N., & Krishna, V. (1993). How informative are the prime time television commercials in India? *Media Asia, 20*(3), 168–172. doi:10.1080/01296612.1993.11727101

Aydın, A. (2015). Küresel Müdacele Politikaları: Orta Asya'da Rusya, ABD ve Çin [Politics of Global Campaign: Russia, USA and China in Central Asia]. *Suleyman Demirel University The Journal of Visionary, 6*(13), 1-11.

Baidya, M., Maity, B., & Ghose, K. (2012). Measuring dynamic effects of advertising: A case study in India. *Journal of Indian Business Research, 4*(3), 158–169. doi:10.1108/17554191211252671

Bailenson, J., Iyengar, S., Yee, N., & Collins, N. (2008). Faical similarity between voters and candidates couses influence. *Public Opinion Quarterly, 72*(5), 935–961. doi:10.1093/poq/nfn064

Bait, M., Baldigara, T., & Komšić, J. (2019). Web advertising messages in Croatian tourism: Exploring qualitative and quantitative perspectives. *TOSEE - Tourism in Southern and Eastern Europe, 5*, 31-45. doi:10.20867/tosee.26

Bakr, N. (2012). The Egyptian revolution. In S. C. Calleya & M. Wohlfeld (Eds.), *Change and opportunities in the emerging Mediterranean* (pp. 57–81). Mediterranean Academy of Diplomatic Studies.

Ballentine, K., & Heiko, N. (2003). *Beyond Greed and Grievance: Policy Lessons from Studies in the Political Economy of Armed Conflict.* Routledge. doi:10.1515/9781685853402

Baloğlu, S., & McCleary, K. W. (1999). A Model of Destination Image Formation. *Annals of Tourism Research, 26*(4), 868–897. doi:10.1016/S0160-7383(99)00030-4

Bansal, D. (2017). Globalization of consumer culture: An empirical survey of consumers in Delhi. *Business Analyst, 38*(1), 213–239.

Bart, L. (1960). Consider Yourself [Song]. On *Soundtrack of Oliver!*.

BBC News. (2017). *Iran Profile – Media.* https://www.bbc.com/news/world-middle-east-14542234

BBC News. (2020, September 16). *Japan country profile.* https://www.bbc.com/news/world-asia-pacific-14918801

BBC News. (2021, 4 October). *Japan's parliament elects former diplomat Fumio Kishida as new prime minister.* https://www.bbc.com/news/world-asia-58784635

BBC. (2017). *United Kingdom profile - Overview.* Retrieved March 1, 2022 from https://www.bbc.com/news/world-europe-18027954

BBC. (2020). *United Kingdom country profile.* Retrieved from https://www.bbc.com/news/world-europe-18023389

BBC. (2021). *Facebook to hire 10,000 in EU to work on metaverse.* Retrieved 22 October 2021, from https://www.bbc.com/news/world-europe-58949867

Beard, F. K. (2005). One hundred years of humor in American advertising. *Journal of Macromarketing, 25*(1), 54–65. doi:10.1177/0276146705274965

Belch, E. G., Belch, M. A., Kerr, G., Powell, I., & Waller, D. (2020). *Advertising: An Integrated Marketing Communication Perspective*. McGraw-Hill Education.

Belch, G. E., Belch, M. A., Kerr, G., Powell, I., & Waller, D. (2020). *Advertising: An integrated marketing communication perspective*. McGraw-Hill Education.

Bellulo, V., & Križman, D. (2000). Utjecaj promjena u dohocima glavnih emitivnih zemalja na turistički promet u Hrvatskoj. *Ekonomski Pregled, 51*(7-8), 681–700.

Belmonte, A., & Rochlitz, M. (2019). The political economy of collective memories: Evidence from Russian politics. *Journal of Economic Behavior & Organization, 168*, 229–250. doi:10.1016/j.jebo.2019.10.009

Bengtsson, M. (2016). How to plan and perform a qualitative study using content analysis. *NursingPlus Open, 2*, 8–14. doi:10.1016/j.npls.2016.01.001

Benoit, W. L. (2001). The functional approach to presidential television spots: Acclaiming, attacking, defending 1952-2000. *Communication Studies, 52*(2).

Benoit, W. L., & Hansen, G. J. (2002). Issue adaptation of presidential television spots and debates to primary and general audiences. *Communication Research Reports, 19*(2), 138–145.

Benoit, W. L., Leshner, G. M., & Chattopadhyay, S. (2007). A meta-analysis of political advertising. *Human Communication, 10*(4), 507–522.

Berger, A. A. (1991). *Media analysis techniniques*. Sage Publications.

Berger, A. A. (1991). *Media analysis techniques*. SAGE.

Berger, J. (1990). *Ways of Seeing*. Penguin Books.

Bernard, L. (2006). *Ortadoğu* (S. Y. Kölay, Trans.). Arkadaş.

Bernstein, D. (1986). The television commercial: An essay. In B. Henry (Ed.), *British television advertising: The first 30 years* (pp. 251–286). Century Benham.

Beteille, A. (2020). *Society and politics in India: Essays in a comparative perspective*. Routledge. doi:10.4324/9781003136262

Bettina. (2020). *Reklámok a szocializmus idejéből! Neked melyik volt a kedvenced?* Retrieved 29 October 2021, from https://www.magyarorszagom.hu/reklamok-a-szocializmus-idejebol-nekem-melyik-volt-a-kedvenced.html

Bhattacharyya, S., & Bose, I. (2020). S-commerce: Influence of Facebook likes on purchases and recommendations on a linked e-commerce site. *Decision Support Systems, 138*, 113383. doi:10.1016/j.dss.2020.113383

Bhorat, H., Naido, K., Oosthuizen, M., & Pillay, K. (2016). South Africa demographic, employment, and wage trends. In H. Bhorat & F. Tarp (Eds.), *Africa's lions, growth traps and opportunities for six african economies* (pp. 229–270). Brookings Institution Press.

Bilić, P., & Primorac, J. (2018). The digital advertising gap and the online news industry in Croatia. *Medijske Studije, 9*(18), 62–80. doi:10.20901/ms.9.18.4

Binet, L., & Field, P. (2012). *The Long and the Short of It: Balancing Short and Long-Term Marketing Strategies*. IPA.

Birkas, P. (2018). *A magyarok közel harmada mobilfüggő*. Retrieved 28 October 2021, from https://24.hu/tech/2018/02/06/a-magyarok-kozel-harmada-tartja-magat-mobilfuggonek/

Blagden, D. (2017). Britain and the world after Brexit. *International Politics, 51*(1), 1–25. doi:10.105741311-017-0015-2

Blunt, E. (2010). *The caste system of northern India*. Isha Books.

Bocock, R. (2009). *Tuketim* [Consumption]. Dost Kitabevi Yayinlari.

Bonsu, S. K. (2009). Colonial images in global times: Consumer interpretations of Africa and Africans in advertising. *Consumption Markets & Culture, 12*(1), 1–25. doi:10.1080/10253860802560789

Booker, A. (2021). *What the World Needs to Learn From Chinese Content Commerce: Part Four*. Accessed from https://jingdaily.com/what-the-world-needs-to-learn-from-chinese-content-commerce-part-four/

Boorstin, D. (1971). *The image: A guide to pseudo-events in America*. Atheneum.

BorgenProject. (n.d.). https://borgenproject.org/womens-rights-in-russia/

Botman, S. (1998). The liberal age, 1923-1952. In M. W. Daly (Ed.), *The Cambridge History of Egypt: Modern Egypt, from 1517 to the end of the twentieth century* (Vol. 2, pp. 285–308). Cambridge University Press. doi:10.1017/CHOL9780521472111.013

Bottomore, T., & Nisbet, R. (1978). Introduction. In T. Bottomore & R. Nisbet (Eds.), A history of sociological analysis (pp. 7-16). Basic Books.

Boudet, J., Gordon, J., Gregg, B., Perrey, J., & Robinson, K. (2021). *How marketing leaders can both manage the coronavirus crisis and plan for the future*. McKinsey. Accessed from https://www.mckinsey.com/business-functions/marketing-and-sales/our-insights/how-marketing-leaders-can-both-manage-the-coronavirus-crisis-and-plan-for-the-future

Bowman, J. (2020). *3 Reasons Why Nike Can Overcome the Coronavirus Crisis*. Nasdaq. Accessed from https://www.nasdaq.com/articles/3-reasons-why-nike-can-overcome-the-coronaviruscrisis-2020-03-29

Brader, T. (2006). *Campaigning for hearts and minds: How emotional appeals in political ads work*. University of Chicago Press.

Bradley, M. (2007). *Iran Open Hearts in a Closed Land*. Authentic.

Braet, A. C. (1992). Ethos, pathos and logos in Aristotle's rhetoric: A re-examination. *Argumentation, 6*(3), 307–320. doi:10.1007/BF00154696

Bratt, M. (2019, June 27). *Mobile advertising soars, but South Africa still a bit sore*. Retrieved 05/07/22 from: https://themediaonline.co.za/2019/06/mobile-advertising-soars-but-south-africa-still-a-bit-sore/

Braund, V. (1978). *Themes in political advertising: australian federal election campaigns 1949-1972*. University of Sydney Department of Government.

Brder, T. (2005). Striking a responsive chord: How political ads motivate and persuade voters by appealing to emotions. *American Journal of Political Science, 49*(2), 388–405.

Briggs, A. (2022). United Kingdom. In *Encyclopaedia Britannica*. Retrieved March 1, 2022, from https://www.britannica.com/place/United-Kingdom

Briney, A. (2019). *Geography of the United States of America*. https://www.thoughtco.com/geography-the-united-states-of-america-1435745#:~:text=The%20U.S.%20borders%20both%20the,called%20the%20Great%20Plains%20region

Britannica. (2022). *Traditional regions of the United States*. https://www.britannica.com/place/United-States/The-South

British Library. (n.d.). https://www.bl.uk/russian-revolution/articles/women-and-the-russian-revolution

Britt, S. H. (2000). Are so-called successful advertising campaigns really successful? *Journal of Advertising Research, 40*(6), 25–31. doi:10.2501/JAR-40-6-25-31

BroadcastPro ME. (2015, June 9). *Image Nation and Discovery to launch new Arabic channel.* Retrieved October 25, 2021 from https://www.broadcastprome.com/news/image-nation-and-discovery-to-launch-new-arabic-channel/

BroadcastPro ME. (2021, November 25). *Emirati action film 'Al Kameen' releases today in Vox Cinemas.* Retrieved October 25, 2021 from https://www.broadcastprome.com/news/emirati-action-film-al-kameen-releases-today-in-vox-cinemas/

Brook, T. V. (2013). *Propaganda that works: Christmas decorations.* https://www.usatoday.com/story/nation/2013/08/13/pentagon-propaganda-information-operations/2646243/

Browne, B. (2020). *Possible, practical, and popular: opprtunities for truth in poliitical advertising laws in australia.* Retrieved November 2, 2021, from The Australia Institute: https://australiainstitute.org.au/wp-content/uploads/2021/10/211025-Truth-in-Political-Advertising-WEB.pdf

Buchkingham-Jones, S. (2021, July 26). *Australian advertising market to grow 9.1% in 2021 to $15.6bn.* Zenith

Bulut, R. (2018). Russian Federation Economy, Opportunities Offered to Foreign and Turkish Entrepreneurs. *Journal of Social Research and Behavioral Sciences, Vol, 4*(6), 345–357.

Burkett, P., & Hart-Landsberg, M. (2003). The economic crisis in Japan: Mainstream perspective and an alternative view. *Critical Asian Studies, 35*(3), 339–372. doi:10.1080/1467271032000109881

Business Setup in Sharjah, UAE | Company Registration in Free Zone - Sharjah Media City (Shams). (2021). *Shams. Ae.* Retrieved September 21, 2021, from https://www.shams.ae/

Business, A. (2020, December 15). *15 years on, how Dubai Studio City has put the emirate on global movie map.* Arabian Business. Retrieved September 28, 2021, from https://www.arabianbusiness.com/industries/media/455930-15-years-on-how-dubai-studio-city-has-put-the-emirate-on-global-movie-map

Businesstech. (2019, February 1). *South Africans spend over 8 hours a day online – and a third of that time is spent on social media.* Retrieved 05/08/22 from: https://businesstech.co.za/news/internet/296716/south-africans-spend-over-8-hours-a-day-online-and-a-third-of-that-time-is-spent-on-social-media/

Buss, T. F., & Hofstetter, C. R. (1976). An analysis of the logic of televised campaign advertisements: The 1972 presidential campaign. *Communication Research, 3*(4), 367–392.

CAA. (2004). *Officer Orations.* China Advertising Association. Accessed from www.iaacongress-china.com/en/about1.htm

Çağlak, E. (2016). Bu toprakların iletişim tarihi. Nobel Yayınları.

Caillat, Z., & Mueller, B. (1996). The influence of culture on American and British advertising: An exploratory comparison of beer advertising. *Journal of Advertising Research, 36*(3), 79–89.

Cameron, S., & McAllister, L. (2019a). *Trends in australian political opinion: Results from the australian election study 1987–2019.* Canberra: Australian Natinal University. Retrieved December 23, 2021, from https://australianelectionstudy.org/wp-content/uploads/Trends-in-Australian-Political-Opinion-1987-2019.pdf

Cameron, S., & McAllister, L. (2019b). *The 2019 Australian federal election: Results from the Australian election study.* Canberra: Australian National University. Retrieved December 12, 2021, from https://australianelectionstudy.org/wp-content/uploads/The-2019-Australian-Federal-Election-Results-from-the-Australian-Election-Study.pdf

Campbell, S., Greenwood, M., Prior, S., Shearer, T., Walkem, K., Young, S., Bywaters, D., & Walker, K. (2020). Purposive sampling: Complex or simple? Research case examples. *Journal of Research in Nursing, 25*(8), 652–661. doi:10.1177/1744987120927206 PMID:34394687

Cao, X., Qu, Z., Liu, Y., & Hu, J. (2021). How the destination short video affects the customers' attitude: The role of narrative transportation. *Journal of Retailing and Consumer Services, 62*, 102672. Advance online publication. doi:10.1016/j.jretconser.2021.102672

Cappo, J. (2003). *The Future of Advertising: New Media, New Clients, New Consumers in The Post-Television Age.* McGraw-Hill.

Carey, J. W. (1988). *Communication as Culture: Essays on Media and Society.* Routledge.

Carr, S. (2021). *How Many Ads Do We See A Day In 2021?* https://ppcprotect.com/blog/strategy/how-many-ads-do-we-see-a-day/

Cashmore, E. (2006). *Celebrity/ culture.* Taylor & Francis e-library.

Castilo, M. (2010). *Colombian military's new weapon against rebels: Christmas trees.* CNN. http://edition.cnn.com/2010/WORLD/americas/12/20/colombia.operation.christmas/index.html

Cele, S., & Vecchiatto, P. (2021). *South African voter turnout slumps in municipal elections.* Retrieved 05/01/22 from: https://www.bloomberg.com/news/articles/2021-11-01/voter-turnout-slumps-in-south-african-municipal-elections

Census. (2021). *About Language Use in the U.S. Population.* https://www.census.gov/topics/population/language-use/about.html

Chadraba, P. G., & Springer, R. (2008). Business Strategies For Economies in Transition Book of Readings on CEE Countries. Cambridge Scholars Publishing.

Chakrabarty, B. (2008). *Indian politics and society since independence: Events, Processes and ideology.* Routledge. doi:10.4324/9780203927670

Chang, C. (2001). The impacts of emotion elicited by print political advertising on candidate evaluation. *Media Psychology, 3*(1), 91–118.

Chang, J., Wan, I., & Qu, P. (Eds.). (2003). *China's Media and Entertainment Law.* TransAsia, Price Waterhouse Coopers.

Chapman, S., & Leask, J. A. (2001). Paid celebrity endorsement in health promotion: A case study from Australia. *Health Promotion International, 16*(4), 333–338. doi:10.1093/heapro/16.4.333 PMID:11733452

Chaudhary, M., Sodani, P. R., & Das, S. (2020). Effect of COVID-19 on economy in India: Some reflections for policy and programme. *Journal of Health Management, 22*(2), 169–180. doi:10.1177/0972063420935541

Chaudhuri, A. (2007). *Indian advertising: 1780 to 1950 A.D.* Tata McGraw-Hill Publishing.

Cheung, M.-C. (2021). *OOH Advertising Returns in China, Bearing New Opportunities.* Accessed from https://www.emarketer.com/content/ooh-advertising-returns-china-bearing-new-opportunities

China Internet Network Information Center. (2020). *The 45th China Statistical Report on Internet Development.* Retrieved from http://www.cnnic.net.cn/hlwfzyj/hlwxzbg/

Christou, L. (2012). Is it possible to combine mass tourism with alternative forms of tourism: The case of Spain, Greece, Slovenia and Croatia. *Journal of Business Administration Online*, 21-23. https://www.atu.edu/jbao/spring2012/is_it_possible_to_combine.pdf

Christou, E. (2011). Exploring online sales promotions in the hospitality industry. *Journal of Hospitality Marketing & Management, 20*(7), 814–829. doi:10.1080/19368623.2011.605038

Chuangqi E-Commerce Research Center. (2020). *China's Social Commerce Consumer Shopping Behavior Research Report 2020*. Retrieved from https://www.sohu.com/a/435530596_120250072

Chung, T. S., Wedel, M., & Rust, R. T. (2016). Adaptive personalization using social networks. *Journal of the Academy of Marketing Science, 44*(1), 66–87. doi:10.100711747-015-0441-x

Çiftci, M. (2021). *Türkiye UNESCO'ya En Çok Kültürel Unsur Kaydettiren 5 Ülkeden Biri.* https://www.trthaber.com/haber/kultur-sanat/turkiye-unescoya-en-cok-kulturel-unsur-kaydettiren-5-ulkeden-biri-556718.html

Ciochetto, L. (2011). Globalisation and Advertising in Emerging Economies Brazil, Russia, India and China. Routledge.

Ciochetto, L. (2004). Advertising and globalization in India. *Media Asia, 31*(3), 157–169. doi:10.1080/01296612.2004.11726750

Ciochetto, L. (2010). Advertising in a globalized India. In K. M. Gokulsing & W. Dissanayake (Eds.), *Popular culture in a globalized India* (pp. 192–204). Routledge.

Ciochetto, L. (2011). *Globalization and advertising in emerging economies: Brazil, Russia, India and China.* Routledge.

Çitlioğlu, E. (2009). İran'ı Anlamak. In *Uluslararası Güvenlik ve Stratejik Araştırmalar Merkezi, Araştırma, Analiz ve Projeksiyon Çalışması.* https://www.academia.edu/2460213/%C4%B0RANI_ANLAMAK

Clawson, P., & Rubin, M. (2005*). Eternal Iran Continuity and Chaos.* Palgrave Macmillan Country Data. https://www.countrydata.com/cgi-bin/query/r-6508.html

Clayton, D. (2010). Advertising expenditure in 1950s Britain. *Business History, 52*(4), 651–665. doi:10.1080/00076791003753194

CNNIC. (2022). *The 49th Statistical Report on Internet Development in China.* China Internet Network Information Center (CNNIC).

Colliander, J., & Dahlén, M. (2011). Following the fashionable friend: The power of social media: Weighing publicity effectiveness of blogs versus online magazines. *Journal of Advertising Research, 51*(1), 313–320. doi:10.2501/JAR-51-1-313-320

Collinson, P. (2020). Panic buying on wane as online shopping takes over, says bank. *The Guardian, 30.*

Constitution of the Arab Republic of Egypt. (2014). Retrieved from State Information Servise: https://www.sis.gov.eg/UP/Dustor/Dustor-English002.pdf

Consumer Protection Law. (2011). https://www.funcionpublica.gov.co/eva/gestornormativo/norma.php?i=44306

Coppock, A., Hill, S. J., & Vavreck, L. (2020). The small effects of political advertising are small regardless of context, message, sender, or receiver: Evidence from 59 real-time randomized experiments. *Science Advances, 6*(36), 1–6.

Corbu, N., & Negrea-Busuioc, E. (2020). Populism meets fake News: Social media, stereotypes and emotions. In *B. Krämer, & C. Holtz-Bacha, Perspectives on populism and the media: Avenues for research* (pp. 181–200). Nomos. doi:10.5771/9783845297392-181

Corley, T. (1988). Competition and the growth of advertising in the U.S. and Britain, 1800–1914. *Business and Economic History, 17,* 155–167.

Çoşkun, G. E. (2015). Use of multimodal critical discourse analysis in media studies. *The Online Journal of Communication and Media, 1*(3), 40–43.

Coursaris, C. K., & Osch, W. V. (2016, July). Exploring the effects of source credibility on information adoption on YouTube. In *International Conference on HCI in Business, Government, and Organizations* (pp. 16-25). Springer. 10.1007/978-3-319-39396-4_2

Covino, W., & Joliffe, D. (2014). Writing about writing a college reader. In E. Wardle & D. Downs (Eds.), *What Is Rhetoric?* (pp. 325–346). Bedford / St. Martin's.

Cox, K., Crowther, J., Hubbard, T., & Turner, D. (2011). *Datamine 3. New Models of Marketing Effectiveness From Integration to Orchestration*. WARC.

Crane, K., Lal, R., & Martini, J. (2008). Iran's Political, Demographic, and Economic Vulnerabilities. Rand Corporation.

Creative City Free Zone Authority. (2021, October 17). *Creative City Free Zone Authority - Business License Registration!* Creative City. Retrieved September 25, 2021, from https://creativecity.ae/

Crescenzi, R., & Rodríguez-Pose, A. (2017). The geography of innovation in China and India. *International Journal of Urban and Regional Research, 41*(6), 1010–1027. doi:10.1111/1468-2427.12554

Croatian National Tourist Board. (n.d.). *Trust me, I've been there*. Retrieved 2021, June 15 from https://www.croatia.hr/en-GB

CroatiaWeek. (2021a, January 22). *Croatian Tourist Board selects five international agencies for advertising activities in 2021*. Travel. Retrieved 2021, June 16 from https://www.croatiaweek.com/ croatian – tourist – board – selects – five – international – agencies -for- advertising – activities -in-2021/

CroatiaWeek. (2021b, May 19). *Croatia launches 'Trust me I've been there' tourism campaign*. Travel. Retrieved 2021, June 16 from https://www.croatiaweek.com/ croatia – launches – trust – me – ive – been – there – tourism - campaign/

Croud.com. (2018). https://croud.com/blog/a-guide-to-advertising-in-russia/

Curti, M. (1967). The changing concept of "human nature" in the literature of American advertising. *Business History Review, 41*(4), 335–357. doi:10.2307/3112645

Cwalina, W. F., & Newman, B. I. (2015). *Political marketing: Theoretical and strategic foundations*. Routledge.

Cwalina, W. F., & Newman, B. I. (2015). *Political Marketing: Theoretical and Strategic Foundations*. Routledge.

Dalyan, M. G., Bayır, Ö. Ö., & Ceyhan, M. Ş. (2018). Understanding Contemporary Woman on Trail of The Past: A Comparative Study on Socio-cultural Statuses of Russian and Armenian Women (Geçmişin izinden Bugünün Toplumsal Kadınını Anlamak). *Tarih Okulu Dergisi, 11*(37), 463–494.

Daly, M. W. (1998). The British occupation, 1882-1922. In M. W. Daly (Ed.), *The Cambridge History of Egypt: Modern Egypt, from 1517 to the end of the twentieth century* (pp. 239–251). Cambridge University Press. doi:10.1017/CHOL9780521472111.011

Damlapınar, Z., & Balcı, Ş. (2014). *Siyasal iletişim sürecinde seçimler, adaylar, imajlar*. Konya, Türkiye: Literatürk.

Danesi, M. (2009). *Dictionary of Media and Communications*. Routledge.

Dash, A. K. (2012). *Advertising strategy and cultural blend: Glocal identities in Indian TV commercials* [Doctoral dissertation, IIT Kharagpur]. DSpace. Retrieved 12/20/21 from: https://www.idr.iitkgp.ac.in/xmlui/handle/123456789/1699

Davenport, R., & Sanders, C. (2000). *South Africa: A modern history*. St. Martin's Press. doi:10.1057/9780230287549

David-Barrett, L., Bracewell, C. W., Lampe, J. R., & Pleština, D. (2022). Croatia. *Encyclopedia Britannica*. Retrieved 2022, January 28 from https://www.britannica.com/place/Croatia

Davies, R. G., & Ikeno, O. (2002). *The Japanese mind: Understanding contemporary Japanese culture*. Tuttle Publishing.

Day, G. S. (1998). What does it to be market-driven? *Business Strategy Review*, 9(1), 1–14.

De Blij, H. J., & Muller, P. O. (1992). *Geography, realms, regions, and concepts*. John Wiley & Sons.

De Mooij, M. (2010). *Global marketing advertising: Understanding cultural paradoxes*. SAGE publications.

De Mooij, M. (2014). Global marketing and advertising: Understanding cultural paradoxes. *Sage (Atlanta, Ga.)*.

Dean, D. (2010). Fear, negative campaigning and loathing: The case of the UK election campaign. *Journal of Marketing Management*, 21(9-10), 1067–1078. doi:10.1362/026725705775194111

Demetriou, D. (2020). Employees in the country whose brutal office culture has led to several deaths are beginning to rethink the tradition. *BBC Worklife*. https://www.bbc.com/worklife/article/20200114-how-the-japanese-are-putting-an-end-to-death-from-overwork

Democratic Alliance. (2019). *Democratic Alliance Youtube channel*. Retrieved 04/28/22 from: https://www.youtube.com/c/DemocraticAllianceSA/videos

Denor Travel. (n.d.). *New advertising spot of the Croatian Tourist Board – Croatia full of life*. Retrieved 2021, July 20 from https://www.orebic-korcula.com/ new – advertising – spot -of-the- croatian – tourist – board – croatia – full -of-life/

Departamento Administrativo Nacional de Estadística - DANE. (2021). *Indicadores relevantes*. https://www.dane.gov.co/files/ses/Indicadores_Relevantes.pdf

Dickenson, J. (2014). "The politics of political advertising" in Australia and Britain, 1970-1989. *The Australian Journal of Politics and History*, 60(2), 241–256.

Dietrich, G. (2014). *PR is More than Media Relations*. Spinsucks. Retrieved 23 October 2021, from https://spinsucks.com/communication/pr-media-relations/

Digital Studio, M. E. (2019, January 9). *Production houses must train next generation of GCC filmmakers, says Image Nation*. Retrieved September 15, 2021, from https://www.digitalstudiome.com/production/31106-production-houses-must-train-next-generation-of-gcc-filmmakers-says-image-nation

DigitalAge. (2020). *Felis Ödülleri'nde İlk Gecenin Kazananları Açıklandı*. https://digitalage.com.tr/felis-odullerinde-ilk-gecenin-kazananlari-aciklandi/

Dinçer, S. (2018). Content analysis in for educational science research: Meta-analysis, meta-synthesis, and descriptive content analysis. *Bartın University Journal of Faculty of Education*, 7(1), 176–190. doi:10.14686/buefad.363159

Djafarova, E., & Trofimenko, O. (2019). 'Instafamous'–credibility and self-presentation of micro-celebrities on social media. *Information Communication and Society*, 22(10), 1432–1446. doi:10.1080/1369118X.2018.1438491

Doland, A. (2015). How Uniqlo doubles its WeChat followers in China: "Style Your Life" push allowed customers to share fun photos in campaign that tapped into China's obsession with all things mobile. *Advertising Age*. Accessed from https://adage.com/article/special-report-women-to-watch-china-2015/uniqlo-doubled-wechat-followers-china/300039

Dongak, E. (2011). *The Role of SMEs in Russian Economy After Transition: The Study of Russian Printing Industry* [Master's thesis]. Yıldız Teknik University Social Science Institute.

Douglas, M., & Isherwood, B. (1978). *The world of goods: Towards an anthropology of consumption*. W. N. Norton.

Dow, J. (2015). *Passions and Persuasion in Aristotle' s Rhetoric.* Oxford University Press. doi:10.1093/acprof:oso/9780198716266.001.0001

Duan, C. (2019). KOC: New marketing outlet in the era of private domain traffic. *China Advertising, 11*, 115–116.

Dubai Media Incorporated. (n.d.). Retrieved October 10, 2021, from https://web.archive.org/web/20111108173917/http://www.dmi.gov.ae/default_En.asp

Dubai Press Club. (2010). *Arab Media Outlook.* Author.

Dubai SME & An Agency of the Department of Economic Development – Government of Dubai. (2010). *A small and medium enterprises development perspective of the Media industry in Dubai.* Dubai SME. https://bit.ly/3wAOAbt

Dubai Studio City. (n.d.). *Global production, broadcasting and entertainment hub.* Retrieved September 21, 2021, from https://dubaistudiocity.ae/

Dubrovnik and Neretva County Tourist Board. (n.d.). *Culture.* Retrieved 2021, June 15 from https://visitdubrovnik.hr/attractions/culture/

Ebiquity. (2018). *Profit Ability: the business case for advertising.* Thinkbox. Retrieved on 28 October 2021, from https://www.thinkbox.tv/Research/Thinkbox-research/Profit-Ability-the-business-case-for-advertising

Eck, D. L. (2012). *India: A sacred geography.* Harmony Books.

Economic and Social Commission for Western Asia (ESCWA). (2015, November 11). *International Media Production Zone.* United Nations Economic and Social Commission for Western Asia. Retrieved September 15, 2021, from https://archive.unescwa.org/international-media-production-zone

EdinburgNews. (n.d.). https://www.edinburghnews.scotsman.com/news/people/international-womens-day-2021-inspirational-quotes-theme-and-why-google-is-celebrating-with-a-doodle-3156358

Eduline. (2021). *Ez a tíz legnépszerűbb alapszak a 2021-es felvételin: vezet a gazdálkodási és menedzsment.* Retrieved 23 October 2021, from https://eduline.hu/erettsegi_felveteli/20210319_legnepszerubb_szakok_a_felvetelin

Effie. (2021a). *Hatékony aktivitásból sikeres pályamű! Effie Awards Hungary 2021. A díj, ami számít.* Retrieved 22 October 2021, from https://effie.hu/2021/downloads/effie2021_hatekony-aktivitasbo-sikeres-palyamu.pdf

Effie. (2021b). Retrieved 19 October 2021, from https://effie.hu/2021/

Egypt. (2022). Retrieved from Minority Rights Group International: https://minorityrights.org/country/egypt/

El Espectador. (2021). *Campaña colombiana para promover la desmovilización se ganó el "Nobel" de la publicidad.* https://www.elespectador.com/judicial/campana-colombiana-para-promover-la-desmovilizacion-se-gano-el-nobel-de-la-publicidad-article/

El Maazouzi, A. (2020). *The impact of official tourism websites on the destination image: The case of Morocco.* Uppsala University. Retrieved 2022, January 29 from https://www.diva-portal.org/smash/get/diva2:1474902/FULLTEXT01.pdf

Elden, M. (2013). Reklam ve Reklamcılık. Say Yayınları.

Elden, M. (2016). Reklam ve reklamcılık. Say Yayınları.

Elder, C. (2005). Immigration history. In M. Lyons & P. Russell (Eds.), *Australia's history: Themes and debates* (pp. 98–115). UNSW Press.

Eldin, H. F., Shahin, M., & Miniesy, R. (2021). The impact of social media adoption on financial & non-financial growth of MSMEs: An empirical comparison of Facebook and Instagram in Egypt. In Egypt's future outlook: The search for a new balances (pp. 1-36). The British University in Egypt.

Electoral legislation amendment (stop the lies) bill 2021: Explanatory memorandum. (n.d.). The Parliament of the Commonwealth of Australia.

Electoral Matters Committee. (2010). *Inquiry into the Provisions of the electoral act 2002 (Vic) relating to misleading or deceptive political advertising* (Parliamentary Paper No 282). Melbourne: Parliament of Victoria.

Elegina, D. (2021). *Advertising in Russia - statistics & facts.* https://www.statista.com/topics/7836/advertising-in-russia/#dossierKeyfigures

Elma, F. (n.d.). Post-Soviet Russia and Central Asia [Sovyet Sonrası Rusya ve Orta Asya]. *Journal of Azerbaijani Studies*, 129-143.

El-Mahdi, R., & Marfleet, P. (2009). *Egypt: The moment of change.* Zed Books. doi:10.5040/9781350219830

Elmeshad, M. (2021). *The Political Economy of Private Media in Egypt.* SOAS University of London.

El-Nawawy, M., & Khamis, S. (2020). Political Activism 2.0: Comparing the Role of Social Media in Egypt's "Facebook Revolution" and Iran's "Twitter Uprising". *CyberOrient, 6*(1), 8–33. doi:10.1002/j.cyo2.20120601.0002

Eltantawy, N., & Wiest, J. B. (2011). Social media in the Egyptian revolution: Reconsidering resource mobilization theory. *International Journal of Communication*, 1207–1224.

Emarketer. (2017, February 17). *Top 10 advertisers in India, ranked by total media ad spending.* Retrieved 12/26/21 from: https://www.emarketer.com/chart/205233/top-10-advertisers-india-ranked-by-total-media-ad-spending-2016

Emerging Markets Information System. (2021). *Sector Publicitario en Colombia Publicidad, Relaciones Públicas y Servicios Relacionados.* https://www.emis.com/

Erbaş, S. (2018, March-April). Kültürlerarası Reklam Araştırmaları: Nike 8 Mart Dünya Kadınlar Günü Reklam Kampanyası Örneği. *Akademik Bakış Dergisi*, (66), 357–375.

Erdogan, Z. (1999). Celebrity endorsement: A literature review. *Journal of Marketing Management, 15*(4), 291–314. doi:10.1362/026725799784870379

Eren, E. (2013). *"Think Small" Işığında Volkswagen Beetle Tarihi.* https://pazarlamasyon.com/think-small-isiginda-volkswagen-beetle-tarihi/

Erkut, A. (n.d.). *Reklam Kampanyasına Dijital Entegre Edilince...* https://www.campaigntr.com/reklam-kampanyasina-dijital-entegre-edilince/

Erlingsson, C., & Brysiewicz, P. (2017). A hands-on guide to doing content analysis. *African Journal of Emergency Medicine, 7*(3), 93–99. doi:10.1016/j.afjem.2017.08.001 PMID:30456117

Eroğlu Yalın, B. (2006). Siyasal iletişimin reklam boyutuna ilişkin kuramsal bir inceleme. *İstanbul Üniversitesi İletişim Fakültesi Dergisi, 25*, 169-180.

Eryiğit, M. (2020). Instagram'da Glokal Yaklaşım Örneği Olarak "Bmw, Volkswagen Ve Mercedes-Benz" Analizi. *Kocaeli Üniversitesi İletişim Fakültesi Araştırma Dergisi*, (15), 140-163. Retrieved from https://dergipark.org.tr/en/pub/kilad/issue/53856/732150

Eser, M. (2017). *Place Of Oligarchs in The Foreign Trade and Politics Of The Russian Federation* [Master's thesis]. Manisa Celal Bayar University, Social Science Institute.

ETBrandequity. (2019, August 7). *Agency reckoner 2018-19: Top 50 most influential people in advertising*. Retrieved 11/30/21 from: https://brandequity.economictimes.indiatimes.com/news/advertising/agency-reckoner-2018-19-top-50-most-influential-people

Etikan, İ., Musa, S. A., & Alkassim, R. S. (2016). Comparison of convenience sampling and purposive sampling. *American Journal of Theoretical and Applied Statistics*, 5(1), 1–4. doi:10.11648/j.ajtas.20160501.11

Etzkorn, K. (2021). *How digital shopping will evolve: Three trends to watch*. Retrieved from https://www.forbes.com/sites/forbestechcouncil/2021/04/09/how-digital-shopping-will-evolve-three-trends-to-watch/?sh=6d43c2e737

European Broadcasting Union. (2017). *About Dubai Media Incorporated*. Retrieved September 20, 2021, from https://www.ebu.ch/files/live/sites/ebu/files/News/2017/02/ABOUT%20DUBAI%20MEDIA%20INCORPORATED.pdf

Eurostat. (2021a). *Population on 1 January by age and sex*. Retrieved 29 October 2021, from https://ec.europa.eu/eurostat/databrowser/view/demo_pjan/default/table?lang=en

Eurostat. (2021b). *Population by age group*. Retrieved 29 October 2021, from https://ec.europa.eu/eurostat/databrowser/view/tps00010/default/table?lang=en

Eurostat. (2021c). *Real GDP per capita*. Retrieved 28 October 2021, from https://ec.europa.eu/eurostat/databrowser/view/sdg_08_10/default/table?lang=en

Eurostat. (2021d). *Adjusted gross disposable income of households per capita*. Retrieved 29 October 2021, from https://ec.europa.eu/eurostat/databrowser/view/sdg_10_20/default/table?lang=en

Eurostat. (2021e). *Employment rates by sex, age and citizenship (%)*. Retrieved 29 October 2021, from https://ec.europa.eu/eurostat/databrowser/view/lfsa_ergan/default/table?lang=en

Eurostat. (2021f). *Unemployment rates by sex, age and citizenship (%)*. Retrieved 29 October 2021, from https://ec.europa.eu/eurostat/databrowser/view/lfsa_urgan/default/table?lang=en

Evans, N. J., Phua, J., Lim, J., & Jun, H. (2017). Disclosing Instagram influencer advertising: The effects of disclosure language on advertising recognition, attitudes, and behavioral intent. *Journal of Interactive Advertising*, 17(2), 138–149. doi:10.1080/15252019.2017.1366885

Eyada, B. (2018). An empirical study of banned advertising in Egypt and violated morals. *International Design Journal*, 8(2), 27–37.

Eyal, G. (2018). *Why influencers fail to disclose commercial relationships and the brands that enable them*. Adweek. Retrieved from https://www.adweek.com/digital/whyinfluencers-fail-to-disclose-commercialrelationships-and-the-brands-that-enablethem/

Facebook Ad Library Report Australia. (2021, December 10). Retrieved December 12, 2021, from Facebook: https://www.facebook.com/ads/library/report/?source=archive-landing-page&country=AU

Fagerstrøm, A., Bendheim, L. M., Sigurdsson, V., Foxall, G. R., & Pawar, S. (2020). The marketing firm and co-creation: The case of co-creation by LEGO. *Managerial and Decision Economics*, 41(2), 226–233. doi:10.1002/mde.3077

Fairclough, N., & Wodak, R. (1997). Critical discourse analysis. In T. van Dijk (Ed.), *Discourse as social interaction: Discourse studies* (Vol. 2, pp. 258–284). Sage.

Fanack.com. (2021, September 6). *Media in the United Arab Emirates - Chronicle.* Retrieved September 11, 2021, from https://fanack.com/united-arab-emirates/media-in-uae/

Fanatics, K. P. (2021). YouTube, Katy Perry x Laudrin Home (Ad), https://www.youtube.com/watch?v=SDtc-SpV92Y

Farivar, S., Wang, F., & Yuan, Y. (2020). Opinion leadership vs. para-social relationship: Key factors in influencer marketing. *Journal of Retailing and Consumer Services, 59,* 102371. doi:10.1016/j.jretconser.2020.102371

Faulconbridge, J. R., Beaverstock, J. V., Nativel, C., & Taylor, P. J. (2011). *Cities and advertising globalization New York, Los Angeles and Detroit in a global perspective.* Routledge.

Favero, P. (2021). *Image-Making-India visual culture, technology, politics.* Routledge.

Feldwick, P. (2007). *Account planning: Its history, and its significance for ad agencies. In The Sage handbook of advertising.* Sage Publications.

Fertik, M. (2020). *Why is influencer marketing such A big deal right now?* Retrieved from https://www.forbes.com/sites/michaelfertik/2020/07/02/why-is-influencer-marketing-such-a-big-deal-right-now/#5be7c9d375f3

Filieri, R., & McLeay, F. (2014). E-WOM and accommodation: An analysis of the factors that influence travelers' adoption of information from online reviews. *Journal of Travel Research, 53*(1), 44–57. doi:10.1177/0047287513481274

Finish 'Yarının Suyu' Hareketi için Türkiye'de İlk Kez İki Diziyi Bir Araya Getirdi. (n.d.). https://pazarlamasyon.com/finish-yarinin-suyu-hareketi-icin-turkiyede-ilk-kez-iki-diziyi-bir-araya-getirdi/

Fletcher, W. (2008). *Powers of persuasion: The inside story of British advertising: 1951–2000.* Oxford University Press.

Flew, T., & Smith, R. (2014). *New media: An introduction.* Oxford University Press.

Florez-Morris, M. (2007). Joining Guerilla Groups in Colombia: Individual Motivations and Processes for Entering a Violent Organization. *Studies in Conflict and Terrorism, 30*(7), 615–634. doi:10.1080/10576100701385958

Forbes Insights. (2011). *Marketing to the New Chinese Consumer.* Accessed from https://images.forbes.com/forbesinsights/StudyPDFs/Marketing_to_the_Chinese_Consumer.pdf

Fortenbaugh, W. W. (1992). Aristotle on persuasion through character. *Rhetorica, 10*(3), 207–244. doi:10.1525/rh.1992.10.3.207

Fourie, L. M., & Froneman, J. D. (2003). Emotional political advertising: A South African case study. *Communicare, 22*(1), 187–211.

Fowler, E. F., Franz, M. M., Martin, G. J., Peskowitz, Z., & Ridout, T. N. (2021). Political advertising online and offline. *The American Political Science Review, 115*(1), 130–149.

Franz, M. M., Freedman, P., Goldstein, K., & Ridout, T. N. (2008). Understanding the effect of political advertising on voter turnout: A response to krasno and green. *The Journal of Politics, 70*(1), 262–268.

Freedom of expression index. (2022). Retrieved from Reporters Without Borders: https://rsf.org/en/index

Freezone Company Setup | Dubai Media City. (n.d.). *Media Hub in Dubai.* Retrieved August 30, 2021, from https://dmc.ae

Friestad, M., & Wright, P. (1994). The Persuasion Knowledge Model: How People Cope with Persuasion Attempts. *The Journal of Consumer Research, 21*(1), 1. doi:10.1086/209380

Frith, K. T., & Wesson, D. (1991). A comparison of cultural values in British and American print advertising: A study of magazines. *The Journalism Quarterly, 68*(1–2), 216–223.

Fuchs, C. (2018). Authoritarian capitalism, authoritarian movements and authoritarian communication. *Media Culture & Society*, *40*(5), 1–13. doi:10.1177/0163443718772147

Fülöp, I. (2021). *Mennyi teret kell engedni a Facebook-hirdetéseknek?* Retrieved 21 October 2021, from https://kreativ. hu/cikk/mennyi-teret-kell-engedni-a-facebook-hirdeteseknek

Gajrani, S. (2004). *History, religion and culture of India*. Gyan Publishing House.

Gallier, E. G. (2021, January 6). *SVOD vs TVOD vs AVOD: What's the Best Content Delivery System?* Retrieved January 10, 2021, from https://www.harmonicinc.com/insights/blog/svod-vs-tvod-vs-avod-whats-the-best-content-delivery-system/

Gamberožić, J. Z., & Tonković, Ž. (2015). From mass tourism to sustainable tourism: A comparative case study of the island of Brač. *Socijalna Ekologija: Časopis za Ekološku Misao i Sociologijska Istraživanja Okoline*, *24*(2-3). Advance online publication. doi:10.17234/SocEkol.24.2.1

Gao, D., Pan, Q., & Xia, L. (2021). *Forecast of China's Media Industry*. Retrieved from https://mp.weixin.qq.com/s/rWmEKAMgDyTzFaVApAK9iA

Gardner, J., & Lehnert, K. (2016). What's new about new media? How multi-channel networks work with content creators. *Business Horizons*, *59*(3), 293–302. doi:10.1016/j.bushor.2016.01.009

Garramone, G. M. (1984). Effects of negative political advertising: The roles of sponsor and rebuttal. *Journal of Broadcasting & Electronic Media*, *29*(2), 147–159.

Gaweesh, K. (2015). Televised political advertising in egypt: The case of 2012 parliamentary elections. *The Scientific Journal of Department of Public Relations and Advertising*, *10*(2), 1–22. doi:10.21608jocs.2015.88997

GDP (current US$). (2022). Retrieved from The World Bank: https://data.worldbank.org/indicator/NY.GDP.MKTP.CD?most_recent_value_desc=true

GDP per capita (current US$) - Egypt, Arab Rep. (2022, May 23). Retrieved from The World Bank: https://data.worldbank.org/indicator/NY.GDP.PCAP.CD?locations=EG

Geçit, E. (2014). William (Bill) Bernbach: Reklamcılıkta Yaratıcı Devrim. In M. Elden & U. Bakır (Eds.), *Reklam Ustaları 1 (pp. 203-240)*. Detay.

Gemius Hungary. (2019). *Trendek az okoseszközök piacán 2019*. Retrieved 13 October 2021, from http://www.gemius.hu/all-reader-news/trendek-az-okoseszkoezoek-piacan.html

GEMO. (2021). *Segment review – Spotlight on India*. Retrieved 10/28/21 from: https://images.assettype.com/afaqs/2021-07/d2232870-68ae-4238-9e7f-71aece3d3033/GEMO_2021___India_Cut_Report___Final.pdf

Gerber, J. (2019, October 9). Explained i what is the DA's federal council. *News24*. Retrieved 04/28/22 from: https://www.news24.com/news24/SouthAfrica/News/explained-what-is-the-das-federal-council-20191009

Ghandeharion, A. & Yazdanjoo, M. (2017). Governmental Discourses in Advertising on Iran's State Television. *CLCWeb: Comparative Literature and Culture*, *19*(3).

Gilboy, E. W. (1932). Demand as a factor in the Industrial Revolution. In Facts and factors in economic history (pp. 620–639). Harvard University Press.

GMA Marketing to China. (2019). *Key Marketing Strategies for China Market*. Accessed from https://marketingtochina.com/key-marketing-strategies-for-china-market/

Göçeri, N. (2004). Ideas Affecting the Women's Movement [Kadın Hareketini Etkileyen Fikir Akımları]. *Ç. Ü. İlahiyat Fakültesi Dergisi, 4*(2), 61-76.

Godin, S. (2020). *Purple cow*. Penguin Books Limited.

Goldschmidt, A. Jr. (2008). *A brief history of Egypt*. Facts On File.

Goodwin, M. J., & Ford, R. (2017). Britain After Brexit: A nation divided. *Journal of Democracy, 28*(1), 17–30. doi:10.1353/jod.2017.0002

Google Blog. (2020). *Building a more private web: A path towards making third party cookies obsolete.* Retrieved 21 October 2021, from https://blog.chromium.org/2020/01/building-more-private-web-path-towards.html

Google Blog. (2021). *An updated timeline for Privacy Sandbox milestones.* Retrieved 21 October 2021, from https://blog.google/products/chrome/updated-timeline-privacy-sandbox-milestones/

Google Transparency Report Australia. (2021, December 12). Retrieved December 12, 2021, from Google: https://transparencyreport.google.com/political-ads/region/AU

Gordon, B. R. G., Lovett, M. J., Shachar, R., Arceneaux, K., Moorthy, S., Peress, M., Rao, A., Subrata, S., Soberman, D., & Urminsky, O. (2012). Marketing and politics: Models, behavior, and policy implications. *Marketing Letters, 23*(2), 391–403. doi:10.100711002-012-9185-2

Government Gazette. (2014, February 17). Regulations on party election broadcasts, political advertisement, the equitable treatment of political parties by broadcasting licence and related matters, *Independent Communications authority of South Africa, 584*(37350), 1-17. Retrieved 05/19/22 from: https://www.icasa.org.za/legislation-and-regulations/party-elections-broadcasts-and-political-advertisement-and-related-matters-regulations-2014

Graham, A. H. (2021). *New Design on Croatia's Coast.* Retrieved 2022, January 28 from New York Times webpage, https://www.nytimes.com/2011/10/23/travel/new-design-on-croatias-coast.html

Green, M. J. (2007). The U.S.-Japan alliance: A brief strategic history. *Education about Asia, 12*(3), 25-30.

Grimal, N. (1994). *A History of Ancient Egypt*. Wiley-Blackwell.

Grinshpun, H. (2012). The city and the chain: Conceptualizing globalization and consumption in Japan. *Japan Review, 24*, 169–195.

Group, M. (2020, November 16). *Covid-19: A game-changer for media and purchasing.* Retrieved 10/22/21 from: https://www.groupm.com/covid-19-a-game-changer-for-media-and-purchasing/

Group, M. (2021). *This year, Next year: China media Industry Forecast.* Retrieved from https://mp.weixin.qq.com/s/NqnxyX8ooOjyNSMc_rAFCw

Group, M. (2021, June 14). *Global advertising to grow by 19%.* Retrieved 12/10/21 from: https://www.groupm.com/this-year-next-year-global-2021-mid-year-forecast/

Güler. (2012). Russia in the Transition Process from Socialism to Capitalism: What Kind of Capitalism? [Sosyalizmden Kapitalizme Geçiş Sürecinde Rusya: Nasıl Bir Kapitalizm?]. *Business and Economics Research Journal, 3*(3), 93–120.

Gunsch, M. A., Brownlow, S., Haynes, S. E., & Mabe, Z. (2000). Differential forms linguistic content of various of political advertising. *Journal of Broadcasting & Electronic Media, 44*(1), 27–42.

Gupta, O. (2005). *Advertising in India: Trends and impact*. Kalpa Publishing House.

Gürel, E., & Bakır, U. (2014). Leo Burnett: İmgeden Zihne Giden Yol. In M. Elden & U. Bakır (Eds.), *Reklam Ustaları 1 (pp. 175-202)*. Detay.

Gurieva, L. K., & Dzhioev, A. V. (2016). *Sustainable development of the Russian economy*. http://science-almanac.ru/documents/77/2016-02-02-Gurieva-Dzhioev.pdf

Guttmann, Y. A. (2021, Mar 15). *Advertising spending in South Africa from 2018 to 2021*. Statista. Retrieved 05/02/22 from: https://www.statista.com/statistics/386540/advertising-expenditures-by-medium-south-africa/

Güven, A. (2020). Siyasal toplumsallaşma aracı olarak youtube: "Mevzular" örneği. In A. Güven (Ed.), Youtube Türkiye'de kültür, siyaset ve tüketim (pp. 1-53). İstanbul, Türkiye: Kriter.

Hacıtahiroğlu, K. (2014). Küreselleşmenin Siyasal Etkileri, Göç ve Ukrayna-Rusya Krizi [Political Effects of Globalization, Migration and Ukraine-Russia Crisis]. *Trakya Üniversitesi Sosyal Bilimler Dergisi, 16*(2), 259-284.

Hackley, C., & Kover, A. (2007). The trouble with creatives: Negotiating creative identity in advertising agencies. *International Journal of Advertising, 26*(1), 63–78. doi:10.1080/02650487.2007.11072996

Haines, H. M. (2021, October 25). *Commonwealth electoral amendment (stop the lies) bill 2021*. Retrieved from Parliament of Australia: https://parlinfo.aph.gov.au/parlInfo/genpdf/chamber/hansardr/25166/0067/hansard_frag.pdf;fileType=application%2Fpdf

Halliday, M. A. (1994). *An introduction to functional grammar*. Edward Arnold.

Hallin, D. C., & Mancini, P. (2012). Comparing Media Systems Beyond the Western World. Cambridge University Press.

Halloran, S. M. (1982). Aristotle's concept of ethos, or if not his somebody else's. *Rhetoric Review, 1*(1), 58–63. doi:10.1080/07350198209359037

Hamilton, B. A. (2007). *Booz Allen Hamilton Finds Television Programming Improving in the Arab World*. Booz Allen Hamilton. Retrieved September 13, 2021, from https://www.boozallen.com/markets/international/middle-east-north-africa.html

Hamilton, M. (2015). *The ad that changed advertising*. https://medium.com/@marathonmilk?p=18291a67488c

He, H., & Harris, L. (2020). The impact of Covid-19 pandemic on corporate social responsibility and marketing philosophy. *Journal of Business Research, 116*, 176–182. doi:10.1016/j.jbusres.2020.05.030 PMID:32457556

Heller, S. (2017). *Earnest Elmo Calkins: Founder of Modern Advertising and a Designer You Probably Don't Know*. https://designobserver.com/feature/earnest-elmo-calkins/39651

Henneberg, S. C., & O'shaughnessy, N. J. (2007). Theory and concept development in political marketing. *Journal of Political Marketing, 6*(2-3), 5–31.

Heywood, A. (2017). *Political idologies: An introduction*. Palgrave.

HINA - State Agency. (2021). *Croatia's tourism industry boasts 2021 figures nearly matching 2019 levels*. Retrieved 2022, January 29 from https://hr.n1info.com/english/news/croatias-tourism-industry-boasts-2021-figures-nearly-matching-2019-levels/

Hiorns, B. (2014, April 2). *Leo Burnett focuses on driving regional growth in the Middle East and North Africa with new appointment*. Creative Pool. Retrieved September 21, 2021, from https://creativepool.com/magazine/inspiration/leo-burnett-focuses-on-driving-regionalgrowth-in-the-middle-east-and-north-africa-with-new-appointment.2765

History.com. (n.d.). https://www.history.com/news/the-surprising-history-of-international-womens-day

Hızal, S.G. (2005). Topography of the advertising industry: an example of Turkey. *Journal of Communication Research,* *3*(1-2), 105-131.

Hızal, S. G. (2005). *Reklam endüstrisinin topografyası: Türkiye örneği.* İletişim Araştırmaları.

Hobolt, S. (2016). The Brexit vote: A divided nation, a divided continent. *Journal of European Public Policy, 23*(9), 1259–1277. doi:10.1080/13501763.2016.1225785

Hofstede, G. (1980). *Culture's Consequences: Comparing Values, Behaviours, Institutions and Organizations Across Nations* (2nd ed.). Sage Publications.

Hofstede, G., & Bond, M. H. (1984). Hofstede's culture dimensions: An independent validation using Rokeach's value survey. *Journal of Cross-Cultural Psychology, 15*(4), 417–433. doi:10.1177/0022002184015004003

Hofstede, G., & Hofstede, J. (2010). *Culture And Organizations-Software of the Mind.* McGraw-Hill International London.

Hofstede, G., Neuijen, B., Ohayav, D. D., & Sanders, G. (1990). Measuring organizational cultures: A Qualitative and quantitative study across twenty cases. *Administrative Science Quarterly, 35*(2), 286–316. doi:10.2307/2393392

Holak, S. L., Matveev, A. V., & Havlena, W. J. (2007). Nostalgia in post-socialist Russia: Exploring applications to advertising strategy. *Journal of Business Research, 60*(6), 649–655. doi:10.1016/j.jbusres.2006.06.016

Holland, D. R. (1974). Volney B. Palmer: The Nation's First Advertising Agency Man. *The Pennsylvania Magazine of History and Biography, 98*(3), 353–381.

Holmes, R. (2019). *The Rules Of Social Media Just Changed. Here's How To Keep Up.* Retrieved from https://www. forbes. com/sites/ryanholmes/2019/04/17/the-rules-of-social-media-just-changed-heres-how-to-keepup

Holtz-Bacha, C., & Kaid, L. L. (2006). Political advertising in international comparison. In L. L. Kaid, & C. Holtz-Bacha (Eds.), The Sage handbook of political advertising (pp. 3-15). Sage Publications.

Hong, C. (1996). Advertising in China: a socialist experiment. In K. T. Frith (Ed.), *Advertising in Asia: Communication, Culture and Consumption. Ames.* Iowa State University Press.

Hootsuite. (2021a). *Digital 2021. Global Overview Report.* Retrieved 21 October 2021, from https://hootsuite.widen. net/s/zcdrtxwczn/digital2021_globalreport_en

Hootsuite. (2021b). *Digital 2021: Hungary.* Retrieved 21 October 2021, from https://datareportal.com/reports/digital-2021-hungary

Hosking, G. (2011). *Russia and the Russians, from the Early to the 21st Century [Rusya ve Ruslar, Erken Dönemden 21. Yüzyıla]* (K. Acar, Trans.). İletişim Yayınları.

House, J. R., Hange, J. P., Javidan, M., Dorfman, W. P., & Gupta, V. (2004). *Culture, Leadership, and Organizations.* https://en.mfa.ir/

Howard, D. J., & Kerin, R. A. (2004). The effects of personalized product recommendations on advertisement response rates: The "try this. It works!" technique. *Journal of User Psychology, 14*(3), 271–279. doi:10.120715327663jcp1403_8

HTZ - The Croatian National Tourist Board. (2020). *Call for expression of interest in the implementation of promotional campaigns with strategic partners in international markets in 2021.* Retrieved 2021, August 05 from https://www.htz. hr/sites/default/files/2020-10/Call%20for%20strategic%20partners%202021.pdf

Huang, Q., Jin, J., Lynn, B. J., & Men, L. R. (2021). Relationship cultivation and public engagement via social media during the covid-19 pandemic in China. *Public Relations Review, 47*(4), 102064. doi:10.1016/j.pubrev.2021.102064

Huang, Y. (1994). Peaceful Evolution: The Case of Television Reform in Post-Mao China. *Media Culture & Society*, *16*(2), 217–242. doi:10.1177/016344379401600203

Hua, Y., Bao, L., & Wu, X. (2020). The product-selling strategy under direct and indirect value Identification. *Journal of Cleaner Production*, *279*, 123591. doi:10.1016/j.jclepro.2020.123591

Hughes, A. (2019, May 6). How digital advertising is shaping this election campaign. *Adnews*. Retrieved November 5, 2021, from https://www.adnews.com.au/opinion/how-digital-advertising-is-shaping-this-election-campaign

Hughes, A. (2018). *Market driven political advertising: Social, digital, and mobile marketing*. Palgrave Macmillan.

Hugo-Burrows, R. (2004). Current trends and future challenges in the South African advertising industry - An introductory review. *Journal of African Business*, *5*(2), 39–52. doi:10.1300/J156v05n02_03

Human Development Reports of UNDP. (2019). https://hdr.undp.org/en/content/broadening-our-thinking-vulnerability

Hungary, I. A. B. (2017). *Hol tart a reklámblokkolás hazánkban?* Retrieved 21 October 2021, from https://blog.iab.hu/wp-content/uploads/sites/3/2017/03/evolution_iab_lfmcs_ag-2.pdf

Hungary, I. A. B. (2021a). *AdExpect 2021*. Retrieved 14 October 2021, https://iab.hu/dokumentum/iab-hungary-adexpect-2021/

Hungary, I. A. B. (2021b). *AdEx IAB Hungary. Digitális reklámköltési adatok*. Retrieved 14 October 2021, from https://iab.hu/wp-content/uploads/2021/04/IAB_HU_Adex_2020.pdf

Hunt, J. D. (1975). Image as a factor in tourism development. *Journal of Travel Research*, *13*(3), 1–7. doi:10.1177/004728757501300301

Hurst, G. C. (2021). Japan. In *Britannica*. https://www.britannica.com/place/Japan

IAB. (2021). http://www.iabcolombia.com/wp-content/uploads/2021/02/5.-Resumen-Ejecutivo-Inversio%CC%81n-en-Publicidad-Digital-Total-An%CC%83o-2020.pdf, accessed on 14/11/2021.

Iepuri, V. (2017). What Makes Russian Advertisements Russian? Contemporary Russian Advertising as a Sociocultural Phenomenon. *Russian Language Journal*, *67*, 55–76.

IGI Global Dictionary. (n. d.) *What is Historical Heritage*. Retrieved 2022, January 29 from https://www.igi-global.com/dictionary/historical-heritage/48689

Iglesias-Sánchez, P. P., Correia, M. B., & Jambrino-Maldonado, C. (2019). Challenges in linking destinations' online reputation with competitiveness. *Tourism & Management Studies*, *15*(1), 35–43. doi:10.18089/tms.2019.150103

Ilić, I. (2021). *Croatia puts safety at heart of 2021 tourism campaign*. Reuters. https://www.reuters.com/article/health-coronavirus-croatia-tourism-idUSL8N2LJ0A1

Imarcgroup. (2021). *Indian advertising market: Industry trends, share, size, growth, opportunity and competitive analysis forecast 2021-2026*. Retrieved 11/09/21 from: https://www.imarcgroup.com/advertising-industry-india

IMF. (2020b, December). *Policy Responses to COVID19*. https://www.imf.org/en/Topics/imf-and-covid19/Policy-Responses-to-COVID-19#C

InfluencerMarketingHub. (2019). *The State of Influencer Marketing 2019: Benchmark Report*. Retrieved from bit.ly/2Ge2xUX

InfluencerMarketingHub. (2021). *Influencer Marketing Benchmark Report 2021*. Retrieved from https://influencermarketinghub.com/influencer-marketing-benchmark-report-2021/#toc-6

Insights, H. (n.d.). *Country comparison*. https://www.hofstede-insights.com/country-comparison/japan/

Internet World Stats. (2008). *Internet World Stats Blog for 2008*. Retrieved November 10, 2021, from https://www.internetworldstats.com/blog.htm#:%7E:text=1%2C574%20Million%20Internet%20Users!&text=A%20new%20year%20and%20new,persons%20for%20year%2Dend%202008

Inversini, A., Brülhart, C., & Cantoni, L. (2011). MySwitzerland.com: Analysis of online communication and promotion. *Information Technology & Tourism, 13*(1), 39–49. doi:10.3727/109830511X13167968595741

Inversini, A., & Cantoni, L. (2011). Towards online content classification in understanding tourism destinations' information competition and reputation. *International Journal of Internet Marketing and Advertising, 6*(3), 282–299. doi:10.1504/IJIMA.2011.038240

Inversini, A., Cantoni, L., & Buhalis, D. (2009). Destinations' information competition and web reputation. *Information Technology & Tourism, 11*(3), 221–234. doi:10.3727/109830509X12596187863991

Inversini, A., Marchiori, E., Dedekind, C., & Cantoni, L. (2010). Applying a conceptual framework to analyze online reputation of tourism destinations. In U. Gretzel, R. Law, & M. Fuchs (Eds.), *Information and Communication Technologies in Tourism 2010* (pp. 321–332). Springer. doi:10.1007/978-3-211-99407-8_27

Ipsos. (2021). *Fizetési Élmény Riport 2021*. Author.

iResearch. (2020). *2020 China Online Advertising Market Annual Insight Report*. Retrieved from https://report.iresearch.cn/report/202007/3614.shtml

İşcan, İ., & Hatipoğlu, Y.Z. (2011). Transition to Free Market Economy in Russia and 2008 Global Crisis. *İstanbul Üniversitesi İktisat Fakültesi Dergisi, 61*(1), 177-237.

İslami, İ. (2016). Political History of Modern Islam. *LIRIA International Review, 6*(1), 189–206.

Ismagilova, G., Safiullin, L., & Gafurov, I. (2015). Using historical heritage as a factor in tourism development. *Procedia: Social and Behavioral Sciences, 188*, 157–162. doi:10.1016/j.sbspro.2015.03.355

İsmayılov, E. (2013). An Evaluation of South Caucasus and Central Asia in 21st Century Russian Foreign Policy Doctrines [Yüzyıl Rusya Dış Politika Doktrinleri'nde Güney Kafkasya ve Orta Asya Değerlendirmesi]. *Marmara Üniversitesi Siyasi Bilimler Dergisi, Vol, 1*(1), 87–105.

Ivanović, Z., Bogdan, S., & Bareša, S. (2018). Portfolio analysis of foreign tourist demand in Croatia. *Ekonomski Vjesnik, 31*(1), 149–162. https://www.proquest.com/scholarly-journals/portfolio-analysis-foreign-tourist-demand-croatia/docview/2066619719/se-2?accountid=15454

Jain, G., Rakesh, S., & Chaturvedi, K. R. (2018). Online video advertisements' effect on purchase intention: An exploratory study on youth. *International Journal of E-Business Research, 14*(2), 87–101. doi:10.4018/IJEBR.2018040106

Jamieson, H. (1996). İletişim ve İkna. Anadolu Üniversitesi Yayınları.

Jamieson, K. H., & Cappella, J. N. (2008). *Echo chamber: Rush Limbaugh and the conservative media establishment*. Oxford University Press.

Jandó, Z. (2020). *Kormányközeli cégeknél landol a magyar reklámpénzek harmada*. Retrieved 17 August 2021, from https://g7.hu/vallalat/20201015/kormanykozeli-cegeknel-landol-a-magyar-reklampenzek-harmada/

Japan News. (2021). *World famous star Katy Perry is reappointed as Randolin's new muse! Appeared in a cute Dalmatian*. Nature Lab. Co. Ltd. https://re-how.net/all/1349144/

Jaspan, C. (2021, July 12). *Australian government vaccine campaign attracts wide criticism on launch.* September 4, 2021 tarihinde Mumberalla: https://mumbrella.com.au/australian-government-vaccine-campaign-attracts-wide-criticism-on-launch-692346

Javidan, M., & Dastmalchian, A. (2003). Culture and leadership in Iran: The land of individual achievers, strong family ties, and powerful Elite. *The Academy of Management Perspectives, 17*(4), 127–142. doi:10.5465/ame.2003.11851896

Jelinčić, D. A., & Žuvela, A. (2012). Facing the challenge? Creative tourism in Croatia. *Journal of Tourism Consumption and Practice, 4*(2), 78–90. http://hdl.handle.net/10026.1/11694

Jelušić, A. (2017). Modelling tourist consumption to achieve economic growth and external balance: Case of Croatia. *Tourism and Hospitality Management, 23*(1), 87–104. doi:10.20867/thm.23.1.5

Jerslev, A. (2016). Media times in the time of the microcelebrity: Celebrification and the YouTuber Zoella. *International Journal of Communication, 10,* 19.

Jiang, T. T., & Xu, Y. R. (2021). Narrowed Information Universe: A Review of Research on Information Cocoons, Selective Exposure, and Echo Chambers. *Intelligence. Information & Sharing, 38*(5), 134–144.

Jing, W. (2008). *Brand New China: Advertising, Media, and Commercial Culture.* Harvard University Press.

Jiwei, L. (2020). *Sector Pulse Under The Epidemic: China's 5G Commercialization Pace is Not Slowing.* Xinhua. Accessed from http://www.xinhuanet.com/tech/2020-03/03/c_1125656066.htm

John, L., Kim, T., & Barasz, K. (2018). Ads That Don't Overstep: How to Make Sure You Don't Take Personalization Too Far. *Harvard Business Review, 96*(1), 62–69.

John, M. E. (2021). Sex selection, family building strategies and the political economy of gender. In S. Mani & C. G. Iyer (Eds.), *India's economy and society lateral explorations* (pp. 355–367). Springer. doi:10.1007/978-981-16-0869-8_13

Johnson-Cartee, K. S., & Copeland, G. A. (2010). *Negative political advertising: Coming of age.* Roudledge.

Johnson, G. D., Elliott, R. M., & Grier, S. A. (2010). Conceptualizing multicultural advertising effects in the "new" South Africa. *Journal of Global Marketing, 23*(3), 189–207. doi:10.1080/08911762.2010.487420

Johnston, A., & Kaid, L. L. (2002). Image ads and issue ads in us presidential advertising: Using videostyle to explore stylistic differences in televised political ads from 1952 to 2000. *Journal of Communication,* 281–300.

Joint Select Committee on Electoral Reform. (1984). *Second report.* Canberra: Parliament of the Commonwealth of Australia.

Joint Standing Committee on Electoral Matters. (2020). *Report on the conduct of the 2019 federal election and matters related thereto.* Canberra: Parliament of the Commonwealth of Australia. Retrieved November 16, 2021, from https://parlinfo.aph.gov.au/parlInfo/download/committees/reportjnt/024439/toc_pdf/Reportontheconductofthe2019federalelectionandmattersrelatedthereto.pdf;fileType=application%2Fpdf

Joseph, S. (2001). *Political advertising and the constitution. In Big Makeover: A New Australian Constitution: Labor Essays 2002.* Pluto Press.

Joshi, M., Joshi, S., Singh, V. K., & Nagar, S. (2010). Challenges of Indian advertising agencies. *Pragya: Journal of Information Management, 9*(1), 20–28.

Kaid, L. K., & Holtz-Bacha, C. (1995). *Political advertising in western democracies: Parties and candidates on television.* Sage Publishing.

Kaid, L. L. (2004). Political advertising. In L. L. Kaid (Ed.), *Handbook of Political Communication Research* (pp. 155–202). Lawrence Erlbaum Associates, Inc., Publishers.

Kaid, L. L., & Johnston, A. (2001). *Videostyle in presidential campaigns: Style and content of televised political advertising*. Praeger Publishers.

Kakwani, N. S., & Kalbar, P. P. (2020). Review of Circular Economy in urban water sector: Challenges and opportunities in India. *Journal of Environmental Management, 271*, 1–15. doi:10.1016/j.jenvman.2020.111010 PMID:32778294

Kala, C. P. (2005). Health traditions of Buddhist community and role of amchis in trans-Himalayan region of India. *Current Science Association, 89*(8), 1331–1338.

Kamrava, M. (2008). *Iran's Intellectual Revolution*. Cambridge University Press. doi:10.1017/CBO9780511756146

Karagiannopoulos, V. (2012). The Role of the Internet in Political Struggles: Some Conclusions from Iran and Egypt. *New Political Science, 34*(2), 151–171.

Karakuş, G. (2019). USSR's Overview of the Women [Sovyetler Birliği'nde Kadının Konumuna Genel Bakış]. *Akademik tarih ve Düşünce Dergisi, 6*(3), 1580-1598.

Karamchandani, S., Karani, A., & Jayswal, M. (2021). Linkages between advertising value perception, context awareness value, brand attitude and purchase intention of hygiene products during COVID-19: A two-wave study. *Vision: The Journal of Business Perspective*, 1-14. doi:10.1177/09722629211043954

Karimifard, H. (2012). Constructivism, national identity and foreign policy of the Islamic Republic of Iran. *Asian Social Science, 8*(2), 239–246. doi:10.5539/ass.v8n2p239

Karp, K. (2016). New research: The value of influencers on Twitter. *Twitter*. Retrieved from https://blog.twitter.com/2016/new-research-the-value-of-influencers-ontwitter

Karp, P. (2020, December 20). Morrison government spent $128m on advertising in 2019-20, figures reveal. *The Guardian*. Retrieved September 23, 2021, from https://www.theguardian.com/australia-news/2020/dec/25/morrison-government-spent-128m-on-advertising-in-2019-20-figures-reveal

Kartajaya, H., Kotler, P., & Hooi, D. H. (2019). *Marketing 4.0: moving from traditional to digital*. World Scientific.

Kassarjian, H. H. (1977). Content analysis in consumer research. *The Journal of Consumer Research, 4*(1), 8–18. doi:10.1086/208674

Katiyar, S. P. (2016). Gender disparity in literacy in India. *Social Change, 46*(1), 46-69. doi:10.1177/0049085715618558

Katunarić, V. (2007). Traditionalism, Modernism, Utopianism: A Review of Recent Works on Transition in Croatia. *Politička misao, 44*(5), 3-27. Retrieved 2022, January 28 from https://hrcak.srce.hr/26397

Katz, H. (2019). *The media handbook: A complete guide to advertising media selection, planning, research, and buying*. Routledge. doi:10.4324/9780429434655

Kawashima. (2006). Advertising agencies, media and consumer market: the changing quality of TV advertising in Japan. *Media, Culture & Society, 28*(3), 393-410.

Kazdin, A. E. (1992). *Research design in clinical psychology* (2nd ed.). Allyn & Bacon.

Keana, M., & Spurgeon, C. (2004). Advertising Industry and Culture in Post-WTO China. *Media International Australia, 111*(May), 104–117. doi:10.1177/1329878X0411100111

Keane, F. (2019, May 11). *South Africa election: ANC wins with reduced majority*. Retrieved 05/03/22 from: https://www.bbc.com/news/world-africa-48211598

Kelly, L. D., & Sheehan, K. B. (2021). *Advertising Management in a Digital Environment*. Routledge. doi:10.4324/9781003107828

Kemaloğlu, İ. (2016). Yüzyılın Başında Rusya Federasyonu. *Marmara Türkiyat Araştırmaları Dergisi, 3*(2), 1-14. Doi:10.16985/MTAD.2016227938

Kemp, S. (2020, February 17). *Digital 2020: Egypt*. Retrieved from Datareportal: https://datareportal.com/reports/digital-2020-egypt

Kerkezi, R. (2018). Transformation of Modernism in Socialist Yugoslavia Architecture. *Prizren Social Science Journal, 2*(3), 18–31. doi:10.32936/pssj.v2i3.61

Kerr, G., Johnston, K., & Beatson, A. (2008). A framework of aorporate social responsibility for advertising accountability: The case of australian government advertising campaign. *Journal of Marketing Communications, 14*(2), 155–169.

Kertai-Kiss, I. (2014). The Fit of National and Organisational Cultures in International ScientificLiterature. In Management, Enterprise and Benchmarking – In the 21St Century. Óbudai Egyetem.

Khairullah, D. H. Z., & Khairullah, Z. Y. (2003). Dominant cultural values: Content analysis of the US and Indian print advertisements. *Journal of Global Marketing, 16*(1-2), 47–70. doi:10.1300/J042v16n01_03

Khairullah, D. H. Z., & Khairullah, Z. Y. (2013). Cultural values in Indian television advertising. *Journal of Promotion Management, 19*(2), 265–281. doi:10.1080/10496491.2013.769477

Khajehpour, B., Namazie, P., & Honari, A. (2013). *A Study on Iranian Values*. NIAC Leadership Conference. Washington DC: The Simorgh Foundation.

Khodair, A. A., AboElsoud, M. E., & Khalifa, M. (2019). The role of regional media in shaping political awareness of youth: Evidence from Egypt. *Politics & Policy, 47*(6), 1095–1124.

Ki, C. W. C., Cuevas, L. M., Chong, S. M., & Lim, H. (2020). Influencer marketing: Social media influencers as human brands attaching to followers and yielding positive marketing results by fulfilling needs. *Journal of Retailing and Consumer Services, 55*, 102133. doi:10.1016/j.jretconser.2020.102133

Ki, C. W. C., & Kim, Y. K. (2019). The mechanism by which social media influencers persuade consumers: The role of consumers' desire to mimic. *Psychology and Marketing, 36*(10), 905–922.

Kim, A. J., & Ko, E. (2010). Impacts of luxury fashion brand's social media marketing on customer relationship and purchase intention. *Journal of Global Fashion Marketing, 1*(3), 164–171.

Kim, D. Y., & Kim, H. Y. (2021). Trust me, trust me not: A nuanced view of influencer marketing on social media. *Journal of Business Research, 134*, 223–232. doi:10.1016/J.JBUSRES.2021.05.024

Kocabas, M., & Elden, M. (1997). *Reklam ve yaratici strateji: Konumlandirma ve star stratejisinin analizi* [Advertising and creative strategy: Positioning and the analysis of celebrity endorsement strategy]. Yayinevi Yayincilik.

Kocasu, N. A. (2019). *Felis'e Göre Entegre Kampanyaların En İyileri*. mediacat.com/felis-2020-entegre-kampanyalar-bolumu-felis-kazanan-tum-isler/

Koloğlu, O. (1999). Reklamcılığımızın ilk yüzyılı: 1840-1940. Reklamcılar Derneği.

Kontsevaia, D. B., & Berger, P. D. (2016). Mobile Marketing in China: Can WeChat Turn Their New Advertising Strategy into a Sustainable Advantage? *International Journal of Marketing Studies*, 8(4), 37–43. doi:10.5539/ijms.v8n4p37

Kordej-De Villa, Ž., & Šulc, I. (2021). Cultural heritage, tourism and the UN sustainable development goals: The case of Croatia. In M. B. Andreucci, A. Marvuglia, M. Baltov, & P. Hansen (Eds.), Rethinking sustainability towards a regenerative economy (pp. 341-358). Springer. doi:10.1007/978-3-030-71819-0_19

Koslow, S., Sasser, S. L., & Riordan, E. A. (2003). What is creative to whom and why? Perceptions in advertising agencies. *Journal of Advertising Research*, 43(1), 96–110. doi:10.2501/JAR-43-1-96-110

KPMG. (2021). *Globális platformok hatása a magyar kommunikációs iparra*. KPMG.

Krajnović, A., Bosna, J., & Jasić, D. (2012). Possibilities and constraints of region branding in tourism: The case of Dalmatia. *Tranzicija, 14*(30), 1-14. Retrieved 2021, August 06 from https://hrcak.srce.hr/94569

Krasno, J. S., & Green, D. P. (2008). Do televised presidential ads increase voter turnout? Evidence from a natural experiment. *The Journal of Politics*, 70(1), 245–261.

Kress, G. (2012). Multimodal discourse analysis. In J. P. Gee & M. Handford (Eds.), *The Routledge handbook of discourse analysis* (pp. 35–50). Routledge.

Kress, G., & Van Leeuwen, T. (2020). *Reading images: The grammar of visual design* (3rd ed.). Routledge. doi:10.4324/9781003099857

Krom, İ. (2019). Reklam ve algı yönetimi: Toplumbilimsel analiz çerçevesinde 2019 yılında Türkiye'de en çok hatırlanan reklamlar. In Ö. U. Yurttaş (Ed.), Reklam perspektifleri (pp. 175-204). Ankara, Türkiye: Nobel Akademik Yayıncılık.

Krom, İ. (2020). Reklam ve algı yönetimi: Toplumbilimsel analiz çerçevesinde 2019 yılında en çok hatırlanan reklamlar. In Ö. U. Yurttaş (Ed.), *Reklam Perspektifleri* (pp. 175–204). Nobel Yayınları.

Kronenberg, K., Fuchs, M., Salman, K., Lexhagen, M., & Höpken, W. (2016). Economic effects of advertising expenditures–a Swedish destination study of international tourists. *Scandinavian Journal of Hospitality and Tourism*, 16(4), 352–374. doi:10.1080/15022250.2015.1101013

Krstinić NižićM.DrpićD. (2013). Model for sustainable tourism development in Croatia. *Tourism in Southern and Eastern Europe, 2nd International Scientific Conference Tourism in South East Europe 2013*, 159-173. https://ssrn.com/abstract=2289408

KSH. (2021a). *Népesség és népmozgalom*. Retrieved 29 October 2021, from https://www.ksh.hu/nepesseg-es-nepmozgalom

KSH. (2021b). *Az adott évben be-, illetve kivándorló külföldi állampolgárok, valamint az adott év január 1-jén Magyarországon engedéllyel tartózkodó külföldi állampolgárok adatai*. Retrieved 29 October 2021, from https://statinfo.ksh.hu/Statinfo/haViewer.jsp

KSH. (2021c). *Egy főre jutó bruttó hazai termék megye és régió szerint*. Retrieved 14 October 2021, from https://www.ksh.hu/stadat_files/gdp/hu/gdp0078.html

KSH. (2021d). *A lakónépesség nem, megye és régió szerint, január 1*. Retrieved 14 October 2021, from https://www.ksh.hu/stadat_files/nep/hu/nep0034.html

KSH. (2021e). *A Magyarországon tartózkodó külföldi állampolgárok megye és régió szerint, január 1*. Retrieved 29 October 2021, from https://www.ksh.hu/stadat_files/nep/hu/nep0050.html

KSH. (n.d.). *A boldog érzelmi állapotok megélésének gyakorisága ország, országcsoport szerint [%]*. Retrieved 30 October 2021, from https://www.ksh.hu/stadat_files/ele/hu/ele0032.html

Kumar, S. (2011). Role of Indian broadcasting federation in preventing inappropriate content in TV programmes. *International Journal of Engineering and Management Research, 1*(1), 33–35.

Kumar, V., & Gupta, S. (2016). Conceptualizing the evolution and future of advertising. *Journal of Advertising, 45*(3), 302–317. doi:10.1080/00913367.2016.1199335

Kumar, V., & Reinartz, W. (2016). Creating enduring customer value. *Journal of Marketing, 80*, 36–68. doi:10.1509/jm.15.0414

Kurucz, I. (2021). *Megkedveltük a home office-t*. NRC. Retrieved 13 October 2021, from https://nrc.hu/nrc-hirek/nrc-kutatas-homeoffice_1/

Kyngäs, H. (2020). Inductive Content Analysis. In H. Kyngäs, K. Mikkonen, & M. Kääriäinen (Eds.), *The Application of Content Analysis in Nursing Science Research* (pp. 13–21). Springer. doi:10.1007/978-3-030-30199-6_2

La República. (2014). *Por campaña para desmovilizados, Lowe-Ssp3 ganó premio en Reino Unido*. https://www.larepublica.co/empresas/por-campana-para-desmovilizados-lowe-ssp3-gano-premio-en-reino-unido-2187706

Ladhari, R., Massa, E., & Skandrani, H. (2020). YouTube vloggers' popularity and influence: The roles of homophily, emotional attachment, and expertise. *Journal of Retailing and Consumer Services, 54*, 102027. doi:10.1016/j.jretconser.2019.102027

Lai, W. H., & Vinh, N. Q. (2013). Online promotion and its influence on destination awareness and loyalty in the tourism industry. *Advances in Management and Applied Economics, 3*(3), 15-30. https://www.semanticscholar.org/ paper/ Online – Promotion -and-Its- Influence -on- Destination -Lai- Vinh/ 821d7 0f1f29 7892 aa 7e277 8d634 73be 52c75 8334

Lambrecht, A., & Tucker, C. (2013). When does retargeting work? Information specificity in online advertising. *JMR, Journal of Marketing Research, 50*(5), 561–576. doi:10.1177/0022243713050000508

Larousse. (n.d.). *Croatie*. Retrieved 2021, September 9 from https://www.larousse.fr/encyclopedie/pays/Croatie/115207

Laudrin' Home. (2021). https://www.laundrin.jp/?_ga=2.147118195.593313241.1638015063-448976400.1637432911

Lau, R. R., Lee, S., Heldman, C., & Paul, B. (1999). The effects of negative political advertisements: A meta-analytic assessment. *The American Political Science Review, 93*(4), 851–875.

Lau, R. R., Sigelman, L., & Rovner, I. B. (2007). The effects of negative political campaigns: A meta-analytic reassessment. *The Journal of Politics, 69*(4), 1176–1209.

LaVoie, N. R., Quick, B. L., Riles, J. M., & Lambert, N. J. (2017). Are graphic cigarette warning labels an effective message strategy? A test of psychological reactance theory and source appraisal. *Communication Research, 44*(3), 416–436. doi:10.1177/0093650215609669

Leading Media Production Zone. (n.d.). *Dubai Production City*. https://dpc.ae/

Lekić R. Franjić T. Mencer Salluzzo M. (2015). Relation between media and tourism – Example of Croatia as a tourist destination. *3ʳᵈ International Scientific Conference Tourism in Southern and Eastern Europe*. https://ssrn.com/abstract=2637285

Leung, S., & Hui, A. (2014). A recent look: Advertising creatives' perceptions of creativity in Hong Kong/China. *Services Marketing Quarterly, 35*(2), 138–154. doi:10.1080/15332969.2014.885366

Levitsky, S., & Way, L. A. (2010). *Competitive authoritarianism: Hybrid regimes after the cold war*. Cambridge University Press.

Levitt, T. (1983). Globalization of Markets. *Harvard Business Review, 61*(3), 92–102.

Levitt, T. (1983). The Globalization of Markets. *Harvard Business Review*, *61*(3), 92–102.

Li, H. (2016). *Advertising in China.* Accessed From https://www.chinacenter.net/2017/china_currents/16-1/advertising-in-china/

Light, D. (2014). Heritage tourism (Book review). *Tourism Planning & Development*, *11*(4), 472–473. doi:10.1080/21568316.2014.900287

Lim, S. (2021). *Digital Ad Revenue in China Grew in 2020 – Despite Coronavirus Spending Cuts.* Accessed From https://www.thedrum.com/news/2021/01/14/digital-ad-revenue-china-grew-2020-despite-coronavirus-spending-cuts

Lipton. (2021). https://www.lipton.com/us/en/home.html

Liu, M. T., Liu, Y., & Zhang, L. L. (2019). Vlog and brand evaluations: The influence of parasocial interaction. *Asia Pacific Journal of Marketing and Logistics*, *31*(2), 419–436. doi:10.1108/APJML-01-2018-0021

Liu, X., Mehraliyev, F., Liu, C., & Schuckert, M. (2020). The roles of social media in tourists' choices of travel components. *Tourist Studies*, *20*(1), 27–48. doi:10.1177/1468797619873107

Llodrà-Riera, I., Martínez-Ruiz, M. P., Jiménez-Zarco, A. I., & Izquierdo-Yusta, A. (2015). A multidimensional analysis of the information sources construct and its relevance for destination image. *Tourism Management*, *48*, 319–328. doi:10.1016/j.tourman.2014.11.012

Lloyd, J. (2005). Square peg, round hole? Can marketing-based concepts such as "product" and the "marketing mix" have a useful role in the political arena? In *Current issues in political marketing* (pp. 24–46). Haworth Press.

Lock, A., & Harris, P. (1996). Political marketing: Vive la diifférence! *European Journal of Marketing*, *30*(10/11), 14–24.

Lodge, T. (1987). State of exile: The African National Congress of South Africa, 1976-86. *Third World Quarterly*, *9*(1), 1–27. doi:10.1080/01436598708419960

Logar, I. (2010). Sustainable tourism management in Crikvenica, Croatia: An assessment of policy instruments. *Tourism Management*, *31*(1), 125–135. doi:10.1016/j.tourman.2009.02.005

Lu, B., Fan, W., & Zhou, M. (2016). Social presence, trust, and social commerce purchase intention: An empirical research. *Computers in Human Behavior*, *56*, 225–237. doi:10.1016/j.chb.2015.11.057

Luo, A. (2019). *Content analysis: A step by step guide with examples.* Retrieved 2021, May 11 from https://www.scribbr.com/methodology/content-analysis/

Luo, T., Chen, W., & Liao, Y. (2021). Social media use in China before and during COVID-19: Preliminary results from an online retrospective survey. *Journal of Psychiatric Research*, *140*, 35–38. doi:10.1016/J.JPSYCHIRES.2021.05.057

Luty, J. (2021). *Number of foreign tourist arrivals in Croatia in 2020, by age.* Retrieved 2022, January 29 from https://www.statista.com/statistics/1275897/croatia-international-tourist-arrivals-by-age/

Lynch, M. (2010). Islam divided between Salafi-jihad and the Ikhwan. *Studies in Conflict and Terrorism*, *33*(6), 467–487.

Mabokela, R. O., & Mawila, K. F. N. (2004). The impact of race, gender, and culture in South African higher education. *Comparative Education Review*, *48*(4), 394–416. doi:10.1086/423359

Mackey, A., & Gass, S. M. (2005). *Second Language Research: Methodology and Design.* Routledge.

Macklin, M. (1984). Dissenting report. In Second Report (pp. 44-50). Canberra: Parliament of the Commonwealth of Australia.

Magna Global. (2021, December 13). *Magna Global advertising forecast.* Mediabrands. Retrieved December 21, 2021, from https://cn.ipgmediabrands.com/magna-global-advertising-forecast-global-advertising-market-reaches-new-heights-and-exceeds-pre-covid-levels/

Magyar Turisztikai Ügynökség. (2021). *Nemzeti Turizmusfejlesztési Stratégia 2030.* Retrieved 9 August 2021, from https://mtu.gov.hu/documents/prod/NTS2030_Turizmus2.0-Strategia.pdf

Maier, J., & Nai, A. (2020). Roaring candidates in the spotlight: Campaign negativity, emotions, and media coverage in 107 national elections. *The International Journal of Press/Politics, 25*(4), 576–606.

Majid, A. (2013). *Cultural influence in Advertising A Comparative analysis between Telenor TV: Advertisements in Sweden and Pakistan* [Master Thesis]. University of Gothenburg.

Mallia, K. L., & Windels, K. (2011). Will changing media change the world? An exploratory investigation of the impact of digital advertising on opportunities for creative women. *Journal of Interactive Advertising, 11*(2), 30–44. doi:10.10 80/15252019.2011.10722183

Mankoff, J. (2009). Russian Foreign Policy: The Return of Great Power Politics. Rowman & Littlefield Publishers.

Marketing & Media. (2021a). *Rekordot döntött a belföldi turizmus.* Retrieved 22 October 2021, from https://mmonline. hu/cikk/rekordot-dontott-a-belfoldi-turizmus/

Marketing & Media. (2021b). *Turizmus: 2020-at már leköröztük, 2019-hez képest hatalmas a lemaradás.* Retrieved 22 October 2021, from https://mmonline.hu/cikk/turizmus-2020-at-mar-lekoroztuk-2019-hez-kepest-hatalmas-a-lemaradas/

Marketing & Media. (2021c). *Jól hajrázott a reklámpiac.* Retrieved 21 October 2021, from https://mmonline.hu/cikk/jol-hajrazott-a-reklampiac/

Marketing & Media. (2021d). Retrieved 21 October 2021, from https://mmonline.hu/cikk/reklampiac-szebb-kepet-festenek-az-adatok/

Marketing, R. (2020a). *Impact of social media influencers on purchasing in China as of October 2020.* Rakuten Marketing. Retrieved from https://www.statista.com/statistics/1200644/china-influencers-impact-on-purchasing/

Marketing, R. (2020b). *Share of consumers who follow social media influencers in Asia Pacific in 2020, by country.* Rakuten Marketing. Retrieved from https://www.statista.com/statistics/1181355/apac-share-of-consumers-who-follow-social-media-influencers-by-country-or-region/

Marketing, R. (2019). *Influencer marketing global survey consumers.* Rakuten Marketing.

Marsh, R. (1996). Women in Russia and Ukraine. Cambridge University Press.

Marsot, A. S. (2007). *A History of Egypt: From the Arab Conquest to the Present.* Cambridge University Press.

Marx, K., & Engels, F. (1970). *Manifesto of the communist party.* Foreign Languages Press.

Masr, M. (2019, June 25). *Arrests target political figures involved in new coalition to run in 2020 parliamentary elections.* Retrieved from Mada: https://www.madamasr.com/en/2019/06/25/feature/politics/arrests-target-political-figures-involved-in-new-coalition-to-run-in-2020-parliamentary-elections/

Massoume, P. (2001). *Culture of Iran: Codes of behavior, Iranian Experience.* https://www.iranchamber.com/culture/articles/codes_behavior.php

Matan, C. (2020). Construction methods and materials in modernist Croatia during the 1930s. *Construction History, 35*, 113–134.

Matusitz, J., & Payano, P. (2012). Globalization of popular culture: From Hollywood to Bollywood. *Sage: South Asia Research, 32*(2), 123–138. doi:10.1177/0262728012453977

Mau, V., & Drobyshevskaya, T. (2012). Modernization and the Russian Economy: Three Hundred Years of Catching Up. SSRN *Electronic Journal*. https://www.iep.ru/files/RePEc/gai/wpaper/0032Mau.pdf doi:10.2139/ssrn.2135459

Ma, Y. (2021). Elucidating determinants of customer satisfaction with live-stream shopping: An extension of the information systems success model. *Telematics and Informatics, 65*, 101707. doi:10.1016/J.TELE.2021.101707

Mazirri, E. T. (2020). Green packaging and green advertising as precursors of competitive advantage and business performance among manufacturing small and medium enterprises in South Africa. *Cogent Business & Management, 7*(1), 1–21. doi:10.1080/23311975.2020.1719586

Mazzarella, W. (2003). *Shoveling smoke: Advertising and globalization in contemporary India*. Duke University Press.

McCarthy, N. (2019). *40 Years On: Iran Before And After The Revolution.* https://www.statista.com/chart/16900/key-economic-social-data-about-iran/

McCarthy, E. J. (1960). *Basic Marketing:A Managerial Approach.* Irwin.

McClintock, A. (2005). Soft-soaping empire: Commodity racism and imperial advertising. In M. Fraser & M. Greco (Eds.), *The body: A reader* (pp. 271–276). Routledge.

McCormack, K. C. (2014). Ethos, pathos, and logos: The benefits of Aristotelian rhetoric in the courtroom. *Washington University Jurisprudence Review, 7*(1), 131–155.

McCracken, G. (1986). Culture and consumption: A theoretical account of the structure and movement of the cultural meaning of consumer goods. *The Journal of Consumer Research, 13*, 71–84.

McKinsey & Company. (2017, 12 April). *The Rise of the African Consumer.* Retrieved 05/20/22 from: https://www.mckinsey.com/industries/retail/our-insights/the-rise-of-the-african-consumer

McKinsey. (2016). *Are you really listening to what your customers are saying?* Retrieved 29 October 2021, from https://www.mckinsey.com/business-functions/operations/our-insights/are-you-really-listening-to-what-your-customers-are-saying

McNutt, L. (2021). Influencer marketing predictions for 2021. *PR Daily.* Retrieved from https://www.prdaily.com/5-influencer-marketing-predictions-for-2021/

Media Diversity in Australia. (2021, March 31). Retrieved September 17, 2021, from Parliament of Austalia: https://www.aph.gov.au/Parliamentary_Business/Committees/Senate/Environment_and_Communications/Mediadiversity

Media Regulation. (n.d.). *The Official Portal of the UAE Government.* Retrieved September 20, 2021, from https://u.ae/en/media/media-in-the-uae/media-regulation

Media Regulatory Office. (n.d.). *Media Regulatory Office. UAE Ministry of Culture and Youth.* Retrieved September 12, 2021, from https://mcy.gov.ae/en/mro/

Mehta, D., Mehta, N. K., & Jain, S. (2017). Advertising industry of India: Problems and prospects. *Asian Journal Management, 8*(3), 491–493. doi:10.5958/2321-5763.2017.00079.8

Melville, I. (1999). *Marketing in Japan.* Butterworth Heinemann.

Mendel, T. (2011). *Politics and Media: Transition in Egypt.* Internews. Retrieved May 23, 2022, from http://hrlibrary.umn.edu/research/Egypt/Internews_Egypt_MediaLawReview_Aug11.pdf

Mengmeng, S. (2020). *Evergrande Projects Going Strong in Online Sales, Beike VR Property Sales Reshapes New Property Sales Value Chain*. Xinhua. http://www.xinhuanet.com/house/2020-03-13/c_1125706856.htm

Merritt, S. (1984). Negative political advertising: Some empirical findings. *Journal of Advertising*, *13*(3), 27–38.

Meyer, D. M. (2017, September 15). *What Is TV Production?* Retrieved December 24, 2021, from https://ourpastimes.com/what-is-tv-production-12190691.html

Meyer, M. (2017). *What is rhetoric*. Oxford University Press. doi:10.1093/oso/9780199691821.001.0001

Miaozhen Systems & China Advertising Association. (2021). *KOL Marketing White Paper*. Retrieved from https://mp.weixin.qq.com/s/Tp_EPqyQG7VMF07Boi_3Yw

Micera, R., & Crispino, R. (2017). Destination Web reputation as "smart tool" for image building: The case analysis of Naples city-destination. *International Journal of Tourism Cities*, *3*(4), 406–423. doi:10.1108/IJTC-11-2016-0048

Middle East and North Africa (MENA). (n.d.). Retrieved December 28, 2021, from https://www.investopedia.com/terms/m/middle-east-and-north-africa-mena.asp

Miller, M. M., & Henthorne, T. L. (2007). In search of competitive advantage in Caribbean tourism websites: Revisiting the unique selling proposition. *Journal of Travel & Tourism Marketing*, *21*(2-3), 49–62. doi:10.1300/J073v21n02_04

Minghetti, V., & Celotto, E. (2015). Destination Web reputation: Combining explicit and implicit popularity to build an integrated monitoring system. *Ereview of Tourism Research*, *6*, 1–5. Retrieved April 20, 2022, from https://agrilifecdn.tamu.edu/ertr/files/2015/02/SP01_RecommenderSession_Minghetti.pdf

Ministerio de Comercio – Mincomercio. (2020). *Contexto Macroeconómico Colombia*. https://www.mincit.gov.co/getattachment/1c8db89b-efed-46ec-b2a1-56513399bd09/Colombia.aspx

Ministry of Foreign Affairs of Japan. (n.d.a). *Web Japan, Japan fact sheet, Economy*. https://web-japan.org/factsheet/en/pdf/e04_economy.pdf

Ministry of Foreign Affairs of Japan. (n.d.b). *Web Japan, Japan fact sheet, Geography & climate*. https://web-japan.org/factsheet/en/pdf/e01_geography.pdf

Ministry of Foreign Affairs of Japan. (n.d.c). *Web Japan, Japan fact sheet, Governmental structure*. https://web-japan.org/factsheet/en/pdf/e08_governmental.pdf

Miskin, S., & Grant, R. (2004, November 24). *Political advertising in Australia* (Research Brief No. 5). Retrieved November 12, 2021, from Parliament of Australia Parliamentary Library: https://apo.org.au/sites/default/files/resource-files/2004-11/apo-nid504.pdf

MMSZ. (2020). *Marketing Indikátor, Ágazati tanulmány*. Retrieved 17 August 2021, from https://marketingindikator.hu/uploads/documentitem/0/marketing-indikator-tanulmany-final-20201207-1607354412.pdf

Mohammadpur, A., Karimi, J., & Mahmoodi, K. (2013). Predicament of identity in Iran: A qualitative meta-analysis of theoretical and empirical studies on identity. *Quality & Quantity*, *48*(4), 1973–1994. doi:10.100711135-013-9875-8

Mohan, K. (2016). Rural and regional development. In R. B. Singh (Ed.), *Progress in Indian geography* (pp. 161-170). Indian National Science Academy.

Moinuddin, S. (2021). *Digital shutdowns and social media: Spatiality, political economy and internet shutdowns in India*. Springer. doi:10.1007/978-3-030-67888-3

Molnár, Cs. (2021). *Őrületes, mi megy az online boltokban - lecserélték a magyarok a karácsonyt.* Retrieved 13 October 2021, from https://www.napi.hu/magyar-vallalatok/jarvany-vasarlas-kiskereskedelem-online-fizetes-utanvet-karacsony.727230.html

Mooij, M. (1998). *Global marketing and advertising - Understanding cultural paradoxes.* Sage Publications.

Morello, J. A. (2001). *Selling the President, 1920: Albert D. Lasker, advertising, and the election of Warren G. Harding* (Vol. 1920). Greenwood Publishing Group.

Moriarty, S., Mitchell, N., & Wells, W. (2012). Advertising: Principles and practice (9th ed.). Pearson.

Morkovkin, D., Shmanev, S., & Shmaneva, L. (2017). Problems and Trends in Innovative Transformation of Russian Economy and Infrastructure Development. *Advances in Economics, Business and Management Research*, volume 32, *3rd International Conference on Economics, Management, Law and Education (EMLE 2017)*, 10-13.

Morosan, C. (2015). The influence of DMO advertising on specific destination visitation behaviors. *Journal of Hospitality Marketing & Management, 24*(1), 47–75. doi:10.1080/19368623.2014.891962

Mostaqbal Watan Party-the official page. (2022, May 10). Retrieved from Facebook: https://www.facebook.com/mostqbalwataneg/videos/321794412854914/

MRSZ. (2021a). *Media and Total Communications pending Hungary 2020.* MRSZ.

MRSZ. (2021b). *MRSZ Barométer – A válság hatásai a reklámiparban. Harmadik lekérdezés.* MRSZ.

MRSZ. (2021c). *Press Release. Figures show an obvious decline for the communications market in 2020: media spending shrank nearly 3 percent, while total communications spending plunged a very significant 16 percent (2021).* Retrieved 17 August 2021, from https://mrsz.hu/cmsfiles/9f/ef/MRSZ_press-release_2020_media-communication-spending_20210414_ENG.pdf

Mshvenieradze, T. (2013). Logos ethos and pathos in political discourse. *Theory and Practice in Language Studies, 3*(11), 1939–1945. doi:10.4304/tpls.3.11.1939-1945

Mubarak, M. K. A. (2021, November 25). *50 years since its founding, the UAE is a more creative place than ever.* The National. Retrieved September 10, 2021 from https://www.thenationalnews.com/opinion/comment/2021/11/25/50-years-since-its-founding-the-uae-is-a-more-creative-place-than-ever/

Mukherji, J. (2005). Maternal communication patterns, advertising attitudes and mediation behaviours in urban India. *Journal of Marketing Communications, 11*(4), 247-262. doi:10.1080/13527260500167223

Müllerb, J., & Christandl, F. (2019). Content is king – But who is the king of kings? The effect of content marketing, sponsored content & user-generated content on brand responses. *Computers in Human Behavior, 96*, 46–55. doi:10.1016/j.chb.2019.02.006

Mulvey, L. (1975). Visual pleasure and narrative cinema. *Screen, 16*(3), 6–18. doi:10.1093creen/16.3.6

Nafees, L., Cook, C. M., Nikolov, A. N., & Stoddard, J. E. (2021). Can social media influencer (SMI) power influence consumer brand attitudes? The mediating role of perceived SMI credibility. *Digital Business, 1*(2), 100008. doi:10.1016/J.DIGBUS.2021.100008

Ndimele, R. (2015). Language use in political advertising: A rhetorical discourse on "see who wants to be president of Nigeria". *Global Journal of Arts, Humanities and Social Sciences, 3*(8), 19–31.

Nelson, K. (2017). *The Greatest Business Secret.* https://swanadvertising.com/blog/greatest-business-secret/

Nelson, M., & Paek, H. (2007). A Content Analysis of Advertising in a Global Magazine Across Seven Countries: Implications for Global Advertising Strategies. *International Marketing Review, 24*(1), 64–86. doi:10.1108/02651330710727196

Nemhauser, M. (2014). *The Real Mad Men: The 1960s—A Golden Age of Advertising.* https://www.academia.edu/7288872/The_Real_Mad_Men_The_1960s_A_Golden_Age_of_Advertising

Nevett, T. (1992). Differences between American and British television advertising: Explanations and implications. *Journal of Advertising, 21*(4), 61–71.

Newman, B. I. (1994). *The marketing of the president: Political marketing as campaign.* Sage Publications.

Newman, B. I. (2002). The role of marketing in politics. *Journal of Political Marketing, 1*(1), 1–5.

Ngo, L. V., Nguyen, T. N. Q., Tran, N. T., & Paramita, W. (2020). It takes two to tango: The role of customer empathy and resources to improve the efficacy of frontline employee empathy. *Journal of Retailing and Consumer Services, 56,* 102141. doi:10.1016/j.jretconser.2020.102141

Niedermeier, K. E., Wang, E., & Zhang, X. (2016). The use of social media among business-to-business sales professionals in China: How social media helps create and solidify guanxi relationships between sales professionals and customers. *Journal of Research in Interactive Marketing, 10,* 33–49. doi:10.1108/JRIM-08-2015-0054

Niray, N. & Deniz, D. (2010). İran İslam Cumhuriyeti: Tarihi, Siyaseti ve Demokrasisi. *Fırat Üniversitesi Orta Doğu Araştırmaları Dergisi, 6*(2).

Nixon, S. (2017). Looking westwards and worshipping: The New York 'creative revolution' and British advertising, 1956–1980. *Journal of Consumer Culture, 17*(2), 147–166. doi:10.1177/1469540515571388

Noelle-Neumann, E. (1974). The spirial of slience: A theory of public opinion. *Journal of Communication, 24*(2), 43–51.

NTI. (2021). *The State of the Russian Economy: Balancing Political and Economic Priorities.* https://www.nti.org/analysis/articles/state-russian-economy-balancing-political-and-economic-priorities/, (08.10.2021)

Nussbaum, M. C. (1996). Essay on Aristotle's rhetoric. In A. O. Rorty (Ed.), *Aristotle on emotions and rational persuasion* (pp. 303–321). Universities of California Press.

Nussbaum, M., & Sen, A. (1987). *Internal criticism and Indian rationalist traditions.* World Institute for Development Economics Research of the United Nations University.

O'Barr, W. M. (2005). *A Brief History of Advertising in America.* Advertising Educational Foundation.

Oates, S., Kaid, L. L., & Berry, M. (2010). *Terrorism, elections, and democracy: Political campaigns in United States, Great Britain, and Russia.* Palgrave Macmillan.

Odabasi, Y. (2004). *Postmodern pazarlama: tuketim ve tuketici* [Postmodern marketing: Consumption and consumer]. Kapital Medya.

Office for National Statistics. (n.d.). *Main Figures.* Retrieved from: https://www.ons.gov.uk/

Ogilvy, D. (1955). *The image of the brand–a new approach to creative operations.* Academic Press.

Ogunsiji, A. S. (2012). The impact of celebrity endorsement on strategic brand management. *International Journal of Business and Social Science, 3*(6), 141–145.

Olaffson, J. B. (2014). *Advertising to the Japanese consumer: Japanese advertising culture examined* [Bacholor's Thesis]. Sigillum University.

Ollman, B. (2011). *Yabancılaşma*. Yordam Kitap.

Onurlu, Ö., & Zulfugarova, N. (2016). Küresel Markaların Yerel Pazarlardaki Reklam Stratejileri İle Kültürel Farklılıklar Arasındaki İlgi Üzerine Bir Uygulama. *Öneri Dergisi*, *12*(45), 491-513. Retrieved from https://dergipark.org.tr/en/pub/maruoneri/issue/17906/187980?publisher=e-dergi-marmara?publisher=e-dergi-marmara

Orsini, K., & Ostojić, V. (2018). *Croatia's tourism industry: Beyond the sun and sea*. Economic Brief of European Commission, No.036. https://ec.europa.eu/info/publications/economy-finance/croatias-tourism-industry-beyond-sun-and-sea_en

Orttung, R. W. (2004, March/April). Business and Politics in the Russian Regions. *Problems of Post-Communism*, *51*(2), 48–60. doi:10.1080/10758216.2004.11052162

Osváth, P. (2021). A COVID–19-pandémia mentálhigiénés következményei. Hogyan tudunk felkészülni a pszichodémiás krízisre? *Orvosi Hetilap*, *162*(10), 366–374. doi:10.1556/650.2021.31141 PMID:33683216

OTT/Over The Top | Definition. (n.d.). Retrieved January 5, 2022, from https://www.adjust.com/glossary/ott-over-the-top/

Ovchinnikov, A. (2020, June 15). *Fujairah Creative City Free Zone Company Formation*. Emirabiz. Retrieved November 21, 2021, from https://emirabiz.com/creative-city-fujairah/

Overview of Culture & Arts. (2022). Retrieved from State Information Service: https://www.sis.gov.eg/section/10/497?lang=en-us

Oxford Business Group. (2021, February 8). *Why have media producers flocked to Abu Dhabi?* Retrieved August 29, 2021, from https://oxfordbusinessgroup.com/overview/ready-prime-time-calculated-investments-and-incentives-aimed-developing-local-production-capacity

Oyedele, A., & Minor, M. S. (2012). Consumer culture plots in television advertising from Nigeria and South Africa. *Journal of Advertising*, *41*(1), 91–108. doi:10.2753/JOA0091-3367410107

Özdemir, A., & Öksüzler, O. (2006). Tourism in Turkey is an economic growth policy toolcould it be? A granger causality analysis. *Balikesir University Institute of Social Sciences Journal, 9*(16), 107-126.

Özdemir, A., & Öksüzler, O. (2006). *Türkiye'de turizm bir ekonomik büyüme politikası aracı olabilir mi? Bir granger nedensellik analizi*. Balıkesir Üniversitesi Sosyal Bilimler Enstitüsü.

Özgür, A. Z. (1994). Televizyon reklamcılığı. Der Yayınları.

Öztürk, E., & Şener, G. (2016). Product Placement in The Social Media Era: A Content Analysis on Instagram and Instabloggers [Sosyal Medya Çağında Ürün Yerleştirme: Instagram ve Instabloggerlar Üzerine Bir İçerik Analizi]. *Global Media Journal TR Edition, 6*(12), 355–386.

PageFair. (2017). *The state of the blocked web*. 2017 Global Adblock Report. Retrieved 21 October 2021, from https://blockthrough.com/blog/adblockreport/

Paltridge, B. (2012). *Discourse analysis: An introduction* (2nd ed.). Bloomsbury Academic.

Papandrea, F., & Tiffen, R. (2016). Media ownership and concentration in Australia. In E. M. Noam (Ed.), *Who owns the world's media?* (pp. 703–739). Oxford University Press.

Papavassiliou, N., & Stathakopoulos, V. (1997). Standardization Versus Adaptation of International Advertising Strategies: Towards a Framework. *European Journal of Marketing, 31*(7), 504–527. doi:10.1108/03090569710176646

Papp-Váry, Á., & Tóth, T. Zs. (2021). Analysis of Budapest as a Film Tourism Destination In Global Perspectives on Literary Tourism and Film-Induced Tourism. IGI Global.

Pariser, E. (2011). *The filter bubble: What the Internet is hiding from you.* Penguin UK.

Park, J. (2018). Celebrity advertising in Japan: Tommy Lee Jones as alien investor in Suntory TV commercials. *Journal of Global Media Studies, 22,* 51–57.

Partners for Livable Communities. (2014). *Cultural heritage tourism.* Retrieved 2021, July 20 from https://www.americansforthearts.org/sites/default/files/culturalheritagetourism.pdf

Paszyc, E., & Wisniewska, I. (2002). Big business in the Russian economy and politics under Putin's rule. *CES Studies,* 45-57. http://pdc.ceu.hu/archive/00002224/01/big_business.pdf

Patrick, H., & Rosovsky, H. (1976). Understanding the Japanese economic miracle [Review of Asia's new giant: How the Japanese economy works]. *Brookings Bulletin (Washington, D.C.), 13*(1), 4–7.

Pattenden, J. (2011). Gatekeeping as accumulation and domination: Decentralization and class relations in rural South India. *Journal of Agrarian Change, 11*(2), 164–194. doi:10.1111/j.1471-0366.2010.00300.x

Patwardhan, P., Patwardhan, H., & Vasavada-Oza, F. (2009). Insights on account planning: A view from the Indian ad industry. *Journal of Current Issues and Research in Advertising, 31*(2), 105–121. doi:10.1080/10641734.2009.10505269

Patwardhan, P., Patwardhan, H., & Vasavada-Oza, F. (2011). Diffusion of account planning in Indian ad agencies. *International Journal of Advertising, 30*(4), 665–692. doi:10.2501/IJA-30-4-665-692

Pauwels, K., Erguncu, S., & Yildirim, G. (2013). Winning hearts, minds and sales: How marketing communication enters the purchase process in emerging and mature markets. *International Journal of Research in Marketing, 30*(1), 57–68. doi:10.1016/j.ijresmar.2012.09.006

Payne, A. (2017). 'The growing practice of calling in continental film groups': The European influence on production of early British TV advertising. *VIEW Journal of European Television History and Culture, 6*(11), 70–80.

Pay-TV. (n.d.). Retrieved December 25, 2021, from https://www.merriam-webster.com/dictionary/pay-TV

Pender, K. (n.d.). *Regulating truth and lies in political advertising: Implied freedom considerations.* Retrieved November 15, 2021, from Australian National University: https://law.anu.edu.au/sites/all/files/pender_-_tpal_paper.pdf

Penney, J. (2011). KEVIN07: Cool politics, consumer citizenship, and the specter of "Americanization" in Australia. *Communication, Culture & Critique, 4*(1), 78–96.

Pénzcentrum. (2020a). *Rengeteg céget számolt fel a járvány: ezek az ágazatok buktak a legnagyobbat.* Retrieved 25 October 2021, from https://www.penzcentrum.hu/egeszseg/20200807/rengeteg-ceget-szamolt-fel-a-jarvany-ezek-az-agazatok-buktak-a-legnagyobbat-1100546

Pénzcentrum. (2020b). *Elképesztő, mennyi kütyüt vettek idén a magyarok: ezeket keresték legtöbben.* Retrieved 13 October 2021, from https://www.penzcentrum.hu/vasarlas/20201229/elkepeszto-mennyi-kutyut-vettek-iden-a-magyarok-ezeket-kerestek-legtobben-1108444

Petty, R. E., Cacioppo, J. T., & Schuman, D. (1983). Central and peripheral routes to advertising effectiveness: The moderating role of involvement. *The Journal of Consumer Research, 10*(December), 135–146. doi:10.1086/208954

Phillip, J. (2018). The Commercial Appropriation of Fame: A Cultural Analysis of the Right of Publicity and Passing Off. *European Intellectual Property Review,* 1.

Pigott, M. B. (1996). The English of advertising: Differences in the British and American languages of television advertising. *Revista de Lenguas para Fines Específicos, 3,* 245–254.

Pinkleton, B. (1997). The effects of negative comparative political advertising on candidate evaluations and advertising evaluations: An exploration. *Journal of Advertising*, *26*(1), 19–29.

Pinkleton, B. E., Um, N.-H., & Austin, E. W. (2013). An exploration of the effects of negative political advertising on political decision making. *Journal of Advertising*, *31*(1), 13–25.

Plasser, F., & Plasser, G. (2002). *Global political campaigning: A worldwide analysis of campaign professionals and their practices*. Praeger.

Pletcher, K. (2011). *The geography of India: Sacred and historic places*. Britannica Educational Publishing.

Podium. (2017). *State of Online Reviews*. Retrieved 23 October 2021, from https://www.podium.com/resources/podium-state-of-online-reviews/

Poljanec-Borić, S. (2017). Prikladni modeli razvojnog korištenja kulturne baštine. In M. O. Šćitaroci (Ed.), *Znanstveni kolokvij Modeli revitalizacije kulturnoga naslijeđa - zbornik radova* (pp. 18–22). HERU. https://www.bib.irb.hr/912433

Pollay, R. W. (1983). Measuring the cultural values manifest in advertising. *Current Issues and Research in Advertising*, *1*, 71–92.

Pope, D. (1983). *Advertising in Britain: A history* by T. R. Nevett; *Dictionary of trade name origins* by Adrian Room. *Business History Review*, *57*(3), 452–454.

Popkova, E. G., Litvinova, T., Mitina, M. A., & French, J. (2018). Social Advertising: A Russian Perspective. *Management*, *39*, 17. https://www.revistaespacios.com/a18v39n01/a18v39n01p17.pdf

Population. (2022). Retrieved from state Infromation Service: https://www.sis.gov.eg/section/10/9400?lang=en-us

Portafolio. (2021a). https://www.portafolio.co/economia/infraestructura/conexiones-a-internet-fija-y-movil-que-hay-en-colombia-segun-mintic-554259

Portafolio. (2021b). *Publicidad exterior una de las que más cae por la COVID*. https://www.portafolio.co/economia/publicidad-exterior-una-de-las-que-mas-cae-por-la-covid-543325

Portfolio. (2021). *Még mindig kevés pláza van Magyarországon, de ez nem biztos, hogy baj*. Retrieved 13 October 2021, from https://www.portfolio.hu/ingatlan/20210917/meg-mindig-keves-plaza-van-magyarorszagon-de-ez-nem-biztos-hogy-baj-501026# Sas

Pottinger, B. (1987). Political advertising in South Africa: Promise and pitfall. *Communicare*, *6*(2), 36–43.

Pradhan, A. (2021). Food substitutes, health supplements and the geist of fitness. In S. Malhotra, K. Sharma, & S. Dogra (Eds.), *Food culture studies in India consumption, representation and mediation* (pp. 3–10). Springer Nature. doi:10.1007/978-981-15-5254-0_1

Praet, C. L. C. (2001). Japanese advertising, The world's number one celebrity showcase? A cross-cultural comparison of the frequency of celebrity appearances in TV advertising. *Proceedings of the 2001 Special Asia-Pacific Conference of the American Academy of Advertising*, 6-13.

Pratt, E. E. (1956). *Building export sales-advertising. In Modern International Commerce*. Allyn and Bacon.

PricewaterhouseCoopers. (n.d.). *Global Entertainment & Media Outlook 2021–2025*. PwC. Retrieved October 21, 2021, from https://www.pwc.com/outlook

Priporas, C. V., Stylos, N., & Kamenidou, I. E. (2020). City image, city brand personality and generation Z residents' life satisfaction under economic crisis: Predictors of city-related social media engagement. *Journal of Business Research*, *119*, 453–463.

Puh, B. (2014). Destination image and tourism satisfaction: The case of a Mediterranean destination. *Mediterranean Journal of Social Sciences*, 5(13), 538–544. doi:10.5901/mjss.2014.v5n13p0538

Puppin, G. (2014). Advertising and China: How does a love/hate relationship work? In *The Changing Landscape of China's Consumerism*. Chandos Publishing. Accesses From https://www.researchgate.net/publication/286113045_Advertising_and_China_How_does_a_lovehate_relationship_work doi:10.1533/9781780634425.177

PwC. (2019). *Outlook: 2019-2023 An African perspective* (10th ed.). Retrieved 05/14/22 from: https://africa.mediaoutlook.pwc.com/dist/assets/pdf/AEMO_entertainment_and_media_2019_final.pdf

Pygmaconsulting. (n.d.). *The change of the advertising medium in South Africa*. Retrieved 05/10/22 from: https://pygmaconsulting.com/the-change-of-the-advertising-medium-in-south-africa/

QuestMobile. (2021a). *2020 China Internet Advertising Market Insight*. Retrieved from https://mp.weixin.qq.com/s/ikrOOmOiKkxl6ZI1b9UHRQ

QuestMobile. (2021b). *New Media in Cross-platform KOL Ecology Research Report*. Retrieved from https://mp.weixin.qq.com/s/xwsovZlbRA94vxGf7AbsIQ

Raddar Forecast. (2021). https://raddar.net/wp-content/uploads/2021/09/Base-Memorias-FORECAST-2021-2022-RADDAR.pdf

Rajaee, F. (2007). *Islamism and Modernism The Changing Discourse in Iran*. University of Texas Press Republic of Turkey Tehran Embassy Commercial Consultancy.

RAKEZ Media Zone. (n.d.). Retrieved August 27, 2021, from https://rakez.com/ar/About/Zones/Zone-Detail/rakez-media-zone

Ramamurthy, A. (2003). *Imperial persuaders: Images of Africa and Asia in British advertising*. Manchester University Press.

Ramanathan, S. (2011). *Advertising self regulation in Asia and Australiasia*. Asian Federation of Advertising Associations. https://icas.global/wp-content/uploads/2011_04_Ad_SR_Asia_Australia.pdf

Ranko, A., & Nedza, J. (2015). Crossing the Ideological Divide? Egypt's Salafists and the Muslim Brotherhood after the Arab Spring. *Studies in Conflict and Terrorism*, 1–23.

Rao, J. (2010). The caste system: Effects on poverty in India, Nepal and Sri Lanka. *Global Majority E-Journal*, *1*(2), 97–106.

Ray, B. J. (2021, November 20). *Law and Order Survives the Pandemic*. Gallup.Com. Retrieved August 20, 2021, from https://news.gallup.com/poll/357311/law-order-survives-pandemic.aspx

Razdan, D., & Arora, J. (2021). Chocolate and the holly factory: Analyzing the "role" of chocolate in select films from Hollywood. In S. Malhotra, K. Sharma, & S. Dogra (Eds.), *Food culture studies in India consumption, representation and mediation* (pp. 85–96). Springer Nature. doi:10.1007/978-981-15-5254-0_9

Rein, Sh. (2015). *End of Copycat China: The Rise of Creativity, Innovation, and Individualism in Asia*. Wiley.

Reisigl, M. (2008). Analysing political rhetoric. In R. Wodak & M. Krzyzanowski (Eds.), *Qualitative discourse analysis the social science* (pp. 96–120). Palgrave, Mcmillan. doi:10.1007/978-1-137-04798-4_5

Reisinger, Y. (1994). Tourist-host contact as a part of cultural tourism. *World Leisure & Recreation, 36*(2), 24–28. doi:10.1080/10261133.1994.9673910

Repiev, A. (2004). *A Glimpse of Russia's advertising and marketing.* Retrieved from http://www.-repiev.ru/articles/ghlimps_en.htm

Republic of Turkey Ministry of Foreign Affairs. (2021). https://www.mfa.gov.tr/iran-kunyesi.tr.mfa

Retnowati, Y. (2015). Challenges in Cross Cultural Advertising. *Humaniora. Volume, 27,* 340–349.

Richards, J., & Curran, C. (2002, Summer). Oracles On "Advertising": Searching for a Definition. *Journal of Advertising, 31*(2), 63–77. doi:10.1080/00913367.2002.10673667

RMAA Agency. (2020). https://russia-promo.com/blog/advertising-market-of-russia-2019-results

Roca, D., Wilson, B., Barrios, A., & Muñoz-Sánchez, O. (2017). Creativity identity in Colombia: The advertising creatives' perspective. *International Journal of Advertising, 36*(6), 831–851. doi:10.1080/02650487.2017.1374318

Rodrigues, S. B., & Singhal, D. (2017). Music placement in Indian television advertisements. *International Journal of Advanced Research in Management and Social Sciences, 6*(3), 116–129.

Rogulj, D. (2021). *Faithful Czech, German, and Polish Tourists Saving the 2021 Tourist Season in Split.* Retrieved 2022, January 30 from https://www.total-croatia-news.com/travel/54825-2021-tourist-season-in-split

Rohanlall, L. (2014). *Party ideology in South Africa.* Retrieved 05/04/22 from: https://wiredspace.wits.ac.za/jspui/bitstream/10539/15787/2/thesis%20361561_05%20SEP%202014.pdf

Roman, K. (2010). *The king of Madison Avenue: David Ogilvy and the making of modern advertising.* St. Martin's Press.

Rozgonyi, K. (2014). *Assessment of Media Legislation in Egypt.* European Union. Retrieved from https://www.menamedialaw.org/sites/default/files/library/material/medmedia_egypt.pdf

Sakr, N. (2012). Social media, television talk shows, and political change in Egypt. *Television & New Media, 14*(4), 322–337.

Sakwa, R. (2008). *Russian Politics and Society.* Routledge. doi:10.4324/9780203931257

Sander, F., & Govender, S. (2018, December 5). *South Africa: The rise and fall of the ANC.* Retrieved 05/07/22 from: https://www.dw.com/en/south-africa-the-rise-and-fall-of-the-anc/a-4260392

Saul, H. (2016). Instafamous: Meet the social media influencers redefining celebrity. *The Independent.* Retrieved from https://www.independent.co.uk/news/people/instagram-model-natasha-oakley-iskra-lawrence-kayla-itsines-kendall-jenner-jordyn-woods-a6907551.html

Saxena, A., & Saxena, V. (2021). Religiosity, ritual practices, and folk deity worship: Bawa Jitto shrine in March Block of Jammu Region. In A. Chauhan (Ed.), *Understanding culture and society in India: A study of Sufis, saints and deities in Jammu Region* (pp. 177–194). Springer. doi:10.1007/978-981-16-1598-6_9

Schofield, A. (1991). International differences in advertising practices: Britain compared with other countries. *International Journal of Advertising, 10*(4), 299–308.

Schomer, A. (2019). Influencer marketing: State of the social media influencer market in 2020. *Business Insider, 18.*

Schouten, A. P., Janssen, L., & Verspaget, M. (2020). Celebrity vs. Influencer endorsements in advertising: The role of identification, credibility, and productendorser fit. *International Journal of Advertising, 39*(2), 258–281. doi:10.1080/02650487.2019.1634898

Schulz-Herzenberg, C. (2020). *The South African non-voter: An analysis, The Midpoint Paper Series*. Konrad-Adenauer-Stiftung.

Scopen. (2021). *Agency Scope*. https://scopen.com/sites/default/files/studies/agency_scope_colombia_2020_-_anexo_informe_tendencias.pdf

Scott, J. (2011). *Conceptualising the social world: Principles of sociological analysis*. Cambridge Unversity Press.

SDAM. (2017). *Yeni Dünya Düzeninde Çin Halk Cumhuriyeti*. Accessed From http://sdam.org.tr/image/foto/2017/12/17/Yeni-Dunya-Duzeninde-Cin-Halk-Cumhuriyeti_1513529142.pdf

Sekhon, J. (2000). *Modern India*. McGraw-Hill.

Sen, C. T. (2004). *Food culture in India*. Greenwood.

Şener, G. (2020). Can Commodified Feminism Empower Women? Feminist Critical Discourse Analysis of International Working Women's Day Advertisements [Metalaşmış Feminizm Kadınları Güçlendirir mi? 8 Mart Dünya Emekçi Kadınlar Günü Reklamlarının Feminist Eleştirel Söylem Analizi]. *Kültür ve İletişim, 22*(2), 146-172.

Sengupta, S., & Frith, K. T. (1997). Multinational corporation advertising and cultural imperialism: A content analysis of Indian television commercials. *Asian Journal of Communication, 7*(1), 1–18. doi:10.1080/01292989709388295

Seong, J., Ngai, J., Woetzel, J., & Leung, N. (2021). *China Consumer Report. Understanding Chinese Consumers: Growth Engine of the World*. Accesses From https://www.mckinsey.com/~/media/mckinsey/featured%20insights/china/china%20still%20the%20worlds%20growth%20engine%20after%20covid%2019/mckinsey%20china%20consumer%20report%202021.pdf

Serrano, A., & Brooks, A. (2019). Who is left behind in global food systems? Local farmers failed by Colombia's avocado boom. *Environment and Planning E. Nature and Space, 2*(2), 348–367.

Seval, H. F. (2017). Japon kalkınmasının temel taşı: Meiji restorasyonu ve Iwakura heyeti [The basic stone of Japan's development: Meiji restoration and Iwakura construction]. *Is ve Hayat, 3*(5), 101–118.

Shabrina, I. (2016). *Persuasive strategies used in Hillary Clinton's political campaign speech* [Undergradute thesis, Universitas Islam Negeri Maulana Malik Ibrahim]. Retrieved 04/29/22 from: http://repositori.uin-alauddin.ac.id/16843/1/NURHIDAYATILLAH.pdf

Shah, K. (2014). *Advertising and integrated marketing communications*. Tata McGraw Hill Education.

Shah, M. K., & Tomer, S. (2020). How brands in India connected with the audience amid Covid-19. *International Journal of Scientific and Research Publications, 10*(8), 91–95. doi:10.29322/IJSRP.10.08.2020.p10414

Shand, K. (2020). *The Advertising Industry in South Africa 2020*. Retrieved 05/21/22 from: https://www.whoownswhom.co.za/report-store/advertising-industry-south-africa-2020/

Shankar, S. (2015). *Advertising diversity: Ad agencies and the creation of Asian American consumers*. Duke University Press.

Shareef, M. A., Mukerji, B., Dwivedi, Y. K., Rana, N. P., & Islam, R. (2019). Social media marketing: Comparative effect of advertisement sources. *Journal of Retailing and Consumer Services, 46*, 58–69. doi:10.1016/j.jretconser.2017.11.001

Shasavandi, L. (2016). *Gender Representation in Iranian Lifestyle Magazine, Green Family: A Semiological Analysis* [Master Thesis]. Eastern Mediterranean University.

Shechter, R. (2003). Press advertising in Egypt: Business realities and local meaning, 1882-1956. *The Arab Studies Journal, 10/11*(2/1), 44-66.

Sheresheva, M. Y., & Antonov-Ovseenko, A. A. (2015). Advertising in Russian periodicals at the turn of the communist era. *Journal of Historical Research in Marketing, 7*(2), 165–18. doi:10.1108/JHRM-09-2013-0055

Sherman, A. (2020). *TikTok reveals detailed user numbers for the first time.* Retrieved from https://www.cnbc.com/2020/08/24/tiktok-reveals-us-global-user-growth-numbers-for-first-time.html

Sheth, J. N., Sisodia, R. S., & Sharma, A. (2000). The antecedents and consequences of customer-centric marketing. *Journal of the Academy of Marketing Science, 28*(1), 55–66.

Shoraka, M. & Omidi, M. R. (2002, Spring). The Internet in Iran. *EEE Technology and Society Magazine*, 28-32.

Shrivastava, P. (2016). Effect of co-creation on customer experience, trust and brand loyalty. *International Journal of Sales & Marketing Management Research and Development., 6*(6), 1–14.

Siddiqui, K. (2020). A comparative political economy of China and India: A critical review. In Y. C. Kim (Ed.), *China-India relations: Geo-political competition, economic cooperation, cultural exchange and business ties* (pp. 31–58). Springer Nature. doi:10.1007/978-3-030-44425-9_3

Silka, D. N. (2014). On priority measures for creating the basis for the development of the Russian economy. *Life Science Journal, 11*(7s), 310–313.

Simpson, J. (2017). Finding Brand Success In The Digital World. *Forbes.* Retrieved 22 October 2021, from https://www.forbes.com/sites/forbesagencycouncil/2017/08/25/finding-brand-success-in-the-digital-world/?sh=17a3b5a626e2

Sinclair, J., & Younane, S. (2007). Government advertising as public communication: Cases, issues and effects. In S. Young (Ed.), *Government Communication in Australia* (pp. 204–226). Cambridge University Press.

Sindane, S. (2010). *The rise of political advertising on television in South Africa and its implications for democracy* [Doctoral dissertation, University of the Witwatersrand]. Retrieved 05/1922 from https://citeseerx.ist.psu.edu/viewdoc/download?doi=10.1.1.927.2315&rep=rep1&type=pdf

Sindane, S. (2014). The commodification of political advertising on television during the 2009 general elections in South Africa. Global Media Journal African Edition, 8(1), 1-29.

Singh, R., & Singh, R. S. (2008). Cultural Geography. In D. K. Nayak (Ed.), *Progress in Indian Geography* (pp. 81-88). Indian National Science Academy. Retrieved 12/15/21 from: http://citeseerx.ist.psu.edu/

Singh, R. L. (1971). *India: A regional geography.* Silver Jubilee Publication.

Singh, R., & Kaur, P. (2014). Maternal Attitude towards TV Advertising in India. *Management and Labour Studies, 39*(2), 160–173. doi:10.1177/0258042X14558182

Singh, S., & Appiah-Adu, K. (2008). Culture, creativity, and Advertising. In M. Vernengo, E. Perez Caldentey, & B. J. Rosser Jr (Eds.), *Business practices in emerging and re-emerging markets* (pp. 133–150). Palgrave Macmillan.

Sivulka, J. (2012). *Soap, sex, and cigarettes: A cultural history of American advertising.* Wadsworth.

Skov, L., & Moeran, B. (1995). Introduction: Hiding in the light: from Oshin to Yoshimoto Banana. In L. Skov & B. Moeran (Eds.), Women, media and consumption in Japan. University of Hawaii Press.

Smith, R., & Xang, X. (2004). Toward a general theory of creativity in advertising: Examining the role of divergence. *Marketing Theory, 4*(1–2), 31–58. doi:10.1177/1470593104044086

Socialblade. (2021). *Top 100 youtubers in India sorted by subscribed.* Retrieved 11/30/21 from: https://socialblade.com/youtube/top/country/in/mostsubscribed

Sokoloff, J. M. (2019). *Advertising for impact: How Christmas lights helped end a war. In Perspectives on Impact.* Routledge. doi:10.4324/9780429452796-15

Solijonov, A. (2016). *Voter turnout trends around the world.* International Institute for Democracy and Electoral Assistance.

Srikandath, S. (1991). Cultural values depicted in Indian television advertising. *The International Communication Gazette, 48*(3), 165–176. doi:10.1177/001654929104800302

Srinivasan, R. (2001). Advertising in India. In I. Kloss (Ed.), *Advertising worldwide* (pp. 149–168). Springer. doi:10.1007/978-3-642-56811-4_7

Srivastava, E., Maheswarappa, S. S., & Sivakumaran, B. (2017). Nostalgic advertising in India: A content analysis of Indian TV advertisements. *Asia Pacific Journal of Marketing and Logistics, 29*(1), 47–69. doi:10.1108/APJML-10-2015-0152

Statista Research Department. (2021). *Major ad agencies Japan 2019: Based on sales revenue.* https://www.statista.com/statistics/1009998/japan-leading-advertising-agencies-by-sales/

Statista Research Department. (2021a). *Global influencer market Size 2020.* Retrieved from https://www.statista.com/statistics/1092819/global-influencer-market-size/

Statista Research Department. (2021b). *Global Instagram influencer market value 2020.* Retrieved from https://www.statista.com/statistics/748630/global-instagram-influencermarket-value/

Statista. (2021). *Gasto anual en publicidad digital en Colombia.* https://es.statista.com/estadisticas/1178729/gasto-anual-publicidad-digital-colombia/

Statista. (2021). *U.S. digital advertising industry - statistics & facts.* https://www.statista.com/topics/1176/online-advertising/#dossierKeyfigures

Statista. (2021, March 14). *Revenue from television advertisements across India.* Retrieved 10/15/21 from: https://www.statista.com/statistics/233489/tv-advertising-revenue-in-india/

Statista. (2021a). *Number of tourist arrivals in accommodation establishments in Budapest, Hungary from 2000 to 2020.* Retrieved 29 October 2021, from https://www.statista.com/statistics/986072/budapest-tourist-arrivals-in-accommodation/

Statista. (2021b). *Distribution of advertising spending worldwide in 2023, by medium.* Retrieved 18 August 2021, from https://www.statista.com/statistics/269333/distribution-of-global-advertising-expenditure/

Statista. (2022). *Retrieved from Distribution of advertising expenditure in Egypt from 2008 to 2015, by medium.* https://www.statista.com/statistics/388242/advertising-expenditures-share-by-medium-egypt/

Stern, E., & Krakower, S. (1993). The Formation of a Composite Urban Image. *Geographical Analysis, 25*(2), 130–146. doi:10.1111/j.1538-4632.1993.tb00285.x

Sultan, N. (2013). Al Jazeera: Reflections on the Arab Spring. *Journal of Arabian Studies: Arabia, the Gulf, and the Red Sea, 3*(2), 249-264.

Sundermann, G., & Raabe, T. (2019). Strategic communication through social media influencers: Current state of research and desiderata. *International Journal of Strategic Communication, 13*(4), 278–300. doi:10.1080/1553118X.2019.1618306

Sunstein, C. R. (2006). *Infotopia: How many minds produce knowledge.* Oxford University Press.

Sur, S. (2020). Family planning and the masculinity of nirodh condoms in India. In S. Sur, R. Kumaramkandath, & S. Srivastava (Eds.), *Stories of desire sexualities and culture in modern India* (pp. 134–151). Cambridge University Press. doi:10.1017/9781108637770.009

SuzukiC. (2021). *China.* Accessed from https://www.britannica.com/place/China/The-eastern-region

Szabó-Kákonyi, A. & Papp-Váry, Á. (2013). *A magyar reklámtudomány kezdetei az 1910-es, 1920-as években és mai napig tartó hatásuk.* A SJE Nemzetközi Tudományos Konferenciája. Komárom.

Szepesi, A. (2021). *Online fizetés: a magyarok megszokták az új rendszert.* https://www.napi.hu/magyar-vallalatok/felmeres-online-fizetes-eros-ugyfel-hitelesites.736849.html

Tafesse, W., & Wood, B. P. (2021). Followers' engagement with instagram influencers: The role of influencers' content and engagement strategy. *Journal of Retailing and Consumer Services, 58.* .jretconser.2020.102303 doi:10.1016/j

Takó, A. (2020). *Effie Awards Analysis by Ipsos.* Retrieved 21 October 2021, from https://effie.hu/2021/downloads/ipsos-pres-effie.pdf

Tan, Z. (2002). Sports Communication in China. China Media Monitor Intelligence (HK).

Tandon, N. (2018). Growth of advertising industry in India. *International Journal of Recent Scientific Research, 9*(1), 23622–23625. doi:10.24327/ijrsr.2018.0901.1502

Tanjung, S., & Hudrasyah, H. (2016). The impact of celebrity and non-celebrity endorser credibility in the advertisement on attitude towards advertisement: Attitude towards brand and purchase intention, *International Conference on Ethics of Business, Economics, and Social Science Proceeding*, 231-45.

TBB. (2021). *Türkiye'nin Coğrafi Yapısı.* http://www.tbb.gen.tr/turkce/cografya/index.html

Teer-Tomaselli, R. (2006). The SAGE Handbook of Political Advertising. In L. L. Kaid & C. Holtz-Bacha (Eds.), Political Advertising in South Africa (pp. 429-444). Sage Publication. doi:10.4135/9781412973403.n26

Telenor. (2021). *Velünk marad a home office egy friss kutatás szerint.* Retrieved 14 October 2021, from https://www.telenor.hu/sajto/kozlemeny/velunk-marad-a-home-office-egy-friss-kutatas-szerint

Thatelo, M. T. (2017). *A social semiotic analysis of the verbal, non-verbal and visual rhetoric of the 2009 and 2014 African National Congress (ANC) political television advertisements: a comparative qualitative content analysis study* [Doctoral dissertation, University of South Africa]. Retrieved 05/20/22 from: https://uir.unisa.ac.za/bitstream/handle/10500/25218/dissertation_mopailo_ma.pdf;jsessionid=9A4E731D7B4E1061473263969B568E89?sequence=1

The Arda. (2015). *South Africa – Religious.* Retrieved 05/15/22 from: https://www.thearda.com/internationalData/countries/Country_207_2.asp

The Economist. (2017). *The world's most valuable resource is no longer oil, but data.* https://www.economist.com/leaders/2017/05/06/the-worlds-most-valuable-resource-is-no-longer-oil-but-data

The official page of President / Abdel Fattah Al-Sisi. (2022, May 14). Retrieved from Facebook: https://www.facebook.com/AlSisiofficial?hc_ref=ARSy4Df0jHID2YDbXqaMVkJ5mcgJMe7kBz4n6SnJm9KNVfzCwjMBkcnIEaRM2n6wLH0&fref=nf&__xts__[0]=68.ARCMs9EXsue6ebQYJY7KNGrlhTgPDw19zkP0LpO1hUfhcOnHY7ELgg_RlMZJ-7c6YVIa1iafKRdjorJGIZH0dey3EQ0XARBDCmSAOwS6t1jGDTI120-KqyK

Themanifest. (2021, November). *Top 100 advertising agencies in India.* Retrieved 09/09/21 from: https://themanifest.com/in/advertising/agencies

Thomas, M. (2021). *Dubrovnik records impressive tourism figures in August.* Retrieved 2022, January 30, from https://www.thedubrovniktimes.com/news/dubrovnik/item/12078-dubrovnik-records-impressive-tourism-figures-in-august

Thomas, A. (2006). *Transnational media and contoured markets.* Sage.

Thomola, L. L. (2020). *Advertising in China - statistics & facts.* Accessed From https://www.statista.com/study/14624/advertising-in-china/

Thomola, L. L. (2021). *Advertising in China - statistics & facts.* Accessed From https://www.statista.com/topics/5604/advertising-in-china/#dossierKeyfigures

Thorelli, H. B. (1968). Its multi-cultural marketing system. *Journal of Marketing, 32*(2), 40–48. doi:10.1177/002224296803200207

Timeanddate. (n.d.). https://www.timeanddate.com/holidays/russia/women-day

Tiryakian, E. A. (1978). Emile Durkheim. In T. Bottomore & R. Nisbet (Eds.), *A history of sociological analysis* (pp. 187–236). Basic Books.

Töre, E. (2011). Türkiye'de reklam endüstrisi değer zinciri ve temel göstergeler. *The Turkish Online Journal of Design, Art and Communication, 1*(2), 34-42.

Tourist Board of Split. (n.d.). *City of culture.* Central Dalmatia: Split-Dalmatia County Tourist Board. Retrieved 2021, June 16 from https://visitsplit.com/en/184/city-of-culture

Treisman, D. (2009). *Russian politics in a time of economic turmoil.* https://www.sscnet.ucla.edu/polisci/faculty/treisman/Papers/RBS%20Final%20Decmeber%2026,%202009%20with%20figures.pdf

Trustpilot. (2020). *Why do people write reviews? What our research revealed.* Retrieved 22 October 2021, from https://business.trustpilot.com/reviews/learn-from-customers/why-do-people-write-reviews-what-our-research-revealed

Tsetsura, K., & Kruckeberg, D. (2021). *Strategic Communications in Russia Public Relations and Advertising.* https://books.google.com.tr/books?hl=tr&lr=&id=efz0DwAAQBAJ&oi=fnd&pg=PT118&dq=History+of+The+Russian+Advertising+Industry&ots=ZtHGatj2FH&sig=KKukAbTxKhS-HnQD268bIDOU8wI&redir_esc=y#v=onepage&q=History%20of%20The%20Russian%20Advertising%20Industry&f=false

Tsutsui, W. M. (n.d.). *Late Twentieth Century Japan: An introductory essay, Imagining Japanese History.* Program for Teaching East Asia, University of Colorado. https://www.colorado.edu/ptea-curriculum/sites/default/files/attached-files/20-essay.pdf

Tucker, C. E. (2014). Social networks, personalized advertising, and privacy controls. *JMR, Journal of Marketing Research, 51*(5), 546–562. doi:10.1509/jmr.10.0355

Tungate, M. (2007). Adland: A global history of advertising (2nd ed.). Kogan Page Publishers.

Turan, M. (2020, June 19). *Business Setup in Dubai | Company Formation in Dubai, UAE.* Emirabiz. https://emirabiz.com

Turkalj, D., Biloš, A., & Deželjin, R. (2019). The effects of digital promotion investment in Croatia's Tourism Product. In *5th International Scientific Conference ToSEE - Tourism in Southern and Eastern Europe 2019 "Creating Innovative Tourism Experiences: The Way to Extend the Tourist Season"* (pp. 715-728). 10.20867/tosee.05.3

Türkiye Kültür Portalı. (2021). *Türk Tarihine Genel Bakış.* https://www.kulturportali.gov.tr/portal/turk-tarihine-genel-bakis

Turner, G. (2013). *Understanding Celebrity.* Sage Publications.

Tuten, T. L., & Solomon, M. R. (2017). Social media marketing. *Sage (Atlanta, Ga.).*

Twofour54 Abu Dhabi media zone | Business Setup & Freelance Visa UAE. (2021, June 2). *Twofour54*. Retrieved September 20, 2021, from https://www.twofour54.com/en/

Tyali, S. M., & Mukhudwana, R. F. (2020). Discourses on political advertising in South Africa: A social media reception analysis. In M. N. Ndlela & W. Mano (Eds.), Social media and elections in Africa, volume 2 challenges and opportunities (pp. 245-270). Palgrave Macmillan. doi:10.1007/978-3-030-32682-1_13

U.S. International Trade Administration. (n.d.). *Croatia - Country Commercial Guide*. Retrieved 2022, January 30 from https://www.trade.gov/country-commercial-guides/croatia-selling-factors-and-techniques

UAE's Media Landscape: An Overview. (2017, March 9). *ICFUAE | International Campaign For Freedom in the UAE*. Retrieved October 20, 2021, from http://icfuae.org.uk/research-and-publications/uae%E2%80%99s-media-landscape-overview

Ugwuanyi, C. C., Okeke, C., & Emezue, L. (2018). Celebrity advertising, brand awareness and brand recognition: A structural equation modelling approach. *European Journal of Business and Management, 10*(28), 17–24.

Ük, Z. Ç. (2019). Evaluation of Gender Stereotypes through Women's Day Advertisements [Toplumsal Cinsiyet Stereotiplerinin Kadınlar Günü Reklamları Üzerinden Değerlendirilmesi]. *UİİİD-IJEAS, 2019*(24), 1-16.

Ultravioleta. (2019). *Así se hizo Ríos de luz, una invitación a la desmovilización*. https://ultravioleta.co/asi-se-hizo-rios-de-luz-una-invitacion-a-la-desmovilizacion/

Umm Al Quwain Free Zone - UAQ. (n.d.). *UAE Free Zones*. Retrieved September 21, 2021, from https://www.uaefreezones.com/uaq_umm_al_quwain_free_zone.html

UNESCO World Heritage Centre. (n.d.). *Properties inscribed on the World Heritage List*. United Nations. Retrieved 2021, July 22 from https://whc.unesco.org/en/statesparties/hr

UNESCO. (2020). *Quadrennial Periodic Report United Arab Emirates 2020 UNESCO Diversity of Cultural Expressions*. Retrieved October 10, 2021, from https://en.unesco.org/creativity/governance/periodic-reports/submission/6975

UNHCR. (2020). *Venezuela Situation*. https://data2.unhcr.org/es/situations/vensit

Unidad para la Atención y la Reparación Integral a las Víctimas. (2019). *Registro Único de Víctimas (RUV)*. https://www.unidadvictimas.gov.co/es/registro-unico-de-victimas-ruv/37394

Union Nations. (2015, October 5-6). *Census of India: Lessons learnt and the way ahead*. Retrieved 11/06/21 from: https://www.un.org/en/development/desa/population/events/pdf/expert/23/Presentations/EGM-S2-Chandramouli%20presentation.pdf

United Nations Conference on Trade and Development. (2020). *COVID-19 and Ecommerce: Findings from a survey of online consumers in 19 countries*. Retrieved from https://unctad.org/search?keys=shopping+more+often+online

United Nations Conference on Trade and Development. (n.d.). *Covid 19 and E-Commerce Findings from a Survey of Online Consumers in 9 Countries*. Accessed From https://unctad.org/system/files/official-document/dtlstictinf2020d1_en.pdf

United Nations Office on Drugs and Crime. (2021). *Global Overview: Drug Demand / Drug Supply*. http://www.odc.gov.co/Portals/1/publicaciones/pdf/WDR21_Booklet_2.pdf

Urošević, N. (2012). Kulturni identitet i kulturni turizam - između lokalnog i globalnog (primer Pule u Hrvatskoj). *Singidunum Journal of Applied Sciences, 9*(1), 67-76. http://scindeks.ceon.rs/article.aspx?artid=2217-80901201067U

Ustinova, I. P. (2006). English and American Culture Appeal in Russian Advertising. *Journal of Creative Communications, 3*(1), 77–98.

Ustinova, I. P. (2008). *English and emerging advertising in Russia*. Academic Press.

Uztuğ, F. (2004). *Siyasal iletişim yönetimi*. İstanbul, Türkiye: Media Cat.

Valentino, N. A., Hutchings, V. L., & Williams, D. (2004). The impact of political advertising on knowledge, internet information seeking, and candidate preference. *Journal of Communication, 54*(2), 37–354.

Vargo, S. L., & Lusch, R. F. (2004). Evolving to a new dominant logic for marketing. *Journal of Marketing, 68*(1), 1–17.

Venngage. (2019). *ROI of influencer marketing infographic*. Retrieved from https://venngage.com/gallery/post/roi-influencer-marketing-infographic/

Vilanilam, J. (1989). Television advertising and the Indian poor. *Media Culture & Society, 11*(4), 485–497. doi:10.1177/016344389011004009

Vitelar, A. (2019). Like me: Generation Z and the use of social media for personal branding. *Management Dynamics in the Knowledge Economy, 7*(2), 257–268. doi:10.25019/mdke/7.2.07

Vivian, J. (2012). *Media of Mass Communication* (11th ed.). Pearson.

W. (2020, November 5). Dubai Media City celebrates 20-year anniversary. *Khaleej Times*. Retrieved August 21, 2021, from https://www.khaleejtimes.com/uae/dubai-media-city-celebrates-20-year-anniversary

Wajid, A., Raziq, M. M., Ahmed, Q. M., & Ahmad, M. (2021). Observing viewers' self-reported and neurophysiological responses to message appeal in social media advertisements. *Journal of Retailing and Consumer Services, 59*, 102373. doi:10.1016/J.JRETCONSER.2020.102373

Wallace, K. (2019, July 11). *The history and future of television advertising*. https://blogs.oracle.com/advertising/post/the-history-and-future-of-television-advertising

Waller, M. (2005). Russian Politics Today. Manchester University Press.

Waller, D. S. (2002). Advertising agency-client attitudes towards ethical issues in political advertising. *Journal of Business Ethics*, (36), 347–354.

Waller, D. S., & Polonsky, M. J. (1996). 'Everybody hide, an election is coming!' An examination why some Australian advertising agencies refuse political accounts. *International Journal of Advertising, 15*(1), 61–74.

WAM. (2021a, April 10). *CNN Academy launches in Abu Dhabi to train region's next generation of journalists*. Retrieved August 21, 2021, from https://www.wam.ae/en/details/1395302871508

WAM. (2021b, April 11). *ADU, twofour54 to train next generation of Abu Dhabi game developers*. Retrieved August 11, 2021, from https://www.wam.ae/en/details/1395302896894

Wang, J. (2005). *From Advertising to Branding: Framing Chinese Consumer Culture*. Routledge Curzon.

Wang, R. Y., & Strong, D. M. (1996). Beyond accuracy: What data quality means to data consumers. *Journal of Management Information Systems, 12*(4), 5–33. doi:10.1080/07421222.1996.11518099

Wang, X., Wang, Y., Lin, X., & Abdullat, A. (2021). The dual concept of consumer value in social media brand community: A trust transfer perspective. *International Journal of Information Management, 59*, 102319. doi:10.1016/J.IJINFOMGT.2021.102319

Wang, X., & Yang, Z. (2011). Standardization or Adaptation in International Advertising Strategies: The Roles of Brand Personality and Country-of-Origin Image. *Asian Journal of Business Research, 1*(2), 25–36. doi:10.14707/ajbr.110009

Wang, Y. (2020). From "online communication" to "offline imitation": Video bloggers on the user's virtual interaction and willingness to buy factors. *Journalism and Communications Review, 6*, 73–85.

Wang, Z., Liu, H., Liu, W., & Wang, S. (2020). Understanding the power of opinion leaders' influence on the diffusion process of popular mobile games: Travel Frog on Sina Weibo. *Computers in Human Behavior, 109*, 106354. doi:10.1016/j.chb.2020.106354

Warc. (2010). https://www.warc.com/newsandopinion/news/russian-advertising-market-set-for-growth/26448

Ward, F. W. (1850). *India and the Hindoos: being a popular view of the geography, history, government, manners, customs, literature and religion of that ancient people, with an account of Christian missions among them.* Baker and Scribner.

Watson, L. (2020). Sustainable influencers: Hypocrites, or catalysts of change. *Sourcing Journal, 20.*

Wattenberg, M. P., & Brians, C. L. (1999). Negative campaign advertising: Demobilizer or mobilizer? *The American Political Science Review, 93*(4), 891–899.

We Are Social & Hootsuite. (2021). *Digital 2021 Colombia.* https://datareportal.com/reports/digital-2021-colombia

We need truth in political advertising laws. (2020). Retrieved November 2, 2021, from The Australia Institute: https://nb.australiainstitute.org.au/truth_in_political_ads

Weber, C. (2013). Emotions, campaigns, and political participation. *Political Research Quarterly, 66*(2), 414–428.

Weiler, J. (2004). *Human Rights in Russia: A Darker Side of Reform.* Lynne Rienner Publisher.

Weissglass, K. (2005). *Image manipulation in political advertisements: How color and music influence viewer attitudes and emotions.* Haverford College.

Welcome to UAE Free Zones. (n.d.). *UAE Free Zones.* Retrieved September 21, 2021, from https://www.uaefreezones.com

Wells, L.G. (1994). Western Concepts, Russian Perspectives: Meanings of Advertising in the Former Soviet Union. *Journal of Advertising, 23*(1), 83-95.

Wells, G. L., & Auken, S. V. (2006). A Comparison of Associational and Claimless-Informational Advertising in Russia. *Journal of East-West Business, 12*(1), 29–48. doi:10.1300/J097v12n01_03

West, B. A., & Murphy, F. (2010). *A Brief history of Australia.* Facts on File Publication.

West, D. (1988). Multinational competition in the British advertising agency business, 1936–1987. *Business History Review, 62*(3), 467–501.

Whang, H., Ko, E., Zhang, T., & Mattila, P. (2015). Brand popularity as an advertising cue affecting consumer evaluation on sustainable brands: A comparison study of Korea, China, and Russia. *International Journal of Advertising, 34*(5), 789811. doi:10.1080/02650487.2015.1057381

What Are Media Productions? (n.d.). Retrieved December 10, 2021, from https://fonktown.es/what-is-media-productions/

White, S., Sakwa, R., & Hale, H. E. (2010). Developments In Russian Politics. Palgrave Macmillan.

White, S. (2010). Soviet nostalgia and Russian politics. *Journal of Eurasian Studies, 1*(1), 1–9. doi:10.1016/j.euras.2009.11.003

WHO. (2021). *Colombia.* https://covid19.who.int/region/amro/country/co

Wictorowicz, Q. (2006). Anatomy of the Salafi movement. *Studies in Conflict and Terrorism, 29*(3), 207–239.

Wiener, J. H., & Hampton, M. (2007). *Anglo-American media interactions, 1850–2000.* Springer.

Wikipedia. (2021). *Women in Russia.* https://en.wikipedia.org/wiki/Women_in_Russia

Wikipedia. (n.d.a). https://tr.wikipedia.org/wiki/D%C3%BCnya_Kad%C4%B1nlar_G%C3%BCn%C3%BC

Wikipedia. (n.d.b). https://en.wikipedia.org/wiki/Perestroika

Willis, K. G. (2014). The use of stated preference methods to value cultural herştage. In V. A. Ginsburgh & B. Throsby (Eds.), *Handbook of the Economics of Art and Culture* (Vol. 2, pp. 145–181). Elsevier. doi:10.1016/B978-0-444-53776-8.00007-6

Wilson, J. L. (2010). The Legacy of the Color Revolutions for Russian Politics and Foreign Policy. *Problems of Post-Communism, 57*(2), 21–36. doi:10.2753/PPC1075-8216570202

Wolf, A. (2020). *Gen Z & Social Media Influencers: The Generation Wanting a Real Experience.* Academic Press.

World Bank. (2020). *Colombia | data.* https://data.worldbank.org/country/colombia

World economic outlook. (2022, April). International Monetary Fund.

World Population Review. (2021). *India population 2021 (Live).* Retrieved 10/10/21 from: https://worldpopulationreview.com/countries/india-population

Worldometers. (2021). *Colombia.* https://www.worldometers.info/coronavirus/country/colombia/

Wu, G. Q. (2018). Official websites as a tourism marketing medium: A contrastive analysis from the perspective of appraisal theory. *Journal of Destination Marketing & Management, 10,* 164–171. doi:10.1016/j.jdmm.2018.09.004

Wunderman Thompson. (n.d.a). *We are not an island.* Retrieved October 2, 2021, from https://www.wundermanthompson.com/work/we-are-not-an-island

Wunderman Thompson. (n.d.b). *Home to so much more.* Retrieved October 2, 2021, from https://www.wundermanthompson.com/work/home-to-so-much-more

Xia, J. (2020). "Loving you": Use of metadiscourse for relational acts in WeChat public account advertisements. *Discourse, Context & Media, 37,* 100416. doi:10.1016/j.dcm.2020.100416

Yamada, M. (2005). *An analysis of Japanese TV commercials that feature foreign celebrities: A content analytic and interview approach* [Graduate Thesis]. University of Oklahoma.

Yegin, A. (2013). *İran Siyasetini Anlama Klavuzu.* Seta.

Ye, M. (2003). *Creativity is Power (Chuangyi jiushi quanli).* Gongye Publishing.

Yılmaz, S. (2015). New Eurasianism and Russia [Yeni Avrasyacılık ve Rusya]. *Sosyal ve Beşeri Bilimler Araştırmaları Dergisi, 2015*(34), 111-120.

Yin, R. K. (2003). *Case study research: Design and method* (3rd ed.). Sage Publications.

Yin, R. K. (2018). *Case study research and applications.* Sage.

Yoon, K., Pinkleton, B. E., & Ko, W. (2007). Effects of negative political advertising on voting intention: An exploration of the roles of involvement and source credibility in the development of voter cynicism. *Journal of Marketing Communications, 11*(2), 95–112.

Yorkie, (2020). YouTube, Spaceman Jones Iron Boss-Japanese AD-Tommy Lee Jones, https://www.youtube.com/watch?v=xHugeSZcJSI

Younane, S. (2006). Protecting 'our way of life': Constructions of national ıdentity in government anti-terrorism advertising. *Australasian Political Studies Association Conference*, 1-19.

Young, S. (2013, August 20). *Here come the negative ads*. Retrieved November 6, 2021, from The University of Melbourne Election Watch Australia: http://past.electionwatch.edu.au/australia-2013/campaign-ads/here-come-negative-ads

Young, S., & Tham, J.-C. (2006). *Political finance in Australia: A skewed and secret system*. Canberra: Democratic Audit of Australia, Australian National University. Retrieved December 3, 2021, from https://apo.org.au/sites/default/files/resource-files/2006-11/apo-nid3933.pdf

Young, C. E. (2000). Creative differences between copywriters and art directors. *Journal of Advertising Research*, *40*(3), 19–26. doi:10.2501/JAR-40-3-19-26

Young, S. (2003). A century of political communication in Australia, 1901–2001. *Journal of Australian Studies*, *27*(78), 97–110.

Young, S. (2004). *The persuaders: Inside the hidden machine of political advertising*. Pluto Press.

Young, S. (2006). Not bitting the hand that feeds? Media reporting of government advertising in Australia. *Journalism Studies*, *7*(4), 554–574.

Young, S. (2007a). A history of government advertising in Australia. In S. Young (Ed.), *Government communication in Australia* (pp. 181–203). Cambridge University Press.

Young, S. (2007b). The regulation of government advertising in australia: The politicisation of a public policy issue. *Australian Journal of Public Administration*, *66*(4), 438–452.

Young, S. (2007c). Following the money trail: Government advertising, the missing millions and the unknown effects. *Public Policy*, *2*(2), 104–118.

Young, S. (2007d). Policy-making in a 'Cold Climate' of ruling party benefit: Party government and the regulation of government advertising in Australia. *Australian Journal of Political Science*, *47*(3), 489–502.

YouTube. (2014). *Retró reklámok*. Retrieved 29 October 2021, from https://www.youtube.com/watch?v=T7cYHrspUQY&t=284s&ab_channel=KrisztinaFeh%C3%A9rv%C3%A1ri

YouTube. (2017). *Croatia full of life - new promotional video 2018*. HTZ. Retrieved 2021, June 20 from https://www.youtube.com/watch?v=0XbIR7e9PYM

Youtube. (n.d.). https://www.youtube.com/watch?v=Y_iCIISngdI

Yu, P., Liu, Z., & Hanes, E. (2022). Supply Chain Resiliency, Efficiency, and Visibility in the Post-Pandemic Era in China: Case Studies of MeiTuan Waimai, and Ele.me. In Y. Ramakrishna (Ed.), Handbook of Research on Supply Chain Resiliency, Efficiency, and Visibility in the Post-Pandemic Era (pp. 195–225). IGI Global. doi.org/10.4018/978-1-7998-9506-0.ch011.

Yüksel, S. (2016). Causal Relationships Between Growth, Unemployment and Inflation in the Russian Economy [Rusya Ekonomisinde Büyüme, İşsizlik ve Enflasyon Arasındaki Nedensellik İlişkileri]. *Finans Politik & Ekonomik Yorumlar*, *53*(614), 43-57.

Yurttaş, Ö. U. (2018). Content Anslysis of Political Ads: 2018 General Elections in Turkey [Siyasal Reklamlara Yönelik İçerik Analizi: 2018 Türkiye Genel Seçimleri]. *Turkish Studies*, *13(26)*, 1171–1186.

Yu, S., & Hu, Y. (2020). When luxury brands meet China: The effect of localized celebrity endorsements in social media marketing. *Journal of Retailing and Consumer Services, 54*, 102010. doi:10.1016/j.jretconser.2019.102010

Yusuf, S., Nabeshima, K., & Perkins, D. (2007). China and India reshape global industrial geography. In A. L. Winters & S. Yusuf (Eds.), *Dancing with Giants: China, India, and the global economy* (pp. 35–66). The World Bank.

Zahed, S. (2004). Iranian national identity in the context of globalization: Dialogue or resistance? *CSGR Working Paper, 162*(5).

Zednik, A., & Strebinger, A. (2008). Brand management models of major consulting firms, advertising agencies and market research companies: A categorization and positioning analysis of models offered in Germany, Switzerland and Austria. *Brand Management, 15*(5), 301–311. doi:10.1057/palgrave.bm.2550096

Zhou, Y. (2020). *IP celebrity Li Ziqi, Interpretation of "KOL map" behind Popular Models.* Retrieved from https://mp.weixin.qq.com/s/yFSoKO1eIBxWDC4Dezfpiw

Zhou, S., Blazquez, M., McCormick, H., & Barnes, L. (2021). How social media influencers' narrative strategies benefit cultivating influencer marketing: Tackling issues of cultural barriers, commercialised content, and sponsorship disclosure. *Journal of Business Research, 134*, 122–142. doi:10.1016/J.JBUSRES.2021.05.011

Zhu, J., & Yang, Y. (2020). Exclusive: TikTok-owner ByteDance to rake in $27 billion ad revenue by year-end: sources. *Retrieved, 11*(14), 2020.

Zhu, Q. (2014). *Research and Application of User Generated Content in the New Generation of Internet Environment.* Science Press.

Zhu, Y., & Chen, H. (2015). Social media and human need satisfaction: Implications for social media marketing. *Business Horizons, 58*(3), 335–345. doi:10.1016/j.bushor.2015.01.006

Zigma8. (2018). *Legal Insights On Marketing And Advertising Laws in Iran.* https://zigma8.com/legal-insights-on-marketing-and-advertising-in-iran/

Zigma8. (2021a). *Rules and Regulations of Out of Home Advertising in Iran.* https://zigma8.com/rules-and-regulations-of-out-of-home-advertising-in-iran/

Zigma8. (2021b). *Why Influencer Marketing in Iran is so popular?* https://zigma8.com/why-influencer-marketing-in-iran-is-so-popular/

Zimmermann, K. A. (2021). *American Culture: Traditions and Customs of the United States.* https://www.livescience.com/28945-american-culture.html

Zubrinić, D. (1995). *Croatian Art.* Retrieved 2022, January 28 from https://www.croatianhistory.net/etf/art.html

Zuiderveen Borgesius, F., Trilling, D., Möller, J., Bodó, B., De Vreese, C. H., & Helberger, N. (2016). Should we worry about filter bubbles? *Internet Policy Review. Journal on Internet Regulation, 5*(1).

About the Contributors

Ipek Krom has studied Communication in Linfield University, OR, USA and has received her Bachelor's degree from Cinema- TV department in Beykent University. She has received her graduate degree and P.h.d. from Marmara University in Advertising and Publicity. She has worked as an Advertising and Public Relations Executive of several shopping malls and business centers. She has worked as Foreign Trade Manager and has marketing experience in this field for six years. She has been working as an Assistant Professor since 2014. Currenly, she works as the Head of Public Relations and Advertising Department in Istanbul Esenyurt University. Her area of interests are advertising, branding and electronic advertising. She has written articles about branding, entrepreneurship and innovation and its relation to brand loyalty; book chapters about brand engagement and postmodern branding and has been recently edited a book called about Viral Advertising: A Perspective from Marketing.

* * *

Ceren Gül Artuner Özder, born in İstanbul (Turkey) in 1972, completed her primary and secondary education at the French Lycée Saint Benoît (İstanbul). She pursued her undergraduate studies at the Faculty of Management, Department of Tourism and Hotel Management at Dokuz Eylül University (İzmir) and graduated as high honor student of the Faculty of Management in 1996. From 1996 to 2016, she worked in private sector companies operating in the fields of import-export, finance, and education. She obtained her Master of Arts (MA) degree in International Relations from Galatasaray University (İstanbul) in 2004 and Master of Management (MBA) degree in Management and Organization from Marmara University (İstanbul) in 2005. In 2011, she completed her postgraduate studies and received the title of Doctor of Management from Marmara University. She started her career as an academician at Yeditepe University (İstanbul) in 2016. Since 2016, she has been an assistant professor and since 2021, an associate professor at Beykent University (İstanbul) in the Faculty of Economics and Administrative Sciences, as the head of the Department of Tourism Management.

Kazım Babacan graduated from Atatürk University English Language and Literature department in 2000. He worked as a teacher of English in a state school in Bursa and then started teaching at Karadeniz Technical University as an instructor in 2001. He completed his MA in Erciyes University Public Relations department in 2013. He started his PhD at the same university in 2017 and has been writing his dissertation thesis on "Perception Management and Digital Diplomacy: The example of YTB on Twitter". His research interests are international public relations, cultural diplomacy, digital diplomacy, advertisements, perception management and language studies. He has still been working as an English instructor at Karadeniz Technical University.

Andrés Barrios Fajardo is an Associate Professor at Universidad de Los Andes School of Management (Bogotá, Colombia). He received his Ph.D at Lancaster University (England). Andrés's research spans marketing, entrepreneurship, and strategy. His interest focuses on the way in which business initiatives can promote social inclusion. Andrés's research has appeared in a wide range of international journals across disciplines, such as Journal of Service Research, Journal of Business Research, Journal of Public Policy and Marketing, Journal of Macromarketing, International Journal of Advertising, among others. Andrés's research has been funded through a variety of international and local grants, including RCUK, Colciencias, USAID, and World Women Bank Foundation.

Selçuk Bazarcı was born in Denizli, Turkey. He completed his undergraduate education at Ege University, Faculty of Communication, Department of Public Relations and Publicity. In 2013, he started to work as a research assistant at Muş Alparslan University. He has been working as a research assistant at Department of Advertising in Ege University since 2015. Selçuk Bazarcı, who completed his master's degree with the thesis titled "Real-Time Marketing as a New Marketing Approach in the Digital Age: A Study on the Brands' Social Media Sharings in Turkey" in Ege University, continues his doctoral studies in the same institution. Selçuk Bazarcı has published articles and book chapters about marketing, digital advertising and influencer marketing.

Onur Serdan Çarboğa received his Bachelor's degree in Advertising from Bahçeşehir University. In 2015 he was hired as a research assistant by Istanbul Bilgi University. After completing his Master's degree in Advertising and Promotion in 2018 in Marmara University, he has started working as a research assistant at Istanbul Bilgi University. His research interests include advertising, cognitive communication, video game advertising and gamification.

Merve Çelik Varol works in the Department of Public Relations and Advertising at the Faculty of Communication of Beykent University. The main areas of her work are Consumer Behavior, Public Relations and Social Media, but she is mainly interested in "Luxury Consumption", "Second-hand Consumption", "Online Shopping", "Digital Consumption" and "Sustainability". In addition, the author's articles, book chapters and research on these topics have been published.

Suzana Dzamtoska-Zdravkovska, PhD in Communication Sciences, MA in Communication, is an Associate Professor at American University of Ras Al Khaimah, United Arab Emirates. She has 12 years of academic experience at universities in North Macedonia and the UAE, teaching a variety of courses related to Communication, Communication Management, Mass Media and Mass Communication. She has more than 17 years of professional media experience as a journalist, public relations advisor, and spokesperson of the Ministry of Education and Science of North Macedonia. She is an active researcher and has published a significant number of scientific papers in international journals (indexed in SCOPUS, EBSCO Publishing Database, Central and Eastern European Online Library (CEEOL), Index Copernicus International, ICI, etc.); as well as in the proceedings of international academic conferences. She is the author and co-author of four peer-reviewed books and university textbooks.

İlkay Erarslan graduated from Istanbul University, Information-Document Management Department in 2002. She has received her MA from Institute of Social Sciences, Department of Management and Organization and P.h.d. from Beykent University, Social Sciences Institute of Business Administration in 2020. In her professional business life, she has worked as the Head of the University Library and Learning Resources Center Department and the Publishing House Manager. She started her academic career as a Vocational School lecturer in 2014 and she is currently working as Assistant Professor Doctor at the Faculty of Economics and Administrative Sciences, Department of Business Administration in Beykent University. Her research areas are business, management organization, information-document management.

Nurdan Güven Toker graduated from Yeditepe University, Faculty of Economy and Administrative Sciences, Department of Political Science and International Relations, and has completed a minor in the History Department of the Faculty of Arts and Sciences in 2009. She recieved her MA Degree in Politics and Society in Siena University in Italy. She holds a PhD in Political Science and International Relations from Yeditepe University with the thesis titled "A Biographical Study of a Utopian Intellectual: Şevket Süreyya Aydemir". Besides working as a Research Assistant at Yeditepe University, she has been working as an Assistant Professor at Haliç University since 2019. She continues her studies in the fields of Turkish Political Life, Turkish Intellectual History, Contemporary Political Thoughts, Comparative Political Systems, and has various publications in national and international refereed journals and books.

Sabir Haque is a multi-faceted media professional with over 18 years of experience in academia, broadcast media & filmmaking. He finished his Master's in Mass Communication from Mass Communication Research Center, Jamia Millia Islamia, New Delhi, in 2003. He completed his Ph.D. in Journalism & Social Media from the School of Communication, Manipal University India, in 2017. His first Documentary film bagged the National Award for Environment & Wildlife Conservation, which was screened at various film festivals worldwide. He joined NDTV, a premiere TV News Channel in New Delhi, India, and later NDTV ARABIA in the UAE. He continues to direct Documentary films and has built up a strong industry profile creating films for Corporates and Govt. UAE agencies. His last production as a Script Writer and Director is a 15 episode Docu-drama telecast on Dubai TV, Sama Dubai, and Dubai One. The docu-drama was produced for the Government of Dubai. He presently teaches Broadcast Media & New Media Technologies at the School of Arts and Sciences, American University of Ras Al Khaimah. He is a certified Avid Media Composer Instructor and creates online training material for Film Production, Graphic Design & Layout, Web Technologies & Social Media Advertising.

Onur Karakaş completed his undergraduate education in Kocaeli University in 2012 majoring in Public Relations and Publicity. He has received his MA in 2015 and P.h.D. in 2020 from Kocaeli University, Public Relations and Publicity Department. His fields of study are new media communication, political communication and advertising.

Ece Nur Kaya Yıldırım received her Bachelor's degree in Public Relations and Advertising from Izmir University of Economics where she also completed a double major in Media and Communication. In 2016 she was hired as a research assistant by Yalova University. After completing her Master's degree in Communication Arts in 2019 in Yalova University, she has started working as a research assistant and studying for her PhD. at Ege University. Her research interests include digital communication, sociology of communication, identity and cultural studies.

Reka Kerti is a Lecturer at Budapest Metropolitan University, Hungary. She has a BSc with a joint specialism in Marketing and Advertising and International Communication from Budapest Metropolitan University and an MSc in Organisational Psychology from City University London. Her research areas are advertising, digital advertising, brand building, and consumer behaviour. Besides her theoretical studies, she has seven years of practical experience working in media agencies as well as in a freelance capacity.

Yuejia Liao is an independent researcher. Her research interests include Advertising, Chinese Economy, and Sustainability.

Ramya Mahendran is a managed innovation consultant. She is certified in design thinking, business modeling and jobs to be done. She has over 10 years of experience in the fields of managed innovation, startup incubation and acceleration, crowd sources idea management systems, design thinking and sustainability. She works with student entrepreneurs to build their business ideas into a successful business model. She works with some of India's leading Technology and Business Incubators, Institution Innovation Councils and Entrepreneurship Cells. She specializes in setting up innovation strategy, opportunity identification, large scale ideation campaigns and facilitating rapid prototyping events like design service jams and hackathons, organizing large-scale Innovation summits and global idea crowd-sourcing events.

Meltem Özel completed her undergraduate education at Işık University, Department of International Relations (English, 100% scholarship), her master's degree at Beykent University, Social Sciences Institute, Business Administration, and her doctorate at Kocaeli University, Social Sciences Institute, Department of Public Relations and Publicity. Özel, who received the title of doctoral faculty member in 2021, has been working at Istanbul Esenyurt University since 2014. She teaches various courses in the Department of Public Relations and Advertising of the Faculty of Private, Arts and Social Sciences, where she served as the assistant coordinator between 2015-2018 and coordinator between 2019-2022 in the Erasmus Coordinatorship. Various works, book chapters and "Cultural Diplomacy and Educational Diplomacy in Turkey" published in the fields of public diplomacy, new media, communication, advertising and political communication. Özel, who has the book titled "On the Axis of International Exchange Programs", gives seminars in the field of "Media and Information Literacy" within the scope of Tübitak Science Talks and European Union Projects.

Başak Özoral received her Ph.D. from the McGill University in 2011. Her research focus on political economy, modernization in the Middle East, economy and culture in Middle East and globalization. She taught in Qatar University and American University in Dubai for five years. She teaches courses on Middle East, political economy, and research methods, and she regularly co-authors papers with graduate students at Istanbul Commerce University.

Rukiye Gulay Ozturk was born in 1981, in Istanbul. She received her bachelor's degree from Marmara University, at the Department of Public Relations and Publicity in 2004 and her master's degree and PhD from the same university at the Deparment of Advertising & Publicity. After PhD, she went to Georgetown University CCT Faculty in Washington DC as a short-term scholar with Postdoctoral Research Scholarship of TUBITAK for her post-doc research. She is working as an Associate Prof Dr. And Head of Public Relations and Advertising Department at Istanbul Commerce University. The research areas are advertising, digital advertising, emotions, product placements, tourism advertising, brand and strategic planning. In addition to this she has a lot of international and national scientific publications in the matter of advertising and public relations.

Árpád Ferenc Papp-Váry is the Dean of the Faculty of Tourism, Business and Communication at the Budapest Metropolitan University, Hungary. He is also the head of the Commerce and Marketing BSc programme and vocational programme, the Marketing MSc programme, and the Digital Marketing executive MBA postgraduate programme. Besides university education, Árpád regularly holds training sessions and provides branding consultancy for cities, companies and professionals. He is serving as Vice President of the Hungarian Marketing Association. His teaching and research areas are country branding, city branding, personal branding, sports branding and branded entertainment. Árpád is the author of six books and several hundred publications, most of which are available online at www.papp-vary.hu.

Burcu Sezen is Assistant Professor of Marketing at the Universidad de los Andes School of Management (Bogota, Colombia). From 2005 to 2010, she worked in the industry in product and brand management in such companies such as Hizli Sistem, Coca-Cola Bottlers Group in Turkey and Nestle Turkey. She oversaw the management of brands as diverse as Logitech, Viewsonic, BenQ, Cappy (Coca-Cola) and Maggi. Her experience in multi-brand companies intrigued her interest in the dynamics of brands within a company's portfolio. Burcu's research has also focused on studying branding in general and brand portfolios and global branding in particular. Having grown up, studied and worked in many different countries, she is sensitive to and fascinated by the role that culture plays in marketing. Burcu holds a PhD in Business Administration from Ozyegin University in Istanbul, Turkey. During her PhD, she also spent a term as Visiting Graduate Student at UCLA in Los Angeles, U.S.A. Her undergraduate major at Middle East Technical University in Ankara, Turkey, was in political science. She holds two master degrees, one in European Studies from a joint program by University of Bath and L'Institut d´Etudes Politiques-Paris and an MBA at Sabanci University in Istanbul. She also completed a Certificate Program in Marketing at UCSD, San Diego, US, where she first discovered her passion for marketing.

Mehmet Sinan Tam graduated from Fırat University Public Relations and Publicity department in 2013. He completed his MA in Marmara University Public Relations department in 2015 and PhD in İstanbul University Public Relations and Publicity in 2020. His research interests are social media, advertisements, influencer and public relations studies. He has still been working as an Assist. Prof. Dr. at Bandırma Onyedi Eylül University Department of Public Relations and Advertising.

Mehmet Cihan Toker completed his PhD in Yeditepe University, Department of Political Science and International Relations. He has been working as an assistant professor at Istanbul Esenyurt University since 2019. His fields of research are political communication, political marketing, voter behavior, comparative political systems. He has various publications in national and international refereed journals and books.

Kıvanç Nazlım Tüzel Uraltaş is Professor of Advertising at the Department of Public Relations, Marmara University, Turkey. Her research areas are marketing, advertising management and consumer behavior. She is also interested in sales promotions and digital advertising. She has published several books, book chapters and articles in different scientific journals.

Erdem Varol was born in Samsun in 1984. He graduated from Ege University, Faculty of Communication, Department of Journalism in 2011. In 2016, he received a Master's degree from Marmara University, Institute of Social Sciences, Master's Program in Public Relations with a dissertation titled "The Relationship between Shopping Centers and Consumer Society in Urban Culture". In the same year, he enrolled in the Doctoral Program of Marmara University, Institute of Social Sciences, Advertising and Promotion, which he won. Since 2013, he has been working as a Research Assistant at Marmara University, Faculty of Communication, Department of Public Relations and Publicity, and has been working on topics such as "Consumer Culture", "Consumer Behavior", and "Advertising".

Poshan (Sam) Yu is a Lecturer in Accounting and Finance in the International Cooperative Education Program of Soochow University (China). He is also an External Professor of FinTech and Finance at SKEMA Business School (China), a Visiting Professor at Krirk University (Thailand) and a Visiting Researcher at the Australian Studies Centre of Shanghai University (China). Sam leads FasterCapital (Dubai, UAE) as a Regional Partner (China) and serves as a Startup Mentor for AIC RAISE (Coimbatore, India). His research interests include financial technology, regulatory technology, public-private partnerships, mergers and acquisitions, private equity, venture capital, start-ups, intellectual property, art finance, and China's "One Belt One Road" policy.

Index

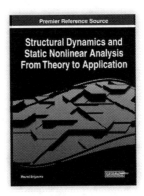

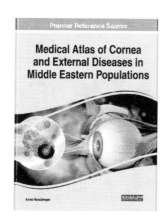

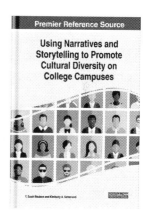

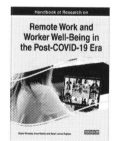

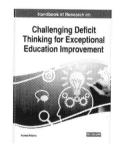

Printed in the United States
by Baker & Taylor Publisher Services